D0088938

Also by Jeffry D. Wert

MOSBY'S RANGERS

FROM WINCHESTER TO CEDAR CREEK:
The Shenandoah Campaign of 1864

JEFFRY D. WERT

Simon & Schuster

New York London

Toronto Sydney

Tokyo Singapore

GENERAL JAMES LONGSTREET

The

Confederacy's

Most

Controversial

Soldier—

A Biography

SIMON & SCHUSTER
ROCKEFELLER CENTER
1230 AVENUE OF THE AMERICAS
NEW YORK, NEW YORK 10020

DESIGNED BY KAROLINA HARRIS
PICTURE SECTION DESIGNED BY BARBARA M. BACHMAN
MANUFACTURED IN THE UNITED STATES OF AMERICA

10 9 8 7 6 5 4 3 2 1

LIBRARY OF CONGRESS CATALOGING-IN-PUBLICATION DATA

WERT, JEFFRY D.
    GENERAL JAMES LONGSTREET: THE CONFEDERACY'S MOST CONTROVERSIAL SOLDIER:
A BIOGRAPHY/JEFFRY D. WERT.
        P. CM.
    INCLUDES BIBLIOGRAPHICAL REFERENCES AND INDEX.
1. LONGSTREET, JAMES, 1821–1904. 2. GENERALS—UNITED STATES—
BIOGRAPHY. 3. GENERALS—CONFEDERATE STATES OF AMERICA—
BIOGRAPHY. 4. UNITED STATES—HISTORY—CIVIL WAR, 1861–1865—
CAMPAIGNS. I. TITLE.
E467.1.L55W46   1993
973.7'3'0092—DC20
(B)   93-28953 CIP
ISBN 0-671-70921-6

For Jason and Natalie,
with a father's love and pride

CONTENTS

LIST OF MAPS

PREFACE

Eleven years after the Civil War, James Longstreet confided in a private letter that "it has been my feeling and opinion, that it would have been better to leave to the historian, and the student of future days, the records of our struggle from which the history should be made; that those of us who bore prominent parts in the struggle should recognize its failure, and should submit to the responsibilities of that failure, as belonging to us all in proportion to our positions and opportunities."

When he wrote the words, the ex-Confederate general and senior lieutenant in the Army of Northern Virginia had been under verbal and printed attack for his alleged failings in the conflict, particularly for his role in the Battle of Gettysburg, the perceived seminal engagement of the war. At first, Longstreet ignored the criticism and the manufactured charges, for he knew them not to be true. But the condemnations of his performance persisted, entwined with his postwar political apostasy. As he stated in the letter, he did not fear history's verdict: "I should have been willing to have any one, who wished to use it, appropriate any or all of my part in the war if it had been done without arraigning me before the world as the person and the only one responsible for the loss of the cause."[1]

History, however, is artificial, a creation framed and defined by participants in the events and by historians. Once wrought, history can be a tenacious muse, with a shadow that envelops decades, even centuries. The history of the Civil War, notably the struggle in Virginia, was fashioned in the early postwar decades amid the formulation of the "Lost Cause" myth. By the 1890s, the tenets of the myth—the Confederacy had been defeated because of the manpower and industrial and material might of the Union—became entrenched, its arguments delineating much of the military historiography of the Civil War.

The recent flood of new campaign studies, biographies, and collections of essays has resulted in fresh, sometimes penetrating, reanalyses and reexaminations. For the most part these new works have been characterized by broad and deep research in manuscript collections and in the printed reminiscences of participants. Major military leaders have been the subjects of the welcomed efforts, with some of the figures warranting more than one book. The treatments of campaigns and battles have added detail, solved riddles, and expanded our knowledge of the strategy and tactics involved in these struggles, while the essays have provided insight into questions and synthesis to the themes of America's greatest tragedy. As a consequence, the "Lost Cause" myth no longer dominates the literature.

A significant—if not the most significant—victim of the "Lost Cause" interpretation of the conflict was James Longstreet. A crucial element of the myth was that the Confederacy nearly attained victory except for the mortal wounding of Stonewall Jackson at Chancellorsville in May 1863 and the defeat of Robert E. Lee's army at Gettysburg two months later. Without the great and brilliant Jackson, the Army of Northern Virginia faltered during the three days' battle at the southern Pennsylvania crossroads village, at the "High Water-Mark of the Confederacy." If Gettysburg were the enduring "if" of Confederate history, then the reasons for Lee's defeat there explained the loss of Southern independence. The burden for Gettysburg fell on James Longstreet, for he was the officer in the army, as he noted, arraigned "before the world as the person and the only one responsible for the loss of the cause."

My biography of Longstreet is the first to appear on him in over a decade and is the most extensive examination of his military career. The three previous studies of his life are neither altogether satisfactory nor buttressed by broad research in manuscript collections. A fine, recent look has analyzed Longstreet's place in Southern history and Civil War historiography but offers only a cursory description of his performance during the war. The focus of my book is on Longstreet during the Civil War, on the battles and campaigns that were the heart of this soldier's life.

The purpose of my work is to present a fresh study based on archival research and recent scholarship. My appraisal will undoubtedly generate controversy among students of the war. The Gettysburg Campaign, for instance, comprises a central feature of my book, for it is that operation which lies at the core of history's judgment of Longstreet. By its nature, a reevaluation of Longstreet's tactical and strategic beliefs, of his performance on battlefields, of the record of his First Corps, and of his relationship with Robert E. Lee must address critical components of the history of Confederate military efforts. Longstreet was foremost a soldier, and this is the story of one of America's most controversial soldiers.

Any written work such as this requires the assistance of numerous individuals; their efforts on my behalf deserve my sincere appreciation and gratitude. Their aid has only made this book better, and all errors of commission and omission are solely the responsibility of the author.

First of all, I wish to thank the archivists and librarians at the various institutions listed in the bibliography for their expertise, patience, and understanding as they guided me through their collections and endured my requests and questions.

Other individuals merit my particular recognition for their contributions:

Michael Musick, an archivist at the National Archives with an unsurpassed knowledge of the depository's Civil War holdings, for supplying me, beyond the call of duty, with important material.

Historians with the National Park Service, notably Ted Alexander and Paul Chiles at Antietam National Battlefield; Robert K. Krick and Donald Pfanz at Fredericksburg and Spotsylvania National Military Park; and Ed Raus at Manassas National Battlefield Park, for sharing with me their knowledge of the engagements and for directing my research at their libraries.

Dr. Gary Gallagher, chairman of the History Department at the Pennsylvania State University, Civil War scholar, and friend, for his guidance and support, and for his generosity in reading several chapters of the book.

Peter Cozzens, a friend and fellow Civil War historian, for supplying me with research material on the Chicakamauga Campaign, for sharing with me chapters of his superb account of that struggle in the West before its publication, and for reading my version of events.

Allan Tischler, a friend and fellow student, for providing me with research material gleaned from his own work.

Jamie Longstreet Paterson, granddaughter of James Longstreet, for sharing with me family material and photographs.

Robert Gottlieb, head of the Literary Department at the William Morris Agency and my agent, for his counsel and for his many endeavors on my behalf.

Bob Bender, vice president and senior editor, Simon & Schuster, for his friendship, his timely encouragement and understanding, and for making me a better writer.

Jason and Natalie, our son and daughter, for assisting with the research, enduring stoically long hours in libraries, and for their love and support.

Gloria, my wife, without whom this book could never have been finished, for her love and for all that makes life fulfilling.

JEFFRY D. WERT
Centre Hall, PA
December 31, 1992

1

SOLDIER'S JOURNEY

The column of men marched up the street in the warmth of a late spring day. Numbering perhaps fifteen thousand and stretching back out of view, the marchers came on without a cadence in their strides or a symmetry to their ranks. Many of them wore tattered old clothes; no two seemed to be dressed alike. At one point in the procession, the shredded remains of a battle flag, held together by red mosquito netting, rose above their heads. The huge crowd of onlookers, however, needed no flag: The sight of these marchers was enough. Everyone sensed that beside each man in the column walked a ghost.

The day was May 29, 1890, in Richmond, Virginia, a time for memories and ghosts. The previous week, the former capital of the Confederacy had been gripped with a "frenzy of Southern feeling," according to a newspaper reporter. Drygoods stores sold Confederate emblems; a huge Confederate flag draped across the facade of city hall; residents decorated their homes; portraits of the South's greatest soldier, Robert E. Lee, hung conspicuously throughout the city; and thousands of invited guests and visitors spilled from railroad cars. The city seemingly resonated with the sounds of the past.

The occasion, long planned and anticipated, was the unveiling of an equestrian statue of Robert E. Lee. Sculptor J. A. C. Mercie had designed and created the monument to the former commander of the Army of Northern Virginia, and a coterie of Lee's lieutenants in the army—Jubal A. Early, Fitzhugh Lee, John B. Gordon, and others

—assisted in the preparations. Invitations were extended to former officers, units, and veterans of the Confederacy's most famous army. In the capital of the long-dead Confederacy, the justness of the Lost Cause and the greatness of Lee's military genius would be affirmed.

At noon on the 29th, the chief marshal and the general's nephew, Fitzhugh Lee, mounted on an iron-gray horse, led the parade down Broad Street. Behind him came bands playing music and ranks of young men in uniform, striding forth with the assurance of their years and with the dreams of untested warriors. The crowds of spectators lining the street watched this passage of youth closely, but they were there to see and honor the veterans of Malvern Hill, Second Manassas, Sharpsburg, Chancellorsville, Gettysburg, the Wilderness, and Appomattox.

As the old soldiers—the youth of an earlier generation who had christened the Confederacy with their sacrifices for four long years —appeared, the onlookers cheered. At the head of the column rode John Gordon, the ramrod-straight Georgian who had led Lee's army in that final march on the road at Appomattox. Behind him and interspersed among the ranks of the veterans came other generals—Early, Joseph E. Johnston, Wade Hampton, Cadmus M. Wilcox, Joseph Kershaw, Charles Field, Joseph Wheeler, and E. Porter Alexander. The crowd greeted each of them with additional cheering.

But as the carriage of one former general passed, the response of the people increased, rippling along the parade route and rising in volume like a volley of musketry fired from one end of a battleline to the other. When former soldiers in the column recognized their old chief, they broke ranks, stopping the procession. A few of the men volunteered to lead the horses throughout the route. At the platform near the covered monument, the general, assisted by one of his former aides, stepped from the carriage and took his place on the stand. The assembled veterans emitted a yell, that eerie Southern battle cry that had echoed across numerous bloody fields.

James Longstreet, former lieutenant general and commander of the First Corps, Army of Northern Virginia, had arrived. His journey to this place and time had been long. For the better part of the past two decades he had been an apostate, a scapegoat for the majority of Southerners. His record in the war had been vilified and falsified, his devotion to the Confederacy had been questioned. He defended himself in print, but did it poorly and only enhanced the efforts of his detractors. The organizers of this event had not invited him until some of his former artillerymen insisted that he attend as their escort, and he accepted. As he sat down, he knew that to many of his former comrades on the platform he was an unwanted presence.

On this day for memories, however, the veterans of the army remembered James Longstreet as a soldier and saluted him. They knew he belonged there, for he had earned their respect and devotion from the beginning at First Manassas to the end at Appomattox. Although he now looked "old, feeble, indeed badly broken up" to one of his former staff officers, they recalled him as a robust, powerful, and tireless man whose battlefield courage and sincere concern for their welfare had few equals in the army. He had the soul of a soldier, and they never forgot it.

So he sat before the men he cared most about, at the foot of a monument dedicated to the general who had called him "my old war-horse." It was as it should have been—a day for memories, a day for ghosts, a day for soldiers.[1]

James Longstreet was born in the Edgefield District, South Carolina, on January 8, 1821, the third son and fifth child of James and Mary Ann Dent Longstreet. His parents owned a cotton plantation in the Piedmont section of northeastern Georgia near what would become the village of Gainesville. Neither parent was a native of the South Carolina–Georgia border region—James was born in New Jersey; Mary, in Maryland. Both belonged to families whose ancestry in America dated from the colonial period.[2]

The first Longstreet in the New World was Dirck Stoffels Langestraet, who emigrated to the Dutch colony of New Netherlands in 1657. Three generations later the family name had been anglicized, and on October 6, 1759, William Longstreet, James's grandfather, was born in Monmouth County, New Jersey. William inherited the independent and roving spirit of the Longstreet males. In the mid-1780s, he married Hannah Fitz Randolph, born on March 23, 1761, the daughter of James and Deliverance Coward Fitz Randolph. The Fitz Randolphs, whose ancestors first settled in Puritan Massachusetts in 1630, had lived in New Jersey for over a century. Following their marriage, William and Hannah moved to Augusta, Georgia, on the Savannah River. Regarded in the family as a "genius," William was a tinkerer and inventor with a keen interest in steam engines.[3]

Within two years of his arrival in Augusta, William had constructed a steamboat and launched it on the nearby river. The craft had no paddle wheel, but a series of long poles driven by the engine against the river's bottom. He utilized the principle subsequently adopted by keelboatmen, but his steamboat was too mechanically complex to be reliable. When he failed to secure local financial backing, he wrote to Georgia Governor Thomas Telfair on September 26, 1790, requesting state funds for his invention. Telfair rejected the proposal, and William's experiment ended.[4]

In his letter to the governor, William wrote: "I make no doubt but that you have often heard of my steamboat, and as often heard it laughed at." In fact, his steamboat had become the subject of numerous jokes and doggerel poetry in Augusta. His fellow townsmen called him "Billy Boy, the dreamer." But despite being regarded as an eccentric, William served as a city commissioner and as justice of the peace.[5]

He continued his tinkering with steam engines, eventually building a steam cotton gin in St. Mary's, Georgia. About 1800, William and Hannah crossed into South Carolina and purchased land for a cotton plantation in the Edgefield District, fourteen miles north of Augusta. They prospered as planters, with William buying a second residence in Augusta that the family lived in periodically until William's death on September 1, 1814.[6]

During their thirty years of marriage, Hannah bore five children. James, their eldest son, was born in New Jersey, while the four other children were born in Georgia. Although devoted parents, William and Hannah fostered in their children the family tradition of independence, self-reliance, and a roving nature. Sometime after the family moved to South Carolina, James struck out on his own, heading north and west to the foothills of the Appalachian Mountains. There he purchased land and began raising cotton.[7]

During the next decade James worked his farm and occasionally visited his parents' home and Augusta. In the latter place, he met Mary Ann Dent. Her father was Thomas Marshall Dent, a cousin of Supreme Court Chief Justice John Marshall, and her mother was Ann Magruder Dent. Native Marylanders whose ancestors had settled in the colony in the 1670s, Mary Ann, her parents. and grandparents—George and Anna Maria Truman Dent—had relocated to Augusta in 1812. How long James and Mary Ann courted is uncertain, but they married in 1814, the year William Longstreet died.[8]

James brought Mary to his growing plantation, and before year's end she gave birth to their first child, a daughter named Anna. Three years later, in 1817, a son, William, was born. During the next three years, another daughter, Sarah Jane, and another son, John, were born, but both of them died in infancy. Then, in 1820, Mary was pregnant for a fifth time. Probably after Christmas, she traveled to her mother-in-law's home in South Carolina and there gave birth to the couple's third son, James. Although the future soldier would be a native South Carolinian, he always regarded Georgia as his home. His mother brought him to that state within weeks of his birth.[9]

The Piedmont section of northeastern Georgia, where the Longstreet farm lay, retained many vestiges of the frontier area that it had been only a few years before. It was a land of few farms, few inhabitants, and fewer towns amid a sea of forests and wilderness clearings. It was a land that required physical labor, patience, and resilience on the part of the settlers who went there to carve a farm or cobble together a village. It was a land that changed adults and shaped children.

Here the newborn son, named for his father, spent the first nine years of his life. With sister Anna and brother William as guides and mentors, young James romped and explored across the family's fields and into the nearby woods. Farm chores shared the children's time with hunting, fishing, riding, and other playful activities. Although young James would not write of his childhood in his memoirs, these early years in northeastern Georgia fostered the characteristics of the future man and soldier. He grew tall, strong, and rugged with a love of the outdoors and of physical activity. From his lineage he inherited independence of thought and self-confidence; from his surroundings, self-reliance, tirelessness, and a work ethic. Although reserved in speech and manner, he learned the value of blunt talk and expressing his opinions in a forthright manner. He possessed little refinement or education.[10]

By the time James was nine years old, the Longstreet children numbered seven. From 1822 to 1829, Mary gave birth to four daughters—Henrietta (1822), Rebecca (1824), Eliza Parke (1828), and Maria Nelson (1829). The elder James provided well for his growing family. In a region where most of the farmers grew tobacco and corn without slave labor, James Longstreet earned a respectable income with cotton, worked by his modest force of slaves. But with such a number of children, the father had to plan ahead for their future education. In 1830, the father decided that his second and namesake son needed a good education if he was to pursue his father's chosen goal—admittance to the United States Military Academy at West Point.[11]

Young James, whom the family called Peter or Pete, spoke often of a military career. Childish dreams of glory filled his head as he read books about Alexander the Great, Caesar, Napoleon, and George Washington. To his practical father, such youthful longings could be gratified with an education at little expense to the family if the nine-year-old warrior gained acceptance to West Point. With this in mind, father and son traveled in the fall of 1830 to Augusta, where James's younger brother and family resided. Here the boy could live with his aunt and uncle and attend Richmond County Academy, the state's finest preparatory school.[12]

The Augusta that welcomed the youthful newcomer had changed measurably since the mid-1780s when grandfather William amused onlookers with his peculiar steamboat. Its population numbered five thousand, making it the second largest city in the state. It bustled with activity, from the numerous commercial establishments along the streets to the noise and sweat found on the Savannah River wharfs. Young James had probably visited the city before, but to live in it, away from his parents, brother, and sisters, must have been daunting for a nine-year-old. Perhaps even more daunting was the knowledge that he would be living with his uncle, Augustus B. Longstreet.[13]

Of all of eccentric William's children, Augustus B. Longstreet was the most remarkable. He was even exceptional from the very beginning of his life, weighing a reported seventeen pounds at his birth on September 22, 1790. After the family moved to South Carolina, his father, William, sent Augustus back to Augusta where he enrolled in the Richmond County Academy. A precocious lad, Augustus did not like the rigid atmosphere at the academy and eventually was expelled. In 1811, he entered Yale University as a junior, graduating two years later with a bachelor of arts degree. From New Haven he went to Litchfield, Connecticut, spending over a year studying at Judge Tapping Reeve's renowned law school. He returned to Georgia and in 1815 was admitted to the bar of Richmond County. His father had died the year before.[14]

A gifted conversationalist with a keen sense of humor, Augustus drew clients to his law practice. On March 3, 1817, he married Frances Eliza Parke of Greensboro, Georgia. Eventually, Augustus and Frances had three children, a son and two daughters. In 1821, he was elected to the state legislature; the following year, he was appointed a judge on the superior court and given a master of arts degree by the University of Georgia. Elective politics still attracted Augustus, and in 1824 he ran for the United States House of Representatives. During the campaign, however, his son was stricken with an illness and died. A deeply grieved Augustus withdrew from the race.[15]

Augustus Longstreet was an enormously talented, well-educated, and personable man. His intellect, perception, and humor, combined with an intense earnestness, made him a formidable presence in a courtroom or on a political stump. A devout individual, he even found time to serve as a licensed lay speaker in the Methodist Church. Into such a man's house, young James Longstreet arrived in the fall of 1830. The nephew would spend the next eight years of his life at "Westover," his aunt and uncle's plantation located at the city's edge. Augustus, Frances, and their two daughters embraced the boy as a member of their family. Although an education at the academy brought him to Augusta, when he departed as a young man, much of the learning he carried with him occurred within the walls of Westover.[16]

Young James Longstreet entered Richmond County Academy on October 7, 1830. Since 1802, the school had occupied a two-story brick building with attached wings on Telfair Street between Centre and Washington streets. During the fall and winter, the school began at 8:30 A.M and concluded at 5:00 P.M. In the warmth and heat of spring and summer, students reported an hour earlier and stayed an hour later. The only vacation from the academic year lasted roughly seven weeks, from mid-August to early October.[17]

The academy had acquired its reputation with a tested curriculum and a strict discipline code. Classes were divided between lower and upper levels. Instruction embodied the accepted course of study of the era—mathematics, grammar, composition, Latin, Greek, and oratory. Breaches of conduct brought stern punishment; teachers even regulated activities outside the classroom. But the academy's regime attracted parents, and by 1830 over three hundred students filed daily into the brick school on Telfair Street.[18]

Like his uncle before him, James Longstreet did not like the

school. For an active nine-year-old recently removed from the freedom of his family's fields and woods, the atmosphere of the academy must have been smothering. He was not alone among the
students in this attitude, but he never seemed to adapt and his
classwork reflected this. He preferred the outdoors where the physical, not the intellectual, counted.[19]

Westover thus beckoned to James every day upon his release
from the academy. There he could romp across his uncle's acres,
enjoying the company of his cousins or that of the slave children
on the plantation. He grew taller and muscular, with a stamina that
seemingly had no bounds. These campaigns in the foothills of the
Appalachians and on the fields of Westover prepared him for future
campaigns. By the time he left for West Point in 1838, he had nearly
attained his adult height of six feet two inches, on a sturdy, powerful
frame.[20]

Before then, however, other lessons were absorbed at Westover,
none more important, perhaps, than the one Uncle Augustus taught
him in the fall of 1832 and the winter of 1833. For a few years
tensions between the sections of the nation had been simmering
over the question of a tariff. Southerners opposed a duty on im-
ported goods, arguing that it imposed financial burdens on them
while it protected Northern manufacturers. In the waning months
of 1832, the issue boiled over in South Carolina.

The guiding spirit and principal architect of this so-called Nullification Crisis was the former vice president of the United States,
John C. Calhoun. Fifty years old in 1832, Calhoun had served in
government in various elective and appointive positions for over
two decades. An outspoken nationalist during his early years, Calhoun's views narrowed into sectionalism during the 1820s. As South
Carolina's cotton economy appeared to stagnate during that decade,
the Palmetto State citizens blamed the federal government's tariff
policy. When Congress passed another duty act in 1828, Carolinians
denounced it as a "tariff of abominations." Many of them advocated
secession from the Union if the measure was not overturned. For
the ambitious Calhoun, it was a challenge to maintain his leadership
among Carolinians while not jeopardizing his opportunity to secure
the prize he coveted—the presidency.

In 1828, the state legislature published his work *The South Carolina Exposition and Protest* anonymously. In it Calhoun argued that
the Constitution had created a compact of sovereign states with the

federal government as their "agent." If Congress passed a law of dubious constitutionality, such as the tariff, each state had the right to nullify that statute. To Calhoun the rights of the individual states had not been subordinated to the power of the federal government with the adoption of the Constitution.

Finally, in 1832, as extremists in South Carolina, persuaded by Calhoun's theory, clamored for action, he resigned as Andrew Jackson's vice president and was elected by the legislature to the U.S. Senate. In the state, "nullifiers" won a referendum on the issue, held a special convention, and voted the tariff law null and void as of February 1, 1833. In Washington, President Jackson erupted in a fury, blaming Calhoun. He called the act of the Carolina convention treason and sought authority from Congress to use the army and navy to enforce the law if necessary. Behind the scenes, Jackson sought a compromise on the tariff, and when Carolinians failed to secure the support of any other Southern state, the crisis ended as South Carolina accepted the law in March 1833.[21]

The controversy gripped the nation and was a portent of civil war. Few if any Americans outside of South Carolina or Washington, D.C., watched the events more closely than Augustus Longstreet. He was a friend of Calhoun; both men had attended Yale and had studied under Judge Reeve, and both were inflamed by the doctrine of states' rights. Westover served as the meeting place for fellow states' rights Georgians in the city. Augustus began publishing a newspaper, the Augusta *State's Rights Sentinel,* in 1833. Although the intensity of the issue subsided, Augustus remained a fervid advocate of the ominous doctrine.[22]

At Westover his nephew surely heard the political arguments and witnessed his uncle's passion. Political theories and constitutional nuances never appealed to him. But what twelve-year-old James imbibed from his uncle was the pure stuff, the states' rights argument undiluted with the countervailing view of the indissolubility of the Union. Years later when James, the man and the officer, faced the choice, he did not hesitate.

Most important for James, however, 1833 brought a personal tragedy. While on a visit to Augusta, his father died during a cholera epidemic. His family—a sixth sister, Sarah Jane, had been born in 1831—briefly resided in Augusta, and then his mother, for reasons unexplained, decided to live permanently in Morgan County in northern Alabama. James had evidently returned each August to the farm near Gainesville, but his mother's decision to move hundreds of miles away almost precluded such visits. Increasingly, Westover became his home, and his mother passed out of his life—he barely mentioned her in his memoirs. Uncle Augustus and Aunt Frances received his affections.[23]

James remained at Westover for another five years. During that time he attended the academy, enjoyed the bustle and color of the city and the plantation, and matured into a fine young man. Uncle Augustus kept active in politics and in the church and published his renowned humorous look at the common folk of the state, *Georgia Scenes*.[24] In 1837, Augustus tried to secure an appointment to West Point for James. The vacancy in the congressional district that included Augusta had already been filled, so Augustus turned to a kinsman, Reuben Chapman, whose First District of Alabama included Morgan County where Mary Longstreet lived. John Calhoun and Governor George McDuffie of South Carolina used their influence, and in December, Congressman Chapman recommended James Longstreet to Secretary of War Joel R. Poinsett. The appointment was offered, and in March 1838, James accepted.[25]

Three months later, in June 1838, James Longstreet left Westover and traveled north to New York and the career he had sought since he was a young boy fascinated by the stories of earlier warriors. Reporting to the academy during the first week of July, he was mustered in as a member of the class of 1842, one of over eighty whose ranks would be depleted during the next four years by the disciplinary and academic rigors of the academy.[26]

The United States Military Academy was one of the finest colleges in the country, but when Longstreet arrived in 1838, it was an institution in transition. Since 1794, a school for the instruction of engineers and artillerists had been located on the bluff above the Hudson River, thirty-seven miles north of New York City. In 1802, President Thomas Jefferson created the Corps of Engineers, directing that it be based at West Point and that the army's chief engineer serve as superintendent of a military academy to be established there.

The academy floundered during its early years, with modest appropriations and few cadets. The War of 1812 demonstrated the need for a trained officer corps, however, and in 1817, Sylvanus Thayer became superintendent. A former instructor at the academy and an engineer during the conflict, Thayer had studied military operations in Europe before returning to West Point. An austere man, his uniform always impeccable, Thayer raised the standards of instruction and instituted a rigid code of conduct. Although the cadets came to have a thorough dislike for the superintendent, he transformed the academy. Unfortunately, Thayer's reforms lapsed under his successor, Major Rene D. DeRussy. When the fourth classmen reported in the summer of 1838, the academy was awaiting a new superintendent.[27]

To novice cadets and first-time visitors, West Point initially appeared as a place of stone, brick, and mortar. Thayer had not only addressed the instructional and disciplinary needs of the academy, he had overseen the construction of new buildings. A library, laboratory, chapel, two barracks that housed the corps of over two hundred cadets, and an enormous mess hall that could feed them all at one sitting comprised the core of the academy. Nearby, small wooden houses served as the residences of the superintendent, professors, and instructors. Within the barracks, cadets shared rooms, sleeping on the floor until 1838 when cast-iron beds were provided. Small fireplaces in each room warmed the residents during the cold Hudson Valley winters.[28]

Cadet life was strictly regimented. Routine characterized the days, weeks, and months. "At West Point all is monotony," wrote a cadet of the era. "What is said of one day will answer for it almost years after."[29]

Nothing typified the sameness of academy life more than the meals. Beef was the staple—boiled, baked, or roasted for dinner; smoked or cold sliced for breakfast and supper. Twice a week the cooks served beef soup. Boiled potatoes, pudding, bread, and coffee supplemented the diet. The quality of the food was so abysmal, however, that cadets often went hungry. They dipped cockroaches from the soup, picked bugs out of the sugar, spread rancid butter on the bread, and covered it with sour molasses.[30]

The menu at the mess hall drove countless cadets to risk punishment by sneaking off the post to the adjacent village of Highland Falls. There, since 1824, Benny Havens and his wife operated a tavern that catered to the cadets. Mrs. Havens's specialities of buckwheat cakes and roast turkey, washed down with liquor, lured the young men. They could relax, carouse, listen to Benny's stories, and purchase their meals and drinks on credit. To academy authorities, the tavern was the source of evil, and when Thayer caught Benny smuggling liquor onto the post, he banished him and his wife from the grounds. They were the only citizens in the country specifically banned from West Point. But Benny Havens outlasted Thayer and a number of successors, remaining in business until after the Civil War.[31]

Academy authorities regulated cadet conduct with a system of demerits. Called "crimes" during this period, demerits were issued to the cadets for various offenses that regulated every aspect of their behavior. The fledgling officers earned demerits for tardiness or absence at roll calls for meals, chapel, drill, and inspections; for dirty quarters or equipment; for visiting after taps; for disturbances during study hours; for unshaven faces and uncut hair; for smoking in the barracks during the evening; for improper behavior toward cadet officers and academy officers; and for altercations or fights. If a cadet earned two hundred demerits in a year, he faced expulsion from the academy. The system was so encompassing that only one cadet had passed through the four years at West Point without a demerit—Robert E. Lee of Virginia, class of 1829.[32]

Although the demanding regime installed by Thayer had waned during the mid-1830s, half of the new cadets who reported in the summer of 1838 would probably be gone before graduation in four years. But the class of 1842 proved to be an exception to the normal attrition rate. In fact, the class proved to be one of the better ones of the decade. Its ranks held ten future Confederate generals, including Longstreet, Daniel Harvey Hill, Richard H. Anderson, Lafayette McLaws, Alexander P. Stewart, Gustavus W. Smith, and Earl Van Dorn; and seven future Union commanders, including William S. Rosecrans, John Pope, Abner Doubleday, George Sykes, and John Newton. Not all of them were brilliant officers in that conflict, but several attained army, corps, or district command.[33]

Longstreet and his fellow classmates' introduction to academy life was the annual summer camp held during July and August. The corps moved from the barracks to the academy plain, where the cadets lived in wall tents during the encampment. The instructors maintained a rigorous daily schedule of artillery and infantry drills, interspersed with fencing and dancing lessons. Dignitaries from Washington, D.C., visited. Parades by the cadets in their gray coats, white pantaloons, and black bell-crowned leather caps attracted throngs of civilians, especially young women. Every Saturday night the female visitors enjoyed the company of the cadets at a weekly ball. At the end of the summer encampment, the young warriors in gray danced with their dates in the candlelight of a grand ball. It was a night long remembered, for within days life at the academy resumed its challenging rhythm.[34]

September ushered in the academic year at West Point, and in 1838 it brought a new superintendent, Major Richard Delafield. A short, pudgy man with an enormous nose, Delafield was devoted to the academy and to the Corps of Engineers. He was appointed to reinvigorate the academic curriculum and to restore the old Thayer code of conduct. Within weeks of his arrival, the corps came to have an abiding distaste for the fidgety superintendent who enjoyed ferreting around, sniffing out delinquent cadets and alleged troublemakers. The cadets soon called him Dicky the Punster because of the sarcasm he frequently used with the corps members.[35]

"Major Delafield," groused cadet Richard S. Ewell, "seems to pride himself upon having everything different from what it used to be." The new superintendent's major innovation in the curriculum was the introduction of cavalry instruction in 1839, with the assignment of a sergeant, five dragoons, and a dozen horses to the academy. A year later Delafield secured thirty horses and harness for a battery of light artillery. The trained engineer's appreciation for the role of the mounted arm and mobile artillery would add measurably to the skills of academy graduates and to the future army.[36]

Delafield also brought his nervous energy to bear on the basic curriculum of the academy and imposed higher standards for classwork. The curriculum for the first two years focused on mathematics, French, drawing, and English grammar. As second classmen, the cadets struggled with philosophy, chemistry, and advanced drawing. Only in a cadet's final year did the instruction address military science, with additional classes in ethics, mineralogy, and geology. Each January and June the cadets endured lengthy examinations that determined their class rank. Failures in the examinations meant expulsion.[37]

The academic demands challenged James Longstreet from the outset, and he struggled in the classroom throughout his four years at West Point. By his own admission in his memoirs, he "had more interest in the school of the soldier, horsemanship, sword exercise, and the outside game of foot-ball than in the academic courses." Longstreet reacted to the course of study at West Point much as he did to his preparatory schooling at the Richmond County Academy —with dislike.[38]

Longstreet ranked in the bottom third of his class in every subject during the four years. In a few subjects he stood near the bottom. At the end of his second year, for instance, he stood seventy-first in drawing and seventy-second in French in a class of seventy-six members. It was not much better in mathematics or English grammar. During his second class year, 1840–41, he ranked sixtieth in chemistry, with only one member of the class below him. In the January examinations of that year, he failed mechanics, arguing later in his memoirs that he saw no sense in pulleys. Two days after he failed, he took a second test and passed. In the June examinations, he scored the highest grade in the use of pulleys.[39]

During his final year at the academy, Longstreet earned mixed grades in the courses devoted to military science—artillery, engineering, and infantry tactics. In artillery he finished the year ranked fifty-first in a class of fifty-six. In engineering he fared slightly better, standing forty-eighth. The engineering course was taught by Dennis Hart Mahan, the academy's most renowned instructor. An academy graduate, ranking first in the class of 1824, Mahan was a "slim skeleton of a man," said a cadet, who was "the most particular, crabbed, exacting man that I ever saw." In his shrill voice, Mahan taught the science of military engineering, devoting only one week to the art of war. To his students, Mahan stressed swiftness of movement, maneuver, and the use of interior lines of operation. He emphasized the capture of strategic points instead of the destruction of enemy armies. Hundreds of cadets left the academy with Mahan's principles, carrying them into campaigns of the Civil War. Although Longstreet's grades in Mahan's class indicated only a modest grasp of engineering principles and the art of war, he had listened and learned.[40]

Longstreet achieved his highest ranking in the course on infantry tactics, standing fortieth in the class that year. In contrast, he stood next to last in ethics. By any measure, Longstreet was a poor to mediocre student at West Point. He never enjoyed the strictures or demands of the classroom; he relished physical activities. When he graduated in 1842, he ranked fifty-fourth in a class of fifty-six.[41]

His disciplinary record was little better than his academic standing. "As I was of a large and robust physique," Longstreet said many years later, "I was at the head of most larks and games." He committed nearly all the common sins of West Point cadets—visiting after taps, absences from roll calls, dirty room, long hair, making a disturbance during study hours, and disobeying orders. He compiled only 58 demerits during his first two years, but as a second classman, he accumulated 164 demerits, ranking 211th in conduct in a corps of 219 cadets. He improved his behavior during his final year, earning only 102 demerits. Longstreet was neither a model student nor a gentleman.[42]

Longstreet was popular with his fellow corpsmen. His leadership in pranks, his sense of humor, his exuberance for the rough-and-tumble, and his open disregard for academy rules made him an appealing companion to his youthful classmates. They came to call him Old Pete, after his family's nickname, and according to his second wife, he was voted the most handsome cadet in the class.[43]

The closest friendships he forged at the academy, in most cases, endured for a lifetime and had profound effects on his career as a soldier. Among upperclassmen, Virginian George Thomas, class of 1840, became a valued companion for two years. Within his own class, his inner circle of friends included William Rosecrans, John Pope, Alexander Stewart, Harvey Hill, and Lafayette McLaws. At one time or another, Longstreet roomed with Rosecrans, Pope, and Stewart. Rosecrans was a studious Ohioan who assisted Longstreet with classwork. Of this group, Longstreet compiled the lowest grades and the most demerits. And of this group, except for Pope, all had a future rendezvous on a terrible battlefield in northern Georgia.[44]

Longstreet found his best friend, however, among the class of 1843—Ulysses S. Grant. An Ohioan, Grant was a reluctant cadet, admitting in his memoirs that "a military life had no charms for me"; he did not expect to remain in the army if he graduated from the academy. What attracted the two cadets to each other is uncertain, and they were an unlikely pair. Grant was reserved and serious; Longstreet was fun-loving and carefree. Grant never joined Longstreet in the pranks and games because, as Longstreet argued, he had a "delicate frame." Despite his physical size and strength, Grant excelled at horsemanship and was regarded as the finest rider in the entire corps of cadets. In his memoirs, Longstreet described Grant, whom his friends called Sam, as "of noble, generous heart, a lovable character, a valued friend." Although they would choose opposite allegiances in 1861, their friendship never wavered. Irony walked with many friends across the grounds of West Point.[45]

James Longstreet was twenty-one years old when he was graduated from the academy on July 1, 1842. Brevetted a second lieutenant of infantry, he had fulfilled a father's hope and a young boy's dreams. It had not come without a struggle, and the training he had received was only a beginning. When he left West Point, he headed home on furlough to Georgia to spend some time with Uncle Augustus and Aunt Frances before reporting to his assignment with the Fourth Infantry at Jefferson Barracks, Missouri. A soldier's journey had begun.[46]

2

SOLDIER'S TRADE

Jefferson Barracks lay hard by the Mississippi River, ten miles south of St. Louis. Established in 1825, the post sprawled across seventeen hundred acres of Missouri meadow, splotched with groves of sycamore and oak. A large parade ground, rimmed on three sides by whitewashed limestone buildings, formed the post's central area. Barracks for the enlisted men abutted the river's edge. During the spring and summer months, a ten-acre garden provided fresh vegetables and flowers for the garrison. Well maintained, Jefferson Barracks was one of the army's finest posts west of the Mississippi.[1]

Brevet Second Lieutenant James Longstreet arrived at the post in the fall of 1842. Twenty-two officers and 449 enlisted men of the Fourth Infantry comprised the garrison, under the command of fifty-year-old Lieutenant Colonel John Garland. Longstreet was assigned to a company commanded by Captain Bradford R. Alden, whom Longstreet described as "a most exemplary man who proved a lasting, valued friend." Under Garland and Alden, Longstreet learned the responsibilities of a regular army officer.[2]

Longstreet spent nearly two years at Jefferson Barracks. Although the post offered pleasant duty for young officers, much of the time was spent in the monotony of drill, training, and inspections common to a peacetime army. As he had at West Point, Longstreet made friends easily, particularly with Captain George A. McCall and Lieutenants Christopher Augur, Alexander Hays, and David A. Russell, all future Union generals. In the spring of 1843, eight companies of the Third Infantry arrived from Florida, expanding the garrison's size.

For Longstreet, the most welcome addition to the officer corps came on September 30, 1843, when Brevet Second Lieutenant Ulysses S. Grant reported for duty with the Fourth Infantry. Soon the two friends were traveling together during duty-free hours, enjoying dances and other social activities. The pair of lieutenants visited nearby White Haven, the family home of Grant's roommate and fellow officer in the regiment, Frederick T. Dent. Longstreet was also warmly greeted at White Haven because his mother was a cousin of the Dents. Here, in February 1844, Grant met seventeen-year-old Julia Dent, who had returned from boarding school in St. Louis. She was not a beautiful woman, but strong, a match for the young Ohioan, and they fell in love. More often, Grant rode alone to White Haven, leaving Longstreet at the post.[3]

Months later it was Longstreet's turn to fall in love after meeting Maria Louisa Garland. The nature of their courtship, his feelings toward her, and their decades-long marriage are difficult to piece together or assess. Longstreet does not even mention her in his memoirs. If the two corresponded during their numerous separations—and in all likelihood, they did—those letters no longer exist. The fire that destroyed their home in Gainesville, Georgia, in 1889 most likely took these letters. Only Longstreet's second wife, Helen Dortch Longstreet, offers hints of the relationship in her memoirs.

Nevertheless, Longstreet met and courted Maria Louisa Garland during the spring or summer of 1844. Called Louise by her family, she was a daughter of Longstreet's regimental commander, Lieutenant Colonel John Garland. The Garlands were a prominent family in Lynchburg, Virginia. Louise's grandfather, Hudson Garland, had been an attorney, a captain in the War of 1812, and a member of the Virginia legislature, and he had held government posts in Washington in the administrations of Andrew Jackson and Martin Van Buren. Hudson's wife, Letitia Pendleton, belonged to another respected Virginia family.[4]

Louise's father, John Garland, born in 1792, was commissioned a lieutenant in the regular army in 1813 and served throughout the War of 1812. He chose to remain in the army and was stationed at various forts. During the 1820s, while in Detroit, he met and married Harriet Smith, daughter of a fur trapper and trader, Jacob Smith, and his wife, a half-, if not full-blooded, Chippewa Indian.

On March 6, 1827, at Fort Snelling, Minnesota Territory, Louise was born, one of five Smith children who would live to adulthood.[5]

Seventeen-year-old Louise was visiting her father at Jefferson Barracks when she encountered the twenty-three-year-old brevet second lieutenant. She was slender, petite, and quite attractive, with high cheekbones and black hair. Lieutenant Richard Ewell saw Louise and her sister, Bessie, at the time and wrote: "I never saw a place so well calculated as Jefferson Barracks is, at present, to cure an Officer of a matrimonial disposition. I must, however, except the Miss Garland's from the number of antidotes as they are so devilish pretty they have rather a tendency the other way."[6]

When Longstreet asked Louise's parents for their permission to marry, they consented but insisted that the couple wait until Louise was older. In her memoirs, Helen Longstreet asserts that the young officer never kissed his fiancée during this time.[7]

In May 1844, "all of our pleasures were broken," wrote Longstreet, when the Third and Fourth regiments were ordered to Louisiana. Longstreet evidently did not leave with the regiment at that time but rejoined his comrades by summer's end. The two regiments formed a part of the Army of Observation, under the command of Major General Zachary Taylor. Months earlier, Congress had annexed Texas to the Union, and Mexico sundered diplomatic relations with the United States. The long-standing strained tensions between the two countries exacerbated, and President James Polk ordered Taylor to Texas's eastern border.[8]

The Fourth Infantry occupied Camp Salubrity, three miles from Natchitoches, Louisiana, on the Red River. The tent site lay on a high sandy ridge covered with pine trees. It was a healthy site, but the troops and officers had little to keep busy. Gambling became the favorite pastime, and Longstreet developed a passion for poker. He could waste an entire day in a game of brag or five-cent ante.[9]

While at Camp Salubrity, Longstreet was promoted to second lieutenant, on March 4, 1845, and transferred to the Eighth Infantry, stationed at Fort Marion in St. Augustine, Florida. He reported about April 1 and was assigned to Company A. In August he traveled to Pensacola, where he served on court-martial duty during the month. The Eighth Infantry, meanwhile, had received orders to depart for Texas and join Taylor's forces. Longstreet followed, arriving at Taylor's camp at Corpus Christi in September.[10]

Corpus Christi was a trading post on the Gulf of Mexico at the mouth of the Nueces River. Taylor's army had occupied it in July when the Polk administration sent it there as an Army of Occupation. Mexican authorities argued that the Nueces River marked the boundary between the two countries, while the government in Washington claimed the Rio Grande as the border. Taylor's command, numbering over thirty-eight hundred by October, had orders to guard the river and patrol the disputed border.[11]

With the Americans came over a thousand camp followers. Gambling and prostitution soon flourished in Corpus Christi. A historian of one of Taylor's regiments described the place as "the most murderous, thieving, gambling, cut-throated, God-forsaken hole in the 'Lone Star State' or out of it." The troops called Taylor "Old Rough and Ready," and he endeavored to keep them busy and away from the town's enticements with constant drill and training. But the allure of quick money and pliable women in this "God-forsaken" outpost posed constant problems for the army.[12]

Longstreet and fellow officers, who had more liberty than enlisted men, enjoyed various off-duty pursuits. Longstreet had plenty of companions to pass the time with—former academy friends and the officers of the Third and Fourth regiments, including Grant. Armed with shotguns, they hunted turkeys, deer, coyotes, wolves, and an occasional cougar. In camp they played brag for hours. Grant, whom Longstreet regarded as a poor poker player, sat in only when the stakes were small.[13]

During the winter, under the direction of Captain John Bankhead Magruder, the officers constructed an eight-hundred-seat theater and formed a joint stock company to present plays, charging admission. Every night enlisted men filled the seats to watch their officers act in various comedies and tragedies, performing both the male and female roles. In *The Merchant of Venice,* Grant played Desdemona after Longstreet was rejected for the role as too tall. The officers earned enough money to pay for the construction of the theater. Longstreet recalled these days in his memoirs, writing that "life through the winter was gay."[14]

The pleasant weeks ended on March 9, 1846, when Taylor's army crossed the Nueces River and marched toward the Rio Grande. Relations between the United States and Mexico had deteriorated over the winter after Mexico rejected President Polk's offer to buy California. The administration consequently ordered Taylor to occupy the disputed territory in Texas. If the Mexicans wanted war, Polk would oblige them.[15]

The advance elements of the American army reached Arroyo Colorado, 130 miles from Corpus Christi, on March 19. Across the arroyo, or ravine, Mexican lancers watched the Americans file in and deploy. When Taylor's main body arrived two days later, Briga- dier General David Worth pushed his troops across the arroyo, and the Mexicans, after protesting the American advance, withdrew. On the 24th, Worth's dragoons rode to the east bank of the Rio Grande, opposite Matamoros, Mexico. Within days Taylor closed with his army; work began on Fort Texas, and a supply line opened to Point Isabel on the Gulf coast. The American camp was within the range of Mexican artillery beyond the river.[16]

For the next five weeks the opponents stalked each other in a tinderbox fashioned by their respective governments. Sparks soon ignited, with increasing frequency and deadliness. Under orders from the minister of war, Mexican patrols crossed the river and raided local farms and ranches. Taylor sent scouts and detachments against the Mexicans. On April 25, sixteen hundred Mexican cavalry ambushed Captain Seth B. Thornton and sixty-three dragoons, kill- ing sixteen Americans and capturing the rest except one man. In another action, Lieutenant George T. Mason, an academy classmate of Longstreet's, died while trying to fight his way through a Mexican trap. Taylor asked the governors of Texas and Louisiana for volun- teer troops and forwarded reports of the engagements to Washing- ton. In Mexico City, meanwhile, the government declared war on the United States on April 23.[17]

By the end of April, the American army needed supplies, and on May 1, Taylor marched with twenty-two hundred men for Point Isabel, leaving behind a garrison of five hundred troops at Fort Texas. The American commander believed that the fort's defenders could withstand a siege until he returned. Two days later, Major General Mariano Arista crossed the Rio Grande with an army of approximately four thousand. The Mexicans passed Fort Texas and at Palo Alto, a water hole on the road from Point Isabel to Matamo- ros, deployed into battle formations and waited for Taylor's army. On May 8, the Americans halted a mile from the Mexican ranks, shifted into lines, and prepared for the action.[18]

Arista opened the engagement with his antiquated cannon that could fire only solid shot. The American artillery responded; its superior armament and range and its better-trained gunners soon ravaged the Mexicans in a storm of metal and smoke. Arista then unleashed his strike force—one thousand mounted lancers. As these superbly uniformed and equally antiquated warriors came on, the American gunners loaded their cannon with grapeshot and the infantrymen formed a square. Taylor's artillery fired first, and when the horsemen closed to within fifty yards, the infantry ranks exploded. The Mexican attack crumbled in a heap of men and horses. The lancers charged a second time, and once again the Americans shredded the assault. After an hour's pause, Arista and Taylor advanced their infantry. The Mexicans were massed in columns, however, not in battle lines, and the American artillery and infantry tore apart the assault force. Arista withdrew, and Taylor bivouacked on the field. American casualties amounted to barely 50; Mexican, over 350.[19]

The Americans pursued the next morning, overtaking the Mexicans at Resaca de la Palma, seven miles from Palo Alto. Arista's army held the western side of a ravine among a tangle of chaparral and trees. Unlike the day before, Taylor attacked with his four infantry regiments. The Americans overran the Mexican artillery, lost the cannon to an enemy counterattack, and finally retook the guns. When the Fourth and Eighth Infantry regiments caved in Arista's right flank, the Mexicans panicked and fled toward the Rio Grande, where scores of them drowned in their headlong flight. Resaca de la Palma cost Taylor thirty-three killed and eighty-nine wounded, while Arista lost over four hundred killed, wounded, and missing. The Americans crossed the river and occupied an abandoned Matamoros.[20]

The American victories marked James Longstreet's first combat experience. In his memoirs he briefly described the two engagements, but wrote nothing about his role or feelings in the fighting, instead focusing on the exploits of a few of his fellow officers. Late in life he visited Mexico and wrote a history of the U.S.–Mexican war that was never published. His second wife, Helen Dortch Longstreet, used this manuscript in her account of the conflict, but offered no insight into his personal reactions to the campaigns and battles. It is an unfortunate void. Like so many future Civil War generals, Longstreet learned tactics and strategy under actual combat conditions on the battlefields of the Mexican War.[21]

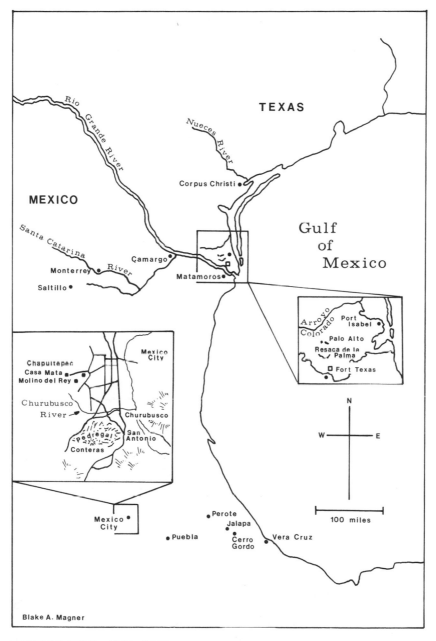

MEXICAN WAR, 1846-1847.
INSETS SHOW THEATERS OF OPERATION IN MEXICO CITY AND
ALONG THE TEXAS-MEXICO BORDER.

Palo Alto and Resaca de la Palma electrified the country and made a hero of "Old Rough and Ready" Taylor. On May 11, Polk asked for a declaration of war, and Congress complied by the next day. The administration had no strategy for waging the conflict except to enlist volunteers and amass supplies and arms.

Back in Matamoros, the new American hero prepared for an advance deeper into Mexican territory. Arista's army had retreated to Monterrey, one hundred miles from the Rio Grande. It took Taylor six weeks to gather transportation and organize the volunteer units that had flocked to his army. By the end of July, most of the Americans had reached Camargo, upriver from Matamoros.[22]

On August 20, the vanguard of Taylor's army, Worth's Second Division, started overland toward Monterrey. Longstreet's regiment, the Eighth Infantry, was in the First Brigade of Worth's division. Longstreet commanded Company A, a post he had held since June 10. It took the Americans a month to reach their target because Taylor had to supply his army from the countryside. Monterrey came into view on September 19.[23]

A beautiful city of ten thousand inhabitants, Monterrey had been turned into a fortress by the Mexicans. To the north of the city, the Citadel, a massive stone fort, stood as a towering sentry; to the south and east, the Santa Catarina River provided a natural barrier; and to the west, two fortified hills—Independence and Federation—loomed above the Monterrey-Saltillo road. Within the redoubts and forts, Major General Pedro de Ampudia had seventy-three hundred troops and forty-two cannon. Ampudia had barricaded the streets and notched loopholes in the one-story, flat-roofed houses. To Taylor's sixty-two hundred troops, Monterrey and its defenders were a formidable opponent.[24]

Taylor and his subordinates conferred and fashioned an attack scheme. Taylor ordered Worth's division to advance against the western defenses while the remainder of the army, under Taylor's direction, demonstrated against the Citadel and the eastern approaches along the river. The Americans moved into position in a heavy rain on September 20. Along Worth's lines no campfires were permitted, and his troops endured a cold, miserable night.[25]

Before daylight on the 21st, a company of mounted Texas Rangers and Companies A and B of the Eighth Infantry, under Longstreet, led the advance of Worth's division toward the Monterrey-Saltillo road. Longstreet strung his men into a skirmish line behind the

Rangers. The Americans plodded through a cornfield, closing on the road. While the ill-disciplined Rangers plundered, two hundred Mexican lancers charged them. Surprised by the onslaught, the Rangers broke, but Longstreet counterattacked with his men, killing or wounding almost half of the Mexicans. His troops pursued, seized the roadway, and cut off the Mexican army within the city. Across the river, cannon on Federation Hill opened fire, driving back the Americans. Late in the afternoon Worth ordered a detachment across the river, and the infantrymen soon overran the Mexican artillery.[26]

During the night, Worth funneled five hundred men into position at the base of Independence Hill. The rain, which had abated, resumed, lashing the Americans in a downpour. At 3:00 A.M. on the 22nd, Longstreet led his company and two artillery companies up the ridge. In a quick assault, his troops seized Fort Libertad, a redoubt on the hill's western point, clubbing and bayoneting the sixty-man garrison in a hand-to-hand melee. Behind them came Texas Rangers, who with Longstreet's contingent advanced along the crest toward the Obispado, the ruins of the bishop's palace. Mexican troops charged from their fortified position, staggered back from the American fire, and abandoned the position as the Rangers, infantrymen, and artillerymen poured over the walls. Worth's division held the high ground west of the city.[27]

To the north and east, meanwhile, Taylor's units breached the walls of the Citadel in bloody fighting. Both wings of the American army closed on the city and, throughout the 23rd, engaged in a vicious house-to-house struggle with the Mexican defenders. Longstreet's company was initially in reserve but, as the combat flared, was ordered forward. Ampudia finally capitulated, and Taylor granted an armistice to the Mexicans. Monterrey had cost Taylor over five hundred men, while Ampudia suffered less than four hundred casualties. The Mexicans evacuated the city on September 26.[28]

Longstreet emerged as a promising young officer at Monterrey. He had reacted skillfully and quickly to the lancer attack and had brought his column up the eight-hundred-foot side of Independence Hill and captured Fort Libertad. He then led his detachment in the assault that cleared the enemy from the Obispado. In this fighting and in the deadly work in the city's streets, one of his men was killed and an officer wounded. As a result of his performance,

Longstreet was promoted to adjutant of the Eighth Infantry, with the responsibility for regimental orders, returns, and correspondence. Months later, on February 23, 1847, he received promotion to the rank of first lieutenant.[29]

Taylor's army occupied Monterrey for several weeks; its presence was marked by incidents of rape, murder, and plundering. By mid-November the Americans had arrived at Saltillo, where they remained until the end of the year. Back in Washington, meanwhile, General-in-Chief Winfield Scott ordered Taylor to stay put while he organized a force for a campaign against Mexico City. Scott planned to land his army at Veracruz on the Gulf coast and then march inland against the Mexican capital. Scott consequently pulled Worth's division from Taylor and directed it to Lobos Island, Scott's rendezvous point, 180 miles north of Veracruz. By the first week of March, Scott's army, including Longstreet and the Eighth Infantry, lay off the coast of Veracruz.[30]

On March 9, 1847, Worth's division spearheaded an amphibious assault by Scott's army. The Americans came on shore in specially built "surf boats," rowed by sailors. The Mexicans offered no resistance but settled in behind their extensive fortifications. Winfield Scott, called "Old Fuss and Feathers" by his men, was the army's most capable officer. In the army since the War of 1812, he had risen to the top rank because of his superb abilities. A fine strategist and tactician, Scott opposed frontal assaults and undertook a siege of the coastal city. He massed his cannon, even borrowing guns from the navy, and began a systematic, day-to-day bombardment of the nine forts. On March 29, the Mexicans surrendered.[31]

Scott started his army westward within ten days, following the historic route of the Spanish conquistador Hernando Cortés. On April 11, the vanguard of the American army found the Mexican army under Antonio López de Santa Anna at Cerro Gordo, a pass through the mountains fifty miles from the coast.[32]

No man had so dominated Mexico during the past dozen or more years than Santa Anna. He had slaughtered the garrisons at the Alamo and Goliad, then suffered the humiliating defeat at San Jacinto that cost his country Texas in 1836. Eventually, he was exiled from his homeland and was living in Cuba when the war began with the United States. He somehow convinced the politically shrewd Polk that he could settle the conflict, so the American administration returned him to his native country. His presence in

Mexico City galvanized supporters, and soon Santa Anna was marching an army northward against Zachary Taylor. Their forces met at Buena Vista on February 23, 1847. Taylor's men fought valiantly and won, and Santa Anna retreated to the capital. Now, less than two months later, he was confronted by another American army on similarly rugged terrain.[33]

Santa Anna had seven thousand troops and artillery to defend the narrow passageway. Arriving on the 14th, Scott spent four days in reconnaissance and planning. When one of his staff officers, Captain Robert E. Lee, found a hazardous trail beyond the Mexican left flank and rear, Scott ordered a double envelopment of Santa Anna's position. On the 18th, the Americans struck—Major General Gideon Pillow's division failed on the left, but Brigadier General David Twiggs's, following Lee's route, poured into the Mexicans' rear. Santa Anna's units dissolved under the attack, with over three thousand soldiers surrendering to the Americans.[34]

The Americans flooded through the pass and advanced to Jalapa, ten miles west of Cerro Gordo, where they halted for a month because of a lack of wagons. Worth's division continued westward, however, occupying Perote, forty miles west of Jalapa. Since the army had landed at Veracruz, Longstreet and his regiment were in reserve and not participating in the combat. But he did witness the tactical value of a flanking movement and the wise reluctance of Scott to launch a frontal assault against an enemy position of fortifications.[35]

On May 15, after a brief engagement, Worth's division occupied Puebla, a beautiful city of seventy-five thousand inhabitants. The remaining units of Scott's army filtered in during the next fortnight. In need of reinforcements, Scott stopped the army for the next three months. By mid-August, Scott had fourteen thousand troops, and severing his supply line to Veracruz, advanced with almost eleven thousand men on Mexico City, a week's march away.[36]

Like Cortés three centuries before, Scott confronted a numerically superior opponent. Santa Anna had thirty thousand troops to defend the capital, which appeared impregnable. Mexico City lay amid a series of marshes and lakes, with stone causeways as the only routes of entry. Scott had to seize the causeways before his army could advance against the city's inner defenses. Unlike the conquistadors, the Americans would not be welcomed into the city.[37]

The Americans approached from the south until they reached the Pedregal, a huge field of hardened lava created a millennium ago by a volcano. The Mexicans held the villages of Contreras, San Antonio, and Churubusco. On August 20, the divisions of Twiggs and Pillow routed the defenders at Contreras while Worth's command advanced against San Antonio. The garrison in the latter village retreated toward Churubusco, only to be caught on the road by the Americans and scattered.[38]

Worth pursued the Mexicans into Churubusco and, without conducting a reconnaissance, ordered an assault. The Mexicans had erected an earthwork on the southern bank of the Churubusco River where a bridge crossed the unfordable stream. The fortification had a ditch with fifteen-foot walls in front and seven thousand troops to defend it. It would not be as easy as Worth expected.[39]

When the Americans appeared, the Mexicans raked them with musketry, wedging them into a cornfield lined with irrigation ditches. Worth's attack stalled for two hours until Scott brought up more troops. Finally, the brigade of Colonel Newman S. Clarke, comprised of the Fifth, Sixth, and Eighth Infantry regiments, charged. The Sixth followed the road into a cauldron of gunfire that slammed it to a halt. To its right, the Fifth and Eighth regiments recoiled before the Mexicans. Suddenly, Captain James V. Bomford of Company H, Eighth Infantry, leaped up and ran toward the earthwork. Close behind was Longstreet, carrying the regimental flag, and behind the lieutenant were the infantrymen.[40]

Bomford, Longstreet, and the men jumped into the ditch. The defenders seared the face of the parapet with musketry, but the Americans were not to be denied and scrambled up the wall, standing on the shoulders of comrades to reach the top. When the attackers rolled over the parapet into the enclosure, the Mexicans broke, fleeing across the bridge. Longstreet was brevetted captain for "gallant and meritorious conduct."[41]

Following the American victories on August 20, Santa Anna requested an armistice, and Scott consented. The Mexicans pulled in their lines and strengthened their defenses during the lull. On September 6, Santa Anna announced that the truce had ended, and two days later the Americans closed on the western defenses of the city. A walled fortress, Chapultepec, or "the Hill of the Grasshopper," anchored the Mexican line. One thousand yards to the west of Chapultepec was Molino del Rey, or King's Mill, where the Mexicans were reportedly recasting church bells into cannon. Another five hundred yards farther west was Casa Mata, a stone building manned by fifteen hundred defenders. Worth convinced Scott to assault Molino del Rey while another column undertook a diversionary attack against Casa Mata.[42]

At dawn on the 8th, as the main attack force drove toward Molino del Rey, Clarke's brigade and other units advanced against Casa Mata. The Mexicans punished the oncoming Americans, including the Eighth Infantry. The attackers' columns melted under the fusillades, flowing rearward. The Eighth lost 27 killed and 132 wounded in the unnecessary slaughter. When Molino del Rey fell, the defenders of Casa Mata abandoned the building. In his report of the day's fighting, Worth commended Longstreet; he was promoted to brevet major for his performance.[43]

Five days later the Americans stormed Chapultepec, the Mexican military academy and the key to the capital. Worth's and Pillow's divisions charged down the San Cosme causeway while Major General John Quitman's division came in on the Belén causeway. Clarke's brigade was in reserve until Pillow's attack stalled. Passing through Molino del Rey, Clarke's regiment came under enemy fire as it neared the fortress on the hill. Longstreet was in front of the Eighth Infantry's ranks, carrying its flag. As he led the men up the hillside, he was hit with a musket ball in the thigh, staggered, and fell. He handed the colors to Lieutenant George E. Pickett, who carried it over the wall. Chapultepec fell and, with it, the city. Santa Anna's army fled in the darkness, and at noon on the 14th, Scott rode into the plaza before the city's magnificent cathedral.[44]

Longstreet's wound was painful and slow to heal. After a stay in an American hospital, he was assigned to the Escandón family, who cared for a number of American officers. The Escandones were proud, wealthy Mexicans whose customs, manners, home, furnishings, and amusements were "altogether European," like their fellow upper-class Mexicans. They tended to the needs of the wounded Americans with graciousness and concern. By early December, Longstreet was fit enough to return to the United States, departing by ship on the 10th. He traveled to Huntsville, Alabama, where he spent the next two months with his mother.[45]

Unknowingly, for Longstreet and his fellow professional officers, the Mexican War served as the training ground for the Civil War. They witnessed the fighting qualities of citizen soldiers trained and led by professionals; the difficulties of supply and transportation across vast expanses of rough terrain; the rising power of artillery, and the declining power of smoothbore muskets; the command methods of two disparate generals, Taylor and Scott; and the costliness of frontal assaults and the effectiveness of maneuver with a numerically inferior army. The conflict also tested the capabilities and courage of the young subalterns in combat. For Longstreet, in particular, the campaigns demonstrated his physical stamina, his skill under the fluid conditions on a battlefield, and his bravery under enemy fire. For those in the soldiers' trade, warfare offered unique lessons.

Throughout his service in the war, Longstreet carried with him a daguerreotype of Louise Garland. When he returned to the States, her family agreed that she was now old enough, and the couple made wedding preparations. Evidently, while John Garland served in Mexico, his family resided part, if not most, of the time with relatives in Lynchburg, Virginia, and it was there Longstreet went during the first week of March 1848.[46]

The ceremony was held on the evening of March 8 in the home of Judge James Garland, uncle of the bride, on Madison Street, on what the locals called Garland Hill. With the house aglow with candles, James and Louise exchanged vows before Reverend William H. Kinckle, minister of St. Paul's Episcopal Church. Captain Joseph Selden of the Eighth Infantry and Lieutenant Edward Johnson of the Sixth Infantry acted as groomsmen; most likely, Louise's sister, Bessie, was maid of honor. Where the newlyweds spent their first night together is unknown.[47]

The couple honeymooned while en route to Longstreet's new assignment, recruiting duty in Poughkeepsie, New York. Longstreet served under Colonel J. B. Crane of the First Artillery at this post into the summer. In July, when he read in the newspaper that the Eighth Infantry would soon return to the United States from Mexico, he requested reassignment to the regiment. The following month he and Louise, who was pregnant with their first child, journeyed to Missouri and attended the August 22 wedding of Ulysses Grant and Julia Dent. Following the ceremony, they returned to the East, with Longstreet reporting for duty at Carlisle Barracks, Pennsylvania.[48]

Here at the old army post in southern Pennsylvania, Louise gave birth to their first child, John Garland Longstreet, on December 26,

1848. Named for Louise's father, the boy, whom the family would call Garland, was the first of ten children born to James and Louise. The only indication of the type of father Longstreet was came from his second wife in her book. She stated that he thought children could be managed like soldiers, and when this method failed, he turned the duties of parenthood over to Louise.[49]

In May 1849, Longstreet and his wife and son journeyed to San Antonio, Texas, where he resumed his duties as adjutant of the Eighth Infantry. San Antonio, a dusty village of one thousand inhabitants, served as headquarters of the Department of Texas. Like other officers and their families, the Longstreets endured life in inadequate quarters, but they were glad to be there because Louise was soon reunited with her parents. John Garland was appointed commander of the Eighth and arrived with his wife in December. Town officials welcomed the Garlands with a supper and ball on January 8, 1850.[50]

The army's main role in Texas was to protect settlements and wagons of immigrants spilling into the state from bands of Comanches and Kiowas. The department had barely fifteen hundred troops to guard a four-hundred-mile frontier against an estimated twenty-five thousand Indians. Small forts or outposts marked the army's presence in the region. The duty was monotonous, hard, and sometimes deadly. A man could learn much about himself in this type of warfare.[51]

Longstreet, however, was initially spared from patrols and counterraids against the Plains warriors. On January 1, 1850, he was relieved as adjutant of the Eighth and appointed chief of commissary for the department. He became responsible for the acquisition and distribution of food and forage for the department's entire complement of personnel and animals. Paperwork filled much of his workday, but he gained valuable experience in the administration of a military force. He served as commissary chief for sixteen months.[52]

In June 1850, Longstreet requested a transfer to the cavalry but was refused. He wanted a promotion from his regular army rank of first lieutenant and its forty-dollars-a-month pay and believed it could be achieved more readily in the mounted arm. His concern for income increased when a second son, Augustus Baldwin Longstreet, was born on December 15, 1850. Finally, shortly after the departmental commander, Brevet Major General George Mercer

Brooke, died on March 9, 1851, Longstreet resigned from his commissary post and returned to the Eighth Infantry.[53]

For the next three years, Longstreet performed scouting duties along the frontier. While Louise and the two boys remained in San Antonio, he led patrols throughout the Comanche territory, moving between Forts Chadburne, Mason, and Marion Scott, and Camp Johnston. Every chance he had, he returned to San Antonio and to his family. On April 19, 1853, Louise gave birth to their third son, William Dent Longstreet. Four months previously, on December 7, 1852, Longstreet had been promoted to captain of infantry in the regular army.[54]

In the late winter or early spring of 1854, Longstreet was ordered to the East Coast, probably as a special courier. While her parents remained in Santa Fe, New Mexico, where Brigadier General Garland commanded the Department of New Mexico, Louise and the boys accompanied Longstreet, traveling by ship from the Texas coast to New York City. From there they went to Washington, D.C., where their one-year-old son William became ill and died on July 19. In her grief, Louise composed a short eulogy, ending with the lines: "He gave thee, He took thee, and He will restore thee. For death has no sting since the Savior hath died." Immediately after the funeral, the parents returned to Texas, arriving at Fort Bliss on July 31.[55]

Fort Bliss was located three miles from El Paso, on the Rio Grande. A detachment of the First Dragoons had established a camp on the site in February 1848; the army designated it a military post in September 1849, with the arrival of six companies of the Third Infantry. A small fort, its adobe quarters had been built on three sides of a square. The alfalfa-covered parade ground, enclosed by an adobe wall, lay across the road from the quarters. Six hundred miles from San Antonio, Fort Bliss lay within the boundaries of the Department of New Mexico, which meant that Longstreet would be serving under the overall command of his father-in-law.[56]

When Longstreet reported at the end of July, four companies of the Eighth Infantry—B, E, I, and K—under Brevet Lieutenant Colonel Edmund B. Alexander manned the post. Alexander assigned Longstreet to the command of Company K, relieving First Lieutenant George E. Pickett, to whom Longstreet had handed the regimental flag when he fell wounded at Chapultepec. Longstreet had always liked Pickett, and their relationship deepened when Pickett served as Longstreet's immediate subordinate until the thirty-year-old Virginian was transferred to Washington Territory in June 1855.[57]

Like the other military posts in Texas, the garrison at Fort Bliss was responsible for protecting farmers, ranchers, and townsfolk from marauding Indians. In this section of the state, Mescalero Apaches raided the homesteads along the road from El Paso to San Antonio. The frequency of their strikes increased during the final months of 1854, forcing the army to react. On January 24, 1855, Longstreet and Captain Edmund B. Holloway, with Companies I and K, left Fort Bliss in search of the Mescaleros. Traveling eastward, Longstreet's column marched toward the Guadalupe Mountains, where it combined with a detachment of the Second Dragoons from Fort Davis, 250 miles to the southeast. The Indians killed Longstreet's civilian guide and eluded their pursuers. The entire operation lasted sixteen days, with the men suffering from ice storms and frigid temperatures.[58]

Longstreet assumed temporary command of the post on April 24 when Alexander was transferred to a new unit. Two months later Major John T. Sprague returned and remained until March 1856, when Captain John G. Walker reported with a company of mounted rifles and assumed command. Walker's captaincy predated Longstreet's, and the senior officer retained his position until October when Garland transferred his company. Longstreet then resumed command at Fort Bliss, holding it until the spring of 1858.[59]

Altogether, James and Louise Longstreet spent nearly four years at Fort Bliss. It was perhaps the happiest period of their lives in the antebellum army. Fort Bliss held many attractions for army personnel and their families. Because of the garrison's small size, the officers, enlisted personnel, and their families socialized together and with the predominantly Mexican villagers in El Paso. At post dances, American soldiers mixed easily with young señoritas. The Longstreets enjoyed the activities, with Louise at the center of the garrison's social life. In the summer, farmers supplied the troops with fresh vegetables and fruits, and the officers, including Longstreet, supplemented the meat supply by hunting the abundant game. Fort Bliss, remembered one officer's wife, was the "most delightful station we ever had."[60]

Fort Bliss's location also allowed Louise to visit her parents in Santa Fe; her father also traveled to the post on official business. The nearness of her parents meant much to Louise during this time.

On March 12, 1856, she gave birth to their fourth child and first daughter, Harriet Margaret Longstreet, but the infant died on August 30. The couple had lost their second child within two years. On July 8, 1857, while on a visit to Santa Fe, Louise bore their fifth child, a son, James Longstreet.[61]

Longstreet's concern for the education of his oldest children— nine-year-old Garland and seven-year-old Augustus (Gus)— prompted him to write to the adjutant general's office in Washington, D.C., on March 29, 1858, requesting an assignment to recruiting duty in the East, preferably in Philadelphia, Pennsylvania. For sixteen years, he stated, he had served on the frontier except for leaves and for a brief period of time in New York and Pennsylvania. He wanted a transfer to "have time, and opportunity for setting my children at some good school."[62]

His request for a six-month leave was granted, and he and the family left Fort Bliss in May. The Longstreets visited with his uncle Augustus and aunt Frances in Columbia, where Augustus served as president of the College of South Carolina. From there they journeyed northward, and while in New Jersey, Longstreet learned of his promotion to major and his appointment as a paymaster beginning July 19. He was directed to report to the paymaster general in Washington for orders. He placed Garland in a boys' school in Yonkers, New York, and then received his orders to report to Fort Leavenworth, Kansas.[63]

While en route to his new station, Longstreet stopped briefly in St. Louis, where he found some former army friends at the Planters' Hotel. They reminisced and decided to play brag, but they needed another player, so one of them left the hotel and returned a short time later with Sam Grant. Longstreet's good old friend had been out of the army for several years and was struggling as a farmer outside the city. Grant, Longstreet said years later, was "poorly dressed in citizen's clothes." The next day, before Longstreet departed, Grant came and handed him a five-dollar gold piece. While cadets at the academy, Longstreet had lent Grant five dollars. Longstreet refused to take it, but Grant insisted, saying, "You must take it. I cannot live with anything in my possession which is not mine." It would be a long time—and after a nation's debt had been paid —before the old comrades met again.[64]

Longstreet spent about a year at Fort Leavenworth. He traveled to the military posts in the department to pay the officers and men. In

October 1859, he was transferred to his father-in-law's department in New Mexico, with headquarters at Albuquerque. A month after the family's arrival there, he wrote to his uncle Augustus: "We are tollerably pleasantly situated out here, and indeed quite comfortable." He added that he would now be able to save money for the boys' education.[65]

The transfer to Albuquerque reunited Louise with her parents and the children with their grandparents. Unfortunately, this reunion did not last long because Harriet Garland fell ill. Her husband took a leave, and they traveled to the springs at Saratoga, New York. Here, after collapsing on a sidewalk, she died on August 30, 1860, and was buried at Oak Hill Cemetery in the Georgetown section of Washington, D.C. General Garland lived less than a year more and died in New York City on June 5, 1861. He was interred beside his wife. But the old veteran of nearly half a century's service lived long enough to witness the dissolution of the Union and the onset of civil war.[66]

With the election of Republican Abraham Lincoln in November 1860, the slide into secession and civil war was precipitated. South Carolina abandoned the Union in December, followed by six other Southern states during the next six weeks. In February 1861, delegates from the seceded states met in Montgomery, Alabama, and formed the Confederate States of America. For millions of Americans allegiance had a terrible new meaning.

Years later James Longstreet remembered the fall and winter of 1860–61 as a time of "painful suspense." Mail service to Albuquerque was irregular, arriving at four- to six-week intervals. Anxiety mounted to such a point that one of the officers or enlisted men stood for hours on the roof of the quartermaster's office—the highest building in the town—to watch for the mail coach. As the events unfolded in the East, the tension mounted until the next mail reached the army post with the news.[67]

For Longstreet the choice came early. When he learned of Lincoln's election, he decided that his allegiance belonged to the South. Although he did not embrace secession, in his mind perhaps he had little choice. He had learned the doctrine of states' rights early in life, had seen his uncle's passion for it, and to oppose that meant to reject the abiding views of a man he regarded as a father. He was a Southerner; his father-in-law's family was Southern. It was, as he said later, a difficult choice—one shared by many Southerners in the army—but he did not hesitate; in fact, he acted with surprising haste.[68]

In December, Longstreet wrote to the War Department to request an escort for him and his family from Albuquerque through Indian territory to San Antonio, Texas. He was concerned for Louise and the children's safety and comfort during travel, particularly because Louise was in the final weeks of another pregnancy. On December 31, 1860, she gave birth to a daughter, Mary Anne Longstreet. Now Louise and the infant would be unable to travel that distance for weeks, perhaps months. Regardless, the War Department, however, denied the request.[69]

About the same time he corresponded with a friend, Congressman J. L. M. Curry of Alabama, asking Curry to tender his services to the governor if the state seceded from the Union. Although born in South Carolina and raised in Georgia, he had received his appointment to West Point from Alabama, and his mother still lived there. He chose Alabama perhaps because of a sense of obligation and perhaps because of ambition. Longstreet was the senior officer in the army from that state who had graduated from the academy, and he could expect to receive a commensurate rank in the state's forces.[70]

When Longstreet received no reply from Curry, he wrote directly to Governor Andrew B. Moore on February 15, 1861. Longstreet stated that he assumed Alabama had seceded. (It had, on January 11, 1861.) He added: "I desire, therefore, to tender through you my services to her, should she need a soldier who has seen hard service. I am the senior officer of the Army, from Alabama, and should be the first to offer her such assistance in my profession as I may be able to render."[71]

In Alabama, meanwhile, Governor Moore had already endorsed Longstreet's letter to Curry, asking the congressman to deliver it to Confederate President Jefferson Davis. When Moore received Longstreet's second letter, he forwarded it to Confederate Secretary of War Leroy P. Walker. Furthermore, seven prominent men in Montgomery wrote to Davis on Longstreet's behalf, stating that "he is an officer of high character, of chivalric bearing, of unquestioned loyalty, patriotism, and courage." Finally, his brother William, after receiving a letter from James, wrote directly to Davis and offered his brother's services to the government "in any capacity that is within the scope of his profession."[72]

Weeks after he sent the letter to Moore, probably around April 1, with Louise and the children able to travel, Longstreet decided to resign his commission and leave Albuquerque for Alabama. About that time, however, two paymasters in the department resigned to join the Confederacy. Colonel William W. Loring, Longstreet's superior, ordered him to assume their duties and close their accounts. Longstreet complied, telling a friend, Bryan M. Thomas, who was leaving to join the Confederacy, to explain his delay to President Davis, adding, "I would rather have my right hand cut off than leave the service owing a cent." He did not undertake the assignment until the middle of April when the payroll arrived.[73]

By the end of the month, Longstreet had learned of the firing on and surrender of Fort Sumter in the harbor of Charleston, South Carolina, on April 12–14. As he recounted it in his memoirs, he made his decision known to his comrades. A group of Northern officers, led by Captain Alfred Gibbs, tried to persuade him to reconsider. In his retelling of it, Longstreet asked Gibbs "what course he would pursue if his State should pass ordinances of secession and call him to its defence." Gibbs, wrote Longstreet, "confessed that he would obey the call."[74]

On May 9, Longstreet submitted his letter of resignation: "I have the honor to tender my resignation as a Major and Paymaster in the Army of the United States." Loring endorsed it and forwarded it to the War Department three days later. On June 1, the department accepted the resignation. A government auditor, however, noted in a circular from the adjutant general's office that Longstreet had incurred an indebtedness of $116.60 during the fourth quarter of 1857 that had not been resolved. The matter was subsequently settled, and Longstreet left the service not "owing a cent."[75]

Longstreet secured a leave of absence and began the preparations for the long journey eastward with his family. A biography of him states that he could now leave the army "with a clear conscience." He had fulfilled his obligations, and his state had called him to its defense. He had waited to the very end, bound by duty, before he resigned "with a clear conscience" to embrace Alabama's cause. Such has been the version of Longstreet's final weeks and days in the army.

The Confederate Adjutant and Inspector General's records in the National Archives provide evidence of a different story, however, a dark story of a man who crossed the delicate line between honor and dishonor. According to the records, Confederate authorities in Montgomery, the secessionist nation's first capital, appointed Longstreet lieutenant colonel of infantry, to rank from March 16, 1861. The commission was confirmed on the same day and evidently forwarded to him in Albuquerque. He accepted the commission on May 1, eight days before he wrote his letter of resignation from the United States Army. As a U.S. Army officer, he accepted a commission in an enemy army. Furthermore, the records contain a voucher signed by Longstreet for $306 in pay as a Confederate lieutenant colonel for the period May 1 to June 24. In the column under "Remarks," Longstreet signed that he had accepted the appointment on May 1.[76]

For obvious reasons Longstreet never revealed this, nor did previous biographers discover it, but his subsequent actions lend additional validity to the records. When he left Texas for the East, he did not head for Alabama to receive a commission in that state's forces, as many other ex-army officers did in their native states before they entered Confederate service, but went directly to Richmond, Virginia, the new capital of the Confederacy. He did not go to answer Alabama's "call" but to answer the Confederacy's, with a commission in hand.

Why did Longstreet not immediately resign when informed of the Confederate offer of a lieutenant colonelcy? Since he never hinted about the commission, his reasons are difficult to explain. Possibly, he had not finished his assignment from Loring and felt compelled, as Bryan M. Thomas related, to settle all his accounts with the army. When he completed the task remains uncertain, but it was most likely during the first week of May. If that was so, why did he not simply wait until he had rectified the books and could resign before accepting the Confederate lieutenant colonelcy? What motivated him or how he justified it to himself remains a mystery; what he did, however, was not the act of an honorable man and officer.

Once he had accepted the Confederate commission and had resigned, all that was left for him and his family were the farewells from old friends. A soldier's trade had been his since he entered West Point in 1838. He had fought in a war, earned commendations, and suffered a serious wound. He had served as both a line and a staff officer, acquiring valuable combat and administrative experience. During those years, he and Louise had lived within the extended army family, amassing friendships. It was, as he wrote later, "a sad day when we took leave of lifetime comrades and gave up a service of twenty years." The Longstreets were not alone—sadness stalked a divided nation.[77]

MANASSAS

The United States Army ambulance bumped along the rutted road eastward out of Albuquerque. Inside rode Confederate Lieutenant Colonel James Longstreet, his wife, Louise, and three of their children. The route carried them past Fort Craig to Fort Fillmore, where they spent a night. At a gathering of old comrades, Longstreet was asked how long the war would last; he predicted that it would be at least three years. In his memoirs he claimed he learned at Fillmore that his resignation had been accepted, effective June 1. For several more days Longstreet could accept the hospitality and privileges accorded an army officer while he was secretly commissioned in the Confederate forces.[1]

From Fort Fillmore the family journeyed to El Paso and Fort Bliss, their former home for four pleasant years. Here Longstreet booked himself on a stagecoach to San Antonio and found lodging for Louise and the children with old friends. He did not want to leave them behind, to follow later on a train of freight wagons, but he believed he had to report to Richmond as soon as possible. With this settled, he said good-bye to his family and climbed into the coach of the San Antonio–San Diego stage line, not knowing when or if he would see them again.[2]

The six-hundred-mile trip through Indian country to San Antonio passed without incident except for finding the Eagle Springs station in charred ruins from a party of Mescalero Apaches. On board with Longstreet was a former colleague, George H. Giddings, superintendent of the stage line. Over a decade before, Giddings had joined Longstreet and his detachment of troops in the pursuit of Indian raiders. When the soldiers overtook the warriors, Longstreet's horse was killed in the fighting, pinning the officer to the ground. Giddings rode to Longstreet's assistance, firing his revolver at the Indians until Longstreet freed himself.[3]

From San Antonio, Longstreet continued on to Galveston to obtain passage on a ship to Louisiana. Leaving on June 10, Longstreet sailed on a fifteen-by-forty-foot "inland sailing craft." Sharing the small quarters with Longstreet were four Texans intent on joining the Confederate army: James A. Wharton, Thomas Lubbock, Frank Terry, and Thomas Jewett Goree. The passengers had plenty of time to converse, and Longstreet was particularly impressed with Goree, a twenty-six-year-old lawyer and native Alabamian whose family had settled in Texas over a decade before. Longstreet thought young Goree was "an intelligent, clever Texan."[4]

The trip along the Gulf coast took over four days. Three squalls lashed the schooner, and the captain sailed cautiously to avoid Union blockading ships. The schooner docked at Brashear City, Louisiana, at night on the 14th. Longstreet and the Texans started for New Orleans the next day, arriving on the 16th. A railroad train took the group through Mississippi and Alabama to Chattanooga, Tennessee, where they boarded the East Tennessee and Virginia Railroad for the final leg of their journey. As they passed through the mountains of East Tennessee, the residents, according to Goree, "looked sour, mean, and glum." These mountain folk never cared for the slaveholding planters of Middle Tennessee and were strongly unionist in sentiment. In less than three years Longstreet and Goree would learn how difficult it could be for Confederates in the rugged region.[5]

When the train crossed into Virginia, they noticed an immediate change in sentiment. The Old Dominion was aflame with war fever. Longstreet and the Texans could not pay for their meals when the train stopped at villages. An engagement had already been fought in the state, and volunteers from all over the South were racing toward Richmond to defend Virginia, win one decisive victory, and then return home as heroes. This was the type of man Longstreet had seen fight so well in Mexico with proper training and leadership. Longstreet was caught in the hurricane that was driving Americans, from both the North and the South, into destruction.[6]

Longstreet arrived at the Confederate capital on June 21. Since the authorities had decided to relocate to Richmond, the city on the James River had been overrun with bureaucrats, office seekers, contractors, and young men en route to war. On the day he arrived, according to his memoirs, Longstreet sought out the War Department offices to request assignment to the paymaster's department. "When I left the line service, under appointment as paymaster," he explained, "I had given up all aspirations of military honor, and thought to settle down into more peaceful pursuits." Either his memory failed him about his desire—he misdated his arrival, placing it on June 29—or he fabricated a story to cover his acceptance of a commission as a lieutenant colonel of infantry. Longstreet came to Richmond not to be a paymaster; he came for a line command that could give him "military honor." [7]

The Confederate lieutenant colonel most likely reported to the War Department. But on June 22, he and the Texans met with President Jefferson Davis at the Executive Mansion. Like Longstreet, Davis was a military man, a West Pointer who had left the army in the 1830s to grow cotton on his Mississippi plantation. During the Mexican War, Davis had served as colonel of the First Mississippi Volunteers in Zachary Taylor's army and earned fame while suffering a wound at the Battle of Buena Vista. He parlayed his military record into a political career as secretary of war in the Franklin Pierce administration and as a United States senator from his adopted state. When the South seceded, he reluctantly accepted the presidency. A proud, honorable man, Davis would labor tirelessly for the cause, while plagued by health problems and mounting criticism, for four years. But as Longstreet and others would learn, Davis never forgot friends and seldom forgave opponents. [8]

On this day the president welcomed Longstreet and the Texans; he needed men of Longstreet's training and experience and of the Texans' ardor for service. Details of the meeting are sketchy. Longstreet had promised his companions that he would use what influence he possessed to assist them in obtaining positions in the army and may have discussed this with Davis. The president informed Longstreet that he had been appointed a brigadier general on June 17, which he accepted on the 25th. [9]

Within days of his acceptance of his new rank, Longstreet was ordered to report to Brigadier General P. G. T. Beauregard at Manassas Junction in northern Virginia. Sometime around July 1, Long-

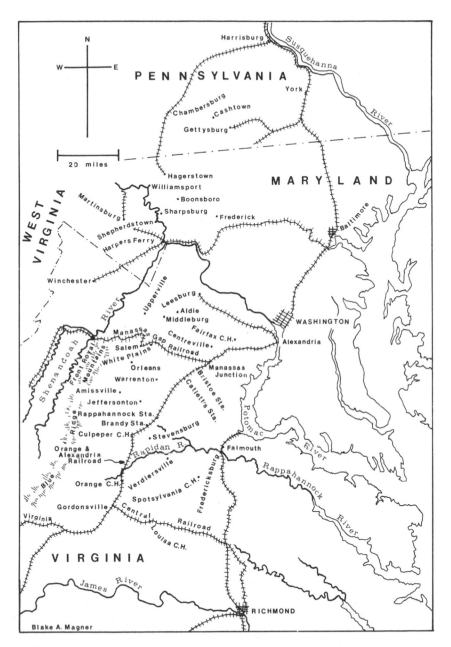

THEATER OF OPERATIONS: NORTHERN VIRGINIA, MARYLAND, AND
PENNSYLVANIA.

street, accompanied by the Texans, left Richmond by train for the front. They rode on the Virginia Central Railroad to Gordonsville, where they boarded a car of the Orange & Alexandria Railroad for Manassas Junction, arriving on July 2. The journey took them through the heart of central Virginia, through land that Longstreet would come to know well during the next four years.[10]

At the time Longstreet reported, the Confederate forces at Manassas Junction numbered roughly eighteen thousand, supported by twenty-nine cannon. It was the largest Southern army in the field, placed at the most critical location along the Confederacy's vast front. Lying twenty-five miles west of Washington, D.C., Manassas Junction guarded the gateway to interior Virginia, across the likely invasion route of Union forces advancing from Washington. The Orange & Alexandria Railroad funneled troops and supplies from the south, while the Manassas Gap Railroad hauled food and forage from the Shenandoah Valley, across the Blue Ridge Mountains to the west. A second Confederate army, under Brigadier General Joseph Johnston, held the lower or northern end of the Shenandoah Valley, barring Federal penetration into the fertile region. If the confrontation were to occur at Manassas Junction, as expected, part or all of Johnston's army could march to the support of Beauregard's men at the railroad junction.[11]

Beauregard's line extended for eight miles along the southern bank of Bull Run, three miles northeast of Manassas Junction. Bull Run was, said a Confederate officer, a "good sized" stream with numerous fords and wooded banks. The Southern battle line ran east to west from the so-called Stone Bridge on the north to Union Mills Ford on the south. Behind the creek, the terrain was rolling with hills and ridges that offered favorable defensive positions. It had been a placid place, home to farmers and tradesmen, made suddenly important by two railroads and men trained in warfare.[12]

The man responsible for the Confederate defenses in northern Virginia was Pierre Gustave Toutant Beauregard, a career soldier, and West Pointer, class of 1838, with a distinguished record in the Mexican War. He had commanded the Southern forces at Charleston, South Carolina, that accepted the surrender of Fort Sumter in April. When the fledgling nation craved a hero, Beauregard became its first. Promotion to brigadier general followed, and on June 2 he arrived at Manassas Junction as commander.[13]

A Louisianan of French descent, Beauregard was, a soldier wrote, "of rather small stature, smooth-faced, and with a swarthy complexion. He was quick-spoken and bright." A vain man, he dyed his hair black and carried himself with the assurance of a man who knew what he was about. Captain E. Porter Alexander, an engineer on Beauregard's staff at the time and a perceptive, extremely intelligent officer who would come to know most of the ranking generals in the East, remarked later that Beauregard "had more courtesy of manner than any of the other generals with whom I ever served." His manner and confidence made him popular with the volunteers, who called him "Old Bory."[14]

Beauregard commanded little more than an armed mob at Manassas Junction. Although the volunteers possessed a fervor for the cause and a passion for battle, they were inadequately armed and barely trained. The commanding general required capable officers, and when Longstreet reported, Beauregard surely welcomed him. Before long these men developed a respect and affection for each other. Longstreet had more of a rough edge about him than the suave Beauregard, but he had always been a reliable subordinate and a personable companion in the regular army. Self-confident in his own right, Longstreet could work well with superiors of similar temperament, offering his judgment and advice on military concerns. Beauregard was the first of four army commanders whom Longstreet would serve under during the war, and of that number, only one, Braxton Bragg, failed to earn his respect and friendship.

Four days after Longstreet's arrival, on July 6, he assumed command of a brigade of three Virginia regiments—First, Eleventh, and Seventeenth. The First Virginia was the state's oldest militia unit, organized in 1851 from individual companies in Richmond and the surrounding counties of Henrico and Chesterfield. Its colonel, Patrick T. Moore, was the son of a British diplomat who had settled in Richmond as a merchant and rose through the ranks of the unit to its commander. The Eleventh Virginia was comprised of volunteer companies from Campbell, Botetourt, Montgomery, Fauquier, Culpeper, and Rockbridge counties. Its colonel was thirty-year-old Samuel Garland, Jr., a cousin of Longstreet's wife. A graduate of the Virginia Military Institute, Garland had been an attorney in Lynchburg and captain of a local militia company when the war began. The Seventeenth Virginia had not traveled far when ordered to Manassas Junction. Men from the surrounding county of Prince William and nearby counties of Fairfax and Loudoun filled its ranks.

A Mexican War veteran, Montgomery D. Corse, a banker in Alexandria, served as its colonel. Because of the militia heritage of many of the companies in the regiments, the troops had some experience with military rules, discipline, and training.[15]

"Incessant drill," according to an artilleryman, marked the daily regimen in Beauregard's army. Longstreet implemented training on the day he took command of the brigade and drilled his units three times each day. The intricacies of regimental and brigade maneuvers tested the best of recruits and required time for the inexperienced volunteers to learn. Units in the Civil War had to march, maneuver, and fight as a whole in the confusion and carnage of a battle. A well-drilled regiment or brigade that could respond at command during combat might save the lives of its members and even alter the outcome of an engagement. The finest officers imposed discipline, demanded "incessant drill," and cared for the needs of the troops. From his first day in command outside Manassas Junction, Longstreet attended to all three, and within two weeks Tom Goree wrote his mother that Longstreet "is considered one of the best genls. in the army."[16]

Goree, who had remained with Longstreet at the latter's request, was a volunteer aide with the unofficial rank of captain. Goree ate at Longstreet's mess and informed his mother that the general "is very kind" to him. G. Moxley Sorrel, who would soon join the staff, later described Goree as "so careful, observing, and intelligent." Among the members that would eventually comprise the inner core of Longstreet's staff, no one earned more of Longstreet's affection than Goree.[17]

Goree typified the caliber of young men whom Longstreet would select for his staff. The general was an excellent judge of talent, seeking individuals of intelligence and perception who had organizational skills. He sought neither sycophants nor fools; men of keener intelligence than himself did not threaten Longstreet. Confidence in his own abilities allowed him to fashion a personal staff that became one of the finest, if not the finest, in the army during 1862 and 1863.

Longstreet made his first official appointment to the staff before he left Richmond for Manassas Junction. On June 26, a day after he accepted his brigadiership, he named Second Lieutenant Peyton T. Manning as ordnance officer. Manning was twenty-three years old, a native of Alabama but residing in Mississippi at the war's outbreak.

Longstreet may have known Manning or his parents before 1861, since his father, Dr. George Felix Manning, lived in Huntsville, Alabama, where Longstreet's mother resided, before relocating to Aberdeen, Mississippi. Young Manning had graduated from the Georgia Military Institute at Marietta in 1859. Upon graduation he hired on as a civil engineer with the New Orleans and Jackson Railroad, working for the company until March 1861 when he was commissioned a second lieutenant in the Confederate army.[18]

Physically, there was not much to Manning. His records listed him as five feet seven inches tall and weighing 125 pounds. Those who came to know him or to serve with him commonly described him as "little." One of his fellow staff officers believed that he could not have weighed over one hundred pounds. Despite his size, Manning impressed people. The superintendent of the institute wrote that he was "one of the best military students" in the school. An individual who recommended him for appointment in the Confederate service noted that he had a "quick, clear mind." And the "little" Mississippian possessed a mettle to his character. While a student at the school, he stabbed a fellow student in an altercation, severely wounding him. His actions must have been justified because he was not dismissed.[19]

After Longstreet's arrival at Manassas Junction, Beauregard assigned Lieutenant Frank Armistead to him as acting assistant adjutant general or chief of staff. Armistead, a graduate of West Point with a few years of service in the regular army, was a temporary appointment and left the staff at the end of the summer.[20]

Longstreet found the final two members of his initial staff in the army's camp. Thomas Walton, like Manning, was a native Alabamian who lived in Mississippi when the war began. A lawyer by profession, he was an acquaintance of Jefferson Davis and came to Virginia with the first contingent of Mississippi troops. Longstreet met him there and appointed him volunteer aide-de-camp with the rank of captain. The second appointment was that of Dr. J. S. D. "Dorsey" Cullen, a surgeon with the First Virginia. Longstreet assigned him as the brigade's medical director.[21]

Longstreet had little time for the organization of a staff and for the training of the troops. On July 16, ten days after Longstreet assumed command of the brigade, Beauregard learned through spies and scouts that the long anticipated Union advance from Washington had begun that day. Public pressure in the North from newspapers and politicians had been mounting for weeks, demanding "on to Richmond" before the Confederate Congress could meet in their capital. Citizens on both sides believed the war's outcome hung on one decisive battle. Driven by romantic illusions of warfare, Bull Run beckoned.[22]

The thirty-five thousand marching Federals greeted the orders with exuberance. A New Hampshire soldier asserted on the day before the movement that if the army did not move this time after previous disappointments, "there will be a mutiny in camp." Despite the high morale, the Northerners were little better prepared for the march than their Southern opponents. They lumbered westward like a huge beast slowed by its own bulk and inertia. By sunset on the 17th, the Federals had barely cleared Fairfax Court House, where they had found the abandoned lines of Beauregard's outpost.[23]

Beauregard reacted swiftly to the oncoming enemy. Only a few days previously he had sent Colonel James Chesnut to Richmond to request a concentration of Confederate forces at Manassas Junction, but President Davis rejected it. Now, with the Federals on the march, Beauregard wrote to Davis on the 17th: "The enemy has assailed my outposts in heavy force. Send forward any reinforcements at the earliest possible instant and by every possible means." The message stirred Davis; he directed five regiments to Beauregard and ordered Joseph Johnston in the Shenandoah Valley to march eastward if he could elude a Federal army at his front. The Confederates were in a race against time and the crawling Union army.[24]

The pace of the Federal march bothered the army commander, Brigadier General Irvin McDowell. A West Point classmate of Beauregard's, McDowell had watched patiently for two days as his raw troops and inexperienced officers lurched ahead, delayed by specters of Rebel defenders in front and by straggling in the ranks. His force was only one prong of a dual Federal movement. In the Shenandoah Valley, eighteen thousand Federals under Major General Robert Patterson, a sixty-nine-year-old fossil who had fought in the War of 1812 and the Mexican War, confronted Johnston's Confederates. If Patterson held Johnston in place as ordered, McDowell would have a numerical superiority over Beauregard.[25]

On the morning of July 18, the main body of McDowell's army pushed cautiously westward on the Warrenton Turnpike, the main road out of Washington, toward Centreville, a village three miles east of Bull Run. McDowell planned to turn the southern or right flank of the Confederate lines with a movement by a division across Occoquan Creek to the Orange & Alexandria Railroad southwest of the junction. When McDowell learned that the terrain and roads precluded such a maneuver, he redirected the division toward Centreville.[26]

The leading unit of McDowell's army, Brigadier General Daniel Tyler's division, entered the crossroads village of Centreville about 9:00 A.M. on the 18th. As the Federals filed in, they cheered. Around them they could see abandoned Rebel works and indications of a hasty retreat. McDowell had ordered Tyler to cover the roads toward Bull Run but not to ignite a fight. Soon after he arrived, Tyler sent Colonel Israel B. Richardson's brigade out on the Centreville-Manassas Junction road to sniff for Southerners. Sometime after ten o'clock Richardson's skirmishers cleared a woodlot into fields that overlooked Bull Run. To their right, the road descended toward Mitchell's Ford on the creek; to their front, a farm lane rolled over the fields to Blackburn's Ford. Tyler wanted to find some Rebels.[27]

The Rebels were not far away, on the southern bank of the creek, waiting. When Beauregard received the reports of McDowell's march on the 16th, he ordered his brigades to the positions along Bull Run. The stream posed no significant barrier to an attack force —infantry could cross along almost any section—but the fords and the Stone Bridge were the vital points. Six fords lay east of the Stone Bridge, and Beauregard posted his units to cover each one. Brigadier General Milledge Bonham's command, the army's largest brigade, advanced to Mitchell's; half a mile to the east, Longstreet's three regiments went into position at Blackburn's, and another half mile beyond Longstreet, Brigadier General David R. Jones's brigade held McLean's Ford. Farther downstream, the troops of Brigadier General Richard Ewell—the young officer who was impressed with the beauty of Louise and Bessie Garland many years before—anchored the Confederate right at Union Mills Ford.[28]

Blackburn's Ford lay at a northward bend or bow of Bull Run. The terrain at the shallows favored an attack force coming from the north. The distant ridge, where the farm lane branched off from the Centreville-Manassas road and where Tyler and Richardson were standing on the 18th, provided a natural platform for artillery that could command opposing cannon south of the stream. At the ford,

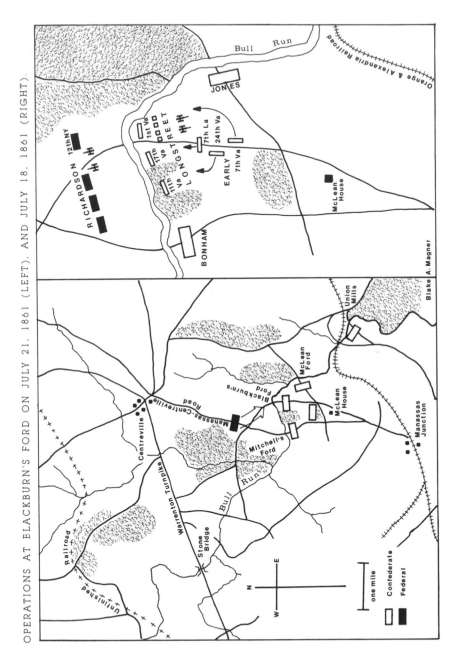

OPERATIONS AT BLACKBURN'S FORD ON JULY 21, 1861 (LEFT), AND JULY 18, 1861 (RIGHT).

Blake A. Magner

a fifteen-foot wooded bluff, lying east of the farm lane, jutted above the creek, dominating the opposite bank. From the creek, the fields north of the ford rose, as Longstreet wrote, in "a pretty ascending plain" to the ridge where Richardson's brigade formed. When he looked at the ground, Tyler was, in his word, "astonished" by the fact that the Confederates did not hold the ground north of the stream.[29]

By the morning of the 18th, Longstreet had only one company, deployed as skirmishers, on the north bank. Beauregard originally directed that Longstreet build fieldworks on the north bank, but the commanding general countermanded this on the 17th after the First Virginia spent the day at the work. When the Federals arrived on the ridge at the farm lane intersection, Longstreet's men had fashioned a line of modest works along the southern bank from logs, rails, driftwood, and dirt. The novice soldiers worked well, complaining only that they had to sleep on the ground without blankets.[30]

Longstreet covered the creek crossing with two of his regiments: The Seventeenth Virginia fronted the fields to the left of the farm lane; the First Virginia, the bluff on the right of the lane. He pulled four companies of the First Virginia out of the line, placing them to the rear as a reserve. Samuel Garland's Eleventh Virginia stretched their pickets westward to connect with Bonham's east of Mitchell's Ford. Garland had had a minor difficulty getting his men into position. When they were marching toward the creek on the 16th, dogs belonging to several men flushed a rabbit. The soldiers joined in the chase until Garland and the officers restored order; the colonel gave the exuberant men a "severe reprimand" for their foolishness. Longstreet had roughly twelve hundred men in line.[31]

Behind the infantrymen, a two-gun section of the Washington Artillery, under Lieutenant John J. Garnett, provided support. Farther to the rear, near the Wilmer McLean residence, Beauregard stationed the brigade of Colonel Jubal Early, whose troops were roughly within a mile of Mitchell's, Blackburn's, and McLean's fords. The commanding general used the McLean house as his headquarters and established a field hospital in the barn and stables. If the brigades at the three fords needed reinforcements, Beauregard could dispatch Early at once.[32]

For Longstreet's men the morning of the 18th seemed like a lifetime. After a breakfast of raw bacon and crackers—the supply wagons with the blankets and rations were far to the rear—they could only stay behind the works and wait. When the Federals appeared in the hazy distance about ten o'clock, the anticipation worsened. "A deathlike stillness prevailed for some time, which was intense and oppressive," W. H. Morgan of the Eleventh Virginia remembered. "All nerves were strung to a high tension." Longstreet was close at hand, sitting on a horse and chatting with Colonel Alexander R. Chisholm, a volunteer aide to Beauregard, and watching the Federals through an opera glass he had borrowed from Chisholm. He was among the few who understood a soldier's apprehension before a battle; he could only hope that his Virginians would stand the test when it came.[33]

Shortly after eleven o'clock, Union artillerymen shattered the "deathlike stillness" with loud cracks from two cannon. Morgan, the Virginian, never forgot the sound of the first shell as it arced toward the creek. The noise, he wrote, "was more like the neigh of an excited or frightened horse than anything I can compare it to; a kind of 'whicker, whicker, whicker' sound as it swapped ends in the air." When Longstreet heard the familiar discharge of the artillery, he jumped from his horse and moved toward his line, dropping and losing Chisholm's opera glass, which had been purchased years before in Paris, France. To his rear, as he had ordered, Garnett's gunners limbered the two brass cannon and withdrew toward the McLean house.[34]

The Federal artillery fire lasted for approximately thirty minutes and failed to disclose the strength of the Rebel position at Blackburn's. Daniel Tyler, over the opposition of two of McDowell's staff officers who were with the division commander, ordered the advance of three companies of the First Massachusetts, Lieutenant Colonel George D. Wells commanding. The Massachusetts men, dressed in gray uniforms, cleared the woods on the ridge, passed the artillerymen, and descended toward the creek, marching toward the wooded bluff above the First Virginia. A few of the Southerners could not endure the tension any longer and fired their muskets at the enemy. Longstreet remounted his horse and prepared for the collision.[35]

Before long, Wells's three companies passed over the crest of the wooded bluff. From the opposite creek bank, the Confederates triggered a volley up the slope; the "bullets," wrote one of the Federals, "screamed over our heads like a hornets nest." Wells shouted the charge, and his men plunged down the bluff, firing as they advanced. "The first pouring-down volleys were most startling to the new troops," Longstreet stated. Numbers of the Virginians broke to the rear; the others wavered, torn between duty and a novel fear. Within minutes Longstreet was among his men, a cigar in his mouth, a saber in his hands, "amid a perfect shower of balls," rallying them. His response and presence stabilized the line, and the Virginians repulsed the attack. The Massachusetts soldiers scrambled back up the bluff and lay down behind the crest to continue the fight.[36]

Wells's effort revealed little of the Confederate strength in Tyler's view. The Union general was a determined man on this day, so he ordered two cannon forward to within five hundred yards of the creek. The Union gunners rammed charges of canister—one-inch iron balls packed in sawdust-filled cans—into the muzzles and fired. A blizzard of iron howled above the heads of the Virginians, slicing off branches and felling limbs of trees. Tyler, meanwhile, at Richardson's recommendation, decided to advance with the latter's entire brigade. It took most of an hour from the repulse of Wells until Richardson's command—soldiers from Massachusetts, Michigan, and New York—went forward.[37]

When Richardson's Federals closed to within range, Longstreet's line exploded in musketry. The Northerners replied, pressing ahead. The gunfire fused into a sheet of unending noise. Tom Goree thought it was incessant for uncounted minutes. A member of the Seventeenth Virginia said, "It was no longer volleys rattling up and down the bank, but a roar, not a dull sound, but precisely like the crackling of the woods when a forest was on fire." Longstreet hurried his reserve companies forward to the bank while dispatching a staff officer to Jubal Early with a request for support. Amid the fury, Longstreet seemed everywhere along the line. One of the Virginians asserted in a letter home that the general was "a good soldier and brave man and won the hearts of the men on all sides."[38]

The Confederates believed afterward that they had repulsed three separate charges by Richardson's brigade, but they were mistaken. The combat possessed an ebb and flow of its own, as the Yankees briefly retired, regrouped, and came on again. Parts of the Union line lay on the ground under the waves of musketry. On each side, individuals and small clusters of men filtered to the rear, drained of courage and the romantic notions of warfare. With each renewal of Union pressure, more Virginians headed for safety in the rear. Although Longstreet's line refused to snap, it was stretched to the limit.[39]

Support for the Virginians, however, was approaching on the farm lane from the McLean house. When Jubal Early received Longstreet's request for assistance, he started forward with his brigade of three regiments. Beauregard also ordered seven cannon of the Washington Artillery in with Early. According to Longstreet's recollection, the commanding general became irritated when a Federal shell plowed through the log summer kitchen of the McLean residence, disturbing his dinner.[40]

The Seventh Louisiana led Early's column, followed by a section of cannon. The Louisianans rapidly formed into a battle line and advanced toward the ford on both sides of the farm lane. The artillerymen wheeled to the right of the lane and unlimbered their pieces. Five additional cannon soon rolled into position, and First Lieutenant Charles H. Squires spurred his horse ahead to find Longstreet. The brigadier "was a heavy man with a large head," wrote Squires. "He was of light complexion." The artillery lieutenant asked for orders. "Advance your guns," replied Longstreet. The Washington Artillery was a proud, old militia command from Louisiana whose service with Longstreet had just begun in the fields south of Bull Run. Before the fighting ended on this day, the gunners fired 310 rounds.[41]

Close behind the Louisiana infantrymen and artillerymen came Early's final two regiments—the Seventh and Twenty-fourth Virginia. The Twenty-fourth Virginia veered to the left, spilling across the field toward Garland's Eleventh Virginia. As the companies shifted into line, one of the captains shouted, "Load in nine times —load!" Early overheard the order and piped in his falsetto voice, "Load in nine times? Hell and damnation! Load in the most expeditious manner possible."[42]

The Seventh Virginia, meanwhile, filed to the right, behind the First Virginia. Longstreet oversaw the regiment's deployment, riding his bay horse in front of the ranks. Before he could clear the Seventh's front, its officers prepared to fire. Longstreet dove from the saddle to the ground, where he lay flat as the regiment's volley passed over him. The Virginians somehow missed his horse, which bolted away. For a moment the men thought that Longstreet had been killed. But he stood up, and if he had any words for the unit's commander, they were unrecorded. On few battlefields of the war would he come so close to death or maiming.[43]

The addition of Early's troops secured Longstreet's line. When the Twelfth New York, on Richardson's left, splintered apart under the increased volume of Confederate fire, the Federal line buckled. Seeing the opportunity, Longstreet ran to the creek, shouting an order to counterattack across the ford. Members of the First and Seventeenth Virginia heard the command—perhaps two companies in all—and in the words of one of them, "like a pack of hounds after a fox, we got across." The sight of the oncoming Rebels finished it for Richardson's troops. Tyler had already ordered a withdrawal, and the Northerners retired under fire. The Virginians soon pulled back to the south bank. Artillerymen on both sides continued their duel, but because of the smoke, the crews could not see much and inflicted little damage on each other. Sporadic fire flashed and crackled until darkness.[44]

During the night, Early's regiments replaced Longstreet's at the ford. Longstreet marched his troops to a stand of pines near the McLean farm where they bivouacked. The day's work had cost them sixty-eight casualties; the Federals lost eighty-three killed and wounded. The smallness of the losses, despite the heavy volume of fire during portions of the engagement, indicated the poor marksmanship of the opponents. Inexperienced troops had a tendency to aim high, and this evidently occurred at Blackburn's Ford. Time and combat corrected this habit.[45]

Beauregard praised the conduct of Longstreet and his men at Blackburn's Ford. In his report of the engagement, Beauregard stated of Longstreet that "by his presence at the right place at the right moment among his men, by the exhibition of characteristic coolness, and by his words of encouragement to the men of his command, he infused a confidence and spirit that contributed largely to the success of our arms on that day." Echoing Beauregard's assessment, Jubal Early reported that when he joined Longstreet on the field, the latter "was actively engaged in the thickest of the fire in directing and encouraging the men under his command, and I am satisfied he contributed very largely to the repulse of the enemy by his own personal exertions." Both generals commended the Virginians and the gun crews of the Washington Artillery.[46]

In his brief report of the engagement, Longstreet cited the "great gallantry" of his troops and the performance of his officers, who "seemed to spring in a body to my assistance at the only critical moment." He added that his staff officers "under a terrific fire . . . seemed to take peculiar delight in having occasion to show those around them their great confidence in our cause and our success."[47]

In a private letter to his uncle Augustus, written nearly four weeks after the fight, Longstreet boasted that his brigade fought alone "because I did not need help." Since his command acted on the defensive, he claimed, "I felt able to hold my position against any force that could be brought against me." His words were certainly self-congratulatory and somewhat inaccurate.[48]

Despite this effusive assessment, Longstreet had demonstrated evident ability. He had prepared well, had his men build fieldworks, and had placed a reserve force that could quickly move to any portion of the line. Once the combat began, he handled the fluid conditions with skill, encouraging his novice soldiers by his presence among them. Longstreet possessed a talent for tactics, for recognizing the changing landscape of a battlefield, and for reacting. Although Tom Goree bubbled with praise for the general, perhaps he came close to the truth when he wrote home: "Gen. Longstreet deserves all the credit."[49]

At the McLean house on the night of the 18th, Beauregard plotted a grand offensive plan. He had learned earlier in the day, in a letter from Jefferson Davis, that Johnston was en route to Manassas Junction. Surmising that Johnston would march overland and arrive on the 20th, Beauregard planned to trap the Federal army in a vise between the two Confederate forces, with Johnston crushing McDowell's right flank while Beauregard assailed his front. Beauregard consequently sent Colonel Alexander Chisholm in search of Johnston to deliver the plan. But Chisholm rode all night and passed through Thoroughfare Gap in the Bull Run Mountains before returning at six o'clock on the morning of the 19th, having covered thirty-five miles without finding Johnston.[50]

Several hours after Chisholm's return, Beauregard gathered his brigade commanders at headquarters for a conference. Longstreet, Ewell, Bonham, Early, Jones, and Colonel Joseph Kershaw met with Beauregard, sitting in the yard under some trees while their staff officers lay on the grass, talking quietly and smoking their pipes. As the generals conferred, Brigadier General Thomas J. Jackson rode up to the farmhouse. Jackson commanded a brigade in Johnston's army and had recently arrived at Manassas Junction with his five Virginia regiments. He and his men had come by train on the Manassas Gap Railroad from Piedmont Station, just east of Ashby's Gap. Jackson's appearance surprised Beauregard, who had expected Johnston's troops to pass through Thoroughfare Gap. Jackson explained that Johnston had decided to expedite his march by utilizing the railroads and that the other brigades would arrive as soon as the single train could return to Piedmont Station. Beauregard remained unconvinced.[51]

Jackson was right, however. Throughout the 20th, the railroad engine and cars rattled back and forth the thirty-five miles between the stations, bringing the brigades of Colonel Francis Bartow and Brigadier General Barnard E. Bee. About noon, Joseph Johnston arrived at the McLean farm. Johnston had executed a brilliant march and had so baffled Union General Robert Patterson that the latter retreated instead of advancing as ordered from Washington. Patterson would be relieved of command on July 22.[52]

Johnston was fifty-four years old, a Virginian, a member of the West Point class of 1829 with Robert E. Lee, and a career soldier who had been quartermaster general of the army until his resignation in April 1861. Commissioned a brigadier general in the Confederate army a month later, Johnston was senior to Beauregard, and when he arrived at the McLean house, he assumed command of the combined Confederate forces. Johnston deferred to Beauregard's knowledge of the terrain, however, and instructed Beauregard to prepare a written battle plan while he snatched several hours of sleep.[53]

While Johnston rested, Beauregard learned that the bulk of the Federal army was massed along the Warrenton Turnpike between Centreville and the Stone Bridge. From that position the Northerners threatened Beauregard's weak left flank, but instead of strengthening that sector of his line, he decided to attack McDowell's army with his units on his right. Milledge Bonham's and Francis Barlow's brigades would cross at Mitchell's Ford and push along the Centreville-Manassas road. To their right the brigades of Longstreet, Jones, and Ewell would cross at the lower fords and cover the right of Bonham and Barlow. Jackson's brigade would support Longstreet, and Colonel Philip St. George Cocke's Virginia command would protect the left of the attack force. Beauregard presented the plan to Johnston at four o'clock on the morning of the 21st. Worried about the weakness of the Confederate left, Johnston altered the arrangement of brigades by holding Cocke in place and sending Jackson and Barnard Bee toward that flank. With that resolved, Beauregard issued the orders to the brigade commanders.[54]

In Centreville, meanwhile, Union General Irvin McDowell had been fashioning a remarkably similar offensive scheme. For the past two days McDowell's chief engineer, Major George Barnard, had been searching for crossings of Bull Run beyond the Confederate left flank. Barnard located a passage at Sudley Ford, two miles beyond the Stone Bridge, and McDowell held a council of war with his division commanders on the night of the 20th. While Tyler's division feinted against Mitchell's and Blackburn's fords, two divisions—thirteen thousand troops supported by five batteries—would follow a route designated by Barnard toward Sudley Ford. One division would cross there and advance southward, clearing Poplar Ford, a mile downstream, and permitting the second division to move on its left toward the Warrenton Turnpike. When the attack force seized the turnpike, Tyler's division would cross at the Stone Bridge and join in the assault. It was a complicated maneuver that required much of inexperienced officers and raw troops.[55]

Sunday, July 21, dawned clear and hot—an ordinary summer day for the extraordinary christening of a divided nation. Neither McDowell's nor Beauregard's plan developed as intended. The Federal flanking column was hours behind schedule; Beauregard's orders to attack on his right never reached Richard Ewell, whose brigade at Union Mills Ford was to initiate the movement. Consequently, despite the delays, the Union troops gained the initiative and ignited the battle on the ground between Sudley Ford and the Warrenton Turnpike, at about 10:30 A.M. For the next six hours the combat caromed across the rolling countryside. The opponents were equally matched, but by fighting on the defensive, the Confederates held a clear advantage. Union attacks slammed into Confederate counterattacks. On Henry Hill in the center of the battlefield, Jackson's brigade of Virginians stood for over two hours, earning its commander his famous sobriquet, "Stonewall." Late in the afternoon, the final contingents of Johnston's army reached the field, sealed the Southern victory, and initiated a Union rout.[56]

Throughout the day Longstreet and his troops heard the sounds of struggle to the left and rear from their position at Blackburn's Ford. Longstreet and D. R. Jones, whose brigade held McLean's Ford, upstream from Blackburn's, had received the orders from Beauregard and advanced their brigades across the creek minutes after seven o'clock. Longstreet deployed his four regiments into two lines—the Fifth North Carolina had been sent to him as reinforcements—pushing them through the field where putrefying Union dead still lay from the fight on the 18th. A Union battery on the ridge to the north opened fire. The Confederates halted, lay down, and endured the artillery bursts for nearly an hour.[57]

Sometime between eight and nine o'clock Frank Terry and Thomas Lubbock, the Texans who had traveled to Manassas with Longstreet and were serving as volunteer aides, cantered up to Longstreet. He had sent them earlier on a reconnaissance toward Centreville, and now they reported that enemy columns were marching toward the Confederate left flank. Longstreet dispatched a courier with the news to headquarters and withdrew the brigade to the south bank.[58]

His men refiled into their works at the ford and with their officers passed the morning relaxing and talking. About noon, Longstreet sent Terry and Lubbock for a second time toward Centreville. Returning an hour or so later, the pair delivered a sketch of the Union position along the Centreville-Manassas road. Longstreet forwarded it to headquarters with the suggestion that his and the brigades on the army's right attempt to capture the position. It took another hour or so before army headquarters replied, approving Longstreet's proposal. He stirred his brigade and reforded the stream. Here Longstreet halted to await the advance of Jones from McLean's. But that officer never received the order, and before long, in Longstreet's words, a "peculiar order" arrived from headquarters to hold his position "*only*."[59]

Earlier that morning, before Longstreet crossed the creek for the first time, Moxley Sorrel rode into the general's camp at Blackburn's Ford. Longstreet had asked Beauregard for additional staff officers, and Sorrel arrived with a three-line note of introduction from Colonel Thomas Jordan, Beauregard's chief of staff. Sorrel was a twenty-three-year-old South Carolinian who had worked as a bank clerk in Savannah before deciding to join the Confederate cause. He was a tall, slender, graceful young man with dark eyes and a friendly disposition. Longstreet welcomed him and appointed him to the honorary rank of captain.[60]

In time Sorrel would become Longstreet's chief of staff and eventually write a valuable memoir of his years in the Confederate army. In that work he described Longstreet as he recalled him on this July Sunday. The brigadier, wrote Sorrel, was

> a most striking figure, about forty years of age, a soldier every inch, and very handsome, tall and well proportioned, strong and active, a superb horseman and with an unsurpassed soldierly bearing, his features and expression fairly matched; eyes, glint steel blue, deep and piercing; a full brown beard, head well shaped and poised. The worst feature was the mouth, rather coarse; it was partly hidden, however, by his ample beard.[61]

But before the day ended, Sorrel witnessed the temper of Longstreet, an anger fueled by frustration. Between 5:00 and 6:00 P.M. a courier splashed across the ford with orders from Johnston for Longstreet to join Milledge Bonham in a pursuit of the routed Union army. Longstreet obeyed at once, starting forward with a section of artillery and the First, Eleventh, Seventeenth and Twenty-fourth Virginia, the latter regiment having reported to him during the afternoon. The Fifth North Carolina remained at the ford, guarding the crossing.[62]

Longstreet's Virginians met Bonham's brigade, coming from Mitchell's Ford, near where the farm lane intersected with the Centreville-Manassas road. Bonham outranked Longstreet, and he ordered the subordinate to deploy his brigade on the right into a woodland. Before long, Terry and Lubbock reported in from another reconnaissance, pointing out the location of a Federal battery. The Union gunners had also seen the oncoming infantry and began shelling the trees. The artillery fire seemingly drained the ardor from Bonham, who halted his brigade and ordered a retreat. Longstreet, with Terry and Lubbock, rode toward the forty-seven-year-old former congressman from South Carolina. Longstreet asked for permission to charge the battery, but Bonham refused, saying: "We must go back, that a glorious victory might [not] be turned into a terrible disaster."[63]

Longstreet argued with Bonham, asserting that his brigade could capture the battery without the loss of a man, reach Centreville, and pursue all the way to Washington. But as the two generals exchanged words, Major William H. C. ("Chase") Whiting of Johnston's staff rode up with the report that the enemy was turning the Confederate right flank, and with orders to retreat. Longstreet exploded, denouncing the intelligence as "absurd," and in Sorrel's retelling, he fumed "in a fine rage. He dashed his hat furiously to the ground, stamped, and bitter words escaped him." He said: "Retreat! Hell, the Federal army has broken to pieces."[64]

Although he halted his brigade, Longstreet did not cool down until after he had eaten supper and received a second order to withdraw. Longstreet's instincts had been correct; his and Bonham's brigades could have inflicted additional damage on the beaten Federals. E. Porter Alexander of the army's staff concurred with Longstreet's assessment, writing afterward that "in fact the battle was treated as over as soon as the Federals retreated across Bull Run. It should have been considered as just beginning—our part of it." But in defense of Beauregard and Johnston, a pursuit by an inexperienced army was a difficult undertaking. Nevertheless, Bonham and Longstreet were in striking distance before their recall. That night, as the brigade pulled back, the Eleventh Virginia gave Longstreet three cheers. They appreciated the mettle of the man.[65]

Bonham, at least, had one thing right—First Manassas or Bull Run had been "a glorious victory" for the Confederates. The morale of the Southern army soared as a result. That night Johnston told Porter Alexander of "his unqualified admiration and surprise at the way our raw troops had behaved." Luck and faulty Union tactics contributed to the victory, but the Southern volunteers had fought valiantly, as did many in the Federal ranks. Confederate casualties amounted to 363 killed, 1,465 wounded, and 12 missing. Union losses totaled 482 killed, 1,126 wounded, and 1,836 missing. It was a modest bill compared to what lay ahead.[66]

On Monday, July 22, rain fell, in downpours at times. Confederate units, including Sam Garland's Eleventh Virginia, scoured the battlefield for discarded arms and matériel. Surgeons worked for hours in the makeshift hospitals as more wounded were located among the trees and grain. The rain helped with the cleansing of the now-hallowed ground. More such work and more verdant fields turned bloody awaited.[67]

4

GENERALS

Ten days after the Confederate victory at First Manassas, Captain E. Porter Alexander wrote to his wife: "Our whole Army is nearly disorganized now for any offensive movements, by overcrowding transportation since the arrival of Johnston, & the disgraceful mismanagement of the railroads in bringing on supplies." Hopes of a glorious march against Washington in the wake of the Union rout vanished almost at the outset. Critics in Richmond and other distant cities may have clamored for action, but the victors were as incapacitated as the vanquished.[1]

Alexander's words only touched on the difficulties within the army. Southern troops began scavenging for food within hours after the battle, with many of them crossing Bull Run and rummaging through abandoned enemy campsites near Centreville. One Georgia soldier asserted that he and his comrades were "literally starved out" at Manassas by July 23, two days after the battle. Advanced contingents of the army occupied Fairfax Court House within a week of the engagement, as much to gather supplies left by the Federals as to shove Confederate lines toward the Northern capital.[2]

Of even greater portent to the Southern army were epidemics of measles and typhoid that swept through the ranks. One officer said that "a deadly fever raged in the camp." It began soon after the battle of First Manassas and stalked the camps into September. Brigades seemed to average four hundred to five hundred absent due to the illnesses, with some units reduced by as much as fifteen hundred men. The troops ate what was available from the supply officers or from local farmers' fields, which compounded the sickness with rampant diarrhea. By the time the scourge ended, hundreds of youthful Confederates were dead.[3]

The sicknesses even felled the robust Longstreet. During the final week of July, he was confined to a house in Centreville because of an unspecified illness. He directed the activities of his brigade, but was so weak physically that he could not leave his quarters. The illness evidently lasted less than a week, and by August 2 or 3 he resumed all of his duties.[4]

Longstreet's brigade now consisted of four Virginia regiments as a result of a reorganization of the army shortly after the battle. He retained command of the original three regiments—the First, Eleventh, and Seventeenth—and was given the Seventh Virginia, Colonel James L. Kemper commanding. Kemper was thirty-eight years old, a veteran of the Mexican War, an attorney, and a former member of the Virginia legislature. Eventually, Kemper would assume command of the brigade and lead it in its most famous operation. Samuel Garland and Montgomery Corse still commanded the Eleventh and Seventeenth Virginia, respectively, while Lieutenant Colonel William H. Fry led the First Virginia, replacing Colonel Patrick Moore, who had been severely wounded at Blackburn's Ford.[5]

While at Centreville, Longstreet reinstituted brigade drill for his command. Although a soldier in the Eleventh Virginia later claimed that the drilling "did not amount to much," contemporary evidence indicated otherwise. Staff officer Thomas Goree wrote home that the unit was the "best brigade" in the army in organization and drill. When Longstreet wanted to conduct a formal drill and review, he followed a specific format. The brigade's standard bearer was placed at a designated spot in a field, then Longstreet and his staff rode to the flag, wheeled into position behind it, and waited for the brigade to pass. The band of the First Virginia, composed of approximately two dozen drummers and brass horn players, led the procession. Goree said that the bandsmen played "the most splendid music I ever listened to." Behind them came the four regiments, with each officer saluting as he passed the colors and Longstreet. A crowd always gathered for the ceremony.[6]

On August 8, the brigade participated in a grand review ordered by P. G. T. Beauregard in honor of Prince Jerome Napoleon, cousin of Napoleon III of France. The prince had come from Washington, passing through each army's lines, to visit the Confederates. He was not, said a Southerner, "an impressive man." An artilleryman described him as the "corpulent and serene Highness," while an infantryman who saw him as he passed in review thought that he "looked like a fat, jolly fellow" who "had on a black suit, white vest, and wore a straw hat." [7]

Two days after the review, on the 10th, Longstreet's brigade marched from Centreville to Fairfax Court House. It was only ten miles, but the day was intensely hot. A veteran of the First Virginia argued: "I suffered more than I did years afterwards on the whole march" to Gettysburg. When the Virginians arrived at Fairfax Court House, they began establishing a campsite, soon named Camp Harrison, south of the village. Longstreet placed his headquarters in a "nice, commodious house" in town.[8]

Longstreet's advance to Fairfax Court House to relieve another brigade was part of a general movement ordered by Beauregard. Altogether, eight brigades moved or would soon move eastward from Centreville toward the Union lines west of Washington. Beauregard, as he told Joseph Johnston, had directed the movement "to prevent a *coup de main*" or surprise attack by the Federals. By holding these positions, Beauregard argued, the Confederates could readily concentrate for offensive or defensive operations.[9]

The enemy, however, was content to remain behind its fortifications and eighty-eight cannon on the Virginia side of the Potomac River. The Federals, in fact, were undergoing a major reorganization under a new commander. In the aftermath of the Manassas debacle, President Abraham Lincoln had summoned Major General George B. McClellan to the capital to assume command of the army. McClellan, a thirty-four-year-old West Pointer with a brilliant antebellum record, had directed a successful campaign in western Virginia culminating in a victory at Rich Mountain on July 11. Although Longstreet's old academy roommate and tutor, William S. Rosecrans, now a brigadier general, directed the fighting on the field at Rich Mountain, McClellan, as overall commander, received the acclaim of the Northern press and populace. When Irvin McDowell lost at Manassas, Lincoln chose the North's new hero.[10]

Arriving on July 26, McClellan was viewed as the savior of the endangered Union. Such adulation suited him, for he was neither modest nor unconfident. He had a messianic view of himself, a belief that he was predestined to command and to save the Republic. He was, however, a gifted organizer and set to work at once to restore morale, institute a rigorous training program, and meet the army's logistical needs. He believed that the army required thousands of additional troops and time. A cautious general, prone to exaggerations of enemy strength, McClellan, despite pressure from the administration, refused to move until ready. The result was a stalemate in northern Virginia that stretched through the winter of 1862.[11]

The killing ground during this period of strategic inertia embraced the countryside between the Southern lines, centered at Fairfax Court House, and the Northern defenses beyond Alexandria, Virginia. Daily directions of the Confederate operations in the area fell upon Longstreet during the latter weeks of August and through much of September. At one point he had authority over the movements of seven infantry brigades, including his own, and the cavalry.[12]

Longstreet's primary responsibility was to ensure against a surprise attack feared by Beauregard by maintaining a constant vigilance and by gathering intelligence information. He accomplished this with a mixture of caution and aggressiveness and of the routine and the creative. Each day Frank Terry and Tom Lubbock, the Texas scouts, went forth on reconnaissance missions, returning at night with an occasional Federal captive. Likewise, pickets at the advanced outposts probed enemy screens, sparking almost daily firefights. Longstreet kept fresh troops in front by rotating infantry companies every two or three days. He garrisoned critical points along his lines with a regiment or even a brigade. The cavalry roamed along the flanks, snaring Union troops and providing early warning of enemy movements.[13]

During the final week of August, Longstreet extended his lines toward the capital, occupying key heights in the vicinity of Annandale on the Little River Turnpike and Falls Church on the Leesburg-Alexandria turnpike. On Mason's Hill, two miles northeast of Annandale, and on Munson's Hill, two miles east of Falls Church, the Confederates built signal stations. The occupation of these two hills brought the Rebels close enough so that from Mason's Hill Porter Alexander counted windowpanes in Washington and, from Munson's, signalmen viewed the Capitol dome and the church spires in Georgetown. Furthermore, each night two officers from the Hampton Legion, including at times its commander, Colonel Wade Hampton, crossed the Potomac River and relayed signals to the station at Munson's. In September, Longstreet reported to army headquarters that "the Balloon is up," indicating that at this early stage the Confederates were using hot-air balloons as observation platforms.[14]

Longstreet's duties included a plethora of administrative tasks that consumed hours of his time each day. He complained frequently to headquarters about the lack of rations for the troops, describing it as "exceedingly annoying." When he did not receive a map of the area, he detailed George N. Wise, a staff officer of the Seventeenth Virginia, to study the topography and road network for a map. The epidemics that began after First Manassas worsened during August, reducing regimental strengths and weakening the picket lines along the front. He kept his staff officers busy, but as he informed headquarters, he had to oversee every detail because they "are all fresh."[15]

The inexperience of Longstreet's staff reflected the youthfulness of its members and the change in personnel after the battle. Peyton Manning, the military school graduate, settled in as the ordnance officer. If he had a weakness, it was his fondness for fast horses that he rode across the countryside, risking life and limb by jumping ditches and fences with abandon. But no other member of the staff had the education and training Manning possessed.[16]

Frank Armistead stayed on until September when Longstreet selected Moxley Sorrel to replace him as assistant adjutant general or chief of staff, with the rank of captain. Longstreet liked the South Carolinian from his appearance on the morning of battle on July 21. Sorrel was a perceptive man with administrative skill. A staff officer from another brigade described him as "a very gallant officer and polished gentleman." Sorrel also possessed a temper that ignited when matters did not suit him, and he could be demanding if not overbearing with those he disliked or who displeased him. But Longstreet had chosen well: Sorrel developed into a excellent chief of staff, one of the finest in the army.[17]

Longstreet also retained another volunteer aide at Manassas, Thomas Walton, the Mississippi attorney. Walton, a difficult man to like, had an explosive temper that could be triggered by minor incidents. Sorrel thought "he could be dangerous at times, and only the greatest firmness held him in check until the humor passed off and then he was all lovely." A proud, even haughty individual,

Walton treated others with scorn. Longstreet probably kept him as a favor to his kinsman, L. Q. C. Lamar, who had been a professor of mathematics at the University of Mississippi before embarking on a political career. Walton had been one of Lamar's finest students, and Sorrel admitted he had "uncommon intellectual attainments." Walton served as an aide-de-camp, but never seemed to be among the inner group on the staff.[18]

Sometime in August, John W. Fairfax reported to Longstreet's headquarters. Fairfax, a tall, middle-aged man, was one of the wealthiest individuals in northern Virginia. He owned "Oak Hill," the plantation of President James Monroe, located ten miles south of Leesburg. The Fairfaxes had been in the Old Dominion since the 1600s and had amassed huge amounts of land. Although he had opposed secession, John Fairfax decided to enlist in the Confederate army and offered his services as a volunteer staff officer.[19]

Why Fairfax sought Longstreet is uncertain, but the latter assigned him as a volunteer aide-de-camp with the honorary rank of captain. It was not long before the "courtly and rather impressive" Virginian was one of the most popular members of the staff. Fairfax was a character and had a zest for the "good things" in life. Sorrel wrote that Fairfax "lacked nothing in courage; was brave and would go anywhere. But Fairfax had two distinctions—he was the most pious of churchmen and was a born bon vivant."[20]

Wherever Fairfax went and despite the rigors of campaigns, he carried his Bible, an ample supply of liquor, and a bathtub "in the shape of a tin hat." Each morning when duty permitted, Fairfax bathed in the tub, reading his Bible and nipping at a bottle of whiskey before breakfast. He kept the book and the bottle in the pockets of a linen "housewife" or sock that seemingly never left his presence. "Sunday," according to a staff member, "was his maudlin day. He would lay down with his bottle and his Bible beside him."[21]

Fairfax soon viewed his duty as attending to the personal needs of Longstreet. He took control of the headquarters mess and worked minor miracles with the variety and quality of the meals. The supply of whiskey never ceased. Whatever Longstreet required or wanted, Fairfax managed, including new horses. The Virginian had a sandy complexion and blue eyes and stood six feet tall, resembling Longstreet in appearance. He was "very much given to show," and in time he enjoyed nothing better than to be mistaken for Longstreet when they arrived at a new location. When a battle beckoned, however, Fairfax dispensed with the mess duties and was "always in front when danger pressed."[22]

Like Fairfax, Tom Goree still served as a volunteer aide with the honorary rank of captain. The Texan's admiration and respect for Longstreet seemingly deepened with each passing day. His letters home to his mother, sister, and uncle provide an intimate and revealing portrait of the general, the headquarters personnel, and events. Perhaps, of all the officers on the staff, Goree became Longstreet's favorite. Even at the end when Longstreet rode away from the war, Goree would be by his side.[23]

On August 19, Goree wrote to his mother:

> Genl. Longstreet is one of the kindest, best hearted men I ever knew. Those not well acquainted with him think him short and crabbed and he does appear so except in three places: 1st, when in the presence of ladies, 2nd, at the table, and 3rd, on the field of battle. At any of those places he has a complacent smile on his countenance, and seems to be one of the happiest men in the world.[24]

As Goree's letter indicated, Longstreet had not lost the roughness of manner and bluntness of speech that had been hewed early in frontier Georgia. To those who knew him well and to women he could be a personable, entertaining individual; to those who saw him briefly or dealt with him officially, he could be laconic, even gruff. He possessed little refinement; there was too much of the old soldier and campaigner about him. When the occasion warranted, however, he could move easily in a parlor, as expected of an officer and a gentleman. But his home was a campsite shared with friends. Except for his absences from his family, Longstreet enjoyed soldier life.

Lieutenant William W. Blackford, a cavalry staff officer, was introduced to Longstreet at a dinner in Fairfax Court House. Longstreet impressed Blackford "as a man of limited capacity who acquired reputation for wisdom by never saying anything—the old story of the owl. I do not remember ever hearing him say half a dozen words, beyond 'yes' and 'no,' in a consecutive sentence, though often in company with his old companions of the old army." Weeks later, however, after Blackford had served temporary duty on Longstreet's staff, he wrote of the general: "He has been very kind to me and has shown me much attention." To those who served closely with Longstreet and came to know him privately, he elicited friendship and loyalty.[25]

Longstreet enjoyed most the renewal of friendships from his antebellum army days and the camaraderie of new acquaintances of fellow generals in the Confederate army. He was a popular companion, as he had been among the regulars, and his headquarters was visited on a frequent basis. An ample supply of whiskey, Fairfax's ability to prepare a fine meal, and the possibility of a good poker game lured numerous generals to his headquarters. Even an irascible man like Jubal Early, who would become one of Longstreet's bitterest postwar enemies, sought the conviviality offered by Longstreet and his staff.

The one subordinate officer who impressed Longstreet and of whom he became quite fond during this period was Colonel James Ewell Brown "Jeb" Stuart, a twenty-eight-year-old Virginian and 1854 graduate of West Point who had served under Johnston in the Shenandoah Valley before distinguishing himself at First Manassas. Since the battle, his cavalrymen roamed along the army's front lines toward Washington. When Longstreet assumed direction of what he termed the "Advance Forces," he and Stuart conferred or exchanged messages on an almost daily basis. Stuart was a superb reconnaissance officer and forwarded a stream of information to Longstreet.[26]

Jeb Stuart, according to an officer, "was as vain and frivolous as he was brave and dashing." He possessed a zest for life and a flamboyance of style that made him the embodiment of a knight errant, a cavalier warrior from an evocative past. But as he had shown in the Shenandoah Valley and at Manassas, Stuart had substance and exceptionable ability as well.[27]

Longstreet liked the cavalryman from the outset, sharing with him a fondness for a good story or joke. Longstreet also recognized the colonel's talent and utilized his skills. On September 11, with a mixed force of cavalry, infantry, and artillery, Stuart routed a Federal infantry brigade and two artillery batteries at Lewinsville, three miles northwest of Falls Church. The next day Longstreet wrote to Beauregard's headquarters that Stuart "has been most untiring in the discharge of his duties at that and other advanced positions." Concluding, he stated: "Col. Stuart has, I think, fairly won his claim to Brigadier, and I hope that the commanding General will unite with me in recommending him to that position."[28]

Beauregard and Johnston endorsed Longstreet's recommendation, with the latter proposing a cavalry brigade for Stuart. On the 13th or 14th, however, Johnston, through Beauregard, expressed a concern for Stuart's use of artillery. Johnston believed it was excessive and that Stuart endangered the guns by pushing them forward so closely to enemy positions. Longstreet immediately defended Stuart, denying the report of "imprudence" by the cavalry officer. Longstreet insisted to Beauregard that he had "the right man in the right place." Then, in interesting words, Longstreet wrote Stuart:

> Yet you should remember that when there is so much at stake, the authorities are of the opinion that too much caution cannot be had. Besides Politics are a little mixed with our cause, and actions. So we cannot be too guarded. Don't give yourself any uneasiness about the matter however: for you have been entirely successful. Rest assured that so long as I can help you, you shall not be depreciated.

On September 24, Stuart was promoted to brigadier general.[29]

One week after Stuart's appointment to brigadier, President Jefferson Davis arrived at Centreville. The chief executive had not been with the army since First Manassas when he arrived as the Confederates were sweeping the field clean of Federals. Davis returned to Richmond two days later, on July 23, and since that time had exchanged views with Beauregard and Johnston through correspondence. He came now to confer directly with the generals and, if the opportunity offered, heal a serious breach between himself and the two commanders. The latter purpose was probably an impossible quest, given the natures of the three individuals. Each of them shared in the blame; each would not bend and never forget, with profound consequences for the Confederate cause.[30]

Joseph Johnston, by universal agreement within the army, looked like a general. Lieutenant John Cheves Haskell, a member of the general's staff, described Johnston as "rather undersized, but the most soldierly looking man in the army." Moxley Sorrel recalled that he was "high-bred, stern-looking of faultless seat and bearing in the saddle." Porter Alexander believed that he "was more the soldier in looks, carriage & manner than any of our generals & in fact more than any man I ever met except Gen. Bob Garnett." Johnston was, Alexander added, of "medium stature but of most extraordinary strength, vigor, & quickness."[31]

Most individuals who knew Johnston well agreed that although he seemed on the surface stiff and formal, he was a man of warmth and generosity. Alexander said that he had a "strong & intellectual face," with thoughtful eyes and a high forehead. His face, asserted Haskell, "was a true index to his character, which was as affectionate and warmhearted, but as quick and passionate as any I ever met; yet his passion, which was sometimes of unseemly violence, was always as quickly followed by regret and acknowledgement so hearty and full that one could never harbor resentment against as true and right-minded a gentleman as ever lived."[32]

As Haskell noted, the passions of the man could be intense. He controlled them with a "disciplined composure," according to a recent biographer. Johnston was a proud man with a prickly sensitivity. The army had been his life since his graduation from West Point in 1829, a world measured by rank. As a staff officer explained, Johnston was "very careful of the observances of military etiquette." Not only did he observe scrupulously the protocols of his world, he expected it from others. If he believed that he had been wronged, he could react with righteousness and obstinancy fueled by pride and emotion.[33]

Rumors and allegations about personal animosity between Johnston and Davis predated their service to the Confederacy. According to some tales, the two men had difficulties from their days together at the academy. Other accounts noted problems in the 1850s when Davis served as Secretary of War and Johnston protested over his rank and seniority. Davis dismissed Johnston's claims, but the Virginian pursued the matter for another four years.[34]

Now, in the summer of 1861, it was again a question of rank and seniority that would result in an irreconcilable split between the two similar individuals. On May 16, the Confederate Congress had authorized the creation of the rank of full general. Davis, in turn, nominated four brigadiers for the new rank: Samuel Cooper, Albert Sidney Johnston, Robert E. Lee, and Joseph Johnston, in that order. (Beauregard's name would be added after First Manassas.) By Davis's list, Joseph Johnston was subordinate to the other three. Neither the president nor the War Department apparently made the list public, but as early as July 24, Johnston suspected a problem.[35]

On that day a staff officer reported to Johnston's headquarters with orders from Lee, Davis's military adviser, assigning the officer to Johnston's staff. Johnston reacted at once, refusing to accept the officer and asserting that he was the senior officer, not Lee. On the 29th, Johnston received more orders from Lee and protested again to Cooper in Richmond. When Davis read Johnston's letters, he endorsed them with "Insubordinate."[36]

Johnston's view that he was the senior general in the Confederacy was predicated upon a congressional enactment on March 14 when the legislature created five brigadierships in the regular army, specifying "that the relative rank of officers of each grade shall be determined by their former commissions in the U. S. Army." Since Johnston had been the quartermaster general of the army with the rank of brigadier, he correctly assumed that Lee and Cooper were his subordinates. Although Johnston's brigadiership was of staff rank, not line rank, the legislation did not make a distinction between the two grades. After Congress passed the act, only Johnston, Cooper, and Lee had been appointed and confirmed in the rank at that time. To Johnston, nothing could be clearer: He was the senior officer in Confederate service.[37]

During the second week of September, Johnston learned with certainty of his ranking beneath Cooper, Albert Sidney Johnston, and Lee. Surprised and mortified, he reacted by penning an ill-advised letter to Davis reciting the justifications for his claim as "the first general in the Armies of the Southern Confederacy." He concluded that it was "a blow aimed at me only." Johnston waited two days before sending it to Richmond, but when he did, he never backed down and never forgave Davis.[38]

Johnston's letter infuriated the president, whose tolerance for criticism was less than the general's and well known. Davis read the letter at a cabinet meeting and then replied to Johnston in writing: "Its language is, as you say, unusual; its arguments and statements utterly one-sided; and its insinuations as unfounded as they are unbecoming." Davis did not provide Johnston with an explanation of the ranking; years later he presented a convoluted rationale that was unconvincing. Davis's reply officially ended the matter; the two proud men never discussed it or corresponded about it again, but it remained like a brooding shadow haunting their relationship during the war.[39]

Another difficulty between Davis and Johnston related to the anomalous command structure in the army since First Manassas. The problem lay with Beauregard, who regarded his command as a separate corps within the army and corresponded directly with

Davis and the War Department. While Johnston tolerated the situation, Beauregard sparked controversy by fighting with Secretary of War Judah Benjamin over the recruitment of a rocket battery. Beauregard feuded with others in Richmond over similarly minor items, taking his cases to congressmen. Davis endeavored to settle the disputes with patience and conciliation, but as Richmond diarist Mary Boykin Chesnut accurately confided, Beauregard was "so puffed up with vanity" that resolution was as unlikely as it had been with Johnston.[40]

While relations were strained, Davis came to Centreville on October 1. About noon the president reviewed roughly twelve thousand troops and spoke briefly to them. Afterward, he and most of the general officers gathered for a "levee" at Beauregard's headquarters in Fairfax Court House. "All of the big bugs of the army" attended, in the words of William Blackford. When the social ended that evening, Davis, Johnston, Beauregard, and Major General Gustavus Smith conferred privately.[41]

At the meeting, Smith acted as spokesman for an offensive movement of the army that smacked of Beauregard's grandiose ideas. Smith proposed a concentration of all available troops in Virginia even if it left other areas temporarily vulnerable; he asserted that fifty thousand men were needed to cross the Potomac. Johnston and Beauregard piped in that sixty thousand was closer to the number required. The president's response was that if he could find additional troops to reach either figure, he could not arm them. Davis rejected the scheme and suggested raids against isolated Federal units. The generals dismissed that idea, which ended the discussion of a forward movement before winter. Before the two-hour conference concluded, Davis reiterated his earlier proposal of a reorganization of the army with regiments from the same state placed in separate brigades with commanders, if possible, from the state. Beauregard had followed that pattern in some units, but neither he nor Johnston ever organized the brigades to Davis's satisfaction. The meeting then adjourned, and Davis returned to the capital two days later.[42]

Longstreet, like many of the subordinate commanders in the army, watched the controversy between the president and the two generals with keen interest. Unlike a number of generals, Longstreet did not remain impartial. By October he counted Beauregard and Johnston among his friends and regarded both as fine officers.

The pair reciprocated in their estimation of the brigadier. In mid-August, Beauregard wrote to Samuel Cooper asking, "Can it not be so arranged as to make General Longstreet second in command?" Two weeks later Tom Goree boasted to his sister and uncle that Beauregard and Johnston "have the greatest confidence in Genl. L., and he is equal to any emergency." In another letter, Goree related that when Johnston visited the front lines, he spent the night at Longstreet's headquarters instead of riding the ten miles to Centreville.[43]

Thus, by the time of Davis's visit, Longstreet and Stonewall Jackson were regarded as the two finest brigadiers in the army. Johnston, Beauregard, and Smith recommended both of them for promotion to major general. Ironically, on September 24, Longstreet wrote to Colonel Thomas Jordan, asking to be relieved of his command. Longstreet had "heard from various and reliable sources" that one or more brigadiers who were his juniors in rank had been promoted over him. Almost echoing Johnston's words to Davis, Longstreet considered it a "great injustice" and contrary to the law. Beauregard denied the request and evidently soothed Longstreet's feelings. On October 7, Longstreet and Jackson were promoted to major general, with confirmation on the 13th.[44]

The probability of Longstreet's promotion had been long conjectured among the Virginians in his brigade. On October 12, he drilled the brigade for the last time. At its conclusion the men "cheered him gallantly before he left." The next day headquarters published the order, and as one member of the Eleventh Virginia remarked, the brigade lost "one of the best brigadiers in the army." His staff had a special dinner in celebration.[45]

A few days later Johnston ordered a withdrawal from the advanced lines to Centreville. During the last week of September, he had pulled in the outposts at Munson's and Mason's hills and at Falls Church. With his army unable to undertake an offensive, Johnston decided to consolidate his lines, lessening the danger to the troops stationed around Fairfax Court House. Not all of the troops welcomed the withdrawal, for duty along the front allowed them to forage among the generous civilians in the area. They had enjoyed, as one Alabamian wrote home, "every thing good." Now it was back to Centreville, "a small village of an antique and dilapidated appearance," according to a Georgian.[46]

Shortly after the Confederates filed into the lines at Centreville, on October 22, Johnston's army underwent a major reorganization into the Department of Northern Virginia. The department consisted of three districts: Aquia, Valley, and Potomac. Longstreet commanded the Third Division in the Army of the Potomac, as it was styled at the time.[47]

Longstreet's division consisted of four infantry brigades and the Hampton Legion, a mixed command of infantry and artillery. The brigades were comprised of North and South Carolinians and Texans under four brigadier generals: Harvey Hill, Longstreet's old friend and academy classmate; David R. Jones, a South Carolinian and West Pointer; Milledge Bonham, whose relationship with Longstreet had been strained since First Manassas; and Louis T. Wigfall, a native South Carolinian who was born in the Edgefield District, like Longstreet, and had emigrated to Texas where he fashioned a political career that culminated in election to the United States Senate. The Legion was named for its creator and benefactor, Colonel Wade Hampton, a South Carolinian of enormous wealth who had organized, armed, and outfitted the command with his own money.[48]

With the withdrawal to Centreville and with the reorganization, the Confederate army settled into the position where it would remain through the winter of 1862. The lines covered the ground north and south of Centreville held by the infantry and artillery. Jeb Stuart's cavalry brigade roamed to the front toward McClellan's lines, which also remained basically static. Porter Alexander organized a storehouse for supplies at Manassas Junction, alleviating much of the shortage that had plagued the army. When the weather turned colder in December, the men began building log huts with canvas roofs for winter quarters. Life at Centreville, groused one Confederate, consisted of "monotony and miserable inactivity, measles and typhoid fever."[49]

The cessation of active operations provided the generals and their staffs with numerous opportunities to relieve the monotony. Dinners and parties abounded among the ranking officers throughout the final three months of the year. As it had during the summer, Longstreet's headquarters served as one of the primary centers for socialization. His enjoyment of a good time, a good meal, and a good drink brought him ample companionship. "He was," Sorrel wrote, "rather gay in disposition with his chums, fond of a glass, and very skilful at poker."[50]

Johnston, Beauregard, Smith, Van Dorn, Jones, Hill, and Wigfall were the most frequent visitors and the ones who invited Longstreet to their dinners. They gathered as often as they could and for any special occasion. The generals, including Longstreet, evidently indulged in wine frequently and some in considerable amounts. Arnold Elzey, Nathan G. "Shanks" Evans, and Louis Wigfall had a problem with alcohol, Tom Goree believed, as they "always are more or less under the influence." Goree grumbled often in his letters during this period about the liquor and the generals. Another staff officer stated that after a dinner on December 11, "Generals Longstreet and Joe Johnston left arm in arm and pretty well soaked." An enlisted man wrote to his father to send more peach brandy as "it is about half gone. General Longstreet took to it amazingly.[51]

Longstreet preferred evenings at headquarters with a few old army friends, playing cards, drinking whiskey, and reminiscing about their youthful days on the frontier and in Mexico. Smith, Van Dorn, and Jones were regulars at these gatherings. Smith and Van Dorn had graduated with Longstreet from the academy in 1842, and Jones was four years younger, a member of the class of 1846. Sorrel wrote that Jones was "a very agreeable, honorable man, tall and stately" who suffered from unspecified health problems. His friends called him "Neighbor" Jones from his West Point days. He came less often than Smith and Van Dorn because his wife stayed in camp with him, and Jones was an "indulgent husband." The four generals spent many evenings together sitting around a table with cards and glasses, swapping tales; they were comfortable with one another and knew one another as "Pete" Longstreet, "G.W." Smith, "Coon" Van Dorn, and "Neighbor" Jones.[52]

Harvey Hill, another classmate of Longstreet's, also came frequently to the latter's headquarters. Hill commanded a brigade in Longstreet's division, and both official duties and unofficial visits brought him to Longstreet. But Hill was unlike the other generals; he was infused with devout religious views and moral rectitude. A North Carolinian, Hill left the army after the Mexican War and went on to teach mathematics at two colleges and serve as superintendent of his state's military academy. He was the brother-in-law of Stonewall Jackson, with whom he shared a fervid devotion to the Presbyterian church.[53]

In many ways Hill was the opposite of Longstreet. Hill stood five feet ten inches tall, but chronic spinal pain forced him to stoop slightly for some relief. He was cursed with dyspepsia, and perhaps it was the suffering that contributed to his sour disposition. He was a bitter, sarcastic critic of the frailties of humans. "I had always a strong perception of right and wrong," he once admitted, "and when corrected from petulance or passion, I brooded over it, did not forget, and I am afraid did not forgive it." He spared few from his bilious wit and sharp tongue. Sorrel said that Hill "was really a good man, but of sharp prejudice and intemperate language."[54]

Despite Hill's "marked and peculiar" personality, Longstreet admired his warrior's soul and enjoyed his wit. One of Hill's staff officers wrote that often the two generals' talk of fellow officers and of military policy was "not intended for the public." When the subject turned to less important topics, Hill usually carried the conversation as Longstreet chuckled at his friend's scathing words. Hill's aide thought that Longstreet possessed a "keen sense of the ridiculous" and, unlike many officers in the army, found entertainment in the odd humor of the serious, vituperative North Carolinian.[55]

The official duties and responsibilities of division command consumed much of Longstreet's days, however. Tom Goree wrote to his mother in mid-December that the general "is exceedingly punctual and industrious. Whatever he has to do, he does well and quickly." Longstreet was the only major general to conduct drills with his division while at Centreville. He conferred frequently with his brigade commanders and lectured both them and their men about the "nonsensical" idea of retreat or defeat. In Goree's words, Longstreet told them that "in every battle somebody is bound to run, and that if they will only stand their ground long enough like men, the enemy will certainly run." Longstreet was, Goree claimed, "very reserved and distant towards his men, and very strict, but they all like him."[56]

Although Goree had seen Longstreet in action only at Blackburn's Ford and late in the day at First Manassas and on fields of drill, the Texan informed his mother that the general's "forte though as an officer consists, I think, in the seeming ease with which he can handle and arrange large numbers of troops, as also with the confidence and enthusiasm with which he seems to inspire them."

Goree added: "If he is ever excited, he has a way of concealing it, and always appears as if he had the utmost confidence in his own ability to command and in that of his troops to execute."[57]

Longstreet, according to Goree, could be a difficult superior to work for at times. His moods fluctuated during those weeks. With the staff, Goree wrote, "he is some days very sociable and agreeable, then again for a few days he will confine himself mostly to his room, or tent, without having much to say to anyone, and is as grim as you please." Goree attributed his grimness to physical indisposition or "something has not gone to suit him." When mistakes were made or someone's conduct displeased Longstreet, "he does not say much, but merely looks grim. We all know now how to take him, and do not now talk much to him without we find out he is in a talkative mood." Goree concluded that Longstreet "has a good deal of the roughness of the old soldier about him, more so I think, than . . . Genls. Johnston, Beauregard, Van Dorn, or Smith."[58]

Finally, throughout these weeks at Centreville as the army prepared for winter, the feud between President Davis and the generals worsened. Longstreet's loyalty to Johnston and Beauregard remained unwavering and drove him increasingly into the antiadministration coterie within the army. The course he selected would not be forgotten in Richmond.

Beauregard had rekindled the controversy when he requested a transfer to New Orleans. When Davis refused, Beauregard proposed a revised command structure for the army, with himself in command of a corps. Davis again refused but tried conciliation with the vain Creole. Then when a synopsis of Beauregard's official report of First Manassas appeared in the newspapers before Davis had read it—with the allegation that the president had vetoed Beauregard's plan for attacking Washington—Davis was outraged, but he sent L. Q. C. Lamar to Centreville to resolve the difficulties.[59]

Lamar, a kinsman of Longstreet, failed in the mission. While at Centreville, Lamar wrote to his wife: "There is some ill-feeling between the Potomac generals and the President. I fear that Cousin James Longstreet is taking sides against the administration. He will certainly commit a grave error if he does. I hope to be able to dissuade his mind, as well as that of General Johnston."[60]

Beauregard backed down somewhat and the troubles subsided, but never disappeared. Grumblings about the administration continued at Centreville. In early January 1862, Goree wrote: "But we are more than all crippled by an unfortunate misunderstanding which unhappily exists between Pres. Davis and the leading generals of this army. I do not [know] all the causes of the difficulty, but I am satisfied from what I know that the blame is not here." From what he had learned or overheard, Goree believed that Davis did not like Longstreet and hardly spoke to Johnston, Beauregard, or Smith.[61]

Within three weeks of Goree's letter, Van Dorn, whom Davis liked, and Beauregard were gone from the army. Van Dorn had argued that his divisional command was not equal to his rank and requested a transfer. Davis appointed him commander of the Trans Mississippi Department. Beauregard soon followed Van Dorn westward, accepting a command in Mississippi. If Davis hoped that the departure of Beauregard would bring a truce with his generals at Centreville, he would not have to wait long to find out otherwise. The war's first autumn and winter witnessed the appearance of discord in the Confederacy. Few, including Longstreet, would be spared from its bitter effects.[62]

TOWARD RICHMOND

Winter settled on Virginia during the first week of January 1862. Rain, snow, and sleet froze and thawed the ground, turning the roads and fields into "seas of red mud." A Confederate soldier, huddled with comrades in a log hut near Centreville, claimed that the sun shone for only two days in a fortnight. Drills and most duties were suspended; sentries still patrolled their posts, but the bustle of army life slowed.[1]

About January 10, under orders from Johnston, Longstreet traveled by train to Richmond. He went as the army's emissary to discuss with President Davis the need for a policy on volunteers and to discuss the implementation of a draft or conscription. By the spring many of the regiments would be depleted or no longer in existence as the twelve-month term of enlistment for most of the troops expired. It was, said Tom Goree, a "very serious matter."[2]

Longstreet spent over a week in the capital, involved with meetings and in the pleasures of his family. Louise and the children boarded with friends in the capital, but Longstreet had seldom been able to visit. Such interludes were cherished, and the days must have passed swiftly. He was back in Centreville on or before the 20th, reporting to Johnston that he "saw nothing encouraging" from his discussions with administration officials.[3]

Longstreet had been back with the army only a day or two before a telegram arrived from Louise urging his immediate return to Richmond. Scarlet fever was raging through the city, and all of the children were stricken. It is uncertain whether any of the children were ill before he left for Centreville, but now all four were grievously sick. Wracked with uncertainty and fear, he hurried to their sides as swiftly as the railroad carried him. He and Louise had already lost two children; could either withstand another loss?[4]

Longstreet reached the city in time to be with Louise when one-year-old Mary Anne succumbed to the fever on January 25. There was no time for grief as the parents and the doctor battled to save the three boys. But the next day four-year-old James died. Six-year-old Augustus Baldwin and thirteen-year-old Garland fought on, their ages and strength aiding in the struggle. Finally, on February 1, Gus died. The depth of their sorrow had no limit.[5]

Sallie Corbell and her beau, George Pickett, Longstreet's old comrade in the Eighth Infantry and now a Confederate brigadier, were with the Longstreets throughout the ordeal. Despite her own grief, young Sallie, who had come to adore the children, and Pickett made the funeral arrangements. James and Louise either could not or chose not to attend the ceremony as the three children were laid to rest in a city cemetery. Garland remained ill but appeared to be out of danger.[6]

Longstreet returned to the army on February 5. Why he left Louise so soon after the tragedy is not known. Perhaps he could find solace only in work and with old comrades. When he arrived, the change in him was apparent. Sorrel said his "grief was very deep," and Goree wrote home on the 9th that "the general is very low spirited." Within a week of Gorce's letter, Longstreet raced back to the capital after being informed that Garland had had a relapse and was "at the point of death." But the teenager rallied and recovered. It would be a long time before James and Louise recovered. He turned more to the church and gave up gambling.[7]

Garland's second crisis occurred as activity in the army quickened after the winter hiatus. When Longstreet resumed his duties during the final week of February, the Confederates were removing provisions, equipment, and other public property and sending it southward on the railroad, preparatory to a withdrawal from the Centreville lines. Although the men were reenlisting in larger numbers than expected, Johnston had perhaps forty thousand troops to confront George McClellan's host of over one hundred thousand. Since he could not assume the offensive with this numerical disparity, Johnston viewed the positions at Centreville as exposed, a weak defensive position. The prudent course, in this thinking, was to retire southward behind the Rappahannock River and, if the Federals followed, offer battle behind that natural barrier. He would relinquish territory to achieve a concentration of force. But Jefferson Davis opposed such a course of action or strategy.[8]

On February 19, Johnston met with Davis and the cabinet in Richmond. The discussion lasted for seven hours. Despite the length of the meeting and the exchange of views, both Davis and Johnston left with different understandings. While the president conceded that a withdrawal should be at Johnston's discretion, Davis believed that such a movement would occur only under impelling circumstances. Johnston, however, thought that the movement would begin as soon as practicable. It was a misunderstanding that would only deepen the mistrust between the two men.[9]

Johnston returned to the army on the 21st, and the removal of stores began the next day. Huge stockpiles of meat and provisions had accumulated at Manassas Junction during the winter although Johnston had opposed the policy. On March 5, Jeb Stuart reported increased Federal activity beyond the Potomac River, and Johnston concluded that the anticipated advance by McClellan was at hand. Two days later the Confederate detachment at Leesburg, northwest of Centreville, started southward. On the 9th, the main army filed into marching columns, leaving behind their quarters of the past four months.[10]

Johnston claimed later that he removed nearly three million pounds of provisions and meat before the withdrawal began, but over a million pounds had to be abandoned, so he allowed local civilians to take all they wanted before squads of soldiers applied the torch. As the troops passed through Manassas, they were permitted to grab whatever they could carry. A South Carolinian remembered that the "whiskey flowed like water," and the men feasted on food for the next few days. When the army cleared the junction, flames lit the night as several thousand barrels of flour, stacks of corn and hay, and a million pounds of bacon were burned. A meat-packing plant in nearby Thoroughfare Gap was also destroyed. As a final measure, Porter Alexander and Major George Duffey blew up the Stone Bridge over Bull Run with five hundred pounds of gunpowder. It was a night of fire, noise, and stench.[11]

The four infantry divisions of the army marched in two columns —Smith's and Longstreet's commands by the Warrenton Turnpike;

Richard Ewell's and Jubal Early's along the tracks of the Orange
& Alexandria Railroad. Stuart's horsemen followed the next day,
protecting the army's rear as the Federals entered Centreville. By
the 12th the Confederates had crossed the Rappahannock River,
and within another week Smith's and Longstreet's troops filed into
position south of the Rapidan River, a tributary of the Rappahannock. Johnston established headquarters at the home of Sidney
James just south of the Rapidan; Longstreet pitched his tents at the
farm of Erasmus Taylor, a mile or so east of Orange Court House.[12]

Johnston did not inform Jefferson Davis of the retreat until March
13, after the army had crossed the Rappahannock. The news
shocked and displeased the president, more so because he learned
about the supplies that had been destroyed. Johnston believed he
had acted under the authority given him in February; Davis thought
otherwise. Regardless, the Confederates were now in central Virginia, the Northerners occupied Centreville, and subsequent movements required clarification. With this in mind, Davis and Robert E.
Lee went to see Johnston and discuss the alternatives.[13]

The trio met at Fredericksburg, fifty miles north of Richmond, on
March 23. Part of the time they rode together, inspecting Johnston's
position along the Rappahannock. When they conferred, they resolved little. Neither Davis nor the two generals knew George
McClellan's plans. Davis had recently learned, however, that a
Union army under Major General Ambrose E. Burnside had appeared off the coast of North Carolina, threatening Roanoke Island
and New Bern. Davis proposed sending Longstreet and his division
to the coast, but Johnston demurred, arguing that G. W. Smith was
ill and he wanted to keep Longstreet, the senior officer in Smith's
absence, with him. It was agreed to dispatch two brigades from
Theophilus Holmes's division.[14]

Of the three men present, Lee was probably the least satisfied
with the discussions. He opposed Johnston's willingness to concentrate forces at the expense of losing territory. Lee appreciated the
strategic importance of uniting commands for battle, but he thought
that when the fighting came, it should be as far away as possible
from Richmond, the symbolic and strategic center of the Confederacy. Furthermore, there was a tension between the two old comrades and friends—Johnston resented Lee's seniority and position.
Ten days before, under the president's direction, Davis had given
Lee the conduct of operations of the Confederacy's armies. As a

result, Johnston's authority over the forces in Virginia had been restricted.[15]

The strategic situation in the Old Dominion changed significantly within days of this meeting. On March 25, reports reached the capital of the landings of Union forces on Virginia's historic Peninsula, slightly over a hundred miles east of Richmond. Since the war began, the Federals had held Fortress Monroe at the Peninsula's tip, and now they were using it as the base for a movement up the James and York rivers toward the capital. Approximately twelve thousand Confederates under Major General John Magruder barred the way at Yorktown, where a British army had been doomed nearly eighty years before. Across the James from Yorktown, Major General Benjamin Huger's thirteen thousand men held Norfolk. But as additional reports filtered in of a massive enemy concentration, it was evident that Magruder and Huger needed reinforcements.[16]

The arrival of the Union flotilla of hundreds of ships, brimming with troops and cannon, marked the beginning of the long-awaited, but delayed, Federal offensive. McClellan had proved to be as difficult a subordinate for Lincoln as Johnston had for Davis. The Northern president had cajoled, prodded, and finally ordered the cautious McClellan to advance. Still the general refused until all details of the operation met his approval. In mid-March, he and his corps commanders at last decided on a campaign up the Peninsula, and the vast Federal army lurched forward. "I had hoped, let me say," McClellan averred, "by rapid movements to drive before me or capture the enemy on the Peninsula, open the James River, and press on to Richmond before he should be materially re-enforced from other portions of his territory."[17]

Ultimately, McClellan's caution gave the Confederates time to concentrate against him, but when the initial contingent of Union troops disembarked at Fortress Monroe, Davis and Lee saw only the danger posed by the movement and needed to react. The Confederate president, with Lee's advice, responded with restraint, however. He asked Johnston to examine personally Magruder's position at Yorktown and report on its merit. About April 1, Johnston and Smith left for Richmond, leaving Longstreet in command of the army.[18]

Longstreet directed the operations of the army for approximately five days. He had had limited knowledge of the discussions between Johnston and Davis during the preceding two weeks. According to his memoirs, however, he took the opportunity while in command to propose an audacious plan in the Shenandoah Valley. It is a strange story whose only source is the general's autobiography thirty years after the events.[19]

According to Longstreet, on April 3 he wrote to Major General Stonewall Jackson, whose command had been defeated at Kernstown on March 23 and had retired southward in the valley to Mount Jackson before a superior Federal force under Major General Nathaniel Banks. Longstreet claimed that he proposed to Jackson that he, Longstreet, with part of the army cross the Blue Ridge Mountains, combine forces, and assail Banks. "I explained," Longstreet recounted, "that the responsibility of the move could not be taken unless I was with the detachment to give it vigor and action to meet my views, or give time to get back behind the Rapidan in case the authorities discovered the move and ordered its recall." But Jackson opposed the idea because, in Longstreet's words, "I had been left in command on the Rapidan, but was not authorized to assume command of the Valley district. As the commander of the district did not care to have an officer there of higher rank, the subject was discontinued."[20]

Unfortunately, Longstreet's dispatch of the 3rd has not been located. He undoubtedly wrote to Jackson at 10:00 A.M. on that day. From Jackson's reply twelve hours later, Longstreet suggested that the valley commander lure the Federals deeper into the region before attacking them. If Longstreet offered to go to the valley with reinforcements, Jackson ignored the offer. The hero of First Manassas requested five thousand additional troops, artillery ammunition, and a battery of six cannon. Two days later he wrote again, stating that he needed seventeen thousand men in total if he were to operate against Banks. He added a list of distances between locations for Longstreet and cautioned against a forced march if reinforcements were to be sent. Their correspondence ended there with Johnston's return to the army.[21]

If Longstreet broached such a scheme, as he alleged in his memoirs, it was at the least an insubordinate plan, at the most a ludicrous one. His words beggar explanation—"to get back . . . in case the authorities discovered the move." Did he believe that temporary command of the army gave him authority to divide that force in a grandiose offensive strategy? Was he willing to undertake a movement without informing Johnston or Davis? If so, Longstreet's motives and judgment need to be seriously questioned. Most likely, however, he concocted the story when he wrote his memoirs to give the illusion that he had conceived of the idea of Jackson's subsequent campaign in the valley before Jackson and Lee, working together, fashioned the brilliant movement. Other statements in his memoirs suffer from similar self-aggrandizement. In the end, the story seems to be the musings of a bitter, elderly man.

Johnston returned from the capital on April 4 or 5. He had barely arrived when a telegram from Lee directed him to begin moving the army to Richmond because advance elements of McClellan's army had started toward Yorktown on the 4th. Five days later Davis wired, summoning the entire army to the capital. Under Davis's orders, Johnston left behind along the river Richard Ewell's eight-thousand-man division as an observation force. The commanding general boarded a train for Richmond; his remaining three infantry divisions, cavalry, and artillery followed.[22]

Johnston's men entered the capital on railroad cars to the cheers of its residents. From there they boarded transports for the trip down the James River to Yorktown. Within days of Davis's orders, the advance elements were filing into the works of Magruder's line across the Peninsula. An artilleryman with the army described the defenses as "these abominable lines." The Peninsula was only four to five miles wide at Yorktown, and Magruder had stretched his lines from the York River to the James River, behind the smaller Warwick River. Magruder had relied upon bluff and the marching back and forth of units to convince McClellan that more Confederates manned the weak lines than really did. It was a bravura performance on Magruder's part.[23]

While the army passed through Richmond, Davis held a conference with Secretary of War George Randolph, Lee, Johnston, Smith, and Longstreet. The meeting began at eleven o'clock on the morning of the 14th and lasted, except for an hour dinner recess, until one o'clock on the morning of the 15th. Smith opened the discussion with the suggestion that troops in Georgia and South Carolina be hurried to Virginia and united with Johnston's army, and together they could pounce on McClellan as Magruder drew him up the Peninsula toward the capital. Johnston concurred, or as he stated in a postwar letter, "I regarded it as the wisest course practicable, and advocated it and represented the danger of attempting to hold the lines near Yorktown."[24]

Secretary Randolph objected, unwilling to evacuate Norfolk and its valuable naval facilities. Lee argued that he doubted if the defenses in the two lower Southern states could be stripped safely of the troops. Davis said little, but asked Longstreet for his views. Longstreet answered that he believed McClellan, a trained engineer, would move deliberately and carefully and not before May 1. According to Longstreet, Davis interrupted him, praising McClellan and not wanting to hear a contrary view. Longstreet said no more, later asserting he concluded that "my opinion had only been asked through polite recognition of my presence, not that it was wanted."[25]

At the meeting's conclusion, Davis announced that the Peninsula would be defended and Magruder reinforced with Johnston's entire army. Johnston accepted the decision, convinced that eventually the Confederates would have to retire before the Union numbers, heavy artillery, and navy. The three generals departed to join the troops en route to Yorktown.[26]

Longstreet's assessment of McClellan's generalship was perceptively accurate. Unwilling to launch bloody frontal attacks against the foe whose numerical strength he vastly overestimated, the Union commander conducted a siege operation, relying upon large-caliber artillery to bombard the Confederate defenses. The Federals had begun the slow work on April 5, and it would not be completed until the first days of May. Caution and careful planning were the lodestones of McClellan's generalship.[27]

Sharpshooting between the opposing lines characterized the combat of the siege. The Confederate lines were mere ditches with the dirt piled in front. Water lay in the ditches, and the men had to stand in it for hours at a time. Longstreet's six brigades, roughly 13,800 men, manned the army's center behind the Warwick River. Harvey Hill's division extended his left to the York; Magruder's, his right to the James. Smith's division acted as the reserve behind Longstreet. Johnston had approximately 70,000 troops in all, confronting over 100,000 Federals.[28]

The Confederates did not have long to wait in the watery lines for Johnston to decide to evacuate the position. On April 27, he informed Richmond that "we must abandon the Peninsula soon." Three days later McClellan's siege artillery lobbed shells into Yorktown. On May 1, Johnston ordered his division commanders to prepare to retreat, sending baggage wagons up the Peninsula to Williamsburg. He told Lee in a dispatch that the withdrawal would begin after dark on the 2nd. "We are engaged," Johnston stated to Lee, "in a species of warfare at which we can never win."[29]

After sunset on May 3, the Confederate army marched away from Yorktown and the muzzles of McClellan's cannon. Unlike the retreat from Centreville, no fires marked their departure, only the black shield of darkness. All night the Rebels slogged along two muddy roads, an ordeal of mired wagons and artillery pieces, shouldered out of the muck by the infantrymen. "And so it went on all night," remembered Porter Alexander, "march or wade two minutes and halt ten or longer." The divisions of Smith and Hill inched westward on the Yorktown-Williamsburg road; Magruder and Longstreet, on a road near the James River. Stuart's cavalrymen prowled along the columns' rear, gathering stragglers and watching for Yankees. When Moxley Sorrel informed Longstreet that Brigadier General Gabriel Rains, a career soldier who had experimented with explosives, was planting artillery shells in the roads as land mines against the Federals, Longstreet, in "a rather severe note" to Rains, ordered it ceased as beyond the bounds of legitimate warfare. Before this war ended, such a view would sound like a fading echo.[30]

The retreat continued on May 4 through Williamsburg where a Confederate soldier remarked that they found "women crying and children squalling." At Yorktown, McClellan's soldiers found the deserted lines and started westward in pursuit. Harvey Hill took time on this day to write a brief letter to his wife: "I think that Genl Johnston has done wisely in saving his troops from a terrible conflict" at Yorktown. Late in the afternoon Johnston instructed Longstreet to send a brigade to relieve the troops in the works at the eastern edge of Williamsburg. The division commander ordered Richard Anderson's and Roger A. Pryor's two small brigades and two batteries back through the town. Arriving at nightfall, Anderson's and Pryor's men filed into position. Before long, rain fell, increased to a downpour, and continued through the night.[31]

The rain had subsided to a drizzle when Union skirmishers appeared through the misty woods on the morning of May 5. Anderson's South Carolinians manned a bastion beside the road that had been constructed previously by Magruder and named for the general. Pryor's troops were scattered among redoubts and rifle pits on either side of Fort Magruder. The Federals closed, and the skirmish fire crackled. Anderson sent a courier into town for reinforcements.[32]

The courier located Longstreet on the campus of The College of William and Mary where he had placed his headquarters the night before and where he stayed throughout much of the day. Cadmus Wilcox, a brigadier in the division, grumbled to Porter Alexander in a postwar letter that the brigade commanders "all thought it strange" that Longstreet was not nearer the firing lines and more accessible during the engagement. Williamsburg marked Longstreet's first real combat as a division commander, and his method of command—demonstrated on this field and future fields—was to issue orders and then leave the fighting to his subordinates. Tom Goree described him as almost phlegmatic in a battle, writing: "In a fight he is a man of but very few words, and keeps at all time his own counsels."[33]

Longstreet's duty on this day was to secure the passage of the army's wagons by keeping McClellan at bay. When Anderson asked for support, Longstreet directed Wilcox and Ambrose Powell Hill with their brigades to the front. Wilcox went first, followed by Hill, whose troops were Longstreet's former brigade. The two commands extended Anderson's right flank where the Federals—Brigadier General Joseph Hooker's division—were pressing the attack. Later, George Pickett joined Longstreet on the college campus. The two friends conferred before Longstreet ordered the brigadier into the action. Pickett's men went forward as a brigade to their first engagement.[34]

With Pickett's entry, Longstreet ordered an attack by Wilcox and Hill, supported by Pickett and two regiments from Pryor. The Southerners advanced across the boggy ground into woods where the combat escalated into "a close musketry fight," according to Wilcox. Artillery from both opponents punctuated the rippling sound of rifle fire with the bellow of cannon discharges. The Confederates drove ahead, shoving the Federal infantry rearward, with the Ninth Alabama of Wilcox's brigade capturing a battery of six rifled cannon. By this time additional Northern troops were replacing Hooker's men, and the action on the Confederate right subsided. One Rebel claimed in a letter home that "it was the prettiest fight I ever saw."[35]

Longstreet, meanwhile, rode forward toward the action, halting at the rear of Fort Magruder. Here he probably found Jeb Stuart, who was directing the artillery fire from the nearby redoubts. The Fourth Virginia Cavalry huddled behind one of the works. At one point in the combat, Stuart cantered by his horsemen as bullets splattered the ground. "Boys, don't mind them," joked Stuart. "They are spent bullets and won't hurt you." A few minutes later Major William Payne of the regiment toppled from his horse, hit by one of the "spent bullets."[36]

Sometime after 3:00 P.M., Johnston joined Longstreet. In his report, Johnston stated that he was a "mere spectator, for General Longstreet's clear head and brave heart left me no apology for interference." Harvey Hill was with Longstreet, having ridden in a short time before. Earlier, Longstreet had asked Hill for a brigade, and then when reports came in of his men running low on ammunition, Longstreet requested the entire division. Behind Hill, his four brigades were shifting into position on the Confederate left, north of the bastion.[37]

Jubal Early's brigade led Hill's division and formed its front line. About five o'clock, Early reported that Union troops were testing the Confederate left and asked for permission to advance against an enemy battery at his front. In his report, Hill asserted that Early made the request in person to Longstreet, who approved the movement, directing Hill to accompany the attack force. "Neither Longstreet nor myself knew the precise position of the battery," wrote Hill, "and both were entirely ignorant of the ground. We, however, agreed in the general plan of getting in rear of the battery by passing through the woods to the left of its supposed position."[38]

The result was a slaughter. Early charged with the Left Wing of the brigade—the Twenty-fourth and Thirty-eighth Virginia—before the Right Wing, under Hill, could join in. Early's Virginians plodded through an open field and were caught in a blizzard of Union musketry and artillery. Early and scores of his Virginians fell before the furnace of gunfire. Hill sent forward the Twenty-fourth Virginia and the Fifth North Carolina, but that only added to the casualties. Porter Alexander later blamed Hill for the debacle, claiming that the division commander was "spoiling" for a fight. "Now the day was practically already gained," wrote Alexander, "& we had no business to do any unnecessary fighting. . . . That was not war."[39]

Most others in the army at the time attributed the bloody repulse to Early's impetuosity. But Alexander was correct that the attack was a needless loss of men. The army's wagons were well beyond Williamsburg, and darkness was settling on the field. The Battle of Williamsburg, a minor rear-guard action, exacted a rather heavy casualty toll—over fifteen hundred Confederates and roughly twenty-two hundred Federals.[40]

In his report, Longstreet praised the officers and men, including his staff officers. He cited Peyton Manning in particular for carrying a regimental flag in an attack and personally killing three enemy soldiers. "My part in the battle," he wrote, "was comparatively simple and easy, that of placing the troops in proper positions at proper times." It was a modest assessment for his first action as a division commander. Years later, perhaps referring in part to Williamsburg, Johnston wrote to Longstreet: "What I *did* notice in you in all the years we served together, was promptness of thought and action equal to your resolution."[41]

The Confederate withdrawal resumed between ten and eleven o'clock that night. The night's march was worse than the one of May 3–4 because the recent rain made quagmires of the roads. The Rebels "struggled out of one mud hole into another." The columns halted on the 6th and strung rear-guard units across the roads and watched. On the 7th, a Confederate brigade engaged a Union force at Barhamsville on the York River after the Federals landed from transports. The Southerners then retired without incident as McClellan trailed at a crawling pace. The march strained body and soul of the Rebels, however. A Georgian growled to his parents that "the past week was the hardest time I ever saw in my whole life." A Virginia artilleryman claimed that his unit's horses sank to their bellies in the mire, and the crew members endured "almost actual starvation." On one occasion, Johnston, an even-tempered man, raged at a teamster, shouting that he wanted to kill the helpless, frightened driver.[42]

On May 15, Johnston's army crossed the Chickahominy River, the last natural barrier between Richmond and the Federals. The stream, northeast of the capital, flowed in a southeasterly direction across the Peninsula to the James River. Normally the river had a width of about forty feet, but the month's rains had caused its waters to spill into the forested, marshy bottomlands on either side. After the Confederates passed over the river, details burned the bridges behind them. Johnston chose not to defend the ground along the river. On the 17th, the army's leading units reached the old field-works—built the year before—three miles from the city and halted. Here, in the shadow of the capital, Johnston would stand.[43]

Jefferson Davis reacted with disbelief when informed that the army was on the city's outskirts. During the past week or so, the president had seen the abandonment of Norfolk and the destruction of valuable naval and army matériel and the scuttling of the ironclad C.S.S. *Virginia.* On the 14th, the cabinet had discussed the possible evacuation of Richmond. During the meeting, when asked where the army could retreat if it had to retire, Robert E. Lee reacted uncharacteristically by exclaiming: "Richmond must not be given up; it shall not be given up! " The fervor of his words stunned the members.[44]

The tension coiled tighter during the next ten days as the Federal army closed on the city. McClellan's advance up the Peninsula had been leisurely, "marked by genuine enjoyment," according to a New Yorker. The soldiers' only complaint was the lack of good water for their coffee. By May 24, parts of the army had crossed the Chickahominy, pushing forward on the Williamsburg Road to Seven Pines, a crossroads named for the loblolly pine trees at the junction. Two of the five Union corps, roughly thirty thousand troops, followed across the repaired bridges to the south side of the river. McClellan strung the other three corps northwestward along the stream's northern bank. It was a dangerous division of the army, but McClellan had been ordered by the administration to extend his right flank to link up with Irvin McDowell's force, which was moving southward from Fredericksburg, fifty miles north of Richmond.[45]

Subsequently, McClellan blamed President Abraham Lincoln and Secretary of War Edwin M. Stanton for the campaign's ultimate failure, attributing it to the separation of the corps along the river. But on May 27, in a letter to his wife, the Union general boasted that "we are getting on splendidly. I am quietly cleaning out everything that could threaten my rear and communications, providing against the contingency of disaster, and so arranging as to make my whole force available in the approaching battle. The only fear is that Joe's [Johnston's] heart may fail him."[46]

Jefferson Davis must have had an even greater concern about Johnston's "heart." While Johnston possessed a soldier's courage, it appeared that he was reluctant to wage war, to give battle and risk a defeat. Before the war, Johnston had visited the plantation of Wade Hampton, who took his guest hunting one day. A companion on the hunt recalled that Johnston proved to be "a dead failure" as a hunter. Whenever they flushed a game bird, Johnston pulled up, arguing that "the bird flew too high or too low, the dogs were too far or too near." "Things never did suit exactly," the gentlemen said of Johnston. "He was too fussy, too hard to please, too cautious, too much afraid to miss and risk his fine reputation for a crack shot." At day's end "Joe Johnston did not shoot at all. The exactly right time and place never came."[47]

Now, during the final days of May 1862, Johnston had to shoot —"the exactly right time and place" had come. If McDowell and McClellan combined forces, his army and the capital it defended were most likely doomed. He understood that, however—McClellan's divided army offered the opportunity for its piecemeal destruction. As Lee said, "Richmond must not be given up."

A "MISUNDERSTANDING" AT SEVEN PINES

On the evening of May 28, Johnston summoned his division commanders to army headquarters, located in the residence of a Dr. Harrison on the Nine Mile Road, about five miles east of Richmond. Johnston had learned the day before of Union general Irvin McDowell's advance from Fredericksburg and prior to that had told Robert E. Lee that the army would attack on the 29th. He brought his ranking subordinates to headquarters to formulate a plan of assault.[1]

As senior officer, G. W. Smith spoke first, recommending an attack against McClellan's right flank at Mechanicsville with three divisions of the army. The proposal generated discussion until a courier arrived from Jeb Stuart with the news that McDowell was not moving on Richmond but retiring toward Fredericksburg. Unknown to the generals, McDowell had been recalled by Abraham Lincoln when Stonewall Jackson routed Nathaniel Banks's command at Winchester in the Shenandoah Valley three days earlier. Since the first week of May, Jackson, with the cooperation of Lee, had been stirring in the valley, bloodying one Union force before turning on Banks. It was an audacious plan by Lee, executed by Jackson. Before it ended in early June, Jackson reforged the strategic landscape in Virginia and emerged as a Confederate hero.[2]

Stuart's information altered the strategic situation along the Chickahominy. With McDowell's threat temporarily removed, the Confederates could act more aggressively. Smith now suggested an offensive against the two Union corps south of the river, in the Seven Pines–Fair Oaks area. Longstreet, whose opinion Johnston valued in these meetings, argued for a turning movement against the Federal right, similar to Smith's original proposal. The generals debated the plans until Johnston, tired of the arguments, walked away. Longstreet joined him; they conferred privately and decided to postpone the attack until Benjamin Huger's division arrived from Petersburg.[3]

On the 29th and 30th, Harvey Hill reconnoitered along the Williamsburg Road toward Seven Pines. He reported to headquarters that the entire Union Third and Fourth Corps were south of the river, but no Federals held the Charles City Road south of Seven Pines. Johnston received Hill's intelligence summary about noon on the 30th. At roughly the same hour he was informed that Huger's division had reached the city's eastern outskirts and was available. Johnston acted.[4]

Longstreet arrived at the Harrison house a short time later. The division commander, according to Sorrel, was "in good humor." If nothing else, the withdrawal to Richmond gave him some time with Louise and Garland. They had visited his headquarters, and he probably stayed in the city with them when duty permitted. Louise still wore mourning clothes, and Harvey Hill noted when he saw her, "she has a very sad, subdued look & has lost all color from her face." For both of them, the healing required more time.[5]

When the general arrived at army headquarters, he and Johnston worked together on an attack plan. Hill's reconnaissance convinced Johnston that the two Union corps south of the Chickahominy were vulnerable. If Federal reinforcements could be cut off across the river, two-fifths of McClellan's army could be isolated and crushed.[6]

Three thoroughfares heading east exited the capital south of the river. From the city's northeastern edge, the Nine Mile Road passed through Fair Oaks Station on the York River Railroad before intersecting with the Williamsburg Road at Seven Pines. Fair Oaks was a mile northwest of Seven Pines and six miles from the capital. South of Nine Mile Road, the Williamsburg Road followed a generally straight course through Seven Pines and across the Chickahominy at Bottom's Bridge. At no point did the distance between the Nine Mile and Williamsburg roads exceed two and a quarter miles. The final highway, the Charles City Road, branched off from the Williamsburg Road roughly two miles beyond the city, coursing south-

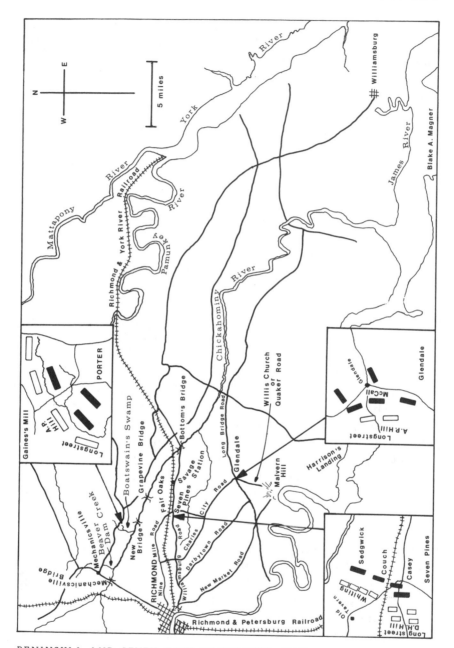

PENINSULA AND SEVEN DAYS CAMPAIGNS, MAY–JULY, 1862.

eastward. As the Charles City Road approached Seven Pines, White Oak Swamp sprawled between the two roads.[7]

Johnston's plan followed the roads. "It was an excellent & well devised scheme and apparently as simple as any plan could be," wrote Porter Alexander after the war. Harvey Hill's division would spearhead the assault on the Williamsburg Road, driving straight ahead to Seven Pines, where the Union divisions of Brigadier Generals Silas Casey and Darius N. Couch covered the ground from White Oak Swamp northward to beyond the York River Railroad. Longstreet's division would advance on Hill's left along the Nine Mile Road to Fair Oaks, converging on the Union right flank and preventing reinforcements from crossing the Chickahominy. On Hill's right, Benjamin Huger's three brigades would march on the Charles City Road, securing the Confederate right flank. Smith's division, under Brigadier General Chase Whiting, would support Longstreet, and John Magruder's command would act as a general reserve. Johnston was committing twenty-three of the army's twenty-seven brigades to the offensive; only Powell Hill's newly organized division, opposite Mechanicsville, would have no role in the operation. Of the army's seventy-four thousand troops, forty-two thousand would assail the two Union corps.[8]

Johnston spent the entire afternoon and part of the evening of the 30th fashioning his first offensive of the war. In his memoirs, Longstreet wrote: "I was with General Johnston all of the time that he was engaged in planning and ordering the battle, heard every word and thought expressed by him of it." He further commented that "the plan seemed so simple that it was thought impossible for any one to go dangerously wrong." Within twenty-four hours, however, the "impossible" had occurred. Had Longstreet listened?[9]

Johnston gave Longstreet verbal instructions, assigning him to command of his own and Harvey Hill's and Huger's divisions. The responsibility for implementing and executing the assault was Longstreet's. Later that night Johnston issued written orders for Hill, Huger, Whiting, and Magruder. He wanted the attack to commence "at an early hour," before 8:00 A.M. on the 31st. Although a careful planner, Johnston neglected details—he never informed Smith, commander of the army's Left Wing and its senior officer, of the offensive, and his instructions to Huger were imprecise as to that officer's role.[10]

After nightfall, a spring thunderstorm lashed the region with vivid lightning and heavy downpours. The men in both armies snatched what little sleep they could in the miserable conditions. The rain ran off the already sodden ground, swelling the Chickahominy and flooding the bottomlands. Before daylight, a dense fog wreathed the woods around Seven Pines.[11]

The dyspeptic warrior and inveterate Yankee hater Harvey Hill ignored the miserable weather and stayed awake the entire night, preparing for the morning's work. Before daylight he sent an aide to Huger's headquarters, a half mile away. The aide found the general and his staff officers asleep and aroused them. Huger soon had his men stirring. Not far away the soldiers in the divisions of Longstreet and Whiting were also busy. The night's rainfall prevented campfires, and the men ate cold breakfasts without coffee.[12]

About 4:30 A.M. the Confederates formed columns and moved out. North of the city, Chase Whiting's division marched southward less than a mile on the Meadow Bridge Road, turned southeastward and followed a crossroad over the tracks of the Virginia Central Railroad to the Mechanicsville Road, where it swung southward toward the Nine Mile Road. When the leading brigade reached the latter road, it found units of Longstreet's division breaking camp at the nearby Fairfield Race Course and in jammed ranks in the roadbed.[13]

The presence of Longstreet's troops surprised Whiting; he had expected the route clear for his march to "Old Tavern," four miles to the east. Whiting sent an aide to Johnston, who replied in writing, "Longstreet will precede you." Whiting waited impatiently for another two hours and then rode personally to headquarters. Here he met Johnston and G. W. Smith, who had arrived at headquarters about daybreak when he learned of the day's operation. Whiting wanted clarification and asked Smith if he would locate Longstreet and get an explanation for the delay.[14]

The wing commander spoke to Johnston, who said that Longstreet should be either on the Nine Mile Road with his division or on the Williamsburg Road with Hill's. With that, Smith sent Captain R. F. Beckham of his staff in search of the general. An hour later, about nine o'clock, an orderly from Beckham returned to headquarters and reported that the staff officer had found neither the general nor his division on Nine Mile Road. Johnston was stunned. Where was Longstreet? Why had the attack not begun an hour earlier? Johnston wanted answers and ordered Lieutenant J. B. Washington to find them, but he stumbled into a picket post of a Maine regiment and was captured. Finally, at ten o'clock, a message from Beckham solved the mystery: Longstreet and his brigades were on the Williamsburg Road at the Charles City Road intersection. When the commanding general read the dispatch, he grumbled: "I wish all the troops were back in camp."[15]

What Beckham had found on the Williamsburg Road was a tangled mess created by Longstreet. In his subsequent private correspondence, official report, and postwar writings, Longstreet never admitted to the blunder he had already committed that day. Although he had spent the entire previous afternoon with Johnston, hearing "every word and thought expressed" by the latter, Longstreet evidently misunderstood his orders. He never offered an explanation of his conduct; instead, he blamed others, writing as if he had done nothing wrong. He may have been confused, or he may have believed that he could modify the battle plan as wing commander. Both seem unlikely. "Gen. Longstreet," asserted Porter Alexander after the war, "entirely misconceived his orders and instead of marching straight down Nine Mile Road massing in front of G. W. Smith [Whiting], *he crosses over to the Williamsburg Road, to get behind D. H. Hill.* Of course he would not have done it had he not conceived himself ordered to do it."[16]

On the night of May 30–31, Longstreet's six brigades were bivouacked on the Fairfield Race Course eastward along Nine Mile Road. According to Johnston's plan, Longstreet had only to march eastward on the roadway to "Old Tavern," where the highway veered southward toward Fair Oaks, two miles distant. His rear brigade at the racecourse had five miles to march to "Old Tavern," his advanced unit less than two. In Johnston's "excellent & well devised scheme," Longstreet's command was in an ideal position at daybreak on the 31st.[17]

Like the other division commanders, Longstreet had his troops in motion by first light. But instead of directing them eastward on Nine Mile Road, he sent them toward the capital on a road that connected with the Williamsburg Road. When Whiting approached Nine Mile Road, he encountered Longstreet's columns heading westward. Johnston's note to Whiting—"Longstreet will precede you"—did not clarify in which direction Longstreet would be moving. Johnston believed that Longstreet was en route to Fair Oaks, not toward Richmond. As Alexander stated, Longstreet could only have "conceived himself ordered to do it."[18]

Longstreet's march brought him into the path of Huger's division, however. After Longstreet's division turned into the connecting road, it reached Gillies Creek, about a mile from the Williamsburg Road. The previous night's thunderstorms had swelled its current, and Longstreet decided to bridge the stream. Details of soldiers constructed a makeshift span from a wagon and planks, but it was so narrow that the men could cross only in single file. The division of nearly fourteen thousand troops started over the bridge one by one.[19]

As the men filed across, Huger's division arrived from its bivouac site at Oakwood Cemetery in Richmond's northeast section. Huger halted his three brigades, inquired about Longstreet's whereabouts, and was directed to Hill's nearby headquarters tent. Here the fifty-six-year-old South Carolinian and career soldier conferred with the two generals. Longstreet explained that his division was moving to attack with Hill's and that Huger should follow to the Charles City Road and act as a support for the main assault. It was the first Huger knew of Longstreet's role. Huger then asked Longstreet who was the senior officer, and the wing commander replied that he was. Huger said that if Longstreet knew that to be the fact, he was satisfied. In his memoirs, Longstreet claimed that he admitted Huger was the senior officer and offered the South Carolinian command but it was declined. Longstreet's version lacks credibility.[20]

Longstreet's troops continued to file across the bridge, insisting that their earlier arrival gave them priority. But Longstreet had instructed Hill the night before not to advance until Huger's division relieved the brigade under Brigadier General Robert E. Rodes, which was posted on the Charles City Road. By keeping Huger waiting, Longstreet contributed further to the delay. Once his division cleared the bridge, he moved them off the road, giving Huger a clear path to the Williamsburg–Charles City intersection. It was about noon when Huger's three brigades turned into the Charles City Road. It would be more than an hour before Rodes closed on Hill's right flank.[21]

Longstreet stated in his report, written within two weeks of the battle, that Huger's division "was intended to make a strong flank movement around the left of the enemy's position and attack him in rear of that flank." Huger disputed that, however, insisting that he never received such instructions. He claimed that his orders from Longstreet directed him to move to an unspecified "designated point" and await further orders. The evidence supports Huger's argument, which in effect meant that Longstreet removed a division of roughly five thousand troops from any active role in the offensive once it began and later implied that Huger had failed to comply with orders.[22]

Longstreet further weakened the assault force by dividing his six brigades. He posted George Pickett's brigade on the York River Railroad with instructions to repulse any Federal sortie along the tracks and be prepared to support the attack force. The brigades of Richard Anderson and Colonel James Kemper, Longstreet's former unit, were marched eastward in direct support of Hill on the Williamsburg Road. Longstreet's remaining three brigades, under the command of Cadmus Wilcox, waited at the Williamsburg–Charles City intersection until 3:30 P.M. when the division commander sent them in support of Huger. After marching and countermarching on the Charles City Road, Wilcox received new orders "to keep abreast" of the combat on Williamsburg Road.[23]

The error-plagued Confederate offensive finally rolled forward at one o'clock, five hours behind schedule. For Harvey Hill it had come none too soon. Hill, wrote an officer, "was a man of considerable capacity and always seemed to go from choice into the most dangerous place he could find on the field." Twice during the morning he asked Longstreet for permission to advance, but the wing commander cautioned patience until Rodes's brigade arrived. When the leading regiment of that command neared Hill's three brigades in the woods west of Seven Pines, the division commander ordered the signal cannon fired. With skirmishers in front, Hill's men went forward.[24]

The attack foundered briefly in the tangled undergrowth and sodden ground, but the Confederates drove ahead. To their front, Federal skirmishers opened with a spattering of gunfire. Behind the screen, Casey's and Couch's divisions manned rifle pits edged with an abatis. A half mile west of the Seven Pines crossroads, a pentagoned open redoubt—subsequently called "Casey's Redoubt" —anchored the Union line. The Northerners had orders to hold the position "at all hazards."[25]

As the Southerners neared the abatis, the Union infantrymen

unleashed "a terrific fire." The musketry from both sides flashed and roared through the woods. One Confederate soldier told his wife a week later that it was a "miracle" he was not hit as "every body else was falling around us." He admitted that the combat "was much the hardest fought battle we have ever been in." Casualties among the Confederates were staggering. A member of the Thirty-eighth Virginia in Samuel Garland's leading brigade said the regiment "suffered very much." Another regiment in the same brigade, the Twenty-third North Carolina, lost all its field officers and eight of ten company commanders.[26]

Hill's men fought the enemy for three hours. When Hill finally coordinated all four brigades in an assault, the Rebels overran the redoubt and swept away the Union line from White Oak Swamp to the Williamsburg Road. The Yankees, however, rallied along a second line of fieldworks north of the crossroads. The fighting still raged, killing and maiming men on both sides. A Confederate artillery officer who witnessed the terrible combat wrote to Hill long after the war to say that, except for the assault on the third day at Gettysburg, Hill's charge at Seven Pines was "under all the circumstances, the most difficult & dangerous that I saw during the war."[27]

By four o'clock Harvey Hill needed assistance, however. Before the attack, Longstreet told the North Carolinian that he would not interfere, but if Hill needed troops, just to request them. Longstreet remained somewhere to the rear along the Williamsburg Road throughout the three hours of fighting. He had Anderson's and Kemper's brigades close at hand but did little more than send Wilcox's three brigades down the Charles City Road. Jeb Stuart spent the afternoon with Longstreet, who stated that the cavalry official rendered "material service by his presence with me." What duties Stuart performed remain unclear because Longstreet did little. He seemingly abdicated his duties as wing commander. After the war in a letter to Hill, he admitted that he "surely had little to do with the battle after the plan of advance and attack was arranged," adding that he made no suggestions except to move Wilcox in support of Huger.[28]

When Hill's request for reinforcements finally came, Longstreet stirred. He sent a message to Johnston's headquarters asking for a division to break the "sack," as he termed it, at Seven Pines. He then ordered Anderson's brigade forward. What Longstreet overlooked at the time was, in Porter Alexander's words, "an opportunity for one of the most brilliant strokes in the war." George Pickett's brigade on the York River Railroad had an unobstructed path to the Union right flank above the crossroads. As events would soon demonstrate, Pickett and Anderson could have rolled up the Union line in a devastating attack. If Longstreet had added Kemper's brigade to the force, the results might have been more dramatic. In Longstreet's defense, the heavily wooded terrain restricted any commander's range of vision, and he had never directed so many units in an engagement. But he remained in the rear, not going forward to get a sense of the unfolding combat. Perhaps he believed that his responsibilities as wing commander dictated such a role and placement of his headquarters. Tom Goree's earlier assessment of his commander's ability to handle troops with ease was not evident on this day.[29]

Anderson's South Carolinians came in on the left flank of Hill's stalled lines. To the east, the Federals clung to their second line, their numbers bolstered by the arrival of Brigadier General Philip Kearny's division of the Third Corps. South of the Williamsburg Road, Hill's right front brigades had repulsed a counterattack by Kearny's men, and to the north of the road, two of Hill's brigades were pressing ahead in another charge. The Union defenders pounded the Confederates back as Anderson's leading regiments entered the fighting.[30]

Anderson advanced the Sixth South Carolina and the Palmetto Sharpshooters, both units under the command of Colonel Micah Jenkins. Twenty-six-year-old Jenkins was a graduate of the South Carolina Military Academy and a favorite of Longstreet. In the fall of 1861, according to Goree, Longstreet pronounced the South Carolinian "the best colonel in the army." Just days prior to this battle, Longstreet presented a flag to Jenkins's regiment. Longstreet expected much from the young officer, and Jenkins more than fulfilled his commander's assessment of him as he led his men toward the fighting.[31]

Jenkins's ranks emerged from the woods on the Nine Mile Road south of Fair Oaks. He wheeled the line to the right, redressed ranks, and charged. The Federal line north of the crossroads exploded in a gale of bullets. Leaning forward, the South Carolinians did not pause, but swept over the works. They unraveled a second line, plunging into a "terrible slaughter" with oncoming Federal reinforcements. The blue-coated enemy broke before the relentless assault, and the South Carolinians scoured the road and woods to Seven Pines.[32]

Although tired and with their ranks grievously thinned, the South Carolinians reached the Williamsburg Road east of the crossroads. More Federal troops advanced to blunt this lance in Confederate gray. At a distance of thirty to forty paces, the two lines raked each other. Jenkins ordered a charge, and with the support of two more Southern regiments, the Federals broke to the rear. Jenkins finally halted his men and led them back to the abandoned enemy camps, where they bivouacked. His command had eliminated Federal resistance around Seven Pines and had captured two hundred prisoners and three cannon. But the cost was dear—seven hundred casualties out of nineteen hundred engaged. It was, remarked a fellow South Carolina officer, "the most brilliant piece of fighting that I ever saw." Goree gushed in a letter that Jenkins and his men *"immortalized"* themselves. That night when Jenkins reported to Longstreet, the general was "very much surprised" to learn how far the South Carolinians had gone. Robert E. Lee subsequently described Jenkins's conduct as "worthy of all commendation."[33]

At army headquarters, meanwhile, Joseph Johnston spent the entire morning and most of the afternoon waiting anxiously for word of the attack at Seven Pines. His conduct on this day is almost inexplicable. He virtually relinquished control of the operation to Longstreet despite knowing as early as 9:00 A.M. that something was wrong. Duty impelled him to ride personally the few miles for an explanation and a possible alteration of the plan to salvage the offensive. Instead, Johnston remained at headquarters, a general wrapped within a cocoon of ignorance and bad luck.

About midday, Johnston relocated headquarters to a house across the Nine Mile Road from "Old Tavern." Men from Whiting's division lounged in the nearby fields and woods. At 2:30 P.M., with his patience frayed, the commanding general dispatched Major Jasper Whiting of Smith's staff to Longstreet for information. Within a half hour Robert E. Lee joined Johnston, and the two officers conferred inside the house. In an adjoining room and outside in the yard, staff officers heard the sounds of combat from the south. But an acoustic shadow or unusual atmospheric phenomenon that disrupted the normal transmission of sound wrapped a pocket of silence around the room in which Johnston and Lee talked, preventing them from hearing the gunfire. Lee thought he heard musketry, but Johnston dismissed it as artillery fire. Sometime after three o'clock a dispatch arrived from Harvey Hill reporting the action, and when Longstreet's request for assistance came in less than an hour later, Johnston finally acted.[34]

Johnston ordered Chase Whiting forward with four brigades down the Nine Mile Road toward Fair Oaks. Johnston directed Whiting's fifth brigade through the woods to Longstreet. Before long the division's lead brigade struck a Federal line north of the railroad station. The Confederates wheeled into line and charged into a wall of artillery and musket fire that stopped them cold. Gustavus Smith arrived and assumed command of his division, bringing two more brigades forward for a renewal of the attack. The Southerners cleared the woods and stepped into the open field beneath the home of a family named Adams.[35]

Opposing the Southerners were an isolated brigade from Couch's division and Brigadier General John Sedgwick's division of the Second Corps. Sedgwick's troops had been across the flooded Chickahominy when the battle opened at Seven Pines. When George McClellan, who was ill from neuralgia, learned of the Confederate offensive, he ordered Brigadier General Edwin V. "Bull" Sumner to cross the river with his Second Corps. Sumner's men filed over the so-called Grapevine Bridge, built earlier by the Federals despite protests from an engineer officer that the rope and plank span would be unsafe. The weight of the troops stabilized the damaged bridge, and Sedgwick's three brigades arrived at the Adams House to assist in the repulse of the initial Confederate attack. They were ready when the second wave of Rebels charged.[36]

The struggle around the Adams House was nearly as fierce and deadly as the combat at Seven Pines. Smith hurled a third brigade into the maelstrom, but the Federals held firm, finishing the action with a counterattack that shoved the Southerners into the woods. The second of Sumner's divisions arrived and secured the position. Twilight began to darken the woods as the gunfire flickered and died.[37]

Joseph Johnston wanted a final look at the terrain and the enemy's position. As he rode toward the railroad station, a burst of gunfire flashed nearby. A bullet ripped into his right shoulder, and seconds later an artillery shell burst above him, its pieces ripping into his chest, breaking some ribs. Staff officers secured a litter, and the painfully wounded general was carried toward headquarters.

Lee and President Davis, who had ridden out to the field, met the litter party and talked with Johnston. The months of feuding between the president and the army commander were momentarily forgotten as Davis said that he hoped Johnston would soon be able to return to duty. The litter bearers carried Johnston to the rear for medical aid, and Davis assigned Smith to command the army.[38]

About one o'clock on the morning of June 1, Longstreet walked into army headquarters. He had already learned of Johnston's fall and reported to Smith. The generals talked for nearly two hours, with Smith ordering a renewal of the attack. Longstreet departed at three o'clock, returned to his headquarters, and rested for an hour; then he remounted and rode toward Seven Pines. Daybreak broke ahead of him.[39]

Longstreet reached "Casey's Redoubt" just as volleys of musketry shattered the morning's quiet. Harvey Hill, who had had a second sleepless night, stood in front of a tent while bullets clipped the air. Longstreet reined up, saying: "You here have taken the bull by the horns and must fight him out." Moments later Brigadier General William Mahone arrived at the head of his brigade from Huger's division. Mahone had never met Hill before, and this was not the best of times for the division commander. Believing Mahone was late, Hill lashed into the brigadier, berating him with what Mahone described as "a harsh and unjust criticism." Hill stopped when an aide galloped in exclaiming that the Federals were coming. Hill ordered Mahone forward.[40]

Mahone's two regiments—a third had been detached—advanced into a furious battle along the railroad north of Seven Pines. Brigadier General Lewis A. Armistead's brigade had already been routed, and the troops of George Pickett, Cadmus Wilcox, and Roger Pryor were taking a pounding from the Union Second Corps's division of Brigadier General Israel Richardson, Longstreet's foe at Blackburn's Ford. The brigades of Armistead, Wilcox, and Pryor had been shifted into the woods north of the Williamsburg Road before nightfall on the 31st. They had been spared the day before, but their good fortune ended on this morning.[41]

For nearly six hours the combat scorched the woods along the railroad and the men caught in there. A Union officer said that their mile-long line "seemed to have become one continuous blaze of musketry." Confederate thrusts recoiled before Federal counterthrusts. Before noon the Southerners withdrew, and the Northerners pursued a short distance before additional enemy troops stopped them. By one o'clock in the afternoon the Battle of Seven Pines had ceased. Both sides had had enough.[42]

The two-day struggle exacted a price of over 11,000 casualties. Of the Confederates, 6,134 were killed, wounded, and missing; of the Federals, 5,031. Over thirteen percent of those engaged fell or were captured. Johnston's fine offensive scheme foundered, and no military objectives were gained. After midnight on June 2, the Confederates retired to the west. Behind them, the woods held only the dead and the wounded amid a debris of discarded arms and equipment.[43]

A Confederate staff officer subsequently described Seven Pines as a "waste of life and a great disappointment." Porter Alexander, whose writings on the war stand unexcelled among officers of the army, stated that the engagement "affords a most striking illustration of how people may misunderstand each other in important affairs; & of the supreme importance, in such matters, not only of having everything thoroughly understood, but of the commanding general supervising by his staff the actual execution of all orders in order to guard against accidents & misunderstandings." In another work, Alexander described Seven Pines as "a monument of caution against verbal understandings."[44]

As Alexander concluded, the misunderstandings between Johnston and Longstreet disrupted the offensive plan and gave shape to the resulting battle. Both men must share the blame, with Johnston taking the primary responsibility. He surely believed that Longstreet knew his role, but once Johnston learned otherwise early on the 31st, he should have responded more expeditiously than sending two staff officers in pursuit of an allegedly lost general and an entire division of troops. Even after Captain Beckham reported Longstreet on the Williamsburg Road, Johnston did not react but waited nearly five more hours before seeking information. For most of the 31st, Johnston was a commander without control of a major portion of his army and did little to rectify the confusion.

Johnston's responsibility for the day's event does not excuse Longstreet. From the evidence and from his actions early that morning, the wing commander made an honest mistake in moving his division to the Williamsburg Road. How he could have misunderstood Johnston's simple and tactically sound battle plan after hours of deliberation remains a mystery. Longstreet never admitted— either in private correspondence that has been uncovered or in his published writings—that he had erred so grievously despite the published accounts of others.

Once Hill advanced, Longstreet, like Johnston, relinquished control of the battle to subordinates. It could be conjectured that he spent a portion of the afternoon chatting and joking with Jeb Stuart, who was a personable companion, while Harvey Hill's men fought in a terrible battle. Longstreet had told Hill beforehand that he should ask for support if his division needed it, and when Hill did, Longstreet responded. But the wing commander mishandled Wilcox's three brigades, ignored George Pickett's brigade, and never pushed Huger to advance or find out if that officer could bolster Hill's right flank. Altogether, May 31, 1862, was perhaps the worst of the war for Longstreet. He did few things correctly and none well.

His performance indicated a general who needed more seasoning in the handling of large bodies of troops. He commanded more units on May 31 than any subordinate officer had in an engagement until then. He directed the movement of thirteen brigades, roughly thirty thousand men, on terrain that hampered, if not precluded, firm control. As he had at Williamsburg, Longstreet granted wide discretion to subordinates in tactical executions, and Hill measured up. Longstreet would have served his good friend better if he had taken a more active role once the fighting commenced.

What cannot be defended, however, was Longstreet's unjustifiable, even reprehensible, decision to blame Benjamin Huger for the day's confusion and problems. Longstreet waited less than a week after the battle to present a case against Huger. On June 7, in a private letter to Johnston, he wrote:

> The failure of complete success on Saturday [May 31] I attribute to the slow movements of Gen. Huger's command. This threw perhaps the hardest part of the battle upon my own poor Division. It is pretty cut up, but as true and ready as ever. Our ammunition was nearly exhausted when Whiting moved, and I could not therefore move on with the rush that we could had his movement been earlier. We did advance however through three other encampments, and only stopped at nightfall. The enemy ran in great confusion. But the troops were arranged [en] echelon, and we encountered fresh troops every few hundred yards. These readily fell back however, as . . . ours came to them closely pursued.
>
> I can't help but think that a display of his forces on the left flank of the enemy, by Gen. Huger, would have completed the affair and

given Whiting as easy and pretty a game as was ever upon a battle field. Slow men are a little out of place upon the field. All together, it was very well, but I cant help but regret that it was not complete.[45]

The letter was filled with misstatements of facts and falsehoods. Three days later, when he wrote his official report, Longstreet paraphrased and reduced his charges in the letter but still attributed the lack of "a complete success" to Huger's not being in position "within eight hours of the proper time." Longstreet further stated that Huger's division "was intended" to make a strong movement around the Union left flank and attack the enemy's rear. Longstreet did not mention why Huger had been delayed.[46]

Johnston, in turn, allowed Longstreet to shift the responsibility to Huger. In his report, he stated that Longstreet's orders were to support Hill on the Williamsburg Road and Huger's were to attack the Federal flank "unless he found in his front force enough to occupy his division." Johnston covered up the misunderstanding of orders between him and Longstreet, probably as much to protect himself as to shield Longstreet. When G. W. Smith filed his report with comments about Longstreet's movement on the 31st, Johnston asked him to delete those remarks.[47]

Johnston wrote his report on June 24. Later he admitted to Smith that he deserved the blame for the "misunderstanding" of orders. When he wrote his memoirs, over twenty years after the battle, he again blamed Huger and his men. Interestingly, however, in two private postwar letters to Harvey Hill, Johnston complained about Longstreet's report, insisting that "in subsequent letters" Longstreet "retracts much said in the report." He described the report as "very unsatisfactory."[48]

Johnston and Longstreet adhered to their story publicly until the end of their lives. When Huger learned the contents of the generals' reports, he wrote to Longstreet, who did not reply. Then when Johnston refused to investigate, Huger asked Davis to order Johnston to prefer charges and convene a court-martial. But Johnston would not prefer charges, and Davis agreed to a court of inquiry "as soon as the state of the service will permit." The court never convened. "Indeed," Porter Alexander wrote afterward, "it is almost tragic the way in which he [Huger] became the scapegoat of this occasion."[49]

This controversy lay in the future. For the Confederates, Seven

Pines marked a change in the course of the war in Virginia. About noon on June 1, Robert E. Lee rode to the headquarters of G. W. Smith. President Davis had appointed Lee to temporary command of the army. Among the officers and men, it was expected that Johnston would return.[50]

CHAPTER

7

"THE STAFF
IN MY RIGHT HAND"

General Robert E. Lee assumed command of the soon-to-be-chris-tened Army of Northern Virginia shortly after noon on June 1, 1862. With the wounding of Joseph Johnston the night before, President Jefferson Davis turned to Lee, his military adviser. The two men had worked well together during the past few months. Lee had earned Davis's trust and confidence, and with no other general in the army capable of replacing Johnston, the president appointed Lee. Davis's decision was the turning point of the war in the East.

Lee, a fifty-five-year-old Virginian, was the son of Henry "Light-Horse Harry" Lee of Revolutionary renown, and a career soldier. He was graduated from West Point in 1829, ranking second in the class with an unblemished demerit record. He rendered distin-guished service in the Mexican War as an officer on Winfield Scott's staff. Scott regarded him as the finest officer in the army, and in April 1861, Union authorities offered Lee command of an army. But Lee resigned his commission when the Old Dominion seceded, reported to Richmond, and served as commander of the state's burgeoning forces. In the fall, he directed a campaign in western Virginia that resulted in disappointment and failure. A trained engi-neer, Lee oversaw the construction of defenses along the south Atlantic coast during the winter until Davis recalled him to Rich-mond as his military adviser in March 1862.[1]

Porter Alexander wrote, "No one could meet Lee and fail to be impressed with his dignity of character, his intellectual power, and his calm self-reliance." He was a strikingly handsome and enormously talented man. Lee possessed an exceptional intelligence of both depth and discernment. He could visualize strategy across a broad landscape and tactics across the terrain of a battlefield. Schooled in the science of warfare, he had an aptitude, an acumen for the art of warfare. Lee saw, as if magnified, opportunities within a theater of operations or on a battlefield where others saw only dim outlines. Lee sifted through reconnaissance reports, Northern newspapers, prisoner statements, captured correspondence, and spy information. From these strands he wove a strategic or tactical fabric. With his deductive reasoning he excelled in the interpretation of data that were often confusing or contradictory.[2]

Lee understood the workings of an army, the requisite administrative details that made an army function before it could be unsheathed as a weapon. Although he loathed paperwork, Lee worked tirelessly at supply, commissary, and organizational problems that comprised the unending functions of army headquarters. As the war lengthened and the army's needs reached critical proportions, the demands on his time and skills multiplied. That the Army of Northern Virginia retained its prowess as long as it did can be attributed to Lee's ample abilities.[3]

As Lee demonstrated in his relationship with Davis, he worked well with even the most difficult people. He was a kind, gentle man by nature who, Moxley Sorrel said, was "approachable by all." Lee dealt courteously and frankly with Davis and members of the cabinet, soothed the fragile egos of officers, expressed a constant concern for the welfare of his men, and inspired loyalty. "No man," an officer remarked of Lee, "was so tender to the faults of others as he was or so ready to assume his own."[4]

His dignified bearing or "calm self-reliance," in Alexander's words, hid Lee's inner passions. He had a temper that could be furious for a brief period of time, but few men ever witnessed it because Lee controlled it with an iron self-composure. What most saw was a general who could be "as calm as a summer cloud" even on the eve of battle. When someone or something displeased or angered Lee, his face and neck reddened and his words came in clips. Such outbursts were uncharacteristic of him, but when they occurred, the recipients and eyewitnesses remembered and recorded them.[5]

Lee's guiding principles were duty and religion. Duty governed a soldier's life, prescribed its limits, and, like a lodestar, led the way. Once Lee decided his duty and obeyed it, however, he left the outcome to Divine Providence. Lee's God interceded and controlled the actions of mankind, who submitted unquestioningly to His will. The two principles guided his command techniques. "I think and work with all my power," Lee once stated, "to bring the troops to the right place at the right time; then I have done my duty. As soon as I order them into battle, I leave my army in the hands of God."[6]

When Lee relieved G. W. Smith of command on that June Sabbath, the Confederate rank and file, sitting around campfires and within headquarters tents, surely speculated about the new commander. His appointment, Longstreet wrote afterward, was "far from reconciling the troops to the loss of our beloved chief [Johnston]." Few had ever spoken with Lee, watched him in councils, or served under him in the antebellum army. Uncertainty about his abilities led to misgivings about his appointment. Only time and battlefield success would change the army's view; for the moment, the officers and men reassured themselves that Johnston would soon return.[7]

Lee responded to the situation in the only manner he could: He went to work. Before his first day in command had ended, he issued a special order: "Commanders of divisions and brigades will take every precaution and use every means in their power to have their commands in readiness at all times for immediate action." He further directed that the men should be well rested and "fresh" and that all excess baggage should be turned in to depots.[8]

Two days later, on June 3, he ordered Major Walter Stevens, the army's chief engineer, to examine the lines, place cannon at commanding points, and oversee the construction of fieldworks. "My object," he informed Stevens, "is to make use of every means in our power to strengthen ourselves and enable us to fight the enemy to the best advantage." The major had the authority to requisition working parties from division commanders.[9]

That same day Lee gathered his division commanders for a meeting. Lee wanted a firsthand description of the army's condition after the Battle of Seven Pines and wanted to discuss a course of action. Little had changed tactically or strategically since the two-day struggle. McClellan's Army of the Potomac held the eastern banks of the Chickahominy River, his various corps divided by the flooded stream. Federal artillery crews lobbed shells into the Confederate lines, but the cautious McClellan, as he had at Yorktown, appeared content to rely on his cannon while awaiting the arrival of reinforcements.[10]

Lee had opposed Johnston's withdrawal up the Peninsula to Richmond, believing that the defense of the capital should be waged away from the city. While Lee concurred with Johnston about the principle of concentration of force, he disagreed with the former commander that territory should be sacrificed or abandoned to achieve the concentration. Lee would give primacy to holding Confederate soil for logistical and political reasons. He understood that if the enemy seized Southern territory, the Confederates lost valuable foodstuffs and livestock. Politically, the expansion of Union control over portions of the Confederacy disheartened the Southern populace and encouraged the Northern citizenry. Before he could retrieve what Johnston had relinquished, however, he had to save the capital.[11]

The division commanders met with Lee at "The Chimneys" on Nine Mile Road, near the headquarters of John Magruder. Present, for certain, were Longstreet, Magruder, Harvey Hill, Chase Whiting, and Robert Toombs, a brigade commander under Magruder. Longstreet stated afterward that some major generals arrived as the meeting ended. After the war, this conference would generate some controversy when Colonel Armistead L. Long, a member of Lee's staff at the time, alleged in a newspaper article that the generals discussed the abandonment of Richmond. The participants denied this, however. Lee would surely not have countenanced such a proposal, given his reaction to the idea at a cabinet meeting in May.[12]

The conference was "quite protracted," according to Major Charles Marshall, one of Lee's aides. Lee posed the question whether the army should withdraw closer to Richmond, await a Federal attack, or assail the enemy. Magruder and Whiting spoke at length, both advocating a retirement away from McClellan's lines. Hill evidently said little, and Longstreet claimed that he did not voice his opinion, preferring to confer with Lee in private. President Jefferson Davis arrived during the discussions, sat quietly, and listened. When Toombs suggested a withdrawal to higher ground for his brigade, Hill, who disliked the former Georgia congressman and senator, chided him about it, and the meeting "took a playful turn." Like Davis, Lee only listened and then dismissed the officers.[13]

In his memoirs, Longstreet stated that when he learned of the meeting, he was not reassured about Lee because "experience had told him that secrecy in war was an essential element of success; that public discussion and secrecy were incompatible." But when Lee revealed nothing of his own views at the council, Longstreet thought it a "wise example." Longstreet and other generals soon learned that "Gen Lee was extremely reticent & seldom communicated his private views & opinions on pending operations to any one."[14]

On the day after the conference, Longstreet rode to army headquarters at the invitation of Lee. Headquarters were at the "High Meadows" farmhouse of Mrs. Mary C. Dabbs, widow of Josiah Dabbs, about two miles from the capital on the Nine Mile Road. Lee's office occupied a rear room on the first floor. His small staff —colonels Robert H. Chilton and Armistead Long, and majors Randolph Talcott, Walter H. Taylor, Charles S. Venable, and Charles Marshall—conducted the army's business in the front room. Taylor, Venable, and Marshall would in time comprise the inner circle of the general's staff.[15]

Lee and Longstreet talked privately. The subject most likely centered on the previous day's discussions. Although he had not said so at the conference, Longstreet opposed a withdrawal closer to Richmond. Instead, he suggested to Lee that the army should turn McClellan's right flank at Beaver Dam Creek near Mechanicsville. He had made a similar recommendation to Johnston before Seven Pines. Lee evidently listened most of the time, impressed with Longstreet's views and advice.[16]

Four days after their meeting, Lee wrote to Davis: "Longstreet is a Capital soldier. His recommendations hitherto have been good, & I have confidence in him." With their headquarters near each other's, the two generals conversed frequently. "It soon became apparent," Moxley Sorrel wrote, "that he [Longstreet] was to be quite close to Lee."[17]

Every day Lee examined the lines that extended from New Bridge on the Chickahominy southward to beyond the Charles City Road. The working parties toiled on the fieldworks, grumbling about the new commander whom they derisively called the "King of Spades."

Despite the digging and filling, the soldiers expected a battle at any moment. Lulls in skirmishing and artillery firing allowed pickets from both armies to meet halfway between the lines and exchange newspapers, canteens, and drinks.[18]

The Federals were as active as their counterparts during those June days. McClellan informed Washington on a regular basis that he would advance soon against Richmond and relayed one more excuse for delaying the offensive. Through the month he shifted all but the Fifth Corps, under Brigadier General Fitz John Porter, south of the Chickahominy. While the massing of the army's corps south of the river indicated an offensive in that sector, McClellan intended to lay siege to the Confederate capital. Porter's corps, however, was isolated and vulnerable.[19]

While McClellan pushed his fieldworks closer to Richmond, Lee formulated an offensive. On June 8, he wrote to Stonewall Jackson in the Shenandoah Valley to ask if his command could leave the valley and unite with Lee's. Three days later Lee sent a second dispatch to Jackson informing him that reinforcements were en route "to enable you to crush the forces opposed to you." When Jackson had accomplished this, Lee directed that he march eastward and "sweep down" on McClellan's right flank and rear when Lee's troops assailed the Union front.[20]

Cavalry commander Jeb Stuart, meanwhile, told Lee that John Mosby, one of Stuart's scouts, reported that McClellan's right flank and supply line were guarded only by cavalry outposts. On June 11, the day he wrote his second letter to Jackson, Lee ordered Stuart to operate against the Federal supply and communication lines and gather information on troop dispositions. Stuart started the next day and was gone until the 15th, riding an entire circuit around the Union army. That spectacular operation garnered the intelligence Lee needed and embarrassed McClellan, and with the loss of only one man.[21]

Lee reacted immediately to Stuart's report. On the morning of June 16, he directed Jackson to move eastward "to unite with this army." Lee cautioned that "the movement must be secret" and asked Jackson to meet with him "at some point on your approach to the Chickahominy." Later that morning, with Colonel Armistead Long, Lee rode to a point opposite Porter's position behind Beaver Dam Creek. Lee studied the ground carefully, and then as much to himself as to his aide, asked: "Now, Colonel Long, how are we to get at those people?"[22]

When Lee returned to the Dabbs house, Longstreet stopped in to propose that Jackson be ordered eastward for an assault against the Union right flank. Lee confided to him that it had already been done and then outlined his plan for an attack north and south of the Chickahominy. Longstreet's response was that if the frontal attack south of the river were delayed, Jackson could be caught between the Pamunkey and Chickahominy rivers, and if the Federals had destroyed the bridges and ferries across the Pamunkey as they should have, Jackson might be "in perilous condition." Longstreet recommended that Lee concentrate the attack on the north side of the river and maintain a defensive posture south of the stream. Lee thought about it and agreed.[23]

After the war, Longstreet publicly claimed that he originated the offensive. His assertion sparked a controversy with former members of Lee's staff and with former generals. Charles Marshall scornfully noted in a private letter that it would be the best course to let Longstreet prove "the existence of that genius that obscured itself so obstinately during the war." Longstreet privately boasted that the operation "was planned by me." That was absurd, but he deserved more credit than Marshall and others gave him. At minimum he helped to refine Lee's plan.[24]

During the next week, the Confederates completed the fieldworks and engaged in picket and artillery exchanges with the Federals. Lee, who had reorganized some units, had eight infantry divisions and Stuart's brigade of cavalry. Longstreet's division still consisted of six brigades, with Brigadier General Winfield S. Featherstone's three regiments of Mississippi troops replacing Raleigh Colston's brigade since Seven Pines. When Jackson arrived with three divisions, including Whiting's that Lee had sent to him, the army numbered nearly eighty-six thousand troops.[25]

About midday on Monday, June 23, Jackson rode up to the Dabbs house. His uniform was dusty, and he looked tired after a sixty-mile ride on horseback. The hero of the Shenandoah Valley Campaign never cared much for appearance, however. A soldier who had seen him just days before described the general as "an awkward, tired, humpshouldered, careworn looking man, dressed in the very plainest garb." His uniform and cap, the soldier thought, looked "very seedy." An Englishman who was visiting the army said Jackson's "wardrobe isn't worth a dollar."[26]

Despite appearances, Jackson was a soldier, an implacable warrior. A stern, fanatically religious man, he was a difficult, unbending taskmaster who pushed his officers and men to the limit. They complained about his relentlessness on the march and laughed about his eccentricities. But he had led them to victory like an Old Testament warrior, and they called him "Old Jack." No officer in the army, including Lee, enjoyed Jackson's renown with the Southern populace.

Lee greeted Jackson when he arrived at headquarters, and they walked together into the house. Lee offered the travel-worn officer a drink, and Jackson accepted a glass of milk. Within a few minutes, Harvey Hill entered the room, followed shortly by Longstreet and Powell Hill. Lee then sketched his plan of the offensive. When he finished, he suggested that the four men discuss the details and excused himself, saying that "he had other matters to look after for a few minutes."[27]

Longstreet turned to Jackson and said: "As you have the longest march to make, and the one likely to meet opposition, you had better fix the time for the attack to begin."

"Daylight of the 25th," replied Jackson.

"You will encounter Federal cavalry and roads blocked by felled timber, if nothing more formidable," argued Longstreet. "Ought you not to give yourself more time?"

Jackson concurred, setting the time for daylight of the 26th.[28]

Lee reentered the room and was informed of the date. The five officers continued the discussion, and then Lee issued verbal orders for each general. Written orders, Lee said, would follow. The meeting adjourned; Longstreet and the two Hills returned to their divisions; Jackson remounted and headed west to hurry his command forward—he had less than forty hours to be in position.[29]

The next morning Lee's confidential orders were delivered to the division commanders. Jackson would initiate the offensive at 3:00 A.M. on the 26th, moving to Pole Green Church, three miles northeast of the Federal position behind Beaver Dam Creek, and communicating with a detached brigade of Powell Hill's division. When Hill learned of Jackson's arrival, he would cross the Chickahominy at Meadow Bridge, march on Mechanicsville, and clear the

Mechanicsville Bridge for the divisions of Longstreet and Harvey Hill. Jackson, meanwhile, would advance "well to his left," turning Porter's position. Once the commands united they would sweep down the river and close on McClellan's rear. The army's other divisions would hold their position "at the point of the bayonet," if necessary. It was a complicated scheme that required timeliness and coordination.[30]

With the orders issued, with the divisions readied, and with the rations cooked, Lee and the army waited. What had been expected for three weeks was at hand. Lee told an acquaintance after the conflict that the only way the Confederates could have won the war was to "crush" the Federals in the field of battle. In his first major campaign of the war, Lee gambled that McClellan would not exploit the Rebels' weak southern front while he moved his units into position to "crush" the Union right flank, save the capital, and if possible destroy the enemy host.[31]

Roughly ten days before, Porter Alexander, the army's ordnance chief, expressed to Captain Joseph C. Ives of President Davis's staff his speculation whether Lee was audacious enough as a commander. The Confederacy, with its inferior manpower and resources, Alexander reasoned, made audacity an "*absolute requisite*" to give "*any chance* at all." Ives turned to his friend and said, "Alexander, if there is one man in either army, Federal or Confederate, who is head & shoulders, far above every other one in either army in audacity that man is Gen. Lee, and you will very soon have lived to see it. Lee is audacity personified. His name is audacity, and you need not be afraid of not seeing all of it that you will want to see."[32]

Before daylight on June 26, Confederate divisions assigned to the attack force moved out. By eight o'clock, Longstreet and Harvey Hill's troops were in position on the plateau above Mechanicsville Bridge; upstream, Powell Hill's brigades rested before Meadow Bridge. Lee and his staff joined Longstreet and Hill on the Mechanicsville Pike. Within an hour or so the president and his aides arrived. All waited expectantly for Powell Hill to cross the river, which was the signal that Jackson had closed on the Union flank. With each passing hour, however, Hill's so-called Light Division remained in place at Meadow Bridge. Lee's concern also rested with the forces south of the river, where McClellan had tested the

Confederate lines the day before, igniting a sharp engagement near Oak Grove. If McClellan enlarged the probe on this day, he might shatter the lines and march into the capital.[33]

Finally, at 3:00 P.M., Powell Hill crossed the river. His patience had ended, and he went forward on his own initiative. Union pickets scattered before the oncoming Confederates, racing through the streets of Mechanicsville. Porter's blue-bloused artillerymen opened fire on the enemy brigades. When Longstreet and Harvey Hill saw the Federals fleeing through the town, they started their columns across the river. Lee rode with them, entered the village, and learned that Powell Hill had advanced without Jackson.[34]

Lee had little choice but to allow Hill to proceed with an attack. Although the army commander did not want to launch a frontal assault, he had to keep McClellan's attention north of the river. At six o'clock Hill sent three brigades forward against the Union right front.[35]

A mile to the east on a plateau behind Beaver Dam Creek, Porter's infantry, supported by sixteen cannon, waited. The Federal position, in Porter Alexander's words, was "absolutely impregnable to a front attack." In May, Johnston's engineers had selected the site as the anchor of the Confederate left flank if Johnston positioned his army north of the river. On this day, however, the Yankees held the ground, and they punished the Rebels. Hill's men charged with yells into a cauldron of musketry and shellfire. The Confederates fell back, charged a second time to within a hundred yards of the enemy works, and retired fighting. At sunset Powell Hill hurled another of his brigades and one from Harvey Hill's division against Porter's left. This attack never had a chance and resulted in additional slaughter. A Union officer said that the Southern dead lay "like flies in a bowl of sugar." The Confederates lost about fourteen hundred; the Federals, less than four hundred.[36]

Where was Jackson? In bivouac between Pole Green Church and Hundley's Corner, approximately three miles from Porter's rear. His three divisions had spent the previous night at Ashland, fourteen miles distant. Although Jackson had ordered the march for 2:30 A.M., his troops did not start until 8:00 A.M., five hours after he was supposed to contact Powell Hill's brigade. The march was slow; Federal cavalry snipped at the vanguard of the column, forcing skirmishers to deploy. By late afternoon Jackson's men heard the sounds of battle, but he ordered a halt before sundown. He did not know what the gunfire meant. "Jackson came up," Longstreet stated, "marched by the fight without giving attention, and went into camp." Moxley Sorrell believed, with justification, that "had Jackson been in position the enemy would have melted before us. He had promised to be there on the morning of the 26th." In his report, Lee attributed Jackson's failure to "unavoidable delays."[37]

The Confederates around Mechanicsville stirred before dawn. At first light, Union artillery and musket fire flashed along the plateau, shielding the retreating Federals who had learned of Jackson's presence. Powell Hill's skirmishers followed, coming under artillery fire from Jackson's cannoneers, who mistook them for the enemy. Lee arrived after a while, found Powell Hill with Jackson at a church, and conferred with the latter. Lee told Jackson to hurry his march to Cold Harbor and to turn at Powhite Creek, where Lee expected Porter to make another stand. Harvey Hill would support Jackson while Powell Hill and Longstreet marched from Mechanicsville.[38]

Powell Hill arrived first before the Union position at Gaines's Mill, at about 1:00 P.M. Longstreet followed shortly, marching on a road on Hill's right. The ground before them and the Union position looked much like the one at Beaver Dam Creek. Instead of being deployed behind Powhite Creek as Lee had anticipated, Porter had massed his infantry and artillery in three lines on a wooded plateau behind Boatswain's Swamp, a small, torpid stream that did not appear on Confederate maps. Nearly thirty thousand Federals held the position, with support approaching from the south.[39]

Lee was now on the field and ordered Powell Hill to attack. The Light Division deployed rapidly, crossed the brow of a ridge, and plunged down the slope toward the swamp. The Federals opened fire as soon as Hill's men passed over the crest. With the spirit they had shown the day before, the Confederates charged into the underbrush along the morass. The Union works exploded in musketry. Some of Hill's units pressed ahead, penetrating the first line, only to be blown back. Other regiments struggled through the swamp, met a wall of flame, and retreated. For two hours, until after four o'clock, Hill's men clung to the ground, fighting until they wrecked themselves in "splendid, but vain & bloody, isolated assaults."[40]

Lee hurried a staff officer to Longstreet, ordering a demonstration against the Union left to relieve the pressure on Hill. Longstreet had his headquarters at the home of Dr. Gaines, west of Powhite

Creek, where he had deployed his brigades behind a hill. About five o'clock, Cadmus Wilcox with three brigades emerged from behind the crest and advanced toward Porter's left front. The Confederates crossed the creek to an open field, a quarter mile in depth and partly planted in wheat. From the plateau in front and from across the Chickahominy, Union cannon raked the three brigades. "I was, in fact," Longstreet reported, "in the position from which the enemy wished us to attack him." He halted the advance; if he were to help Hill, he would have to order an assault.[41]

Longstreet selected George Pickett's and Richard Anderson's brigades for the task. The Virginians and South Carolinians marched over the crest and down the slope toward Powhite Creek, on the left of Wilcox's stalled brigades. Simultaneously, to their left, Chase Whiting's two brigades—men from five states under Brigadier General John B. Hood and Colonel Evander Law—appeared. Lee had ordered them forward and directed that Jackson's remaining units, which had filtered onto the field throughout the afternoon, press the Union right. As the four brigades closed, they merged into one line.[42]

The Union ranks exploded in flame and smoke. "The roar of musketry was so terrific," recounted a Virginian with Pickett, "that it was impossible to hear anything else." Tom Goree described the Federal fire as a "perfect hail." The Rebels screamed their yell and drove forward. Like a wave they crashed over the first line, sustaining their power, and seized the second tier of works halfway up the slope. Now it was the Southerners' turn: They triggered a volley that rolled up and over the crest. The musketry slammed in the Union ranks like a hammer, pounding a hole in the line. The attackers swarmed over the crest.[43]

Clubbing and bayoneting, the Confederates seized fourteen cannon. Union cavalrymen spurred toward the Rebels in a counterattack that ended in a heap of dead and dying men and horses. Behind the Southerners, their comrades in the other divisions were advancing as Lee finally cobbled together a coordinated assault. For two days Fitz Porter's Yankees had fought valiantly and virtually alone, with only limited support from McClellan. The Federals now retreated before this onslaught, leaving behind twenty-eight hundred prisoners and twenty-two cannon. Porter's corps crossed during the night—the Confederates had swept the enemy from north of the Chickahominy.[44]

The Battle of Gaines's Mill cost Lee's army roughly eighty-seven hundred men. Powell Hill's division and the four brigades that spearheaded the final assault incurred the largest losses. Longstreet's friend George Pickett was unhorsed during the attack with a bullet in the shoulder. Soon afterward a staff officer found Pickett in a hollow "bewailing himself," asking for litter bearers because he was mortally wounded. The officer examined the wound, saw it was slight, and rode away since Pickett was "perfectly able to take care of himself." As darkness set in, a Texan said that "friends walked and looked for friends, and brothers knew not the fate of each other living or dead."[45]

For a second consecutive day Lee had to refashion an attack plan. He had not expected Porter to be in line behind Boatswain's Swamp, which negated the turning movement Lee had plotted. But for a second day Jackson was late; his division had taken the wrong road because of a guide's error. During the afternoon, Lee was anxiously awaiting Jackson's arrival, and when he learned the general was on the field, Lee galloped to meet him. Lee's staff believed, in Porter Alexander's words, that Lee was "deeply disappointed" with Jackson's performance during the two days. "Jackson," Alexander argued, "simply *was not Jackson*."[46]

As they had at Beaver Dam Creek, the Confederates attacked piecemeal and suffered for it. The attack of Whiting's and Longstreet's brigades—"The charge of these troops through the open field was the grandest sight I ever saw," wrote Goree—salvaged the victory. In his report, Lee praised Longstreet, writing that the general "resolved with characteristic promptness to carry the heights by assault" after he realized the futility of the demonstration Lee had ordered. Walter Taylor of Lee's staff stated afterward that "no more creditable performance can be found in the history" of the army than the charge of these four brigades. Taylor believed that where Longstreet's troops hit the Union line was the initial breach.[47]

Saturday, June 28, was a day of rest and speculation for the Confederates around Gaines's Mill and Cold Harbor. At daylight Longstreet sent skirmishers probing southward toward the Chickahominy, bagging more prisoners who had fallen asleep during their retreat. When they approached the stream, Union artillery opened fire. Throughout the morning Lee searched for evidence of McClellan's next move. Lee could not believe that the Union general would abandon his supply base on the Pamunkey River at White

House. Lee ordered Jeb Stuart's cavalry and Richard Ewell's infantry division eastward toward the York River Railroad, McClellan's supply line to White House. Toward midday clouds of dust rolled northward from beyond the river, indicating a retreat. When a courier from Stuart reported that the Federals had burned the railroad bridge over the Chickahominy and a message from one of Ewell's brigadiers confirmed the southward march of the enemy, Lee thought that McClellan was retreating either back down the Peninsula or toward the James River. But Lee needed more evidence before he would issue marching orders.[48]

Lee spent the night at Longstreet's headquarters in Dr. Gaines's house. Before he went to bed, he ordered two of Longstreet's engineers, Major R. K. Meade and Lieutenant Samuel R. Johnston, to cross the river during the night on a reconnaissance mission. The two engineers returned soon after sunrise with the news that the Federals had evacuated a key position south of the river. McClellan must be in retreat toward the James River, Lee reasoned, and issued orders for the pursuit. A short time later he wrote to Davis that "though not certain" of McClellan's route, "the whole army has been put in motion upon this supposition."[49]

The entire Confederate army—all the units north and south of the Chickahominy—had an assignment on the 29th if Lee were to interdict McClellan's withdrawal the next day. Longstreet's and Powell Hill's divisions under Longstreet's command marched first because they were ready when Lee's orders came. They moved, back across the river at New Bridge to the outskirts of Richmond, swinging into the Darbytown Road. By sunset they bivouacked at the intersection of the Darbytown–Long Bridge roads at Atlee's farm, roughly four miles southwest of the road on which the Federals were retiring. The two divisions had covered thirteen miles, a "forced march," in torrid heat and humidity.[50]

While Longstreet and Hill looped behind the Confederate units south of the river, Magruder, Huger, and Theophilus H. Holmes with their divisions pushed eastward toward the Union columns. Huger and Holmes accomplished little, advancing a few miles on the Charles City and New Market roads, respectively. To their north, on the Williamsburg Road, the flamboyant "Prince John" Magruder —"He was fond of pomp and show and always dressed in full uniform with all attendants allowed," wrote a soldier—struck Federal troops near Savage Station. Magruder engaged the enemy for over two hours in what Lee termed a "severe action." The Confederates incurred casualties of about 450, primarily from Major General Lafayette McLaws's division. After nightfall the rear elements of the Union army marched away from Savage Station, leaving behind twenty-five hundred sick and wounded soldiers and piles of charred supplies. By the next morning all of McClellan's troops had passed White Oak Swamp and had partially destroyed the bridge.[51]

Contrary to Lee's expectations, Magruder's men fought alone at Savage Station. Huger failed to support Magruder's right flank on the Charles City Road, and more important, Jackson failed to cross the Chickahominy and attack the Federal rear. Before the battle flared at the railroad stop, D. R. Jones, commanding Magruder's left flank division, requested assistance from Jackson, who replied that he had "other important duty to perform." In his report, Jackson never explained those duties, but as Walter Taylor noted, "certainly there is no room for misunderstanding as to his orders"—to repair the bridge, cross the river, and in Lee's words, "to push the pursuit vigorously."[52]

Jackson's performance on this day—in fact, for the entire campaign—generated controversy that has not abated. Partisans and critics in the army and historians have debated it without resolution. Regardless, Jackson's men did not begin crossing the repaired bridge until after two o'clock on the morning of the 30th. It was not what Lee expected.[53]

Longstreet stirred his and Hill's men early on the morning of June 30. The day broke cloudless after a drenching rainstorm overnight. Longstreet had orders from Lee to march eastward on Long Bridge Road toward Glendale, where the road intersected Charles City Road and Willis Church Road, down which the Federals were retreating. He had to find the enemy and engage them when he heard the guns of Huger's division closing in on Charles City Road. Beyond Huger, Jackson was ordered to cross brackish White Oak Swamp and assail the Federal rear. To Longstreet's right, Holmes was directed to occupy New Market Heights, guarding the army's flank. Magruder's troops were directed to countermarch to Darbytown Road and support Longstreet. If the trap were sprung, McClellan's army could be wrecked.[54]

Longstreet's division, under Richard Anderson, led the march, followed by Hill's brigades. Before eleven o'clock, the troops filed into position on both sides of the road, about two miles west of the crossroads. One of Longstreet's aides arrived with orders for Hill to take command of the field. Hill and Anderson surveyed the ground, but woods and underbrush limited vision. Beyond the Rebels, the dark figures of Union skirmishers fired sporadically.[55]

Some time later, probably after midday, Longstreet found Hill and Anderson. For unexplained reasons, Longstreet had apparently remained behind at the campsite when the troops marched. Upon his arrival, he reassumed command and examined the lines and terrain. About 2:30 P.M., artillery fire was heard in the direction of the Charles City Road, where Huger was to signal his advance. Longstreet had batteries rolled forward to test the woods up ahead. Within minutes Lee, President Davis, and their aides joined Longstreet in a clearing of broomstraw and small pines where he had his headquarters behind his right front.[56]

Before the Confederate artillerymen could respond to Longstreet's order, a Union battery of cannon bellowed, arcing shells toward the Southern lines. One of the rounds exploded above the clearing, killing some horses and wounding one or two men. Davis and Lee moved out of range at the urging of Powell Hill. The Rebel artillery returned the fire, and Longstreet instructed Micah Jenkins, commanding Anderson's brigade, to charge the enemy cannon. "With great suddenness and severity," said Moxley Sorrel, the battle began.[57]

Jenkins's South Carolinians disappeared into the woods, and into a hellish furnace of Union gunfire. The South Carolinians reeled before the blasts delivered by Pennsylvanians in Brigadier General George McCall's division. Jenkins spurred along the line, the men looking at him, their faces saying, "We can go no farther." At one point the colonel paused for a prayer, asking for a bullet in the heart; he did not want to live with so many of his men dying beside him. Longstreet regarded Jenkins as "the best officer he ever saw," but he could not overcome an enemy division with a solitary brigade.[58]

Support was coming on his right as James Kemper's Virginians plunged into the difficult terrain. These had been Longstreet's men at Manassas, and they honored their old commander on this day. The Virginians overran two Union batteries and part of the infantry line. Exultant, the Southerners drove on and into a second line manned by troops from another enemy division. They could go no farther, clinging to what they had taken, dying where they stood.[59]

Cadmus Wilcox's Alabamians followed the Virginians, their ranks overlapping Long Bridge Road on Jenkins's left. As a cadet at West Point, Wilcox had put rubber soles on his shoes so he could sneak undetected into a room and steal a fellow cadet's pipe. On this day he and his men had a bigger prize to steal—a six-gun Union battery.[60]

The Alabamians charged into the blasts of the cannon, yelling and firing, driving the gunners away. But the Yankees counterattacked. For a few minutes the fighting was hand to hand, with the opponents using their muskets as clubs. The Federals prevailed, retaking the battery, only to have the Alabamians rally and force them back. Wilcox's men could not endure the musketry, however, and retired into the woods. The cannon stood abandoned, neither side able to secure the prizes. The Southerners lost nearly half their number in the struggle.[61]

Longstreet could only hear the combat among the timber. Jenkins, Kemper, and Wilcox had advanced in succession with perhaps a thirty-minute interval between each brigade. Longstreet had hesitated in the commitment of his entire division and Hill's, anticipating the attacks of Huger and Jackson. But his three units needed support, and he ordered his remaining brigades and one of Hill's into the battle. Pickett's brigade, under Colonel Eppa Hunton, and Brigadier General Lawrence Branch's command of the Light Division went in on the right behind Jenkins and Kemper. On the left of the road, Longstreet's troops under Roger Pryor and Winfield Featherston bolstered Wilcox's flank. The Federals, in turn, were piling additional brigades into their lines.[62]

The whirlpool of fury pulled in the four Confederate brigades. Featherston went down with a severe wound, and his men soon needed help. Longstreet called on Hill, who brought four more brigades forward. On the left, Brigadier General Maxcy Gregg spoke briefly with Longstreet before entering the woods. As Gregg's South Carolinians neared Featherston's ranks, Major John Fairfax, mounted on a gray thoroughbred, galloped along the line, shouting for the men to "charge, charge, charge." It was a moment the staff officer savored.[63]

Hill's rested troops secured numbers of the Union cannon, punched holes in the enemy line, and captured scores of prisoners. One of those bagged was Union general McCall. As he was being led to the rear, Longstreet rode up, dismounted, removed his glove, and offered his hand. Longstreet had served under McCall in the Fourth Infantry twenty years before. McCall stiffened, refusing his former comrade's hand, and said: "Excuse me, sir. I can stand defeat but not insult." The guards hustled him away, and Longstreet went back to work.[64]

The combat had one more spasm. When Federal reserves plugged the gaps, "the volume of fire that . . . rolled along the line was terrific," reported Hill. The Confederates held, and within minutes the roar of musketry, like the bellow of a giant, suddenly ceased in the darkening woods. Weary men fell to the ground, welcoming the silence. Enough had been asked of them.[65]

The Battle of Glendale or Frayser's Farm involved upward of sixty thousand men, two Federals for every one Confederate. Total casualties approached sixty-five hundred. Longstreet's and Hill's brigades opposed four Union divisions, fighting "for all they were worth," in Porter Alexander's view. Alexander claimed afterward that the engagement had the most hand-to-hand combat he knew of in the war. The Confederates captured eighteen cannon and a few stands of colors, but the Northerners kept Willis Church Road open, saving McClellan's army. During the night, the final elements of the Union army reached Malvern Hill, a forbidding defensive position south of Glendale.[66]

"But when one thinks of the great chances in General Lee's grasp that one summer afternoon," Alexander contended years later, "it is enough to make one cry to go over the story how they were all lost." He firmly believed that "never, before or after, did the fates put such a prize within our reach." It was on this day at Glendale, not on three July days at Gettysburg, Alexander alleged, that the Confederates missed the finest chance for a victory to end the war.[67]

Lee knew that night what had been missed, and he reacted in anger. His foremost biographer, Douglas Southall Freeman, wrote that the battle was "one of the great lost opportunities in Confederate military history. It was the bitterest disappointment Lee had ever sustained, and one that he could not conceal." In his report, Lee stated: "Could the other commands have co-operated in the action the result would have proved most disastrous to the enemy." For Lee, it was a rebuke.[68]

While Longstreet's and Hill's divisions, roughly twenty thousand men, fought "for all they were worth," nearly fifty thousand Confederates, all within a few miles of the field, rendered virtually no assistance. Huger advanced so feebly on Charles City Road that Federal units opposing him were removed and added to the ranks at Glendale. On New Market Road, Holmes came under enemy artillery fire and stopped as if in a state of paralysis.[69]

While Holmes and, in particular, Huger performed miserably, the key rested with Jackson and his 27,500 troops. His performance on this day, even more than on the 29th, has undergone scrutiny without resolution. Jackson biographers and partisans maintain that by the afternoon of the 30th, he was exhausted and ill. When John Fairfax arrived with a message from Longstreet, evidently asking for assistance, Jackson walked away from the aide without replying. When reports came in of other possible crossing sites instead of the destroyed bridge across White Oak Swamp, protected by Union artillery and infantry, Jackson ignored them, sleeping much of the time. His artillery engaged the Federals, but Porter Alexander later termed that an "absurd farce." Even his opponent, Brigadier General William B. Franklin, commander of the Sixth Corps, argued subsequently that had Jackson attacked simultaneously at the bridge and Brackett's Ford, a mile upstream, the Confederates "would have embarrassed us exceedingly." Jackson never investigated conditions at the ford.[70]

Porter Alexander also thought that Lee must share some of the blame for Jackson's efforts. Although the commanding general was less than an hour's ride away from Jackson's position, he never sent a staff officer to either prod Jackson or ask for an explanation. Once Lee issued orders, Alexander maintained, he had to *supervise their execution.* That was not Lee's method of command, but when the evidence of a problem mounted, he needed to learn the reasons. Instead, Jackson bedded down for the night, having told his staff that they would "rise with the dawn and see if tomorrow we cannot do *something.*" Perhaps Jackson's brother-in-law, Harvey Hill, said it best when he wrote afterward: "Had all our troops been at Frayser's Farm, there would have been no Malvern Hill." It was to this latter place the Confederates marched on July 1.[71]

On the morning of Tuesday, July 1, the troops of Jackson, Huger, and Magruder converged on the Glendale crossroads. Magruder's command, which had reached the battlefield early in the morning after an arduous eighteen-mile march, relieved Longstreet's and Hill's men. Lee had spent the night near Longstreet and Hill and was discussing with them and Magruder the previous day's battle when a Federal surgeon, N. F. Marsh, found them. Marsh had been left behind with the wounded at Willis Church and was sent by Jackson to ask Lee for supplies and protection. Lee agreed at once, and Longstreet asked Marsh what he knew about the fighting and the Union troops engaged. Marsh replied that he was in McCall's division and knew nothing of other units. Longstreet said: "Well, McCall is safe in Richmond; but if his division had not offered the stubborn resistance it did on this road, we would have captured your whole army. Never mind; we will do it yet."[72]

With that, Lee asked Longstreet to accompany him as they rode to Willis Church. Here the two generals met Harvey Hill, who earlier had asked a local minister about Malvern Hill. The division commander repeated the civilian's description of the terrain, concluding: "If General McClellan is there in force, we had better let him alone." Still optimistic, Longstreet laughed and jokingly responded to his old friend: "Don't get scared now that we have got him whipped." Hill said no more, but if a fighter like him had doubts, his words should have been heeded.[73]

Unwell and ill-tempered, Lee, too, said nothing. He ordered the pursuit. Jackson's, Huger's, and Magruder's units led the march, with Longstreet's and Hill's trailing in reserve. The northern tip of Malvern Hill was less than three miles from the church, but it took the Confederates hours to close on the position and deploy. By early afternoon most of the Confederate brigades had formed into line—Jackson on the left, Huger and Magruder on the right.[74]

Before the Southerners, Malvern Hill rose 150 feet above the surrounding terrain. The crest was open ground, extending one and a half miles in length and over a half mile wide. The ground sloped to the north and northwest, and the hillsides were clear for several hundred yards. An extensive field with ripened grain and shocks of harvested wheat lay beneath the northwestern crest. Ravines and marshes protected the flanks, so the Federals massed their artillery and infantry above the open ground—the direction from which the Confederates were to attack. The position had "elements of great strength," stated Fitz Porter, and with McClellan's army defending it, it was a nearly impregnable fortress against frontal assaults. Harvey Hill's advice was an omen of disaster.[75]

The Confederates stumbled into one of the greatest mistakes of Lee's career. Inaccurate maps, the heavily wooded terrain, faulty troop dispositions, no concert of action, and incompetence combined to pull the army into a bloodbath.[76]

Lee assigned to Longstreet the responsibility of reconnoitering the army's right front and posting Huger's and Magruder's troops. Longstreet soon discovered that Magruder's divisions were moving westward, away from Jackson's. Longstreet questioned Magruder, who said he had orders to follow the Quaker Road. Magruder called forward his three guides, natives of the region, and they assured the generals that they were correct to move west. None of the guides seemed to know that the Willis Church Road, the route intended by Lee, was also known as the Quaker Road. Longstreet refused to redirect the march when Magruder offered but instead rode away.[77]

Apparently Longstreet soon became convinced that Magruder was wrong and overtook the column. The two officers debated a second time until Colonel Robert Chilton, Lee's chief of staff, brought orders for Magruder to countermarch down a road through some woods near the Willis Church Road. Magruder's mistake brought his three divisions into position not on Jackson's immediate right but to the rear and right of the brigades of Brigadier Generals Lewis Armistead and Ambrose R. Wright of Huger's division. Magruder's division trickled in during the afternoon, with Prince John arriving about four o'clock.[78]

Longstreet, meanwhile, continued his reconnaissance. He located an "elevated point" that could serve as a platform for artillery, accommodating forty to sixty cannon. He reported to Lee that guns from this site and from a field along Jackson's line could rake the plateau of Malvern Hill in a crossfire and prepare the way for an infantry assault. Lee ordered it, but before the Rebel artillerists rolled their pieces into position, Union batteries on Malvern Hill opened fire. When the Confederate cannon returned fire, the superior Federal armament shattered the enemy guns. Less than thirty cannon—few at the same time—opposed the Federals. Lee's artillery reserve, more than twenty batteries, remained idle in the woods south of Willis Church because their commander, Brigadier General William N. Pendleton, by his own admission, could not find Lee for orders.[79]

By three o'clock in the afternoon, the Federal artillery had silenced or controlled the Confederate cannon. In his report, Longstreet stated that he "understood" no attack would be attempted. A short time later, a request came from Lee to join him on a reconnaissance along the left of the line. After the two generals had surveyed the ground for a possible turning movement and were starting back, Lee received two reports that indicated McClellan was retiring. Earlier, Lee had designated Armistead's brigade as the unit for initiating the attack, and when told Armistead was making progress, he instructed Magruder to "press forward your whole command and follow up Armistead's success."[80]

Magruder complied, hurling, as he stated, "about 15,000 men against the enemy's batteries and supporting infantry." A soldier who saw the general at this time thought that he "was the reddest, hottest looking man I ever saw." But Magruder's fervor for action doomed thousands of soldiers. He had neither knowledge of the terrain nor of troop dispositions. The information given to Lee was wrong: The Yankees had only shifted troops; they had not begun a withdrawal. When Magruder instructed Armistead and Wright to advance, Lee's army was committed.[81]

For the next four hours fifteen Confederate brigades, men from seven Southern states, charged up the slopes of Malvern Hill in a magnificent display of courage. The brigades attacked in pairs or alone, pulled successively into what one participant described as a "perfect hail storm of shell, grape, canister." Lee put it tersely in his report: "For want of concert among the attacking columns their assaults were too weak to break the Federal line."[82]

But Malvern Hill can only be understood in the words of the officers and men in the commands of Harvey Hill, Magruder, and Huger. In them can be found the horror and sadness of war. A Georgia lieutenant, after visiting the silent slopes a few weeks later, remembered "that a tempest of iron and lead was sweeping over it cutting down every living thing." He thought, "Oh what a terrible consuming fire is man's passions when it has full sway." "Nothing," he concluded, "but a kind Providence saved any of us alive." A Virginian said, "At no other time did I so realize the horrors of a battle field."[83]

Another Virginian believed that during his regiment's charge "the roar of the artillery was such that our firing was hardly audible." Lafayette McLaws, a division commander under Magruder, also remembered the deafening sound. "The Boom, Boom, of the guns was nearly a continuous roar," he wrote. "The sounds of each gun, though distinctive, were so mixed with the next, that there was not more than a quarter of a second between. Gettysburg did not compare with it." McLaws never saw so many men panic, adding, "It was but a slaughter pen" before the massed firepower of the Union artillery. The general said in a postwar letter to Longstreet: "As for Malvern Hill, who is going to tell the truth about it, the whole truth. If I [were] ever to write what I saw . . . I would be denounced by our own people as a caluminator."[84]

Another division commander, Harvey Hill, confessed to Jackson's chief of staff in a letter two years after the battle that "my recollections of Malvern Hill are so unpleasant that I do not like to write about it. It was a mistake to fight & the battle was fought in detail just as Gettysburg was." In a postwar published account, Hill said bluntly: "It was not war—it was murder."[85]

Eyewitnesses to the "murder" wrote of Malvern Hill's "bloody fields and crest," of the "useless slaughter," and of "the rivers of good blood that flowed that evening all in vain." A Virginia artillerist concluded: "The battle ought never to have been fought where it was."[86]

The cleansing of the ground at Malvern Hill began the next day with a drenching rainstorm. The Federal army retreated to Harrison's Landing on the James River under the protection of gunboats. During the morning, Longstreet visited army headquarters and found Lee and Jackson in the dining room of the Poindexter family home. Lee was dictating a letter to Walter Taylor when Longstreet asked if Lee was sending someone to the capital. "Yes," answered the commander. "An orderly will set out soon. Can we do anything for you?"

"Yes. Send Mrs. Longstreet word I am alive yet; she is up at Lynchburg."

Lee preferred not to have an orderly telegraph an officer's wife, however, so he suggested that Longstreet write her a note, which he did.

Then Lee inquired: "General, has your morning's ride led you to see anything of the scene of awful struggle of the afternoon?"

"Yes, General. I rode over pretty much all of the line of the fighting," Longstreet said.

"What are your impressions?"

"I think you hurt them about as much as they hurt you."

Knowing the battle's cost to his army, Lee replied: "Then I am glad we punished them well, at any rate."[87]

Before Longstreet departed, Jeb Stuart and President Davis walked into the room. Davis had been with the army since the 30th, sharing quarters with William Pendleton. They discussed the army's condition and the pursuit. When they finished, Charles Marshall of Lee's staff offered a flask of whiskey presented to him by Union general George McCall at Glendale. Lee, Jackson, and Stuart declined; Davis drank "very lightly," while Longstreet took "a good soldierly swig." Marshall then shared it with his fellow staff members, who drained the contents.[88]

Because of the weather and the scattered units in the army, the pursuit did not begin until the 3rd. Jackson initially led, but Lee ordered Longstreet to the front. Longstreet reached the Federal position at nightfall, delayed by a guide who took a wrong road and by the muddy conditions. The next morning he and Jackson surveyed McClellan's lines on Evelington Heights, the commanding ground that Stuart was driven from on the 3rd when he had fired on the Union camps with a small howitzer. The Yankees had then seized the ground. Longstreet believed an assault could succeed and sent a message to Lee. Before long, the commanding general arrived and with Longstreet and Jackson carefully studied the position. Enemy skirmishers fired on the generals. Supported by Jackson, Lee concluded that McClellan's army was secure from attack. When they walked away, the campaign ended.[89]

The Seven Days Campaign, as it came to be called, altered the course of the war in Virginia. With a masterful strategy of concentration and turning movements, Lee removed the immediate danger to Richmond and gained the strategic initiative for the summer. In numerical terms, the Confederates inflicted 15,849 casualties, including prisoners, and captured 52 cannon and 35,000 muskets and pistols. For a week, with little to eat and without a change of clothing, Lee's men displayed the fighting spirit that would soon make them one of the finest armies in American military history.[90]

To Confederates, however, the Seven Day Campaign became an operation of missed opportunities. "Under ordinary circumstances," Lee stated in his report, "the Federal Army should have been destroyed." Inaccurate maps, inadequate staff, organizational flaws within the army, and the difficult terrain crippled Lee and his commanders' efforts in the offensive operation. At critical moments, subordinate officers failed him. Forced to refashion tactics, Lee hurled his divisions against Union troops in defensive positions. The result was a loss of a fourth of the army—3,286 killed, 15,909 wounded, and 946 missing; in all, 20,141. For every man McClellan lost in killed or wounded, Lee lost nearly two. Writing after the war, Harvey Hill argued: "The attacks on the Beaver Dam intrenchments, on the heights of Malvern Hill, at Gettysburg, etc., were all grand, but of exactly the kind of grandeur which the South could not afford."[91]

Within Lee's army the blame for the missed opportunities centered on Jackson. Porter Alexander subsequently argued that not to fault Jackson did an injustice to Lee because the campaign was "perhaps his [Lee's] greatest achievement." Rumors abounded as to the cause of Jackson's performance—illness with the "gripp"; Jackson wanted to spare his men; he refused to act on the 29th because it was the Sabbath. Casualties testified to the burden carried by Jackson's command. His brigades accounted for roughly twenty-three percent of the army's total, but they incurred less than six percent of the loss. Longstreet's and Powell Hill's troops suffered the worse in proportion, with Cadmus Wilcox's brigade sustaining the heaviest unit losses, 1,055, mostly at Glendale.[92]

According to Alexander, Lee's staff members "knew at the time" that the commanding general "was deeply, bitterly disappointed." Frederick Colston, who would serve in time on Alexander's staff, jotted on the back of a postwar letter that Robert Chilton "always said after the war that Jackson ought to have been shot for his failure there." In his memoirs, Alexander remarked pointedly that the Southern press throughout the postwar years wrote "nothing at all" on Jackson's failures during the Seven Days "as compared with Longstreet's alleged shortcomings at Gettysburg."[93]

Lee responded to the command failures with tact and with a carefully worded report. He much preferred to avoid official or public condemnation of an officer. Magruder, Huger, and Holmes left the army for new assignments. As for Jackson, Lee reorganized the army in July, reducing Jackson's command from fourteen brigades to seven and increasing Longstreet's from six to twenty-eight.[94]

Longstreet emerged from the campaign as Lee's most reliable subordinate commander. At Gaines's Mill and at Glendale he had handled his command with a confidence and calmness that became a hallmark of his battlefield leadership. Less than a month after his performance at Seven Pines, Longstreet had redeemed himself. Moxley Sorrel described him as "that undismayed warrior," adding, "He was like a rock in steadiness when sometimes in battle the world seemed flying to pieces." In his report, Lee praised the men in the ranks and the division and brigade commanders as a whole, only briefly singling out Longstreet for Gaines's Mill. Privately, when congratulated for the campaign, Lee repeated his estimation for the rank and file and then said, "Longstreet was the staff in my right hand."[95]

8

RETURN TO MANASSAS

Reputations are seldom cast from pure metals. They are alloys extracted from disparate ores. Except for a rare, particularly brilliant vein, they result from a fusion of elements dug from a number of mines. For generals, battlefields are those mines. Combat is the crucible into which the ores are poured, heated, and tempered. Once cast, shining reputations, like precious metals, are coveted.

For James Longstreet the Seven Days Campaign yielded a valuable ore. Lee had come to welcome Longstreet's counsel, to trust his judgment. As a consequence, Lee augmented Longstreet's responsibilities, adding units to his command. Seven Days enhanced Longstreet's reputation within the army, counterbalancing his performance at Seven Pines. He had earned Lee's confidence and that of his men and officers.

Consequently, Longstreet was incensed when he read the July 8 edition of the Richmond *Examiner,* the city's most interesting newspaper, which was widely read by residents and the members of Lee's army. This issue featured in the third article of a series on the recent campaign a description of the Battle of Glendale or Frayser's Farm. "The battle," the *Examiner* stated in part, "was fought under the immediate and sole command of General A. P. Hill, in charge of both divisions. . . . The heroic command of General Hill pressed on with unquailing vigor and a resistless courage, driving the enemy before them." It concluded: "One fact is very certain, and that is that the battle of Monday night was fought exclusively by General A. P. Hill and forces under his command."[1]

John M. Daniel, the newspaper's editor, penned the series of articles. Daniel had served as a volunteer aide on Hill's staff during the campaign until Gaines's Mill, where he suffered a minor arm wound and retired gloriously from the field to the capital. His first article glorifying Powell Hill appeared on June 28, followed by a second one on July 2. Daniel was a strange but gifted man whose columns had previously engendered controversy. Although he was safely back in the city when the Battle of Glendale occurred, Daniel filled two columns with his description of the engagement.[2]

Daniel's exaggeration of Hill and the Light Division's role in the battle of June 30 ignored the bloody fighting of Longstreet's brigades and implied that Longstreet was absent from the field during the combat. Not only was Longstreet furious about the articles, but his staff members were "all fighting mad." The day after the newspaper published Daniel's account, Longstreet gave Major Moxley Sorrel a "sketch of a short letter," asking his chief of staff if he would sign it as assistant adjutant general and submit it to the Richmond *Whig,* a competitor of the *Examiner.* Sorrel said that he was "only too willing" and sent it to the *Whig.* In it, Longstreet argued that "no one in the army has any objections to Major Gen'l. A. P. Hill being supplied with all the notoriety that the 'Examiner' can furnish, provided no great injustice is done to others." Longstreet dismissed Daniel's casualty claims for Hill's division and rebutted Daniel's allegation that Hill, not Longstreet, commanded on the field. Sorrel labeled the response a "flat contradiction" of Daniel's article. The *Whig* printed Longstreet's letter, signed by Sorrel, on July 11.[3]

Like Longstreet, Powell Hill was a proud man, but he had a fiery temperament and a prickly sense of honor. He had had nothing to do with Daniel's articles, but neither had he recanted them. When he saw the letter in the *Whig,* he, too, reacted in anger, believing that Longstreet had unfairly criticized his men in public. On the 12th, Hill wrote to Lee: "I have the honor to request that I may be relieved from the command of Major-General Longstreet." When the note crossed Longstreet's desk en route to Lee, Longstreet endorsed it: "Respectfully forwarded. If it is convenient to exchange the troops, or to exchange the commanders, I see no particular reason why Maj. Gen. A. P. Hill should not be gratified."[4]

At the same time Sorrel sent an order to Hill requesting some information. Hill returned it without complying, scribbling across the bottom: "Maj. Gen. Hill declines to hold further information with Major Sorrel." When the staff officer showed the message to Longstreet, the general "was at once on fire at such disobedience." Longstreet stormed: "Write him again and say that note was written by my command and must be answered satisfactorily." But Hill refused a second time, and the two generals exchanged letters. Neither man budged, and Longstreet ordered Sorrel to place Hill under arrest "with orders to confine himself to limits of his camp and vicinity."

Sorrel confessed later in a letter that he had a "natural trepidation" when he rode to Hill's headquarters to execute the order on July 13. Dressed in his full uniform, with sash and sword, Sorrel found the explosive Powell Hill inside a tent on a chair. The major entered, Hill stood, and they exchanged stiff salutes. When Sorrel informed the general of his mission, Hill said nothing but saluted and sat down as Sorrel turned to leave. The meeting, Sorrel wrote, was "smooth, formal and courteous." Brigadier General Joseph R. Anderson assumed temporary command of the Light Division.[5]

The arrest provoked Hill even more, and he and Longstreet corresponded again. The feelings between the two officers became so antagonistic that Hill challenged Longstreet to a duel. At this point Lee, who had ignored Hill's request for a transfer, intervened. Although the precise events are cloudy, Lee apparently used mutual friends of the generals to stop the duel and granted Hill's request. On July 26, Hill returned to duty, and the next day Lee ordered him and the division to Gordonsville to join Stonewall Jackson's command. Sorrel asserted that Longstreet and Hill subsequently resolved the animosity, saying that "the difference left no sores." But Sorrel was mistaken; the relationship between the generals remained professional and cool.[6]

While the dispute festered throughout July, Longstreet was burdened with the responsibilities of commanding five divisions. Although the army remained inactive after its withdrawal to the Richmond lines on July 8, administrative duties kept Longstreet and his staff busy. Union general George McClellan's Army of the Potomac still huddled under the protection of gunboats at Harrison's Landing, requiring constant reconnaissance by the Confederates. When Federal units occasionally debouched from their lines, probing forward, Longstreet's troops countered the movement. Few casualties resulted from the actions, since McClellan had no intention of testing the Southern lines.[7]

The Confederate soldiers enjoyed the respite during the month. The army healed itself as the recovered wounded and ill absentees rejoined the ranks. "We have always been at our post, ready and willing," a Georgian wrote his sister on July 16, "but not very anxious, as we have seen a few battlefields." In one camp, at month's end, a local farmer pulled up with a wagonload of ducks, chickens, and vegetables for sale. The "old skin-flint," as a soldier called him, demanded "outrageously high" prices for his goods. The men angrily refused to pay and stormed the farmer, overturning the wagon and taking the birds and produce without paying. When the irate civilian appealed to the regiment's commander, the colonel told him that if he did not like the way the troops did business, to stay away from the camp.[8]

While not at their posts or cleaning out an "old skin-flint's" wagon, the troops relaxed. Sorrel said that many of the men enjoyed singing religious hymns and plantation chanteys. Many more relieved the boredom by gambling. It was endemic within the ranks. On one occasion, Lee rode through the camps with Longstreet and saw circles of soldiers engaged in games of "chuck-a-luck" with dice. Lee disliked the habit and asked Longstreet if something might be done to end it. Although he promised Lee he would look into the matter, poker player Longstreet knew the men would gamble despite orders to the contrary, so he did nothing about it.[9]

The inactivity on the Peninsula continued until the second week of August. During that time Lee carefully watched for any indication of a Union withdrawal from Harrison's Landing. To the northwest of Richmond, along the Orange & Alexandria Railroad, however, a newly organized Union force, the Army of Virginia, was advancing southward toward the Rappahannock River. Federal authorities had created this three-corps army during the final week of June by merging the Mountain, Shenandoah, and Rappahannock departments. The force numbered roughly fifty thousand, with one eleven-thousand-man division posted at Fredericksburg.[10]

Major General John Pope, one of Longstreet's West Point roommates, commanded the Army of Virginia. Pope had achieved modest success in the West, and when the government reorganized the three departments, the administration appointed Pope. Egotistic, fractious, and loudmouthed, Pope quickly alienated his subordinate officers and earned the scorn of the men in the ranks. He proclaimed to the army that he came from the West "where we have always seen the backs of our enemies." "Let us look before and not behind," Pope asserted. "Success and glory are in the advance."[11]

Pope energized the army and, as he promised, advanced. On July 12, the vanguard of the army occupied Culpeper Court House between the Rapidan and Rappahannock rivers, thirty miles north of Gordonsville, a vital Confederate railroad junction where the Orange & Alexandria and Virginia Central railroads intersected. The Virginia Central hauled the foodstuffs of the fertile Shenandoah Valley to Richmond, and Lee could not allow the rails to be severed. When the Federals reached Culpeper, Lee dispatched Jackson with two infantry divisions and an artillery battery—approximately ten thousand troops—to Gordonsville, on the 13th. Two weeks later Powell Hill's Light Division followed. Lee had informed Jackson: "I want Pope to be suppressed." On August 9, Jackson attacked Major General Nathaniel Banks's Second Corps troops at Cedar Mountain, eight miles south of Culpeper. Jackson held the field at nightfall, claiming victory in the tactically flawed engagement.[12]

Although Jackson's action pleased Lee, it was evident that more troops were required if Pope was "to be suppressed." A day after Cedar Mountain, preparations began for a movement to Gordonsville. Lee committed Longstreet's and D. R. Jones's divisions and two brigades under John Hood to the operation. The troops began filling the cars of the Virginia Central on August 11, a "scorching hot" day. By the 13th most of the brigades had reached Gordonsville. Longstreet and his staff departed on the 12th, arriving on the morning of the 13th. Jackson soon reported to Longstreet, offering command to the latter. Longstreet declined, however, arguing that Lee would soon join them and Jackson knew the terrain and the situation.[13]

Lee entrained for Gordonsville at four o'clock on the morning of August 15, arriving later in the day. Before leaving Richmond he learned that portions of McClellan's army had embarked from Harrison's Landing and floated down the James River. After receiving orders on the 3rd from Washington to transfer his army to Northern Virginia, McClellan stalled until the end. Lee surmised that the entire Federal army would evacuate the Peninsula, so he requested that Richard Anderson's division be forwarded to Gordonsville. Jef-

ferson Davis consented at once, leaving only three divisions under
G. W. Smith to guard the capital.[14]

When Lee reached Gordonsville, he met with Longstreet and
Jackson at the residence of a Mrs. Barbour in the town. Earlier,
Longstreet had written to Lee proposing a movement against Pope's
flank. The Army of Virginia was tucked in a large "V" laid on its
side, formed by the Rappahannock and Rapidan rivers. The apex of
the "V" pointed eastward and toward Fredericksburg, located nine
miles from the apex or confluence of the two rivers. Longstreet
wanted to assail the open or westward part of the "V"; Lee, the
closed end, to isolate Pope from possible reinforcements from
Fredericksburg.[15]

Lee's view prevailed, and the three generals discussed the details.
Longstreet would cross the Rapidan at Raccoon Ford; Jackson, upstream at Somerville Ford. Jeb Stuart and the cavalry would splash
over at Morton's Ford, east of Longstreet, march through Ste-
vensburg, and seize the railroad bridge at Rappahannock Station.
Jackson advocated an advance the next day to the fords, followed
by the attack on the 17th. Longstreet evidently argued for an additional day, needing the time to supply his troops with rations after
their rapid movement to Gordonsville. More important, however,
the cavalry was not and probably could not be concentrated by the
16th. Lee designated the 18th and issued the orders. If the plan
worked, Pope's army could be trapped in the "V" and destroyed.[16]

The Confederates were on the move throughout the 17th. The
infantry and artillery filled the country roads, marching north and
east from Orange Court House into their positions. Stuart rode in
and reported to Lee at headquarters, located this day at Erasmus
Taylor's "Meadow Farm," outside Orange Court House. Stuart informed Lee that he had ordered Brigadier General Fitzhugh Lee's
brigade toward Raccoon Ford. Stuart gave no indication that the
brigade would not cover the thirty-seven miles from Beaver Dam
Station and be in position by the next morning.[17]

D. R. Jones's division led Longstreet's command on this day, de-
ploying south of Raccoon Ford. That evening when Fitzhugh Lee
did not appear, Longstreet assigned two Georgia regiments from
Robert Toombs's brigade as pickets along the road to Raccoon Ford.
Toombs was absent when the order arrived, visiting his former
congressional friend Jeremiah Morton, whose residence, "Morton
Hall," lay between Raccoon and Somerville fords. On his return

ride to the brigade, Toombs discovered his pickets, and learning that they had been sent at Longstreet's instruction, sent them back to camp. According to one of Jones's staff officers, Toombs thundered that the road could be guarded "with an old woman and a broomstick."[18]

The next morning a detachment of Union cavalry clattered down the vacated road and galloped into Verdiersville, nearly bagging Jeb Stuart, who had spent the night there. The Yankees, however, nabbed Major Norman Fitzhugh of the staff and the copy he had of Lee's orders to Stuart. When Longstreet learned of the circumstances, he had Toombs arrested.[19]

Robert Toombs, Porter Alexander remarked, "was not entirely a subordinate & respectful brigadier" and frequently sparked trouble within the army. Fifty-two-year-old Toombs was a Georgian of wealth and political power who had nearly secured the presidency of the Confederacy. Although he disliked Jefferson Davis as a result of political disputes when both were United States senators, Toombs served as Davis's first secretary of state until he was appointed a brigadier general in July 1861. According to a staff officer, Toombs possessed "extraordinary mental powers," but "his faults were bluster and a vivid imagination that was not always hampered by facts. He was decidedly given to boasting. Allegations abounded that he was drunk at Malvern Hill, and Harvey Hill particularly loathed him. Moxley Sorrel stated that Toombs was unquestionably a talented man but was "in the wrong shop with a sword and uniform on."[20]

Characteristically, Toombs fulminated over his arrest. According to him, he saw Longstreet and Lee at the head of his brigade on the 19th, and while riding forward to protest his arrest, his troops cheered, "which so incensed the magnates Lee and Longstreet" that the latter refused to listen to Toombs and ordered him to Gordonsville. According to Sorrel, Toombs, wearing his sword contrary to orders, delivered "a violent speech" to his men that Sorrel overheard and recounted to Longstreet, who then sent the brigadier to Gordonsville. Regardless, Toombs left the brigade and about a week later wrote to Longstreet explaining his speech and requesting that he be restored to duty. Longstreet "always had a decided liking for Toombs," Sorrel wrote, and relented. A chastened Toombs overtook his brigade on the field at Manassas. From that time on he "knew better than to disobey Longstreet."[21]

Lee, meanwhile, learned of Stuart's near capture on the morning of the 18th. Later, a telegram arrived from Fitzhugh Lee informing the commanding general that his nephew's brigade was en route from Louisa Court House where the horsemen had secured rations and ammunition. Stuart subsequently criticized the brigadier in his report, and Longstreet after the war blamed the failure of the offensive on Fitzhugh Lee. The cavalry officer apparently misinterpreted his orders or they were so loosely written that he did not understand his arrival initiated the attack. Later in the day the commanding general postponed the movement until the 20th.[22]

On August 19, Longstreet joined Lee on the crest of Clark's Mountain, eight hundred feet above sea level, which served as a natural watchtower in the area. From its peak Lee and Longstreet looked northward across the Rapidan. Before them, Pope's army moved in long columns toward the Rappahannock. The orders taken from Stuart's aide revealed the danger that Pope faced beyond the Rapidan. The Union general had begun the withdrawal on the night of the 18th, and the two Confederate generals saw the final elements pass to safety beyond the second river. As they watched, Lee turned to Longstreet and said, "General, we little thought that the enemy would turn his back upon us this early in the campaign."[23]

The Confederate pursuit started at first light on the 20th—Stuart at three fords to the east; Longstreet at Raccoon; Jackson at Somerville. A Georgian described the scene at Raccoon Ford to his mother two days later: "An army fording a river is a sight worth seeing. Some of the men just walked in with shoes & all on, but most of them were guiltless of any clothing below waist." By day's end the columns approached the Rappahannock where the Yankees had burned the bridges and protected the fords. If Lee was to cross the river and get at Pope, he would have to move upstream with his left flank.[24]

The Rebels probed ahead toward the Rappahannock fords on Thursday, August 21. While Jackson tested Pope's defenses at Beverly's Ford, Longstreet closed on Kelly's Ford with Cadmus Wilcox's division. The Federals held the higher ground along the river, and the Confederates acted cautiously. When Wilcox retired, Union infantry crossed the river, igniting a brief skirmish with some Mississippians. The Rebels repulsed the Northerners, who returned to the opposite bank. During the day, pickets from a Georgia regiment captured a Federal spy, who gave his name as Charles Mason. The

Lieutenant General James Longstreet, CSA, commander of the First Corps, Army of Northern Virginia. Photo probably taken in 1863.

1

Maria Louisa "Louise" Longstreet, first wife of James Longstreet, and two of their sons, Augustus Baldwin, on the left, and James Longstreet, on the right. Photo was probably taken in 1860.

2

Postwar photo of Longstreet, probably taken in 1872. His right arm remained crippled from his wound at the Wilderness in May 1864.

General Robert E. Lee, CSA, commander of the Army of Northern Virginia, whose relationship with Longstreet was one of mutual respect and affection.

Lieutenant Colonel Osmun Latrobe, CSA, a Marylander who joined Longstreet's staff in the autumn of 1862 and succeeded Sorrel as chief of staff two years later, serving until the end of Appomattox.

5

6

G. Moxley Sorrel, CSA, Longstreet's chief of staff for three years, who served his commander faithfully and bravely in all of the major campaigns. Photo taken after Sorrel's promotion to brigadier general in October 1864.

7

Left, Lieutenant Thomas Jewett Goree, CSA, a Texan who traveled to Richmond with Longstreet in the spring of 1861 and became one of his most devoted and capable staff officers.

Left, John W. Fairfax of Longstreet's staff, CSA. Although portrayed with the rank of colonel, Fairfax was a major and one of the general's favorite aides. A wealthy Virginian, Fairfax was renowned in the army for his sumptuous meals and ample whiskey at Longstreet's headquarters.

8

9

Postwar view of the sunken road or "Bloody Lane" at Sharpsburg or Antietam, defended by troops under Longstreet's command on September 17, 1862. On this field Lee called Longstreet "my old war-horse."

Artist's sketch of
Lee and officers
watching the Battle
of Fredericksburg,
December 13, 1862.
Longstreet is the
third officer from
the left, behind Lee.

10

11

Section of the stone wall at
Fredericksburg, defended by
Longstreet's troops on December
13, 1862. During the fighting,
Longstreet remarked to Lee that
if the Federals continued the
attacks and his men had enough
ammunition, "I will kill them all
before they reach my line."

Major General Joseph Hooker,
USA, one-time commander of
the Army of the Potomac whose
troops opposed Longstreet's
command in Lookout Valley in
Tennessee in October 1863.

12

Colonel E. Porter Alexander, CSA, the artillery officer who served under Longstreet from the fall of 1862 until Appomattox. The two men remained friends until Longstreet's death. Alexander was promoted to brigadier general in 1864.

13

E. P. Alexand

14

Lieutenant General Ambrose Powell Hill, CSA, commander of the Light Division and later the Third Corps, Army of Northern Virginia. A proud, fiery man, Hill had a serious feud with Longstreet in the summer of 1862.

Major General James Ewell Brown "Jeb" Stuart, CSA, commander of the cavalry troops, Army of Northern Virginia, whom Longstreet described as "endowed by nature with the gifts that go to make a perfect cavalryman."

15

Lieutenant General Thomas J. "Stonewall" Jackson, CSA, famous commander of the Second Corps, Army of Northern Virginia. His death as a result of wounds at Chancellorsville in May 1863 left Longstreet as Lee's only reliable corps commander.

16

Major General George G. Meade, USA, a Pennsylvanian, who assumed command of the Army of the Potomac three days before the Battle of Gettysburg. His generalship in that pivotal engagement contributed to the Union victory.

17

Above, artist's drawing of the attack by Longstreet's troops at Gettysburg on July 2, 1863. Longstreet is pictured in the lower left center, conferring with two officers.

Left, Major General George E. Pickett, CSA, who commanded a division in Longstreet's corps. When Pickett asked permission to lead his division forward at Gettysburg on July 3, 1863, his old friend Longstreet could only nod his head.

Lieutenant General John B. Hood, CSA, division commander in the First Corps, who rose to eventual command of the Army of Tennessee. Seriously wounded at Gettysburg and Chickamauga, Hood was one of the finest combat officers in Lee's army and highly regarded by Longstreet.

21

Artist's drawing of the assault by Longstreet's infantry and artillery on the Federal line at Chickamauga on September 20, 1863.

22

Group photo of Civil War veterans, taken on the battlefield of Chancellorsville in 1884, at the stone that marked the spot where Stonewall Jackson fell mortally wounded on May 2, 1863. Longstreet stands in the rear, second from right. To his right, the second man, with arm on stone, is William S. Rosecrans, Longstreet's West Point roommate and the opponent he defeated at the Battle of Chickamauga.

General Braxton Bragg, CSA, commander of the Army of Tennessee, whom Longstreet and other generals plotted to remove from command in the autumn of 1863.

(Below) Major General Ambrose E. Burnside, USA, commander of the Army of the Potomac at Fredericksburg on December 13, 1862, and Longstreet's opponent at Knoxville in the fall of 1863.

23

Fanciful sketch of the attack on Fort Sanders at Knoxville on November 29, 1863. It ended in a debacle for Longstreet's troops and sparked a bitter controversy in his command.

24

25

A postwar photo of
Erasmus Taylor of
Longstreet's staff, CSA.
A Virginian, Taylor
joined the staff in the
fall of 1863 and served
as quartermaster
during the difficult
winter of 1864 in East
Tennessee.

26

Major General
Lafayette McLaws,
CSA, childhood friend
and West Point
classmate of
Longstreet's. Longstreet
removed him from
command of his
division during the
bitter winter of 1864 in
East Tennessee.

27

An artist's sketch of Longstreet, probably drawn from a photo in 1863 or 1864.

28

Below, artist's rendition of Longstreet's accidental wounding at the Wilderness on May 6, 1864. To Longstreet's right, Brigadier General Micah Jenkins reels in the saddle with a mortal head wound. Two other officers were slain by fire from Confederate troops.

29

30

Longstreet's home in Gainesville, Georgia. Constructed in 1875–76, the house was destroyed by fire in April 1889.

31

Lieutenant General Ulysses S. Grant, USA, Longstreet's best friend at West Point and in the antebellum army. As president he appointed Longstreet to a postwar government position. When Grant died, Longstreet described him as "the truest as well as the bravest man that ever lived."

32

The Piedmont Hotel in Gainesville, Georgia. It was purchased by Longstreet in 1875, who owned it until his death. The hotel was torn down around 1916.

Photo of Longstreet taken in the 1890s when the former general was in his seventies. He had the "Burnside" style of whiskers for many years.

33

Longstreet's casket on a horse-drawn hearse during the funeral procession in Gainesville, Georgia, on January 6, 1904.

The decorated gravesite of Longstreet in Alta Vista Cemetery in Gainesville, Georgia, on January 6, 1904.

Helen Dortch Longstreet, Longstreet's second wife, shown during the 1940s. Longstreet married her in September 1897; he was 76 years old, she, 34. After his death, she devoted her life to his memory and the rehabilitation of his reputation. She died in 1962.

night before, one of Longstreet's couriers had been shot in the back
and killed. His documents were found on Mason, and Longstreet
ordered his execution. Members of the general's escort, Company
E, Seventh South Carolina Cavalry, known as the Kirkwood Rangers,
hanged Mason and buried his body beside a road.[25]

The tactical dance along the Rappahannock continued through
the 22nd and 23rd. Longstreet shifted Hood's and Jones's divisions
upstream to Freeman's and Beverly's fords, respectively. Hood repulsed a Union advance across the stream late on the 22nd. Jackson,
meanwhile, sidled leftward for an unguarded crossing. He found
one opposite Warrenton Sulphur Spring. The Federals had burned
the bridge, but Jackson eventually pushed eight regiments and two
batteries under Jubal Early onto the Union side. During the night
a pounding thunderstorm struck, and the freshets caused Early's
command to be isolated.[26]

Jackson labored throughout the 23rd to extricate Early's troops
while Longstreet demonstrated against Pope's position at Rappahannock Station. Longstreet rolled part of his artillery, nineteen cannon, into range and opened fire. Federal gunners responded, and
the duel lasted most of the day. The Confederates suffered the
worst in the exchanges. The Washington Artillery, according to an
eyewitness, was "badly cut up," losing eight horses to one shell
alone. Late in the afternoon, while Longstreet and Cadmus Wilcox
watched the action in the rain, an enemy shell plowed into the
ground a few feet from the generals but did not explode. When
another round burst nearby, Longstreet heard a Texan exclaim:
"Dad drat those Yankees! If I had known that they were going to
throw such things as that at a fellow, I would have stayed in Texas."
Before nightfall the Northerners withdrew, torching the railroad
bridge and a building.[27]

While the Southern infantry and artillery engaged the Yankees,
Stuart's cavalry struck in the enemy's rear. Circling behind Pope's
right flank, Stuart and fifteen hundred men rode into Catlett's Station, a railroad stop, on the night of the 22nd when the rainstorm
blew in. Although the troopers could not burn the bridge, they
captured hundreds of men and horses and Pope's personal baggage, including a dispatch book. Stuart had a staff officer deliver
some of the captured documents to Lee the next day, with more
arriving later.[28]

Pope's dispatches confirmed Lee's suspicions. He could not assault Pope in front or wait until McClellan's troops arrived from the Peninsula. He outlined his strategic goal to Davis on the 23rd, writing: "If we are able to change the theater of the war from James River to the north of the Rappahannock we shall be able to consume provisions and forage now used in supporting the enemy. This will be some advantage and prevent so great a draft upon other parts of the country." Lee wanted to avoid an engagement by maneuvering Pope farther away from Fredericksburg and reinforcements while at the same time reclaiming lost territory.[29]

The leftward sidle of Lee's army resumed on the 24th. Longstreet's divisions marched upstream, the leading units reaching Jeffersonton. Jackson's artillery, meanwhile, scattered a Federal infantry force at Warrenton Springs Ford where Early's command had recrossed earlier in the morning. After midday, Lee met with Jackson in Jeffersonton and instructed him to take his three divisions and artillery, approximately twenty-four thousand men, march up the Rappahannock, swing beyond the Union flank, and sever the Orange & Alexandria Railroad, Pope's communications and supply link. Lee did not specify a target, leaving it to Jackson's discretion. Longstreet later joined the two generals and learned of the movement. One of Jackson's staff members prepared a sketch of the region for Longstreet, whose troops would occupy Pope's attention while Jackson marched.[30]

After the war, Lee justified his bold plan, explaining that "the disparity . . . between the contending forces rendered the risks unavoidable." Lee hoped to maneuver Pope out of the region without a battle and, if the circumstances permitted, to advance the army toward the Federal capital. To Lee, the approach of McClellan's troops dictated either the need for an operation or the abandonment of territory and supplies. As he had during the Seven Days, Lee implemented a strategic offensive within the framework of a defensive policy.[31]

Lee entrusted the crucial initial movement to Jackson. Stonewall's performance since the Peninsula Campaign had reconfirmed Lee's opinion of the general. Independent operations seemingly invigorated Jackson—he had acted aggressively in his confrontation with Pope. One of his men wrote perceptively after the war that "Jackson was always a surprise. Nobody ever understood him, and nobody has even been quite able to account for him." He was a driven, exacting soldier when aroused, a taskmaster of unbending will-power. Colonel Armistead Long of Lee's staff compared Longstreet and Jackson in his memoirs. Long believed that Longstreet possessed "superior intelligence" but Jackson had an "iron mind," characterized by determination and perseverance. One of Longstreet's officers in a letter home during August asserted: "I think Gen. Jackson is the most efficient & energetic Gen in our army, the glory of belonging to his army is great & so is the *labor*."[32]

Before dawn on August 25, Jackson's command—the divisions of Richard Ewell, Powell Hill, and William B. Taliaferro, twenty-one batteries and a cavalry regiment—started its march. From Jeffersonton to Amissville, across the Rappahannock at Hinson's Mill Ford, through Orleans toward Salem, the miles-long column moved. All day long, officers prodded the men, closing the ranks, maintaining the pace. As the troops approached Salem they saw "Old Jack," as they called Jackson, standing on a rock beside the road. His "foot cavalry" began to cheer, but the general quieted them. Then, as the men filed past with hats off in salute, Jackson turned to his staff and remarked: "Who could not conquer with such troops as these?"[33]

The march resumed again at first light on the 26th. From Salem the route led eastward through Thoroughfare Gap in the Bull Run Mountains to Gainesville on the Warrenton Turnpike. Turning south, the Confederates trudged to Bristoe Station on the railroad, arriving about sunset. Here Stuart's cavalrymen overtook the infantry and artillery, and Jackson derailed a train. That night two infantry regiments and some cavalry seized Manassas Junction, Pope's main supply base five miles up the tracks. The Army of Virginia's supply and communications line had been severed. Jackson and his men had followed a glory road—fifty-four miles in thirty-six hours. Moxley Sorrel thought that their labors and marches "in swiftness, daring, and originality of execution, were almost extraordinary."[34]

Meanwhile, to the south, along the Rappahannock, Longstreet's command had skirmished with the Federals and had exchanged artillery fire. By midday on the 26th, Lee had decided that Pope was pulling back from the river. Although Lee did not know whether Pope had learned of Jackson's movement, he summoned Longstreet to headquarters. Lee wanted Longstreet to march as soon as possible to join Jackson and gave Longstreet the selection of a route. Following deliberation the wing commander chose Jackson's roundabout circuit to avoid delaying tactics by the enemy.[35]

Late on the afternoon of the 26th, Longstreet's twelve infantry brigades and sixteen artillery batteries began fording the Rappahannock at Hinson's Mill. "The crossing was ruff and took some time," wrote a Virginian, "the ascent on opposite side of river steep & rocky." When the units reached Orleans, the men bivouacked for the night. Lee, Longstreet, and their staffs enjoyed dinner and stayed the night at "Edgeworth," the plantation of Mrs. Rebecca Boyd Marshall, located two miles north of the village. Richard Anderson's infantry division and Colonel Stephen D. Lee's artillery battalion remained south of the river with orders to march when relieved by Harvey Hill's and Lafayette McLaws's divisions, which were en route from Richmond.[36]

Longstreet's men, a Texan remembered, "plodded along" the following morning, covering the ten miles from Orleans to Salem by midday. Lee and Longstreet, with their staffs and escorts, rode at the head of the column, trailed by the Washington Artillery and then the infantry. As the generals and their aides approached "Vermont," the estate of Mrs. Benjamin Rixey, outside of Salem, a contingent of Union cavalry rode up near Mrs. Rixey's barn and outbuildings. The Confederate horsemen hurried Lee and Longstreet to the rear, forming a line across the road. The Yankees withdrew, however, taking Mrs. Rixey's carriage horses with them. After an hour's delay, the march resumed through Salem to White Plains. Lee and Longstreet boarded at the home of James W. Foster, and the troops bedded down along the road to Salem. During the evening, Anderson's division and Lee's artillery battalion arrived at Salem after a grueling march. Longstreet now had thirty thousand troops with him.[37]

Years later, Longstreet's critics, notably fellow officers in the army, alleged that his march to Manassas was slow, forcing Jackson to fight alone for two days. Fostered by postwar political differences, the charge has no merit. When the vanguard of Longstreet's column bivouacked for the night at White Plains, his troops had covered roughly thirty miles in a little over twenty-four hours. If Jackson was at Manassas Junction, Longstreet was twenty-two miles distant, a difficult day's march to be sure, but attainable. More important to the controversy, Lee, not Longstreet, regulated the pace of the movement. Lee evidenced no outward anxiety, having learned on the afternoon of the 27th, in a message from Jackson, of the capture of Bristoe Station and Manassas Junction. Even more indicative of Lee's satisfaction with Longstreet's efforts was the speed of the march on the 28th. The troops did not start eastward toward Thoroughfare Gap until eleven o'clock in the morning.[38]

D. R. Jones's Georgians and South Carolinians led the march, followed by the divisions of Hood, Wilcox, and Kemper. One of the Georgians recalled the 28th as "one of the hottest days I ever experienced." Fortunately for the men, the pace was slow, even leisurely. Lee and Longstreet rode side by side at the front, trailed by a cloud of aides and escorts. About three in the afternoon, Jones's leading brigade, under Colonel George T. Anderson, halted at the foot of Thoroughfare Gap. Anderson's Georgians shook out a skirmish line and stalked forward. In the defile, Federal cavalry videttes sniped at the oncoming Rebels. Behind the Georgians, Jones deployed his three brigades in a battle line, ordering the men to lie down. Lee and Longstreet, standing at the mountain's base among Anderson's troops, peered through their glasses.[39]

As the Georgians climbed the western face of the mountain, the Federal cavalrymen disappeared behind the crest and fell back to the eastern foot of the gap where Brigadier General James Ricketts's five-thousand-man division was deployed. Ricketts had been ordered to resist the Confederate advance through the gap, but the directive came too late for his infantry to hold the high ground. It now belonged to Anderson's Georgians, who were pressing down the eastern side, slowed by felled trees and boulders placed in the road by the cavalrymen. Ricketts advanced a brigade, supported by artillery, toward the Southerners, many of whom clustered behind the stone Chapman's Mill. The gunfire escalated as the Rebels stalled before the Union fire.[40]

Lee and Longstreet viewed the action from the crest. They decided that the Federal position had to be flanked, so Lee ordered John Hood to send one brigade north of the gap, up rugged Mothercoat Mountain, and directed Colonel Henry L. Benning, commanding Toombs's brigade, to scale Pond Mountain south of the defile with two regiments. Lee also instructed Cadmus Wilcox to lead his division northward six miles to Hopewell Gap and come in from that direction. With this done, Lee descended the mountain, leaving Longstreet to direct the fighting.[41]

The entry of Colonel Evander Law's brigade, part of Hood's division, and Benning's two regiments settled the issue. With both flanks threatened, Ricketts held his ground until nightfall and then retreated. The Confederates had cleared the gap, and many of them slumped to the ground and slept. No fires were permitted, and the men ate cold bread and beef. Longstreet retired to a nearby mountain cabin while Lee slept at "Avenel," the beautiful residence of Robert Beverley outside White Plains. Tomorrow the Army of Northern Virginia would be reunited.[42]

While the Confederates struggled in Thoroughfare Gap during the afternoon, they heard musketry and cannon fire to the northeast in the direction of Manassas Junction. Since the night of August 26 when Pope learned of Jackson's seizure of Bristoe Station, the Union commander had been searching for the elusive Southern general and his "foot cavalry." On the morning of the 27th, Pope abandoned the Rappahannock line and ordered a convergence of his corps on Jackson. Pope now had six corps under his direction, with the arrival of the Third, Fifth, and Sixth from the Army of the Potomac. If his scattered units responded with alacrity, Jackson's command could be destroyed.[43]

The Yankees stumbled forward, slowed by the heat and dust, and confusion at army headquarters. On the afternoon of the 27th, one division collided with Ewell's troops at Bristoe Station, resulting in a skirmish until Ewell disengaged and retired to Manassas Junction. During the day, Jackson's men feasted on the foodstuffs at the junction, including lobster and oranges. Under the cover of darkness, Jackson headed westward, filing into a position behind a wooded ridge near Groveton, north of the Warrenton Turnpike; all his units were in place by midday on the 28th. Pope, meanwhile, redirected his corps toward Manassas Junction and then Centreville. The Confedcrates seemingly vanished until late on the afternoon of the 28th when Jackson attacked a Union division at the Brawner farm. In a vicious engagement, Jackson lost thirteen hundred men, including Ewell and Brigadier General Isaac Trimble, who were seriously wounded. To Jackson's right rear, Longstreet's men slept in Thoroughfare Gap.[44]

Lee joined Longstreet in the mountain defile as the troops descended the eastern slope at daylight on Friday, August 29. As they had on the three previous days, the generals rode at the head of the column. Before them, sharpshooters from the Fifth Texas screened the march, probing for enemy skirmishers. Hood's, Kemper's, and Jones's divisions followed, their ranks extending across the mountain's crest. As the sun rose higher in the sky, the heat intensified. In the distance, artillery rumbled and, in Long-street's words, "the men involuntarily quickened step." The noise and scent of battle rippled upward from the plain below.[45]

Just west of Gainesville, the marchers met Confederate cavalry-men from the brigade of Brigadier General Beverly Robertson. Lee and Longstreet spurred forward, and within minutes Jeb Stuart and his staff reined in. Stuart described Jackson's location and advised Lee to turn left in Gainesville onto the Warrenton Turnpike toward Groveton. Couriers scurried along the column, giving the instruc-tions. Lee then ordered Stuart to the right to patrol that flank, and after Robertson's horsemen passed to the south, Hood's men en-tered Gainesville and swung onto the turnpike.[46]

Lee with his staff cantered ahead of the column to reconnoiter the front. After pausing at the edge of a woodlot, the commander walked forward alone, his attention focused on the skirmish fire billowing below him. According to Major Charles S. Venable, one of Lee's aides, the general returned within a few minutes and said quietly. "A Yankee sharpshooter came near killing me just now." Lee's face bore the mark of the bullet that grazed his cheek.[47]

Longstreet, meanwhile, conducted his own reconnaissance. Cap-tain Edmund Berkeley of the Eighth Virginia claimed in an unpub-lished account that he accompanied Longstreet, having been sent forward earlier as a guide at the general's request. Like Lee, ac-cording to Berkeley, Longstreet came under enemy fire as he stood on a ridge examining the terrain. After returning to the foot of the elevation, he met Lee, followed minutes later by Jackson. The three generals conferred in the hollow before walking to the ridge's crest. From there Jackson pointed out his position behind the embank-ment of an unfinished railroad and the ground south of the War-renton Turnpike for Longstreet's troops. Longstreet then left to place his units.[48]

Mounted on a large bay horse, Longstreet preceded the troops, looking "like a king leading his hosts to battle" in the opinion of one of Jackson's men. For the next two hours, from ten o'clock until noon, Longstreet oversaw the deployment of his command. Hood's division filed into position first—Law's brigade to the left of the Warrenton Turnpike, Hood's Texas Brigade to the right. Once in line, Hood's men advanced and shoved Union skirmishers before them, bagging some prisoners and connecting with Jackson's right flank. Brigadier General Nathan "Shanks" Evans's Independent Brigade formed behind the Texas Brigade, acting as a reserve.[49]

James Kemper's three brigades extended the line southward from Hood's right. D. R. Jones's division came next, forming behind Kemper's right and rear, its right flank touching the Manassas Gap Railroad. Cadmus Wilcox's division arrived about midday, its march delayed from Hopewell Gap by the passage of Longstreet's other units. Wilcox's three brigades settled in behind Hood's and Evans's troops on the Confederate left. Except for Hood's men, who were engaged in a skirmish with the enemy, the Southerners relaxed; they were footsore, weary, and thirsty. Finally, about 1:00 P.M., Longstreet had nineteen cannon posted on the low ridge between Jackson's right and Hood's left. Shortly afterward the Confederate artillerists opened a duel with Union batteries near Groveton.[50]

With Longstreet's dispositions completed, the Confederate front covered roughly three miles, divided almost equally between Jackson and Longstreet. Jackson's line offered an excellent defensive position; Longstreet's had no natural strength but was more like a platform from which to launch an attack. Woods concealed Longstreet's ranks. If the Federals stumbled into the ground between the two wings, Lee could snap the blades together like a giant scissors slicing the enemy ranks into pieces. By a strategic maneuver Lee had placed his army in one of the greatest tactical opportunities of the war.[51]

About noon Longstreet reported to Lee that the deployment had been completed. *"We all were particularly anxious to bring on the battle after 12m;* General Lee more so than the rest," asserted Longstreet in a postwar letter. Lee "expressed his wish" that an attack be made at once. Longstreet, however, cautioned against an immediate assault. He wanted to conduct a more thorough examination of the ground in front and of the Federal strength and position south of the turnpike. Also, Stuart had earlier informed Lee that an unknown enemy force was approaching on the Gainesville-Manassas road beyond Longstreet's right flank, requiring Lee to send Colonel Montgomery Corse's brigade from Kemper's division to Stuart as support. Longstreet believed these matters deserved attention and requested a personal reconnaissance, which Lee approved.[52]

Longstreet rode to Brewer's Spring, east of the Hamilton Cole house, and surveyed the situation from horseback and on foot. He saw that the Federal position south of the turnpike—occupied by the divisions of Brigadier Generals John F. Reynolds and Robert C. Schenck—covered half of his front. "The position was not inviting," Longstreet argued later, and after an hour's inspection, "I so reported to General Lee."[53]

It was not welcome news to Lee—he "was quite disappointed," according to Longstreet. Lee was also not convinced and insisted that the enemy left could be turned with some brigades. The commander further considered sending his engineers to reconnoiter, but then a courier from Stuart arrived with the message that the Federals along the Gainesville-Manassas road were in considerable numbers and were threatening the army's right flank. Lee relented for the moment until further study could be undertaken.[54]

During the next two hours—from 2:00 to 4:00 P.M.—both Lee and Longstreet conducted individual reconnaissances on the right front. To the north, the clamor of battle escalated as Jackson's defenders clung to the embankment against a series of Union assaults. At points along the line, the fighting was hand to hand, muzzle to muzzle, vicious and deadly. The final Federal attack crashed into Jackson's left. The Yankees belonged to Major General Philip Kearny, a superb combat officer who exhorted his men: "Fall in here, you sons of bitches, and I'll make major generals of every one of you!" Kearny's "sons of bitches" stormed up a rocky knoll and met a furnace of gunfire. Confederate reserves repulsed the Northerners, ending the combat on Jackson's sector for the day.[55]

The reconnaissances by Lee and Longstreet, meanwhile, confirmed that the Union force on the right flank amounted to at least one corps—Fitz Porter's Fifth Corps of the Army of the Potomac, the Confederates' opponent at Beaver Dam Creek and Gaines's Mill. Lee, in turn, shifted Wilcox's division to the right behind Jones's brigades. The Yankees maintained a defensive position, however, their skirmishers and artillery batteries exchanging desultory fire with the Rebels. After watching the action for some time and seeing a dust cloud that indicated a march of other Federal units toward Manassas, Longstreet concluded that Porter posed no immediate threat to an assault. Returning to the Warrenton Turnpike, Longstreet found Lee and stated his views. It was approximately five o'clock.[56]

For a third time Lee urged an attack south of the turnpike, and for a third time Longstreet demurred. "Though more than anxious to meet his wishes, and anticipating his orders," wrote Longstreet in his memoirs, "I suggested, as the day was far spent, that a reconnaissance in force be made at nightfall to the immediate front of the enemy, and if an opening was found for an entering wedge, that we have all things in readiness at daylight for a good day's work." Hesitating, Lee reluctantly acceded to Longstreet's proposal, and orders were issued.[57]

Longstreet selected Hood's division to spearhead the operation. Although this command held the obvious position from which to advance, Longstreet could not have chosen better troops or commander to execute it. The Texas Brigade had stormed up the slope of Gaines's Mill in the charge that broke the Union line. They were wild, rugged men devoted to Hood, a strapping, raw-boned man of six feet two inches who seemingly relished combat. He and his troops had a unique bond. "Few generals have possessed the warm personal love of his men as Hood did," claimed a staff officer. "This attachment was something different from any feeling I have ever known to exist between men and commander; there was more of an element of comradeship in it." It was understood between them that Hood would make no demand beyond the brigade's ability or power to attain, and they would accomplish all that he asked of them. Hood was "one of the best brigadiers" in the army, in the opinion of an officer.[58]

The Texas Brigade aligned itself immediately south of the turnpike; Evander Law's four regiments, across the roadway. Longstreet brought Shanks Evans's South Carolinians forward as a reserve and ordered Colonel Eppa Hunton's brigade from Kemper's division to act as support for Hood's right. Finally, he recalled Wilcox's division from the right to add weight to the advance if needed. In all, Longstreet assigned seven of his twelve brigades to the reconnaissance force.[59]

Hood's troops stepped out at 6:30 P.M., sunset. They emerged from the woods, plunged down the slope, and drove toward Groveton, a handful of houses along the turnpike. Within minutes they collided with two brigades of Union Brigadier General John Hatch's division. Believing that the Confederates were retreating, Pope had earlier directed Irvin McDowell to pursue toward Groveton, and

McDowell gave the duty to Hatch. Instead of finding a retreating foe, Hatch's men ran headlong into Hood's veterans.[60]

The collision stunned the Federals, who cobbled together a battle line under fire. The combat rapidly lost its form in the enveloping darkness. The Confederate pressure shoved the Union line backward. The Rebels seized one cannon and several battle flags in the confusing struggle. Men flailed at each other with muskets and bayonets. It became "so dark that one flag could not be distinguished from another, nor the Yankee troops from Southern soldiers," remembered a Texan. By eight o'clock most of the fighting had subsided, snuffed out by the darkness and the retreat of the Federals. Hood's and Evans's brigades halted a mile in front of Longstreet's line.[61]

Cadmus Wilcox and his division arrived after the struggle had ceased. He and Hood conferred and agreed they were too far in advance of the main Confederate line and should be withdrawn. Wilcox's papers at the Library of Congress contain a handwritten copy of his original report of the campaign, with notations added later. In these notations, Wilcox stated that he sent Hood to the rear between 10:00 and 10:30 P.M. to report the situation to either Lee or Longstreet. Hood found Lee and relayed the two generals' conclusions. Lee objected, however, and replied that he did not want to abandon the ground taken. When Hood informed Wilcox of this, Wilcox rode back, located Longstreet, and persuaded the wing commander to order a withdrawal. In an account published after the war, Longstreet implied that Lee issued the directive after Longstreet talked with him about midnight. It would seem from Wilcox's version, however, that Longstreet acted on his own initiative and then explained it to Lee. Regardless, the proposed dawn assault was canceled and the brigades drawn back.[62]

The operations south of the Warrenton Turnpike on August 29 eventually generated bitter controversy in both armies. Union general Fitz John Porter became Pope's scapegoat in the aftermath of the debacle. At 4:30 P.M., Pope sent orders for Porter to advance against the Confederate right, but the Fifth Corps commander did not receive them until sunset. When he forwarded them to his leading division commander, that officer protested because of the evident Confederate strength in the area; Porter canceled the attack and bivouacked on the ground. Pope, whose myopia about the tactical situation throughout the battle seemingly had no limits, formally charged Porter afterward. In January 1863, Porter, a loyal McClellan man, was found guilty by a court-martial and cashiered from the army.[63]

The disgraced general spent the next fifteen years seeking vindication. After the war, Porter corresponded with various Confederate officers, including Lee, Longstreet, and Wilcox. His former enemies agreed that had Porter attacked Longstreet's command, the Federals would have been, in Wilcox's words, "easily and thoroughly repulsed." Porter had approximately ten to eleven thousand men while Longstreet counted twice that number. Porter eventually achieved his exoneration from all charges and had his name restored to the list of army officers.[64]

Porter lived to see his vindication, but not so his opponent on the 29th, James Longstreet. The accusations against Longstreet began years after the war and after the death of Lee, and they persisted for over a century. His critics within the former officer ranks and future historians charged him with slowness, thwarting Lee's desire for an attack, and even complained of his domination of the commanding general. They linked his conduct on the first day at Second Manassas with that on the second day at Gettysburg. The best example of this reasoning came from the pen of Douglas Southall Freeman in his seminal biography of Lee. The great Confederate historian wrote: "The seeds of much of the disaster at Gettysburg were sown in that instant—when Lee yielded to Longstreet [on August 29] and Longstreet discovered that he would."[65]

To be sure, Longstreet fueled the criticism with his own intemperate postwar writings, often according himself more distinction than warranted. Facts should butt hard against myths woven from political differences and personal animosities, however, and the facts sustain Longstreet's judgment on the 29th. Porter told Longstreet in a letter that the Federals wanted the Southerners to attack. Porter had his infantry and artillery posted, and for much of the afternoon, McDowell's corps was in immediate supporting position. "I am very sure if you had attacked me," wrote Porter, "your loss would have been enormous." Longstreet had either to assail Porter or detach brigades from his force to protect his flank, weakening the thrust against the enemy units in his front. Porter's presence could not be ignored.[66]

Longstreet's conduct on this day revealed a deliberate, careful tactician who was unwilling to throw his men into a situation without knowledge of the terrain or enemy dispositions. Circumstances at noon necessitated a reconnaissance, and once Longstreet reported his findings, Lee postponed the offensive. Then, as new concerns arose, Lee and Longstreet discussed each development. Although Lee displayed reluctance and disappointment, he accepted Longstreet's advice. To argue that Longstreet dominated Lee is to presume that Lee could be controlled. It would be accurate to say that the commanding general utilized Longstreet's talents, listened to his counsel, and concurred.

The relationship between the two men had been evolving since Lee assumed command on June 1. Longstreet described it in his memoirs, noting that by the Seven Days Campaign it was one of "confidence and esteem, official and personal, which ripened into stronger ties as the mutations of war bore heavier upon us." Longstreet then added: "He always invited the views of the latter in moves of strategy and general policy, not so much for the purpose of having his own views approved and confirmed as to get new light, or channels for new thought." It was this command arrangement of a superior to a trusted subordinate, not overbearing influence, that transpired on the afternoon of August 29. Finally, the events of the 30th sustained Longstreet's judgment.[67]

Saturday, August 30, dawned clear—"a lovely day," recalled a Virginian. "The morning was so still and quiet that everybody seemed to be on his good behavior." At Confederate army headquarters, situated in a stand of trees south of the Warrenton Turnpike, Lee took time to write to Jefferson Davis:

> The movement has, as far as I am able to judge, drawn the enemy from the Rappahannock frontier and caused him to concentrate his troops between Manassas & Centreville—my desire has been to avoid a general engagement, being the weaker force & by manoeuvring to relieve the portion of the country referred to—I think if not overpowered we shall be able to relieve other portions of the country, as it seems to be the purpose of the enemy to collect his strength here.[68]

The silence noted by the Virginia soldier perplexed Lee. He anticipated, even desired, a renewal of Federal assaults against Jackson. He consequently deferred any action and summoned Longstreet, Jackson, and Stuart to headquarters. The generals decided to await

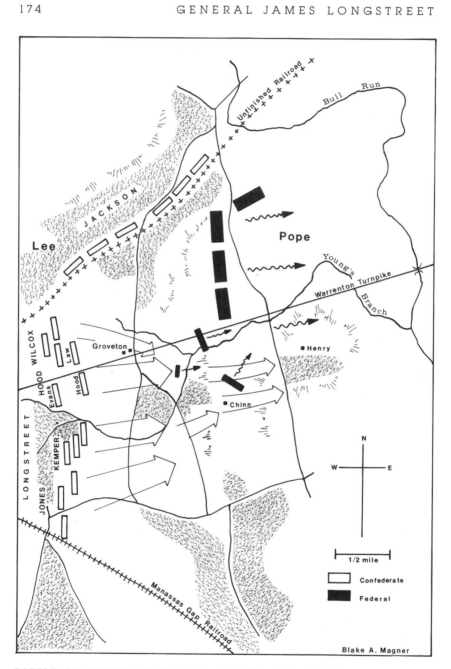

BATTLE OF SECOND MANASSAS, OR BULL RUN, AUGUST 30, 1862.

a movement by Pope, and if the Union commander did not attack again, Jackson would withdraw after darkness and march beyond the Union right flank, interposing his troops between the enemy and Washington. Longstreet would demonstrate against Pope's left while Jackson disengaged and then follow if the Northerners retreated. As he told Davis, Lee preferred maneuver to battle. If Pope resumed the offensive, the Confederates were prepared to fight.[69]

When the meeting adjourned, Longstreet returned to his lines. His units needed realignment, and he restored the lines, closed gaps, and shifted a few brigades. During the night Anderson's division had reached the battlefield following what one soldier called "the most terrible march yet." Longstreet neglected to post a staff officer to guide them into position, however, and instead of halting behind the lines, Anderson's men moved ahead, past Hood's and Wilcox's sleeping men, until they stumbled onto the debris of the previous evening's combat. The troops collapsed on the ground and slept. When Hood discovered this at daybreak, he alerted Anderson to the danger of his location, and the bone-weary soldiers retraced their march to a position behind Hood.[70]

On Longstreet's left, on the ridge above Groveton where the Washington Artillery had been deployed, Colonel Stephen D. Lee's battalion rolled into position. Lee and his artillery pieces had preceded Anderson's division. When the colonel arrived, he conferred with Hood, who suggested placing the cannon there. It was, said Porter Alexander, a "beautiful position" from which Lee's gunners could sweep the ground in front of Jackson's right. When Lee finished the deployment of his eighteen cannon, he notified army headquarters. The commanding general—no relation to the artillery officer—replied: "You are just where I wanted you—stay there."[71]

Lee's artillerists indicated their presence with the discharge of several cannon. The fire was sporadic, never sustained; the army commander had cautioned against the wasteful expenditure of ammunition. The crackling fire of skirmishers blended with the booms, but for most of the time, quiet prevailed on the field. As the morning hours passed into the afternoon, the Confederates increasingly doubted if the Federals would attack. Longstreet believed since early morning that his former academy roommate would not give battle, and Jackson pulled out some of his frontline brigades for a rest.[72]

The inactivity along the Union lines resulted from confusion at army headquarters. Since early morning, Pope had wrestled with conflicting information that had the Rebels retreating or still in force along the railroad bank. Like Lee, Pope met with his senior officers, who reluctantly assented to a renewal of the offensive. Pope had known of Longstreet's presence on the field since the previous night but mistakenly concluded that his old friend's troops had moved behind Jackson's line, not as an extension to the south. Porter and John Reynolds both tried to convince Pope otherwise, but the commander, in Porter's words, "put no confidence in what I said."[73]

Reports filtered back to Pope throughout the morning, their contents as bewildering as the earlier ones. About noon, however, Pope concluded, without creditable evidence, that the Southerners were in flight and ordered Porter's corps, supported by Reynolds's and Hatch's divisions, to pursue. It took the better part of three hours for the pursuit column to form, but at about three o'clock the Yankees emerged from the woods beyond Groveton, charging toward Jackson's line. Above them and to their left, Stephen Lee's gunners scrambled to their cannon and prepared to fire.[74]

Jackson's ranks exploded in a flash of musketry, and Lee's artillery pieces roared. The Federals drove ahead, however, displaying bravery in the fury. "The first line of the attacking column," averred a Southerner, "looked as if it had been struck by a blast from a tempest and had been blown away." The cannon on the ridge scorched the ground, gouging holes in the Union ranks. But the Yankees kept coming, penetrating Jackson's ranks at points. Some of the defenders hurled rocks, their ammunition expended. Jackson sent an aide to Longstreet for help.[75]

Longstreet had just reached his front line along the turnpike when Major Henry Kyd Douglas of Jackson's staff galloped up with the request. Longstreet immediately dispatched Major Peyton Manning for additional batteries to bolster Stephen Lee's eighteen guns. Manning secured two batteries from Hood's division and Captain William H. Chapman's Dixie Artillery. When Chapman's four gun crews rumbled in, Longstreet personally placed them and then instructed Douglas to post the next one. Chapman's cannon enfiladed the Union ranks, increasing the destructive firepower of the Confederate artillery on the ridge. Although Longstreet discreditably attributed the breakup of Porter's attack to the batteries he ordered forward, Lee's battalion wreaked the greatest havoc upon the enemy.[76]

To his credit, Longstreet recognized the opportunity before him. Porter's serried lines were dissolving under the blanket of shellfire, streaming into the shelter of the woods. He decided to counter-attack with his entire command, and his staff officers went racing along the front, transmitting the orders. At army headquarters Lee concluded the same, sending a staff officer to Longstreet. The moment had come, and Longstreet seized it.[77]

Longstreet hurried to John Hood; he designated his division as the column of direction and cautioned the subordinate not to outpace his support. The target, Longstreet said, was Henry Hill, a mile from Hood's position but a mile and a half from D. R. Jones on the right. The divisions would advance successively, and if the Confederates secured the hill, Pope's retreat route would be severed and his army destroyed. Longstreet was confident, as he boasted later, that he commanded "over 30,000 of the best soldiers the world ever knew." (In fact, he had only slightly more than twenty-five thousand in the attack.)[78]

"My whole line," Longstreet stated in his report, "was rushed forward at a charge. The troops sprang to their work, and moved forward with all the steadiness and firmness that characterizes war-worn veterans." Each regimental color bearer stepped in front, ahead of the battle lines—"the spectacle was magnificent," admitted an onlooker. When some of Jackson's men saw the battle flags moving eastward, they cheered. A Mississippian with Longstreet asserted that when the general "went to fight he was a whole team." At least on this day the Mississippian had it right.[79]

For the next four hours Longstreet's veterans fought magnificently. Like a giant hammer they pounded Union defenders in a series of blows—first Hood, then Evans, Kemper, Jones, Anderson, and Wilcox. The combat flowed across Young's Branch onto the bloody crest of Chinn Ridge to the climax at Henry Hill. The Federals battled as if the fate of the army hung in the balance, and it did. One "murderous volley" followed another, and cannon belched waves of iron; men fell in clusters. Longstreet trailed the fury along the turnpike, rushing artillery batteries forward and directing infantry brigades toward the struggle. Lee accompanied Longstreet, and both of them came under Union artillery fire. Longstreet and his men accomplished all that could be expected of them, but Pope and his generals funneled enough brigades into the action to secure the army's retreat route.[80]

It was one of the finest counterattacks of the war. That Longstreet's troops did not ultimately succeed in destroying the enemy army can be attributed, in part, to the failure of Jackson to lend assistance. When Longstreet charged, Lee sent a message to Jackson: "General Longstreet is advancing, look out for and protect his left flank." For reasons unexplained, Jackson did not move forward until 6:00 P.M., nearly two hours later. By then his delay had allowed the Federals to shift brigades to their left against Longstreet and to enfilade the latter's units with artillery. The Confederates would never come so close again.[81]

Rain fell during the night of August 30–31, discomforting the sleeping and tormenting the wounded. It was, said Longstreet, a "nasty and soggy" morning. His troops began the gruesome work of burying the dead. While on a reconnaissance along Bull Run, Lee injured his hands in a fall, spraining his left and breaking a small bone in his right one. With his hands in splints, the general would have to ride in an ambulance for over a fortnight.[82]

Despite the weather and the mud, Lee stirred the army. He hoped to intercept Pope's retreating forces between Centreville and Washington. Jackson marched across Bull Run at Sudley's Ford, followed the Little River Turnpike, and reached Fairfax Court House. The Federals, however, moved ahead of Jackson. On September 1, in an afternoon thunderstorm, Jackson struck Pope's rear guard at Chantilly. In a nasty firefight, the Federals repulsed Jackson's thrust but lost Philip Kearny, who was killed. That night Longstreet relieved Jackson's men, and the Second Manassas Campaign concluded.[83]

The campaign and battle fashioned by Lee had been a strategic masterpiece. "Gen. Lee," wrote Brigadier General William Dorsey Pender, "has shown great Generalship and the greatest boldness. There never was such a campaign, not even by Napoleon." By a timely, brilliantly executed turning movement, Lee nearly crushed Pope's army before it and all of McClellan's units could combine. Although Pope's glaring ineptitude contributed markedly to the outcome, once Lee seized the initiative, he never relinquished it. His army inflicted a total of 13,824 casualties, while suffering 8,353 losses. Of that number, Longstreet's command incurred more casualties in roughly four hours of fighting than Jackson's troops did in two days.[84]

Longstreet described the campaign as "clever and brilliant," giving the entire credit to Lee. On the battlefield, Lee "displayed the most brilliant tactical ability." Longstreet came to regard it as Lee's finest operation—an ideal blend of the strategic offensive and the tactical defensive. To him, Second Manassas became the model. As the Army of Northern Virginia, forged into a splendid weapon at the old killing ground along Bull Run, turned northward, James Longstreet remembered what he had been a crucial part of and what he had witnessed.[85]

"MY OLD WAR-HORSE"

The Potomac River, remembered Georgian William Ross Stillwell, was as "clear as crystal" when he and his comrades crossed it at White's Ford on September 6, 1862. For two days the Army of Northern Virginia, in columns that snaked back to Leesburg, Virginia, had been wading through the neck-high water to enter Maryland. A young boy who watched the procession for hours said the Rebels "were the dirtiest men I ever saw, a most ragged, lean, and hungry set of wolves." Regimental bands played "Maryland, My Maryland." According to their commander, the Confederates had come to remove the "foreign yoke" of the Federal government from the oppressed citizenry of the state.[1]

The victory at Second Manassas opened the path for an invasion of the border state. Since the Seven Days Campaign, Robert E. Lee had held the strategic initiative in Virginia, and with Union general John Pope's defeat at Manassas and his army's retreat into the defenses of Washington, Lee had a major opportunity to extend the war beyond the Old Dominion's borders. "The present," Lee informed Jefferson Davis on September 2, "seems to be the most propitious time since the commencement of the war for the Confederate Army to enter Maryland." While the general admitted that such a movement was "attended with much risk," an advance across the Potomac would give Virginia a respite from the ravages of the conflict, perhaps force the Federals into a crucial battle, and bring supplies and additional recruits into the army from the Maryland citizenry.[2]

Lee cautioned the president in another letter, however, that the army was "not properly equipped for an invasion." The men needed shoes and clothing, and the march to Manassas had outpaced the commissary. The lack of ammunition, supplies, and animals concerned Lee, but the army could purchase supplies in Maryland and conserve ammunition. Although numerically weaker than the Federals, Lee argued that the Confederates "must endeavor to harass, if we cannot destroy" the enemy. If the operation proceeded well, Lee planned to extend the raid into Pennsylvania, perhaps as far north as Harrisburg, the state capital, where vital railroad bridges spanned the Susquehanna River.[3]

Longstreet endorsed Lee's proposed invasion of Northern territory. "The situation called for action," Longstreet subsequently asserted, "and there was but one opening—across the Potomac." Like Lee, the major general believed that the army could forage for food and grain in Maryland, sparing the farmers in Virginia. Longstreet also remembered that the army "was then all that its leaders could ask, and its claim as master of the field was established, but it was worn by severe marches and battles, and in need of rest." The men in the ranks needed time to "refresh," but the strategic situation dictated the offensive thrust beyond the Potomac. As Longstreet had come to understand, opportunism characterized Lee's operations.[4]

Lee started his fifty-three-thousand-man army northward on September 3. The troops marched leisurely to Leesburg, where the residents welcomed their heroes with cheers and offers of food. While in Leesburg, Longstreet attended to administrative details, ordering an inspection of all artillery batteries, their horses, limbers and cannon, and a reduction in the number of wagons. A soldier who saw the general in the town described him as "a large fine looking man." On the 6th, he and Lee followed the troops to the ford, crossing into Maryland and arriving at Frederick the following day.[5]

The entire Confederate army stopped at Frederick, its campsites sprawling across the surrounding farmland. Lee established his headquarters south of the small city at Best's Grove, a stand of oak trees; the tents of Longstreet, Stonewall Jackson, and Jeb Stuart were nearby. Lee paused at Frederick to formulate the next phase of the operation. With the Union army still within sight of Washington's spires, he had time to rest the troops and confer with his ranking generals.[6]

While en route to Frederick, Lee had told Longstreet that he wanted to force surrender of the Federal garrison at Harpers Ferry, Virginia, located at the confluence of the Shenandoah and Potomac rivers. If the Confederates were to march into Pennsylvania, Lee proposed to eliminate this threat to his communications and rear by dividing the army during the passage through Maryland. "I objected," Longstreet related, "that the move would be very imprudent as we were then in the enemys country, that he would be advised within ten or twelve hours of our movement, and would surely move out against us in our dispersed condition."[7]

Lee evidently dropped the subject, and the two generals did not discuss it again until September 8 when Longstreet visited army headquarters. Here he found Jackson and Lee at work on the campaign and, at Lee's request, joined them.[8]

The three generals presented an odd appearance. Lee still had his hands in splints, and Longstreet was hobbled by a chafed heel that forced him to wear a carpet slipper. Two days earlier Jackson had been thrown from his horse and "considerably hurt." A member of the Washington Artillery who saw the famous Stonewall at Frederick remarked that "Jackson looks as if wading the Potomac and other streams has in no wise improved his appearance." The troops joked that the peculiar warrior had not changed his shirt since leaving his home in April 1861.[9]

Lee and Jackson were at work on the details of the movement against Harpers Ferry. Much of the plan had been agreed upon by the time Longstreet arrived. He listened to the proposal and, as he said later, "I offered no opposition." He suggested that the entire army be utilized in the operation instead of the five divisions indicated by Lee. The commanding general rejected Longstreet's recommendation, so Longstreet counterproposed that Richard Anderson's division be added to the attack force and that his two divisions be kept in close supporting distance of D. H. Hill's five brigades, which would act as the army's rear guard. Lee agreed, and the meeting concluded.[10]

Lee's biographer, Douglas Southall Freeman, wrote that Longstreet "sulked at the decision," implying that Jackson supported the division of the army. A biographer of Jackson stated that "he looked forward to it eagerly," and a recent historian of the campaign argued that "it was a plan to Jackson's liking." By contrast, Harvey Hill, Jackson's brother-in-law, related in an 1864 letter to one of Jackson's staff officers that in December 1862, Stonewall told Hill: "At the council held at Frederick, I opposed the separation of our forces in order to capture Harper's Ferry. I urged that we should all be kept together." If Hill was accurate in his recollection of the conversation, the allegedly eager Jackson concurred with the allegedly sulking Longstreet. Furthermore, in a postwar letter to Hill, a former officer in the army recalled that on the night of September 5 he heard Jackson tell Hill that he wanted to invade Pennsylvania and "give them a taste of war." When Hill responded that the Federals could attack the Confederate rear, Jackson rebutted that there were two rears.[11]

Hill's wartime letter poses some intriguing questions. Had Jackson voiced opposition to Lee before the arrival of Longstreet, who believed that Jackson endorsed the plan? If Jackson did so, would Lee have overruled both of his trusted lieutenants? When Longstreet objected to the dispersal of the divisions, why did Jackson remain silent if he held a similar view?[12]

The answers remain elusive. Jackson did not live to write a memoir; Longstreet did. Perhaps it was his published criticism of the operation and of Lee—"we then possessed an army which, had it been kept together, the Federals would never had dared attack," averred Longstreet—that moved Freeman to his harsh judgment. More evidence exists that Jackson shared Longstreet's concern than exists that Longstreet "sulked."[13]

Lee's plan was predicated on the tactical vulnerability of Harpers Ferry. The village, the scene of John Brown's famous raid on the government arsenal in October 1859, lay at the bottom of a bowl formed by three heights. If the Confederates could seize the high ground, the Federal garrison of approximately thirteen thousand troops was doomed. By eliminating the Union force at Harpers Ferry and by pulling his army behind the mountain ranges west of Frederick, Lee could secure a supply line into the Shenandoah Valley and advance into Pennsylvania, while drawing the Union Army of the Potomac farther away from Washington and its base.[14]

Lee incorporated his strategic ideas in Special Orders No. 191, issued to the army on September 9. Jackson and three divisions would spearhead the movement against Harpers Ferry by recross-

ing the Potomac River upstream from the village and turning eastward, sealing the western approaches to Harpers Ferry. The
divisions of Major Generals Lafayette McLaws and Richard Anderson
would march down Pleasant Valley and seize towering Maryland
Heights across the Potomac from the target. Brigadier General John
G. Walker's division would reenter Virginia, swing westward, and
occupy Loudoun Heights, east of the Shenandoah River. Longstreet's two divisions would cross the mountains to Boonsboro,
guarding the reserve and the supply and baggage trains. Major
General Harvey Hill's division would serve as the rear guard near
Boonsboro while Jeb Stuart divided the cavalry among Jackson,
McLaws, and Longstreet. Once Harpers Ferry fell, projected for Sep-
tember 12, the army would reunite at Boonsboro or Hagerstown,
Maryland.[15]

The Confederates departed from Frederick before daylight on
the 10th, with Jackson marching on the National Road followed by
Longstreet, McLaws, Anderson, and Hill. As the columns passed
through the city, regimental bands played "The Girl I Left Behind
Me." "Much speculation as to our destination," an officer scribbled
in his diary. By nightfall Longstreet and Hill bivouacked near
Boonsboro at the western base of South Mountain, with Jackson
closing on Williamsport, Maryland, and Walker on the Potomac
River. McLaws and Anderson had entered Pleasant Valley, but Lee's
timetable had already been disrupted as Jackson moved farther west
to capture the Federal detachment in Martinsburg, West Virginia, at
the northern end of the Shenandoah Valley.[16]

Lee rode with Longstreet and during the day received a report
that a Federal force was moving toward Hagerstown, thirteen miles
north of Boonsboro. To meet this alleged threat, Lee ordered Longstreet to Hagerstown on the morning of the 11th. Once again Lee
accompanied his subordinate, who did not like the further separation of the army. As they traveled together, Longstreet grumbled to
Lee: "General, I wish we could stand still and let the damned Yankees come to us!" Longstreet's frustration was evident in his choice
of words, for few officers cursed in Lee's presence.[17]

Longstreet's concern was well founded, however. The army was
weakening with every mile it marched. Men left the ranks in droves,
unable or unwilling to continue because of illness and exhaustion,
compounded by the lack of food and shoes. For three weeks, since

the army had crossed the Rappahannock in the movement against Union general John Pope's command, the Rebels had marched scores of miles, fought a major engagement, and trekked into Maryland. The men of McLaws's and Harvey Hill's divisions had endured forced marches to overtake their comrades after Manassas. One of their men, writing home, commented: "The march up to Maryland liked to have ruined me." The pace was so killing that Brigadier General Howell Cobb, one of McLaws's commanders, claimed that Hill should be charged with "incapacity and inhumanity," describing him as "a weak, self-conceited heartless & cruel ass."[18]

While McLaws's and Hill's troops may have been extreme in their physical exertions, the soldiers from other divisions also endured hardships. They suffered from hunger, reduced in some instances to chewing tobacco to alleviate stomach pangs. Enlisted men and officers foraged, even plundered, for food. In fact, the officer ranks had been so reduced that the officers still with their regiments were insufficient in numbers to stem the flood of stragglers and deserters. Lee admitted to Davis that the draining away of men was "one great embarrassment." He estimated that from one-third to one-half of the troops had abandoned their commands. A regimental captain termed the straggling "a great curse of the army."[19]

The Confederates, in turn, encountered shut doors or exorbitant prices when they sought food at the homes of western Marylanders. Although Lee's proclamation of September 8 to the people of the state announced that the Rebel army had come to assist them in their efforts to secure liberty, much of the citizenry of western Maryland was pro-Unionist in sentiment and, as a Southern officer remarked, "turned the cold shoulder *every where.*" The civilians who sympathized with the Confederate cause hid their views. "The Marylanders," wrote a Georgian on the 13th, "cannot be made to believe that we intend to help them, they think that this movement of ours is simply a raid to get supplies & provisions & they are afraid to make much show of their feelings because they will suffer for it after we leave." Lee's hopes for recruits likewise never materialized in large numbers.[20]

A woman who lived in Shepherdstown, Virginia, across the Potomac from Sharpsburg, Maryland, left a graphic description of the Rebels' physical condition during the campaign. Mary Bedinger Mitchell wrote:

When I say that they were hungry, I convey no impression of the gaunt starvation that looked down from their cavernous eyes. . . . I saw the troops march past us every summer for four years, and I know something of the appearance of a marching army, both Union and Southern. There are always stragglers, of course, but never before or after did I see anything comparable to the demoralized state of the Confederates at this time. Never were want and exhaustion more visibly put before my eyes, and that they could march or fight at all seemed incredible.[21]

When respites came, as at Frederick, the soldiers welcomed them. For Longstreet's men the two days spent in Hagerstown—the 12th and 13th—accorded them a chance to rest. The community had more residents of Southern sympathies than Frederick, and some of them extended an open hand to the famished Rebels. The reports of a Union advance from Pennsylvania proved erroneous, so no compelling duties interrupted the men's relaxation. Lee received reports from the Shenandoah Valley that Jackson had passed through Martinsburg and was approaching Harpers Ferry. No word came from McLaws or Walker, but on the evening of the 13th, Hill relayed Stuart's afternoon message that the Federals had crossed the Catoctin Mountains and were within seven miles of South Mountain. If the Yankees shoved their way through the gaps on South Mountain, the dispersement of the army, the straggling in the ranks, and the delay in capturing Harpers Ferry would combine to jeopardize Lee's army.[22]

Part of Lee's rationale for the Maryland expedition and the Harpers Ferry operation was his assessment of the Federal army following its defeat at Manassas. Lee believed the Union troops were disorganized and demoralized, and when he learned that Major General McClellan had resumed direction of the forces, he calculated that the enemy's pursuit would be slow and cautious. McClellan had been given command of the Army of the Potomac and John Pope's Army of Virginia by a reluctant Abraham Lincoln on September 2. The Northern president and his secretary of war, Edwin Stanton, thought that McClellan had deliberately withheld units from Pope. Lincoln's secretary John Hay noted in his diary at the time of Second Manassas that the president "said it really seemed to him that McC. wanted Pope defeated." But Pope's defeat and the condition of the army forced Lincoln to offer McClellan the command—the president had no one else.[23]

If the administration had doubts about McClellan, the men in the ranks did not. When he rode among the troops on the 2nd, they responded with thunderous cheers. Although he had serious flaws as a commander, "Little Mac," as the men called him, had fused them into an army, and they never forgot it. No future commander of the army secured the men's affection as did McClellan, a bond that battlefield defeat could not sever. Perhaps the tragedy of McClellan's Civil War career was that he never fully appreciated the weapon he had forged.[24]

As it had been on the Peninsula it would be initially in Maryland —McClellan's army crawled in pursuit, not starting northward from the capital's defenses until the 7th. Five days later the vanguard of the army entered Frederick. On the 13th, while lounging in a field outside the city, two members of the Twenty-seventh Indiana found a copy of Lee's Special Orders No. 191 wrapped around three cigars. It was addressed to D. H. Hill and evidently lost by a staff officer. (After the war the so-called Lost Order generated heated controversy among former Confederates.) The two soldiers took it to their commander, who sent it through channels to McClellan. Their discovery gave the Union general one of the greatest intelligence coups in American military history. When he read it, McClellan, waving the copy, vowed: "Here is a paper with which if I cannot whip Bobbie Lee, I will be willing to go home."[25]

But the cautious McClellan frittered away precious time before responding to this remarkable opportunity. He received the copy before noon but then waited another eighteen hours, until the morning of the 14th, before marching the bulk of his army toward South Mountain. Earlier in the day, before he learned of the Confederate dispositions, McClellan had sent his cavalry, supported by infantry, westward from Frederick. These Yankees probed westward, engaging Stuart's horsemen in skirmishes. Stuart relayed the news to Lee at Hagerstown. Lee, in turn, reacted at once to this sudden increase in the tempo of McClellan's pursuit, even before his opponent advanced in force the next day.[26]

The courier with Stuart's message reached Hagerstown shortly after nightfall on the 13th. When Lee read the contents, he sent an order to Harvey Hill to defend Turner's Gap, where the old National Road crossed South Mountain, and he summoned Longstreet to headquarters. Longstreet limped into the tent as Lee was studying a map. The commanding general summarized the situation and then

requested Longstreet's advice. The danger Longstreet had counseled about now seemed a reality—Harpers Ferry had not capitulated, and if McClellan drove forward with energy, the Federals
could sever Lee's army, crushing each segment in detail. Longstreet
responded that it was too late for his troops to march to the gap
and aid Hill; instead his divisions and Hill's should be concentrated
at Sharpsburg, Maryland, a mile or so north of the Potomac, and
take a defensive position. If the Yankees moved against the Confederate divisions at Harpers Ferry, Longstreet and Hill could assail
their flank or rear.[27]

Lee "would not agree," as Longstreet stated afterward. The army
commander replied that he preferred to make a stand on the mountain; accordingly, he directed Longstreet to march at daylight for the
gap, leaving Robert Toombs's brigade behind to guard the army's
wagon train. With that understood, Longstreet returned to his tent,
prepared the orders, and lay down to sleep. Lee's decision still
gnawed at him, so he arose, lit a cigar, and wrote a note to his
commander restating his argument for a concentration at
Sharpsburg. To Lee the matter was settled, and he did not reply.
Writing the note, Longstreet asserted later, "relieved my mind and
gave me rest."[28]

Longstreet's eight brigades and artillery batteries filled the road
to Boonsboro at first light. The late summer's sun rapidly heated
the air, and clouds of dust from the dry roadbed hung above the
men, who gasped for clean air. Longstreet and the officers pushed
the pace and endeavored to close the ranks. With each mile, however, the column stretched farther apart; men fell exhausted by the
roadside; gaps between regiments and brigades widened. Up
ahead, the sound of gunfire boiled over the crest of South Mountain. About 3:00 P.M., the leading brigade stumbled into Boonsboro
and was directed up the mountainside.[29]

Lee had preceded the troops in an ambulance and awaited them
at the foot of the mountain. When John Hood's division, under
Shanks Evans, saw the general, the men shouted: "Give us Hood!"
Their beloved general had been under arrest since Second Manassas when he and Evans had become embroiled in a dispute over
captured ambulances. Longstreet sided with Evans, who had the
senior rank, had Hood arrested, and ordered him to Culpeper
Court House. Lee wisely intervened, countermanding Longstreet's
directive, which would have removed Hood from the army. Since

then, Hood's veterans buzzed with anger and resentment, finally swarming forth on this day. Lee knew Hood's ability and temporarily suspended the arrest. When the Texans heard the news, they bellowed: "Hurrah for General Lee! Hurrah for General Hood! Go to hell, Evans."[30]

Longstreet rode ahead of his panting men to find his old friend Harvey Hill. It had been a long September sabbath for the devout North Carolinian, of whom Porter Alexander believed the army had no "more honest fighter." An artilleryman described Hill as "a born fighter—as aggressive, pugnacious and tenacious as a bull-dog, or as any soldier in the service, and he had a sort of monomania on the subject of personal courage."[31]

The situation on South Mountain required of Hill every characteristic the gunner attributed to him. The division commander had been on the crest since sunrise, gazing down on the plain as it filled with masses of dark figures, seemingly giving the ground life, like a huge colony of ants on the march. The mountainside was heavily wooded, its face scarred with ravines and hollows. Mountain laurel intertwined beneath the trees; a handful of farmers' fields and pastures, edged by rail fences and stone walls, provided a few clearings amid the swath of green. The terrain favored the defenders, but it could not aid a solitary division against corps of Federals.[32]

McClellan advanced on two fronts—against Turner's Gap and Fox's Gap, less than a mile to the south. The fighting ignited about 9:00 A.M. at Fox's and continued throughout much of the day. Brigadier General Samuel Garland, Jr., Louise Longstreet's cousin, was killed in the combat while leading his North Carolinians. Hill, as he wrote later, "played the game of bluff" after Garland fell, until his other brigades reached the summit. Longstreet's troops arrived in time to stabilize Hill's beleaguered lines and retain the Confederate grip on the mountain until dark. The combat cost the Federals eighteen hundred men; the Confederates, perhaps twenty-three hundred. Six miles to the south, one Union corps punched through Crampton's Gap into Pleasant Valley, threatening Lafayette McLaws's Rebels as they closed on Maryland Heights above Harpers Ferry.[33]

When Longstreet scaled South Mountain, he superseded Hill in command. He assisted in the deployment of the brigades and scribbled a message to Lee that they could not hold another day without reinforcements and that the units should be withdrawn after nightfall. Upon its receipt, Lee sent majors Charles Venable and Randolph

Talcott up the mountain. When they found Longstreet, "that imperturbable old soldier," in Venable's words, they informed him that the retreat could begin under cover of darkness. Shielded by the blackness, the Rebels filed down the western face. In Moxley Sorrel's telling, it was "a bad night" on the mountain, and Hill's men "made a magnificent defense, but [were] terribly mauled and broken up." Longstreet's brigades went last, replaced on the crest by Confederate cavalry.[34]

In Boonsboro that night, Lee conferred with several of his generals, including Longstreet, Hill, and Hood. "After a long debate," according to Hood, the council decided to retreat to Sharpsburg the next morning. Later, Lee received news of the seizure of Crampton's Gap by McClellan's troops. A note from Jackson indicated that Harpers Ferry would fall on the 15th. Finally, Lee sent Charles Venable and Lieutenant Samuel Johnston, an engineer officer, to Sharpsburg to determine if the village was in Union possession. The aides found the town full of Federal cavalry, and they returned to Boonsboro and informed Lee, who directed one of Hill's brigades toward Sharpsburg. The soldiers marched all night, arriving before daylight. The Yankees had vanished.[35]

The Union horsemen seen in Sharpsburg by Venable and Johnston were a contingent from Harpers Ferry that had eluded Confederate videttes and escaped. Led by Colonel Benjamin F. "Grimes" Davis of the Eighth New York Cavalry, the troopers refused to surrender with the garrison. Crossing a pontoon bridge, the riders skirted the base of Maryland Heights and then headed north through Sharpsburg toward Pennsylvania and safety. Beyond Sharpsburg they scurried across fields to the Williamsport-Hagerstown Turnpike, where they suddenly encountered Longstreet's ordnance train en route from Hagerstown. Acting quickly, Davis, a native Mississippian, stood in the road and in his distinctive drawl detoured wagon after wagon into another roadway where his men, with pistols drawn, pointed the teamsters in a different direction. The Northerners netted forty wagons before the Confederates discovered the ruse. By 9:00 A.M. on the 15th, the cavalrymen and their prizes rolled into Greencastle, Pennsylvania. It was one of the most daring exploits of the war.[36]

Longstreet learned of the loss of the wagons later that day when Toombs's brigade arrived at Sharpsburg. Since early in the morning, his and Hill's men had been spilling onto the ridges, hills, and fields around the village. "Men in grand humor for fight," an officer jotted in his diary. There were probably not much over twelve thousand troops in all, but as Lee told some Virginians, "We will make our stand on those hills."[37]

Sharpsburg and the encircling farmland lay between the Potomac River to the west and Antietam Creek to the east. The smaller stream, spanned by four stone bridges, meandered less than a mile from the village, a modest barrier to an army. The hills pointed out by Lee jutted 150 feet or so above the creek, natural towers for a defending force. A ridge extended northward from Sharpsburg, ending in wooded knolls and ravines that could conceal bodies of troops. The Hagerstown Turnpike followed this ridge, with sections of its roadbed framed by rail fences. Stone outcroppings, hollows, and little ripples in the ground provided additional protection amid the fertile landscape of lush green crops. A land blessed by nature's richness, it was made important now by man because of its location. If Lee were to fight a battle before he abandoned Maryland, it had to be here.[38]

Lee's decision to make a stand "on those hills" was arguably the worst decision of his career. Porter Alexander believed it to be "the greatest military blunder that Gen. Lee ever made." Alexander argued that with the army's reduced strength Lee could expect little more than a drawn battle as the best *possible* outcome." Furthermore, if McClellan's army succeeded in breaking the Confederate lines, forcing a retreat by Lee, the Southerners had only one avenue of escape—Boteler's Ford on the Potomac, a deep, rocky crossing. Lee risked the destruction of his army but, in Longstreet's words, "he found it hard, the enemy in sight, to withhold his blows."[39]

For Lee to give battle at Sharpsburg, he needed time for his army to reconcentrate. About midday on the 15th, a courier galloped up with a message from Jackson that announced the surrender of the Union garrison at Harpers Ferry earlier that morning. The Confederates had netted over 11,500 prisoners, seventy-three cannon, thirteen thousand small arms, roughly two hundred wagons and a stockpile of supplies, at a loss of approximately two hundred casualties. Lee immediately relayed orders for the divisions to rejoin the army as soon as possible.[40]

The courier had barely departed for Harpers Ferry when Lee's cavalry videttes reported the approach of McClellan's army. All

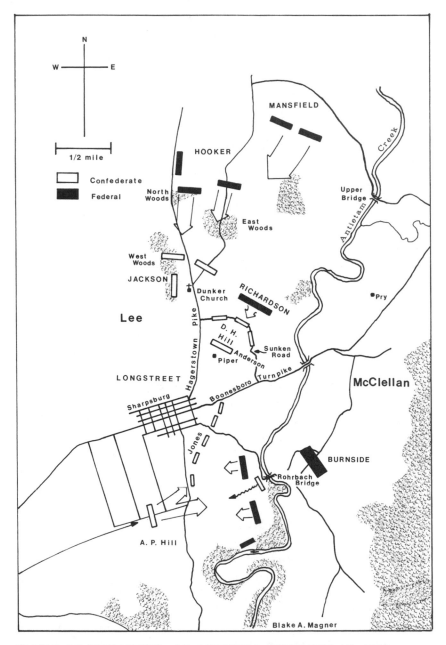

BATTLE OF SHARPSBURG, OR ANTIETAM, SEPTEMBER 17, 1862.

through the afternoon dust clouds indicated the oncoming Yankees, whose numbers eventually swelled to 71,500, supported by three hundred pieces of artillery. Lee stated, however, that the cautious, careful McClellan would not attack until Wednesday, the 17th, giving the Rebels one vital day for the absent divisions to march to Sharpsburg.[41]

Longstreet, meanwhile, spent the 15th overseeing the deployment of the divisions on the field. Hood's and Jones's troops settled in on the hills east and south of the town, with Hill's brigades extending the line north of the Boonsboro Turnpike to a sunken lane that zigzagged across the farmland between the Boonsboro and Hagerstown roads. Longstreet instructed his battery commanders to "put them all in, every gun you have, long range and short range."[42]

During the morning, Longstreet and Hill established their headquarters at the stone and log farmhouse of Henry and Elizabeth Piper, located in a swale approximately five hundred yards south of the sunken road. The Pipers and their five children farmed 231 acres of land and welcomed the two generals and their staffs. Elizabeth Piper and her daughters prepared dinner for their guests and offered them home-brewed wine with the meal. Believing it might be poisoned, Longstreet declined until Hill drank a glass, and then he said, "Ladies, I will thank you for some of that wine." The two generals and their aides slept in the family's nearby orchard.[43]

After breakfast with the Piper family on Tuesday, September 16, Longstreet rode along his lines, surveying the Federal position across Antietam Creek. Sporadically, the opposing artillery crews banged away at each other. At one point in his reconnaissance Longstreet passed behind a brigade of Georgians as the cannon fire pockmarked the air above with black, smoking explosions. To one of the Georgians the general seemed "perfectly indifferent to the bursting shell," looking through his glasses, with his bay horse moving at a slow walk. Later, Longstreet met Lee, and together they watched for evidence of an enemy advance. According to a staff officer with D. R. Jones, Lee had brush cut and dragged behind the horses to create dust to fool McClellan until the troops from Harpers Ferry arrived.[44]

About midday, to the relief of Lee, Jackson and John Walker rode up and reported that two of Jackson's divisions and Walker's were trailing behind and would soon be on the field. Jackson had left

Powell Hill and the Light Division at Harpers Ferry to parole the prisoners and to gather the supplies. As for the commands of Lafayette McLaws and Richard Anderson, they were en route, marching south of the Potomac instead of coming via the difficult road from Maryland Heights to Sharpsburg. These two divisions would not arrive until daylight on the 17th, with a forced march over the final six miles.[45]

Lee summarized the situation and the army's position for Jackson and Walker, explaining his reasons for confronting the Federals. Jackson "emphatically concurred with me," Lee wrote afterward. The commanding general then ordered Jackson's two divisions to the left along the Hagerstown Turnpike and told Walker to rest his men until further instructions. By this time the artillery duel had subsided, and Jackson's veterans took their places during the lull. Finally, about 4:00 P.M., Walker's division moved south of the town, forming on Longstreet's right flank.[46]

East of Antietam Creek, meanwhile, at his headquarters at the brick residence of Philip Pry, McClellan slowly fashioned an offensive for the next day. He held no council of war, either for advice or for the issuance of specific orders. He decided to launch his main attack against Lee's left or northern flank where the terrain appeared from the Pry house to be most favorable for such a maneuver. On his left, where the hills rose above the creek, he intended to force a crossing at the Rohrbach Bridge—soon rechristened Burnside's Bridge—although he was not altogether sure if it would be a diversion or a full-scale assault. Finally, if the attacks on the flanks succeeded, he planned to assail the Confederate center astride the Boonsboro Turnpike. The battle scheme was patched together from limited knowledge of the ground beyond the creek and from a miscalculation of Lee's strength. Despite having a copy of Lee's orders in hand, McClellan convinced himself that the entire Rebel army waited west of Antietam Creek.[47]

His main attack force—the First, Second, and Twelfth Corps— shifted toward the Confederate left during the afternoon and night. The First Corps, under Major General Joseph Hooker, crossed Antietam at the Upper Bridge late in the afternoon, sparking a skirmish with John Hood's Rebels, who had been moved there earlier in the day. The combat amounted to little, a false harbinger of the fury that was to consume both armies in another day.[48]

A gentle rain began falling after dark. Along the four-mile Confederate line, many of the men bedded down with hunger, having had only ears of green corn and apples to eat during the day. Some lucky Georgians, however, had dined on beef after a cow strayed into their campsite. At Longstreet's bivouac site on the Piper farm, horses from an artillery battery stampeded through the trees, scrambling the officers from their blankets. But mostly it was a night of silence in Miller's Cornfield, the East and West Woods, Bloody Lane, at Dunker Church and Burnside's Bridge—places to be given new meaning before another nightfall. For roughly thirty-nine hundred Americans near Antietam Creek and Sharpsburg, it was also the final sleep before the unending darkness.[49]

The Battle of Sharpsburg or Antietam exploded about 6:00 A.M. on Wednesday, September 17, amid a dissipating fog when "Fighting Joe" Hooker's Federals charged southward along the axis of the Hagerstown Turnpike. Before them were the two divisions of Jackson's and Hood's brigades. From the beginning the combat seared the land, consuming unharvested crops and soldiers in both armies. Attacks crumbled before flaming musketry and thunderous artillery fire. The fury embraced Miller's Cornfield, East Woods, West Woods, and the plateau where the whitewashed brick church of the pacifist German Baptist Brethren or Dunkers stood.[50]

The slaughter drew more and more units into its grip. Lee ordered Walker's division from the right flank; Harvey Hill sent three of his brigades to support Jackson. On the Federal side, Major Joseph K. F. Mansfield's Twelfth Corps followed Hooker's divisions. The rifle and cannon fire scythed through the Cornfield, leveling the stalks and the men caught among them. One of Hood's Texans thought that "doomsday had come." Stretched, broken, cobbled back together, the Confederate line held for three hours, but the end was far away. Union Major General Edwin Sumner brought one of his Second Corps divisions forward, pointing it toward the conspicuous church outlined against the foliage of the West Woods. Sumner's troops advanced bravely where he indicated, only to be annihilated by additional Confederate brigades rushed to the front by Lee. Nearly sixteen thousand Southerners fought to a momentary standstill an equal number of Northerners.[51]

As Sumner's troops streamed rearward, Lee and Harvey Hill halted near the ridge along the Hagerstown Turnpike south of the church. A short time before, Lee, now back on horseback but with his right arm in a sling, had ridden behind Hill's troops in the sunken road. As the generals prepared to spur ahead, Colonel John B. Gordon, Sixth Alabama, exclaimed to his officers: "These men are going to stay here, General, till the sun goes down or victory is won."[52]

Longstreet, who had spent the earlier hours superintending his line and conferring with Lee at headquarters west of Sharpsburg, soon joined the commanding general and Hill at the base of the rise. Lee and Longstreet walked to the crest, followed by Hill on horseback. Turning to his friend, Longstreet said to Hill: "If you insist on riding up there and drawing the fire, give us a little interval so that we may not be in the line of fire when they open on you." Minutes later Longstreet saw a puff of smoke from a cannon and jokingly told Hill it was aimed at him.[53]

Before Hill could respond, a cannon ball clipped off the forelegs of his horse. Hill tried to get off, but the wounded animal wavered back and forth. Amused by Hill's predicament, Longstreet nettled: "This side, Hill. No, the other. Get off over his head, Hill, slide off behind." Finally, the general extricated himself and then shot the animal.[54]

One of Hill's aides who had witnessed the scene remembered Longstreet's bearing under fire. The general was, the staff officer wrote, "as cool and composed as if on dress parade. I could discover no trace of unusual excitement except that he seemed to cut through his tobacco at each chew."[55]

Hill borrowed another mount and with Longstreet rode toward his line in the sunken road. Remounting Traveller, his iron-gray horse, Lee went to speak with Jackson. Hill and Longstreet reached the Rebel position not long before the focus of the Union offensive shifted to this sector. Hill had perhaps twenty-five hundred men with him to hold the army's center across a front of six hundred yards or more. His troops had piled fence rails on the northern bank of the lane, whose bed lay from three to six feet below the farmland on each side. Years of farmers' wagons, loaded with grain for a mill on Antietam Creek, had eroded the roadway. For the Southerners the roadside bank was a natural parapet.[56]

The initial Federal assault rolled down the hillside north of the sunken road. On signal, Hill's line erupted, a rippling flash of smoke and flame that "brought down the enemy as grain falls before the reaper," in the words of a North Carolina colonel. The Yankees belonged to Brigadier General William H. French's Second

Corps division, and there were more behind this first line. In fact, French had over twice Hill's numbers and sent a second brigade forward, then a third. The Confederates repulsed each successive thrust, killing and maiming over seventeen hundred of the enemy. Hill, said a soldier, "was the coolest man in our army," and he demonstrated it along what would come to be called Bloody Lane.[57]

Brigadier General Israel Richardson's Union division replaced French's with the famous Irish Brigade in the forefront. When these Federals descended the slope, they, too, staggered under the killing fire from the roadbed, losing 550 of their comrades within minutes. Streaming rearward behind the crest, the Irishmen joined other Northerners in returning the Southerners' fire. Hill's casualties, likewise, had been escalating and he needed help, which Longstreet was able to provide.[58]

When the struggle for the sunken road began, Longstreet stationed himself on the Piper farm, most likely in or near the orchard. According to Major Sorrel, Longstreet's "eyes were everywhere." He sent orders for Richard Anderson's division to rush forward to support Hill. The four brigades, thirty-five hundred men in all, arrived at the Piper cornfield and orchard as the Irish Brigade withdrew. Before the units could be deployed, Anderson went down with a wound; he was succeeded by Brigadier General Roger Pryor. Union artillery from the opposite side of Antietam Creek hurled shells into the ranks. Soon an orderly came from Pryor to ask Longstreet for artillery support. Longstreet scribbled a hurried note: "I am sending you the guns, my dear General. This is a hard fight and we had all better die than lose it."[59]

When Richardson's Irish Brigade had initially charged, Longstreet instructed Colonel John R. Cooke to take his Twenty-seventh North Carolina and the Third Arkansas and attack toward the Federal flank across the sunken road. Cooke's 675 men and roughly 250 soldiers from another brigade drove gamely ahead, surprising the Northerners and penetrating their flank. Union reinforcements stopped the thrust in a bloody slugfest, and with ammunition nearly expended, Cooke ordered a retreat. The North Carolina colonel lost half of his command, and the other unit counted only fifty survivors.[60]

By this time the fight for the sunken road and Piper farm had reached a climax. In the lane a Confederate officer mistakenly withdrew his regiment, and the Yankees stormed down the hillside into the gap, raking the defenders and splintering apart their line. The

Confederates scrambled out of the deathtrap into the Piper fields, carrying with them three of Pryor's brigades who had advanced into or near the road. "The slaughter was terrible," recalled a Georgian. "When ordered to retreat, I could scarcely extricate myself from the dead and wounded around me." Behind them, shouting and firing, the Northerners swarmed into the cornfield, charging toward the orchard.[61]

Longstreet wrote in his memoirs of this awful day that the artillery and musketry were "multiplied and confused by the reverberations from the rocks and hills . . . in this great tumult of sound." Although he did not specifically refer to this moment, it applied as the center of Lee's army reeled on the edge of destruction amid a "great tumult of sound." To stop the surge of the enemy Longstreet had only Captain W. B. Miller's battery of the Washington Artillery, a section of a South Carolina battery, and remnants of infantry units.[62]

The Union fire toppled the gunners until two of Miller's brass cannon were silenced. Longstreet and his staff hurried forward, with aides replacing the fallen artillerists. Sorrel, Tom Goree, Tom Walton, John Fairfax, and Peyton Manning loaded the pieces and pulled the lanyards. Longstreet sat calmly on his horse, chewing on a cigar, holding the reins of his officers' mounts, and ordering charges of canister. One of D. R. Jones's aides soon appeared and later wrote in his diary: "Gen. Longstreet working like a man god in center."[63]

Additional artillerymen soon relieved the staff members, and Hill launched a counterattack with two hundred men but was repulsed. Other Confederate batteries concentrated fire on the Federals in the Piper cornfield and along the sunken road. Without fresh troops, the Union assault stalled; of the nearly ten thousand Yankees involved in this fearful combat, roughly three thousand were down. In the sunken road, their bodies lay on top of the Rebel dead and dying. Longstreet, Hill, and their officers and men had saved Lee's army—at least for the moment.[64]

"Longstreet's conduct on this great day of battle was magnificent," asserted Sorrel. "He seemed everywhere along his extended lines, and his tenacity and deep-set resolution, his inmost courage, which appeared to swell with the growing peril to the army undoubtedly stimulated the troops to greater action, and held them in place despite all weakness." A Virginia captain claimed simply that the general was "one of the bravest men I ever saw on the field of battle."[65]

To Longstreet, however, the day's hero was his friend and academy classmate Harvey Hill. In a postwar letter to Porter Alexander, Longstreet argued that there was "never a more plucky or persistent fighter" than Hill, who fought all day with a "handful" of exhausted men. "Had the fight made by D. H. Hill been made by a Virginian," added Longstreet, "it would have been heralded as a wonderful achievement, and to all time. But Hill was from far down in Dixie."[66]

But this "dreadful day," as Alexander termed it, had not concluded with the struggle in the center. As the gunfire flickered on the killing fields north of Sharpsburg, it escalated east of the town where Major General Ambrose Burnside's Union Ninth Corps was finally rolling toward the village, endangering the Confederate army's right flank and retreat route. Throughout the late morning and early afternoon, Burnside had been thwarted by Robert Toombs's Georgians at Rohrback Bridge. Finally, two Federal regiments knifed across the arched stone structure and cleared the way for their comrades. Burnside needed another two hours to move over the span and deploy for battle, but at 3:00 P.M. fifty-five hundred men in two divisions advanced on Sharpsburg.[67]

To confront Burnside's troops, D. R. Jones had approximately twenty-eight hundred men in five brigades. Jones's Rebels fought stalwartly and slowed the Union onslaught, buying time for support to arrive. When it came, as the Yankees closed on the village, it was Powell Hill's Light Division from Harpers Ferry. To secure Lee's flank, Hill's veterans had marched seventeen miles in eight hours, a grueling pace. Three of Hill's brigades counterattacked, reversed the tide, and with Jones's units, shoved the enemy back to the hills above Antietam Creek. The firing subsided and then ended. The "long, exciting, amazing day" of "*terrible* battle," in the words of a Confederate, was done.[68]

Darkness settled in, mercifully. The carnage surpassed any previous day's slaughter in the nation's experience; in fact, it stands today as the bloodiest single day in American history. By a recent calculation, the casualties exceeded 24,000: 11,500 Confederates, 12,800 Federals. Over 3,700 soldiers lost their lives in the combat, with another 18,300 wounded. Lee's casualties amounted to twenty-eight percent of his army; McClellan's, twenty-four percent. Major

Henry Douglas of Jackson's staff described the night as "a fearful one. Not a soldier, I venture to say, slept half an hour. Nearly all of them were wandering over the field, looking for their wounded comrades, and some of them, doubtless, plundering the dead bodies of the enemy left on the field. Half of Lee's army were hunting the other half."[69]

Casualties among Confederate infantry units reached staggering proportions. Longstreet's and Jackson's commands suffered a casualty rate of slightly over forty percent, with the divisions of McLaws, Harvey Hill, John R. Jones (Jackson's former command), and Anderson incurring the greatest number. While Longstreet emerged unscathed, Sorrel and Walton of his staff were wounded. Walton took a bullet in the shoulder while serving the cannon in the Piper orchard, and Sorrel was knocked unconscious and bruised by the concussion of a shell burst. John Fairfax lost Saltron, his "superb gray stallion" during the fighting at the Piper farm. Distraught by the animal's death, Fairfax rushed to Longstreet and exclaimed, "General, General, my horse is killed. Saltron is shot; shot right in the back!" Turning to his aide, Longstreet gave him a "queer look" and replied, "Never mind, Major. You ought to be glad you are not shot in your own back!"[70]

Despite the army's condition, Lee concluded on the night of the 17th to hold the field another day. He gathered his senior lieutenants at headquarters in a field west of Sharpsburg. Stonewall Jackson, both the Hills, Hood, Jubal Early, and D. R. Jones joined the army commander. When Longstreet did not report with the others, Lee became concerned and inquired among the officers if anyone had seen the general. Smoking a cigar, Longstreet finally rode in, having been detained in the village as he assisted a family whose house was on fire from an artillery shell. When Lee saw him, the army commander walked forward, grasped his subordinate's hand, and said: "Ah! Here is Longstreet; here's my old *war-horse!* Let us hear what he has to say." The two generals then talked quietly with each other.[71]

Lee's decision to remain on the defensive for another day amazed his subordinate commanders. Most of them anticipated a retreat across the Potomac during the night. Instead, Lee issued orders for rations to be cooked and delivered to the men along the front lines, for artillery to be redeployed, and for stragglers to be herded back to their units. Once again Lee risked the destruction of his army, but he did so "without apprehension," as he stated. Lee's refusal to abandon the field except at his own choosing resulted from practical reasons and from a contempt for his opponent. In the end, Lee —as equally as McClellan—could claim victory at Sharpsburg.[72]

September 18 passed quietly on the battlefield. A truce allowed burial details and stretcher parties to gather the awful harvest of the dead and the maimed. Wagonloads of wounded Southerners rolled toward the Potomac throughout the day. After midnight Lee's infantry and artillery units pulled out for Boteler's Ford and Virginia. The cavalry brushed aside Federal pursuers on the morning of the 19th and then crossed the river. The Yankees followed that evening, touching off an engagement on the 20th at Shepherdstown. The Northerners were driven into the river in a bloody debacle. Within a week the Army of Northern Virginia had established its campsites in the Shenandoah Valley near Winchester.[73]

"The fight of the 17th," wrote Major Walter Taylor of Lee's staff to his sister four days after the Battle of Sharpsburg and Antietam, "has taught us the value of men—who can even when weary with constant marching & fighting & when on short rations, contend with and resist three times our number." Echoing Taylor publicly, Lee stated in his official report that "nothing could surpass the determined valor with which they [the troops] met the large army of the enemy, fully supplied and equipped, and the result reflects the highest credit on the officers and men engaged." In time, Lee regarded the engagement as the army's finest hour and took the greatest pride in its accomplishment.[74]

Other voices, in time, also attested to the army's courage and skill at Sharpsburg but questioned the decision to fight. Longstreet privately argued, "All that we can claim is that we got across the Potomac with an organized army." Porter Alexander believed that Lee's "overdone" audacity governed the commander's judgment along Antietam Creek. Defeat, Alexander wrote, "would have meant the utter destruction of his army." Alexander concluded, "So he fought where he could have avoided it, & where he had nothing to make & everything to lose—which a general should not do."[75]

On no other major battlefield in the East did the Confederate army face such a disparity in numbers in such a vulnerable position —with the Potomac River at its back. Calculations of Rebel strength on that day vary, but evidence indicates that Lee had barely thirty thousand troops on the field, if that, a ratio of less than two to one in McClellan's favor. One North Carolina officer described the battle as *"a complete game of bluff,"* with battle lines reduced to skirmish lines. Lee thought the raid into Maryland and its goals justified his willingness to give battle. He told Stonewall Jackson's widow after the war, paraphrasing her husband's words, that "it was better to have fought the battle in Maryland than to have left it without a struggle."[76]

Lee made his stand and jeopardized his army because he was certain he could beat McClellan in a battle, and he was correct. Although McClellan eventually considered Antietam the highlight of his career, the Union commander squandered the finest opportunity given a Federal general to destroy the Army of Northern Virginia. The Northern corps and divisions entered the action, as General Edwin Sumner said, in "driblets." In fact, once the battle was joined, McClellan acted more like a spectator than an army commander. One of his men perceptively commented that McClellan "never realized the metal that was in his grand Army of the Potomac." Consequently, the Confederates repulsed one uncoordinated assault after another and won a tactical victory. Lee's decision to fight and then retreat, however, gave the Northern administration a political victory.[77]

The ultimate meaning of Sharpsburg and Antietam came not from within either army but from Abraham Lincoln. Five days after the battle, on September 22, the Union president issued the preliminary Emancipation Proclamation. The document sparked heated debate and controversy, but its message would reshape the struggle. The trumpet now heralded freedom.

"I WILL KILL THEM ALL"

Members of the Ninth Virginia of the Army of Northern Virginia dubbed their bivouac site near Winchester in the Shenandoah Valley "Barefooted Camp." The nickname provoked laughter and enlivened morale, but it also testified to a bitter truth about the condition of not only many within the ranks of one regiment but of thousands in the army.[1]

From Barefooted Camp to army headquarters, the officers and men knew they needed time to heal and to refit. Since mid-August the army had fought two major battles and had endured countless miles of marching without shoes and adequate food. When they recrossed the Potomac River following the fearful slaughter at Sharpsburg, they were little more than a specter of an army. The autumn of 1862 brought a pause in the warfare in the Old Dominion, an interlude of two months for the refashioning of the army.

Soldiers' letters to loved ones at home spoke of the ordeal. The men wrote of diets of apples and green corn in Maryland, and of rags clotted in blood wrapped around swollen feet. A North Carolinian informed a friend on October 3, two weeks after they reentered Virginia, that "our men are nearly exhausted, and greatly need the rest they are now enjoying." "We are a dirty, ragged set," admitted a Georgia lieutenant. Another soldier told his wife that even after a week back in Virginia he could "scarcely walk" because of his feet. As the days lengthened into weeks, shoes, pants, and coats arrived "in degrees," but a Virginian stated in mid-November that many of his comrades were still barefoot.[2]

Despite the shortages and the suffering, the men retained their morale. An Alabamian boasted on October 1: "I am barefooted and have been for about 6 weeks and I never was in better health and spirits in my life." Likewise, one of the Virginians in the Barefooted Camp noted that his comrades were "in very good spirits." The campaigns of Second Manassas and Sharpsburg had stretched the physical limits of the army, but its members had a resiliency that sustained them through the forced marches and the bloody engagements. It was a bedrock fused from victory, belief in the cause, and faith in Robert E. Lee.[3]

The restorative power of the army became evident within a fortnight of the army's return to Virginia. The "evil" of straggling, as Lee termed it, had reduced regiments to shadows of themselves and "greatly paralyzed" the army's efficiency. On September 22, Lee reported 41,520 troops present. But the stragglers began returning in droves, and on September 30 the aggregate present had increased to 62,713. Ten days later officers counted 78,204 within the ranks, and by the month's end, the number had surpassed 80,000, almost a doubling of strength within six weeks. A staff officer remarked that brigades once again looked like brigades.[4]

While the absentees refilled the regiments, Lee, Longstreet, Jackson, and their subordinate officers refitted, retooled, and reorganized the command. Foodstuffs, clothing, footwear, and equipment arrived from supply depots, but still not in the numbers required. The artillery had incurred serious losses, especially in Longstreet's command, and the worst batteries were disbanded, their serviceable cannon and equipment dispersed to other units. Officers reinstituted regimental and brigade drills while the senior commanders held periodic reviews. Because of these efforts, the army had a "renewed confidence that we could not be whipped," in Porter Alexander's words. "We are now beginning to feel like farm cocks again," wrote Longstreet in a letter on October 6, "and some begin to wish for the chance to convince the Yanks that Sharpsburg is but a trifle to what they can do."[5]

The final change in the army involved the organization of Longstreet's and Jackson's commands into official corps. On September 18, President Jefferson Davis signed into law an act that provided for the appointment of lieutenant generals and the creation of army corps. Once the army had returned to Virginia, Davis wrote to Lee and asked for his recommendations for the new rank and for promotions of major and brigadier generals. Lee replied on October 2, "confidently" recommending Longstreet and Jackson for the position of lieutenant general. His endorsement of Longstreet was without reservations. Of Jackson, Lee stated: "My opinion of the merits of General Jackson has been greatly enhanced during this operation." Davis forwarded the two generals' names to the Senate, and both were soon appointed—Longstreet to rank from October 9; Jackson, from October 10. Longstreet was the senior subordinate officer in the army.[6]

The rank and seniority given Longstreet reflected Lee's estimation of him. While Jackson had redeemed himself at Second Manassas and Sharpsburg for his performance during the Seven Days, Longstreet had been the most dependable subordinate since Lee's accession to command on June 1. With each successive campaign and engagement, he had matured as a general—the contrast between his performance at Seven Pines and at Second Manassas or Sharpsburg was keen. His direction of large numbers of troops in combat, his tactical acumen, and his courage and composure under fire had been distinguished. Lee had valued Longstreet's advice, had sought it on a regular basis, and had enjoyed his company during the operations. After all, it was Lee who called Longstreet "my old war-horse."

Lee also recognized the diverse talents of his two senior lieutenants. In the Second Manassas Campaign, Jackson again demonstrated his particular genius for the execution of a strategic combination and his relentlessness as a general. Semi-independent operations seemingly infused Jackson, unleashing his manifest abilities. He embraced warfare as he did his religious faith—with fervor. "As a leader he was fire," Longstreet wrote of Jackson. He drove his men as few, if any, generals did, demanded absolute obedience to orders and duty, and did not countenance failure. To Jackson, duty implied fighting; fighting implied death. Jackson accepted casualties as war's consequence; he harbored no romantic illusions about warfare. He was a remorseless enemy, a warrior in the mold of a biblical Joshua.[7]

By contrast, Longstreet approached war dispassionately. No moral imperatives, no testings of men's characters drove his generalship as they did Jackson's. To Longstreet, victory resulted from preparation—deliberate, thoughtful planning. He believed in the strategic offensive and the tactical defensive. If Jackson was the army's hammer, Longstreet was its anvil. To overcome the disparity in numerical strengths between the two opponents, Longstreet wanted to conserve his men's lives, not expend them in assaults. Risks had to be measured by costs. While he supported Lee's bold strategic movements, he became increasingly committed to the tactical defensive; he preferred the counterstrike to the attack. He believed that ultimately organization and the conservation of resources, manpower, and matériel, more than the fighting qualities of the troops, would result in Confederate independence.[8]

On October 6, Longstreet wrote a revealing letter to Joseph Johnston in response to information or rumors that his former superior and friend might be sent to the western theater upon his recovery from his Seven Pines wound. After describing the Sharpsburg engagement and the army's present condition, Longstreet wrote, "Although they [the officers and men] have fought many battles and successfully under another leader, I feel that you have their hearts more decidedly than any other leader can ever have. The men would now go wild at the sight of their old favorite."

Then Longstreet addressed the question of Johnston's assignment to another theater, writing: "I can't become reconciled at the idea of your going west. I command the 1st Corps in this Army if you will take it you are more than welcome to it, and I have no doubt but the command of the entire Army will fall to you before Spring." He added, "If it is possible for men to relieve you by going west don't hesitate to send me. It would put me at no great inconvenience. On the contrary it will give me pleasure if I can relieve you of it. I fear that you ought not to go where you will be exposed to the handicaps that you will meet with out there. I am yet entirely sound and believe I can endure anything."[9]

A recent biographer of Longstreet charged that his letter "represented an extraordinarily unfavorable assessment of Robert E. Lee." The author asserted that Longstreet regarded Lee's "bloody offensive tactics" as a failure and "expected" Lee's eventual removal from command because of them. He also alleged that Longstreet's words hint of his dissatisfaction with the treatment accorded him by the newspapers. To Longstreet, Jackson's renown smothered his accomplishments, and if he could not secure appreciation for his achievements with the army, he would willingly transfer to the West, where the opportunities for fame would not be overshadowed by Jackson and Lee. It was thus a "period of disenchantment" for Longstreet, according to the biographer.[10]

This assessment seems strained, however. Unquestionably, Longstreet's esteem for Johnston had not wavered. Johnston's careful generalship suited Longstreet, while Lee's willingness to take risks disturbed Longstreet, particularly Lee's division of the army in Maryland. But Longstreet did not then or later voice opposition to Lee's bold strategic movements during the Seven Days and Second Manassas campaigns. As noted previously, Longstreet criticized subordinates, not Lee, for the resultant attacks at Gaines's Mill, Glendale, and Malvern Hill, and regarded the Second Manassas operation as Lee's finest. Admittedly, the army had suffered heavy casualties since Lee assumed command—forty-seven thousand in all, a figure larger than the entire Confederate Army of Tennessee at the time. The evidence does not indicate, however, that Longstreet indicted Lee for those losses. Of the three campaigns, Lee utilized the tactical defensive in two of them, resorting to offensive tactics only in the Seven Days.[11]

There is some merit to the charge that Longstreet resented the praise accorded others, notably Virginians. A native of the Deep South, Longstreet had seen the acclaim given Virginians by Richmond newspapers. His difficulties with Powell Hill resulted from such stories. But Longstreet was not alone in this feeling; other non-Virginians believed the same. An anti-Virginia sentiment was present within units of the army, but it was still not an open source of controversy. Nevertheless, Lee had accorded Longstreet high praise with the recommendation for promotion. Longstreet could not have been unhappy with this.[12]

Finally, was Longstreet's offer to relinquish corps command to Johnston and go west in his stead a sincere one? It may have been sincere but not realistic, and Longstreet surely knew that. A proud man who was jealous of Lee, Johnston would not have consented to serve as a corps commander in an army he once directed under a commander who still retained only temporary authority as his replacement. Furthermore, Johnston had no authority to transfer Longstreet to the West. It would appear that Longstreet flattered his valued friend and endeavored to remind Johnston of his and others' high regard for the general. Although Longstreet undoubtedly considered Johnston a superior general to Lee, he was not, as the biographer claims, "so distressed by Lee's performance" that he sought assignment elsewhere. The Maryland campaign troubled Longstreet, but he had respect and affection for Lee. His differences with Lee over tactics would arise in the future.[13]

Curiously, about the same time Longstreet wrote to Johnston, Jackson evidently was displeased with Lee. According to Harvey Hill, Jackson told him in December that he had contemplated resignation. "While at Fredericksburg, General J.'s feelings were not kind toward General Lee," Hill stated in a July 1864 letter to Robert Dabney, Jackson's former chief of staff. "He thought that the latter had shown partiality to Longstreet in the distribution of guns, clothing, camp & garrison equipment etc. He had felt this keenly after the battle of Sharpsburg & once said that he feared he would be compelled to resign." By the time Hill wrote to Dabney, he was no longer with the army and was disenchanted with Lee's generalship, and his words should be accepted with caution. But Hill had no apparent reason to fabricate the story, and Jackson possessed a sensitivity to such perceived unfairness. If it were as Hill related, Jackson could remain incensed with Lee for months over relatively minor grievances.[14]

During this period, Lee worked closely with Longstreet and Jackson, seeking their advice and recommendations in the promotions of junior officers. The summer campaigns had thinned the officer ranks; brigadiers and colonels were commanding divisions, and majors were at the head of brigades. Those who demonstrated ability and promise needed to be rewarded; those who failed needed to be shunted aside. On November 6, Lee announced the appointment of Longstreet and Jackson to lieutenant general and the official organization of the First and Second Corps, including two new major generals and ten new brigadiers.[15]

The final details of the reorganization required another month to complete, but once finished, Longstreet's First Corps consisted of five divisions, comprised of twenty-one brigades and twenty-four artillery batteries—approximately forty-one thousand troops in all. Jackson's Second Corps counted thirty-eight thousand men in four divisions of nineteen brigades and twenty-three artillery batteries. Jeb Stuart commanded four cavalry brigades and five batteries of horse artillery, totaling ten thousand troopers and gunners, while the army's Reserve Artillery, under Brigadier General William Pendleton, had fourteen batteries and eight hundred artillerists.[16]

The First Corps of the Army of Northern Virginia contained infantry units from eight of the eleven Confederate states. Of the corps's ninety-one regiments and battalions, fifty-eight came from Georgia, South Carolina, and Virginia. Only one division—Brigadier General Robert Ransom, Jr.'s, two-brigade command—had troops from one state, North Carolina. There were three regiments each from Florida and Texas, and one from Arkansas.[17]

The senior division commander was Major General Lafayette McLaws, whose command had five brigades of South Carolinians, Georgians, and Mississippians. McLaws and Longstreet had been childhood friends in Augusta, Georgia, and fellow classmates at West Point. A career soldier, McLaws had received his current rank in May 1862 after leading a division during three campaigns. He was a stout man of modest height with a round, bearded face. He attended to the needs of his troops as few others and earned their respect and affection. "He was an officer of much experience and most careful," noted Moxley Sorrel. "Fond of detail, his command was in excellent condition, and his ground and position well examined and reconnoitered; not brilliant in field or quick in movement there or elsewhere, he could always be counted on and had secured the entire confidence of his officers and men." His deliberateness and fussiness had given McLaws a reputation for slowness, but his attention to his men made him and his division a reliable command.[18]

Second in rank to McLaws was another member of the West Point class of 1842, Richard Anderson. A native South Carolinian, Anderson commanded a brigade under Longstreet on the Peninsula before leading a division at Second Manassas and Sharpsburg, where he fell wounded in the action at the Piper farm. Of Anderson, Sorrel stated: "His courage was of the highest order, but he was indolent. His capacity and intelligence excellent, but it was hard to get him to use them. Withal, of a nature so true and lovable that it goes against me to criticize him." Sorrel added, however, that Longstreet could get "a good deal out of him, more than any one else."[19]

The third division belonged to the "very striking" John Hood, who was one of the two new major generals in the army. His promotion could not be denied after Sharpsburg, and Longstreet recommended him. His combat record as a brigade commander and temporary division commander equaled any in the army. Tom

Goree predicted in a letter of October 10 that Hood would be promoted: "No man deserves it more. He is one of the finest young officers I ever saw." Sorrel thought that the tall, somewhat gangly general was an "ideal" soldier. Hood's division consisted of the two brigades he had directed and two others from D. R. Jones's division, which was divided up. Jones had left the army after Sharpsburg because of a serious heart problem that would result in his death on January 15, 1863.[20]

The second newly commissioned major general was thirty-seven-year-old George Pickett, who was also endorsed by Longstreet. Few officers, if any, enjoyed Longstreet's favor more than the "very dashing" Pickett. Their friendship extended back to the Mexican War and was cemented with his and Sallie Corbell's kindness upon the death of the Longstreet children during the previous winter. Pickett, remarked a staff officer, "was very foppish in his dress and wore his hair in ringlets. He was what would be called a dapper little fellow but brave as they ever make men." He owed his promotion to Longstreet, although his conduct at Gaines's Mill had won the plaudits of many. The shoulder wound he incurred there still bothered him and kept him from placing his arm in his coat sleeve. With limited experience and a flashing temper, Pickett needed seasoning and maturing. He would receive much attention from Longstreet.[21]

Longstreet's fifth division had been John Walker's during the Maryland campaign. A Missourian, Walker was transferred to the Trans-Mississippi Department upon his promotion to major general in November and was replaced by Robert Ransom, Jr. A thirty-four-year-old North Carolinian and West Pointer, Ransom had served under Longstreet since the spring. As senior brigadier in Walker's division, he assumed command while retaining direction of his brigade.[22]

One officer in the corps angered by the promotions of Hood and Pickett was Brigadier General Cadmus Wilcox. He believed, with justification, that he deserved a major generalcy ahead of either Hood or Pickett, who were both junior in rank to him. On a number of battlefields since Seven Pines, Wilcox had directed more than one brigade with capability. But Wilcox was a victim of pro-Virginia sentiments and Longstreet's preference for Pickett. Hood's promotion was undeniable, while Pickett benefited from Longstreet's advocacy and being a Virginian. The division given to Pickett had been for the most part Longstreet's, comprised of five brigades—four

Virginian and one South Carolinian. Wilcox, however, was a North Carolinian in a corps with only two brigades from that state, both under Ransom. He did not fit into the politics of the reorganization.[23]

Consequently, Wilcox wrote to Lee asking to be relieved from command and transferred to the western theater. "I cannot consent to it," replied Lee, "for I require your services here. You must come and see me to tell me what is the matter. I know you are too good a soldier not to serve where it is necessary for the benefit of the Confederacy." Wilcox evidently spoke with Lee and did remain with Army of Northern Virginia. He also blamed Longstreet for his failure to attain higher rank and would in time become one of the corps commander's harshest critics.[24]

As part of the organization of the First Corps, Longstreet expanded the size of his staff. By the end of November the staff consisted of eighteen. During these weeks he added majors Raphael J. Moses, Osmun Latrobe, John J. Garnett, and Dr. Randolph Barksdale. In a short time, Moses and Latrobe joined the inner circle of Sorrel, Goree, John Fairfax, Peyton Manning, and Dr. Dorsey Cullen.[25]

Longstreet brought Moses and Latrobe from the staff of D. R. Jones when that general left the army. Fifty years old, a native South Carolinian, Moses had been a wealthy "commercial lawyer" in Columbus, Georgia, when the war began. He served initially as the commissary officer in Robert Toombs's brigade and later in that capacity in Jones's division. He soon became a favorite with the younger members of Longstreet's staff because of his wit and seemingly endless string of stories and anecdotes. Many nights he entertained them at the dinner table or around the campfire with his humorous tales. Moses was also, in Sorrel's description, a "most intelligent, efficient officer" whose reputation as Longstreet's chief commissary officer extended beyond the corps.[26]

Like Moses, Osmun Latrobe had rendered valuable service on Jones's staff before joining Longstreet. Latrobe was twenty-eight years old and a member of a prominent Maryland family. His father, John H. B. Latrobe, was an attorney, inventor, author, and public servant; his grandfather, Benjamin H. Latrobe, had been a renowned architect in Baltimore. When the war came, Latrobe traveled to Virginia and volunteered as an aide to Jones. A tall, robust man, nearly as large as Longstreet, the Marylander became "an ardent

Confederate" whose gallantry under fire and courteous manner attracted Longstreet's attention. The general appointed the captain an assistant adjutant and inspector general. In time, Latrobe would assume more duties and greater responsibilities.[27]

Dr. Randolph Barksdale was named the corps's medical inspector, serving under Dr. Cullen. His duties required the inspection of the medical departments in each unit, from the regimental to divisional levels. Similarly, Major John Garnett, who as an artillery lieutenant fought under Longstreet at Blackburn's Ford on July 18, 1861, acted as inspector of ordnance and artillery. Under Peyton Manning's direction, Longstreet's ordnance department was one of the army's finest.[28]

No addition to the First Corps pleased Longstreet more, however, than the appointment of Lieutenant Colonel Porter Alexander to the command of Stephen Lee's artillery battalion on Lee's promotion to brigadier and reassignment to Mississippi. An 1857 graduate of West Point, the twenty-seven-year-old Georgian was an excellent engineer and a thoughtful officer, with a talent for artillery. Alexander had served as the army's ordnance chief for over two years and possessed one of the keenest intellects in the army. An intense, demanding individual, he was also an amiable companion and well liked by those who knew him. Longstreet managed to find officers of ability and promise, and in Alexander he had one of his most valuable officers. The Georgian became a familiar figure at corps headquarters as Longstreet utilized his engineering and reconnoitering skills frequently. Their admiration for each other deepened with time.[29]

Lee, Longstreet, and Jackson had not completed the army's reorganization when their opponents began stirring. For nearly six weeks after Sharpsburg, McClellan and his Army of the Potomac remained encamped north of the Potomac River. Like its Confederate counterpart, the Federal army needed a period of rest and rehealing. But once the inactivity extended into the first week of October, President Lincoln visited the campsites and urged McClellan to undertake an offensive south of the river. The Union general refused to budge, citing his usual litany of more time, more supplies, and more men. Then when Jeb Stuart and eighteen hundred cavalrymen raided northward to Chambersburg, Pennsylvania, and encircled the Federal army for a second time, on October 9–12, Lincoln's patience frayed. Additional telegrams passed between army headquarters and the capital in an exchange depressingly familiar to Lincoln. Finally, on October 26, the Northerners began crossing the Potomac east of the Blue Ridge Mountains. The autumnal interlude had ended.[30]

Anticipating an enemy movement for some time, Lee reacted quickly to McClellan's advance. When the reports came in of the Federal crossings, Lee directed Longstreet eastward while keeping Jackson's corps in the Shenandoah Valley until the extent of McClellan's operation could be determined.[31]

The First Corps started for the mountains on the same day, the 26th. The pace, recalled a Texan, was "unhurried" in the cool autumn weather. Longstreet's men marched via Front Royal and the gaps east of the village. Once over the mountains, the Confederates averaged roughly twenty miles a day, and by November 5 most of the brigades had reached Culpeper Court House. Longstreet established headquarters in the home of a Pendleton family in the town, and Lee joined him there on the 5th. The commanding general had preceded the troops, journeying to Richmond for a conference with the administration.[32]

On the day Lee arrived at Culpeper Court House, Abraham Lincoln relieved McClellan of command and replaced him with Major General Ambrose Burnside. The president had learned on the 4th that once again the Confederates had outmarched the Federals— McClellan had covered only thirty-five miles in eleven days. Lincoln's order reached army headquarters at Rectortown on the night of the 7th. Three days later McClellan bid farewell to the army, exiting the conflict as a general beloved by the troops. When Lee heard of McClellan's removal, he joked to Longstreet that he had become so used to his oppontent's methods "he hated to part with him.[33]

For the next week the opposing armies remained in place, separated by the Rappahannock River. Jackson's corps was still beyond the Blue Ridge Mountains; Longstreet's was bivouacked around Culpeper; Stuart's cavalry probed along the river for indications of a Federal advance. Burnside, who believed himself unfit for army command, moved swiftly to formulate an offensive scheme. Within days the Union general decided to march to Fredericksburg beyond Lee's right flank, cross the Rappahannock on pontoons, and advance overland toward Richmond, with his supplies ferried by the navy. Burnside secured Lincoln's approval on the 14th and started one of his newly formed Grand Divisions toward Fredericksburg the next day.[34]

Stuart's horsemen detected the Federal march within hours and forwarded the news to army headquarters. Lee hesitated, however, until more definite information could be ascertained. Throughout the 16th conflicting reports filtered back to Culpeper. Finally, the next day, Burnside's movement toward Fredericksburg was confirmed, and Lee directed McLaws's and Ransom's divisions toward the little river city. Longstreet ordered his remaining units ready to march "at an instant notice." On November 18, while McLaws's and Ransom's troops plodded eastward in a rainstorm, Stuart forded the Rappahannock, pushed northward to Warrenton, and discovered the entire Union army in motion. Stuart's intelligence settled the matter, and Lee instructed Longstreet to leave the next morning.[35]

The rain of the previous day resumed on the 19th and continued into the night and through the following day. The roads from Culpeper to Fredericksburg turned into tracks of mire. A Georgia lieutenant described them as "the meanest, muddiest roads you ever saw." Longstreet's men struggled through them. Thousands of the soldiers still had no shoes and wrapped their feet in rags of cowhide moccasins that soon fell apart. At night Longstreet rode among the campfires, telling the men to rake the ashes and coals into beds and sleep on them to keep themselves dry and warm. Despite the conditions, the divisions covered forty-five miles in three days, and by the 22nd, four of the divisions were posted on the hills west of Fredericksburg.[36]

The inclement weather and the delayed arrival of the pontoon train conspired to thwart Burnside's design to cross the river at Fredericksburg and occupy the heights beyond the town. Instead, all the Union general could do was watch the waters rise and wait on the portable bridges. The vanguard of the army had arrived at Falmouth, across the Rappahannock from Fredericksburg, on the 17th and stopped. Although some of his subordinates argued for a crossing at one of the numerous fords, Burnside demurred. When Longstreet's leading Confederates appeared on the 21st, Lee barred the path to Richmond. Women and children fled the city in wagons, in carriages, and on foot, driven away by the threat of a Union bombardment.[37]

Lee, Longstreet, and their staffs preceded the bulk of the First Corps troops to Fredericksburg. The commanding general did not expect to make a stand at the historic community. Although the ground west of the city offered fine defensive positions, Stafford Heights, where the Federals lay, dominated the Southern lines, and if Burnside attacked, Lee had no room for a counterstrike. Lee thought that the North Anna River, thirty-odd miles to the south, accorded his army better tactical opportunities. Ultimately, however, Lee summoned Jackson's corps to Fredericksburg. As Lee later stated, he remained at Fredericksburg because of "an unwillingness to open more of our country to depredation than possible, and also with a view of collecting such forage and provisions as could be obtained in the Rappahannock Valley."[38]

History had walked the streets of Fredericksburg many times before December 1862 but never with such portent as when Lee decided that the Army of Northern Virginia would stand here. With the arrival of Jackson's corps during the month's first days, nearly two hundred thousand troops sprawled along the heights, hills, woods, and plain around the city. Drama hung as heavy as the early morning air in anticipation of "a great battle to commence," in the words of a Rebel. This time it seemed that history intended to stay.[39]

The suspense ended before daylight on December 11 when two Confederate cannon boomed, the signal that the Yankees were crossing the river. The alarm had been given by Brigadier General William Barksdale's Mississippians, who occupied the city. Although a thick fog blanketed the river, the Mississippians heard the sounds of Federal engineers at work on pontoon bridges. The Northerners worked feverishly behind the shield of mist, laying sections at three points on the Rappahannock—at the foot of Hawk Street, below the railroad bridge opposite Fredericksburg, and at the mouth of Deep Run a mile below the city's limits.[40]

By six o'clock the fog had lifted enough to reveal the Northern work parties, and Barksdale's men, aided by a Florida regiment, scorched the unfinished bridges with musketry, driving back the engineers. The Federals bravely returned to work, then ran back before the fire, repeating the effort several times. At Deep Run, where no Southern infantry contested the construction, the engineers finished the bridge by nine o'clock; opposite the city, the Rebels still defied all attempts.[41]

The enemy's stubbornness drained Burnside's patience. He reluctantly ordered a bombardment of Fredericksburg. About midday, approximately 150 cannon on Stafford Heights unleashed their fury on the city. The soldiers and residents huddled in cellars as homes, stores, and churches shook under the concussions and shell bursts. Fires ignited; brick walls collapsed; mothers clung to children in terror. War showed its hellish face.[42]

The guns ceased after two and a half hours, and the engineers rushed forward. Despite the barrage, Barksdale's men emerged nearly unscathed, pounding back the workers another time. Finally, blue-coated infantry piled into pontoon boats and poled across the water in an amphibious assault. Spilling out into the barricaded streets, the Federals engaged the Southerners in house-to-house fighting that lasted until nightfall. During the combat, Barksdale sent a message to Longstreet, asking if his men should douse the fires. "You have enough to do to watch the Yankees," Longstreet shot back. About 7:00 P.M. the Southerners withdrew; Burnside had the city and his bridges.[43]

The horrors of the 11th were followed by war's magnificence on the 12th. All day long, in cords of unbroken blue set against a backdrop of newly fallen snow, Burnside's troops filed over the bridges, entered Fredericksburg, and filled the plain south of town. Brigades were stacked behind brigades; artillery batteries were aligned in rows of iron and bronze. Within the city, the soldiers ransacked the damaged buildings, taking what they wanted, breaking what they did not. Artillery exchanges and skirmish fire characterized the limited fighting. By nightfall Burnside had eighty thousand troops massed before the enemy's lines.[44]

The Confederates watched the pageantry before them. Their lines extended from the river above Fredericksburg to Hamilton's Crossing, a distance of roughly six miles. Longstreet's divisions held the front from Taylor's Hill on the left to beyond the valley cut by Deep Run. From there, Jackson's troops manned a woodland west of the Richmond, Fredericksburg and Potomac Railroad. Beyond Jackson's right flank at Hamilton's Crossing, Stuart's cavalry and horse artillery prowled.[45]

Longstreet's position behind the city embraced three hills: Taylor's, Marye's, and Telegraph (or Lee's, as it was known afterward). Anderson's division held Taylor's; McLaws's brigades covered Marye's; Pickett's troops curled around Lee's; and Hood's command lay across the valley of Deep Run. Ransom's two brigades acted as a reserve behind Anderson and McLaws. The corps's artillery supported the infantry, its cannon bristling from the natural platforms.[46]

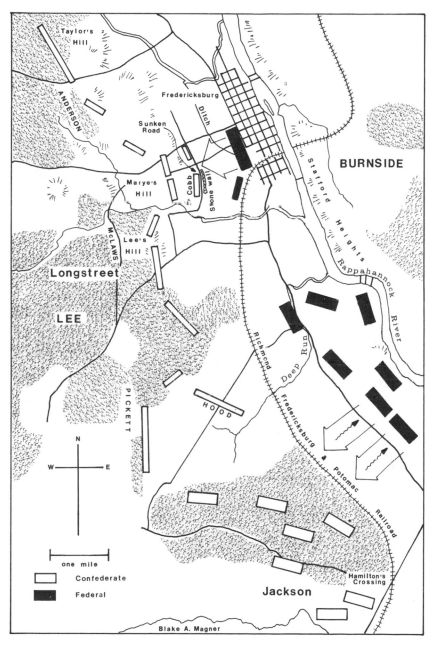

BATTLE OF FREDERICKSBURG, DECEMBER 13, 1862.

At the center of the position and closest to the city loomed Marye's Heights, its crest crowned with "Brompton," the Marye family mansion. Beneath the brow, Lee's engineers and Porter Alexander had artillery pits dug for cannon. At the base ran a sunken road, its track edged by two stone walls. Between the city and the roadbed lay an open plain dotted with a few houses and gardens and sliced by a millrace, five hundred yards from the stone walls. The plain's contour was flush with the top of the eastern stone wall, making the natural trench invisible to the Yankees in Fredericksburg. Lee's Hill, where the commanding general and Longstreet had their headquarters, rose above Marye's Heights, half a mile to the right and rear.[47]

Longstreet had not been satisfied with the terrain's evident strength, however, and in the days before the battle he ordered trenches, abatis, and fieldworks constructed. Perhaps the slaughter at Sharpsburg, where no works were built by the Rebels, had convinced him of their merits. For Lee's army, Longstreet's efforts were a tactical innovation and a harbinger of the future. During one of his inspections, Longstreet, accompanied by Alexander, suggested to the artillery officer that additional guns be placed on Marye's Heights. Turning to Longstreet, Alexander remarked, "General, we cover that ground now so well that we will comb it as with a fine-tooth comb. A chicken could not live on that field when we open on it."[48]

When Burnside's troops crossed the Rappahannock on the 12th, Longstreet's men finished their labors. On Marye's Heights, the gunners of the Washington Artillery readied nine cannon while fellow artillerists in several batteries to the rear prepared. Behind the stone wall, Brigadier General Thomas R. R. Cobb's Georgians of McLaws's division stockpiled ammunition, provisions, and water. In the other commands, similar efforts marked the day's passage. By nightfall Longstreet and his men were waiting for the enemy, in McLaws's words, "with perfect calmness and with confidence in our ability to repel them.[49]

Longstreet arose before dawn on Saturday, December 13, mounted his horse, Hero, and with Osmun Latrobe rode along his lines. Once more a heavy cold fog clung to the snow-covered ground. As he and his aide neared Hood's lines at Deep Run, they heard the voices of Union officers in the distance. Finding Hood, Longstreet directed the division commander to attack the Federals' flank when they advanced against Jackson. He would have Pickett ready to cooperate, Longstreet told Hood. The corps commander believed the enemy would attack both his and Jackson's positions simultaneously, but Hood should not worry about supporting Longstreet's left because the position was so strong that the troops there could hold it. With this done, Longstreet joined Pickett, whose nine thousand troops were already under arms, repeated the instructions, and returned to Lee's Hill.[50]

Arriving at headquarters shortly after sunrise, Longstreet waited for Lee's return from a similar reconnaissance. Nearby, a Virginia artillery lieutenant watched the general; three days later he described him in a letter to his wife: Longstreet had on a gray frock coat and gray pants, with no marks of insignia or rank. "A gray or lead colored shawl" covered his shoulders and arms, warming him in the morning's chill. The officer believed Longstreet stood six feet two inches tall and estimated his weight at 190 pounds. His "strong round frame [is] portly and fleshy but not corpulent or fat. His hair is dark auburn, and his long whiskers and beard are the same color and thick and heavy. His forehead is broad and full, his brows heavy. His nose, straight and rather fleshy, and his eyes, which are set in close to his nose, are dark and steady in their movements and gaze."

Longstreet paced much of the time, "apparently intensely thinking." When he spoke, he did so "in a rather low tone." "He had a very intellectual appearance," concluded the lieutenant, "is certainly a very industrious man and an energetic, skillful officer. Next to Lee I should prefer entrusting the chief command of our armies to him."[51]

McLaws joined Longstreet on the hill, followed by Lee. The commanding general, the Virginia artillerist stated, appeared older than his years but was "a fine magnificent looking man," dressed in a plain blue overcoat. The fog lifted at about ten o'clock, and Jackson reined in on the crest. The generals briefly conferred, and as Jackson turned to leave, Longstreet jokingly said to him; "Are you not scared by that file of Yankees you have before you down there?"

Jackson, who seldom found humor in anything, grimly replied, "Wait till they come a little nearer and they shall either scare me or I'll scare them."[52]

The dissipation of the fog brought the bellow of artillery from both sides. About noon, Union Major General George G. Meade's division of Pennsylvania Reserves led the attack against Jackson's lines. From Lee's Hill, Lee, Longstreet, and others watched the Northerners' steady advance into the trees that sheltered Jackson's ranks. The smoke of thousands of muskets billowed up from the woodland as the treble of rifle fire mixed with the roar of cannon. Meade's men found a six-hundred-yard gap in Jackson's line at a marsh and poured through. Jackson, who "*never* indulged in rhetorical heroics on a battlefield," rushed reserves into the breach. A second Union division added its weight, and the fighting was fearful in its carnage. But the Rebels held, driving the Northerners rearward.[53]

When George Pickett witnessed the onset of the attack on Jackson, he galloped to John Hood to urge him to advance as Longstreet had instructed. Hood, wrote Pickett the next day, "was afraid to assume so great a responsibility" and sent an aide to Longstreet for permission. The corps commander granted it for a second time. Hood pushed some troops forward, but it was too late to aid Jackson. In his report, Longstreet said that "General Hood did not feel authorized to make more than a partial advance." In a postwar letter to Alexander, however, Longstreet asserted that he "made a mistake in not bringing the delinquent to trial." If he had, the corps commander believed, he would have created "official trouble," so he dropped the matter.[54]

Longstreet's attention was not focused on Pickett and Hood, however, but along his lines at Marye's Heights. As Longstreet guessed, the Federals in Fredericksburg advanced in conjunction with the attack on Jackson. The first Union assault force cleared the city's edge about midday and marched toward the millrace and Marye's Heights beyond. The Northern division came on with three brigades stacked in a column, a two-hundred-yard interval between each of them, the troops carrying their muskets at shoulder arms. Porter Alexander later admitted: "I never conceived for a moment that Burnside would make his main attack right where we were the strongest—at Marye's Hill."[55]

In the sunken road, behind the stone wall, a rooster crowed, the mascot of Cobb's Georgians, trained for such moments. It was the only sane sound on this insane field. Above the rooster, the cannon of the Washington Artillery exploded, and Marye's Heights was "fringed with flame." Other artillery pieces from Taylor's and Lee's hills joined in, creating "a sea of fire," according to a Rebel. When the Georgians leveled their muskets atop the wall and pulled the triggers, the Federals reeled before a gale of death. Within thirty minutes, one thousand Yankees lay dead or maimed; the survivors either ran to the rear or lay in a depression one hundred yards from the wall. The white ground had lost its purity; it was now red with the blood of brave men.[56]

A second Union division followed, and for a second time the rooster crowed. One of the Georgians boasted that he "never saw men more cool and more deliberate" than his comrades, who fired, loaded, and passed rifles forward. The unending flame from the wall created "the most fearful carnage," said Longstreet. The Union division commander exclaimed that his ranks "melted like snow coming down on warm ground." His second unit was the famed Irish Brigade, whose attack "was beyond description," in Pickett's view. But they fared no better than their fellow Northerners before the wall and the heights. As they stumbled back, a third division braced for the storm.[57]

Watching his brave men go forward across the fearful plain, one Union general declared that "it was a great slaughter pen . . . they might as well have tried to take Hell." But four more divisions were led into the "great slaughter pen," their ranks torn apart by the Southerners. One Confederate officer believed that "the gods" had made the enemy attack and "that their destruction might surely follow." After the third assault failed, Lee said to Longstreet from their vantage point on Lee's Hill, "General, they are massing very heavily and will break your line, I am afraid."

"General," replied Longstreet, "if you put every man now on the other side of the Potomac on that field to approach me over the same line, and give me plenty of ammunition, I will kill them all before they reach my line. Look to your right; you are in some danger there but not on my line."[58]

Longstreet spoke a tragic truth for the Federals. As he added more troops to the stone wall and replaced the Washington Artillery with Alexander's guns, the killing mounted. Cobb's Georgians slowed down only when they had depleted their ammunition and when their beloved general had fallen mortally wounded, his femoral artery sliced by a piece of shell. Longstreet and his subordinates' preparations had funneled a whirlwind of destruction onto the plain.[59]

By Lafayette McLaws's estimate, only one Federal lay within thirty yards of the wall. "The piles and cross-piles" of Union dead and wounded covered the ground in a blanket of blue. Longstreet and others remarked that they had never seen so many fallen men on a battlefield. What had been "a grand spectacle . . . like some great panoramic picture of a battle" to the Confederates had been a tragedy to Burnside and the Army of the Potomac. In Porter Alexander's opinion, Fredericksburg was "the easiest battle we ever fought."[60]

During the night, Lee met with Longstreet, Jackson, and a few division commanders at headquarters. Some argued that Burnside would renew the assaults with another morning's sun; some were not so sure. When one of Longstreet's scouts brought a message from Burnside that he had taken from a Federal courier, Lee's belief in a renewal of battle was confirmed. He ordered the lines strengthened and the ammunition replenished. If Burnside meant to destroy his army, the Southerners would oblige.[61]

The planned assault never came on the 14th. Burnside's generals, particularly Edwin Sumner, convinced the commander that it would only result in a disaster. Instead, the Federals entrenched. On the plain before the wall, the wounded pleaded for water and suffered in the frigid weather.[62]

On December 15, Burnside requested a truce to gather his dead and wounded, and Lee consented. Northerner joined Southerner in the harvest. Among the civilians who assisted was a "woman of abandoned character and an outcast of society" whose run-down log cabin stood on the plain before Marye's Heights. Her kindness restored her "to respectability" in the city, according to a Rebel officer. During the night, Burnside pulled his army across the river and had the bridges dismantled. Before they departed, Confederate general Jubal Early told a companion that he wished the Yankees "were all dead and in hell." Many were gone, and all had at least seen hell.[63]

The heaps of Union dead indicated the staggering proportions of Burnside's losses. His casualties amounted to over 12,600 killed, wounded, and missing. Lee lost roughly 5,300 men, of which Longstreet's First Corps incurred nearly 1,900. No colonels and only two Confederate generals were killed—Thomas Cobb and Maxcy Gregg. Like Cobb, Gregg fell mortally wounded and died on the 15th at "Belvoir," the Yerby family residence.[64]

Five days after the battle, Longstreet issued congratulatory orders to the corps, commending them for "the remarkable firmness with which they defended Marye's Hill," adding that "you stood by your post and filled the field before you with slain." He also asked his troops to contribute money for the residents of Fredericksburg. In his official report, the general singled out McLaws "for his untiring zeal and ability" while praising other subordinates.[65]

In his report, Lee had much to say about the performance of his two corps commanders:

> To Generals Longstreet and Jackson, great praise is due for the dispositions and management of their respective corps. Their quick perception enabled them to discover the projected assaults upon their positions, and their ready skill to devise the best means to resist them. Besides their services in the field—which every battle of the campaign from Richmond to Fredericksburg has served to illustrate—I am also indebted to them for valuable counsel, both as regards the general operations of the army and the execution of the particular measures adopted.[66]

At one point in the battle on the 13th, as Jackson's men counterattacked and Longstreet's troops ravaged the Union attack columns, Lee turned to Longstreet and said; "It is well that war is so terrible —we should grow too fond of it." If Longstreet replied, it was not recorded. Most likely he said nothing. He, too, saw war's pageantry and terribleness below them, and whether he shared Lee's penchant for it or not, he, too, had chosen it as a profession. James Longstreet was a superb soldier.[67]

11

INDEPENDENT COMMAND

The train from Richmond screeched and hissed to a halt south of Fredericksburg, Virginia, on December 28, 1862. At the station Longstreet waited for the passengers to step from the cars. He probably paced with impatience and excitement, for on board was Louise, whom he had not seen in months. When he found her, the couple embraced, and he led her to his nearby ambulance. With the general and his wife inside the vehicle, the driver prodded the four gray horses, and bells on the harness jingled in the winter air.[1]

Longstreet had made arrangements for Louise to board at "Forest Hill," the fine residence of the Hamilton family near Hamilton's Crossing. The general's commissary chief, Raphael Moses, had discovered the hospitality of the Hamiltons before the battle at Fredericksburg. He had dined with the civilians and paid for his meals with commissary stores. Moses slept in a nearby schoolhouse and seized every chance to seat himself at their dinner table. Whether Longstreet knew of Moses's method of payment is unknown, but the staff officer may have spoken to him of the family's generosity. To Forest Hill, then, he brought Louise three days after Christmas.[2]

The owner of the house and family patriarch, George Hamilton, had died in 1858. His forty-five-year-old daughter, Matilda Hamilton, presided over Forest Hill. For Matilda, Louise Longstreet's presence in the house offered her companionship and security. After she met the couple, Matilda wrote that "General Longstreet is a fine-looking man, though shy and embarrassed in manner. She is lady like in appearance but not otherwise striking."[3]

Longstreet had his headquarters about a mile from Forest Hill and visited during the day when duty permitted. He kept the ambulance available for the ladies, assigning a staff officer as an escort. On some evenings a regimental or brigade band serenaded the general and his wife. Longstreet spent each night with Louise.[4]

Between Longstreet's headquarters and Forest Hill was the winter campsite of the Texas Brigade. Each morning the corps commander passed through under a barrage of snowballs from the playful Texans. He endured the joke "with his usual imperturbability" for several days until one morning when he saw a line of troops with snowballs in hand. Riding up to them, Longstreet exclaimed: "Throw your snowballs, men, if you want to, as much as you please. But if one of them touches me, not a man in this brigade shall have a furlough this winter. Remember that." Longstreet was untouched.[5]

Like the Texans and other troops, Longstreet's staff officers sought diversions and amusements while in winter quarters. Moxley Sorrel recalled that the old aristocratic families in the area had "cellars of old Madeira" that they shared with the officers. According to one of the general's aides, the staff members indulged in "hard drinking" and nightly poker games. One evening, Thomas Walton, an in-law of Longstreet and "a very smart man," took nearly two thousand dollars in notes from a surgeon. On one occasion Longstreet joined in the festivities, and after evidently drinking too much, he rode around the tent on the back of a staff officer who was on his hands and knees, until both rolled onto the ground.[6]

At Fredericksburg, Lieutenant Francis W. Dawson rejoined the staff as an ordnance officer. Dawson had been with the ordnance train captured by the Federal cavalry before Sharpsburg. He spent a month in prison, was paroled, and following a leave of absence, reported for duty with Longstreet. Dawson was twenty-two years old and British. His real name was Austin John Reeks. In late 1861, he changed his name to Dawson in honor of a deceased uncle and signed on as a blockade runner before securing an appointment to the staff in August. Dawson served under Peyton Manning, the only member of the staff the Britisher seemed to like. Dawson stated in his memoirs, "The staff had 'no use' for me, which was perhaps not surprising, as I was a stranger and a foreigner."[7]

The pleasures open to generals, their staff and field officers in winter quarters were unavailable to ordinary soldiers. For most of the time the enlisted men endured "a very dull life," in the view of one Georgian. They did not miss the forced marches or the combat, but the daily routine could become numbing. They grumbled about the biscuits and beef given to them twice a day, about the scarcity of furloughs, about the extortionist prices for wood and food charged by the local residents, and about the drills and picket duty in the cold weather. But their morale remained high, bolstered by the confidence that resulted from victory.[8]

Years later Robert Toombs remembered the weapon he had seen forged that summer and fall, and his words echoed back, describing these men and their officers outside Fredericksburg. "I had served with the army nearly a year," the former brigadier told Longstreet, "had an extensive general acquaintance with its general field & company officers and I [do] not believe a finer army or one in better fighting conditions ever faced an enemy."[9]

Across the Rappahannock, where the Americans in Union blue camped, the mood was starkly different. Although better fed and clothed than the Rebels, the Northerners had only defeats to ponder, except for Sharpsburg or Antietam. Discontent filled the huts of the Army of the Potomac. Finally, on January 19, 1863, the commander, Ambrose Burnside, undertook a turning movement up the river. The fates abandoned this unfortunate general, however, and a winter rainstorm swept in, miring the army in its tracks. The Federals returned to their camps five days later, and on the 25th, President Lincoln replaced Burnside with Major General Joseph Hooker.[10]

If Burnside had crossed the Rappahannock, he would have found Longstreet's men behind a network of fieldworks and rifle pits. Since the battle in December, the Confederates had constructed them along their entire front. Only Longstreet had strengthened his lines before the battle with some fieldworks, but according to a British newspaperman with the army, Lee remarked afterward: "If I had only thrown up these works before, I should have saved many valuable lives." Perhaps Lee said something to that effect; if not, he had witnessed the worth of Longstreet's efforts on the day of battle.[11]

Roughly ten days after Burnside's ignominious "Mud March," Longstreet wrote a letter to Confederate Senator Louis Wigfall, with whom he had been friends since Wigfall's service as a brigadier in the summer and fall of 1861. Joseph Johnston had convalesced at the senator's home in Richmond following his wounding at Seven Pines. Like Longstreet, Wigfall had been born in South Carolina's Edgefield District. He studied law and later moved to Texas where he won election as a state legislator and then as a United States senator.[12]

Sam Houston had dubbed the nervous, intemperate transplanted Texan "Wiggletail." Forty-six years old in the winter of 1863, Wigfall was a flamboyant, combative individual who had the eye of a "Bengal tiger," according to a British newspaper correspondent. He and Jefferson Davis had enjoyed a cordial relationship until Wigfall's election to the Senate in February 1862; then the senator, often fortified by alcohol, publicly criticized the president. In the fall, the two men had "an unpleasant interview," apparently over Davis's refusal to consult with the senator about a cabinet change.[13]

As a member of the military affairs committee, Wigfall was a powerful voice in the Senate against the administration, allying himself with fellow members of the same persuasion. When Longstreet learned of the autumn clash with Davis, he wrote to caution his friend: "It is no business of mine, but I would like to take the liberty to beg you not to allow to bring about any difference between you." He added, "We think that all our hopes rest upon you and the hopes of the country rest upon the army."[14]

Longstreet knew well at the time he wrote this letter, on November 7, that Johnston had no firmer supporter in Congress than Wigfall. Longstreet evidently wanted the senator to maintain a cordial relationship with Davis for the benefit of Johnston, at least, and perhaps himself. Johnston still had not been restored to duty by the president, and Longstreet may have believed that his friend might return to the Army of Northern Virginia, as he had written Johnston in October. If so, Wigfall could influence the decision. Regardless, Davis appointed Johnston commander of the Department of the West and, by November's end, the recovered general was in Tennessee.[15]

Wigfall continued his labors on behalf of Johnston and, to some extent, Longstreet. When Confederate general Braxton Bragg and the Army of Tennessee suffered a defeat at the Battle of Murfreesboro or Stones River at the beginning of the new year, the anti-Davis faction clamored for the removal of one of the president's favorite generals. It was this news from Tennessee that motivated Longstreet to correspond with Wigfall on February 4, 1863. The

First Corps commander stated that he desired to go west because there seemed to be "opportunities for all kinds of moves to great advantages."[16]

To Longstreet "moves to great advantages" meant a strategic concentration of troops in Tennessee. Several days prior to this letter to Wigfall, Longstreet suggested to Lee "that one army corps could hold the line of the Rappahannock while the other was operating elsewhere." The lieutenant general thought that the line behind the Rappahannock, strengthened by the fieldworks, could be held by Jackson's troops while his divisions moved by railroad to reinforce Bragg. Once joined, the Confederates could assail the Federal army of General William Rosecrans, Longstreet's academy roommate, and recover Middle Tennessee. Perhaps, too, personal ambition nudged Longstreet, for he would be under the overall command of Johnston, and if Bragg faltered again, he might expect command of the army. He may have been motivated by such a prospect, or he may have given only a trained soldier's assessment of the situation and a recommended course of action. Lee rejected the proposal, but Longstreet did not abandon the plan.[17]

Within a fortnight of Longstreet's letter to Wigfall, Lee detached two First Corps divisions from the army and ordered them not to Tennessee but to Richmond. For a month the administration had voiced concern over developments in southeastern Virginia and North Carolina. There, in December, the Federals held Suffolk, Virginia, sixteen miles west of Norfolk, and had occupied Kinston and Goldsboro, North Carolina. Lee and authorities in the capital suspected that the enemy's real target was the vital seaport of Wilmington, North Carolina, and the railroad from the south to Virginia. With Lee's assent, Davis sent Harvey Hill, a North Carolinian, to his native state to oversee the defense and to rally the citizenry. Lee even traveled to Richmond for a conference with the president and his advisers.[18]

Then, on February 14, Lee received reports that a Union corps— the Ninth Corps—was on transports steaming down the Potomac. The Confederate general could not be certain of its destination, but he believed it would be either Charleston, South Carolina; Wilmington; or southeastern Virginia. Lee issued orders the next day for George Pickett's division to start for the capital. Additional intelligence indicated the Peninsula, east of Richmond, so Lee directed John Hood and his division to follow Pickett. Finally, when further information placed more Federal units in motion, the commanding general assigned Longstreet to personal command of the two First Corps divisions.[19]

A winter snowstorm blew across Virginia on the night of February 16–17, dumping eight to nine inches on the ground before turning to rain that fell throughout the 18th. Through it slogged the men in Pickett's and Hood's commands; the "worst marching I ever saw during the war," remembered a veteran Alabama officer. The men had no tents because they could not be loaded on wagons in time to accompany the troops. The soldiers passed through Richmond on the 21st and 22nd, crossing the James River and bivouacking on the south side. On the 22nd, snow began to fall again.[20]

Longstreet and his staff boarded a train on Thursday, February 19, with orders from Lee to report to Secretary of War James Seddon in Richmond. Longstreet met with the secretary, remaining in the capital four days, and Seddon outlined the troop dispositions and the situation. Whatever Longstreet said reassured the secretary, who informed Lee that "General Longstreet is here, and under his able guidance of such troops no one entertains a doubt as to the entire safety of the capital." While in the capital, Longstreet was told of G. W. Smith's resignation as commander of the Department of Virginia and North Carolina and his assignment to the command. On the 23rd, he left Richmond for Petersburg, twenty miles south of the capital, where he established his headquarters. Two days later Longstreet's appointment was officially announced.[21]

The Department of Virginia and North Carolina embraced an area from Richmond to Wilmington, North Carolina. With the arrival of Pickett's and Hood's sixteen thousand men, Longstreet had forty-three thousand troops in his command. Under Davis's instructions, the new department commander had to protect Richmond and the approaches to the capital from the south and east. His units were distributed on the Peninsula, at Petersburg, behind the Blackwater River, forty miles east of Petersburg, and with Harvey Hill and Brigadier General Chase Whiting in North Carolina. On March 1, Longstreet informed Lee that his force was "quite sufficient."[22]

With his characteristic energy and efficiency, Longstreet dealt with a myriad of problems. He sifted through intelligence reports, corresponded with his subordinates, requested a cavalry commander, and kept Lee and the War Department posted. His immediate concerns centered on the forces along the Blackwater River,

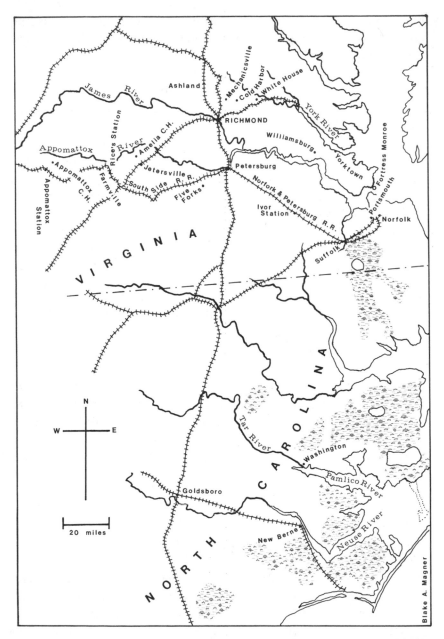

THEATER OF OPERATIONS: SOUTHEASTERN VIRGINIA AND EASTERN
NORTH CAROLINA.

which was twenty miles west of the Union garrison in Suffolk, and Hill's operations in North Carolina. With Pickett's division in Petersburg, Longstreet sent Brigadier General Raleigh Colston's brigade to bolster the Blackwater line. He assigned Colston to command there; this elicited a four-page letter of protest from Brigadier General Roger Pryor, who outranked Colston. As for his old friend Hill, he suggested a movement against the Federals at New Bern.[23]

Initially, Longstreet had to balance the wishes of Davis, Lee, and Seddon. Longstreet complied with Davis's orders to protect the capital and its approaches, with Pickett at Petersburg and the dispatch of Colston to the Blackwater. Lee, however, wanted Hood and Pickett readily available if Hooker undertook an offensive along the Rappahannock. Lee had roughly sixty-two thousand troops with him to confront an enemy of twice that number. Longstreet complied by keeping Hood along the railroad at Falling Creek, seven miles south of Richmond. He promised Lee: "I shall keep you advised of matters here that you may, by comparing notes, satisfy yourself of the enemy's position, &c. I shall be guided by the information that I may receive from you of the enemy's movements more than by what I hear here, for the present at all events."[24]

Secretary of War Seddon, meanwhile, urged an advance against Suffolk and the gathering of foodstuffs and subsistence. The shortage of food and forage in Lee's army was reaching critical levels. Lee had sent artillery batteries southward toward the capital to winter there. Untouched counties in southeastern Virginia and in North Carolina brimmed with an abundance of grain and meat. If those areas could be made secure from Federal incursions, the Rebels could forage and fill wagons with the larder. As the weeks passed, this supply operation became the focus of Longstreet's duty.[25]

Consequently, Longstreet acted during the first week of March. He instructed Chase Whiting to send half his forces at Wilmington to Hill for foraging service, and then journeyed to Goldsboro for a meeting with Hill. Longstreet had wanted to visit earlier, but a serious throat infection confined him to Petersburg. The two friends agreed on a movement against New Bern, with Longstreet releasing one brigade from Petersburg for the offensive. Upon his return, Longstreet ordered Richard Garnett's brigade to Hill and Micah Jenkins's to the Blackwater. He also placed the young Jenkins in command along the river.[26]

Within days Hill's operation began against New Bern, located at the mouth of the Neuse River, on the Atlantic coast, fifty-odd miles east of Goldsboro. The second largest town on the North Carolina coast, New Bern had fallen into Federal hands in March 1862. Outnumbered—Garnett did not reach him, and Whiting sent no troops —Hill tried but failed to take the garrison. His troops garnered wagonloads of supplies before withdrawing.[27]

From New Bern, Hill, under Longstreet's instructions, advanced against Washington on the Tar-Pamlico River, thirty miles north of New Bern. Longstreet added James Kemper's brigade to the force and pried one brigade from Whiting. The siege of Washington began on March 30 and continued for over two weeks. When Union supply ships ran past the Confederate batteries along the river, Hill abandoned the effort and retreated to Goldsboro. But the presence of Confederate troops at various locations in the state thwarted Union incursions, opening the supply-rich counties.[28]

At Petersburg, meanwhile, Longstreet balanced the concerns of Lee with the need for gathering supplies and Seddon's interest in Suffolk. On March 16, Lee wrote to his corps commander stating that he anticipated an advance by the Federals on the Rappahannock and that Longstreet should "be prepared" to return Hood and Pickett. Longstreet replied the next day: "I shall be ready to join you with Hood's division at any moment unless there is a fine opportunity to strike a decided blow here, in which case I think I had better act promptly and trust to your being able to hold the force in your front in check until I can join you."[29]

The call for Hood came from Lee on the 18th. Federal cavalry had crossed a ford upstream from Fredericksburg, and Lee could not be certain if it was a preliminary thrust or a major movement. When the order arrived—"took us all by surprise," an Alabamian soldier recorded in his diary—two of Hood's brigades scrambled into ranks and started northward. They halted at Ashland, north of Richmond, and bivouacked as another storm barreled in, covering the ground with nearly ten inches of snow. Hood's men stayed there throughout the 19th until Longstreet recalled them on Lee's authority. The Federal attack was isolated and repulsed. When the soldiers passed through the capital the following day, the Texans scattered to enjoy the city's pleasures. Their commander, Brigadier General Jerome B. Robertson, rode back and forth on the streets, cursing and inquiring where "is the Texas Brigade?" Hood, who had experienced the Texans' shenanigans, assured the angry officer that they would reappear before the next battle.[30]

For the next two weeks Lee and Longstreet exchanged a series of correspondence, discussing the department commander's mission in the region and the utilization of his units. On March 19, following the repulse of the Yankees on the Rappahannock, Lee wrote that Longstreet should "turn all the energies of your department" to "obtaining all the supplies possible of forage and subsistence from North Carolina." In a letter dated the same day, Longstreet asserted, "I can, I think, get all of the supplies in that State if I can use my forces; but if the two divisions are to be held in readiness to join you, or even one of them, I can do nothing." He estimated enemy strength in the region at forty thousand.[31]

Continuing, Longstreet said, frankly:

> I know that it is the habit with individuals in all armies to represent their own positions as the most important ones, and it may be that this feeling is operating with me; but I am not prompted by any desire to do, or to attempt to do, great things. I only wish to do what I regard as my duty—give you the full benefit of my views. It seems to me to be a matter of prime necessity with us to keep the enemy out of North Carolina in order that we may draw out all the supplies there, and if we give ground at all it would be better to do so from the Rappahannock. It is right, as you say, to concentrate and crush him; but will it be better to concentrate upon his grand army rather than on his detachments and then make a grand concentration on the grand army? [He concluded,] If we cripple him only, a little at one place and then another, we may mutually produce grand results. I hope that I have gone into details sufficiently to give you my views, but I am always ready to do and to say all that I can.[32]

More letters passed between Fredericksburg and Petersburg. Lee was reluctant to restrict operations in the department if a harvest of supplies could be obtained. If Longstreet saw an opportunity for striking a blow against the Federals, Lee wrote, "do not be idle, but act promptly." For his part, Longstreet argued for an advance on Suffolk that would bottle up the garrison at that place and open additional territory for Confederate commissary wagons. Both generals agreed that if the enemy remained on the defensive behind its works at Suffolk, Longstreet could only procure supplies, but in Lee's view it was "of first importance to draw from the invaded districts every pound of provision and forage we can." Finally, on

April 2, Lee reported that Burnside and part of the Ninth Corps were in Ohio. With this force no longer in southeastern Virginia, Lee stated to Longstreet, "I leave the whole matter to your good judgment." On that day in Richmond, residents looted stores in the so-called bread riots.[33]

In the end, the decision for an operation against Suffolk was driven by desperate conditions in Lee's army. For weeks the men had survived on half rations, with scurvy afflicting many of them. Lee appealed constantly for food and forage while the railroad system and commissary department in Richmond faltered through inefficiency and incompetence. If the cornucopia of supplies within Longstreet's department could be further tapped by an advance on Suffolk, Lee would risk a movement by the Federals opposite Fredericksburg. Although Longstreet held out the prospect, with the cooperation of the navy, of capturing the river town and its garrison, neither he nor Lee expected it. The Suffolk movement was a supply expedition.[34]

Before daylight on April 8, the troops at Petersburg awoke to the "rolling of drums, the shrill piping of the fife, and the sweeter, richer music of horn bands." Filing into columns, the men with Hood and Pickett marched eastward. They covered twenty-one miles that day; eighteen the next. Speculation in the ranks agreed that the destination was Suffolk. On the 11th, the Confederates crossed the Blackwater River—"a small but deep stream," a Mississippian said—on pontoons, and by nightfall some units encamped within three miles of the Union works. Rain fell on the 12th, as Longstreet brought the brigades into line. "The men are as careless as if nothing of importance was on hand," jotted an Alabamian in his diary. Hood's four brigades held the left, Major General Samuel French's two-brigade command manned the center, connecting with Pickett's reduced division on the right. Before he left Petersburg, Longstreet had reminded Lee: "I do not propose to do anything more than draw out the supplies from that country, unless something very favorable should offer."[35]

Located seventeen miles southwest of Portsmouth, Virginia, Suffolk protected the approaches to Norfolk that lay across Hampton Roads from Portsmouth. The Federals had placed a force in Suffolk when they occupied Norfolk in May 1862 and had held it ever since. In September, Union Major General John J. Peck, a New Yorker who had attended West Point in the class behind Longstreet's, took command there to oversee the construction of the defenses. When Longstreet's troops appeared, the works encircled Suffolk in a fourteen-mile perimeter, with eight forts interspersed at strategic locations. Peck had slightly more than seventeen thousand defenders in the forts and rifle pits.[36]

Longstreet knew beforehand from scouts' reports the strength of Peck's handiwork. To him the only chance to capture the garrison and the town rested with the Confederate navy. Suffolk lay at the head of navigation of the Nansemond River, a crooked, narrow, marshy channel deep enough for gunboats. If the CSS *Richmond,* an ironclad, could seal the river's mouth to prevent the ascent of enemy ships, Longstreet argued, he could outflank the Federal defenses and force Peck to give battle on open terrain. He had requested naval assistance before he left Petersburg, but did not receive a satisfactory answer. Finally, on April 18, Seddon informed the general that President Davis refused to open the obstructions across the James River that would allow the passage of the ironclad to the Nansemond, fearing a sudden enemy attack with gunboats through the cleared channel. All the secretary could promise was that engineers would study the matter.[37]

Confronted with the formidable defenses and enemy gunboats, Longstreet resorted to a siege. He estimated casualties at three thousand in an assault, so he dismissed that idea. Consequently, from the outset, skirmishing and artillery exchanges marked the fighting at Suffolk. The Confederates dug their own fieldworks, and with both sides sheltered from the fire, casualties were modest—the Southerners incurring three times as many as the Northerners.[38]

The sharpest combat of the siege occurred along the Nansemond between Confederate artillery units and Union gunboats. To the Federals, one of the most troubling enemy batteries was posted in an old earthwork at Hill's Point on the river. The Rebel unit was Captain Robert M. Stribling's Fauquier Artillery of five cannon, supported by infantry from Evander Law's brigade. Twice the Yankees had tried to capture it and failed. Then at 6:00 P.M. on April 19, roughly 270 men from Connecticut and New York, piling off a transport, stormed the battery and overran the gunners and two companies of Alabama troops. In ten minutes the Federals had all five guns and 130 prisoners. Before other Southern troops could react, the attackers redeployed the ordnance toward the Rebels and hauled away the prisoners. Their comrades cheered from the lines around Suffolk.[39]

The loss of the cannon and the men infuriated Longstreet, who blamed Samuel French for the debacle. French commanded all the Confederate artillery, and twice Longstreet had ordered him to position the seven-hundred-man Fifty-fifth North Carolina from his division in close support of Stribling's battery. Like his North Carolinians, Colonel John Kern Connally was unseasoned, and he kept his companies a mile to the rear of the cannon. In turn, French was ill on the 19th, confined to bed, though he had instructions forwarded to Connally to be alert. The result was, in Moxley Sorrel's words, "a most remarkable and discreditable instance of an entire absence of vigilance." Longstreet considered a counterattack but dismissed it when Hood and Law "strenuously" objected because of the enemy artillery and gunboats. French relinquished command of that sector of the line to Hood. When Richmond newspapers criticized him, French suspected Longstreet and eventually asked President Davis for a court of inquiry. Davis denied the request. In his endorsement to French's report, Longstreet stated: "This lesson, it is hoped, will be of service to us all."[40]

The affair at Hill's Point was an aberration in the routine of the operation. On many days neither command engaged in serious firing of either cannon or musketry. The Federals preferred shelling the Confederate works and camps at night. Rain and cold weather restricted the action on a number of occasions. On April 24, one Union brigade attacked Pickett's troops on the Confederate right but were slammed back. Otherwise, death came from an unseen sniper's bullet or a bursting artillery shell. Few of the soldiers, Northern or Southern, probably thought when they volunteered that their lives might end so ingloriously.[41]

By contrast, George Pickett enjoyed the relatively quiet operation —it brought him close to his beloved seventeen-year-old Sallie Corbell. She lived in nearby Chuckatuck, and the dashing general visited her as frequently as his duty permitted. Although Longstreet liked Pickett perhaps above all others, his patience with these romantic rides evidently ended, and he told the major general. Not to be denied, Pickett turned to Sorrel for permission. "No," responded the chief of staff. "You must go to the lieutenant general."

"But he is tired of it and will refuse," pleaded the lovestruck general, "and I must go, I must see her. I swear, Sorrel, I'll be back before anything can happen in the morning."

Sorrel would not budge, and Pickett went without authority. "I don't think," grumbled Sorrel, "his division benefited by such carpet-knight doings in the field."[42]

During the siege, Longstreet received information on Federal activities in the region from a scout, Henry Thomas Harrison. "Altogether an extraordinary character" to Sorrel, Harrison went to Longstreet's headquarters, most likely while at Petersburg, with a letter of introduction from Seddon. Nicknamed "Harry," Harrison had performed similar service in Mississippi and Virginia before he met with Longstreet, who hired him and sent him on to Hill in North Carolina. The scout was paid in United States greenbacks, not Confederate notes, but he was worth the money; as Sorrel said, he "always brought us true information." While in North Carolina or southeastern Virginia, however, Harrison's identity as a Rebel agent was exposed, and he barely eluded capture. But his services with Longstreet were just beginning.[43]

While the Confederate soldiers kept the Yankees within the works at Suffolk, the campaign's primary objective—the collection of foodstuffs and supplies—rolled on unimpeded. Longstreet impressed every wheeled vehicle he could find, including crude ox carts. The harvest began as soon as his divisions arrived before Suffolk, with Brigadier General Henry Benning's brigade of Georgians detached as guards for the wagons. Major Raphael Moses, the First Corps commissary chief, directed the operation.[44]

Moses's net extended into the counties drained by the Blackwater, Nottoway, and Meherrin rivers. The rich valley soil yielded tens of thousands of bushels of corn and an estimated million pounds of bacon. Wherever the details roamed, the residents welcomed them. The citizens had been plagued by pro-Union marauders, and when they could, Benning's men hunted down the "Tories." One Georgian wrote home that he saw many "pretty girls" and suffered from "a rascally little varmint commonly known as the *Seed Tick* which exists in enormous numbers & has a peculiar way of presenting its bill."[45]

The work, in Moses's judgment, "accomplished all that had been contemplated." His officers and men gathered "all accessible supplies" from three North Carolina counties—enough bacon and grain to feed Lee's soldiers and animals for an estimated two

months. When Lee learned of the amounts, he was completely satisfied with the results. Moses only abandoned the collections when
Longstreet recalled the wagons at the end of April.[46]

The suspension of the supply operation resulted from events
along the Rappahannock. On April 29, Union general Joseph
Hooker began his spring offensive, with units of his army crossing
the Rappahannock on pontoons south of Fredericksburg, while the
bulk of his force marched upstream beyond the Confederate left
flank. Lee wired Richmond for Longstreet's two divisions. Samuel
Cooper forwarded the telegram, directing Longstreet to be prepared to march "with the least practicable delay." Seddon followed
with a message the next day, echoing Cooper's words: "Move without delay with your command to this place to effect a junction with
General Lee." Longstreet responded that he would comply as soon
as possible, but the wagons were scattered across the countryside.
The secretary then modified his instructions on May 1: "The order
sent to you was to secure all possible dispatch without incurring
loss of train or unnecessary hazard of troops."[47]

Longstreet hurried couriers to the supply details, urging that the
trains be pushed as rapidly as possible across the Blackwater River.
He notified his chief quartermaster that compliance was a "matter
of greatest importance." At Suffolk the infantry and artillery units
prepared for the withdrawal. By the morning of May 3, Longstreet
learned that the wagons were either in camp or approaching the
river. At 10 P.M. the Rebels lifted the siege and marched westward
in the Virginia night. On the afternoon of the 4th, they passed the
river, bivouacked, and resumed the retreat the next day in a rainstorm, halting at Ivor Station on the Norfolk and Petersburg Railroad. When the rain ceased, the men built "huge fires" to dry their
clothes—they had covered forty-two miles in less than forty-eight
hours.[48]

On May 6 the troops piled onto railroad cars for the journey to
Petersburg and then to Richmond. Longstreet left French and two
brigades, including Micah Jenkins's, behind along the Blackwater
River. The department commander preceded the troops and ar-
rived in the capital on the night of the 5th. Securing a room at the
Spottswood Hotel, he met with Seddon in the hotel the next day.[49]

Fifty miles to the north of Richmond, the Battle of Chancellorsville ended as Longstreet journeyed to the city. Hooker had

executed a fine turning movement around the Confederate flank, but instead of clearing a forbidding stretch of trees and scrub brush known as the Wilderness, he recoiled before Lee's counterthrust and pulled his units into the difficult terrain, negating his numerical and artillery strength. Late on the afternoon of May 2, Stonewall Jackson rolled up Hooker's right flank, and the Confederates sealed the victory the next day. It was a tactical masterpiece by Lee, but it cost his army and the Confederate cause the great Stonewall, who was accidentally shot by his own men. Surgeons amputated Jackson's left arm, but he would succumb to pneumonia on May 10.[50]

Longstreet's failure to reach Lee in time for the battle has been condemned. Two of his biographers, H. J. Eckenrode and Bryan Conrad, for example, blamed Longstreet, arguing that "his ambition to become an independent commander" foiled a brilliant opportunity to crush Hooker's army. They further alleged that Longstreet "did not move because he did not wish to move. He had no desire to join Lee." Their assertions are without foundation, even ludicrous in part.[51]

Lee had endeavored to balance his strategic concerns at Fredericksburg with the army's dire need for supplies. In Porter Alexander's opinion, the commanding general "miscalculated" the time necessary for Longstreet to rejoin the army. Lee told his First Corps commander on May 7: "I did not intend to express the opinion that you could reach me in time, as I did not think it practicable." There was little glory to be won by Longstreet in southeastern Virginia, just vital foodstuffs that his country required. In that he succeeded to the satisfaction of Davis, Seddon, and Lee. He may have missed an opportunity to cross the Nansemond River and envelop the Union flank at Suffolk during the first few days of the operation; instead, he unwisely hoped for cooperation from the navy. When he did not get it, he refused to sacrifice men's lives in an assault.[52]

Longstreet was "closeted" with Seddon on May 6. The secretary and the general discussed the situation in the West, in Mississippi and Tennessee. As they conferred, a Union army under Longstreet's antebellum best friend, Ulysses S. Grant, had made a lodgment in Mississippi, south of Vicksburg, threatening either that river city or Jackson or Port Hudson. Major General John Pemberton's Confederate forces at Vicksburg opposed Grant, with Joseph Johnston, overall commander in the region, gathering additional forces to reinforce Pemberton. In Tennessee, William Rosecrans's Union forces still held the middle section of the state against Braxton Bragg's Rebels.[53]

A capable administrator, cursed with frail health, Seddon had been moderating a debate within the administration over a strategy course for the past month. Davis, Seddon, Samuel Cooper, and Lee engaged in the discussions. The persistent question was whether Lee could reinforce Bragg or Johnston with Pickett's and/or Hood's divisions. Lee countered with several arguments—the enemy could send troops more rapidly west than the Confederates; if Pickett or Hood or both went, Longstreet would have to suspend the supply efforts; and the "readiest method" of relieving the pressure in Mississippi and Tennessee would be another raid down the Shenandoah Valley and into Maryland. But the matter was still unresolved when Seddon sought Longstreet's views.[54]

As he had in February, Longstreet advocated a concentration in Tennessee against Rosecrans's army. He suggested to Seddon that Johnston's troops march to join Bragg while his two divisions travel by railroad to link up in Tennessee. Once Rosecrans was defeated, Longstreet argued, the Southern force could invade Kentucky, then move toward Cincinnati and the Ohio River. Grant's army in Mississippi would be the only Union command that could be withdrawn to meet the Rebel threat, thus relieving Pemberton at Vicksburg. "It was mainfest before the war was accepted," as Longstreet stated his views subsequently, "that the only way to equalize the contest was by skilful use of our interior lines, and this was so impressed by two years' experience that it seemed time to force it upon the Richmond authorities."[55]

That evening Seddon and Longstreet met with Davis. The secretary doubted that Grant could "be induced" to abandon his campaign except by incurring "terribly hard knocks." Longstreet countered that as a soldier Grant would obey orders, and if Lincoln directed him to move toward the Ohio River, Grant would comply. To Davis, in Longstreet's retelling, "foreign intervention was the ruling idea . . . and he preferred that as the easiest solution of all problems."[56]

But Longstreet's memory of Davis's position seems uncharitable regarding the president. Admittedly, foreign recognition by Great Britain and France offered the Confederacy its best hope, but that had been stillborn since the autumn of 1862 when Lee retreated from Maryland. Previously, Davis had organized departments to expedite the transfer of troops from one section to another. As noted, he had also sought Lee's counsel and, for the moment, accepted Lee's rationale against a detachment. To the president, Johnston held the solution if he would combine with Pemberton. Thus, when they conferred, Davis thought it best that Longstreet's divisions return to Lee, and he so ordered it.[57]

The reconstruction of the meetings between Longstreet and the two officials relies on the general's postwar recollections and some correspondence. Longstreet undoubtedly recommended the course of action, and historians have stressed the departure in views between Lee and his senior general. A recent biographer of Longstreet has contended that he wanted out from under Lee's strategic and tactical views, which he vigorously opposed as wasteful of life. That argument is not supported by contemporary evidence, however. Longstreet's support of a "western strategy" was not as firm at the time as his postwar writings portrayed it. His break with Lee would come in a southern Pennsylvania village.[58]

Longstreet stayed in Richmond two additional days as Federal cavalry raided toward the capital. On the morning of May 9, he and his staff boarded a train for Fredericksburg and the Army of Northern Virginia. Unknowingly, the engine pulled him toward a distant battlefield that would define his military career and history's judgment of him.[59]

COLLISION IN PENNSYLVANIA

The commander of the First Corps, Army of Northern Virginia, stepped down from a train at Hamilton's Crossing before noon on Saturday, May 9, 1863. From the station Longstreet went to army headquarters and reported to Robert E. Lee. The two generals had not seen each other for nearly three months. Lee appeared tired and distracted, with the commanding general expressing concern about Stonewall Jackson's wound, terming it "a great calamity." They shared a midday meal before Longstreet departed to establish his headquarters near Lee's at the residence of a Garnett family. In an adjoining field, his staff members pitched tents.[1]

May 10 dawned with the warmth of a spring day, of the renewal of life. South of Fredericksburg, at Guiney's Station—Longstreet had passed by it the day before—Stonewall Jackson struggled against the pneumonia that was taking his life away. With his wife, infant daughter, devoted chief of staff, and surgeons with him, Jackson died at 3:15 P.M. He rallied momentarily at the end, called out an order, and then quietly said, "Let us cross over the river and rest under the shade of the trees." It was as this devout warrior wanted it—he went to his Lord on a Sabbath.[2]

When the news of his death reached the army and the public, the grief poured forth. Secretary of War James Seddon correctly described Jackson as "the hero of the war." Lee wrote to Jeb Stuart: "I regret to inform you that the great and good Jackson is no more." To one of his sons the commander admitted: "It is a terrible loss. I do not know how to replace him. Any victory would be dear at such a cost. But God's will be done." And to a British newspaperman he claimed: "Such an executive officer the sun never shone on." A government employee in Richmond recorded in his diary: "No name in the state was so electrical to his troops as his, none so terrible to the enemy, so inspiriting to his own. He had left a name second to none these times have evoked."[3]

In his memoirs, Longstreet described his fellow corps commander's death as a "great misfortune." Now, he added, "we seemed to face a future bereft of much of its hopefulness." The two men had never been close—they were so different in personality and temperament. Both brought qualities of generalship to the army that under Lee's leadership made that command an incomparable force for nearly a year. Lee had no one to replace Jackson and no one to replace Longstreet, should that prove necessary.[4]

While Lee could say to his brother two weeks later: "I write you in mourning at the death of Genl Jackson," the concerns of the army and future endeavors demanded Lee's immediate attention following that sad Sabbath. To assist him, Lee turned to Longstreet. For three days—from May 11 to 13—they conferred at headquarters. From these meetings arose the army's summer campaign, and from them, as detailed by Longstreet after the war, came the basis for his disagreement with Lee at Gettysburg.[5]

Longstreet devoted numerous pages in various publications to his and Lee's discussions. At the time he wrote, Longstreet had already been singled out as the scapegoat for Gettysburg, the defeat that allegedly led to Appomattox and the end of the Confederacy. Longstreet presented a case in his defense that seemed to distance him from Lee's plans, to show that Lee, not Longstreet, changed the operational understanding that the two men agreed on in May. He knew that his reputation—even his place in history's long reach— was at stake, and he began his version with the meetings outside Fredericksburg.

The talks between Lee and Longstreet were lengthy and involved. Longstreet reiterated the proposal he had broached to Seddon— detach two divisions from the army, send Johnston's troops to Tennessee, and, combined with Bragg's army, assail Rosecrans, and then advance into Kentucky. In a published account, he wrote: "I laid it before him [Lee] with the freedom justified by our close personal and official relations." Back and forth the two generals examined the idea. Lee countered with a plan for a large-scale offensive or raid into Pennsylvania. Longstreet objected, arguing that the "extensive preparations for a campaign" in Northern territory might take too long to conclude, and Vicksburg might fall in the interim.[6]

Lee would not be swayed by Longstreet's arguments, however. Opposed to a division of the army, the commanding general adhered to his idea for a summer offensive. "His plan or wishes announced," recalled Longstreet in his memoirs, "it became useless and improper to offer suggestions leading to a different course. All that I could ask was that the policy of the campaign should be one of defensive tactics; that we should work so as to force the enemy to attack us, in such good position as we might find in his own country, so well adapted to that purpose—which might assure us of a grand triumph. To this he readily assented as an important and material adjunct to his general plan." In another published version, Longstreet claimed that his "assent" to the operation was given "upon this understanding"—a defensively fought battle similar to Fredericksburg.[7]

This was how Longstreet reconstructed the meetings years later. But he wrote a more revealing and more accurate description on the last day he and Lee conferred. On May 13, Longstreet penned a lengthy letter to his confidant in Richmond, Senator Louis Wigfall. The senator was an advocate of a "western policy" and had spoken to Seddon about the subject. As such, Longstreet's letter is of major import in an examination of his and Lee's contemporary views.

At the top of the letter in awkward words Longstreet cautioned: "Some of these matters by me to anyone beyond Gen. Lee and yourself." He then proceeded:

> There is a fair prospect of forward movement. That being the case we can spare nothing from this army to re-enforce in the West. On the contrary we should have use of our own and the balance of our Armies if we could get them. If we could cross the Potomac with one hundred & fifty thousand men, I think we could demand Lincoln to declare his purpose. If it is a christian purpose enough of blood has been shed to satisfy any principles. If he intends extermination we should know it at once and play a little at that game whilst we can.

As for Mississippi and Tennessee, continued Longstreet, reinforcements would not be of much worth with Pemberton at Vicksburg. One or two divisions would be insufficient, "Grant seems to be a fighting man," he stated, "and seems to be determined to fight. Pemberton seems not to be a fighting man." If Pemberton chose not to engage Grant, "the fewer the troops he has the better." It would be better, if it were decided to detach units from Virginia, to give them to Johnston with orders to advance into Kentucky. If Vicksburg fell, "we would be no worse off than we are now" because the Confederates were already cut off from the states west of the Mississippi River. "In fact," the general asserted, "we should make a grand effort against the Yankees this summer, every available man and means should be brought to bear against them."

Summarizing his viewpoint, Longstreet declared:

> When I agreed with the Secy & yourself about sending troops west I was under the impression that we would be obliged to remain on the defensive here. But the prospect of an advance changes the aspect of affairs to us entirely. Gen. Lee sent for me when he recd the Secy's letter. I told him that I thought that we could spare the troops unless there was a chance of a forward movement. If we could move of course we should want everything, that we had and all that we could get.

In ending, Longstreet emphasized that "after mature reflection" he doubted the army in Virginia could be of assistance to Pemberton in Mississippi. Lee would travel to Richmond in a day or two "to settle matters," Longstreet informed Wigfall, and "I shall ask him to take a memorandum of all points and settle upon something at once."[8]

The contrast between this letter and Longstreet's postwar versions is significant. In both the contemporary and later writings, Longstreet stated that if a detachment were sent from Virginia, it should be combined with Johnston's and Bragg's, not with Pemberton's. But he added a critical disclaimer in his contemporary letter to Wigfall—that his support for such a movement was contingent upon Lee adopting a defensive posture in the East. Once Lee revealed his strategy for an offensive, Longstreet supported an operation beyond the Potomac. Contrary to his later assertions, the evidence indicates that Longstreet, like Lee, saw the opportunity for Confederate victory beyond the Potomac River, where "we could demand of Lincoln to declare his purpose." Longstreet was not yet —if he ever had been—a firm member of the so-called western concentration bloc of Seddon, Wigfall, Johnston, P. G. T. Beauregard, and others.[9]

Another facet of Longstreet's reasoning to Wigfall—the indictment of Pemberton's generalship—hints of Lee's views. It would appear from the letter's contents that the commanding general argued that "Pemberton seems not to be a fighting man." In the course of their conversations, Lee unquestionably presented countervailing points. "After mature reflection," Longstreet concluded that they could not help the Vicksburg commander. While not definitive, the implication was that Lee broached it to Longstreet for consideration.

Nowhere in the correspondence to Wigfall is a cornerstone of Longstreet's postwar analysis, namely that Lee agreed to use the tactical defensive in an engagement. In April 1868, when asked if he had consented to fight a defensive battle in Pennsylvania, Lee replied that "the idea was absurd. He [Lee] had never made any such promise, and had never thought of doing any such thing." But the expectation, perhaps the understanding, by numbers of Lee's officers was to wage a defensive fight. Walter Taylor of his staff stated afterward that Lee's design was to select "a favorable time and place in which to receive the attack which his adversary would be compelled to make on him, to take the reasonable chances of defeating him in a pitched battle." And Lee wrote in his own post-battle report: "It had not been intended to fight a general battle at such a distance from our base, unless attacked by the enemy."[10]

Lee's operational plan for the Pennsylvania campaign included avoiding an offensive battle, if possible. It may have been discussed during the three days of meetings in May, but no conclusive evidence indicates that. Longstreet's subsequent allegation that "upon this understanding [of a tactical defensive] my assent was given" has no credence. In an 1873 letter to Lafayette McLaws, Longstreet insisted that his objection to an invasion of Pennsylvania which he had voiced to Lee in May was "the delay that extensive preparations for a campaign in the enemys country would entail." The subject was discussed later, if not then, and Lee's intent was to maneuver the Federals into a position from which they would have to be the assailant. Longstreet and others expected this to be the course of action, but as a soldier he understood that circumstances on a battlefield dictated decisions.[11]

Longstreet was committed to the tactical defensive. He thought that the victory at Chancellorsville brought only barren results, and at a high cost—Lee's army lost twenty-one percent of its men; Joseph Hooker's, fifteen percent. "This was one of the occasions where success was not a just criterion," he wrote. To Longstreet the defensive battles of Second Manassas and Fredericksburg, not the brilliant tactical offensive at Chancellorsville, were the model engagements, victorious struggles that spared men's lives.[12]

By May 1863, in Longstreet's view, the Confederacy had reached its limits. In a postwar article, he analyzed the situation as he saw it in the war's third spring:

> One mistake of the Confederacy was in pitting force against force. The only hope we had was to outgeneral the Federals. We were all hopeful and the army was in good condition, but the war had advanced far enough for us to see that a mere victory without decided fruits was a luxury we could not afford. . . . The time had come when it was imperative that the skill of generals and the strategy and tactics of war should take the place of muscle against muscle. Our purpose should have been to impair the *morale* of the Federal army and shake Northern confidence in the Federal leaders.[13]

The assessment was astute, and "to impair" Northern morale became an aim of the offensive Lee and Longstreet debated at Fredericksburg. All that was left for Lee was to convince Confederate authorities in Richmond, and he traveled there on May 14. The army commander stayed in the capital until the 18th, sequestered in meetings with Davis and cabinet members. Lee argued that an invasion of Northern territory would bring a harvest of supplies, spare the Old Dominion from the conflict's ravages for a period of time, and disrupt Union campaign plans for the summer. It might offer relief to the forces at Vicksburg, but Lee did not stress that aspect. The proposal sparked lengthy debate, with objections from at least one cabinet officer. At length, the cabinet voted five to one in favor, and Davis approved. Lee's opinion, Secretary of War Seddon revealed afterward, "naturally had great effect in the decisions of the Executive." To Joseph Johnston the decision was expected; he subsequently grumbled that Lee's army and Virginia "absorbed the interest of the government, and therefore occupied the attention of the country."[14]

Upon his return to Fredericksburg, Lee began the preparations for the major operation. His first priority was a restructuring of the two corps. For months Lee had been deliberating a reorganization, and with Jackson's death, he believed the time had come. On May 20 he wrote to Davis: "I have for the past year felt that the corps of this army were too large for one commander. Nothing prevented my proposing to you to reduce their size and increase their number but my inability to recommend commanders." Each corps had approximately thirty thousand troops, and "these are more than one man can properly handle and keep under his eye in battle in the country that we have to operate in. They are always beyond the range of his vision, and frequently beyond his reach."[15]

Lee recommended the creation of a third corps and Richard Ewell and Powell Hill as corps commanders. Ewell would replace Jackson at the head of the Second Corps, and Hill would get the new Third Corps. Ewell had been away from the army for nearly a year, since he had lost a leg in the Second Manassas Campaign in August 1862, but Lee regarded him highly, writing that he was "an honest, brave soldier, who has always done his duty well." To Lee, Powell Hill had been the army's best division commander, "the best soldier of his grade," since the previous summer.[16]

Confederate authorities approved, and on May 30 the reorganization was announced to the army in a special order. Three corps necessitated a reshuffling of divisions and brigades; Lee chose to assign three divisions to each corps. Longstreet retained the commands of Lafayette McLaws, John Hood, and George Pickett in the First Corps. Jackson's, now Ewell's, Second Corps consisted of the divisions of Jubal Early, Robert Rodes, and Edward Johnson. For Hill's Third Corps, Lee took Richard Anderson's division from Longstreet and divided the Light Division and added brigades to create two divisions for William Pender and Henry Heth, both of whom gained promotion to major general.[17]

The reorganization and promotions brought questions and stirred discontent. The initial concern focused on Ewell and Hill: Could they handle the increased responsibilities? Had Lee elevated them above their abilities? Had the amputation of a limb hindered Ewell's generalship? Could Hill act as decisively as a corps commander as he had at the head of a division? Longstreet, for instance, regarded Ewell highly but opposed the selection of Powell Hill, preferring Harvey Hill for the post. Longstreet said that Ewell was superior to Powell Hill "in every respect." Perhaps his opinion of the latter officer was colored by their dispute in July 1862.[18]

The fact that Ewell and Hill were both Virginians rekindled a festering resentment within the army. While the bulk of the troops hailed from outside the Old Dominion, two of the three corps commanders, six of the ten division commanders—including Jeb Stuart with the cavalry—and sixteen of forty-seven brigade commanders were natives of Virginia, along with the army commander and the chief of artillery. The favoritism perceived by non-Virginians ignited as early as July 1862, smoldered the following October with the changes, and now heated again. Longstreet remarked that "no little discontent" resulted from the choice of Virginians.[19]

The level of disgruntlement is difficult to assess. For months non-Virginians had grumbled privately and among themselves about the praise accorded Virginians in the state newspapers. When Lee chose Ewell, Hill, Heth, and Johnson—all Virginians—for the new commands, the ill feelings toward natives of the Old Dominion deepened. Lafayette McLaws, for instance, sought a transfer. His case was not a simple matter of failure to secure promotion but involved complexities that remain somewhat clouded.[20]

Longstreet's senior division commander had been ill during the previous winter, and his performance at Chancellorsville had been less than Lee expected. These two factors prompted Lee to discuss with Longstreet his desire for assigning McLaws to "other service." The commanding general asked Longstreet to inquire about McLaws's health and physical capacity for an extended campaign in the field.[21]

Longstreet spoke to McLaws, who evidently assured his superior that his health was fine. One of them broached the possibility of a reassignment for the division commander. A short time later, on June 3, Longstreet wrote an intriguing letter to McLaws. "You spoke of going South the other day," he noted. "If you wish to go I expect that I may make the arrangement for you I was speaking of for myself. That is for you to go there and let Beauregard come here with a Corps. We want everybody here that we can get and if you think of going south one must agree to send us every man that you can dispense with during the summer particularly."

Longstreet then stated that it was his understanding that Beauregard, who served as commander of the coastal defenses along the lower Atlantic with headquarters at Charleston, South Carolina, was "anxious to join this army, and if he is I believe that I can accomplish what I have mentioned." At the end he promised McLaws "to make the effort if it is desirable to you."[22]

Ultimately, McLaws retained command of his division in the First Corps. Longstreet's idea of a switch never transpired for unknown reasons. He may never have discussed it with Lee, or the latter opposed it. But Lee's concern for McLaws's health and its effect on his generalship remained. According to Longstreet, he promised Lee that he would give personal attention to McLaws and his division. "I thus became responsible for anything that was not entirely satisfactory in your command from that day," Longstreet subsequently informed McLaws, "and was repeatedly told of that fact [by Lee]." At the time, however, McLaws knew nothing of the arrangement between Lee and Longstreet, and as a consequence, the command relationship portended trouble within the First Corps.[23]

The internal dissensions and strained egos never surfaced openly as the army finalized preparations for the Northern campaign. Lee prodded the authorities in Richmond for additional brigades, conferred with his senior officers, and finished the reorganization of the artillery; he assigned five battalions to each corps and relegated Brigadier General William Pendleton, artillery commander, to administrative direction of the command. By June 2 the army was ready, and orders were issued for the march. Within the ranks, confidence and anticipation characterized the men's feelings. "I believe there is a general feeling of gratification in the army at the prospect of active operations," an officer contended in a letter to his father.[24]

On June 3—"a beautiful bright" day—the Army of Northern Virginia started northward. While Powell Hill's Third Corps watched the Federals along the Rappahannock River at Fredericksburg, Longstreet and Ewell's divisions led the march. Lee knew the terrible weapon he commanded; a fortnight before he asserted in a letter that "the country cannot overestimate its [the army's] worth. There never were such men in any army before & never can be again. If properly led they will go anywhere & never fail at the work before them." By June 8 the units of the First and Second Corps were encamped around Culpeper Court House, a pause in the initial leg.[25]

Lee joined the two corps and reviewed Stuart's cavalry brigades on a nearby plantation. A day after the impressive display, on June 9, Union horsemen pushed across the Rappahannock, surprising the Confederates in a swirling battle around Brandy Station. The Yankees came on with a newfound grit and gave as good as they took. While Stuart's men held the field at the end, the fight embarrassed the flamboyant cavalry commander, who came under criticism from the press. But his men's defense kept the strategic initiative with Lee, and the march resumed on the 10th.[26]

Ewell's Second Corps spearheaded the movement toward the Shenandoah Valley. The pace of their march harked back to the days when Stonewall Jackson prodded on his "foot cavalry." On June 13 and 14, Ewell's veterans routed an enemy force at Winchester, seizing cannon, wagons, supplies, and nearly four thousand prisoners. On the day following Ewell's victory, Longstreet's corps resumed its march in scorching heat. By the 17th, Longstreet had cleared the Blue Ridge Mountains, with three of Stuart's cavalry brigades patrolling the gaps; Ewell had a division across the Potomac in Maryland; and Hill's corps was en route to the Shenandoah Valley from Culpeper. Like a huge gray-and-butternut serpent, Lee's army stretched back across the heart of Virginia for over one hundred miles.[27]

In the Confederate wake, moving east of the mountains through Virginia's Piedmont, came Union Major General Joseph Hooker's Army of the Potomac. Hooker had been slow, even reluctant, to react to Lee's advance; instead he proposed a movement on Richmond, but Lincoln rejected that idea. Finally, two days after Brandy Station, Hooker pulled away from Fredericksburg, once again chasing the elusive Rebels toward some distant rendezvous. The Yankees reestablished contact with the enemy east of the Blue Ridge gaps. From June 17 through June 21, Northern and Southern cavalrymen battled each other at Aldie, Middleburg, and Upperville, with Stuart's troopers holding the mountain passages and screening Lee's infantry and artillery.[28]

Beyond the Blue Ridge—"to look at them when the sky is clear is a beautiful sight never to be forgotten," marveled a soldier—Longstreet shuttled two divisions back across the Shenandoah River as support for Stuart. The infantrymen carved some works on the mountain with rocks and trees but never engaged the Federals because Stuart's horsemen repulsed the attacks. Longstreet spent one entire day on the Blue Ridge, examining his lines and reconnoitering. When he returned about eleven o'clock at night, Major Raphael Moses said that he must be tired. "No," responded the general. "I have never felt fatigue in my life."[29]

Longstreet had his headquarters at Millwood, west of the Shenandoah River; Lee's tents were several miles beyond, at Berryville. Lee had traveled with Longstreet throughout the march from Fredericksburg. Almost daily the two men conferred. "I think he [Lee] relied very much on Longstreet," said Moses. Harvey Hill thought Longstreet was Lee's "confidential friend, more intimate with him than anyone else." Longstreet described their meetings and letters as "almost always of severe thought and study." As each stage of the campaign unfolded, Lee stayed close to Longstreet, seeking the latter's advice and counsel.[30]

While halted beyond the Shenandoah River, Lee, with Longstreet's concurrence, consented to an operation that altered the course of the campaign. In orders of June 22 and 23, Lee granted permission to Stuart to take three brigades and "pass around" the Federal army. He expected Stuart to move on the Confederate right flank, collecting information and supplies, but his instructions were vague and discretionary. For his part, Longstreet approved, believing that it would conceal their intentions as the main army marched northward. At 1:00 A.M. on June 25, Stuart began the "ride," disappearing to the east and out of the campaign for the next week.[31]

Longstreet's and Hill's corps, meanwhile, headed for the Potomac River. The troops were "in highest spirits" and "cheering and yelling most vociferously." Throughout the 25th and 26th the columns forded the Potomac River. When Hood's division finished the passage, Hood issued orders for the distribution of a gill of whiskey to each man, and within thirty minutes, many were drunk. "It kept the sober boys busy to keep the drunk ones from killing each other," recalled a Texan. By nightfall of the 26th, advance units had entered Pennsylvania. "We breakfasted in Virginia, dined in Maryland and took supper in Pennsylvania," boasted an Alabamian in his diary.[32]

Longstreet watched his veterans pass on the march toward the Keystone State. He was proud of them and described his feelings later in his memoirs: "The First Corps was as solid as a rock—a great rock. It was not to be broken of good position by direct assault, and was steady enough to work and wait for its chosen battle." A sense of invincibility permeated the army's ranks.[33]

To the residents of Chambersburg, Pennyslvania, it began as a rivulet and swelled to a flood on June 27 as thousands of Rebels poured into their community. Other Southern troops—Ewell's Second Corps—had passed through days before, but not in these numbers. The townsfolk were strongly pro-Union, and United States flags hung from posts and houses; the town "had the appearance of a city of banners," to one Confederate. Behind shuttered windows and closed doors the citizens looked on. On one street, however, four "old spinsters" and a string of schoolgirls stretched from sidewalk to sidewalk, singing "John Brown's Body." When a Confederate brigade reached them, its commander directed the men onto the sidewalks, passing by without incident. When Lee arrived, he issued orders forbidding anyone under the rank of general to remain in town. His and Longstreet's headquarters tents were pitched in a grove of trees, used as a picnic area by locals and known as Shatter's Woods, roughly three-fourths of a mile east of the square on the road to Gettysburg.[34]

To the north and east, beyond South Mountain, Ewell's infantrymen and Brigadier General Albert Jenkins's cavalry brigades probed toward the Susquehanna River and the state capital of Harrisburg, occupying York and harvesting the plenty of south-central Pennsylvania. A major objective of the campaign was the collection of supplies and livestock, and the Rebels emptied barns and outbuildings, rustled horses and cattle, and cleaned out stores. Although Lee issued two orders warning against depredations, his men plundered. Most of the effort, however, was executed as official requisitions that garnered food, medicine, clothing, and cash. Jubal Early had the Caledonia Iron Works, owned by Pennsylvania Congressman Thaddeus Stevens, destroyed, but the Confederates restrained themselves and spared private residences and barns. As one Southerner noted in a letter home: "We are living very well."[35]

From Chambersburg, Lee directed the operations through June 29. Six tents and a solitary Confederate flag marked his headquarters east of town. A Virginia lieutenant colonel saw Lee during these days and told his brother that the army commander "looks the general every inch of him & is in fine health." A visitor with the army, Lieutenant Colonel Arthur James Lyon Fremantle of Her Majesty's Coldstream Guards, later described Lee as "almost without exception, the handsomest man of his age I ever saw." The British officer thought him to be "a perfect gentleman."[36]

During the march northward, Fremantle attached himself to Longstreet's staff, sharing a tent with Moses and seeing much of the general. Fremantle found Longstreet's aides to be "all excellent good fellows, and most hospitable," arguing that they lived "more luxuriously than their generals." As for Longstreet, the foreigner described him as "a thick-set, determined-looking man" of "iron endurance" who "seems to require neither food nor sleep." Longstreet and Fremantle chatted one evening about Texas, through which the latter had journeyed, but the Britisher stated that the general was "generally a particularly taciturn man."[37]

Longstreet, wrote Fremantle, "is never far from General Lee, who relies very much upon his judgment. By the soldiers he is invariably spoken of as 'the best fighter in the whole army.'" Expanding on the Lee-Longstreet relationship, Fremantle contended: "The relations between him and Longstreet are quite touching—they are almost always together. Longstreet's corps complain of this sometimes, as they say that they seldom get a chance of detached service, which falls to the lot of Ewell. It is impossible to please Longstreet more than by praising Lee. I believe these two generals to be as little ambitious and as thoroughly unselfish as any men in the world." Neither general carried a pistol or wore a sword, and from what Fremantle learned in conversations, both men desired an end to the war.[38]

Although he did not mention it, Fremantle probably witnessed or heard of the concern at army headquarters about Stuart's whereabouts and the lack of information about movements of the Union army. Lee had not received any intelligence from Stuart since the cavalry officer's departure on June 25. While Lee had two of Stuart's brigades with the army, he had not pushed them to the front for reconnaissance, perhaps because he expected word from Stuart at any time. When none arrived, anxiety mounted; in Walter Taylor's words: "The absence of that indispensable arm of the service was most seriously felt by General Lee."[39]

About ten o'clock on the night of June 28, the Confederate high command received its first solid piece of intelligence about the enemy, brought by Longstreet's spy, Henry Harrison. Sometime during the first week of the month, Longstreet had instructed the operative to travel to Washington and secure any information he could obtain, giving him gold coins for expenses. "Where shall I find you, General, to make this report?" inquired Harrison.

"With the army," Longstreet replied. "I shall be sure to be with it."[40]

As Longstreet predicted, Harrison found the general when he located the army. Harrison "was dirt-stained, travel-worn, and very much broken down" when a staff officer led him to Longstreet's tent. His report startled the general—the Yankees were in Maryland, moving toward Pennsylvania. Longstreet sent him at once with either Moxley Sorrel or John Fairfax—both claimed they escorted the spy, and Longstreet named each officer in different versions—to Lee's tent. The commanding general did not trust Harrison, but when the aide vouchsafed for Longstreet's confidence in him, Lee accepted the intelligence. With the vanguard of Ewell's troops near the Susquehanna River, Lee had to concentrate his scattered divisions before the Federals overtook them.[41]

"Excitement" at army headquarters was evident after Harrison appeared out of the darkness. Later that night Lee issued orders recalling Ewell's three divisions and Jenkins's horsemen to Chambersburg. He countermanded the directive the next day, redirecting them toward either Cashtown or Gettysburg across South Mountain from Longstreet's and Hill's corps. Johnson's division received the new instructions too late, however, and it marched toward Chambersburg with the corps' wagon train. If Lee needed to hurry troops to either concentration site, seven of the army's nine divisions and most of the artillery and wagons would have to rely on the Chambersburg Pike that ran to Gettysburg.[42]

The atmosphere at army headquarters on June 30 indicated that confidence in the army's prowess and position had not been darkened by the news from Harrison. Conversation by Lee's and Longstreet's staff members was "unusually careless and jolly." Belief in themselves and Lee permeated the ranks of the army. As Porter Alexander remarked: "We looked forward to victory under him as confidently as to successive sunrises." Sometime during the day, probably after noon, the Confederates learned that Major General George Meade had succeeded Joseph Hooker in command of the Union army. Hooker had resigned in a dispute with the administration over the abandonment of Harpers Ferry. When Hooker refused to comply and tendered his letter, Lincoln accepted it. When Lee heard the news, he allegedly said: "General Meade will commit no blunder in my front, and if I make one, he will make haste to take advantage of it."[43]

Late on the 30th, Lee and Longstreet rode eastward toward Cashtown and Gettysburg. At Greenwood, west of South Mountain, Lee established headquarters at a deserted sawmill for the night; Longstreet set up his tents nearby. Earlier in the day, Lee had told a group of staff officers: "Tomorrow, gentlemen, we will not move to Harrisburg as we expected but will go over to Gettysburg and see what General Meade is after."[44]

Beyond South Mountain, two divisions of Powell Hill's Third Corps bivouacked near Cashtown, roughly eight miles west of Gettysburg. Searching for a reported cache of shoes, one brigade had marched to Gettysburg during the day, encountered Union cavalry, and withdrawn. Division commander Henry Heth informed Powell Hill of the incident and asked: "If there is no objection, General, I will take my division tomorrow and go to Gettysburg and get those shoes."

"None in the world," replied Hill.[45]

Wednesday, July 1, dawned cloudy, but the overcast skies cleared. Lee greeted Longstreet "in his usual cheerful spirits" and asked the First Corps commander to ride with him. Mounted on Hero, his favorite horse, Longstreet accompanied Lee up the western slope of South Mountain. As they climbed the ascent, an indistinct rumble, like the growl of a distant giant, could be heard ahead, indicating artillery fire. When they reached the crest, the sound from the east was unmistakable and incessant. Leaving Longstreet behind to expedite the march, Lee spurred forward to Cashtown where he met Powell Hill, who knew little more than that Heth had gone toward Gettysburg with instructions not to bring on an engagement until the other divisions came up. At no time since his accession to command had Lee heard such ominous gunfire. He rode toward Gettysburg.[46]

Longstreet, meanwhile, worked to hasten the crawl on Chambersburg Pike; its roadbed was jammed with the troops and wagons of Edward Johnson's, Lafayette McLaws's, and John Hood's divisions. About two o'clock in the afternoon, Longstreet followed Lee, accompanied by some aides and Fremantle. Passing Johnson's ranks, the party of horsemen drew spectators. Many of the veterans had never seen Longstreet before and ran toward him, inquiring if it was he. When he passed some Florida troops who had served under him, a shout went up: "Look out for work now, boys, for here's the old bulldog again." With each mile the clatter of musketry and the bellow of artillery increased in volume, while clots of wounded men stumbled rearward. Whether Lee planned it or not, his army had been drawn into a battle.[47]

About five o'clock, Longstreet found the commanding general near the Chambersburg Pike on Seminary Ridge where the buildings of the Lutheran Theological Seminary graced the crest. Longstreet had arrived as the soldiers of Hill's and Ewell's corps were driving the broken elements of Federal units through the streets of Gettysburg. What had begun as a routine encounter escalated into a fierce struggle west and north of the town. Two Union corps— the First and Eleventh—fought valiantly until Hill and Ewell coordinated assaults and swept the Northerners before them to hills and a ridge south and east of the community. Lee witnessed and countenanced the attacks and ordered Ewell to press the enemy, securing the heights if possible.[48]

When Longstreet arrived, Lee "was engaged at the moment," and the corps commander surveyed the terrain through field glasses for several minutes. He did not like what he saw—the ground on which the Federals were regrouping appeared naturally strong. He had not enough time for a thorough examination, but his initial survey, experience, and instincts led him to conclude that assaults on the position should be avoided. When Lee finished, Longstreet turned to him and said: "We could not call the enemy to position better suited to our plans. All that we have to do is file around his left and secure good ground between him and his capital." Lee did not like the idea of a flank movement, and Longstreet noticed it immediately. Perhaps Lee's face flushed or his neck and head jerked, as was his habit when upset or angry. Jabbing a fist toward the enemy, Lee exclaimed: "If the enemy is there tomorrow, we must attack him."

"If he is there," Longstreet shot back, "it will be because he is anxious that we should attack him—a good reason, in my judgment, for not doing so."[49]

Longstreet had disagreed more openly and forthrightly with Lee than he probably ever had. He admitted that he "was not a little surprised" at Lee's "impatience" and decision to attack the enemy. Longstreet had not expected a tactical offensive, believing that the commanding general was committed to the defense once the opponents met. Longstreet wanted a duplication of either Fredericksburg or Second Manassas, not the bloody assaults of Chancellorsville or Malvern Hill. He was undoubtedly disturbed by the prospects indicated by Lee. While Longstreet's words had an edge to them, he uttered them because of the relationship between the two of them and his judgment that Lee was committed to a grievous mistake. Too many times in the past, in many councils lost to history, Longstreet had either voiced opposition or proposed a different plan, and for him not to express his views on this day would have been contrary to how the generals had operated together.[50]

After the war, in words that would make ex-Confederates bristle, Longstreet explained Lee's reaction to the day's results and his desire for a resumption of the offensive on the 2nd. Lee, wrote Longstreet, "seemed under a subdued excitement, which occasionally took possession of him when 'the hunt was up,' and threatened his superb equipoise. The sharp battle fought by Hill and Ewell on that day had given him a taste of victory."[51]

Longstreet's assessment had elements of truth in it, but there was more to it than that. Certainly, combat rejuvenated Lee, stirred his emotions. Furthermore, his men possessed "an overweening confidence," in Walter Taylor's opinion; "a profound contempt for an enemy whom they have beaten so constantly, and under so many disadvantages," in Fremantle's judgment. Since the Seven Days Campaign, they had not failed Lee, and as he had written less than two months before, they could "go anywhere" if properly led. And they had done so again on this day, wrecking two Union corps, inflicting heavy casualties, killing a major general—John F. Reynolds, commander of the Union First Corps—and capturing hundreds of prisoners. The Confederates, argued staff officer Henry Kyd Douglas, "never seemed to me as invincible as on the 1st July 1863."[52]

Above all else, however, Lee found himself in a battle he had not wanted. He knew little of the Federal dispositions or of the location of his opponent's other corps. As Longstreet subsequently said, "The first collision was an unforeseen accident," and Lee had to react to those circumstances. Longstreet's proposal of a vague flank movement was impractical, and Lee rightly dismissed it at the time. Without Stuart's cavalry he could not agree to a movement into the unknown. While he had not expected such a fight on this day, Lee had won a clear victory and was reluctant to relinquish the initiative to George Meade. In history's glare, Lee had choices on this afternoon, but Douglas Freeman's description of him as "a blinded giant" seems fair. Fate or chance or human error had pulled the army to Gettysburg, and without intelligence, Lee could only react to what he saw.[53]

Lee asserted in his report that "it had not been intended to fight a general battle at such a distance from our base, unless attacked by the enemy." But once the combat had been joined, Lee argued that "a battle thus became, in a measure, unavoidable. Encouraged by the successful issue of the engagement of the first day, and in view of the valuable results that would ensue from the defeat of the army of General Meade, it was thought advisable to renew the attack."[54]

Longstreet remained with Lee for approximately two hours. During that time Colonel Armistead Long of Lee's staff reported in from a reconnaissance of the Federal position on Cemetery Hill, counseling against an attack. An aide from Ewell rode up with a request from his commander for support in an assault. Lee reiterated his wish for Ewell to advance if possible but could not promise assistance from Hill's corps. At some point Longstreet recommended that the effort should be undertaken at once if Lee intended to assail the enemy. Lee, however, preferred to wait until McLaws's and Hood's divisions arrived. With that settled, Longstreet remounted Hero and rode westward toward his oncoming troops. Lee went to visit Ewell, met with that commander, Jubal Early, and Robert Rodes, and learned that Ewell had neither advanced nor supported an assault the next morning against the position. The commanding general left it at that and returned to army headquarters in a field across the Chambersburg Pike from the stone cottage of Maria Thompson.[55]

Longstreet camped near the troops of McLaws and Hood, who were stretched out beside the roadway a few miles west of the town. At his headquarters he could not hide his displeasure with the prospect of an offensive the next day. As he shared a meal with his staff and guests, he shook his head and described the enemy position as "very formidable." He told Dr. Dorsey Cullen that they would need the "whole army" to take the heights and "then at a great sacrifice." Lee's senior officer and most trusted subordinate was a troubled man as he lay down for a few hours' sleep.[56]

GETTYSBURG, JULY 2, 1863

Longstreet arose early on the morning of Thursday, July 2, 1863, a day that in time would haunt both his life and Confederate history. He had slept but a handful of hours; if restlessly, he never said. He breakfasted with his staff and headquarters guests before mounting his horse and riding eastward toward Gettysburg. Stars glistened in the clear morning darkness. In the fields on both sides of the Chambersburg Pike still lay the dead of yesterday's combat—the silent sentries of a battlefield. Beneath his mount the roadway rose and fell—across Herr and McPherson's ridges, into the swale and up the western shoulder of Seminary Ridge. Once on the crest, he nudged his horse southward, continued a short distance, stopped, and dismounted. Longstreet walked toward Robert E. Lee.[1]

Like Longstreet, Lee had awakened hours before daybreak, eaten breakfast, and returned to Seminary Ridge. When Longstreet arrived, Lee had not formulated a specific plan for the day except for a determination to resume the offensive. The commanding general needed to wait until after sunrise, however, to examine the Federal position, assess its strength, and send reconnaissance parties to explore the ground and enemy dispositions. The two generals conferred in the darkness, and at some point Lee indicated that he wanted to attack the Union army and needed the First Corps divisions of Lafayette McLaws and John Hood.[2]

Longstreet opposed the idea of an offensive strategy, and for a second time within twelve hours voiced his objection. He again suggested a broad turning movement around the enemy's left flank that would place the Confederate army between the Federal capital and George Meade's army. Meade's Yankees, Longstreet argued, would have to assail the entrenched Southerners. To Longstreet this could result in a slaughter similar to Fredericksburg and/or to a crushing counterattack reminiscent of Second Manassas. But once again Lee rejected the proposal.[3]

The commander's refusal silenced Longstreet, and Lee turned to the task at hand. Before daybreak Lee detailed Captain Samuel Johnston, an engineer officer on his staff, to conduct a reconnaissance of the Federal left flank south of Gettysburg and to report back as soon as possible. The instructions were vague, but Johnston knew from experience that Lee "wanted me to consider any contingency which might arise." Longstreet was either present when Lee spoke with Johnston, or Lee informed him of the reconnaissance, because the corps commander assigned Major John J. Clarke of his staff to accompany Johnston. A civil engineer from Petersburg, Virginia, Clarke had joined Longstreet's staff in May after serving under him around Suffolk. After they departed with one or two unidentified individuals, Lee ordered Major Charles Venable to ride to Richard Ewell's headquarters on the Confederate left and direct the Second Corps commander to examine the enemy lines for a possible attack along that sector.[4]

Before long, members of both generals' staffs and generals Powell Hill, Henry Heth, and John Hood joined Lee and Longstreet at their post located near a log or fallen tree trunk that was probably north of the seminary buildings. Later, the foreign observers with the army—the Britisher, Arthur Fremantle; Major Justus Scheibert of the Prussian Royal Engineers; Captain Fitzgerald Ross, a native of Britain serving in the Austrian Hussars; and Francis Lawley, a correspondent for the London *Times*—came in at one time or another during the morning. To get a better view of the Union position from the ridge, Fremantle climbed an oak tree.[5]

While the officers and guests conversed with one another, Lee waited for the return of Venable, Johnston, and Clarke. Several of those present noted that Lee appeared impatient and uncharacteristically restless. Scheibert, who had been with the army at Chancellorsville, remarked that Lee throughout the battle's final two days did not have the "quiet self-possessed calmness" he had shown at Chancellorsville. He was "not at his ease" and looked "care-worn" to Scheibert. Writing six weeks later, Lawley described Lee on the 2nd as "more anxious and ruffled than I had ever seen him before, though it required close observation to detect it." Likewise, Hood thought the commander was "seemingly anxious " for an attack. When Hood asked about the enemy's position, Lee responded: "The enemy is here, and if we do not whip him, he will whip us."[6]

Between seven and eight o'clock, Johnston and Clarke returned from the reconnaissance, having been gone over three hours. When they arrived, Lee, Longstreet, and Hill were sitting on a log and talking while Lee pointed to a map. Johnston joined the generals and, using the map, described the route that led them all the way to Little and Big Round Top. The engineers had viewed the Peach Orchard, crossed Emmitsburg Road, and rode along the bases of the two hills. Except for four Union cavalrymen they saw on their return ride, the Confederates had found no enemy troops in the area.[7]

The report surprised Lee, who inquired: "Did you get there?" pointing to the Round Tops. When Johnston assured the general that they had, Lee "showed clearly that I had given him valuable information." With that, the staff officer stepped back while the generals conferred for several minutes. Longstreet and Hill soon walked away, and Johnston then sat down beside Lee to discuss the topographical features of the terrain. When they had finished, Lee told Johnston to join Longstreet, which the captain inferred to mean to "aid him in any way that I could."[8]

The information assured Lee that his army had an opportunity to strike the Union flank and roll it up toward Gettysburg. But the reconnaissance report was inaccurate. For reasons that remain inexplicable if Johnston had gone where he said he had, the Southerners had not seen hundreds of Union infantry in the area near the Round Tops. Units of the Third Corps had bivouacked in the fields north of Little Round Top and were stirring when Johnston's party was reportedly nearby. The morning mist may have obscured the Yankees from view, but Johnston should have detected the noise of men and animals, drums and bugles. A historian of the day's action has concluded that Johnston's reconnaissance was "somehow a victim of grave misfortune" and that his information "was to have serious consequences later in the day."[9]

Soon after Johnston gave his report, Major General Lafayette McLaws arrived at the crowded observation post on Seminary

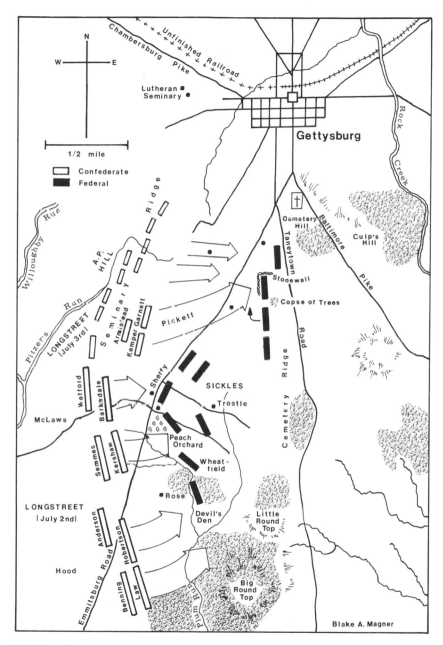

BATTLE OF GETTYSBURG, JULY 2-3, 1863.

Ridge. The division commander had ridden in advance of his troops, who were halted in a lengthy column along the Chambersburg Pike. Although McLaws's accounts of his activities on this morning imply that he reached the ridge before Johnston returned, the reconstruction of events indicates otherwise. The conversation as recounted by McLaws makes little sense if Lee had not had the information supplied by the staff officer. Either McLaws misunderstood what Lee meant or remembered the meeting inaccurately.[10]

McLaws reported to Longstreet and Lee. Contrary to other eyewitnesses, McLaws thought Lee "was as calm and cool as I ever saw him." Still sitting on the log and holding the map, Lee pointed to the Emmitsburg Road and a line drawn perpendicularly across it, and said to McLaws: "General, I wish you to place your division across this road, and I wish you to get there if possible without being seen by the enemy." He paused, then asked: "Can you get there?"

"I know of nothing to prevent me," replied McLaws. He requested permission to reconnoiter the ground, but Lee responded that Captain Johnston had been ordered to do that. Misunderstanding Lee's words, McLaws volunteered to accompany the engineer officer. At this point Longstreet, who had been pacing while listening to the conversation, stopped and exclaimed: "No, sir, I do not wish you to leave your division." Then, leaning down, Longstreet traced a line on the map with his finger that was parallel, not perpendicular, to the Emmitsburg Road and remarked: "I wish your division placed so."

"No, General," interjected Lee. "I wish it placed just perpendicular to that."

For a second time McLaws made the request to examine the terrain, and Longstreet denied it for a second time. With the instructions given, McLaws returned to his command, which he had posted along Herr Ridge, roughly a mile and a half west of Seminary Ridge. Here his men rested among trees beside a country lane until ordered forward. During the wait, McLaws and his staff members watched Federal units in the distance march up the Emmitsburg Road toward Gettysburg.[11]

The time was approximately nine o'clock when McLaws headed back to start his division for Herr Ridge. During the previous hour or two, Lee had settled on an attack scheme against the Union left flank believed to be located on Cemetery Ridge, north of Little

Round Top. The final details could not be resolved, however, until Lee heard from Ewell on the opposite flank. Since Venable had not returned from his mission, Lee decided to talk personally with the Second Corps commander. The commanding general spent nearly two hours on the army's left flank, surveying the enemy positions on Cemetery and Culp's hills and discussing an assault with Ewell and subordinates. At Ewell's suggestion Lee agreed to keep the corps on the ground opposite the hills and have it undertake a diversion when Longstreet began the attack south of the town. Lee then rode back to Seminary Ridge and arrived about eleven o'clock.[12]

Longstreet met Lee and received orders to advance with the infantry divisions of McLaws and Hood and the corps artillery battalions. Longstreet requested a delay until Brigadier General Evander Law's brigade of Hood's division, known to be en route, arrived from New Guilford, where it had been stationed, and Lee acceded. As understood, Longstreet's command would march to a position beyond the Union flank, avoiding detection from a Union signal station on Little Round Top and, once deployed, would attack northward along the Emmitsburg Road, rolling up the enemy line on Cemetery Ridge. When McLaws's division charged, Major General Richard Anderson's division of the Third Corps, posted in the Confederate center along Seminary Ridge, would continue the assault against the Union position. On the left, Ewell would "make a simultaneous demonstration" to hold enemy units in place, preventing reinforcements from being shifted against Longstreet and Anderson. Lee's plan encompassed an en echelon assault that required coordination and could involve most of the brigades on the field.[13]

Finally, after several hours of deliberation and study, Lee committed the army to a specific attack. The primary responsibility for its execution rested with Longstreet, who had argued against this operation. In fact, the corps commander had been unable to hide his displeasure with Lee's renewal of the offensive. Moxley Sorrel admitted later that Longstreet "failed to conceal some anger." With Pickett at Chambersburg, Longstreet had only two of his three divisions on the field, and he said to Hood: "The General is a little nervous this morning; he wishes me to attack. I do not wish to do so without Pickett. I never like to go into battle with one boot off."[14]

Longstreet believed that Lee was making a grave mistake and scrapping their prior understanding of fighting a defensive battle.

In a postwar letter to McLaws, written in 1873, Longstreet stated that "Lord will now understand my surprise at finding all of our previously arranged plans so unexpectedly changed, and why I might wish and hope to get the Gen. to consider our former arrangements."

Longstreet then detailed those "former arrangements" for McLaws. He claimed in the letter that "almost every day from the 10th May 63 until the Battle" he and Lee discussed strategy. Longstreet proposed a defensive battle during their talks, arguing the Napoleonic maxim that an invading army should maneuver to force an enemy to assail it in a chosen position. "We agreed," wrote Longstreet, "that this was a good maxim, and particularly applicable to the Confederate army." To Longstreet such a strategy was not only sound military thought but a necessity because of the South's limited manpower pool. "Our losses were so heavy when we attacked that our army must soon be depleted to such extent that we should not be able to hold a force in the field sufficient to meet our adversary."[15]

He and Lee reexamined previous engagements—First and Second Manassas, Seven Days, and Fredericksburg—and "concluded even victories such as these were consuming us, and would eventually destroy us." After the many discussions, the two generals concurred on "the ruling idea of the campaign," in Longstreet's phrase. "Under no circumstance were we to give battle," as he described it to McLaws, "but exhaust our skill in trying to force the enemy to do so in a position of our own choosing. The 1st Corps to receive the attack and fight the battle. The other corps to then fall upon and try to destroy the Army of the Potomac."[16]

The letter is significant. It lends credence to his subsequent published writings on the campaign, and it explains the rationale behind his and Lee's thinking in the weeks before the battle. It repeats Longstreet's strong commitment to the tactical defensive and explains his reaction when Lee adopted the tactical offensive. To Longstreet the flanking movement that he recommended on the 1st and 2nd reflected the strategy they had thoroughly discussed—compelling the Federals to attack them. When Lee chose otherwise, Longstreet was disturbed because he thought the commanding general was wrong and was putting the army at too great a risk.

From history's perspective, Longstreet was right. At Gettysburg the Federals held, in Porter Alexander's opinion, a "wonderfully strong position" that "could never have been successfully assaulted." On no other battlefield in the East during the war did the Army of the Potomac defend a position of such natural advantage and with interior lines for troop movements. By contrast, the Confederate line extended in an exterior arc for nearly five miles. In a postwar letter, Alexander described it as "the *utter absurdity* of our position. It was simply preposterous to *hope* to win a battle when so strung out & separated that cooperation between the three corps was impossible except by a miracle. And comparatively little pains was exercised to bring it about either."[17]

Like Longstreet, Alexander believed that Lee should not have resumed the offensive on July 2 but should have fashioned a defensive line on Seminary Ridge. In his judgment, Meade would have been compelled for both military and political reasons to attack the Confederates. "I think it a reasonable estimate to say," Alexander wrote afterward, "that 60 per cent of our chances for a great victory were lost by our continuing the aggressive." But if Lee intended "to fight aggressively," Alexander argued, he should have attacked the "sharp salient" at Cemetery Hill on the 2nd, "with both Hill & Ewell, with Longstreet right behind Hill, & Johnsons Divn behind Early. It was the weakest point of the enemys line, all the time."[18]

In his report, Lee contended that "we were unable to await an attack, as the country was unfavorable for collecting supplies in the presence of the enemy, who could restrain our foraging parties by holding the mountain passes with local and other troops." Alexander countered, however, that the Confederates supplied themselves for nearly another two weeks north of the Potomac and extricated the wagon train. Lee may have been correct in his assessment, but he seems never to have considered seriously waging a defensive battle at Gettysburg. From the afternoon of July 1, Lee was committed to the offensive and refused to listen to alternative proposals. Like his men, Lee possessed supreme confidence in his generalship and believed in the army's invincibility. As Alexander noted, he "never paid his soldiers a higher compliment than in what he gave them to do" at Gettysburg.[19]

Could the Federal army's position have been outflanked, as suggested by Longstreet on July 2? After the war, Lee's opponent, George Meade, stated that "Longstreet's advice to Lee was sound military sense; it was the step I feared Lee would take." But the difficulties of such a movement were evident and, without the cavalry of Jeb Stuart, probably insurmountable. On the afternoon of the 1st and on the morning of the 2nd, Lee had little choice but to reject the idea. Confronted with an unexpected battle and without reliable information about enemy troop dispositions, Lee had to improvise during the first two days of fighting. The improvisation, however, was consistently framed within an offensive tactical plan.[20]

In turn, Longstreet deserves censure for his performance on the morning of July 2. He allowed his disagreement with Lee's decision to affect his conduct. Once the commanding general determined to assail the enemy, duty required Longstreet to comply with the vigor and thoroughness that had previously characterized his generalship. The concern for detail, the regard for timely information, and the need for preparation were absent. Or, as Moxley Sorrel admitted, "there was apparent apathy in his movements. They lacked the fire and point of his usual bearing on the battlefield."[21]

While Lee did not order the advance until eleven o'clock, Longstreet knew at least two hours earlier that his two divisions would, in all likelihood, attack the Union left flank. Before Lee rode to visit Ewell, at approximately nine o'clock, Colonel Porter Alexander reported to Longstreet on Seminary Ridge. When the artillery officer arrived, Longstreet informed him of the First Corps's role and directed him to assume command of the artillery on the field, to find a route by which to move the batteries into position that would not be detected by a Union signal station on Little Round Top, and then to bring up the cannon. He could not have issued such instructions to Alexander without knowing what was expected of him and his command.[22]

But once Longstreet gave his orders to Alexander, he evidently did nothing else to expedite the movement during Lee's two-hour absence. He did not confer with McLaws and Hood, send Clarke or any staff member on a more timely reconnaissance, confirm whether a concealed route had been found to the enemy flank, or check with Alexander whether that officer had fulfilled his instructions. He stayed at the observation post and waited for Lee's return. Lee apparently expected Longstreet to do something during his visit with Ewell, although what is unclear. In Longstreet's defense, Lee had not finalized the plans, and both men had accepted Johnston's report, believing that the route of march had been examined by the engineer officers. What was lacking in Longstreet was the energetic and careful preparation that had been a hallmark of his generalship at Second Manassas, Sharpsburg, and Fredericksburg. The failings on this day, however, were not solely Longstreet's; like an ungainly beast the Confederate army stumbled into battle on July 2.[23]

Longstreet left Seminary Ridge shortly after eleven o'clock. It would be another hour before Law's brigade arrived from New Guilford, and Longstreet began attending to the movement. He ordered Colonel John L. Black of the First South Carolina Cavalry, whom Lee had assigned as a guard for Longstreet's right flank and rear, to send two trustworthy lieutenants to scout the front. Around noon Law's Alabamians reached the field, and one of Black's lieutenants reported that he had ridden to Seminary Ridge and found no enemy troops. About the same time, gunfire crackled to the front as Richard Anderson's Third Corps division collided with Union sharpshooters on the lower end of Seminary Ridge as Anderson moved into position.[24]

The march began between noon and one o'clock—probably closer to the latter hour—when Captain Samuel Johnston led McLaws's division forward. From their rest area on Herr Ridge, the Confederates followed a lane down the slope, struck a road along Marsh Creek, turned left, crossed the Fairfield Road at the Black Horse Tavern, and entered a road that led southeasterly to Pitzer's Schoolhouse. A short distance beyond the tavern, reaching the crest of a small hill, McLaws halted the column. Little Round Top, with its signal station, could be seen in the distance. The division could not pass over the crest without exposing its ranks to the enemy. While the one-and-a-half-mile-long column halted, McLaws and Johnston searched for an alternate route. The division commander soon returned to the head of the column "saying things I would not like to teach my grandson," according to a nearby soldier.[25]

Riding with the vanguard of Hood's column, Longstreet spurred ahead as soon as McLaws's men stopped. He joined McLaws, and when he learned the reason for the delay, he exclaimed: "Why, this won't do. Is there no way to avoid it?" McLaws replied that during the morning he had reconnoitered a route that would avoid the hill, but it required a countermarch. "Then countermarch," barked Longstreet. According to Brigadier General Joseph Kershaw, whose brigade led the division, the two generals were displeased, "both manifesting considerable irritation."[26]

McLaws later blamed Johnston for the "dilemma," asserting that the two divisions "had been placed by an error of his [Lee's] staff officers." Johnston, who refused to become involved publicly in the postwar contention about the battle—"I do not want to be a party to controversy with any one," he wrote to McLaws, "certainly not with General Longstreet, who always treated me with so much kindness and consideration when we were thrown together"—denied in private correspondence that he had guided the march to the hill, but he undoubtedly was mistaken. If he and Major Clarke had examined the roads during their reconnaissance as he stated, how could the trained engineers have overlooked the crest? He may have become confused and led McLaws down the wrong road, but the record offers no explanation. Johnston claimed that he recommended to Longstreet that the troops skirt the hill by marching across the fields, but the general "preferred the road." Hours earlier Porter Alexander had faced the same problem at the rise and detoured through the fields without exposing his batteries to Union view. The tracks of the artillery wheels must have been visible, but Longstreet and McLaws chose not to follow them, which would have saved valuable time. They never gave the reasons; perhaps Johnston was correct—Longstreet thought it better to stay on the roads.[27]

More problems plagued the countermarch. Hood's column jammed into the rear of McLaws's, causing additional lost time. In turn, McLaws insisted that his division continue to lead, and Longstreet reluctantly acquiesced. The Southerners tramped back to near the starting point, on a lane to Fairfield Road, up it several hundred yards before turning right into another road along Willoughby Run. During part of the march, Lieutenant George W. Peterkin of Brigadier General William Pendleton's staff joined the column as a guide. When Kershaw's South Carolinians, still leading McLaws's division, again hit the road from Black Horse Tavern, they turned left, passed Pitzer's Schoolhouse, and ascended the western slope of Seminary Ridge. It could not have been much before three o'clock when the Confederates approached the staging area.[28]

As the South Carolinians climbed the ridge, Longstreet overtook McLaws. Halting beside his division commander, Longstreet asked, "How are you going in?"

"That will be determined when I can see what is in my front," McLaws replied.

"There is nothing in your front," Longstreet stated. "You will be entirely on the flank of the enemy."

"Then I will continue my march in columns of companies," rebutted McLaws, "and after arriving on the flank as far as is necessary will face to the left and march on the enemy."

"That suits me," Longstreet replied, and with that he turned and rode to the rear.[29]

Minutes later Kershaw's men cleared the treeline and immediately came under enemy artillery fire. Startled by the sudden explosions, McLaws ordered his other brigades hurried forward and, dismounting, walked ahead for an examination of the Federal position. "The view presented astonished me," he wrote years later. Instead of being in the rear of the Union line and confronted with only two infantry regiments and a battery at the Peach Orchard as he had expected, McLaws saw brigades of blue coated infantry backed by batteries of cannon stretched from the Peach Orchard to near Little Round Top. Behind them, additional Federal units were marching across the fields to extend the line northward from the Peach Orchard along Emmitsburg Road. The Yankees, numbering about eleven thousand, belonged to the Third Corps under Major General Daniel Sickles, who had advanced them on his own initiative.[30]

Kershaw, meanwhile, pushed forward skirmishers and deployed his brigade behind a stone wall west of and roughly parallel to the Emmitsburg Road. Lee had originally intended the division to align itself perpendicularly to the road, but changed circumstances on the field dictated otherwise. On his left, Brigadier General William Barksdale's Mississippians closed, with the brigades of Brigadier Generals Paul Semmes and William Wofford filing into a second line 150 yards to the rear of the stone wall. An artillery battery from Colonel H. G. Cabell's battalion rumbled into position and began engaging the enemy gun crews. Soon all of Cabell's eighteen cannon were involved in the duel.[31]

Behind McLaws's veterans, Hood's soldiers marched to the right, having been ordered ahead by Longstreet, whose patience had finally unraveled at the delays. Longstreet also sent Major Osmun Latrobe to McLaws with a message to "proceed at once to the assault." If McLaws had any patience left, it, too, was spent when Latrobe delivered the instructions. There was more than "a small force of the enemy in front," he grumbled to Latrobe; he asked Longstreet to come forward and see for himself. Latrobe spurred back only to return shortly with a second command to advance, commenting: "General Lee was with General Longstreet and was impatient that the charge was delayed." Left with no choice, McLaws said he would be ready in five minutes and passed the word to his brigadiers. But before the division could move, another courier from Longstreet arrived with orders to wait until Hood was in position and had charged.[32]

From McLaws's account and from a later version from Longstreet, it was Lee who agreed to or personally altered the attack scheme when confronted with the new Federal position. Three other eye-witnesses placed Lee either with Longstreet or in the area at the time, adding credence to the two generals' descriptions of the events. As such, the refashioned attack that soon rolled forward had Lee's approval if not his imprint.[33]

Leaving Lee behind, Longstreet then rode to the front and joined McLaws. The corps commander, in McLaws's words, "was very much disconcerted and annoyed" when he saw the situation before them. Both men's tempers had frayed by now, and Longstreet asked sharply why a battery had not been placed where the road crossed the ridge. McLaws responded that if deployed there, it would draw the enemy's cannon fire and would be in the path of his attack. Longstreet, however, seemingly wanted neither explanations nor excuses and ordered that gun crews be brought up. McLaws did as instructed, and as he predicted, the Federals howled shells and shots toward the exposed pieces, sawing limbs off trees and knocking men over.[34]

The pounding endured by the one Rebel battery was shared up and down the line. By now Alexander had placed most of his fifty-four cannon in position, and their crews were sending their own rounds toward the Union artillery pieces. While the opposing gunners killed and maimed each other, Longstreet moved to the right front of McLaws's line, near Kershaw's brigade. Here he watched the action from behind the stone wall with several staff members. A South Carolinian thought that the general "had more the look of gloom than I had ever noticed before." His mood was also seen in the faces of others, for there was an "air of heaviness hanging around all," said the soldier.[35]

John Hood, meanwhile, brought his four brigades into line on McLaws's right. Like McLaws, Hood deployed into two lines—Jerome Robertson's and Evander Law's troops in the front, George Anderson's and Henry Benning's in support. Part of the front line overlapped the Emmitsburg Road, with Law's five Alabama regiments on the right entirely east of the road. As the soldiers shifted into battle formation, Hood sent several Texans on a scout toward Big Round Top. When they soon reported back that the Confederates could swing around the hill and into the Federal rear where only wagons were parked, Hood rushed an aide to Longstreet with the news and with a request for permission to turn the flank. It was a proposal similar to Longstreet's to Lee, but the corps commander had his orders and denied the request.[36]

Hood tried a second and a third time to persuade Longstreet, even using Moxley Sorrel, the latter's chief of staff, in the effort. Each time Longstreet said no. Finally, Longstreet sent Major John Fairfax to tell Hood to advance. But Hood persuaded the staff officer that the flanking movement could succeed, and Fairfax hurried back to his commander. Longstreet must have bristled when Fairfax voiced support for Hood's idea. From the beginning, Longstreet had opposed the attack, arguing against it, but time had run out— Lee had issued specific orders for an assault up the Emmitsburg Road, and further delay would not be welcomed. "It is General Lee's order—the time is up—attack at once."[37]

Longstreet followed Fairfax to the right and spoke to Hood, whom the corps commander later described as "a splendid fighting soldier without guile." The conversation lasted only a few minutes, with each general riding away—Hood to initiate the attack, Longstreet to the center of his line to watch. As he headed back, Longstreet paused, and in the words of a Texan who saw him, astride "his horse like an iron man with his spyglass to his eye, coolly watching the effect of our shots. Limbs of trees fell and crashed around him, yet he sat as unmoved as a statue."[38]

A year after the war and three years after Gettysburg, Hood allegedly said of his commander: "Of all the men living, not excepting our incomparable Lee himself, I would rather follow James Longstreet in a forlorn hope or desperate encounter against heavy odds. He was our hardest hitter." Hood may have been thinking of a number of battlefields, but his words resonated with haunting clarity back to this July afternoon in southern Pennsylvania. The major general and the thousands of soldiers with him knew that the task before them would be difficult, desperate, perhaps forlorn. They may have been reassured, for the battle now belonged to them and the army's "hardest hitter."[39]

If nothing else, they seemingly had come to expect such a moment. "There was a kind of intuition, an apparent settled fact, among the soldiers of Longstreet's corps," one of them put it, "that after all the other troops had made their long marches, tugged at the flanks of the enemy, threatened his rear, and all the display of strategy and generalship had been exhausted in the dislodgement of the foe, and all these failed, then when the hard, stubborn, decisive blow was to be struck, the troops of the first corps were called upon to strike it." It was that time once again.[40]

Minutes after four o'clock the veterans of the First Corps, Longstreet's "great rock," rolled forward. Law's Alabamians and Robertson's Texans and Arkansans spearheaded the charge, followed by Anderson's and Benning's Georgians. Across the fields and woods, Union artillery fire roared with a deeper, more deadly defiance. The shellfire ripped into the ranks, knocking men down at every step. "I could hear bones crash like glass in a hail storm," wrote a Rebel six days later. Twenty minutes into the attack, a shell piece found Hood, tearing into an arm and punching him off his horse. Aides carried him to the rear and informed Law that he now commanded the division. Hood's fall was a grievous loss as his division closed on the enemy infantry.[41]

The Union artillery was merciless, but the Southerners kept coming. "I never saw troops move more steadily & in better order than these did on that occasion," remembered a colonel. "There was no wavering, disorder or want of confidence on the part of the troops." Past the Rose farm and up the slope of Houck's Ridge, the Confederates drove against a wall of musketry and artillery. They found themselves on the lower slope of Big Round Top, called "Devil's Kitchen," in the forsaken landscape of Devil's Den, down in the swale of the soon-to-be-christened "Valley of Death," and up the side of Little Round Top. The attack on Little Round Top reminded a Texan of "a devil's carnival." Federal reinforcements hammered back the assaults, only to be splintered by counterattacks. Six times the triangular-shaped Wheatfield changed hands. The Rebels "did all men can do," a Georgian told his wife afterward.[42]

Longstreet watched Hood's sixty-nine hundred troops advance from a post near Kershaw's brigade. To him, Union general Daniel Sickles's line "was, in military language, built in the air." With Hood's men fighting against the Federal left, it was McLaws's turn to advance against the Peach Orchard salient and line along the Emmitsburg Road. About five o'clock, at a signal, Kershaw's South Carolinians stepped over the stone wall and charged. Longstreet walked with them to the Emmitsburg Road and, hearing Barksdale's drummers beat assembly, mounted and rode toward the Mississippians.[43]

Longstreet found Barksdale "chafing" to enter the battle. The redoubtable politician-turned-warrior "had a thirst for battle glory," said one of his men. Barksdale's Mississippians had held on to Fredericksburg during that long day in December and, in the words of an artillerist, were "the finest body of men I ever saw. They were almost giants in size and power." On this afternoon they had suffered under the Union cannon fire and, like their commander, wanted to go in. Longstreet finally released them, and Barksdale shouted, "Forward, men, forward." The Mississippians emitted a yell and, swinging their line to the left, passed through a Virginia battery.[44]

From the Peach Orchard and along the Emmitsburg Road, the Yankees unleashed a "terrible" flame of musketry and artillery. The fourteen hundred Mississippians plowed ahead in what an eyewitness claimed was "the most magnificent charge I witnessed during the war." Relentlessly the Rebels came, swarming into the Peach Orchard and among the buildings of the Sherfy farm, decimating two Pennsylvania regiments, overrunning a battery, and capturing a Union general. Three of Barksdale's regiments wheeled northward and scoured the ground east of the Emmitsburg Road, while the fourth regiment plunged down the Wheatfield Road and seized another battery. Dan Sickles's salient at the Peach Orchard had been blown away by a Mississippi whirlwind.[45]

In the wake of the Mississippians came Wofford's Georgians. When these Southerners passed through the battery, the sight of them "filled my eyes with tears," stated the battery's captain. Instead of moving directly behind Barksdale, Wofford swung southeastward and charged in on the right of the Mississippians astride the Wheatfield Road. On their right front, Kershaw's South Carolinians, supported by Semmes's Georgians, drove through the Wheatfield toward the Valley of Death. The onslaught of McLaws's division of seventy-three hundred troops had crushed the remnants of Sickles's line from the Peach Orchard to the Wheatfield and wrecked additional enemy units thrown into the fury. Farther to the Confederate rear, Alexander rolled his batteries into position west of the Emmitsburg Road, their fire bracing the infantry. "The smoke was at this time so dense," reported a Union general on Cemetery Ridge, "that but little could be seen of the battle."[46]

Longstreet rode ahead with Wofford's Georgians. When the men yelled, he shouted to them: "Cheer less, men, and fight more." As Longstreet and the Georgians advanced, they passed by a knot of Federal prisoners taken by the Mississippians. One of the Yankees inquired about the identity of the general, and when told it was Longstreet, he allegedly growled: "No wonder we are thrashed upon every field, there is not in the whole of our army a lieutenant general who would have risked his life in such a charge." Since no officer in Meade's army held that rank, the soldier's statement was undoubtedly truthful, but its meaning testified to the Northerners' perception of their leadership and that of the Confederates.[47]

Longstreet halted near the Peach Orchard and watched the combat on the smoke-swept field. Not since the Seven Days, except for the stand in the Piper Farm at Sharpsburg, had he been so close to the fighting. Contrary to his habitual method of command, which gave his subordinates battlefield direction of their units, he had personally ordered Barksdale's and Wofford's brigades into the action and then followed them to the front. His conduct on the field lends credence to his postwar claim to McLaws that he had promised Lee to assume personal responsibility for the performance of McLaws and his division.[48]

Lafayette McLaws knew nothing of Longstreet's pledge; all he saw on this afternoon was his corps commander meddling in the operations of the division. Five days later, in a letter to his wife that has become a favorite piece of evidence of anti-Longstreet historians, McLaws vented his outrage:

> I think the attack was unnecessary and the whole plan of battle a very bad one. General Longstreet is to blame for not reconnoitering the ground and for persisting in ordering the assault when his errors were discovered. During the engagement he was really excited giving constantly orders to every one, and was exceedingly overbearing. I consider him a humbug, a man of small capacity, very obstinate, not at all chivalrous, exceedingly conceited, and totally selfish. If I can it is my intention to get away from his command. We want Beauregard.[49]

The words had a harshness of a general infuriated, perhaps even embarrassed, by the loss of his authority on the battlefield. Longstreet deserved criticism for the failure to reconnoiter the terrain and enemy dispositions before the divisions reached the attack area, but it was Lee and, in turn, Longstreet who persisted "in ordering the assault." Longstreet might have served his command better had he overseen the direction of Hood's division after its commander fell wounded. Its attack lost cohesion under Law, and with Longstreet in control, it might have achieved more. But Lee wanted the corps commander near McLaws, and there he stayed.

Longstreet's instincts on a battlefield were outstanding, and not long after he reached the Peach Orchard he saw that the assault had gone as far as could be expected. Union general George Meade had rammed one successive wave of troops after another into the Confederate attackers. The conduct of the Rebels had been "magnificent," but as Longstreet wrote afterward:

> We felt at every step the heavy stroke of fresh troops—the sturdy regular blow that tells a soldier instantly that he has encountered reserves or reinforcements. We received no support at all, and there was no evidence of co-operation on any side. To urge my men forward under these circumstances would have been madness, and I withdrew them in good order to the peach orchard that we had taken from the Federals early in the afternoon.[50]

In a postwar letter to McLaws, Longstreet disclosed privately that "this attack went further than I intended that it should, and resulted in the loss of your gallant Brigadier Barksdale. It was my intention not to pursue this attack if it was likely to prove the enemys position too strong for my two divisions. I suppose that Barksdale was probably under the impression that the entire Corps was up." Although this letter does not contradict his published statements, it indicates that he had planned to halt the assault if the lives of his men were needlessly sacrificed but that the momentum and success of the charges forced him to continue. Once he moved to the front, he reasserted direction and signaled a retirement. Had he decided beforehand to follow the letter of Lee's orders but not its spirit? It would appear so until his veterans took the decision out of his hands, delivering "the best three hours' fighting ever done by any troops on any battle-field."[51]

Longstreet initiated the retrograde movement by pulling Wofford's brigade out of an exposed position beyond Trostle's Woods. Couriers and aides raced to the other units, and the Confederates withdrew toward the Peach Orchard and the Emmitsburg Road. They clung to Devil's Den and the woods south of the Wheatfield. Fortunately for them, the Yankees had had enough, and the fearful combat subsided. The Southerners bedded down on the bloody ground.[52]

Longstreet's casualties exceeded four thousand, including William Barksdale and Paul Semmes, both mortally wounded. A Mississippian with Barksdale asserted later that Mississippi had "lost many of her best & bravest sons," words that could be echoed for Texas's, Arkansas's, Georgia's, and South Carolina's sons. They had fought and bloodied upward of twenty thousand Federals in what Porter Alexander subsequently thought "not only contests with Pickett's Charge the palm of being the most brilliant & desperate part of the whole battle of Gettysburg, but that it is not excelled in these qualities by any record of the war." It seemed to one of Longstreet's men that the enemy never ran out of troops during the combat, which moved him to exclaim to his comrades: "Great God! Have we got the universe to whip?"[53]

Longstreet shared the soldier's assessment, writing afterward that "this was an unequal battle." Lee's planned en echelon attack of one division following another into action faltered when it reached the division of Richard Anderson, who sent in disjointedly only three of his five brigades. On Anderson's left, Major General William Pender's division never advanced once its commander suffered a wound. On the Confederate left flank, Richard Ewell had his artillery engage the enemy, but not until 6:30 P.M. did he advance his infantry against Culp's Hill. The attack foundered from the outset, and an hour later two of his brigades stormed up Cemetery Hill in a valiant but doomed charge. Ewell's efforts allowed Meade to shift troops to the Union left against Longstreet.[54]

After the war, Major Walter Taylor of Lee's staff wrote of the battle of July 2: "The whole affair was disjointed. There was an utter absence of accord in the movements of several commands, and no decisive results attended the operations of the second day." The command system of the army cracked under the strain of Lee's loose battlefield direction and the extended line. Once the fighting began, Lee received only one report and sent only one message.

Ewell and Powell Hill needed firmer supervision, but that was not Lee's method. Had the commanding general duplicated the active role taken by his counterpart, George Meade, the outcome might have been different.[55]

Longstreet's performance during the morning deserves criticism, as noted previously. Had he attended to the details that were his responsibility and not allowed his disagreement with Lee to affect his judgment and effort, the afternoon assault would have begun sooner, but not several hours earlier. The attack plan ordered by Lee—an advance up the Emmitsburg Road—had little chance of success if Union general Daniel Sickles kept his corps on Cemetery Ridge. Once Sickles moved to the Peach Orchard and Emmitsburg Road, he jeopardized the entire Federal army and increased the likelihood of a Confederate victory. Only the conduct of Meade and other subordinates and the valor of Northern soldiers salvaged the day.[56]

July 2, not 3, 1863, was the pivotal day of Gettysburg. The Army of Northern Virginia nearly achieved a victory. That it did not can be attributed to internal problems and human failings, and to the performance of the Army of the Potomac. While disappointed with the day's outcome, Lee thought that night, as he reported, "the result of the day's operations induced the belief that, with proper concert of attack, and with the increased support that the positions gained on the right would enable the artillery to render the assaulting columns, we should ultimately succeed, and it was accordingly determined to continue the attack." The agony of Gettysburg was not finished for the First Corps and James Longstreet.[57]

14

"NEVER WAS I SO DEPRESSED"

The nearly fifty-eight hundred Virginians of Major General George Pickett's infantry division arrived at Gettysburg on the afternoon of July 2, 1863. While the other divisions of the army coverged on the battlefield on July 1, Pickett's three brigades remained in Chambersburg, destroying public property and workshops. Relieved by a cavalry brigade that night, the Virginians started for Gettysburg early on July 2. The day's heat and the march's length wilted the troops, and when they halted near Marsh Creek, they were "almost exhausted." To the east, artillery fire growled, hinting of the fury that was soon to engulf their comrades in the First Corps.[1]

While the men rested in the fields, Pickett directed Major Walter Harrison to report the division's arrival to Robert E. Lee and then spurred ahead to find his commander and old friend, James Longstreet. Pickett located the lieutenant general while the latter was watching the attack against the Union Third Corps. Longstreet *"was mighty glad to see me,"* wrote Pickett. The two officers chatted briefly, with Pickett describing the location and condition of his troops. Before long Harrison rode up to inform Pickett that he had met with Lee, who said to the staff officer: "Tell General Pickett I shall not want him this evening, to let his men rest, and I will send him word when I want them."[2]

Pickett and Harrison lingered in the area, spectators to the combat that raged in the fields between the Emmitsburg Road and Cemetery Ridge. As the fighting subsided with the repulse of Major

General Richard Anderson's Confederate brigades, the division commander and his staff officer headed back to their fellow Virginians. Pickett issued orders for an early start the next morning. Sleep came easily for the weary men. Circumstances had spared them for two days, but such fortune could sometimes exact its price. A terrible accounting awaited when the word came from Lee.[3]

With Pickett's division at hand, Lee finally had his army on or near the battlefield. An hour or so before Pickett rode up, the long-absent cavalry commander, J. E. B. Stuart, had reported to Lee on Seminary Ridge. Stuart had been out of contact with the invading Confederates since the morning of June 25. While the Southern infantry and artillery had stumbled into the collision at Gettysburg, Stuart's three brigades had become entangled with the Union army en route northward; they captured an enemy wagon train that further slowed their march and engaged enemy horsemen at Hanover, Pennsylvania. A courier from Lee located Stuart at Carlisle on the night of July 1. The orders directed the cavalry officer to Gettysburg, and he moved his tired men there hours later.[4]

When Stuart joined Lee, the commanding general, as was his habit, said little, but his deameanor indicated his disappointment with the cavalry commander. While others in the army would castigate Stuart then and later for his "ride" Charles Marshall, Lee's aide, even suggested that he should be shot—Lee only mildly rebuked the subordinate in his report. Although Stuart did not violate Lee's orders, he exercised poor judgment that undoubtedly crippled the army as it maneuvered in southern Pennsylvania and affected Lee's decisions on the battlefield. In the cobweb of controversy surrounding the Gettysburg Campaign, Stuart's performance still engenders heated debate.[5]

For Lee, however, the present mattered, and the results of the July 2 combat shaped his decision for the 3rd. With coordination among the corps, he believed that an assault would ultimately achieve victory, so he issued orders for a renewal of the offensive at daylight on the 3rd. He directed Stuart to operate on the left flank and sent couriers to Longstreet and Richard Ewell instructing them to attack the Federal flanks simultaneously. Pickett's division should be in position at the appointed hour to augment Longstreet's force. Lee might have eliminated any misunderstandings had he spoken personally to Longstreet and Ewell, but he did not, and neither of them came to army headquarters on the night of the 2nd.[6]

Longstreet stated later that his headquarters that night in a field west of the Emmitsburg Road was four miles from Lee's, and instead of riding that distance, he sent an aide with a brief report of the day's action. His decision not to confer with Lee was probably due more to his mood than to the necessity for a short horseback ride. He had watched his two divisions fight magnificently only to suffer heavy losses in an attack he never wanted. He had been unable to conceal his anger with Lee's plan, and after the sacrifice he had witnessed, his dissatisfaction could only have been worse that night. He remarked to Captain Fitzgerald Ross of the Austrian Hussars: "We have not been so successful as we wished."[7]

Sometime after dark the orders came from Lee for the resumption of the attack at first light on Friday morning. In his memoirs, Longstreet denied that he received such a directive from Lee, but he either forgot or deliberately lied when he wrote that thirty years after the battle. Porter Alexander's version of events makes it clear that Longstreet had been informed:

> During the evening I found my way to Gen. Longstreet's bivouac, a little ways in the rear, to ask the news from other quarters & orders for the morning. From elsewhere the news was indefinite, but I was told that we would renew the attack early in the morning. That Pickett's division would arrive and would assault the enemy's line. My impression is the exact point for it was not designated, but I was told it would be to our left of the Peach Orchard. And I was told too to select a place for the Washington Artillery which would come to me at dawn.[8]

Alexander's reminiscences reveal that not only did Longstreet have Lee's instructions, but the corps commander had begun to implement the orders. Longstreet most likely sent the orders to the Washington Artillery, but whether he directed Pickett to be in position by daylignt is uncertain. It would appear that neither Lee nor Longstreet informed Pickett of a specific time, for the division commander's troops did not awaken until 3:00 A.M., ate breakfast, and then marched, not arriving until hours past daylight. Perhaps Lee expected Longstreet to take that responsibility, or perhaps the latter assumed that Lee had done so. In either case, evidently no one told Pickett that his command would be needed at daylight. To meet this timetable, Pickett should have stirred his men about midnight; that he did not indicated he had not received a message to do so.[9]

Consequently, when Lee rode to the Confederate right at sunrise, he found neither Pickett's division nor preparations under way for an assault. Instead, the commanding general found Longstreet at work on a movement around Big Round Top and beyond the Union left flank. This was not what Lee expected or ordered, and he sought an explanation. "General," Longstreet offered, "I have had my scouts out all night, and I find that you still have an excellent opportunity to move around to the right of Meade's army and maneuver him into attacking us."

Longstreet saw at once that Lee had heard enough about a flank movement. "With some impatience," Lee rejected the proposal and, pointing toward Cemetery Ridge, said that he was going to attack the Federals there with the three divisions of the First Corps. "I felt then," Longstreet related afterward, "that it was my duty to express my convictions; I said, 'General, I have been a soldier all my life. I have been with soldiers engaged in fights by couples, by squads, companies, regiments, divisions, and armies, and should know, as well as any one, what soldiers can do. It is my opinion that no fifteen thousand men ever arranged for battle can take that position."[10]

It was a defining moment between the two men. For two days Lee had endeavored to impose his will on the battle. Hampered by a lack of intelligence, he had fashioned an offensive scheme that required coordination among his corps, confident that if it could be attained, his incomparable infantry would succeed. The men accomplished all that could have been asked of them on July 2, but it was not enough because the Union army fought with tenacity. But Lee refused to relinquish the initiative to his opponent despite the casualties and the natural strength of the enemy position. Now, on the morning of the 3rd, the audacious general ordered one more assault, a final reckoning on these bloody fields.

For Longstreet, the commanding general wanted too much. As the senior and most experienced and trusted subordinate, Longstreet had opposed the plan on the 2nd, believing it was a mistake. He knew by Lee's reaction that his counterarguments—his recalcitrance—had wearied his superior, but still he pressed for an alternative. "He was a trained soldier," a historian has written of Longstreet, "who dealt in human life with a conservatism lacking in most military men. In the intangibility of battles he took no chances. Life was too precious to gamble needlessly." He could order men to death and had done so, but only when it made sense. And on this third morning at Gettysburg, when Lee proposed another attack, Longstreet could not accept it.[11]

That Longstreet responded precisely with the words as he subsequently recounted them is unlikely, but he must have uttered some version of them. In a postwar letter he stated that his opposition to Lee's decision on the 3rd was "strong against the attack." He meant what he wrote later in a published account: "I should not have been so urgent had I not foreseen the hopelessness of the proposed assault. I felt that I must say a word against the sacrifice of my men; and then I felt that my record was such that General Lee would or could not misconstrue my motives." A man of physical and moral courage, he had a warrior's soul, but he could not unquestioningly approve "the sacrifice of my men." Lee had asked for too much.[12]

The exchange between Lee and Longstreet—the third in as many days—could have been construed as insubordination on Longstreet's part. That Lee evidently did not regard it as such testified to his character and to the relationship between the men, later described by Longstreet as "affectionate, confidential, and even tender, from first to last." Longstreet's response manifestly irritated Lee, but the commanding general listened, and when the subordinate had finished, Lee jabbed a fist toward the ridge, indicative of his impatience, and said firmly: "The enemy is there, and I am going to strike him." The talking ceased, and as Longstreet put it: "Nothing was left but to proceed."[13]

Lee then rode with Longstreet to a point near the Emmitsburg Road, north of the Peach Orchard, and dismounted. They walked together into a field and focused their field glasses on Cemetery Ridge. In time, members of their staffs and generals Powell Hill and Henry Heth joined them. A discussion ensued, with Lee still advocating an assault with the First Corps. Longstreet again objected, arguing that the previous day's fighting had exacted much from Lafayette McLaws's and Evander Law's troops—Hood's division—and that if they advanced, the enemy could enfilade their exposed right flank. Lee was persuaded, and after further talk, the generals resolved to use Pickett's unscathed division and brigades from Hill's Third Corps, supported by McLaws and Law.[14]

The attack force as finalized consisted of Pickett's three brigades, Heth's four brigades—under Brigadier General J. Johnston Pettigrew because Heth had not fully recovered from a wound received on July 1—two brigades from William Pender's division, and two from Richard Anderson's. The latter two units were ordered to protect Pickett's right flank while the other nine brigades acted as the spearhead of the attack. If they succeeded, Lee could augment the force with brigades from Pender and Robert Rodes. Altogether in the eleven brigades there were fifty regiments from six Southern states, numbering perhaps as many as fourteen thousand, although the figures conflict. To prepare the way for the infantry, Lee directed an artillery bombardment of the Federal position that included over 170 cannon. Not since Malvern Hill, a year before, had the Confederate army undertaken such a frontal assault.[15]

Preparations consumed the entire morning. While Lee had hoped to coordinate an attack with Longstreet and Richard Ewell on the Confederate left, the latter's troops had been engaged on Culp's Hill since 4:30 A.M. when the Federals opened with artillery. The combat raged all morning and could easily be heard on Seminary Ridge where the troops filed into ranks for the assault. Pickett deployed his three brigades into two lines among the woods on the ridge and in a swale in front that stretched southward beyond the H. Spangler farm—Richard Garnett's and James Kemper's regiments in front; Lewis Armistead's in support. On Pickett's left, Pettigrew aligned his four brigades in a single line through the trees. Behind his right front, the two brigades of Pender's command were posted. Minutes before the cannonade began, Major General Isaac Trimble, a redoubtable sixty-one-year-old fighter who had rejoined the army as a supernumerary in June after recovering from a severe wound at Second Manassas, was given the direction of these latter two brigades.[16]

While the infantrymen settled in and the artillerymen rolled the cannon forward, Lee and Longstreet—sometimes together, at other times separately—passed back and forth along the lines. Why neither general saw nor anyone reported the weakened condition of Pettigrew's command and the faulty alignment of the left units in the assault force remains a mystery. On July 1 the division had incurred losses of roughly one-third of its strength, and now, on the 3rd, three brigades had colonels in charge, and Pettigrew had no experience at divisional command. The corps commander, Powell Hill, evidently never reported the situation to Lee. Perhaps no one regarded it as significant, but as Longstreet noted afterward, it was "a grievous error."[17]

Compounding this "grievous error" was the position and formation of the six brigades on Pickett's left. The Third Corps troops were deployed farther to the rear than Pickett's Virginians, and if they advanced at the same time, they would trail, exposing Pickett's flank to artillery fire. Furthermore, the left two brigades of Pettigrew's line—the weakest in the division—had no immediate support and were vulnerable to an enfilade. The odds against the Confederates were formidable from the beginning and were increased by the flawed deployment of the units.[18]

Responsibility for the assault column rested with Longstreet—Lee assigned it to him. He saw to the placement of Pickett's division but apparently did not supervise the positioning of the brigades from Hill's corps. In his report, he described Pettigrew's units as deployed in two lines, supported by Trimble's brigades, which would have given the attackers depth and more power. But he was mistaken because he either did not know the alignment or reported it wrongly. He may have thought that Hill had attended to his troops, and since the relations between the two men remained strained, he may not have endeavored to impose his authority or will on Hill. For his part, Hill stated afterward that he ordered his brigades to report to Longstreet, implying that the duty fell to the latter. Although Hill was with Lee and Longstreet throughout much of the morning, did he mean that he neither had nor assumed any responsibility? At Gettysburg, Powell Hill somehow disappeared.[19]

In his memoirs, Longstreet tried to excuse his conduct on this morning. Lee, wrote Longstreet, "should have put an officer in charge who had more confidence in his plan." He added: "Knowing my want of confidence, he should have given the benefit of his presence and his assistance in getting the troops up, posting them, and arranging the batteries; but he gave no orders or suggestions after his early designation of the point for which the column should march."[20] This assertion was both inaccurate and disreputable. Lee may not have issued additional orders or superintended the location of the infantry and artillery—it was not the duty of an army commander to do so—but he spoke frequently with Longstreet. The obligation assigned to Longstreet by Lee demanded the subordinate's proper execution. To shift the blame to Lee was wrong and unworthy of Longstreet. When he wrote his memoirs in the 1890s, Longstreet had been under vehement attack for nearly two decades about his conduct at Gettysburg, and he made unwise statements.

This was probably the case here, a countercharge delivered by a tired, even bitter, but proud old man.

Indisputably, Longstreet believed that the assault was doomed, and his mood darkened throughout the morning. Major Walter Harrison of Pickett's staff thought the general "seemed to be in anything but a pleasant humor at the prospect 'over the hill.' " Despite his ill disposition, however, Longstreet attended to his duty, overseeing in particular the arrangement of Pickett's brigades and the corps artillery; and when the time came, he inspired the troops by personal example. At one point in the morning he told Lee that he and his staff "had been more particular in giving the orders than ever before," conferring with the unit commanders and designating the point of attack. He may have been too parochial in his attention to his men and may have neglected his wider responsibility for Hill's units. The failure to address the tactical problems of the left wing deserves criticism, but this failure should be shared with Lee, perhaps even with Hill. As Porter Alexander remarked about the situation, Lee's "not interferring with it stamps it with his approval." Like the day before, Longstreet did as ordered but without spirit and with grave concerns.[21]

Longstreet was not alone in his judgment about the strength of the Federal position and the task before the Confederates. He said later that the "opinion expressed on the field" was that thirty thousand fresh troops, supported by additional units, would be required for success. Walter Harrison described Cemetery Ridge and the target area, a clump of trees, as "frightful to look at," while Walter Taylor of Lee's staff informed his sister four days after the attack that the "position was impregnable to any such force as ours." When brigadiers Richard Garnett and Lewis Armistead saw it, Garnett remarked: "This is a desperate thing to attempt." Armistead predicted that "the slaughter will be terrible." At one point during the morning, Brigadier General Cadmus Wilcox, whose brigade had charged the ridge on the 2nd, visited with Garnett and avowed that it was "twice as strong as Gaines's Mill." Wilcox estimated that he had lost between four hundred and five hundred men in less than twenty minutes "without making the slightest impression." A Virginian with Garnett probably spoke for most if not all his comrades in the ranks when he admitted that he "never expected to get out alive."[22]

Preparations for the bombardment and assault were completed

between eleven o'clock and noon. At 11:45 A.M., Colonel Porter Alexander received a note from Longstreet: "If the artillery fire does not have the effect to drive off the enemy or greatly demoralize him so as to make our effort pretty certain I would prefer that you should not advise Gen Pickett to make the charge I shall rely a great deal upon your good judgment to determine the matter, and shall expect you to let Gen Pickett know when the moment offers."[23]

Alexander had been at work before daylight. Once the decision was made to attack Cemetery Ridge, he supervised the placement of the batteries, careful not to move them forward in bunches, thereby avoiding Union counterfire. He believed that Lee would use every brigade in the army and expected the assault to be a success. Now, when he read Longstreet's message, he received a "sudden shock," in his words. It seemed that Longstreet had doubts about the operation and was shifting the responsibility to the artillery officer. Although Longstreet treated Alexander "as if he were my father," according to the younger man, the colonel was upset and asked Brigadier General Ambrose Wright, who was with him, for advice. They discussed the matter, and then Alexander scribbled a reply:

> General: I will only be able to judge the effect of our fire on the enemy by his return fire as his infantry is but little exposed to view & the smoke will obscure the whole field. If as I infer from your note there is any alternative to this attack it should be carefully considered before opening our fire, for it will take all the arty ammunition we have left to test this one thoroughly & if the result is unfavorable we will have none left for another effort & even if this is entirely successful it can only be so at a very bloody cost.[24]

As Longstreet read Alexander's response, he must have realized how close he had come to relinquishing his duty to a subordinate. He hurriedly wrote a second note, which Alexander received about 12:15 P.M. "The intentions is to advance the Inf," stated the lieutenant general. "If the Arty has the desired effect of driving the enemy off or having other effect such as to warrant us in making the attack. When that moment arrives advise Gen P. and of course advance such artillery as you can use in aiding the attack."[25]

Although ambiguous, this second message sought Alexander's opinion as to the most opportune time for the advance of the infantry. It still bothered Alexander, who spoke with Wright before riding to feel Pickett's "pulse." When Alexander found the Virginian "in excellent spirits & sanguine of success," he was reassured. At 12:30 P.M. he jotted to Longstreet: "When our arty fire is at its best I will advise Gen Pickett to advance."[26]

About thirty minutes later, Longstreet directed Colonel J. B. Walton, his artillery chief, to "let the batteries open." Within minutes two guns from the Washington Artillery fired in succession, signaling the cannonade. The line of Confederate cannon exploded in a deafening roar. A watching Alabamian thought he had seen Judgment Day. "When the heavens are rolled together as a scroll in the last days," he marveled, "I doubt whether it will present a more awe inspiring spectacle."[27]

Across the valley, Union artillery crews, numbering about 118, responded in kind, and for the next hour and forty minutes "it was a hellish scene" of flame, smoke, and explosions. The bombardment reminded James Kemper of John Milton's description of the artillery conflict between the contending forces of Heaven. The brigadier had his men lie down, but that did not spare all of them. The men could not move, for "it seemed that death was in every foot of space," according to one of them caught in the fury, "and safety was only in flight, but none of the men did that."[28]

Kemper recounted in a postwar letter:

> While this was going on, Longstreet rode slowly and alone immediately in front of our entire line. He sat his large charger with a magnificent grace and composure I never before beheld. His bearing was to me the grandest moral spectacle of the war. I expected to see him fall every instant. Still he moved on, slowly and majestically, with an inspiriting confidence, composure, self-possession and repressed power in every movement and look, that fascinated me.

As Longstreet approached, Kemper walked toward him and said: "General, this is a terrible place."

"What! Is your command suffering?" asked Longstreet.

"Yes. A man is cut to pieces here every second while we are talking; sometimes a dozen are killed at one shot."

Kemper saw the sadness in Longstreet's face as he spoke: "Is it possible? Can't you find any safer position for your men?"

"No," answered the brigadier. "We are exactly behind the line of this crest—the very safest place about here."

"I am greatly distressed at this," Longstreet replied, "greatly distressed at this; but let us hold our ground a while longer; we are hurting the enemy badly, and we'll charge him presently."

He said no more and moved on in "his stately course." Kemper stated that he would never forget that display "of the truest heroism."[29]

Elsewhere along the line, men of lesser rank than Kemper watched in admiration of Longstreet as he passed in front of them through the storm of Union fire. A staff officer claimed that the general "was as unmoved as a statue." A Virginia captain attested that he was "one of the bravest men I ever saw on the field of battle." A soldier in the Fifty-sixth Virginia thought "he did not seem to notice the Federal lines at all." With each shell burst, the troops shouted at Longstreet "to go to the rear," admonishing him: "You'll get your old fool head knocked off," and "We'll fight without you leading us."[30]

Eventually Longstreet reined up in the woods on the ridge, dismounted, and rested in the shade. As a corps commander he need not have exposed himself so dangerously. Perhaps he was impelled to do so, to share with his men the fury into which they would soon march. He was a troubled man—"Never was I so depressed as upon that day," he admitted afterward. "I felt that my men were to be sacrificed and that I should have to order them to make a hopeless charge." All that remained for him was to inspire, and by his effort he saluted them for what they had been chosen to do once the firestorm ceased.[31]

But for both Longstreet and his men time was running out. As the cannon fire melted into a deafening thunder, Alexander scribbled a note to Pickett: "If you are to advance at all you must come at once or we will not be able to support you as we ought, but the enemy's fire had not slackened materially and there are still 18 guns firing from the cemetery." Minutes later, through the smoke, Alexander thought he saw Union gun crews removing their pieces from near the clump of trees, and wrote again to Pickett: "The 18 guns have been driven off For Gods sake come on quick or we cannot support you ammunition nearly out."[32]

The courier from Alexander found Pickett with Longstreet in the woods. The younger man was unmistakable, with his "long ringlets" of hair that "flowed loosely over his shoulders, trimmed and highly perfumed." Pickett was "altogether rather a desperate-looking character" in the opinion of the Britisher Fremantle. Longstreet "was

exceedingly fond of him," wrote Sorrel, and gave him special attention. "Taking Longstreet's orders in emergencies," added Sorrel, "I
could always see how he looked after Pickett, and made us give him
things very fully; indeed, sometimes stay with him to make sure he
did not get astray." On this day Longstreet personally assisted Pickett with the division and gave "him things very fully." What he could
not do for his good friend was stop time.[33]

Pickett read Alexander's first note and handed it to Longstreet. "I
have never seen him so grave and troubled," Pickett wrote of his
commander. As Longstreet finished, Pickett asked, "General, shall I
advance?" Longstreet turned his face away, unable to speak. Despite
his training, his years as a soldier, the self-confidence that marked
the man and the general, the responsibility assigned to him, he
could not find the words to send his men into the slaughter pit he
knew awaited them. He could only nod. Pickett saluted, mounted
his horse, and said: "I shall lead my division forward, sir."[34]

While Pickett returned to his division, Longstreet rode to Alexander. When he arrived, Alexander reported that the battery crews
had depleted the ammunition chests and that the nine howitzers he
had planned to advance could not be located. The news seemingly
stunned Longstreet, but neither he nor Lee had checked on the
supply of ammunition during the morning. Longstreet quickly directed Alexander to halt Pickett and to replenish the chests. The
colonel replied that the trains had been nearly emptied before the
bombardment, and if the Confederates had any rounds, it would
require over an hour to restock, giving the Federals time to recover
from the losses.[35]

"I don't want to make this attack," Longstreet said slowly to Alexander, looking at the enemy position through field glasses. "I believe it will fail—I do not see how it can succeed—I would not
make it even now, but that General Lee has ordered it & expects
it." Alexander said later he thought that if he had encouraged the
general, the attack would have been stopped. But Longstreet stated
in his report that "the order for this attack, which I could not favor
under better auspices, would have been revoked had I felt that I
had that privilege." When someone later suggested that he should
have used his discretion and canceled the assault, he explained
that he "never exercised discretion" with Lee present and after a
movement had been ordered. Against his judgment and with the
lack of artillery support, the infantry advanced.[36]

By now Pickett's men were clearing the batteries, marching as if on review, accompanied by music from a band. Pickett's favorite hymn was "Guide Me, O Thou Great Jehovah," and if the musicians played it, its words would have been most appropriate. Before the men went forward, one of them jotted in his diary: "With our trust in God, we fear not an earthly enemy. God be with us!" An officer confided that as they received the order to move, he knew "that it was almost sure death." It had come to this—prayers and valor.[37]

Sitting on a rail fence at the woods' edge, Longstreet watched as the veteran troops advanced into "the *cul-de-sac* of death," in James Kemper's words. "I never saw men march more steadily up to their work than our line," affirmed an officer of the Eighth Virginia. But it was as Longstreet said it would be. Federal infantry and cannon loaded with canister erased ranks of the oncoming Southerners. The furnace of fire scorched the Rebel line and, in the words of a Union general, "melted it away." Longstreet rushed staff officers forward to warn Pettigrew of the danger on the left flank and to hurry support to Pickett's right flank. Late in the attack, Colonel Fremantle joined Longstreet, bubbling that he would not have missed this for anything. "The devil you wouldn't," barked Longstreet. "I would have liked to have missed it very much; we've attacked and been repulsed. Look there."[38]

As he spoke, Longstreet pointed toward Pettigrew's troops streaming rearward along with Pickett's. The weak left flank of the attack formation had caved in first under a counterattack. On Pickett's front, Vermont troops swung out and ravaged the Virginians with an enfilade. Hundreds of Confederates had driven to near the clump of trees and to the stone wall north of the grove. But Union reserves poured into the gap and sealed it. The assault was magnificent, and doomed. Perhaps half of the attack force was either killed, wounded, or captured. "We gained nothing but glory," asserted a Virginian, "and lost our bravest men."[39]

When the smoke cleared, "Pickett's division was gone," in Longstreet's words. He and Lee rode among the survivors, reassuring them and asking them to rally before the Yankees counterattacked. To Cadmus Wilcox, Lee admitted that *all this has been my fault— it is I that have lost this fight, and you must help me out of it in the best way you can.* Pickett was in tears and bitter. Years later he allegedly blamed Lee for having "massacred my division." Longstreet sent Sorrel to have McLaws and Law withdraw their divisions to Warfield Ridge. Before they could pull out, however, the Federals advanced cavalry against Law's infantrymen and suffered a bloody repulse. Finally, farther to the east, Jeb Stuart's horsemen collided with Union troopers, were stopped in a spirited engagement, and the Battle of Gettysburg ended.[40]

Longstreet and Lee rode together along the lines on Seminary Ridge during the night and conferred with other generals. Lee ordered preparations begun for a retreat. Both armies spent Saturday, July 4, waiting for something to occur. During the afternoon a drenching rainstorm swept in. After dark, the Confederate infantry and artillery marched away on the Hagerstown-Fairfield road. Lee's wagon train—seventeen miles long—followed the Chambersburg Pike, the vehicles filled with wounded. Altogether the battle exacted approximately fifty thousand casualties from both armies. Of fifty-two Confederate generals, seventeen, or almost one-third, fell in the battle, including Armistead and Garnett killed in the assault, and Trimble and Kemper, seriously wounded. Lee's losses probably reached thirty percent of his army. While fighting on the defensive, George Meade's Federals suffered roughly twenty-three thousand casualties. As a North Carolinian put it: "Both sides got the worst of it at Gettysburg."[41]

The Rebels slogged through the mud during the night of July 4–5, endeavoring to outdistance the enemy. When Longstreet and the staff halted, the general "walked ceaselessly backward and forward like a sailor on his quarterdeck." The march resumed during the afternoon, and by the 7th, the Rebels pulled up north of the Potomac River. The rains had swollen the stream and prevented a crossing. Meade's Yankees appeared on the 10th, but by then the Southerners had finished fieldworks. When Lee's engineers completed a pontoon bridge, the Southerners filed across during the wet night of July 13–14. Union cavalry struck the rear guard after daylight, and Johnston Pettigrew, who had been spared in the attack on the 3rd, fell mortally wounded. When President Lincoln learned that Lee had escaped, he was furious at Meade, who tendered his resignation. Lincoln did not accept it, but he never quite forgave the army commander for the timid pursuit.[42]

Gettysburg and the surrender of Vicksburg, Mississippi, to the Union army of Ulysses S. Grant on July 4 marked a turning point in the war. The import of the twin defeats was not lost on Lee's soldiers. A North Carolinian informed his family only days after the army's return to Virginia that "our solders are very near give up all hope of ever whipping the Yanks" with the losses in Pennsylvania and in Mississippi. A Georgian in Longstreet's corps voiced a similar view in a letter to his parents:

> I am willing to fight them as long as General Lee says fight. But I think we are ruined now without going any further with it. One thing convinced me: that is when we went into Maryland and Pennsylvania. The [low] prices of everything showed they did not feel the effects of this war, and I saw a great many men that are fit for service. . . . This war is hard to account for. It is no telling how it will end or when it will end.[43]

Within the ranks of the Army of Northern Virginia, the men regarded the invasion and the battle as mistakes. A Georgia lieutenant, on July 16, described the operation as "evidently a failure, that is nothing was accomplished." The men thought Lee had erred at Gettysburg in waging an offensive fight. A South Carolinian argued: "I think our wise Gen. Lee made a great mistake in making the battle." A Floridian claimed that "we fought the Yankees at a great disadvantage." Writing to his wife at the time, a Georgia officer stated: "We found the enemy posted in a terribly secure position. Now I know, we should not have attacked him there on high hills and mountains, but we did so. The Yankees were impregnably posted and on their own soil they fought undoubtedly well. . . . Our men were rushed at their positions, performed heroic deeds, and died heroic deaths." As he looked back on the battle after the war, another soldier believed that the spirit of the men "never seemed to be exactly the same" after July 3. From that day the troops preferred the defensive to an assault.[44]

Lee, as was his magnanimous habit, faulted himself. He wrote to President Jefferson Davis on July 31:

> No blame can be attached to the army for its failure to accomplish what was projected by me. . . . I am alone to blame, in perhaps expecting too much of its prowess & valour. . . . With the knowledge I then had, & in the circumstances I was then placed, I do not know what better course I could have pursued. With my present knowledge, & could I have foreseen that the attack on the last day would have failed to drive the enemy from his position, I should certainly have tried some other course. What the ultimate result would have been is not so clear to me.[45]

It was an honest and accurate evaluation. The Confederates stumbled into an unwanted battle at Gettysburg, and after the first day's results, Lee chose an audacious course, relying on his splendid infantry to achieve victory. In Porter Alexander's judgment, the offensive was an "example of the forcing game." As Lee admitted, he expected too much of the troops because of the strength of the Union position. His confidence in his army's prowess undoubtedly affected his judgment. As a result, according to Alexander, Lee "unnecessarily took the most desperate chances & the bloodiest road" at Gettysburg.[46]

About the same time Lee confided in Davis, Longstreet offered a similar assessment in a letter. On August 2 he wrote to Senator Louis Wigfall: "Our failure in Pa was due I think to our being under the impression that the enemy had not been able to get all of his forces up. Being under this impression Gen. Lee thought it best to attack at once and we did attack before our forces got up and it turned out that the enemy was ready with his whole force, and ours was not." He described it as the "principal" reason for the defeat.[47]

And like Lee, Longstreet assumed his share of the responsibility for the battle's outcome. In a July 24 letter—which he subsequently had published—Longstreet told Uncle Augustus that he "would prefer that all the blame should rest upon me. As General Lee is our commander, he should have the support and influence we can give him." "The truth will be known in time," he added, "and I leave that to show how much of the responsibility of Gettysburg rests on my shoulders."[48]

In time, of course, much of the "responsibility of Gettysburg" would fall on Longstreet's shoulders. In turn, Longstreet sought vindication, preparing published accounts that offered detailed reasons for the defeat that went far beyond his explanation to Wigfall and that shifted blame from himself to Lee and others, in contradiction to his statement to his uncle. He was justified in some of his charges but not many of them. Nothing inflamed the anger of veterans and comrades more than his assertion in his memoirs that Lee being "excited and off his balance was evident on the afternoon of the 1st, and he labored under that oppression until enough blood was shed to appease him." It was uncharitable, even disreputable, of Longstreet to resort to such hyperbole against his commander and friend.[49]

Alexander contended in a postwar letter that "Longstreet's *great* mistake was not in the *war,* but in some of his awkward & apparently bitter criticisms of Gen. Lee in his own books." Alexander believed that Longstreet's conduct and behavior at Gettysburg could be vindicated. "It is true that he [Longstreet] obeyed *reluctantly* at Gettysburg, on the 2nd & on the 3rd, but it must be admitted that his judgment in both matters was sound & he owed it to Lee *to be reluctant,* for failure was *inevitable* do it soon, or do it late, either day."[50]

In an 1893 newspaper interview—three years before the publication of his memoirs—Longstreet gave one of the most revealing and truthful evaluations of Lee, of himself, and of Gettysburg. Lee, Longstreet argued, "outgeneraled himself" during those three July days thirty years before. As a general, Lee possessed profound learning and "in all strategical movements he handled a great army with comprehensive ability and signal success. . . . On the defensive Gen. Lee was absolutely perfect." In Longstreet's view, however, Lee was not a "master" of offensive battle. "In this field," he told the reporter, "his characteristic fault was headlong combativeness; when a blow was struck, he wished to return it on the spot. He chafed at inaction; always desired to beat up the enemy at once and have it out. He was too pugnacious."

Continuing, Longstreet said: "It was entirely different with me [as compared to Lee]. When the enemy was in sight, I was content to wait for the most favorable moment to strike—to estimate the chances, and even decline battle if I thought them against me."[51]

In the end, at Gettysburg, Longstreet thought the chances were against the Southerners and opposed Lee's tactics, recommending a different course of action. When the "pugnacious" Lee ordered striking blows, Longstreet objected more forcibly, certain that victory could not be attained. As Longstreet told former Union general Daniel Sickles in 1902, Gettysburg became "the sorest and saddest reflection of my life for many years."[52]

In the winter of 1864, Lee allegedly admitted to Major Thomas Goree of Longstreet's staff that he should have taken Longstreet's advice and executed a flanking movement around the Federal position. While the accuracy of this confession cannot be confirmed, Goree stated in a postwar letter that he was "willing if necessary to make affidavit" to its truthfulness. Goree claimed that Lee confided to him when the staff officer delivered correspondence from Longstreet in East Tennessee to Lee in Virginia. Another of Longstreet's staff members, Captain Erasmus Taylor, asserted that Longstreet showed him a confidential letter from Lee during this time in which Lee wrote: "Oh, General, had I taken your advice, instead of pursuing the course that I did, how different all would have been." Taylor said he committed the words to memory and never forgot them.[53]

Whether Lee admitted as much to Goree or wrote to Longstreet, he recognized within minutes of the repulse of Pickett and Pettigrew that he had been mistaken. As Alexander stated, Longstreet's judgment on the 2nd and 3rd was "sound," but as Lee told Davis, if he had known the outcome, "I should certainly have tried some other course." Lee and the army might have succeeded if he had followed Longstreet's advice. Or they might not have. For the Confederacy, the tragedy of Gettysburg lay not with what might have been but with what was—the windrows of the fallen that Longstreet had foreseen.

Seventy-five years after the battle, at a reunion of veterans on the battlefield, a former officer in Pickett's division had his own opinion of Longstreet, of the battle, and of the controversy. "Longstreet opposed Pickett's charge, and the failure shows he was right," the Virginian stated to a newspaperman. "All these damnable lies about Longstreet make me want to shoulder a musket and fight another war. They originated in politics and have been told by men not fit to untie his shoestrings. We soldiers on the firing line knew there was no greater fighter in the whole Confederate army than Longstreet. I am proud that I fought under him here. I know that Longstreet did not fail Lee at Gettysburg or anywhere else. I'll defend him as long as I live."[54]

"LONGSTREET IS THE MAN"

"Meadow Farm" lay a few miles outside of Orange Court House, Virginia. Owned by Erasmus Taylor, the fertile homestead had welcomed Confederate soldiers often during the previous year as they passed through or encamped in this strategically important section of Old Dominion south of the Rapidan River and west of Fredericksburg. Taylor was thirty-three years old, a graduate of the University of Virginia and a kinsman of former Presidents James Madison and Zachary Taylor. He had served as a volunteer aide on the staff of General D. R. Jones from First Manassas until the winter of 1862 when he returned to his wife and children at Meadow Farm. He and his wife, Roberta Ashby Taylor, were generous hosts whose cupboards were always open to members of the army.[1]

It was here that Longstreet came on August 5, 1863. Longstreet had likely met Taylor when the staff officer was in the army and, in August 1862, had visited Meadow Farm in the early days of the Second Manassas Campaign. The lieutenant general and his staff members always sought a hospitable house, and when the troops of the First Corps returned to the region south of the Rapidan River, Longstreet found a welcome at the Taylors' home.[2]

The arrival of the Army of Northern Virginia in the Virginia Piedmont marked the conclusion of a fortnight of movement. After the Southerners crossed the Potomac River on July 14, Lee held them in the Shenandoah Valley until Union Major General George

Meade's army pushed southward into Virginia, east of the Blue Ridge Mountains. The Rebels stirred on the 19th, marching eastward toward the mountains. For a few days it was a race, and the opponents clashed at Snicker's, Chester, and Manassas gaps in the Blue Ridge. The Confederates held, allowing the passage of their columns through the mountains ahead of the Northerners. By August 5, when Longstreet set up temporary headquarters at Meadow Farm, the entire Confederate army, except for units of Jeb Stuart's cavalry, had passed the Rapidan, with the Yankees posted north of the Rappahannock River.[3]

Here the two armies stayed in relative quiet for the next six weeks. To alleviate supply problems, Lee stretched his lines from Fredericksburg to Gordonsville. Longstreet's three divisions manned the army's right front toward Fredericksburg. The soldiers enjoyed the respite, and enough rations arrived to keep them well fed. Hundreds of men deserted, however, so Lee granted furloughs to those with the "most meritorious and urgent cases." The rigors of the Pennsylvania invasion and the defeat at Gettysburg still exacted a toll.[4]

Moxley Sorrel remembered this interlude as "those . . . lovely days." For most of the time, corps headquarters was five miles outside of Orange Court House along the Plank Road, but toward the end of August, Longstreet shifted it back to Meadow Farm. While at the Taylors' his staff and other officers enjoyed picnics, parties, excursions, and dances on a daily basis. Lee, who had his headquarters at the farm for a number of days, wrote to his wife that Mrs. Taylor brought buttermilk, loaf bread, ice, and vegetables every day to his tent. "I cannot get her to desist," admitted Lee, "though I have made two special visits to that effect."[5]

Lee and Longstreet evidently shared in little of the festivities at Meadow Farm. Both men struggled with inner conflicts. Bothered by the public criticism of the defeat in Pennsylvania, on August 8 Lee asked President Davis to relieve him of command. Lee argued that he had lost the confidence of his men and that he had not fully recovered from the effects of the illness which had afflicted him in the spring. "Everything, therefore," Lee stated, "points to the advantages to be derived from a new commander."[6]

Davis responded at once, writing on the 11th and saying he could not do it for it would be "an impossibility" for him to find "some one in my judgment more fit to command, or who would possess more of the confidence of the army, or of the reflecting men of the country" than Lee.[7]

Gettysburg also haunted Longstreet. While he esteemed and remained personally fond of Lee, Longstreet could not accept, as he saw it, the needless sacrifice of life that had resulted from Lee's tactics in the battle. If Lee continued to adhere to such a costly strategy and tactics, Longstreet wanted no part of it. Consequently, sometime between August 5 and August 17, he wrote a *"private letter"* to Secretary of War James Seddon requesting a transfer to the West where he could serve under his old friend General Joseph Johnston.[8]

On August 18, Longstreet confided to Senator Louis Wigfall that he had approached Seddon, and he asked his ally in Congress "to urge this" with the secretary. "If I remain here," Longstreet asserted, "I fear that we shall go, little at a time, till all will be lost. I hope that I may get west in time to save what there is left of us. I dislike to ask for anything, and only do it under the impression that if I do not, our days will be numbered." He then assured Wigfall that he had "no personal motive in this for with either Bragg's or Pemberton's army I shall be second to Johnston and therefore in the same relative position as I am at present. I am not essential here, on the contrary, and I am satisfied that it is a great mistake to keep me here."[9]

Longstreet's proposal was a reiteration of his suggestions made during the previous January and May. On those two occasions the scheme was rejected, and as noted before, he changed his mind after Lee convinced him of the value of a movement across the Potomac into Pennsylvania. This time, however, other motives impelled him, as his letter to Wigfall indicated. While Longstreet still believed in the strategic merit of a concentration in the West, he also saw a way in which he could honorably leave the Army of Northern Virginia, reunite with Johnston, and perhaps attain command of an army. It was disingenuous of him to compare his position of corps commander under Lee with accession to army commander under Johnston as "the same relative position." Wigfall undoubtedly knew the difference, but the senator had long considered Longstreet a possible replacement for Braxton Bragg, commander of the Army of Tennessee.[10]

In Richmond at this time, the situation in the West was of primary concern. The loss of Vicksburg and the defeat at Gettysburg had shifted the balance in the conflict. A retrieval of Confederate fortunes appeared to rest temporarily with Bragg's army in Tennessee. The Rebels held Chattanooga, the strategic gateway to northern Georgia, but Union general William Rosecrans's army was advancing against the city and threatening to force Bragg to abandon the place. The crisis had to be met, and President Davis summoned Lee to the capital for a conference.[11]

Lee traveled to Richmond during the last week of August. Earlier, the president had suggested that Lee replace Bragg, but Lee declined. Davis now argued for a detachment of troops either from Lee's army or from southwestern Virginia. Reluctant as he had been in the past to weaken his army, Lee proposed another offensive against Meade's Federals along the Rappahannock. In fact, on August 31, Lee directed Longstreet, who commanded in Lee's absence, "to prepare the army for offensive operations." "I can see nothing better to be done," added Lee, "than to endeavor to bring General Meade out and use our efforts to crush his army while in its present condition."[12]

The letter disturbed Longstreet, who responded in length from Meadow Farm on September 2:

> I don't know that we can reasonably hope to accomplish much here by offensive operations, unless we are strong enough to cross the Potomac. If we advance to meet the enemy on this side, he will in all probability go into one of his many fortified positions. These we cannot afford to attack.
>
> I know little of the conditions of our affairs in the west, but am inclined to the opinion that our best opportunity for great results is in Tennessee. If we hold the defensive here with two corps and send the other to operate in Tenn. with that army I think that we could accomplish more than by an advance from here.
>
> The enemy seems to have settled down upon the plan of holding certain points by fortifying and defending whilst he concentrates upon others. It seems to me that this must succeed unless we concentrate ourselves, and at the same time make occasional show of active operations at all points.
>
> I know of no other means of acting upon that principle at present except to depend upon our fortifications in Va. and concentrate with one corps of this army and such as may be drawn from others, in Tennessee and destroy Rosecranz army. I feel assured that this is practicable, and that greater advantages will be gained than by any operations from here.[13]

Three days later Longstreet followed with another letter, restating his argument for sending the First Corps to Tennessee: "If my corps cannot go west, I think that we might accomplish something by giving me [Micah] Jenkins's, [Henry] Wise's, and [John] Cooke's brigades, and putting me in General Bragg's place, and giving him my corps. A good artillery battalion should go with these brigades. We would surely make no great risk in such a change and we might gain a great deal."

And then in words similar to those in his August 18 letter to Wigfall, Longstreet declared: "I feel that I am influenced by no personal motive in this suggestion, and will most cheerfully give up, when we have a fair prospect of holding our western country." Furthermore, he argued: "I doubt if General Bragg has confidence in his troops or himself either. He is not likely to do a great deal for us."[14]

These two letters, particularly the second one on the 5th, have been used as evidence of Longstreet's desire for independent command. One historian has charged that he "hungered for Bragg's command" because he advocated over a period of months a concentration in the West. Ambition, self-confidence in his own abilities, and disdain for Bragg's are evident in the letter, but Longstreet's desire for promotion was understandable. Months earlier, in March, Joseph Johnston thought Longstreet must be frustrated with his rank and position, writing to Wifgall about his friend and former subordinate: "It is, indeed, a hard case for him, the Senior Lieut. Genl. & highest in reputation, to be kept in second place." But Johnston misjudged Longstreet at that time—neither his correspondence nor subsequent writings indicate that he sought promotion. Even with Stonewall Jackson alive, Longstreet appears to have been proud to be commander of the First Corps and content as Lee's senior officer.[15]

Gettysburg changed his views, however, and now in early September, with authorities in Richmond pursuing a solution to the problems in Tennessee, he saw an opportunity for possible advancement and transfer, and acted. He also was not alone in the advocacy of a concentration in the West, and if his personal gain coincided with the strategic considerations of the Davis administration, so much the better for him. The timing of his proposal must have seemed appropriate to Longstreet. If neither Johnston nor Lee would succeed Bragg, then who was more experienced and capable in the service than himself? He may have been correct in his judgment. Tennessee attracted Longstreet with motivations more complex than the hunger of ambition.

On the day Longstreet wrote the second letter, September 5, Davis and Lee agreed to dispatch Longstreet with two infantry divisions to Bragg. The situation in Tennessee had reached a crisis—a Union force under Ambrose Burnside had seized Knoxville on the 2nd, severing the direct rail line to Virginia, and Rosecrans's army was closing on Chattanooga. If Longstreet's command was to arrive in time, they had to leave as soon as possible since with the fall of Knoxville the route had to be through the Carolinas—roughly 775 miles. The next day Lee issued the orders for the organization of the transportation and directed Longstreet to prepare the troops for movement.[16]

Dubbed "Westward Ho," the operation taxed the logistical and transportation resources of the Confederacy in a magnitude not previously known. Government agents coordinated the efforts of sixteen railroad companies, altering schedules, rerouting trains, stranding freight and passengers. On September 9 the first contingent of troops from the divisions of Lafayette McLaws and John Hood climbed on board the passenger, baggage, mail, coal, box, and flat cars—"crazy cars" to Moxley Sorrel—that were confiscated for the movement. "We all disliked very much to see this splendid section of our army leave us," stated Walter Taylor of Lee's staff. "No better troops could be found anywhere than those under General Longstreet, and he was so strong in defense.... There was never any doubt about the security of a position that was held by him."[17]

Longstreet remained another day at Meadow Farm, overseeing the loading of additional regiments. Before he boarded the train, he visited Lee's headquarters to give his farewells. Despite the disparate views of the two men, they had deep affection and respect for each other. As Longstreet placed a foot in a stirrup to mount his horse, Lee put a hand on his shoulder and said: "General, you must beat those people out there." It was not enough just to attain a victory, Longstreet replied, but Bragg must understand that he had to push the Federals "to the wall." Lee assured him that he had written to Bragg about that very matter. They shook hands, and Longstreet spurred away. It would be seven months before they saw each other again.[18]

Longstreet traveled to Richmond where he established temporary headquarters at the Spotswood Hotel. He stayed in the capital until the 14th, coordinating the movement of the troops. He dined with President Davis on the night of the 11th and secured permission to augment his force with Porter Alexander's twenty-six-gun artillery battalion. He also shuffled some brigades, taking Henry Wise's command from the capital defenses, detaching George Anderson's Georgia regiments from Hood's division for service in South Carolina, while replacing Anderson's men with the brigade of Micah Jenkins, one of his personal favorites.[19]

The assignment of Jenkins, who was the senior brigadier in the division, resulted in discontent among the command's officers, however. While passing through the city, a number of these officers urged a convalescing Hood to return to duty. Although not fully recovered from his Gettysburg wound, Hood consented. For Hood it was a difficult personal decision, for he had fallen in love with the vivacious Sally "Buck" Preston. He proposed marriage before he left, but she gave no answer. With a crippled left arm and a full heart, John Hood returned to the war.[20]

Longstreet entrained from Richmond on Monday, September 14. Before he departed, he wrote to Lee and to Wigfall. Both letters were dated the 12th, and both letters offer insight into Longstreet's thoughts as he left for Tennessee. To Lee, he stated:

If I can do anything there, it shall be done promptly. If I cannot, I shall advise you to recall me. If I did not think our move a necessary one, my regrets at leaving you would be distressing to me, as it seems to be with the officers and men of my command. Believing it to be necessary, I hope to accept it and my other personal inconveniences cheerfully and hopefully. All that we have to be proud of has been accomplished under your eye and your orders. Our affections for you are stronger, if it is possible for them to be stronger, than our admiration for you.[21]

To Wigfall, Longstreet admitted:

I have learned after much experience that one must after expressing views, fight for them if he hopes to have them adopted. So I shall hereafter contend with more pertinacity for what I know to be right. Yet I yield it in the very outset.

I don't think that I should be under Bragg. And would fight against it if I saw any hope of getting anyone in the responsible position except myself. If I should make any decided opposition the world might say that I was desirous of a position which would give me fame. So I conclude that I may be pardoned if I yield my principle under the particular circumstances.[22]

Together the letters reveal a man plagued by doubts as to the prospects ahead of him. While he was less than frank with Lee in his desire to leave the army and his "regrets" may not have been as "distressing" as he indicated, his sincerity should not be doubted in his expression of feeling toward Lee. As he told Wigfall, his problems with Lee resulted from opposing views. But the idea of serving under Bragg rankled Longstreet deeply, because he regarded the abrasive Bragg as unfit for army command. Worse yet, he saw no solution unless he actively undertook "decided opposition" to a general he held in disdain. At this time he refused to take such a course of action because of the perception it might create with the public. His state of mind portended trouble.

The journey of Longstreet and his First Corps veterans to Bragg's army was long remembered. Although the men endured crowded boxcars, hardtack, and uncooked bacon, the welcome they received from civilians compensated for the conditions on the train. "The reception of the troops all along route," Lafayette McLaws informed his wife, "was enthusiastic in the extreme dinner and supper for all comers were provided with the greatest liberality." At Sumter, South Carolina, the townsfolk fed Porter Alexander's entire battalion at one long table. Some of the artillerymen exclaimed that they had never seen so many sweet potatoes. In other villages and cities, the people shared as much as they could with the soldiers.[23]

Problems hampered the operation throughout the route. The poor condition of the tracks and the various gauges slowed the trains and caused delays. A northbound train collided with a southbound train on the Western and Atlantic Railroad north of Atlanta, killing eighteen, injuring sixty-seven, and closing the track for a day. In Raleigh, North Carolina, Georgia troops attacked the offices of the Raleigh *Standard,* a newspaper noted for its criticism of the war effort. A conductor on one of the trains demanded fares from the troops until they pointed their rifles at him and one of them barked: "I paid my fare at Gettysburg."[24]

The entire effort would take nearly three weeks to complete, but the lead elements of the First Corps reached Bragg's army by September 17. Longstreet and staff officers Moxley Sorrel and Peyton Manning arrived two days later, detraining at Catoosa Station outside Ringgold, Georgia, at two o'clock in the afternoon. When Longstreet arrived, the clamor of battle could be heard from the northwest, about fifteen miles distant. No guides or mounts awaited, and Longstreet spent another two hours on the platform until his and his aides' horses came in on a second train. "It would appear that if Bragg wanted to see anybody, Longstreet was the man," reasoned Sorrel. "But we were left to shift for ourselves." It was an inconspicuous, even embarrassing, beginning for the renowned general.[25]

Riding on the road to Ringgold, the trio snaked their way through the flotsam of a battle—the walking wounded, the stragglers, the wagons. The din of combat was unrelenting, like the bellow of two giants locked together. About sunset they veered into a seeming maze of trails through the forest. As darkness settled in, the three officers stumbled on a Federal picket post, exchanged words, and hurried away as a volley clipped through the trees behind them. "Another road was taken for Bragg, about whom by this time some hard words were passing," Sorrel recalled. About eleven o'clock, Longstreet found Bragg's headquarters at Thedford's Ford on Chickamauga Creek. An aide awakened the army commander, who was asleep in an ambulance.[26]

Bragg stirred from the ambulance and greeted Longstreet. The forty-six-year-old commander of the Army of Tennessee was an 1837 academy graduate, veteran of the Mexican War, and a favorite of President Davis's. Before Fort Sumter, Bragg secured a brigadiership in the Confederate army, followed by his promotion six months later to major general. In June 1862, he replaced P. G. T. Beauregard in command of the main western army, retaining the post through a series of defeats at Perryville, Kentucky; Stone's River or Murfreesboro, Tennessee; and the recent loss of Chattanooga. Controversy followed each setback, haunting Bragg and his senior generals, but the army commander knew he had the confidence and support of Davis in Richmond.[27]

Bragg was cursed with a personality that irritated his few friends and enraged his many enemies. A cold, even sour man, devoid of compassion, Bragg seemingly never understood people. He never refrained from blistering a subordinate in private or humiliating an officer in public. He hunted for faults in others while admitting to few in himself. He always had scapegoats for his defeats until the

number of generals and officers in the anti-Bragg faction could fill
a large room. In turn, they harbored grievances that festered like
rancid sores. Under Bragg's direction, the army knew defeat while
stewing with dissension.[28]

As a general, Bragg combined rigidity with indecisiveness. Devoted to the cause, he labored tirelessly and demonstrated ability
in strategic and tactical planning. But once a battle was joined, he
could neither adjust to the fluid nature of combat nor commit his
units at crucial moments when a battle's outcome hung in the balance. Although he had earned the troops' respect as a disciplinarian
and drillmaster, he never garnered their affection. He probably
would not have known how to react if he had.[29]

Bragg's personal and professional flaws were exacerbated by his
deteriorating physical and mental condition. A nervous individual,
he suffered particularly from headaches and dyspepsia. His ailments
worsened the natural sourness of his personality. The defeats and
imbroglios with subordinates further strained his health and mental
well-being. In June 1863 he admitted to "a general breakdown,"
and a month later his corps commanders thought him unable to
exercise field command. The recent setbacks only added to the
pressures on this ill, weary, and bitter man and general.[30]

From the time authorities in the capital had ordered the movement of Longstreet's troops to the West until this night, Bragg and
his opponent, Union Major General William Rosecrans, Longstreet's
former academy roommate, had stalked each other across the rugged terrain south of Chattanooga. When Rosecrans seized the city,
he pushed his columns in pursuit of the Confederates, dangerously
separating the corps of his army. Bragg recognized the opportunity,
but, as had been so true with this star-crossed army, the Rebels
failed to spring the traps. As usual, Bragg blamed others, and the
army retired to La Fayette, Georgia. Here, on September 15, he and
his senior officers decided to turn around and endeavor to outflank
Rosecrans, interposing their forces between the enemy and Chattanooga. Bragg vacillated again, however, and the Southerners did
not close on the Yankee army, which was deployed in the valley
of West Chickamauga Creek, until September 18. By nightfall the
Confederates encamped in the woods east of the creek, huddling
against the cold and awaiting another day's light.[31]

It was into a nightmarish landscape for warriors that the Confederates plunged on the morning of September 19. Forests and thick-

ets covered much of the bottomland along the Chickamauga, which a Rebel thought was "too large for the appellation of creek and yet does not rise to the dignity of a river." Cleared farmers' fields broke the solidity of the trees, and a network of roads crisscrossed the ground. While the roads provided avenues of march and the fields offered open firing spaces, the terrain hampered coordination among units and defied the efforts of the best of generals. The battle would belong to the men in the ranks.[32]

Bragg's assault plan was predicated on faulty intelligence and initiated under imprecise orders. Believing that the left flank of Rosecrans's army lay opposite Lee and Gordon's Mill, Bragg directed a sweep up the creek against the flank, crushing the position and driving for the La Fayette Road. If that road and the Dry Valley Road fell into Confederate hands, the Yankees' most viable retreat routes to Chattanooga would be severed. But confusion at headquarters and among subordinates, and aggressiveness on the part of Rosecrans, disrupted Bragg's plans from the outset. The Southern commander never had control of the combat, but his units still cut the Federal lines in half late in the afternoon. The attackers could not sustain their penetration, however, and retired. The fighting was consuming and deadly. Darkness ended the bloodletting, but with it came plunging temperatures that increased the suffering of the thousands of wounded.[33]

Well after nightfall, Bragg's ranking officers began filtering in to army headquarters. Lieutenant General Leonidas Polk, a trained soldier and a bishop in the Episcopal Church, arrived first, about nine o'clock. Bragg told Polk that the army was to be reorganized into two wings for the next day's action, and Polk would command the Right Wing while Longstreet would be given direction of the Left Wing when he arrived. The decision relegated Lieutenant General Harvey Hill, Longstreet's comrade and friend who had been serving in the West since late summer, to corps command under Polk. The proud and quarrelsome Hill could not possibly welcome such a change. Of the two generals, Hill was the better officer and more redoubtable fighter.[34]

The Right Wing, Bragg added, was to renew the attack at daylight against the enemy's left flank. Polk rebutted that the day's combat had shown Rosecrans had piled units into that sector, and one Federal corps overlapped Polk's flank and rear. The bishop asked for more troops, but Bragg assured him they would not be neces-

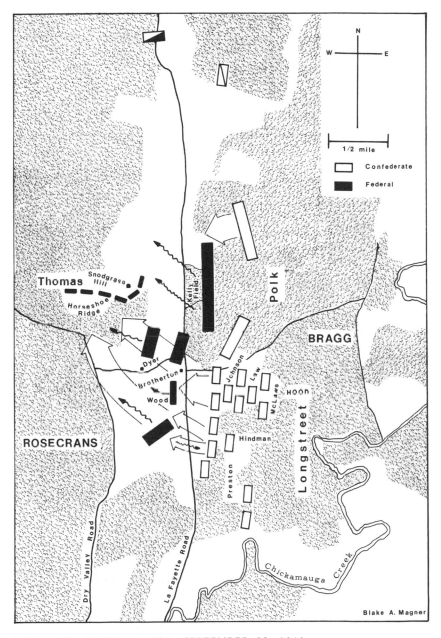

BATTLE OF CHICKAMAUGA, SEPTEMBER 20, 1863.

sary. That settled it, and Polk departed with his oral instructions. Bragg then crawled into the ambulance for a few hours' sleep, not knowing the whereabouts of the commander of the army's Left Wing.[35]

This was the situation into which Longstreet reported. His dark assessment of Bragg's generalship had merit. He and Bragg conferred privately for nearly an hour. The commanding general handed Longstreet a crude map of the area, noted the general positions of the antagonists, and summarized the plan for the morning's contest. Longstreet would command Major General Simon Buckner's corps, Major General Thomas Hindman's division of Polk's corps, Brigadier General Bushrod Johnson's provisional division, his own troops on the field under John Hood, who had led them in the day's fighting, and three artillery battalions. Longstreet would begin his advance once Polk's en echelon attack—each division advancing after the unit on its right moved forward—reached the Left Wing. According to Sorrel, Longstreet was evidently satisfied with the plan, and after Bragg retired to the ambulance, he and his aides lay down on a bed of leaves for some sleep.[36]

Longstreet returned to the saddle at daylight, riding in search of his command. One of the first officers he found was his former academy classmate, Major General Alexander P. Stewart, whose division of Buckner's corps held the right front of the wing. Longstreet described the plan to his old friend and instructed him to move forward and make contact with the Right Wing. From there Longstreet moved along his lines, meeting Buckner, Hindman, and Brigadier General William Preston, a division commander under Buckner. When John Hood met his superior, the subordinate welcomed him warmly and asserted that "the feeling of the officers and men was never better." Longstreet, Hood recalled later, "responded with that confidence which had so often contributed to his extraordinary success, that we would *of course* whip and drive him from the field. I could but exclaim that I was rejoiced to hear him so express himself, as he was the first general I had met since my arrival who talked to victory." When Bragg's veterans saw Longstreet, they gave him a new nickname, "Bull of the Woods."[37]

The generals briefed Longstreet on the situation as they knew it. Roughly six hundred yards through the woods to the front, or west, lay the La Fayette Road, beyond which the Federals were deployed behind crude breastworks in the forest. To understand the terrain better, Longstreet talked to a Confederate soldier, Tom Brotherton, whose family's farm abutted the roadway and in whose woods the enemy was posted. After further discussion, Longstreet decided to concentrate his assault force against that point in the Union lines, placing Tom Brotherton's homestead in the direct path of the attackers.[38]

Although the alignment of his units as he found them favored such a deployment, Longstreet would pack eight brigades into a deep column of attack on a narrow front. Two of Bushrod Johnson's brigades formed the front line, with his third brigade in direct support to the rear. Behind Johnson, Hood's three brigades, stacked in a similar formation, lengthened the column. For the final line, Longstreet designated the two brigades of Lafayette McLaws's division, which were en route to the field and would arrive before the advance. He gave Hood overall command of the force, with Brigadier General Evander Law directing Hood's brigades.[39]

On the left of Johnson's troops, Thomas Hindman aligned his brigades in a similar formation—two brigades in the front, one in reserve. William Preston's division of three brigades extended Hindman's line to the south, completing the front of the Left Wing. Once the other units advanced, Preston's command would act as the pivot in a projected wheeling movement to the left. Longstreet also planned to support the assault with whatever cannon could be rolled forward in the confining terrain.[40]

The scheme fashioned by Longstreet on this morning illustrated his tactical thought and demonstrated his skill as a battlefield commander. He believed that if an attack was to be delivered, it required depth to preserve its momentum. Its striking power could be sustained either with an en echelon assault, which he had used at Second Manassas and on the second day at Gettysburg, or with a narrow column, which he would use on the field at Chickamauga. Battlefield conditions, terrain, and enemy dispositions dictated which mode should be employed, but Longstreet preferred a column of assault. He thought that no defenders without fortifications could withstand the pounding from successive waves of attackers.[41]

In a postwar letter to Porter Alexander, he explained his thinking: "With a column say of four or five brigades, if the 1st and 2nd are broken or dispersed by the assault, the 3rd, in turn, finds itself in full strength and force, and near enough the enemies lines to break thru. The force is strong enough in itself to give it confidence as long as it is in order." The size of contending forces, the distances covered by the battlefields, and the rifled musket, he added, re-shaped his views from what he had learned in Mexico. Attacks during the Civil War were delivered across hundreds of yards of ground against opponents who could kill and maim at greater ranges. To negate those advantages of defending forces, the assault column must possess numerical strength and depth. Chickamauga, he concluded, exemplified the evolution of his tactical views during the war.[42]

Shortly after 11:00 A.M., Longstreet's giant lance of Confederate infantry—eight brigades tiered in five lines—rolled forward. While he had seen to the details of his attack, he had waited all morning for the noise of Leonidas Polk's legions going into battle. But confusion, undelivered orders, apathy, and bungling delayed the advance of the Right Wing for hours. Finally, at 9:30 A.M., Major General John C. Breckinridge's troops initiated the error-plagued offensive, and the sound of the gunfire drifted toward Longstreet. He dispatched a courier to Bragg, suggesting that he "had probably better make my attack." The Confederate commander, meanwhile, had hurried a staff officer to the Left Wing with orders for an advance. Suddenly, to Longstreet's surprise, he heard the explosion of musketry from the direction of Alexander P. Stewart's division, his right front unit. Minutes later someone informed him that Stewart had been directed forward by Bragg, so Longstreet immediately sent his staff officers to start Hood's command.[43]

Johnson's Tennesseans drove through the timber, spearheading Longstreet's attack. Ahead of them, beyond the Brotherton farm and fields, Union Brigadier General Thomas Wood was pulling his division out of line, shifting it to the north. Wood had reacted to an order sent from army headquarters that directed him to move to the left and seal an alleged gap in the line. Some of Wood's subordinates questioned the wisdom of the movement, but the division commander was adamant in his decision to obey. Skirmish fire from the front indicated the presence of the enemy, but Wood began the withdrawal despite the ominous crackle. It was, as Wood supposedly described it, "the fatal order of the day."[44]

Clearing the woods east of La Fayette Road, Johnson's Rebels swept across the Brotherton property and poured into the gap created by Wood's retirement. Federal units on either side of the breach fought stubbornly. The Confederates, however, surged through the woods and into a large field owned by the Dyer family. Behind Johnson, Law's three brigades were closing, swinging to the right where they slammed into a Federal division. These veterans of the Army of Northern Virginia had tangled with the enemy the day before and told their comrades in Bragg's army that they had "come down from Virginia to help you fellows." Their assistance was welcomed as the woods near the Dyer field erupted in gun-fire.[45]

Longstreet, meanwhile, had ridden with Simon Buckner to Thomas Hindman's division to order it forward. A lieutenant in the brigade of Brigadier General Zachariah Deas watched Longstreet and six days later remarked in a letter: "Longstreet is the boldest and bravest looking man I ever saw. I don't think he would dodge if a shell were to burst under his chin." Deas introduced himself to the wing commander, and Longstreet explained where he wanted the brigadier's Alabamians to go in on Johnson's left. As Deas's troops advanced, followed by Hindman's other brigades, Longstreet watched and then turned back toward the Brotherton farm.[46]

The entry of Hindman's division into the fighting resulted in the collapse of the Federal right. In forty minutes the Southerners hammered into pieces two Union divisions, whose members streamed westward and northward away from the carnage. The plan was for the Confederates to swing to the south once they had pierced the enemy lines, but when Johnson knifed through the gap and Law veered northward toward the collapsing enemy front, the Rebels wheeled northward. Two of Hindman's brigades—Deas's and Patton Anderson's—came within three hundred yards of the vital Dry Valley Road when Union regiments smashed into Brigadier General Arthur Manigault's brigade on Deas's left. Manigault's men broke under the onslaught, stopping Hindman's advance.[47]

Longstreet soon learned of Manigault's rout and concluded that a swing to the left would uncover his right flank. He agreed to Hood's request to advance with Johnson's and Law's troops against Federal cannon and regrouped infantry in the woods north and east of the Dyer field, sent instructions for Hindman to move northward as support for Johnson, and dispatched a courier to Major General Joseph Wheeler with orders for the cavalry officer to cross Chicka-mauga Creek and secure the left flank of the infantry. He then rode ahead to follow the action of Hood's troops.[48]

The Confederates charged across Dyer field into a wall of resistance. The combat surged in intensity. On Law's right, Brigadier General Henry Benning's Georgians routed one brigade only to be struck on the right flank by an enemy counterattack. The Georgians scampered back, with Benning riding off the field on an artillery horse, seeking Longstreet. He soon found the wing commander and exclaimed: "General, I am ruined. My brigade was suddenly attacked and every man killed. Not one is to be found. Please give orders where I can do some fighting."

Longstreet looked at the excited officer, who he knew was a good brigadier, and calmly said: "Nonsense, General. You are not so badly hurt. Look about you. I know you will find at least one man, and with him on his feet, report your brigade to me, and you two shall have a place in the fighting line." Benning recovered his composure and hurried away to rally his men.[49]

At some point in the action, perhaps before the Benning incident, Colonel Thomas Claiborne, who was serving temporarily on Buckner's staff, located Longstreet. He had been searching for the lieutenant general along the line because he had brought a message from Buckner that the corps commander was holding William Preston's division in reserve. When they met, according to Claiborne, Longstreet "had sort of a toothpick in his mouth, and thoughtfully gazed at me." When the staff officer began relaying the message, an artillery shell whirled past, and he ducked. "I see you salute them," joked Longstreet.

"Yes, every time," responded Claiborne.

"If there is a shell or bullet over there destined for us," Longstreet drawled, "it will find us."

Longstreet then directed Claiborne to tell Buckner that "if I send again, to send a Brigade."[50]

It was approximately one o'clock, and John Hood was being carried off the battlefield. The splendid fighter had been with his troops from the outset, and as he was riding away from his old Texas Brigade to rush Brigadier General Joseph Kershaw's South Carolinians into the combat, he was hit in the right leg, the bullet smashing into the bone just below the hip. A courier and some Texans put him on a litter, and he was carried to the rear, where a surgeon amputated the leg. Without Hood, the Confederate assault lost cohesion.[51]

Longstreet was close at hand—in the Dyer field. Here Brigadier General Benjamin G. Humphreys, leading the Mississippi brigade

behind Kershaw, met Longstreet. Humphreys had commanded the
Mississippians since William Barksdale's death at Gettysburg. As the
two generals reined up, Humphreys saluted and looked at Longstreet's face. "I never saw him wear so bright and jubilant a countenance," remembered the brigadier. Longstreet returned the salute
and jokingly said: "Drive them, General. These western men can't
stand it any better than the Yankees we left in Virginia. Drive 'em."[52]

Humphreys spurred away to "drive them" as Longstreet rode
eastward toward the Brotherton farm. Kershaw's and Humphreys's
brigades assailed the so-called Horseshoe Ridge beyond the Dyer
field. On this crest the Federals had rallied under the direction of
Major General George Thomas, commander of the Fourteenth
Corps. Thomas was a Virginian who had remained loyal to the
Union despite his family's vehement objection. There was no better
general in Rosecrans's army than this redoubtable warrior, and if
the day could be salvaged, it fell to Thomas. On Horseshoe Ridge
and to the north on Snodgrass Hill and in Kelly Field, Thomas made
his stand against both wings of Bragg's army.[53]

When Kershaw and Humphreys advanced toward the ridge, they
encountered a "terrific fire" and recoiled. It would be nearly another hour before the Confederates tried again, and when they did,
the result was the same, a bloody repulse for Johnson's brigades
and Kershaw's South Carolinians. A lull followed as the Confederates regrouped and brought up reinforcements. It would be after
three o'clock before they reentered the fury.[54]

During this interlude, Longstreet left the direction of the battle
to his subordinates. In his memoirs, he stated that he ordered
Bushrod Johnson to allow the men to rest and to reorganize the
units before resuming the attack. He had already instructed Hindman to move into position on Johnson's left and must have thought
that he could do little more. He directed that lunch be prepared
while he rode with Buckner along the lines.[55]

The two generals and their staffs rode northward "to view the
changed conditions of the battle." Skirmishers from both armies
sniped at each other. Passing beyond his right flank, Longstreet and
the others went forward into the woods, believing that they had
gone beyond the Federal lines. Instead, they approached the right
flank of the Union line in Kelly Field that opposed Polk's wing and
came under picket fire. Turning around, the Rebels headed south,
toward Humphreys's position. Longstreet ordered Buckner to bring

up the reserve artillery of twelve cannon to secure his right flank. But the generals and their aides had missed a half-mile gap in the Federal lines between Kelly Field and Horseshoe Ridge. The heavily forested terrain limited the range of vision, but neither Longstreet nor Buckner seemed to grasp the importance of their collision with the Federals. "I saw enough, however, to mark the ground line of his field-works," Longstreet wrote in his memoirs. If he had conferred with Humphreys, he must have learned of the extent of the enemy line in front of the Mississippians. In the end, why Longstreet did not recognize the significance of his encounter with the enemy "is something of a mystery," according to a historian of the battle.[56]

Longstreet and Buckner returned to the vicinity of the Brotherton farm, where they sat down to a lunch of bacon and sweet potatoes. "We were not accustomed to potatoes of any kind in Virginia," Longstreet remembered, "and thought we had a luxury." Before they finished, an artillery shell howled in and exploded above their heads. A fragment grazed Peyton Manning's scalp, and he began gasping for breath. Officers rushed to his assistance, believing that he had been mortally wounded. Instead, he was choking on a piece of potato that he had bitten off just before the shell burst. Someone removed it, and Manning revived quickly.[57]

A short time later, Major William Miller Owen of the Washington Artillery, who was acting as chief of artillery for Preston's division, came upon the lunch party. Recognizing Owen, Longstreet called him over to the log on which he and Buckner were seated. Longstreet asked for some tobacco, and Owen handed him his bag, from which the general filled a meerschaum pipe. The artillery officer asked if the Federals had been beaten. "Yes," answered Longstreet, "all along the line. A few are holding out upon the ridge up yonder. Not many, though. If we had had our Virginia army here, we could have whipped them in half the time." He then continued: "By the by, don't you want some guns for your command? I think my men must have captured fifty today." Owen replied that he did, and Longstreet said: "Well, you can have as many as you want."

"General," Owen remarked, "hadn't you better put that in writing?"

Laughing, Longstreet told Osmun Latrobe to write the order, and Owen departed. He had new cannon; Longstreet had some tobacco.[58]

This exchange between Owen and Longstreet, if accurately recounted, revealed a commander confident of success. He had Preston's fresh division nearby to augment the assault force, and despite the repulse of two attempts, he evidently believed that a coordinated thrust would secure the ridge. But Longstreet underestimated the numerical strength and grit of the blue-coated defenders and knew nothing of the squabbling between Hindman and Johnson about who was in command on the front line. Without Hood's spirit and talent, the odds for a concerted push had diminished. Longstreet should have personally directed the effort. He relinquished control of the offensive to subordinates, a method of command similar to Robert E. Lee's, which he had used on previous battlefields. If he had intended to return to the front and oversee the attack, however, his plans changed when a courier brought a message from Bragg to report to army headquarters.[59]

When Longstreet rode up, he briefly summarized the situation on his front to Bragg and requested reinforcements from Polk's wing for a final push that could secure the Dry Valley Road and seize the McFarland and Rossville gaps, cutting off the Federals from Chattanooga. But Longstreet saw at once that Bragg was in no mood "to hear suggestions from subordinates for other moves or progressive work." Bragg seemed to think that the battle had been lost and growled in response to Longstreet. "There is not a man in the Right Wing who has any fight in him." "From accounts of his former operations," Longstreet wrote afterward, "I was prepared for halting work, but this, when the battle was at its tide and in partial success, was a little surprising." Longstreet said nothing more, and Bragg rode away, a general blinded by the Furies that consumed his soul. To Longstreet "there was nothing for the left wing to do but work along as best it could."[60]

The Left Wing began to "work along" at 3:30 P.M. when Bushrod Johnson ordered Thomas Hindman's brigades to renew the assault against Horseshoe Ridge. For the next four hours, even after nightfall had darkened the woods, the combat between the opponents engulfed the battlefield. Confederate attackers endured the withering musketry, grabbed footholds on the ridge and knolls, only to be punched back. Nearly every brigade of the Left Wing, including Preston's unscathed units, was engaged in the fighting. The Federal grip on the ridge weakened, and at five o'clock Union general George Thomas ordered the divisions east of the La Fayette Road in the Kelly Field to withdraw incrementally to secure the escape route to Chattanooga. Against these units, Polk's Right Wing was applying pressure. Casualties on both sides reached staggering levels as the Confederates mounted new assaults. The final Southern effort against Horseshoe Ridge went forward amid the shadows at seven o'clock.[61]

Longstreet assumed little personal direction of the combat, but he acted in response to the conditions as he grasped them. Shortly after five o'clock he instructed Thomas Claiborne to write a dispatch to Joseph Wheeler, ordering the cavalry commander to move "with celerity" down the Dry Valley Road and enfilade the Federal line with artillery. But it came too late for Wheeler, whose path had been blocked by enemy horsemen. The Yankees' resistance secured strings of wagons and kept the vital road open long enough.[62]

Just after Longstreet sent the message to Wheeler, Moxley Sorrel galloped up. The chief of staff reported that he had been to the front near the Kelly Field and saw Federal infantry retreating northward on the La Fayette Road. Sorrel urged Stewart to attack at once, but, Sorrel related, Stewart refused "unless assured the orders came direct from Longstreet." He told Stewart to prepare to move and that he would be back with confirmation from the wing commander. "Longstreet's thunderous tones need not be described" when he heard of Stewart's refusal. Sorrel raced back with the orders, and Stewart's men went in, bagging prisoners and assisting in pushing the enemy out of Kelly Field. Shielded by darkness, the Federals abandoned the battlefield.[63]

Longstreet wrote in his memoirs that "like magic the Union army had melted away in our presence." In fact, contrary to his subsequent assertions, he and many other Confederate officers thought the Yankees remained on the field. Fatigue, confusion, entangled commands, and the forested terrain contributed to the uncertainty and mistaken beliefs among the Confederates. It was not until well after daylight on the 21st that the Southerners knew with assurance the enemy had fled.[64]

Braxton Bragg joined Longstreet at the latter's campsite about sunrise on the 21st. Bragg asked for advice, and according to Longstreet, he urged that the army march at once to Chattanooga, cross the Tennessee River north of the city, and force Rosecrans's beaten army out of its fortifications. If the Rebels could not pursue the retreating enemy, they should advance against Union general Ambrose Burnside at Knoxville. Bragg, wrote Longstreet, concurred and "stated that he would follow that course."[65]

In his report, Bragg implied that Longstreet had advised this operation, but he argued that "such a movement was utterly impossible for want of transportation." Bragg was correct in his judgment, for the army suffered from a critical shortage of wagons, livestock, and rations. The addition of Longstreet's units to the army only worsened the situation because they arrived without wagons. Furthermore, asserted Bragg, the proposition "abandoned to the enemy our entire line of communication and laid open to him our depots of supplies." Finally, the army did not have the means either to cross the river or to operate at length in the rugged terrain. Bragg acidly referred to it as "a visionary scheme." For the present, Bragg rightly judged that the Confederates could pursue the enemy only to Chattanooga.[66]

The army commander vacillated throughout the 21st, however, and did not authorize a full pursuit by the entire army until the next day. During the 21st, he learned of the shattered condition of the Federal army from Brigadier General Nathan Bedford Forrest. A superb cavalry officer and relentless foe, Forrest dogged the enemy rear toward Chattanooga. At 9:00 A.M. he wrote to Leonidas Polk: "I think they [the enemy] are retreating as hard as they can go." The Northerners were felling trees to slow down the Rebels, added Forrest, and "I think we ought to press forward as rapidly as possible." When he heard nothing in response, Forrest sent a second, more urgent message and then rode back to the army. He met Bragg and argued for an immediate pursuit, but Bragg hesitated because of a shortage of supplies. Allegedly, Forrest stormed: "General Bragg, we can get all the supplies our army needs in Chattanooga."[67]

The Confederate infantry marched after the Federals on the 22nd, led by Lafayette McLaws's division. McLaws approached the Union works outside the city and threatened an assault. According to one of Longstreet's staff officers, Longstreet ordered McLaws to drive the enemy, but McLaws demurred, arguing that he would incur heavy losses and needed more ambulances. When the aide reported this to Longstreet, his "only remark was a wish that the ambulances were in a hotter place than Chattanooga." The staff officer concluded: "Longstreet did not love McLaws."[68]

The Confederate army filed into position on Missionary Ridge, south of Chattanooga, on September 23. Below them, the enemy manned the city's defenses. Two weeks of maneuver and two days of fearful battle had brought them back to Chattanooga. The Chickamauga Campaign had ended.[69]

Chickamauga, in the words of Francis Lawley, the British newspaperman, was "another American massacre." In the number of casualties, the two-day battle was exceeded by only four other Civil War engagements. Federal losses exceeded sixteen thousand; Confederate, eighteen thousand. A Georgian with Longstreet attested in a letter: "I never saw so many wonded men in my life." One of Hood's Texans described it as "the meanest, most unsatisfactory place I struck during the war." It was a sentiment shared by thousands of other men, whether in Union blue or Confederate gray.[70]

Longstreet subsequently called the battle "a tussle in the wilderness. . . . Simply a test of physical forces without a chance for strategical manoeuvre or brilliant assault." He believed that Chickamauga was notable because of "the sanguinary severity of the fight and the heroism of the troops." In his report, he stated that the conduct of his officers and men was "worthy of the highest praise and admiration." To him, the Confederate victory belonged to the soldiers in the ranks and to the officers who led them into the terrible fury.[71]

To many in the army, however, the battle's outcome resulted from Longstreet's generalship. According to a story that circulated in Richmond days afterward, Major General John Breckinridge rode along his line on September 21, and his men cheered him. Halting, Breckinridge allegedly exclaimed: "Longstreet is the man, boys, Longstreet is the man." Newspaperman Lawley reported later that the sentiment in the army was that "never in the war has any General been found who was superior to General Longstreet in the art of what is here called 'putting in his men.'" Lawley averred that "his well-known and inspiring presence" on a battlefield was "equivalent to a thousand fresh men."[72]

From Virginia, Robert E. Lee wrote Longstreet five days after the battle: "If it gives you as much pleasure to receive my warmest congratulations as it does me to convey them, this letter will not have been written in vain. My whole heart and soul have been with you and your brave corps in your late battle. It was natural to hear of Longstreet and [Harvey] Hill charging side by side, and pleasing to find the armies of the east and west vying with each other in valour and devotion to their country." Then Lee added: "Finish the work before you, my dear general, and return to me. I want you badly and you cannot get back too soon."[73]

Contemporary praise for Longstreet has echoed down through the years since Chickamauga. Some biographers of the general have regarded the battle as his finest performance of the war. In one work, it was claimed that "Chickamauga was the high-water mark in Longstreet's career." In another, a biographer regarded the engagement as "the greatest achievement of his career. A lesser soldier might not have been able to launch an attack of any kind; Longstreet's action gave the Federals one of their worst defeats of the war. Luck, in the form of an accidental gap in the Union lines, played a major role. But if we describe this as the primary reason for the victory we ignore the valor and skill of both Longstreet and his men."[74]

Indisputably, Longstreet's presence on the battlefield on September 20 was the decisive factor on the Confederate side. He imposed his will and, most important, order on the Left Wing of the army. His tactical arrangement of the units—a narrow, deep column of attack—proved to be the ideal formation for the terrain and conditions on the field. While he lost firm control of the units once the attack began in the forests, he managed to send additional units into the fighting at timely intervals. His was not a flawless performance, but it was unequaled in the Confederate army.

Longstreet, however, merits further recognition. The orderliness and the mode of attack rank him as one of the preeminent combat generals of the war. Few officers of that rank grasped the realities of or situation on a battlefield better than Longstreet. He saw what would not work at Gettysburg and fashioned what would work at Chickamauga. He had advocated the strategic combination that brought him and his troops to Chickamauga and then utilized his intellect and experience to formulate the tactical scheme that brought victory. It was the performance of a first-rate soldier, of a man who knew his trade.

Nearly a century later, a soldier of another of America's wars offered his assessment of Longstreet at Chickamauga. A combat general of World War II wrote to a Civil War historian:

> There were two kinds of officers in the Civil War, on both sides. Neither were schooled beyond the basic training at West Point. One

sort never learned anything—kept making the same mistakes over and over again. The other sort had the intellectual capacity to reason; to calculate what would work and why. Such was Longstreet. His attack in depth was the perfect solution. Today army schools teach the attack in depth for an envelopment (which Longstreet made), and when the situation is obscure. But no one taught it to him. He figured that one himself.[75]

16

"NOTHING BUT THE HAND OF GOD CAN SAVE US"

Long ago fortune had abandoned the Confederate Army of Tennessee, and now, after its greatest victory, fortune returned as mockery. Chickamauga's dead had not been buried before its ghosts haunted the command. Within days of the battle's conclusion, the months of dissension within the officer's ranks boiled over into a bitter, enervating controversy. The Army of Tennessee's corps commanders plotted to remove their commander, while he suspended from duty two of the army's senior generals. The affair enhanced none of the participants' reputations as the fate of thousands of troops and perhaps the Confederacy hung in the balance. At the center of it stood Braxton Bragg, Jefferson Davis, and Longstreet.

The controversy embraced a period of roughly three weeks, but its roots were sunk deeply in the soul of the army. Bragg was a figure of nearly universal contempt within the upper ranks. In the view of Major J. W. Ratchford of Harvey Hill's staff, the commanding general "possessed the faculty of alienating every able man whom he came in contact." Bragg's own chief of staff, Brigadier General William Mackall, who had known him since their days together as classmates at West Point, confessed in a letter that "he is very earnest at his work, his whole soul is in it, but his manner is repulsive and he has no social life. He is easily flattered and fond of seeing reverence for his high position. . . . If he don't want news to be true, he will listen to nothing."[1]

Bragg had an appalling lack of insight into the frailties of the human condition. "He is as much influenced by his enemies as by his friends," declared Mackall, "and does not know how to control the one or preserve the other." Reluctantly, Mackall conceded a little over a week after Chickamauga that "frankly, I am afraid of his Generalship, and would think the cause of the country far better, placed in other hands. That he may have success I pray and wish, but he has not genius, and if our circumstances make this call upon him, he will fail in our hour of need. His mind is not fertile nor his judgment good."[2]

Captain Charles Blackford, who had come west with Longstreet's troops, saw enough to be convinced, as he wrote his wife, that "Bragg ought to be relieved or disaster is sure to result. The men have no faith." The reason for the army's low morale was evident, Blackford believed. He stated:

> The difference between this army and Lee's is very striking. When the men move in the Army of Northern Virginia, they think they are doing the proper thing, whether it be backward or forward, and if all the success anticipated is not secured, at all events it is not Lee's fault. Down here the men seem to feel the wrong thing is being done whatever it be and when success is secured they attribute it to anybody else than Bragg. Thus they give the whole credit of Chickamauga to Longstreet.[3]

Ironically, then, it was the victory at Chickamauga that ignited the grievances that had been simmering since the beginning of the year. Bragg viewed himself as a victim, as a commander cursed by subordinates who had disobeyed orders, who refused to cooperate, and who neglected their duty. In his mind, the campaign and battle could have been a more decisive achievement if his plans had been executed as prescribed. On September 28, he struck at the two main culprits—Lieutenant General Leonidas Polk and Major General Thomas Hindman—suspending both men from duty and ordering them to Atlanta. Bragg charged Polk with "failure to attack the enemy at daylight" on the 20th, and Hindman with disobedience of orders in not assailing a Federal force in McLemore's Cove in the operations prior to the battle. Before Bragg acted, Mackall warned him "there will be great dissatisfaction." But, Mackall testified, "he is hard to persuade when in prosperity."[4]

Bragg should have heeded Mackall's advice, but in his myopia, he most likely underestimated the opposition, both in numbers and influence. Even before Bragg suspended Polk and Hindman, his corps commanders—Longstreet, Polk, Harvey Hill, and Simon Buckner—met secretly on September 26. To them, the victory at Chickamauga had been squandered because of Bragg's incompetency—he had issued vague orders during the battle, had little or no grasp of the situation on the field, and had failed to pursue a defeated foe, missing an opportunity to retake Chattanooga and possibly Middle Tennessee. At the meeting, Longstreet and Polk consented to write authorities in Richmond and Robert E. Lee, arguing for Bragg's removal from command, with either Lee or Beauregard as his replacement.[5]

The anti-Bragg faction had finally coalesced. For months the group had needed a leader, a catalyst, and it seemed that Longstreet was that man. He was the senior lieutenant general; he possessed a stature and reputation unmatched by the others; his voice would be listened to in the capital and by Lee; and he shared the others' personal and professional disdain for Bragg. Although he carefully underplayed his role in the affair, Longstreet served as the faction's leader, or as Lafayette McLaws described him, "the nominal head of [the] cabal."[6]

His letter of September 26 to Secretary of War James Seddon, for instance, was a damning indictment of Bragg's generalship. "May I take the liberty to advise you of our condition and our wants?" began Longstreet. Chickamauga, he asserted, was the "most complete victory of the war," except perhaps for First Manassas. Then, after briefly recounting the operations since the 21st, he went to the heart of the matter: "To express my convictions in a few words, our chief has done but one thing that he ought to have done since I joined his army. That was to order the attack upon the 20th. All other things that he has done he ought not to have done. I am convinced that nothing but the hand of God can save us or help us as long as we have our present commander."

Longstreet continued: "Now to our wants. Can't you send us General Lee?" The Army of Northern Virginia could remain on the defensive, Longstreet argued, while the army in Tennessee assumed the offensive until the state was recovered. "We need some such great mind as General Lee's (nothing more) to accomplish. You will be surprised to learn that this army has neither organization nor mobility, and I have doubts if its commander can give it them." As for himself, the lieutenant general stated:

In an ordinary war I could serve without complaint under one whom the Government might place in authority, but we have too much at stake in this to remain quiet under such distressing circumstances. ...When I came here, I hoped to find our commander willing and anxious to do all things that would aid us in our great cause, and ready to receive what aid he could get from his subordinates. It seems that I was greatly mistaken. It seems that he cannot adopt and adhere to any plan or course, whether of his own or of someone else. I desire to impress upon your mind that there is no exaggeration in these statements.[7]

While Longstreet's evaluation of Bragg's generalship may have been accurate, the letter reflected duplicity and self-promotion on his part. It was, as McLaws wrote afterward, "simply preposterous" to think that President Davis and Secretary Seddon would transfer Lee without the general's accord. Earlier, Lee had rejected that idea. Furthermore, Longstreet had preconceived notions about Bragg, had not wanted to serve under him, and consequently was not an impartial judge of his abilities. Contrary to what he told Seddon, he expected difficulty with Bragg when he came west. Finally, his role was motivated, in part, by his willingness to accept command of the army. McLaws subsequently alleged that one of the "conspirators" recommended Longstreet as a successor to Bragg.[8]

Longstreet, however, did not stop at official correspondence. If Mackall is to be believed, and there exists no reason to suspect otherwise, Longstreet undermined Bragg's authority and respect among the generals through conversations. Longstreet, wrote Mackall, "is talking about him [Bragg] in a way to destroy all his usefulness." In another letter, Mackall informed Joseph Johnston: "I think Longstreet has done more injury to the general than all the others put together. You may understand how much influence with his troops a remark from a man of his standing would have to the effect that B. was not on the field and Lee would have been."[9]

On October 4, Longstreet, Buckner, and Hill met for a second time in secrecy. They agreed to prepare a petition for Davis that requested the removal of Bragg and to secure the signatures of generals who supported them. Authorship of the petition has been debated ever since, but the evidence indicates that Hill wrote it and Buckner made alterations in the document. Each general, however, kept the paper at his headquarters for a period of time to gather signatures. In all, a dozen generals signed, and it was forwarded to the president.[10]

Bragg learned of the meeting and the petition that night, causing him "much distress and mortification," in the words of Mackall. "I do believe," wrote the chief of staff of his commander the next day, "he thought himself popular. . . . Bragg has the misfortune of not knowing a friend from a foe, and taking subserviency as evidence of friendship." That same day, October 5, Bragg telegraphed Davis, importuning the president to intercede.[11]

In Richmond, Davis read Bragg's telegram and another one from Colonel James Chesnut, the president's trusted aide whom he had sent to Tennessee to assess the situation. Hoping that Chickamauga would silence the bickering and soften the rancor within the army, Davis had counseled Bragg against the suspensions of Polk and Hindman. When Bragg could not be dissuaded, Davis had ordered Chesnut to Tennessee. Now he had the aide's wire: "Your immediate presence in this army is urgently demanded." The beleaguered president left the capital by train the next morning, October 6. Before he departed, Davis hinted to Seddon that Bragg would remain in command.[12]

Davis arrived at his destination on the afternoon of October 9. He closeted himself at once with Bragg, who asked to be relieved of command, but the president rejected the request for the present until he had conferred with the corps commanders. Soon Longstreet, Buckner, Hill, and Major General Benjamin Cheatham, the senior division commander in Polk's corps, joined Davis and Bragg at army headquarters. While en route to the army, Davis had spoken with Polk in Atlanta and had heard the suspended officer's views. With Bragg sitting in a corner of the room, the president asked each general for his opinion of the conduct of the recent campaign.[13]

Longstreet spoke first, but reluctantly, and only after prodding from Davis. The general presented an assessment of the campaign and then stated that Bragg "was incompetent to manage an army or put men into a fight," adding that the commanding general "knew nothing of the business." Buckner and Cheatham followed Longstreet, endorsing his views. It was probably not what Davis expected to hear, at least not with Bragg present, listening to every word.[14]

Harvey Hill, meanwhile, like Bragg, sat in a corner, silent, "apparently trying to be overlooked," in Longstreet's words. Davis, however, "forced" Hill to speak, and the North Carolinian moved his chair into the center of the circle. Hill replied slowly, admitting how proud he had been upon his promotion to lieutenant general and how willing he had been to serve under Bragg, whom he had known in the antebellum army. But, avowed the caustic general, "he was never so mistaken in his estimate of a man's character as a soldier." When Hill finished, Davis adjourned the meeting. As the generals rode away, Buckner told Longstreet that he was certain Bragg would be relieved of command.[15]

On October 10, Davis visited the army's lines—a Georgia lieutenant thought the president "looks like the God of famine. He is a dried up specimen of humanity"—and conferred privately and individually with Longstreet and Buckner. "The interview was exciting, at times warm," remembered Longstreet. The general volunteered to resign at once or take a leave of absence and then resign, but Davis rebuffed both proposals. When the president started to leave, the two men walked together a short distance and shook hands. Longstreet sensed trouble ahead for him and his corps.[16]

The next morning on Missionary Ridge, the president, Bragg, and the corps commanders discussed strategy. Little was resolved except to maintain the siege of Chattanooga and await developments. Davis gave no intimation whether Bragg would be retained. On October 12, in a brief speech, Davis removed all speculation, endorsing Bragg and dismissing all the "shafts of malice" aimed at the army commander. He stayed with the army another day, then boarded a train for Alabama on the 14th. With the president was Major General John Pemberton, the disgraced loser of Vicksburg, whom Davis had brought along to secure a command in the army. The opposition to Pemberton was so intense, however, that Bragg could not accept him. "Mr. Davis got more than he came for," concluded Moxley Sorrel.[17]

Within hours of Davis's departure, Bragg exacted his revenge. He relieved Hill of command, citing the corps commander for weakening "the morale and military tone" of his command and for "a want of prompt conformity to orders of great importance." Outraged, Hill demanded specifications, but Bragg refused to provide any because he had no creditable grounds for the charges. Davis had consented to the removal of Hill, and when the North Carolinian later sought redress from the president, he received no satisfaction, only equivocation and lies. On October 16, William Mackall resigned as chief of staff; he had predicted earlier that "if Mr. D. sustains him [Bragg], he will be too elated to listen to reason." By month's end, Simon Buckner was reduced to division command, and the Department of East Tennessee, which he had directed, was disbanded. For the other malcontents, Bragg dispersed their units and reassigned them. "I do not know a single contented general in this army; a very sad fact in the presence of the enemy," wrote Mackall before he left.[18]

Bragg reduced Longstreet's corps, leaving him with only the two infantry divisions and artillery battalion he had brought with him from Virginia. Within the rank and file of the Army of Tennessee, Longstreet was regarded as the prime leader of the faction, motivated by his desire to supplant Bragg as commander. In the end, Longstreet and his fellow generals may have been correct in their judgment of Bragg's generalship, but their action shredded whatever cohesiveness there was in the army. For this, Longstreet must bear a major responsibility. Bragg never forgave Longstreet.[19]

An immediate consequence of the feuding was the paralysis of the army's high command. As the events unfolded, Bragg ignored the Federals in Chattanooga, his attention diverted. When the Confederates filed into position south of Chattanooga, Bragg decided to stockpile supplies, wagons, and a pontoon bridge for a movement across the Tennessee River, outflanking Union Major General William Rosecrans's army in the city. On September 29 and October 3, he informed the administration in Richmond that he was preparing for such an offensive operation. Until the Southerners amassed the foodstuffs and matériel, Bragg would besiege the Federal defenders, who reportedly had only six days' rations.[20]

The key for the Confederates was the interdiction of supplies into the city. Chattanooga lay on the south bank of the river, linked to other towns and cities by three railroads—the Nashville and Chattanooga, the East Tennessee and Georgia, and the Western & Atlantic. The latter two rail lines had been severed by the Confederate occupation of Missionary Ridge. The Nashville and Chattanooga Railroad crossed the river thirty miles downriver from Chattanooga, at Bridgeport, Alabama, with its tracks following the river until it entered Chattanooga under the western brow of Lookout Mountain, an eleven-hundred-foot crag that rose opposite a huge U-shaped bend in the river. If the Confederates shut down this railroad and closed the river to steamboat traffic, Rosecrans and his army would have to rely on a miserable road that went into the city from the north through Sequatchie Valley and across rugged Walden's Ridge. Even in good weather, the road was barely passable.[21]

Bragg assigned the Lookout Mountain sector of the Rebel lines to Longstreet. During the first week of October, Colonel Porter Alexander's artillerists began hauling their cannon up the sides of Lookout Mountain. The gunners mounted the pieces on skids and pulled and heaved them to the crest. The work was exhausting and time-consuming, and the Southerners toiled at it for days. Once Alexander had some cannon in place, he began shelling the city and the Federal works. Below the mountain, Confederate gunners rigged platforms for their cannon to give them a steeper angle for vertical fire. Defective ammunition, however, hampered the effectiveness of the Rebels' fire.[22]

The occupation of Lookout Mountain by the Confederates could not seal the Federal supply route along the river or through Lookout Valley at the western foot of the mountain. That could only be accomplished by Confederate infantry stationed in the valley. Lookout Valley was four miles in width, butted on the east by Lookout Mountain and on the west by Raccoon Mountain. A road from Trenton, Georgia, ran the length of the valley, roughly following the course of Lookout Creek, to Brown's Ferry on the river and, from there, across Moccasin Point into Chattanooga. By holding Lookout Valley with infantry, Longstreet would close the main Union supply route.[23]

On October 9, Brigadier General Evander Law's brigade of Alabamians crossed Lookout Mountain and entered the valley. During the next two days, Law strung his regiments along the river, posting pickets at Brown's Ferry and upstream toward Chattanooga. Rain began falling heavily on the 12th and continued through the 13th. Lookout Creek flooded, isolating the Alabamians from their comrades beyond the mountain. "Rations are scarce," jotted one of them in his diary on the 14th, as the men killed every sheep and hog they could find. Some of them built rafts from the walls of an old cabin, floated across the flooded valley, walked back across the mountain, and returned with boxes of hardtack and bacon, carried on the backs of pack mules. When the creek waters subsided, Law's men settled in, their hold on the valley dependent on the supplies brought by the mules.[24]

For the next two weeks the siege of Chattanooga followed a

monotonous pattern. The Confederates continued to lob shells into the defenders' lines, while the Federals scrounged for every morsel of food. Rosecrans cut rations to one-quarter and limited the forage for animals. The downpours of October 12 and 13 turned the road across Walden's Ridge into an impassable trough, further reducing the trickle of supplies into the city. In the Southern camps, "the two great events of the day are breakfast & supper," a Georgian wrote to his parents. The routine and the siege "disheartened hundreds, and they deserted by the scores," according to a Tennessean. Bragg adopted harsh measures to stanch the flow of deserters, which "made him the most hated commander in the army."[25]

During this time period, Longstreet spent the days on Lookout Mountain or with the bulk of his troops at the eastern base of the heights. He and Bragg kept their distance from each other, communicating only by written correspondence. At his own head-quarters, Longstreet and his staff enjoyed evening meals washed down with peach brandy that the general drank from a pewter quart mug. As they had in Virginia, he and his aides invited guests to the meals. The most joyous event of these days was the news of the birth of a son at Petersburg, Virginia, on October 20; he and Louise named him Robert Lee Longstreet. The father wrote a letter to his child's namesake in Virginia, announcing the occasion. It had been less than two years since he and Louise had lost three of their children to scarlet fever.[26]

About the time Longstreet learned of his son's birth, activity around Chattanooga quickened, initiated by a new Federal com-mander, Major General Ulysses S. Grant, Longstreet's best friend in the old army. Conditions had become so critical in the city, with Rosecrans undertaking no plans to alleviate the near starvation, that Union authorities in Washington relieved him of command on October 19, assigning Grant to the post. The victor of Vicksburg arrived on the 23rd and began at once to open a new supply route. Within two days Grant adopted a proposal of Brigadier General William F. "Baldy" Smith, an engineer officer whom Grant had known since their West Point days.[27]

Smith recommended a three-pronged attack on Brown's Ferry at the northern end of Lookout Valley. A column of infantry would march across Moccasin Point to the ferry while another infantry force would float down the river in pontoon boats and launch an amphibious assault against the Confederates on the south bank,

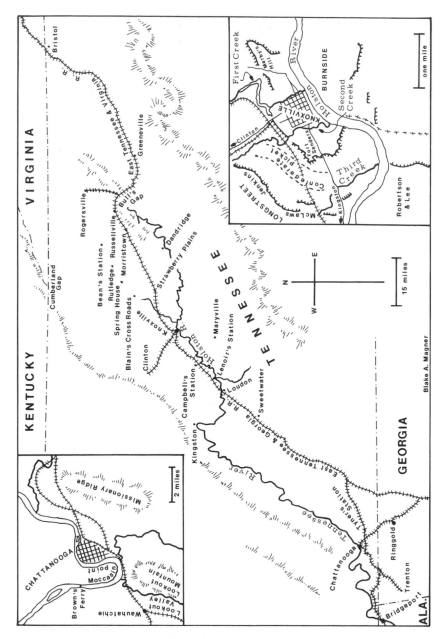

EAST TENNESSEE OPERATIONS, OCTOBER 1863–APRIL 1864.

providing cover until the pontoon bridge was constructed. The third prong would be the Eleventh and Twelfth Corps under Major General Joseph Hooker, advancing from Bridgeport down Lookout Valley and linking up with the troops at the ferry. After an inspection tour of Moccasin Point and Brown's Ferry, Grant approved Smith's plan and ordered its implementation for daylight on October 27.[28]

At the northern end of Lookout Valley, meanwhile, Evander Law's Alabamians guarded the southern bank of the river at Brown's Ferry. Law had stretched three of his regiments along the stream, placing two regiments and a two-gun section of artillery in reserve. In a postwar memoir, Law claimed that he informed Longstreet soon after his arrival that an entire division would be required to hold the valley. "I was satisfied from the first," wrote Law, "that an effort would be made to reopen communication in this direction." On October 25, despite indications of enemy activity across the river, Law left on an approved two-day leave of absence to visit his friend and former commander John Hood, who was convalescing in a house about thirty miles south of Chattanooga. Later that day, Brigadier General Micah Jenkins, Law's acting division commander, withdrew three of the regiments of Alabamians to the east side of the mountain.[29]

Law returned from his visit with Hood on the night of the 26th and found his three regiments with the division. He and Jenkins disliked each other; both men coveted promotion and command of the division. Although his criticisms of Jenkins must be accepted cautiously, Law's subsequent assertion seems fair: "The withdrawal of these troops [was done] without 'rhyme or reason' for there was no earthly necessity for them, on the east side of Lookout." Informed that he would have temporary command of the division in Jenkins's absence on the 27th, Law prepared to recross the mountain with his three regiments. He would be too late.[30]

The Federals struck at Brown's Ferry as planned at daylight on the 27th. Shielded by fog, the Yankees in the pontoon boats landed on the south bank, surprised the Rebel pickets, and seized the high ground beyond the ferry. The two Confederate regiments, the Fourth and Fifteenth Alabama, and the artillery section contested the landing but were overwhelmed by the enemy's strength. One of the Alabamians noted in his diary that the Northerners "had us in a trap and could have captured us with ease had they pushed on." But the Federals' role was to secure a bridgehead while engineers cobbled together the pontoon bridge. The Alabamians retired up the valley, meeting Law and their comrades at Lookout Creek. Here Law deployed the brigade on a hill near a destroyed railroad bridge that had once spanned the creek, and waited.[31]

The musketry from the combat at the ferry alerted the Confederates on Lookout Mountain. Longstreet rode to the crest and, as the fog dissipated, watched the Federals at work on the pontoon bridge. For some reason he did not report the action to army headquarters. In time, Law and Lafayette McLaws, in particular, blamed Longstreet for the loss of the vital valley, alleging that their commander ignored signs and warnings of a probable Federal effort to reopen the supply line through the area. McLaws claimed that he and some aides rode personally to Brown's Ferry—days before the attack— saw the enemy at work across the river, and recommended that another brigade and one or two batteries be sent there. When McLaws spoke to Longstreet about his findings, the latter responded that one of his staff officers had already reconnoitered and "reported it impracticable to station troops there, that it was an untenable place." McLaws stated that the identity of the staff officer was never ascertained.[32]

In his memoirs, Longstreet insisted that he kept army headquarters posted of developments on the mountain and in the valley but that Bragg dismissed the reports and "treated them with contempt." He also contended that he received scant intelligence from the cavalry units that Bragg had sent into the valley to patrol toward Bridgeport and on Raccoon Mountain. In fact, while Longstreet did not receive the support and attention of Bragg that the importance of the sector warranted, the army commander ordered a reconnaissance toward Bridgeport on October 25 that Longstreet never undertook. Furthermore, the cavalry officers sent warnings of enemy activity on Raccoon Mountain and from the south, but Longstreet evidently did not pay much attention to them. In his postwar account, Longstreet endeavored to shift the responsibility to Bragg and others, but he was the commander on that portion of the line.[33]

On October 26, Longstreet wrote to Bragg's chief of staff: "I have no doubt but the enemy will cross below and move against our rear. It is his easiest and safest move." Why then did he permit Jenkins to pull out three of Law's regiments the day before? Why did he not require a second reconnaissance of Brown's Ferry after McLaws recommended that reinforcements be sent there? Why did neither he nor Jenkins personally ride down into the valley? And why did he not assume a more active direction of operations? Apparently, Longstreet did not appreciate the strategic importance of Lookout Valley or the vulnerability of Law's handful of troops. He seems not even to have demonstrated serious interest in the region until it was too late. McLaws argued afterward that Longstreet "neglected to provide in any manner against such a disaster." It is a fair judgment.[34]

When Bragg learned of the Union attack at Brown's Ferry from one of his officers who had been on Lookout Mountain, he was incensed. The next morning he wrote to Longstreet that "the loss of our position on the left is almost vital; it involves the very existence of the enemy in Chattanooga." What did Longstreet plan to do, Bragg asked. After he sent the message, Bragg decided to speak personally with Longstreet and rode to the crest of Lookout Mountain. The two generals had not seen each other since Davis's visit, and the personal animosity between them had not abated. It undoubtedly contributed in part to the loss of Brown's Ferry.[35]

While the two commanders conferred, a signalman rode up to report that a long column of Union infantry and artillery were marching through Lookout Valley from the direction of Trenton. Bragg was skeptical but agreed to accompany Longstreet to the western rim of the mountain. When they arrived, they saw below the dark line of soldiers on the move toward the river. The Yankees belonged to the Eleventh and Twelfth Corps, "Fighting Joe" Hooker's command, the third contingent of Grant's operation. As Bragg and Longstreet watched, one Union division halted at Wauhatchie, a railroad station, while the other two divisions encamped three miles beyond, near Brown's Ferry. Law's Alabamians skirmished with the enemy before pulling back to a position between the two Federal forces.[36]

Bragg soon started back toward army headquarters after giving Longstreet permission to launch a night assault on the Federals. Despite Longstreet's later claims, Bragg authorized the use of Jenkins's, McLaws's, and Major General William H. T. Walker's divisions in the offensive, but Longstreet chose only Jenkins's four brigades, including Law's. Longstreet also decided to attack the solitary division at Wauhatchie, while Bragg believed the thrust would be against the larger contingent near the ferry. These misunderstandings were indicative of the relationship between the two generals. That night, as Jenkins's three brigades snaked down the mountainside into the valley, Bragg groused bitterly to an officer at headquarters "of Longstreet's inactivity and lack of ability."[37]

Between midnight and 1:00 A.M., Jenkins's veterans went forward —they were Hood's men and some of the best fighters in the army. Colonel John Bratton's South Carolinians led the assault, supported by Brigadier General Henry Benning's Georgia brigade. A volley of musketry from the Rebels ignited the darkness, staggering the Federals at Wauhatchie. These Yankees were also veterans, however, New Yorkers and Pennsylvanians under Brigadier General John Geary, and they expected an attack. The Northerners responded in kind, slowing the Rebels. But the South Carolinians plunged ahead into the park of wagons and ambulances.[38]

The combat lasted for nearly two hours, at times raging "with vehemence," in Geary's words. The Hampton Legion and the Fifth South Carolina crushed the Federal left flank, only to be swept back by a combined fire of musketry and artillery. During the fighting, Captain Edward R. Geary, an artillery officer and the Union general's son, was slain. About three o'clock, Jenkins ordered Bratton to withdraw, ending the engagement. The Confederate losses exceeded 400, and Union casualties amounted to 216.[39]

When the gunfire erupted at Wauhatchie, Union Major General Oliver O. Howard at Brown's Ferry rushed a brigade to Geary's assistance. Jenkins had prepared for such a movement, however; he posted Law's Alabamians on a wooded hill beside the road and deployed part of Brigadier General Jerome Robertson's brigade on Law's right to secure the Confederate retreat route. Law's troops built log works, and when the Yankees appeared out of the darkness, they unleashed a volley. The Northerners counterattacked, fell back, and charged a second time, breaking through on the left center of Law's line. The Alabamians shoved them down the hill, and the fighting subsided. A courier from Jenkins arrived with orders to retire, so Law extricated his regiments, followed by Robertson's brigade, which had been guarding a bridge over Lookout Creek. The Northerners did not pursue, and after sunrise on the 29th, Jenkins's men filed into their camps on the eastern side of the mountain. Grant had his supply line through Lookout Valley.[40]

The faultfinding and grumbling about who was to blame for the abortive assault began almost at once. Jenkins blamed Law and Robertson for not securing the flank of Bratton and Benning and for pulling out before ordered. On October 30, Jenkins complained to his wife in a letter that "for a few [more] minutes [we] would have had the whole Yankee force routed and their guns captured." Law countered that he had not abandoned the hill until so instructed by Jenkins. In his report, written on November 3, Law stated that he sent a courier to Jenkins, informing his superior that he was under attack and that Bratton "might be placed in a dangerous position" if the enemy passed beyond Law's flank. Minutes later an order arrived from Jenkins to hold the hill until Bratton and Benning retired. Law complied until notified that the two brigades had reached the bridge. Although not a model of clarity, Bratton's report, dated November 1, supported Law's reconstruction of the events.[41]

Longstreet sided with Jenkins. More than anyone else, Longstreet was responsible for the feuding within the division. Since he had first met Jenkins after First Manassas, Longstreet regarded the South Carolinian as the finest young officer in the army and urged his promotion. When his two divisions traveled to Tennessee, Longstreet secured the assignment of Jenkins's brigade to Hood's division. As senior brigadier, Jenkins would have commanded the division at Chickamauga had Hood not returned to duty at the urging of officers in the unit. With Hood's fall, Jenkins succeeded him, and Longstreet endeavored to have the brigadier promoted and given permanent command. On October 18, Longstreet wrote McLaws that he "very strongly recommended Gen. Jenkins for Hood's Divn. In case another Maj. Gen. may be appointed there. Of all the Brigadiers in the Army, Gen. Jenkins is my first choice as the most active and zealous officer."[42]

The officers and men of the division disliked Jenkins, however, preferring Law instead. McLaws intimated that Hood "did not hesitate to denounce" Longstreet for this and other matters. Very likely that was why Law rode thirty miles to see Hood when his duty required him to be with his troops. But Longstreet neither cared for Law personally nor wanted him in command of the division. When he prepared his report months later, Longstreet attributed the failure at Wauhatchie to Law, blaming his "want of conduct" on "a strong feeling of jealousy among the brigadier-generals." Longstreet's conclusion, if true, was a sad commentary on the effectiveness of Hood's once splendid division.[43]

For the present, Longstreet took no official action against Law but instead moved against Jerome Robertson, almost assuredly at the urging of Jenkins. On November 1, Longstreet wrote to Colonel George William Brent, army chief of staff, requesting that Robertson be relieved of command. "This officer," Longstreet charged, "has been complained of so frequently for want of conduct in time of battle that I apprehend that the abandonment by his brigade of its position of the night of the 28th may have been due to his want of hearty co-operation." On Bragg's order, Brent relieved Robertson the next day and assigned a board of inquiry to examine the case. The board began taking testimony on the morning of the 4th. The proceedings were suspended on the 8th, and Brent returned Robertson to duty with the brigade.[44]

Brent postponed the inquiry because the board members were needed with their commands. What had been rumored in the camps for a few days was now true—Longstreet's divisions were leaving the Army of Tennessee. On November 3, Bragg had met with Longstreet, Lieutenant General William Hardee, who had joined the army after the dispute in October, and Major General John Breckinridge to discuss the sending of Longstreet's troops into East Tennessee against Union general Ambrose Burnside's forces. Bragg had detached two divisions, roughly eleven thousand men, to the region, but a few days earlier, Jefferson Davis had proposed using Longstreet, which would bring him and his command closer to Virginia for a return to Lee's army. Bragg wanted to know the generals' opinion about such a movement.[45]

Longstreet spoke first, advocating a crossing of the Tennessee River below Bridgeport, Alabama, and a march into Middle Tennessee against Grant's supply bases. Bragg and perhaps Hardee and Breckinridge opposed it because of the enormous logistical and supply problems that the Rebels would encounter in a march across the barren country. Longstreet accepted the argument against his plan and then endorsed the movement into East Tennessee. Bragg stated that Union reinforcements were en route to Chattanooga, but if Burnside could be defeated swiftly, Longstreet could return before the Federals arrived. If not, the generals concluded that Grant would be compelled to detach units from his army at Chattanooga or reroute the oncoming force to assist Burnside.[46]

The generals finally settled on a plan that detached Longstreet's two infantry divisions, two artillery battalions, and Major General Joseph Wheeler's two small cavalry divisions. The Confederates would follow the East Tennessee and Georgia Railroad, relying on it for transportation and supplies, and attack Burnside's command. The primary object was, as Bragg told Longstreet two days later, "to get possession of East Tennessee, and in doing so, to destroy or capture the enemy if possible." No agreement was reached, however, on whether Longstreet would return to the army once the Federals had been defeated. Longstreet requested maps, scouts, staff officers who knew the region, and additional wagons. Bragg assented and ordered Longstreet to begin preparations.[47]

With the detachment of Longstreet's units, Bragg now faced an opponent with a numerical advantage of roughly two to one. It was a serious gamble, but Bragg was motivated in part by his desire to have Longstreet away from the army. He had written to Davis on October 31 of Longstreet's "disrespectful and insubordinate" correspondence and stated that detaching him from the army would be a "great relief to me." To another general, Bragg admitted that he sent Longstreet to East Tennessee "to get rid of him and see what he could do on his own resources." Unfortunately for Bragg, his greatest enemy at Chattanooga was not Longstreet but that general's old friend Grant.[48]

Very likely Longstreet welcomed the separation as much as Bragg. He hurried the preparations, and on the 5th the leading contingents of his command started for the railroad. Later in the day he and his staff followed. He may have thought of his journey through East Tennessee in the spring of 1861 and remembered the strong unionist sentiment of its residents. Now it offered him an escape. It was one month and a day since he, Simon Buckner, and Harvey Hill had plotted together and agreed to the petition.[49]

17

KNOXVILLE

Tyner's Station was a stop on the East Tennessee and Georgia Railroad, located roughly eight miles east of Chattanooga, Tennessee. Since 1861, the elements of war—men, arms, animals, uniforms, food, and equipment—had passed through it, en route to and from the city to the west. Rarely had the station been a center of activity, a rendezvous for thousands of men and wagonloads of matériel. But here on November 5, 1863, the vanguard of Longstreet's command came, eddies of Confederates that soon flooded the fields along the tracks. From Tyner's Station the railroad stretched into East Tennessee.[1]

When Braxton Bragg and his corps commanders approved the operation into East Tennessee against Burnside's forces, Longstreet planned for a swiftly executed movement that used the East Tennessee and Georgia Railroad for its initial leg. But like many other Southern lines, the railroad had deteriorated under the burdens of the conflict. By the time Longstreet's troops arrived at Tyner's Station and at Tunnel Station, a few miles to the west at Missionary Ridge, the railroad was in a deplorable condition. A staff officer with Longstreet described it as "a complete failure." He could not understand why no one had checked the company's reduced capacity beforehand.[2]

Carloads of troops did not begin rolling from Tyner's Station until November 7. For two days the men had waited in the cars, with little to eat and without their winter coats. An accident on the

6th closed the tracks for a day, and once the trains lurched out of the station, one of them collided into the rear of another. Colonel Porter Alexander's artillerymen, with their cannon, did not leave until the 10th, and by then most of them were "nearly starved." The gunners rode on open flatcars, huddled together against the cold wind. By November 11, the bulk of the command had reached Sweetwater, Tennessee, approximately fifty miles from Tyner's Station.[3]

Longstreet had preceded the men to Sweetwater, where he expected to find rations, supply wagons, and draft animals. On November 8, before he left Tyner's Station, Longstreet had complained to Bragg's chief of staff: "I understood from the general that preparations were already made or would be made for all our wants." Instead, little or nothing had been stockpiled or requisitioned. Major Raphael Moses, Longstreet's chief of commissary, groused in his report that "the department, on our arrival at Sweet Water, was utterly unprovided for, and its condition as bad as it could be in a country not utterly exhausted."[4]

For a second time within a week, the movement halted. Moses and other staff officers sent details of troops into the countryside to confiscate wheat and mill it into flour, and to impress livestock. Major General Carter Stevenson's division had been stationed in the area, and when Longstreet's troops arrived, it began marching back to the main army. Before it departed, Moses wangled a supply of fresh pork from its commissary officer. A few days later a supply train finally rolled in from Bragg, but it numbered only thirty-five wagons when it should have been seventy.[5]

Another critical shortage was wagons and teams of animals. The command had brought neither with them from Virginia and relied on the generosity of Bragg. By the time they reached Sweetwater, the train consisted of 113 wagons, 30 short of their allotted number. "The condition of what we had," wrote Captain Frank Potts, Longstreet's assistant quartermaster, "was beyond all question the worst I ever saw; wagons frequently breaking down, mules just able in a large proportion of cases to carry their harness, harness much worn, and many teams without collars and saddles." In time, Bragg sent an additional 64 wagons and teams of equally inferior quality. As the troops penetrated deeper into East Tennessee, their lifeline for supplies and ordnance increasingly depended on these vehicles and "feeble animals."[6]

Longstreet, meanwhile, exchanged a series of messages with Bragg, protesting what he termed "the entire failure of the preparations" ordered by Bragg. The army commander blamed Longstreet, however, for not utilizing his authority and taking the wagons that were along the road. "I cannot understand your constant applications to me to furnish them," replied Bragg. Longstreet shot back that Bragg had not given him that authority. "Instead of being prepared to make a campaign," Longstreet argued, "I find myself not more than half prepared to subsist." On November 12, he promised that "as soon as I find a probability of moving without almost certain starvation, I shall move."[7]

By the 12th, Longstreet had received fairly accurate information about enemy dispositions in East Tennessee. Union Major General Ambrose Burnside, the former commander of the Army of the Potomac who had hurled his Grand Divisions against the Confederates at Fredericksburg in December 1862, had the Ninth and Twenty-third Corps and two cavalry divisions strung out along a line roughly eighty miles in length from Cumberland Gap northeast of Knoxville to Loudon southwest of the city. In all, Burnside counted approximately twenty-three thousand—a figure Major General Joseph Wheeler reported to Longstreet on the 8th—with over half the number in Knoxville or along the East Tennessee and Georgia Railroad toward Loudon. Burnside had orders from Major General Ulysses S. Grant to delay Longstreet's advance as he fell back to Knoxville. In Grant's estimation, time favored the Federals as Major General William T. Sherman and the Fifteenth Corps were en route to Chattanooga.[8]

The advanced elements of Burnside's command were stationed behind the Holston River at Loudon, fifteen miles from Sweetwater. Longstreet decided to force a crossing at Loudon and dispatched Porter Alexander and Major John Clarke of his staff to find a pontoon crossing site below the town. Late on the 12th, he issued orders directing the infantry and artillery to Loudon and detaching Wheeler with three brigades of cavalry on a raid via Maryville to Knoxville to seize the heights south of the city or to prevent reinforcements from the garrison being sent against Longstreet. The Confederates finally had patched together enough wagons and garnered enough supplies for the advance.[9]

The march from Sweetwater began early on the 13th, with Brigadier General Micah Jenkins's division in the lead. By the afternoon the Southerners had closed on Loudon, Jenkins swinging below the town and Major General Lafayette McLaws demonstrating above it. Alexander and Clarke had selected Huff's Ferry, six miles downstream from Loudon, as the crossing point. After nightfall, a detachment from the Palmetto Sharpshooters rowed boats across the Holston, "a beautiful river," according to a Georgian, and secured the northern bank. Behind them, work crews began stringing the pontoon bridge across the stream. No fires were permitted, and the waiting troops braced against the cold night without any cooked food.[10]

In a heavy rain, Jenkins's veterans tramped across the bridge on the morning of the 14th, veering upstream toward Loudon. McLaws's division and the artillery remained on the southern side of the river as the Federals abandoned their works opposite the town and retired eastward along the railroad tracks. Late in the afternoon, a small Union force attacked Jenkins's skirmish line and was repulsed. Throughout the wet, miserable day, details of Rebels foraged for food and ground more wheat into flour at nearby mills.[11]

The pursuit of the Federals began early the next day. The Confederates slogged through the mud on a road from Huff's Ferry to Lenoir's Station on the railroad. Two miles from the station the road forked, and Jenkins turned right, moving directly on the railroad. At Lenoir's, the Yankees had built a permanent camp of log houses with plaster walls and glass windows. Burnside intended to oppose the Rebel advance as long as possible and then withdraw toward Knoxville, pulling the Southerners farther away from Chattanooga. He had the Ninth Corps and a division of the Twenty-third Corps with him and deployed them west of the station. When Jenkins's skirmishers appeared, gunfire crackled.[12]

The weather and wet ground abated Burnside's designs. It was not until nearly dark that Jenkins wrestled his brigades into position on some hills southeast of the station. Longstreet watched the deployment from a nearby knoll. Here McLaws found him, and together they saw the road to Knoxville filled with wagons. McLaws asked for orders and was told to bivouac his troops for the night at the fork of the road, three or four miles to the rear. McLaws departed, and Longstreet directed Jenkins to send a brigade around the right to be in position to cut off the enemy retreat. Local guides missed the road, however, and it was after midnight before the brigade was in position near the road to Knoxville. By then Burnside had pulled out his infantry and artillery and most of his wagons, leaving behind nearly one hundred vehicles filled with supplies and ammunition.[13]

During the night, McLaws learned from a courier who had resided in the area before the war that if he followed the left fork road, he could reach Campbell's Station, several miles northeast of Lenoir's, and strike the enemy retreat route to Knoxville. McLaws checked with local farmers, who confirmed the courier's information, and then sent a note to Longstreet. "I am not aware wheather or not he received it," McLaws wrote afterward, "as no reply was received." McLaws asserted later that Longstreet missed a splendid opportunity to crush Burnside's force by not moving that night. If Longstreet had received McLaws's note and ignored it, McLaws's criticism seems valid. It was not until daylight that McLaws received orders to march to Campbell's Station and, once there, communicate with the commander, who would be with Jenkins's division on the main road from Lenoir's.[14]

McLaws started his division on the road as Jenkins's troops swarmed over the abandoned Federal wagons and through the cabins. The Yankees had destroyed the running gear of the wagons but left their contents untouched. The Confederates captured over one hundred thousand rounds of rifle ammunition and several hundred artillery rounds. In the cabins and among the wagons, the soldiers, according to a South Carolinian, "got all kinds of good things." Rations were still in short supply, and back at Sweetwater, Raphael Moses was making extraordinary efforts to move the foodstuffs forward. When a railroad engineer refused to haul supplies to Loudon, Moses commandeered the train, picked a crew from a Tennessee regiment, and had it rolling to Loudon.[15]

Longstreet sought a fight on November 16. By noon, McLaws and Jenkins had closed on Campbell's Station, finding the Yankees deployed in a "beautiful position" across the narrow valley east of the station. Longstreet directed McLaws to deploy in line behind some woods to the left of the station and not advance until Jenkins engaged the enemy. On the Confederate right, Jenkins's skirmishers ignited the fighting and pushed back the enemy. Behind Jenkins, Alexander rolled seventeen cannon into position in a broad meadow.[16]

While the skirmishers dueled, Longstreet marched two of Jenkins's brigades—Brigadier Generals Evander Law's and George Anderson's—along a concealed route to outflank the Union left. Law commanded the force and brought the line in short of the enemy flank. When the Yankees saw the Rebel brigades, they began withdrawing from their position. Alexander had his cannon open fire, but their effectiveness was limited because of defective ammunition. One twenty-pound Parrott cannon exploded, injuring its crew members. Later, rumor within the command alleged that Law had deliberately exposed his troops to the enemy to deny Jenkins, his bitter foe, an opportunity for victory. An artillery officer with Alexander subsequently contended "if our infantry had been handled with anything like the skill and dash with which the artillery was handled that the greater part of Burnside's force would have been captured before he got to Knoxville."[17]

Longstreet evidently agreed with the artillery officer, telling his staff that Campbell's Station was their chance to destroy the Federals. Like Jenkins, he attributed the failure "to some mismanagement of General Law." Undoubtedly, Law botched his assignment, but once again Burnside had extricated his troops in a timely manner, retiring only a short distance and then redeploying. The Union general had managed his retreat from Loudon with skill, only abandoning Lenoir's Station with some evidence of panic. Conversely, the Confederates battled poor weather, muddy roads, supply problems, and worn animals in their effort to overtake the enemy. The result was that by nightfall on the 16th, the Federals were on the march to Knoxville and the safety of the city's defenses.[18]

The Rebels stirred at daylight on the 17th, with McLaws's division leading the pursuit. During the day, Wheeler's three cavalry brigades rejoined the main body after probing the fortifications at Knoxville and bagging about 140 Yankees in a brief engagement. Burnside's horsemen contested the Confederate march to the city, finally disengaging as the Southerners pushed them into their works. By nightfall, Longstreet had his infantry and artillery posted along a line on Knoxville's western outskirts.[19]

The city of Knoxville sat on a half-mile-wide plateau that rose 150 feet above the Holston River on the city's southern edge. First Creek divided the city proper from East Knoxville, and Second Creek flowed along the western edge of the plateau. West of Second Creek, a second plateau rose above the valley, and beyond it, roughly three-fourths of a mile away, another plateau extended back from the river along Third Creek. The Union defenses—a series of earthworks, redoubts, battery positions, and forts—encircled the city from East Knoxville to the plateau beyond Second Creek, which local citizens called College Hill, the site of the University of East Tennessee. To man the defenses and serve the cannon, Burnside had approximately twelve thousand troops.[20]

On the morning of November 18, after a dense fog dissipated, skirmishers from the brigade of Brigadier General Joseph Kershaw probed eastward and collided with dismounted Union cavalrymen behind a work of stacked rails on the plateau beyond Third Creek. The Federals, under Brigadier General William Sanders, a close friend of Porter Alexander when they were together at West Point, stalled the Rebels for hours. Sanders had been ordered by Burnside to hold on as long as possible while work details strengthened the main works on the plateau between Second and Third creeks. Finally, at 3:00 P.M., with orders from Longstreet, McLaws sent Kershaw's infantrymen forward in an attack, supported by a battery from Alexander's battalion. Sanders's weary men buckled and then broke under the onslaught, and as the young Union brigadier tried to rally them, he fell with a mortal wound, dying the next afternoon in the bridal suite of the Lamar Hotel in the city.[21]

Behind Kershaw's men, McLaws's other brigades, Jenkins's division, and the artillery filed into position north and south of the Kingston-Knoxville road. Using shovels captured from the Federals at Lenoir's Station, the Rebels dug in. McLaws's troops held the line from the river northward across the road, where Jenkins's units extended it northeastward to cover the road to Clinton, Tennessee. Alexander selected the artillery positions and had the crews begin work on the gun pits. Longstreet and McLaws established their headquarters in the brick "Bleak House," the home of Robert H. Armstrong, on the Kingston Road.[22]

For the next several days Confederate operations were marked by uncertainty and indecision. On November 20, Longstreet wrote Bragg that Burnside's position "is stronger than at Chattanooga." "I cannot invest him completely, but have closed all the avenues to the town pretty well, and have them strongly guarded. It seems to be a question of starvation with the enemy, or to re-enforce." But Longstreet wanted to attack before the Yankees either ran out of food or received additional troops. The problem was to find a vulnerable point and to organize an assault force.[23]

Initially, Longstreet thought an advantage might be gained on the south side of the river if the Confederates could seize some high ground and bring their artillery to bear on Burnside's works on the opposite side. Using flatboats pulled by a wire cable, the Confederates ferried the brigades of Jerome Robertson and Evander Law of Jenkins's division across the Holston, and the two units occupied a hill opposite the mouth of Third Creek. When Major John Fairfax reported to Longstreet that he found a position from which they could enfilade the enemy works, Longstreet ordered Alexander to take a battery to the south side. Alexander ferried it across on the 23rd and had the gunners toil at digging gun emplacements throughout that day and the next. As Fairfax predicted, the artillerists had a favorable field of fire, but the ammunition was so unreliable that Alexander withheld testing it. Instead, on the morning of the 25th, Law's brigade, supported by the battery, attacked a Union earthwork close to the city, but they suffered a repulse and retired with about fifty casualties. The Southerners abandoned further effort on the south side.[24]

North of the Holston, meanwhile, Longstreet and other officers were focusing their attention on a Union-bastioned earthwork shaped like a truncated star, located on a hill "of considerable elevation" approximately one thousand yards in front of McLaws's lines. Fort Loudon, which the Federals renamed Fort Sanders in honor of the fallen brigadier, squatted on a 198-foot elevation northwest of College Hill and roughly three hundred yards north of the Kingston Road. Originally constructed by the Confederates, it had been strengthened since Burnside occupied the city.[25]

Fort Sanders had been constructed as an "irregular quadrilateral," with salients at the northwest and southwest corners. The eastern front had been kept open to expedite the movement of troops into or out of the fort. Each of the three other sides had a steep parapet topped by cotton bales that were covered with rawhide to prevent their igniting from gunfire. A ditch that varied in width from eight to twelve feet and in depth from six to eight feet edged the base, creating a face of twenty feet in depth at numerous spots. In front of the ditch, the Federals had strung telegraph wires from tree stumps. A garrison of approximately 440 infantrymen and artillerymen, with a dozen cannon, manned Fort Sanders. The garrison's band often played songs at night that could be heard by the Southerners. Its favorite was "When This Cruel War Is Over."[26]

On November 21, Longstreet informed McLaws that Bragg had telegraphed to urge a battle at Knoxville. "The only chance that I see of doing anything in time to do good is an assault upon the redoubt," wrote Longstreet. He suggested that McLaws use three brigades in a moonlight assault on the night of the 22nd, but "I am loath," he added, "to put the troops at it when there is a disinclination to it." McLaws agreed to examine the Union fort and discuss the attack with his brigade commanders. The officers conferred on the 22nd, concluded that they could not direct their men in a night operation, and opposed the idea. Longstreet postponed it.[27]

Further discussions ensued, and Longstreet set another attack date on Fort Sanders for the 25th. He directed Alexander to place the artillery of his and Major A. Leyden's battalions, thirty-four cannon in all, for a bombardment of the Union redoubt. Alexander labored day and night, even rigging four howitzers on skids to serve as mortars. The artillery colonel reported to Longstreet that he would be ready by sunrise on the designated day. But before the attack went forward, Longstreet received a message from Bragg that Brigadier General Danville Leadbetter, the army's chief engineer, and Brigadier General Bushrod Johnson's thirty-five-hundred-man division had been sent to Knoxville. For a second time Longstreet delayed the assault.[28]

Leadbetter reached Knoxville on the night of the 25th. A fifty-two-year-old West Pointer, he had served primarily as an engineer officer throughout the war, including the overseeing of the construction of the defenses at Knoxville. Leadbetter told Longstreet that Bragg wanted the lieutenant general to attack Burnside "very promptly." Longstreet probably responded that he had been endeavoring for days to fashion a plan—it was a matter of where and when. They agreed to conduct additional reconnaissances of the Federal works and to select a target. In Alexander's subsequent estimation, Leadbetter's "advent cost us three as valuable days as the sun ever shone upon." The delayed attacks, he added, had been "a bitter disappointment to the artillery."[29]

Leadbetter favored an assault on the Confederate left against Burnside's fortifications in East Knoxville, and he and Longstreet rode there on the morning of the 26th. For hours the two generals studied the works and the terrain, with Leadbetter proposing an attack on Mabry's Hill, the northeast anchor of the Union defenses. Returning to headquarters late in the afternoon, Longstreet ordered

Alexander to return the battery from the south side. When Alexander read the note, he was "never more disgusted in my life." Earlier, he had surveyed the same ground and dismissed it as too exposed. "Leadbetter evidently had no appreciation of ground," stated Alexander. "Longstreet had some, but was misled in some way I have never [been] able to understand."[30]

Longstreet and Leadbetter conducted a second reconnaissance the next day, bringing along McLaws, Jenkins, Alexander, and Bushrod Johnson, who had arrived that morning. The party of officers studied the ground before Mabry's Hill. The attackers would have to cross a creek and mill pond while subjected to Union artillery and musketry fire. No one said anything, and they rode back to a point opposite Fort Sanders. McLaws's skirmishers had advanced to within four hundred yards of the Federal rifle pits outside the fort, so if the assault force could be brought into line behind them, it would require only a short dash to the fort. The Confederates knew of the ditch and discussed its depth. While they examined the works, a Yankee crossed the ditch, and Longstreet remarked that the lip of it "catches him to his waist." (The soldier they observed evidently walked across a plank that straddled the ditch.) The officers agreed the target would be the northwest salient of Fort Sanders, with McLaws's troops leading the charge, supported by units from Jenkins's and Johnson's commands. If preparations were completed, the attackers would go in the next day, November 28.[31]

A heavy rain poured down on the morning of the 28th, limiting the prospects of an assault that day. Longstreet, however, instructed McLaws to double his picket lines and reserve, drive in the enemy skirmishers, and complete preparations for a general attack. McLaws hesitated to execute the orders because of the weather, and eventually Longstreet joined him at the Armstrong house. The commanding general reaffirmed his previous directive, designating 2:00 P.M. as the hour. When Longstreet departed, McLaws gathered his brigade commanders—Joseph Kershaw, Benjamin Humphreys, William Wofford, and Goode Bryan—at headquarters to arrange the details of the operation.[32]

The generals decided that two regiments, acting as sharpshooters, would precede the main force, overrun the Union rifle pits, and provide a cover fire. Behind them, deployed in columns of regiments, the brigades of Wofford, Humphreys, and Bryan would charge. If they seized the fort, Kershaw would advance on the right, securing that flank. The attackers would advance with fixed bayonets and would not fire or halt until on the parapet. They then discussed the need for ladders to scale the walls and for fascines— bundles of sticks—to fill in the ditch; they concluded that the ditch would not be an obstacle because of the observations of the previous day. But the brigade commanders preferred to postpone the assault until daylight on the 29th and asked McLaws if he would speak with Longstreet. The meeting adjourned, and McLaws relayed his subordinates' request to Longstreet, who acceded one more time.[33]

Later in the day, McLaws scribbled a note to Longstreet, repeating the rumor of a battle at Chattanooga, and asked for another postponement until it could be verified. If the Confederates captured the fort, McLaws argued, the enemy would retreat across the Holston River and occupy the heights south of the city. Longstreet replied that he also had been informed of the news but could not be certain of its validity. The report he received indicated that Bragg had been defeated and was in retreat. Longstreet wrote to McLaws:

> I am entirely convinced that our only safety is in making the assault upon the enemy's position to-morrow at daylight, and it is the more important that I should have the entire support and co-operation of the officers in this connection, and I do hope and trust that I may have your entire support and all of the force you may be possessed of in the execution of my views. It is a great mistake to suppose that there is any safety for us in going to Virginia if General Bragg has been defeated, for we leave him at the mercy of his victors, and with his army destroyed our own had better be disgraced. There is neither safety nor honor in any other course than the one I have chosen and ordered.[34]

Sometime during the afternoon, Micah Jenkins rode to the Armstrong house to confer with Longstreet. Jenkins was troubled by the attack scheme and the ditch around Fort Sanders. He had been told by Brigadier General Archibald Gracie, Jr., of Johnson's division that the ditch was four to five feet deep and the parapet eleven to twelve feet high. Longstreet was away when Jenkins arrived so he talked with McLaws, suggesting that the attackers carry fascines. McLaws responded that "he knew nothing about such things," and if the ditch was too deep, "they would trust to luck in getting around or over." That did not reassure Jenkins, who thought McLaws "was rather indifferent" during the conversation.[35]

Hours later, after nightfall, Jenkins encountered Porter Alexander and repeated his concern about the ditch. Jenkins wanted Alexander to ride with him to Longstreet's headquarters and persuade the commanding general to order McLaws to provide ladders for his men. The artillery officer admitted it was a good idea, but he was so weary that he demurred. Tell Longstreet, Alexander said, that "I most heartily concur in your opinion." Alexander then headed for his camp, and Jenkins decided to write to Longstreet, recounting his meeting with McLaws and the information he had learned from Gracie. Longstreet replied shortly thereafter, reassuring Jenkins that the ditch was probably "not more than 3 feet deep." Then, like a father to a favorite son, Longstreet stated that "if we go in with the idea that we shall fail, we will be sure to do so. But no men who are determined to succeed can fail."[36]

At the Armstrong residence, meanwhile, McLaws held a second meeting with his brigade commanders. They finalized the details of the plan—the sharpshooters to advance about midnight, and the assault force to charge at the fire of signal cannon from Leyden's battalion. The brigadiers returned to their units, repeated the instructions to their regimental commanders, and waited until the sharpshooters went forward. The day's rain had slowed to a fine mist, but in Alexander's words, "the night was wretched, the temperature freezing." With no fires permitted, the soldiers suffered through the long hours.[37]

Minutes before midnight, the sharpshooters—two regiments of Mississippians—raced across the frozen ground. The Federal pickets in the rifle pits fired a round and then fled into the fort. As the Rebels occupied the abandoned line, cannon from Fort Sanders scorched the field with canister. The Federal artillery fire subsided, only to resume periodically throughout the night. Farther west, the Mississippians and Georgians of Humphreys, Bryan, and Wofford formed into attack columns. Officers from McLaws's staff assisted in overseeing the deployment. Finally, shortly after daylight, three cannon rang in succession, and the infantrymen stepped out. A captain in Wofford's brigade wrote later that the men went forward "without a doubt in our minds of going right over."[38]

From Fort Sanders, the parapet flashed with musketry and shell fire, the discharges guiding the attackers toward the northwest salient. Led by Humphreys's troops, the Rebels stepped over the wire and drove ahead. With the discipline of veterans, they withheld their fire as ordered. Then, as they reached the ditch, the cohesion of the units disappeared as the men plunged into the deep trench. On Humphreys's right, Bryan's Georgians piled in; men jammed together, unable to ascend the icy parapet. Minutes later Wofford's Georgians, hit by fire on their left, veered to the right and into the ranks of Humphreys's Mississippians.

Suddenly, the Confederates were caught, as one of them described it, in a "death pit." Union fire from above and on either flank raked the packed ranks. Some of the Rebels shoved comrades up the slope of the parapet, only to see them tumble back, dead or wounded. The enemy rolled lit artillery shells down the incline. Without ladders or fascines, the attackers were doomed in the cauldron, and Humphreys ordered the withdrawal. Southern casualties exceeded eight hundred in only twenty minutes in the ditch; Federal losses amounted to fifteen. "I have witnessed many terrible conflicts," Humphreys asserted later, "but I know of none where more daring, bravery, and perseverance were exhibited by both Federal and Confederate."[39]

Longstreet followed the assault by accompanying the support brigades of Bushrod Johnson's division. As these troops marched forward, Major James Goggin of McLaws's staff reported to Longstreet that the Mississippians and Georgians had been stopped. Longstreet halted Johnson's units and hurried an officer to Jenkins to suspend his advance. Afterward, Longstreet attributed the failure of the assault to his "order of recall." He believed that had he pushed the brigades into action, the fort would have fallen. In fact, Humphreys had probably ordered the withdrawal from the deathtrap before Goggin found Longstreet. By the time the additional troops reached the ground before the fort, the slaughter in the ditch would have been even more horrendous. Without a means to cross the ditch and scale the parapet, the Mississippians and Georgians were doomed."[40]

Fort Sanders was a tragic debacle, and for this Longstreet bears responsibility. In his memoirs, Porter Alexander declared that plans for the assault in "some of its features were crazy enough to have come out of Bedlam"; he added: "I will go to my grave believing that Leadbetter devised it & imposed it upon Longstreet, & he afterward preferred to accept the responsibility rather than plead that he had let himself be so taken in." It may have been as Alexander portrayed it, but that does not excuse Longstreet for implementing a scheme marked by shoddiness in preparation, by the dismissal of serious questions about the size of the ditch, and by haste at the end. Careful, thoughtful planning, attention to detail, and a disposition against frontal attacks—long-standing characteristics of Longstreet's generalship—were absent in the attack on Fort Sanders.[41]

At Knoxville, Longstreet seemed hesitant, even indecisive. For ten days he and his subordinates fashioned plans for an assault, only to postpone or cancel them. With the arrival of Leadbetter, who impatiently urged an attack, Longstreet acquiesced and approved it. In his defense, others, including Alexander, maintained that the ditch would be no impediment to the attackers. But when McLaws and particularly Jenkins, for different reasons, suggested further delay, Longstreet responded that the spirit of the men would ensure success. The men went forward with spirit and became caught in a trap of death. McLaws complained subsequently, with some justification, that Longstreet's "orders were so often changed, and were given with such an evident want of purpose, that it was impossible for any one to know what he really wanted or intended doing." Longstreet's performances at Knoxville and at Lookout Valley had disturbingly similar qualities.[42]

Within an hour of the repulse at Fort Sanders, a telegram from Jefferson Davis to Longstreet was delivered by a staff officer of Major General Robert Ransom, Jr. The president had wired Ransom, who commanded the District of Southwestern Virginia and East Tennessee, about Bragg's defeat at Missionary Ridge and directed that Longstreet abandon the siege of Knoxville and join Bragg in Georgia. Davis's message confirmed the rumors.[43]

In time, Longstreet and his men would learn of the magnitude of the Confederate defeat at Chattanooga. By ridding himself of Longstreet and adding Bushrod Johnson's division to the operation at Knoxville, Bragg had stretched his line too thin. On November 24 the Federals clawed their way up Lookout Mountain. A day later the Yankees stormed up Missionary Ridge and routed the Rebels. Eventually, the Southerners retreated to Dalton, Georgia, nearly thirty miles south of Chattanooga. Bragg asked to be relieved, and when his request was granted, he relinquished command to William Hardee on December 2.[44]

Davis's telegram spurred Longstreet into action. Initially, he thought that the siege should be lifted at once, and he had the wagons started to the rear. In the afternoon he received two messages from Bragg suggesting that Longstreet march across the mountains and rejoin the Army of Tennessee, if practicable. He then met with his division commanders, and the generals decided to remain at Knoxville until Union reinforcements approached. To counter one possible Federal advance, Longstreet ordered Brigadier General William Martin, who had commanded Joseph Wheeler's cavalry divisions since the latter officer's recall by Bragg on November 24, toward Cumberland Gap, and instructed Brigadier General John Vaughn at Loudon to destroy locomotives, railroad cars, boats, and bridges, and to begin a withdrawal to Knoxville.[45]

For the next three days Longstreet held consultations with his senior officers at the Armstrong house. Logistics precluded a march across the mountains to Georgia, and the officers voted to retreat to Bristol, Virginia, and encamp for the winter. On December 1, Confederate cavalrymen grabbed a Union courier with a letter from Grant to Burnside with information that three relief columns were en route to Knoxville. (The dispatch was bogus; the messenger a decoy whom Grant wanted to be captured.) Longstreet directed the wagon train, with infantry guards, to begin moving eastward the next day. The main body of troops would follow after nightfall on the 4th, and Longstreet issued detailed instructions for the movement.[46]

With campfires ablaze, the Confederates stole away from Knoxville in a downpour on the night of December 4–5. Swinging north of the city, the Southerners plodded eastward through the mud. The Rebels marched all night. In Henry Benning's brigade, whenever exhausted soldiers fell to the ground, the general cursed at them and had a picked detail of men prod them to their feet with bayonets. One of those unlucky men bellowed to comrades that Benning was "the damnedest, most aggravating old cuss that was ever seen upon a march." When the Confederates were beyond earshot of the enemy, some of them sang "Carry Me Back to Ole Virginny." Longstreet's proud First Corps had had few, if any, worse nights in its experience.[47]

The retreat continued for the next several days, through Blain's Cross Roads, Spring House, Rutledge, and Bean's Station to Rogersville, where the Southerners finally halted on December 9. The next day Longstreet received a letter from President Davis granting him discretionary authority over troops in the region. He immediately recalled Martin's cavalry command, which had been ordered to the Army of Tennessee. While the commissary officers impressed foodstuffs from the local farmers, the troops rested and foraged. The Confederates remained encamped until the 13th, with the cavalry roaming to the north and west, skirmishing with the advance elements of a Union force.[48]

The Federal pursuit of Longstreet's troops began on December 7, under orders from Grant at Chattanooga. Earlier, Burnside had sent part of his cavalry after the Southerners but hesitated to follow with his infantry until the column from Grant's army, under William Sherman, reached Knoxville. Major General Gordon Granger's Fourth Corps arrived on the 6th, and Burnside ordered Major General John Parke to march with the Ninth and Twenty-third Corps and Brigadier General James Shackelford's cavalry division in pursuit. Burnside had done everything Grant had asked of him. But on December 12, Burnside left Knoxville, relieved of command at his own request and replaced by Major General John G. Foster. On January 28, 1864, Congress voted Burnside its "thanks" for his defense of the city.[49]

Shackelford's horsemen led the Federal march, and it was his troopers that skirmished with Martin's cavalrymen between Rogersville and Bean's Station. Parke halted the infantry at Rutledge, about eight miles west of Bean's Station, where Shackelford maintained his camps and headquarters. Bean's Station, an old stagecoach stop, lay between Clinch Mountain and the Holston River, seventeen miles southwest of Rogersville. Parke's entire force numbered approximately ten thousand.[50]

When Martin reported the enemy dispositions at Bean's Station, Longstreet decided to bag Shackelford's cavalry and an infantry brigade at the station. On the afternoon of the 14th, the Confederates struck. But like other operations during the past two months, the execution failed. Martin was ordered to ford the Holston River below the enemy camp and march his four brigades into the mountain gap behind the Federals. The cavalry commander managed to cross only part of his force, however, and then halted, his men firing long-distance at the Yankees. Worse yet, Brigadier General William Jones and two brigades, moving along the mountain north of the station, reached the gap, found a park of Federal wagons, looted them, and then withdrew.[51]

At Bean's Station, meanwhile, Bushrod Johnson's twenty-four-hundred-man division bore the brunt of the fight. Johnson's men charged the village, surprising the Federals. The Yankees used the buildings for cover, with the three-story brick tavern the center of the resistance. At one time the hotel was reportedly the finest between New Orleans and Baltimore. On this day it served as a fortress. The combat—"the briskest little fight of the war," according to Major Osmun Latrobe—flowed among the buildings. Union artillerists delivered a killing fire that slowed the Southerners. The defenders in the hotel hung on until a Confederate battery slammed two cannon balls into the brick walls. Porter Alexander unlimbered his cannon in an old graveyard, but Longstreet ordered him not to fire when Joseph Kershaw's brigade marched across the battalion's front against the enemy's left flank. Alexander grumbled afterward that "it was one of the disappointments of my life not to have turned my whole battalion loose there that evening." When the sharpshooters scampered from the hotel, the Federals retreated. The Northerners reported 115 casualties; Johnson, 222.[52]

Few things worked better for the Confederates on the 15th. When Longstreet told McLaws to march his division into the gap and round up Federal stragglers, the subordinate objected, citing the hunger of his men, who had had no bread rations for two days. Displeased, Longstreet ordered one brigade forward, called for rations to be hurried to the soldiers, and assigned Jenkins's division to the pursuit. Three miles beyond Bean's Station, Jenkins's men encountered the Yankees behind rail defenses. Supported by Martin's horsemen, the Confederate infantry skirmished with the enemy. But Parke rushed additional units from Rutledge, and the line held. Earlier, Longstreet had directed the brigades of Evander Law and Jerome Robertson of McLaws's division, who had been guarding the trains, to march to Jenkins's assistance, but the two commands took hours to cover the eight miles. When Longstreet appeared on the scene late in the afternoon, Law grumbled to him about the hardships and lack of food.[53]

During the night, Parke pulled back from Rutledge, retreating to Blain's Cross Roads. Here, Martin's cavalrymen found the Yankees and probed their line throughout the 16th. Jenkins marched to Rutledge and encamped there for the next two days. On the 19th, Longstreet started his troops eastward to winter quarters. The entire operation frustrated and angered him. His men had secured only sixty-eight wagons, forty of which were loaded with coffee and sugar. In his report, he claimed that among several generals "there seemed so strong a desire for rest rather than to destroy the enemy." He wrote that the movement only pushed the enemy closer to Knoxville and gave "us foraging grounds."[54]

Three days before Christmas, the Confederates—"poorly clad, scantily fed, and many of them barefooted," in the description of an officer—were settling into winter quarters south of the Holston River around Russellville, Morristown, and Rogersville, along the tracks of the East Tennessee and Virginia Railroad. They had their "shanties" built by Christmas and had foraged through the country-side for their holiday meals. Although an officer thought the region "a bleak, desolate, inhospitable country," the soldiers found it for the present brimming with foodstuffs and "moonshine." On Christmas Day they dined on turkey, chicken, ham, molasses cake, ginger-bread, and cornpone. It was a welcome feast for men who had been hungry since they had left Tyner's Station. Moxley Sorrel remembered the troops as "happy and cheerful," despite the shortages of winter clothing and shoes. Ample supplies of oak and hickory logs warmed the shanties, but winter had only begun—long nights to think of home, families, and the diminished hopes of the cause.[55]

If the men remained "happy and cheerful," as Sorrel later attested, it resulted from those inner qualities shared by veterans. They knew that the recent campaign had been a failure or, as a Georgia lieutenant informed his parents after Bean's Station: "Gen Longstreet's whole campaign in Tennessee has been a mystery to me & to all the rest of us." A cavalryman with Martin claimed that the Knoxville operation "raised a bitter feeling in the army against" Longstreet. As far away as Richmond, criticism of the general could be heard in conversations. Mary Boykin Chesnut, the wife of Colonel James Chesnut, President Davis's adviser, and an astute observer of the social and political scene in the capital, recorded in her diary in December: "Detached from General Lee, what a horrible failure, what a slow old humbug is Longstreet." The rumor in the city, according to Mrs. Chesnut, was that his own men called him "Peter the slow."[56]

Longstreet sensed the discontent with his generalship. The previous three months had exacted their price. The compelling charac-teristic of the man—his self-confidence—had deserted him. The glory of Chickamauga, when soldiers chanted "Longstreet is the man," had been tarnished by the derisive joke, "Peter the slow."

Instead of accepting his responsibility, however, he chose denial, attributing the blame to others. On December 17, he relieved from duty his childhood friend, West Point classmate, and senior subordinate Lafayette McLaws for "a want of confidence in the efforts and plans which the Cmdg Genl has thought proper to adopt." Tennessee was a bitter place.[57]

"THE IMPOSSIBLE POSITION THAT I HELD"

The scene has been lost to history, but it may be conjectured. Alone in a room of a widow's house, Longstreet sat at a table writing a letter to request that he be relieved of command. He appeared broken by the burdens of independent command, by the knowledge of his failures at Lookout Valley and at Knoxville; he was a general without direction and a man without self-assurance. At no other time during the war, except for the months after the deaths of his children and perhaps on the third day of Gettysburg, did he seem so depressed. By his own admission, he felt isolated from the counsel of superiors and bereft of authority. The overcast skies of a winter's day may have added to the darkness within the man.[1]

He may have sensed it, but he could not have known with certainty that he was at the nadir of his Confederate career. Thirteen days before, he had relieved from duty Major General Lafayette McLaws, and now he was preparing formal charges against his long-time friend and fellow officer. With the cold of winter at hand, his troops suffered from shortages of clothing, shoes, and food. His officer corps seethed with dissension, some of it of his own making. As he saw it from his headquarters, it was an "impossible position that I held."[2]

The letter that Longstreet prepared, dated December 30, 1863, was addressed to General Samuel Cooper, Adjutant and Inspector General of the Confederacy. "If this field is to be held with a view to future operations," declared Longstreet, "I earnestly desire that some other officer be sent to the command." The recent campaign at Knoxville, he argued, failed because of a combination of circumstances. "It is fair to infer," he confessed, "that the fault is entirely with me, and I desire, therefore, that some other commander be tried." In conclusion, "I believe that this is the only personal favor that I have asked of the Government, and I hope that I may have reason to expect that it may be granted."

Longstreet also informed Cooper that he had relieved McLaws from duty and requested a court-martial for Brigadier General Jerome Robertson, charged with "incompetency" by his division commander, Brigadier General Micah Jenkins. McLaws had not been arrested, stated Longstreet, "for the reason that it was supposed that his services might be important to the Government in some other position. If such is the case, I have no desire that he should be kept from that service, or that his usefulness should be impaired in any way by a trial." With the letter Longstreet submitted a formal charge of "Neglect of duty" with three specifications against McLaws. The specifications cited him for the assault on Fort Sanders.[3]

When the correspondence arrived in the capital, Cooper endorsed it with the notation that Longstreet had no authority to relieve the two officers and send them beyond the limits of his command but could have arrested them and requested courts-martial. He then forwarded the documents to Secretary of War James Seddon, who passed them on to President Davis. Seddon was willing to accept Longstreet's request that he be relieved, but Davis opposed it until a successor could be found. As for McLaws and Robertson, Davis ordered courts-martial assembled when the "interests of the service will permit." By January 16, 1864, Seddon had approved a court to be held at Russellville, Tennessee, and delegated Cooper to recommend the generals for it. Cooper then informed Longstreet, McLaws, and Robertson that the court would convene on February 3 or "as soon thereafter."[4]

Delays ensued, and the courts did not convene until February 12 at 10:00 A.M. in Morristown instead of Russellville. Major General Simon Buckner, Longstreet's accomplice in the effort to remove Braxton Bragg, served as president of the court. The other members were Major General Charles Field, Brigadier Generals John Gregg, Francis T. Nicholls, George Anderson, Benjamin Humphreys, and James Kemper, who had not fully recovered from his Gettysburg wound and required crutches. Major Garnett Andrews acted as judge advocate or prosecutor for the court.[5]

The proceedings began with the trial of Jerome Robertson, commander of the Texas Brigade, charged with "conduct highly prejudicial to good order and military discipline" at Bean's Station. During the engagement, his division commander, Micah Jenkins, ordered Robertson to advance his brigade on the Confederate right. When a courier relayed the verbal instructions, Robertson assembled his regimental commanders and ranted about the lack of food and shoes, snorting that "God only knows where more are to come from." He was tired of unkept promises from superiors, had no confidence in the campaign, and exclaimed at the end that he would need written orders before they marched. By the time Robertson finished the tirade and sent the brigade forward, the fighting had ended.[6]

The seven-member court evidently heard testimony from the three regimental commanders of the brigade and from Jenkins. The trial concluded before the end of the day. Three days later Longstreet granted permission to Robertson to travel to Richmond and "await there the promulgation of the sentence." If the court rendered a verdict and forwarded it to the capital, no record of it has been found. Davis and Seddon apparently dismissed the charges. A staff officer with Longstreet's command, while admitting that Robertson was not "considered a good officer," told his mother that "I am satisfied he has been unjustly dealt with, and is 'more sinned against than sinning.'" Nevertheless, Robertson would never again serve with the First Corps. Afterward, he asked for a transfer to Texas, and in June assumed command of the state's reserve forces.[7]

Buckner reconvened the court the next morning, February 13, to hear McLaws's case. Before testimony could be heard, a courier arrived with orders from Longstreet to adjourn until March 15 "or as soon thereafter as possible." Longstreet had begun a movement on Knoxville and wrote that he "shall need not only the witnesses that your court wants, but the members of the court who belong with us." Buckner complied; the court adjourned, and the generals returned to their commands. Longstreet directed McLaws to proceed to Abingdon, Virginia, and remain there until summoned by Buckner.[8]

In Abingdon, McLaws prepared extensive "Notes for Defence"

for the trial. From the beginning, on December 17, 1863, when Moxley Sorrel presented him with the order of his relief from duty, McLaws determined to fight the action. On December 18 he wrote to his friend and fellow Georgian Brigadier General Henry Benning, stating that "it is a real Lincolnite affair prompt and positive without reasons given further than the order." He continued: "That I have differed from Gen. Longstreet in his military measures there can be no doubt, but that I have been influenced in my conduct because of this difference or that my command has been influenced by it is totally without foundation." McLaws then asked Benning for any information the brigadier might possess, concluding, "I am as much in the dark as ever as to the particular cause of the order."[9]

Before he departed for Augusta, McLaws, according to a postwar letter, confronted Longstreet and asked why he had been relieved. "I had not co-operated cordially with him," as McLaws recounted Longstreet's answer, "& he was afraid that my influence would extend to the troops that one of us must go, that he could not & therefore I must & I could." McLaws then demanded that Longstreet file formal charges, and once the latter did on the 30th, McLaws wrote a lengthy letter to Cooper, dismissing each specification. He called upon Cooper to order a court-martial.[10]

Then, while in Abingdon, McLaws sought advice and assistance from various individuals. Brigadier General William Martin, the cavalry commander, assured McLaws that he would be vindicated and offered any correspondence he had that McLaws might need. Major John F. Edwards, McLaws's chief of commissary, who was serving temporarily on Longstreet's staff, relayed headquarters gossip to the general's brother, W. R. McLaws, and journeyed on leave to Richmond, where he argued McLaws's case before government officials and members of Congress. Like Edwards, Benning repeated rumors or alleged conversations about the attack on Fort Sanders, gave advice, and approached Buckner about serving as his friend's counselor. Benning believed that the defense hinged on whether they could demonstrate "that Gen. Longstreet regarded the ditch as a trifling affair not requiring ladders."[11]

It was in the capital, however, that McLaws had his most important ally, Braxton Bragg. Despite the disgraceful rout of his army at Missionary Ridge and his subsequent resignation, Bragg was serving as nominal general-in-chief of the Confederacy, appointed to the post in February by President Davis. To Bragg, McLaws's case offered a chance for revenge against Longstreet and others for "the treasonable act" of trying to remove him from command. When McLaws wrote Bragg two letters in February, the general-in-chief willingly responded.[12]

"The case was so extraordinary and involved so much calculated to destroy the integrity of the service," Bragg informed McLaws on March 4, "that I determined to use the information." He had ordered Buckner, whom Bragg described as "a tool in interest against you," to expedite the trial without "further delay and annoyance" to McLaws. "The irregularities already committed cannot be commented on until the official proceedings are received," added Bragg. "They will not then escape attention." Finally, "This matter has been carried so far that self-defence may require you to attack, and I can assure you the evidence in my possession is ample to convict [Longstreet] of disobedience of orders, neglect of duty, and want of cordial co-operation and support, which resulted in all the disasters after Chicamauga. This matter is worthy of your consideration!"[13]

McLaws welcomed Bragg's advice and assistance, although the motives of the general-in-chief were evident. By now the Georgian believed, as he told his wife on March 8, "the charges are malicious I am more and more convinced every day." A day later McLaws replied to Bragg, writing: "I honestly think that the interest of the country demands that the cause of failure of this campaign should be known." He would in time prepare a list of charges and specifications against Longstreet, related not to the campaign but to the latter's efforts, as McLaws saw it, to prevent a trial.[14]

McLaws's suspicions about Longstreet and the trial had some basis in fact. The lieutenant general acted as if he never wanted the case to be heard. He granted thirty-day leaves of absence to Micah Jenkins, a key witness, and to Benjamin Humphreys, a member of the court. He also offered a leave to George Anderson, another member, but the brigadier declined. The leave to Humphreys evidently prompted Cooper to inquire of Buckner whether Longstreet was endeavoring to undermine the court. On March 12, one day after the court reconvened, Buckner wrote to Cooper: "It is proper for me to say that every facility has been rendered to the Court, in the transaction of its business, by the Dept. Cmdr.—and no interference has been designed with its proceedings." Humphreys, asserted Buckner, needed a leave because of matters "of the most urgent character." Then, when the court met, Longstreet was absent, having been ordered to the capital for consultations.[15]

Snow lay on the ground in Greenville, Tennessee, when Simon Buckner ordered the court into session before noon on March 11. Longstreet had charged McLaws with "Neglect of duty" in the Fort Sanders assault. The first specification cited the division commander for leaving the attack column unprotected by failing to place sharpshooters "within good rifle range." The second specification alleged that he did not issue correct instructions to the force, and the third claimed that he directed the assault units toward the section of the fort where the ditch "was impassable" and did not supply the troops with ladders or other means of crossing the barrier.[16]

The court heard witnesses for the next two days, including Colonel Porter Alexander and Dr. Dorsey Cullen of Longstreet's staff. A three-day adjournment followed, with the court reconvening on the 16th in Midway, Tennessee. Five other officers testified that day and the next. Major Garnett Andrews asked for a delay until Longstreet and Jenkins returned. On March 19, with only three members of the court present, Buckner adjourned it for a final time. Major Joseph Ganahl, a surgeon in McLaws's division, served as defense counselor throughout the proceedings. Why Henry Benning, who requested the duty, did not act as an attorney for McLaws is unexplained.[17]

Several weeks later, on May 5, Cooper's office published the court's finding. The court acquitted McLaws on the first two specifications but found him guilty of the third specification—"failing in the details of his attack to make arrangements essential to his success." McLaws was suspended from rank and command for sixty days. Cooper overturned the verdict and sentence, however, citing the leave of absence granted to Humphreys and the adjournment of the court in February as "irregularities . . . fatal to the record." Cooper dissolved the court and ordered McLaws returned to duty with his division. At the end of the month, however, the War Department assigned McLaws to the Department of South Carolina, Georgia, and Florida. He protested the transfer to Seddon, but, like Robertson, McLaws was gone from the First Corps.[18]

McLaws believed he was a victim of "a combination against me," so Longstreet could secure the promotion of Micah Jenkins to permanent command of John Hood's division and of Joseph Kershaw to McLaws's. To McLaws, Longstreet also needed a scapegoat for his own failures in East Tennessee and chose him. The deposed commander blamed not only Longstreet but Buckner, Jenkins, and others, "the commander and his clique," as McLaws described them.[19]

McLaws departed a bitter man, and with some justification. The sentiment among the officers and men of the First Corps was divided over the matter, however. A South Carolina officer in his division argued later that McLaws "was not the man for the times— not the man to command such troops as he had." In April, President Davis sent Lieutenant Colonel Archer Anderson on a secret mission to Longstreet's command to investigate the situation. Although he conducted a perfunctory survey and did not consult with officers in McLaws's division, Anderson reported on the 14th that he could "discover no dissension of moment among the officers of Longstreet's Corps. Assurances have everywhere been given me that no feeling was aroused in McLaws's division by the arrest and trial of its commander. . . . If opinion may be expressed after such limited observation as I made, I would say that General Longstreet possesses the confidence and affection of his officers and men."[20]

Decades later, in his memoirs, Longstreet admitted that he should not have filed charges against McLaws, stating that the dismissal by Cooper "was very gratifying to me, who could have taken several reprimands to relieve a personal friend of [an] embarrassing position." In July 1873, after he and McLaws had reconciled to some extent, Longstreet wrote to him that he had relieved the subordinate "in an unguarded moment." The action was rooted in McLaws's health problems and Longstreet's responsibility for his division given to him by Robert E. Lee before Gettysburg. "I know as well as you," Longstreet continued, "that Mr. Davis would be pleased to have you make charges against me, and that Gen Bragg would be more than pleased to join you, and I will say frankly that I would rather have had you make charges against me than to be obliged to make them against you. I was anxious to be rid of the impossible position that I held."[21] In time, the breach healed between the two aging warriors, although McLaws never fully forgave Longstreet.

While the legal proceedings transpired during the winter weeks, Longstreet attended to the myriad of responsibilities of independent command. The daily duties, the efforts to supply his men's needs, the activities of the Federals, and the formulation of plans and strategies seemingly rejuvenated him in late December. As Anderson's report indicated, despite the difficult conditions endured by the troops, Longstreet maintained morale.

Hardships stalked the camps around Russellville and Morristown. The weather was bitterly cold—the worst in a decade—and the soldiers had only shelter tents or "shanties" for protection. They slept on beds of leaves and straw, covered with oilcloth. For much of the time they had inadequate clothing, until a shipment of fourteen thousand uniforms arrived from North Carolina in late February or early March. Many men went barefoot or wore rags on their feet. Some of the soldiers retrieved fresh cow hides, cut out a piece for each foot, and molded shoes. "They were better than nothing for a time," recalled an Alabamian. The officers formed work details to produce "moccasins," at a rate of roughly a hundred pairs a day, while other squads raided local tanyards for leather. On February 1, a brigade of South Carolinians received a shipment of fifteen hundred pairs of shoes from civilians in their home state.[22]

The most critical shortage was food; a soldier remembered that he and his comrades were "constantly hungry." The diet consisted mainly of coarse cornbread and bacon. Vegetables were a rarity because the local populace, many of whom were Union sympathizers, refused to accept Confederate currency. A Georgia officer joked to his wife that he and fellow officers enjoyed each night "a very royal snack" of two or three biscuits and "a flitch or so" of bacon cooked over a fire. The scarce rations were supplied in uneven quantities, and some weeks were worse than others. A South Carolinian grumbled that he "lived on lye hominy" for many days, and another veteran from the same state asserted later that all his comrades had was an ear of corn each day for a week. Tobacco was in such short supply that when the men wanted to smoke, they walked away from the campfires in order not to share what little they possessed.[23]

The primary responsibility for gathering foodstuffs fell to Major Raphael Moses, Longstreet's chief of commissary. "A very able man," in the view of Captain Charles Blackford of the staff, Moses used ingenuity and blackmail to extract supplies from civilians. He confiscated the books of local wheat thrashers and identified each farmer with the grain. When farmers hid their bacon from the troops, Moses collected their sheep, then swapped two pounds of sheep for one pound of bacon. "This unlocked the secret places in which bacon was hid," he chuckled later. He traded for nearly all the bacon the men required, but on occasion he had the sheep butchered and the mutton distributed. The meat, however, was thin and "very distasteful" to the troops. With some exaggeration Moses boasted in his memoirs that he "kept the army supplied six weeks after Longstreet thought he would be obliged to retreat for want of supplies."[24]

The weather, the scarcities, and the inadequate shelters took their toll. A Georgian expressed to his sister a sentiment shared by thousands of his comrades when he wrote: "I think if I could only start home I would be the happiest mortal that Ever lived." While he did not "start home," scores of others deserted. If captured, the men were court-martialed, and several were executed. The sick and wounded, meanwhile, filled hospitals, with the worst cases sent to hospitals in Virginia. Longstreet frequently visited the local hospitals, spoke to each man, and, on one recorded occasion, helped dress one of the patients. The men appreciated his visits and acts of kindness.[25]

The wounded men were the result of skirmishes and minor engagements with the enemy. In mid-January, a month after Bean's Station, the Federals stirred from Knoxville, marching to Dandridge and Strawberry Plains between the Holston and French Broad rivers. About the first of the month, Major General Ulysses S. Grant had visited Knoxville and ordered Major General John Foster to drive the Confederates farther eastward, at least beyond Bull's Gap, southeast of Russellville. Grant pulled additional cavalry units from elsewhere in the state to augment Foster's command. On the 14th, the Yankees advanced, with three cavalry divisions and three corps of infantry. Foster, who was ill, remained in Knoxville, and the command devolved on Major General Gordon Granger.[26]

When the Federals reached Dandridge on the 15th, Brigadier General William Martin, Confederate cavalry commander, notified Longstreet. The next morning the Rebels marched toward the Northerners—two infantry divisions to support Martin's horsemen at Dandridge and two infantry divisions toward Strawberry Plains. Longstreet rode ahead and joined Martin outside of the town. Despite Grant's directive, the Federals advanced cautiously, and Martin's cavalrymen attacked, driving the enemy through the town. Longstreet personally led one of Martin's brigades in the charge. That night McLaws and his staff enjoyed drinks of whiskey from a flask left behind by Granger.[27]

Granger's units retired behind their fortifications at Knoxville, and some of the Confederate units returned to camp. Longstreet, however, remained at the front with Martin's cavalry. When another Federal sortie was repulsed a week later, he began thinking in terms of an offensive against Knoxville. He had repair crews increase their efforts on the railroad and ordered the pontoon train brought forward. He posted Jenkins's division at Strawberry Plains and relocated his headquarters there. He requested ten thousand reinforcements from Richmond and telegraphed his old friend General Joseph Johnston, who now commanded the Army of Tennessee in northern Georgia, to see if he could sever Union communications between Chattanooga and Knoxville. He asserted subsequently in a letter to Davis that if he had more troops and Johnston had been able to assist him, he could have starved the Federals out of Knoxville. But he received no additional units, and Johnston could not undertake the proposed movement.[28]

On February 20, Longstreet received a telegram from Davis that directed him to send Martin's cavalry to Johnston's army. The president informed Longstreet that no troops could be spared for another operation against Knoxville and concluded that Johnston required the services of the cavalry more than Longstreet. Johnston also reported to Longstreet that the enemy was reinforcing Knoxville. Although he objected to the loss of Martin's command, Longstreet knew he would have to withdraw eastward, perhaps as far as Bristol. He wired Davis that he would dispatch Martin and that he would retire to a safer position.[29]

The Confederates began the withdrawal on the 22nd, marching toward Bull's Gap beyond Russellville. Here Longstreet halted the bulk of his command, and the troops barricaded and fortified the defile. One infantry division and a number of artillery batteries encamped eighteen miles from the gap at Greeneville, where Longstreet established his headquarters. Pickets extended beyond the gap to Russellville. Longstreet maintained later that the position was "unassailable."[30]

"Greeneville is perhaps the most intensely disloyal town in E. Tenn.," a Virginian wrote to his mother, "and indeed is to a considerable extent deserted by its people who could not abide the return of the C. S. troops." The town was the former home of Andrew Johnson, soon to be Lincoln's vice president and a former United States senator who opposed his state's secession. When the troops learned that Johnson had lived there, some of them looted his home, law office, and tailor shop. But Thomas Goree of Longstreet's staff stopped the men and forced them to return the items. The staff members located a few loyal Southerners and enjoyed their stay in the village.[31]

On March 8, Longstreet boarded a train for Virginia. (On this day in Washington, Grant accepted his appointment as general-in-chief of the Union armies, with the reauthorized rank of lieutenant general.) For weeks Longstreet had exchanged letters with Lee and Johnston about strategic operations in the western theater. He offered several proposals, including a plan to mount his corps on horses and mules for a raid against the Federals' line of communication in Kentucky. Lee countered that the animals could not be gathered without stripping them from other Confederate armies, which would immobilize those commands. Finally, before Longstreet left for Virginia, Lee wrote that a joint offensive by Johnston and Longstreet in Tennessee was under study and asked Longstreet to consider the plan.[32]

Longstreet journeyed initially to Lee's headquarters at Orange Court House. The two men had not seen each other since September, and the welcome must have been warm. After serving under the detested Braxton Bragg, Longstreet could only have had a deeper appreciation for Lee's qualities as a man and as a commander. For his part, Lee had not wavered in his estimation of his senior officer and respected his counsel.[33]

As Lee had requested, Longstreet gave thought to an operation in Tennessee. He envisioned a more ambitious stroke, suggesting that P. G. T. Beauregard with twenty thousand troops be moved by rail from South Carolina to Abingdon, Virginia. From there Beauregard could march into Kentucky, followed by Longstreet's command, toward Louisville and the Union railroad that supplied the troops in Tennessee. Johnston, meanwhile, could pull troops from Alabama and Mississippi to augment his army and then sweep across Tennessee into Kentucky, where the forces could unite in a "grand junction" and accept battle. Such a movement, Longstreet believed, could "break the entire front of the Federal forces."[34]

Lee approved and recommended that Longstreet continue on to Richmond and present the idea to Davis. Although Davis had requested proposals from Longstreet earlier, the latter knew that if he presented the plan, the president and Bragg, his inveterate enemy, would reject it. He asked Lee to accompany him and submit the plan as his own. Lee would not do that but consented to go with Longstreet. Together they boarded a train, passed through country both men knew well and had ably defended during the previous two years, and arrived in the capital on March 12.[35]

The next morning, a Sunday, Davis, Lee, Longstreet, and several other generals attended church services together. On Monday morning, the 14th, Lee met with the president, Seddon, and Bragg. The details of the discussion were not recorded, but Longstreet subsequently described it as "not conclusive." That afternoon Longstreet went with Lee for another meeting. Bragg, who was plotting with McLaws against Longstreet, suggested a combined movement of Johnston and Longstreet against Nashville. A debate ensued, with Lee wanting to know if Johnston approved of the idea. Longstreet said that he did not because of the logistical difficulties of supplying his army as it marched through the mountains of Georgia and Tennessee. Davis and Bragg had been urging such an operation to Johnston for weeks, but the president hesitated to implement it over the general's objections. The meeting adjourned without resolution.[36]

Longstreet left the city that night or the next morning for Petersburg, twenty miles south of the capital. When he left for Georgia in September 1863, Louise had moved in with a Mrs. Dunn in Petersburg. Longstreet spent two days with Louise, fifteen-year-old Garland, and Robert Lee, the infant son he had not seen. The time surely passed too swiftly, for Longstreet was on board a train for Tennessee on the 17th.[37]

Before he returned to his command, Longstreet wrote to Davis, Lee, and Johnston. His letter to the president was fifteen pages in length and detailed the proposal he had outlined to Lee of a combination of his, Beauregard's, and Johnston's forces for a movement into Kentucky. There were, Longstreet informed Davis, "great moral advantages" to retaking Tennessee, "but there can scarcely be a doubt but we can advance into Kentucky and hold that state if we are once united." He asserted that "my troops can start out upon this or any other move in three days," but if the Confederates were to achieve the initiative, any operation must begin by April 1. "These ideas are given under the supposition that if they are thought worthy to be adopted," he continued, "it will be done with a determination to execute the movements with such undivided vigor as to insure great results."[38]

To Lee and Johnston, Longstreet repeated his request for their support for the plan. "You complain of my excess of confidence," he acknowledged to Lee, but the union of his and Beauregard's troops could be, he argued, "the beginning of the end of this war." To Johnston he voiced similar optimism, writing: "I think it the strongest effort thus ... attempted during the war and have confidence in its resulting in a speedy race." He admitted to his former commander, however, that "we don't know what will be done. All agree in the idea that we should take the initiative."[39]

Longstreet reached Greeneville, Tennessee, on Friday, March 18. During the next three weeks, events quickened, bringing a resolution to the strategic dilemma. On March 20, Confederate authorities ordered Longstreet's one cavalry division to Johnston's army, and the Federals advanced from Knoxville, demonstrating against his lines at Bull's Gap. When the enemy retired, Longstreet decided that he had to concentrate his infantry near the railroad, so on the 28th he started them toward Bristol. Three days later he reported to Lee that the Union Ninth Corps was en route to Virginia. Longstreet confirmed the intelligence on April 2, and Lee asked Davis for Longstreet's command. The president finally abandoned the plan for an offensive in Middle Tennessee—Johnston had continued to raise objections—and issued orders on the 7th for Longstreet's return to the Army of Northern Virginia.[40]

Longstreet's bold strategic proposal had been dismissed. Although Davis worked tirelessly to fashion an offensive in the West, the difficulties of achieving a concentration plus Johnston's opposition doomed the effort. Johnston's arguments about supplying his army with food and forage while on the march across the mountains had merit. In fact, logistics rendered Longstreet's plan an impossibility. Even his more modest scheme of a mounted raid by infantry foundered because of the shortage of horses and mules. Increasingly, Confederate operations were strangled by inadequate transportation and resources.[41]

The impracticalities of Longstreet's plans should not overshadow their strategic vision. He was convinced that the policy of scattering forces across the breadth of the Confederacy or placing "our troops just where he [the enemy] wants them" would result in ultimate defeat. The nation's most important advantage—interior lines of operations—must be utilized as it had been for the Chickamauga Campaign in a grand concentration of forces that could regain the initiative in the conflict. Biding their time and waiting for a massed Union strike meant a slow death for the Southerners. While his raid by mounted infantry did not involve a concentration, he grasped the value of raiders and anticipated Grant's use of infantry as a raiding force during the war's final year.[42]

The invasion of Kentucky, moreover, reflected the astuteness and prescience of Longstreet's strategic thinking. Although a conquest of this critical border state would have been of inestimable military value, Longstreet predicated the move on political consequences. In his view, Confederate independence would result only with the electoral defeat of Lincoln in the fall. If the Rebels held Kentucky, he contended in a March 27 letter to Colonel Thomas Jordan, "it would be a powerful argument against Lincoln and against the war. Lincoln's re-election seems to depend upon the result of our efforts during the present year. If he is re-elected, the war must continue, and I see no way of defeating his re-election except by military success." To Longstreet the stakes necessitated risks, a gamble against the long odds and the deepening darkness moving across the Confederacy. It was the judgment of a general with strategic insight.[43]

The return of Longstreet's command to Lee's army was delayed for several days because of problems with the railroad. The first contingent of troops piled into cars on April 11. One of the trains derailed west of Lynchburg, injuring a number of soldiers and slowing the movement. By the 22nd most of the units had reached Mechanicsville, five miles west of Gordonsville, and their comrades in the Army of Northern Virginia. A Georgian with Longstreet exclaimed in a letter to his sister that they were now back with "the great and much beloved chieftain Gen R E Lee." Colonel Walter Taylor of Lee's staff wrote to Longstreet a few days after his arrival that "I really am beside myself, General, with joy of having you back. It is like the reunion of a family." A soldier of lesser rank than Taylor also rejoiced, pleased that Lee's "right-hand man" had rejoined the army. Weeks earlier Congress had voted its "thanks" to

Longstreet and the troops "for their patriotic services and brilliant achievements in the present war."[44]

The First Corps units that came back to Virginia had undergone key personnel changes during their final weeks in Tennessee. Since Hood's fall at Chickamauga in September 1863 and since McLaws's removal in December, command of the two divisions had been unresolved and the cause of turmoil among the officers. As noted previously, McLaws believed that Longstreet's action against him had been predicated on the latter's desire to have Micah Jenkins and Joseph Kershaw promoted and assigned permanently to the respective divisions. Unquestionably, Longstreet's maneuvering to place Jenkins at the head of Hood's division resulted in an acrid dispute with Evander Law and impaired the efficiency of this excellent unit. For McLaws's brigades, he preferred Kershaw and warmly endorsed the appointment.

Jefferson Davis, however, chose to resolve the issue with Hood's command by appointing Major General Charles Field to the post on February 12, 1864. Field, a thirty-five-year-old Kentuckian, was an 1849 graduate of West Point; he had led a brigade in Powell Hill's Light Division until seriously wounded at Second Manassas. During his lengthy convalescence, Field served for a time as superintendent of the Bureau of Conscription. He had been a capable brigadier and, more important, available for field duty when Davis assigned him permanently to Hood's division.[45]

When Longstreet learned of Field's appointment, he endeavored to thwart Davis's decision by placing Simon Buckner, who was on temporary duty with Longstreet, in command of Hood's brigades and shifting Field to Buckner's division. If Buckner was transferred to another post, direction of the division would again devolve on Jenkins, the senior brigadier. Once he implemented the change, he informed the War Department. Cooper responded at once: "The order from this office assigning Field to [Hood's] Division will be carried out." Unbowed, Longstreet asked if the department would approve giving Field McLaws's division. Again, Cooper telegraphed back immediately that "it does not suit the views of the President to assign Major General Field to the Division lately commanded by Major General McLaws. He is to take the Division to which he was assigned in orders from this office."[46]

Field reported for duty at Greeneville during the first week of

March. His appointment gnawed at Longstreet, however, until he again allowed his displeasure to affect his judgment. On March 20 he wrote an indignant letter to Cooper inquiring which distinguished services and "high recommendations" of Field had "induced the Government to make this unusual promotion and assignment." Cooper passed the letter on to Davis, who reacted furiously to Longstreet's temerity and insubordination, and instructed Cooper to send a stern reprimand. Cooper complied, writing to Longstreet: "The advice you have asked is considered highly insubordinate and demands rebuke. It is also a reflection upon a gallant and meritorious officer, who has been severely wounded in battle in the cause of the Confederate States and deemed unbecoming the high position and dignity of the officer who thus makes the reflection." Cooper then reminded Longstreet of the regulations and stated: "Your inquiry is a direct reflection upon the Executive." Longstreet was no match for Davis in such matters—Field took Hood's division; Jenkins resumed command of his brigade.[47]

The appointment of Field did not end the controversy within the division, however. Although Jenkins was denied the promotion and command that he coveted, so, too, was his rival, Evander Law. The jealousy and dislike between the two brigadiers and Longstreet's transparent preference for Jenkins had originally ignited the dispute, impaired the efficiency of the command, and contributed to its performance in Lookout Valley, at Campbell's Station, and at Bean's Station. On December 19, 1863, Law tendered his resignation, unwilling to serve under Jenkins any longer.[48]

Law presented his resignation personally to Longstreet and asked for a leave of absence with the privilege of carrying the letter to Richmond. Law told Longstreet that he was making this unusual request so he could seek service in the cavalry. The proposal seemed to Longstreet a fine opportunity to rid himself of Law and secure the division for Jenkins. "The favor," as Longstreet termed it, was "cheerfully granted," and Law left Tennessee. Once in the capital, Law conferred with his friend and former commander John Hood, who convinced the brigadier to allow him to take the resignation to Secretary of War Seddon. Hood showed the letter to Seddon but did not formally submit it. Instead, Hood convinced Law to reconsider and destroyed the letter. Law assumed that because he had not officially tendered his resignation, he retained command of his brigade and boarded a train for Tennessee.[49]

Longstreet, meanwhile, heard rumors that the officers of Law's Alabama brigade were circulating a petition for transfer to their native state and that their commander had sought leave to expedite acceptance of it by the War Department. Longstreet fumed with outrage, and when Law returned from Virginia, he had the brigadier arrested and filed a charge against him for "conduct highly prejudicial to good order and military discipline," alleging that he obtained his leave under "false pretenses" and accusing him of "deceiving his commanding general to his real intentions." Approximately two weeks later, Longstreet added a second charge: the failure to deliver his resignation and that he "did purloin or clandestinely do away with said communication." As a final measure, as the corps prepared to leave for Virginia, Longstreet transferred the brigade to Simon Buckner's division, which was to remain in East Tennessee. Colonel William Oates, commander of the Fifteenth Alabama and one of Law's counsels, contended later that "the effort to punish the men of that brigade to gratify his malice against Law, its commander, was too small a thing for a man of Longstreet's position to have stooped to perform. But he was brim-full of malice."[50]

The patience of the president and the War Department with Longstreet had been frayed—first McLaws, then Robertson, and now Law. On April 18, Cooper ordered Law relieved from arrest and replaced in command of his brigade, which should be sent to Charlottesville, Virginia. Eight days later Lee informed Longstreet that Davis "had declined to entertain the charges" and directed that Law be restored to command. Longstreet now challenged Davis's authority for a second time within two months: He ordered Law rearrested upon his appearance and put the matter bluntly to Lee on April 27, writing:

> If my efforts to maintain discipline, spirit, and zeal in the discharge of official duty are to be set aside by the return of General Law and his restoration to duty without trial, it cannot be well for me to remain in command. I cannot yield the authority of my position so long as I am responsible for the proper discharge of its functions. It is necessary, therefore, that General Law should be brought to trial upon the charges that have been preferred against him, or that I be relieved from duty in the Confederate States service.[51]

Lee could not afford to lose Longstreet because active operations were about to begin. On April 30 the commanding general recommended "that General Law be relieved from duty until an investigation can be had." This placated Longstreet, but within two weeks Law had been restored to command by Davis. By then Longstreet was not with the First Corps, and on June 3, Law fell wounded in battle. Upon his recovery he was transferred, at his request, to the cavalry. Somewhere, perhaps in the fields and woods southwest of Little Round Top on July 2, 1863, a shadow of misfortune enveloped this outstanding division and did not dissipate until nearly a year later.[52]

In McLaws's former division, meanwhile, the senior brigadier, Joseph Kershaw, retained temporary command. A forty-two-year-old South Carolinian, Kershaw had been an attorney, Mexican War veteran, and state legislator before the war exploded in his native state. Appointed colonel of the Second South Carolina, he led it with distinction at First Manassas and was subsequently promoted to brigadier general in February 1862. Intelligent, devout, with striking features and blond hair, Kershaw possessed "steady courage and military aptitude," in the words of Moxley Sorrel. He also had "boundless ambition" and, like Jenkins, desired promotion and divisional command. When he initially went off to war, his beautiful wife, Lucretia, so missed him that she wore a necklace and bracelets woven from locks of his hair.[53]

The months of turmoil, of shortages, and of winter's cold were forgotten for a few hours on April 29 when the two divisions of the First Corps, with Field and Kershaw at their heads, passed in review for General Lee and a crowd of civilians, including ladies. "No one who was present could ever forget the occasion," claimed Porter Alexander. Lee and his staff entered the one-hundred-acre field through large square gateposts, spurred their mounts up a knoll, and halted beneath a panoply of tall oak trees. As Lee—"he had aged a great deal more than a year in the past twelve months," a South Carolinian thought—and his entourage rode to their posts, Alexander had a bugle sounded, and his cannon bellowed in salute. Lee removed his hat, and the ranks of infantrymen echoed with shouts, while flagbearers waved their scarred colors. "For sudden as a wind, a wave of sentiment, such as can only come to large crowds in full sympathy . . ." remembered Alexander, "seemed to sweep the field. Each man seemed to feel the bond which held us all to Lee. There was no speaking, but the effect was that of a military sacrament, in which we pledged anew our lives."[54]

Lee, Longstreet, and their staffs rode along the length of the line, so closely they could see each man's face. A chaplain asked Colonel Charles Venable of Lee's staff: "Does it not make the general proud to see how these men love him?" "Not proud," remarked Venable, "it awes him." When the generals and aides finished the ride, they returned to the knoll. The infantrymen and artillery crews shifted into columns and marched past. So many times before, Lee and Longstreet had watched these units go by on roads that led to Second Manassas, Sharpsburg, Fredericksburg, and Gettysburg, bloody fields where "the bond" had been fused. "All were certainly glad to see General Lee," wrote a Georgian. "And I expect he was glad to have us again under his Banner." He was—another road and another field awaited.[55]

19

T W O   R O A D S

To Americans in 1864, spring brought not nature's renewal and the reaffirmation of life but death—in numbers that staggered a nation already numbed by the casualties of three years of war. Under the direction of Lieutenant General Ulysses S. Grant, the might of the Union was unsheathed as a terrible swift sword against the Confederacy. In Georgia, Major General William T. Sherman and three armies advanced on the heartland's citadel, Atlanta, and its defenders, General Joseph Johnston's Army of Tennessee. In Virginia, the Federals struck along three lines—in the Shenandoah Valley, up the James River east of Richmond, and against the Army of Northern Virginia in its lines south of the Rapidan River. On roads firmed after the spring thaw, the Yankees came.

The Confederates expected them. On May 2, General Robert E. Lee met with his corps commanders—Longstreet, Richard Ewell, and Powell Hill—and the army's eight division commanders on Clark's Mountain, northeast of Orange Court House. From the crest the generals surveyed the winter campsites of Major General George Meade's Army of the Potomac beyond the Rapidan River. Lee told his ranking subordinates that he expected the Federals to march on the Confederate right flank, crossing the river downstream at Germanna and/or Ely's fords. All preparations for a swift movement should be completed, cautioned Lee. He had approximately sixty-five thousand troops to oppose a force nearly twice that number.[1]

The Southerners had less than forty-eight hours to wait. At dawn on May 4 signalmen on Clark's Mountain detected the Federal movement as they looked north and saw roads jammed with endless columns of cavalry, infantry, artillery, and wagons. The Yankees had started toward the river after midnight, and some mounted units had already forded the stream. The Rebels on the mountain flagged a message to Ewell's headquarters, which was relayed to Lee's. Before midday, Lee had Ewell's and Hill's corps on the march eastward to intercept the Union army—Ewell by the Orange Turnpike, Hill on the Orange Plank Road. "It is apparent," Lee telegraphed Jefferson Davis, "that the long threatened effort to take Richmond has begun, and that the enemy has collected all his available force to accomplish it."[2]

Longstreet at his headquarters in Mechanicsville, five miles west of Gordonsville, learned of the developments along the Rapidan sometime before nine o'clock. Moxley Sorrel alerted the commanders of the infantry divisions—Charles Field and Joseph Kershaw—and the artillery battalions, now under Porter Alexander, who had been promoted to brigadier general and named the corps's artillery chief. Longstreet wired Lee's headquarters that his command would be ready to move when "called upon," and at 10:30 A.M. he sent a dispatch to Lee advising: "I fear the enemy is trying to draw us down to Fredericksburg. Can't we threaten his rear, so as to stop his move?" Half an hour later Sorrel issued orders to the infantry divisions to be "ready to move at once." Sorrel designated the route of march—via Forest Hill and Brock's Bridge toward Richards Shop at the intersection of the Old Fredericksburg and Lawyer's roads, and requested notification of "the earliest hour" the commands could march.[3]

In his memoirs, Longstreet stated that his orders from Lee to march arrived at his headquarters about 1:00 P.M. The commanding general instructed him to use the Orange Plank Road, following Hill's units to Parker's Store. Longstreet wrote back to Lee seeking permission to redirect his units on the route Sorrel had indicated earlier to Field and Kershaw. He also proposed that his command should advance to Brock Road where, as Longstreet noted later, "we could look for and hope to intercept the enemy's march, and cause him to develop plans before he could get out of the Wilderness." Lee consented to the change in route and destination.[4]

The Wilderness was an area of scrub trees and brush covering dozens of square miles south of the Rapidan. The two armies had fought each other in its confines a year before in the Battle of Chancellorsville. If the Federals cleared the Wilderness and went into the open terrain beyond, in the direction of Fredericksburg, the Confederates might be forced to assail the enemy's lines at a serious disadvantage. If Lee could bring the Yankees to battle amid the tangled terrain, however, he could negate their numerical strength and artillery superiority. Union Major General Joseph Hooker had allowed himself to be trapped there the year before, and Lee and Stonewall Jackson had inflicted a bloody defeat on him. But on this day Lee could not be certain whether Grant, who accompanied Meade's army and had overall direction of it, would endeavor either to march through it toward Fredericksburg or turn westward, as Meade had done the previous fall, and confront the Southerners head-on.[5]

With this uncertainty, Longstreet's recommendation made tactical sense. While Longstreet's knowledge of the terrain and distances may have been sketchy—he had not been present at Chancellorsville—he surely knew that his corps had too far to march to intercept the Northerners before they reached Brock Road. But if Grant planned to engage the Confederates along Mine Run, where they had sparred in November 1863, Longstreet's command would come in on the Federal left flank and, as he said, force Grant "to develop plans before he could get out of the Wilderness." Although Lee expected and hoped that Grant would pass directly through the Wilderness, where the Yankees could be ensnared again, he had to cover the other contingency for the present and approved Longstreet's alternate route. Finally, the Southerners would be racing to engage the enemy on three avenues of advance instead of two.[6]

The First Corps started eastward at four o'clock on the afternoon of May 4. According to a Georgian, the men were "confident and in high anticipation of success." The column marched all night and halted at Brock's Bridge on the morning of the 5th to rest and feed the animals. While at the bridge, Captain Erasmus Taylor of Longstreet's staff rode in with James Robinson, a former sheriff of the county, who agreed to serve as a guide. With Robinson at the front, the troops resumed the march down the Old Fredericksburg Road past Richard's Shops to near Craig's Meeting House on the Catharpin Road, where they stopped a second time about 5:00 P.M.

Longstreet placed his headquarters at the nearby residence of a Faulkner family.[7]

Soon after the troops encamped, Colonel Charles Venable of Lee's staff reached Longstreet's headquarters. Venable came with orders for Longstreet to redirect his march to Parker's Store on the Orange Plank Road, to arrive as soon as practicable but at least "by daybreak" on the 6th. The change in plans was the result of the day's fighting in the Wilderness, which Venable recounted. The Federals, said Venable, collided with Ewell's troops on the Orange Turnpike during the morning. Although Lee wanted to avoid a general engagement until all his units were on the field, Grant had forced the issue and the combat escalated, pulling in more and more troops from both armies. In the nightmarish terrain, the struggle was between shadows in the woods; regiments and brigades lost their cohesion and sense of direction, entangling lines of battle. By nightfall each army was entrenching in anticipation of another day's slaughter.[8]

Longstreet's veterans started toward the battlefield between midnight and 1:00 A.M. on the 6th. Field's division led, followed by Kershaw's and Alexander's batteries. The column marched on a seldom used road through the woods. At a fork in the road, the guide, an unidentified individual sent from army headquarters, proceeded in the wrong direction until the road disappeared in the foliage. Field's brigade retraced the route, and Longstreet doubled up the column, placing Kershaw's troops abreast of Field's. Only Field lost time because of the mistake, and when the Rebels struck the Plank Road at Parker's Store, Field moved on the left of the road, Kershaw on the right. It was daylight; the battlefield was three miles away. The pace quickened; they could hear the familiar din of battle, loud and sustained, like "the roar of water," as one of them jotted it in his diary. Unknowingly, they were on a road and in a race to save the Army of Northern Virginia.[9]

The clamor of cannon fire and musketry signaled an impending disaster for Lee's army. At first light, about 5:00 A.M., the Federals—elements of three corps—rolled forward in a massive offensive. On the Confederate left, Ewell's soldiers initiated the fighting, attacking before the enemy advanced, but then ran into a wall of resistance, staggered, and retired when the Yankees countercharged. On the Confederate right, however, the Northerners struck first, nine bri-

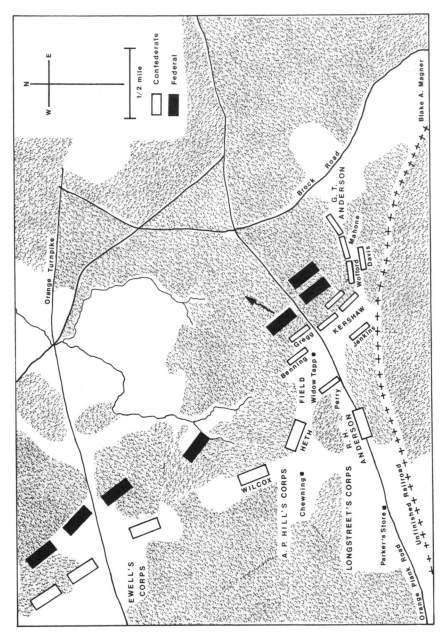

BATTLE OF THE WILDERNESS, MAY 6, 1864.

gades, roughly twenty thousand troops, spearheading the assault. Opposing them were the divisions of Major Generals Cadmus Wilcox and Henry Heth, with less than ten thousand men aligned on both sides of Plank Road. During the night, Wilcox and Heth had been informed that their battered ranks would be relieved before daylight by Longstreet's command and the Third Corps division of Major General Richard Anderson. Neither general rectified his lines, replenished ammunition, or had his men entrench even though evidence mounted throughout the night that the enemy was preparing something. "We expected an attack in overwhelming numbers at the first blush of dawn," recalled Colonel William Palmer, Hill's chief of staff.[10]

Wilcox's and Heth's men consequently never had a chance before the onslaught. Brigade after brigade of Confederates dissolved, the soldiers streaming to the rear in a rout. North of the road, the Southerners burst out of the woods into a field on the Widow Tapp farm. Lee was at hand, witnessing the collapse of his right flank and the "imminent" destruction of his army. According to Venable, he "was exceedingly disturbed" that Longstreet had not reached the field before the enemy attacked. Lee rushed Venable up Plank Road to hurry Longstreet and ordered Colonel Walter Taylor to ride to Parker's Store and ready the army's wagon train for a retreat. He then spurred Traveller toward the troops and when he met Brigadier General Samuel McGowan of Heth's division, Lee exclaimed angrily: "My God, General McGowan, is this fine brigade of yours fleeing like wild geese?" "Sir, my men are not beaten," McGowan snorted back. "They want only a place to reform and fight."[11]

Charles Venable found the heads of Field's and Kershaw's columns less than half a mile from the bedlam around the Widow Tapp farm and delivered to Longstreet the order from Lee to rush forward. Minutes later Cadmus Wilcox reined up and voiced similar instructions. Staff officers galloped to the infantry units; officers shouted commands, and the veteran soldiers shifted into battle formation. The ranks opened and shut to allow the passage of Wilcox's and Heth's men. Suddenly, the deluge of sound was hyphenated by the explosions of Confederate ordnance wagons parked in the clearing. On the western fringe of the field, an artillery battalion of Hill's unleashed a howling curtain of canister into the Union brigades. Moxley Sorrel had watched these First Corps units on many battlefields and marveled at what he witnessed this morning, writing afterward: "I have always thought that the forming line, in the dense brush, under fire of the enemy, amid the routed men of A. P. Hill, and the beating of the enemy under these circumstances was the steadiest and finest thing the corps ever did. To their chief was due that steadiness as always."[12]

North of Plank Road, Brigadier General John Gregg's Texas Brigade doubled-quicked to the front. Lee saw them coming and hurried to meet them. In Porter Alexander's words, Lee "was in the most desperate strait he had ever known." When the Texans and Arkansans saw Lee in their front, they halted and several yelled, "Go back General Lee. We will not go on if you don't go back." Lee consented and spurred Traveller across the road where he met Longstreet. They talked briefly about dispositions and separated as Longstreet rode ahead to oversee the attack.[13]

When Gregg's eight hundred men cleared the cannon on the edge of the field, the Federals met them with a volley. The musketry ravaged the ranks of the Texans and Arkansans. On their left, Brigadier General Henry Benning's Georgians entered the clearing and were hammered back. Behind them, Colonel W. F. Perry led Evander Law's Alabamians toward the enemy line, pressing through the Tapp farmland. South of the road, Joseph Kershaw—"who always looked like a gamecock, & now more so than ever," wrote Alexander—waved three of his brigades forward, surging ahead with the Alabamians. The Confederates triggered a volley that "seemed to shake the earth itself," claimed an eyewitness. The Federal ranks buckled, then broke and fled rearward. The Southerners hit like "a whirlwind," in Alexander's estimation. "It was superb," Venable remembered fifteen years later, "and my heart beats quicker to think about it at this distance of time."[14]

Longstreet and members of his staff rode forward with the battle line. The corps commander was, thought Major John Haskell, "always grand in battle, [and] never shone as he did here." Osmun Latrobe was hit in the right hand and thigh at the outset of the counterattack and left the field for assistance. The Texan Thomas Goree passed a group of wounded soldiers from Gregg's brigade and discovered his brother among them. Goree was with Longstreet at the time, and the general had tears in his eyes when he saw his aide's grief.[15]

The momentum of Longstreet's counterthrust slowed before the Federal resistance and the wooded, entangled ground, but it did not cease. Longstreet had adapted his tactics to the terrain. "As full lines of battle could not be handled through the thick wood," he wrote in his memoirs, "I ordered the advance of the six brigades by heavy skirmish lines, to be followed by stronger supporting lines." This formation was unconventional and contrary to the tactical manuals of the era. By dispersing the front units as skirmishers, the troops delivered a continuous fire into the massed ranks of the enemy and were elusive targets to their opponents' volleys. Longstreet then sustained the force of the attack by adding brigades from his command and Anderson's division.[16]

The struggle along Plank Road lasted for over two hours; Confederates seized one line of Union breastworks and pounded against a second. With the Yankees shoved into their works, "the fight became steady and very firm," as Longstreet described it, "occasionally swinging parts of my line back and compelling the reserves to move forward and recover it." Lee's army had been saved and the Union assault wrecked in one of the war's most dramatic counterattacks. A historian of the battle attributed much of the Confederate success to "the display of tactical genius by Longstreet which more than redressed his disparity in numerical strength." No other subordinate commander on the field matched his skill in handling troops on a battlefield.[17]

While the fighting continued, Brigadier General Martin L. Smith, Lee's chief engineer, reported to Longstreet. An able engineer and tactician, Smith had been sent by the commanding general to give Longstreet any advice or assistance that he required. The two officers knew each other well—they had been classmates together at West Point. Longstreet ordered Smith to ride through the woods south of Plank Road to an unfinished railroad bed and scout for a route around the Union left flank. Shortly after Smith left on his mission, Longstreet instructed Sorrel to gather an attack force for the operation.[18]

Smith returned before ten o'clock, reporting that he had located a concealed route through the woods that led to the enemy flank. Sorrel, meanwhile, had located three available brigades—Brigadier Generals George Anderson's, William Wofford's, and William Mahone's from the divisions of Field, Kershaw, and Anderson, respectively. When Smith finished his report, Longstreet directed Sorrel to guide them into position. In Sorrel's account, the general said: "Hit hard when you start, but don't start until you have everything ready. I shall be waiting for your gunfire, and be on hand with fresh troops for further advance." Longstreet then told Smith to conduct a second reconnaissance toward Brock Road, where the main Union works were located, and determine if that line could be turned.[19]

"No greater opportunity could be given to an aspiring young staff officer, and I was quickly at work," recalled Sorrel. Following the railroad bed for part of the distance, Sorrel brought the brigades into line beyond the right flank unit of Kershaw's division and faced them to the north. When the attackers started the march, three regiments of Mississippians, Brigadier General Joseph Davis's brigade, attached themselves to the column and participated in the charge. Before noon the Rebels plunged ahead toward the exposed Federal flank.[20]

Yelling and firing, the Rebels slammed into the enemy units and "rolled them up like a scroll," in Alexander's words. Some Northern regiments were hit by fire from three directions and dissolved under the musketry. The attackers drove through the woods, and the gunfire rolled between the lines in sheets, igniting dried leaves and underbrush. Islands of Federal resistance formed and then disappeared as the Southerners reached Plank Road, where they halted to reorder their ranks. To their front, Field's other brigades were engaged, applying pressure to the collapsing Union front. Amid the fury, north of the road, Union Brigadier General James Wadsworth, while endeavoring to rally his shattered division, was cut down with a mortal wound. Only clusters of Yankees remained.[21]

As Longstreet had promised Sorrel, he was "on hand," directing additional units into the assault. While he watched, Smith rode up from his second reconnaissance and brought the news that the enemy line on Brock Road could be turned in a similar fashion. Longstreet asked the engineer officer to conduct the brigades of Wofford, Anderson, and Mahone to the position, moving by "inversion"—pulling the left unit out of line by its left flank and marching it behind the other brigades to the right end of the line and duplicating the maneuver with the other commands. Smith hurried away, and Wofford's regiments soon pulled out of line and filed eastward.[22]

When Wofford's troops began their march, Longstreet decided to ride down Plank Road to the front. With him were several of his staff officers, including Sorrel, who had ridden in moments earlier,

Field, Kershaw, Micah Jenkins, and numbers of their aides. The cavalcade of generals and officers filled the roadbed as they clattered onward. Jenkins, whose brigade was advancing through the woods south of the road, exclaimed to Longstreet: "I am happy. I have felt despair of the cause for some months, but am relieved and feel assured that we put the enemy back across the Rapidan before night." If Smith succeeded, Jenkins had good reason for his confidence.[23]

The mounted party approached the brigade of William Mahone halted on the south side of the road. When Mahone's regiments had reached the roadbed, the Twelfth Virginia continued into the woods across the roadbed. The fighting had not altogether ceased, and when its colonel saw that his men were isolated, he ordered it back. As the Virginians neared the road, their comrades on the opposite side mistook them for Federals and triggered a volley. In the road, between the Twelfth Virginia and Mahone's ranks, was Longstreet's group.[24]

Kershaw quickly saw Jenkins's troops level their rifles to fire and shouted, *"Friends!"* The soldiers held up, but it was already too late. The gunfire had hit and killed Captain Alfred E. Doby and orderly Marcus Baum of Kershaw's staff. Another bullet struck Micah Jenkins in the skull, and he lay on the roadbed, his life ebbing away. Nearby, Longstreet reeled in his saddle, his right arm hanging limp at his side. He had been struck in the throat by a bullet that passed through his shoulder and severed nerves. "He was actually lifted straight up and came down hard," according to Sorrel.[25]

Sorrel, Peyton Manning, and Francis Dawson lifted the general gently from the saddle and lay him against a tree. Longstreet "bled profusely," nearly choking. An officer rushed to find a surgeon. Speaking only in a whisper and blowing bloody foam from his mouth with each word, Longstreet told Sorrel to report his wounding to Lee. He relinquished command of the corps to Charles Field and described the proposed flank attack to the major general. Within minutes Dr. Dorsey Cullen arrived and attended to his friend and commander, stanching the bleeding. Aides laid him on a stretcher and carried him toward the rear. One of the officers covered his face with his hat, and when the troops saw Longstreet, they shouted that he was dead. With his left hand he lifted the hat, and "the burst of voices and the flying of hats in the air eased my pains somewhat." He was soon placed in an ambulance, and it rolled away from perhaps the triumph of Longstreet's career. Not far away, a year earlier, Stonewall Jackson had also fallen from the fire of his troops at a similar moment. The Wilderness seemed to be a place for ghosts.[26]

The ambulance and escort of staff officers proceeded up Plank Road, passing by various bodies of troops. An artillery officer who was near the road wrote afterward: "I never on any occasion during the four years of the war saw a group of officers and gentlemen more deeply distressed. They were literally bowed down with grief. All of them were in tears. . . . It was not alone the general they admired who had been shot down—it was, rather, the man they loved." The ambulance stopped briefly, and the lieutenant looked inside and saw the stricken general; his undervest was bloodstained and his face was ashen white. When the vehicle lurched forward, Longstreet opened his eyes and tried to examine his wound. "He is not dead, I said to myself," remembered the onlooker, "and he is calm and entirely master of the situation—he is both greater and more attractive than I have heretofore thought him."[27]

In the aftermath of the tragic accident, Longstreet's planned flank assault was delayed. In Porter Alexander's view, "Longstreet's fall seemed actually to paralyse our whole corps." It was not Field who postponed the operation, but Lee. When Lee saw the entangled ranks and overlapping lines, he stopped the attack and ordered Field to rectify the alignments and to form the brigades into a parallel line. Lee's decision, in the words of historian Edward Steere, was "a fatal mistake of judgment—one that cost him his last chance of winning a decisive victory." When the Confederates went forward again at four o'clock, the Federals had regrouped and had more troops in position. The Rebels charged with spirit and courage but could not breach the Union works in a frontal assault and fell back. The battle possessed one more spasm as brigades from Ewell's corps hit the Federal right flank two hours later and suffered a similar repulse. The Battle of the Wilderness had ended, at a price of 17,666 Union casualties and an estimated 8,000 Confederate.[28]

In time the Southerners concluded that the fall of Longstreet denied them a decisive victory that would have swept the Army of the Potomac back across the Rapidan. Colonel Walter Taylor of Lee's staff termed his wounding "this catastrophe." "A strange fatality attended us," Taylor thought. Porter Alexander also believed that the removal of Longstreet was the critical juncture in the battle.

"Gen. Longstreet," wrote Alexander, "soon appreciated that he had the enemy 'on the jump,' & determined to press the panic to the utmost. The time was ripe for it & the opportunity far more favorable than the one presented to Jackson." Longstreet "intended to play his hand for all it was worth, & to push the pursuit with his whole force." Alexander was confident that the panic among the Federals who opposed Longstreet's troops would have been extended to the other units of the Union army.[29]

Northern accounts provide evidence of the disorganization of the regiments and brigades and the demoralization of the rank and file. Longstreet grasped this, and, as Alexander phrased it, "intended to play his hand for all its worth." It was not a sure thing, for fresh Union brigades were nearby, but whether they could have withstood a flank and frontal assault appears unlikely. In the most difficult of terrain, Longstreet modified his tactical formations, salvaged the army from disaster, routed one enemy line with a rapidly conceived and executed flank attack, and was preparing a final offensive when misfortune denied him. His performance was brilliant, a confirmation of his consummate ability as a tactician. Nearly three quarters of a century after the battle, one of his veterans had not wavered in his estimation of his old commander and, like Alexander, was certain the Rebels would have achieved a great victory in the Wilderness because, as he put it, "we always gave them hell when Longstreet was along."[30]

One aspect of Longstreet's performance in the campaign has been criticized. In an interview after the war, Lee allegedly charged his subordinate with being "slow coming up" on May 6. Before Longstreet arrived on the field that morning, Lee was, as Charles Venable stated, "exceedingly disturbed" when the First Corps did not arrive before the enemy attacked. They made it by the slimmest of margins but only after covering forty-three miles, by Alexander's estimation, in thirty-six hours. As Alexander saw it, the problem was not Longstreet's slowness but Lee's failure to shift the three corps in the direction of Grant's anticipated movement prior to May 4. Instead, when finally ordered, Longstreet marched with commendable swiftness, and when his troops reached the field, they were not exhausted from a forced march. Lee's criticism has little merit.[31]

On May 7, Dr. Dorsey Cullen, John Fairfax, Thomas Goree, Erasmus Taylor, Osmun Latrobe, and Andrew Dunn accompanied Longstreet's ambulance as it traveled westward to Orange Court House.

Cullen and Latrobe rode inside with the general while the others trailed on horseback. At noon they stopped at a house and secured food, whiskey, and sugar. In Taylor's words, they then "traveled the twenty miles in fair comfort." By nightfall they arrived at "Meadow Farm," where Taylor's wife, Roberta, attended to the general. The next morning Cullen, Goree, and Taylor helped Longstreet onto a train and rode with him to Charlottesville. Meanwhile, Lee assigned Richard Anderson to temporary command of the First Corps, whose units were marching toward Spotsylvania Court House.[32]

Longstreet and his aides spent a day or two in Charlottesville, staying at a private residence. Mrs. Charles Blackford, wife of a member of his staff, visited the general and noted: "He is very feeble and nervous and suffers much from his wound. He sheds tears on the slightest provocation and apologizes for it. He says he does not see why a bullet going through a man's shoulder should make a baby of him."[33]

From Charlottesville, Longstreet journeyed by train to Lynchburg, where he was briefly placed in Taliaferro Hospital, one of the thirty-two in the city that had nearly ten thousand patients. Lynchburg was Louise Longstreet's hometown, and her husband found ample attention from her relatives. Before long he was moved to "Garland Hill," the home of Samuel and Caroline Garland, parents of Confederate general Samuel Garland, Jr., who had been killed on South Mountain in September 1862. Louise and the children soon joined him, and she and Caroline saw to his needs. Dorsey Cullen evidently roomed with the Garlands and was assisted in his treatment by Dr. R. Kidder Taylor and a Dr. Houston, surgeons from one of the hospitals. During the second week of June, a Union army, under Major General David Hunter, approached the city, forcing the doctors and Louise to relocate Longstreet to "Lotus Grove," the residence of Colonel John D. "Jack" Alexander near Campbell's Court House, twelve miles east of the city.[34]

On the night of June 13, Yankee cavalrymen burned a railroad depot near the village and early the next morning passed by Lotus Grove as Longstreet slept in a bedroom. Two days later, Longstreet telegraphed Samuel Cooper that the wound had healed, but his right arm was paralyzed. He requested permission to travel to Georgia and visit friends, which Cooper approved. The general, Louise, and the children remained at Lotus Grove until at least month's end; Cullen apparently returned to the army, so doctors Taylor and

Houston visited frequently. In a postwar letter to his former patient, Taylor remembered the "pleasant times under shade trees" at Alexander's and "the elegant and refreshing mint julep that Jack always ordered as soon as the Doctor and I arrived from Lynchburg."[35]

Sometime in July, Longstreet and his family left Virginia for Georgia. Tom Goree stayed behind in Lynchburg to attend to his brother, Edward, who was recuperating from his Wilderness wound. The Longstreets spent the entire summer in his home state, initially with kinsfolk in Augusta, and later with friends at Union Point, thirty miles south of Athens. Goree rejoined them at a later time, staying with the general until his return to the army.[36]

While he mended, Longstreet corresponded periodically with Lee in Virginia. Following one of the letters, his commander replied on August 29: "You will soon be as well as ever & we shall all be rejoiced at your return. You must not however be over impatient at the gradual progress you must necessarily make, but be content with the steady advance you are making to health & strength. Your programs will be more certain & your recovery more confirmed. Do not let Sherman capture you & I will endeavour to hold Grant till you come.

"I am glad," continued Lee jokingly, "to hear such good accounts of my little namesake. Good lungs are a great blessing & nothing expands them better than a full hearty yell." He hoped that Louise was well and enjoying Georgia's peaches and melons. "We had but little enjoyment here," he admitted. "Our enemy is very cautious & he has become so proficient in entrenching that he seems to march with a system already prepared." Longstreet's friends in the army inquired often about his condition, Lee added, and headquarters staff sent "sincere wishes for your welfare & happiness." In conclusion, Lee extended his regards to Louise and "love to my namesake."[37]

Lee devoted little of the letter to the military situation for he knew that Longstreet had probably received correspondence from the army and surely read newspapers. Since the Wilderness, Confederate fortunes had deteriorated. In Georgia, Sherman's armies had nearly encircled Atlanta. Joseph Johnston had slowed the Union advance on the city for weeks, but when he was not forthcoming with a plan for Atlanta's defense, Jefferson Davis replaced him on July 17 with John Hood, who had undermined Johnston's support with letters to the capital. The aggressive Hood soon launched bloody assaults on Sherman's lines that fatally crippled the Confederate army. When Lee wrote to Longstreet, it was only days before Hood abandoned the city and Sherman's troops entered.[38]

In Virginia, Grant and Lee had engaged in a classic confrontation —Grant as the unrelenting aggressor, Lee as the masterful defender. For forty days the two armies were virtually locked together in a campaign from the Rapidan to the James River—Wilderness, Spotsylvania Court House, North Anna, and Second Cold Harbor. In mid-June, Grant crossed the James in a brilliant movement that nearly secured Petersburg, twenty miles south of the capital. Lee's army raced to the vital railroad center, and Grant began siege operations. Trenches, bombproofs, and forts began scarring the landscape from north of the James to west of Petersburg, Grant had locked Lee and the Army of Northern Virginia into place and planned to strangle the Confederates to death. West of Richmond and Petersburg, another Union army, under Philip H. Sheridan, had descended on the Shenandoah Valley to lay waste to this granary.

Lee and the nation required the services of all its able-bodied men, and in mid-September, Longstreet and Goree boarded a train for Richmond, while Louise and the children returned to Lynchburg. The general still had no use of his right arm, holding it in a sling, and could not ride a horse. He reached the capital by September 25, for on that day he attended services at St. Paul's Episcopal Church—he had been confirmed as a member of the Episcopal Church on May 1, 1864, at Orange Court House—with Lee, who "seemed worn" to Longstreet, and several other generals. They witnessed a baptism and heard a sermon based on Jesus' words in Matthew 6:34: "Take therefore no thought for the morrow: for the morrow shall take thought for the things of itself. Sufficient unto the day is the evil thereof."[39]

By month's end Longstreet could mount and ride Fly-By-Night, a horse sent to him by Lee while he was in Georgia. On October 7, he wrote Colonel Walter Taylor of Lee's staff to request authority to return to duty, willing to serve wherever assigned. In his memoirs, Longstreet stated that his concern for Lee's health and burdens prompted him to accept duty elsewhere. "Although anxious to assist in his severe trials," he wrote, "and relieve him of part of his work, I feared that he might think a cripple an additional incumbrance." But Lee desired his services, for, as Goree correctly argued earlier, "Genl. Lee needs him not only to advise with, but Genl. Longstreet has a very suggestive mind and none of the other Lt. Genls. have this." He reported to the First Corps on October 13 and six days later officially resumed command.[40]

Despite his concern for his physical limitations, Longstreet was pleased to be back with the army and heartened by the welcome accorded him. On October 21 he telegraphed his friend P. G. T. Beauregard: "I am now on duty with my Corps and Genl. Lee thinks he cannot spare me." Goree wrote home the same day that Lee "seems delighted to have him back again" as were the staff and the troops. When Longstreet rode along the lines for the first time, the men reacted with "wild enthusiasm," standing on the fieldworks and cheering for "'the old bull of the woods' as they love to call him." The outburst by his veterans visibly gratified Longstreet. "He is a tower of strength to our cause," Captain Francis Dawson wrote of Longstreet in a letter to his mother, "and he returns at a good time." Lieutenant Andrew Dunn hosted a party in the general's honor, which was attended by many officers in the corps.[41]

Longstreet's return coincided with personnel changes at First Corps headquarters. From his initial command at First Manassas, Longstreet had sought and found talented and loyal men to serve on his staff. In time he possessed perhaps the finest staff of any subordinate commander in the army. They demonstrated their intelligence, bravery, and devotion to the cause and their commander on a number of battlefields. They prepared the paperwork, organized the departments, carried his messages and orders, attended to his personal needs, and shared good meals, fine whiskeys, and warm fires with him. The pain and grief in their faces, as witnessed by the artillery officer in the Wilderness, testified to their respect and affection for Longstreet. Now, like the nation itself, the staff was breaking apart.

The first to leave was Major Raphael Moses, the chief of commissary, whose wizardry of swapping confiscated sheep for bacon, of running mills day and night, and of commandeering trains had fed the men in those difficult weeks in East Tennessee. Moses requested and was granted a transfer to Georgia. Major Thomas Walton, the intelligent, opinionated Mississippian, was reassigned to duty with Richard Ewell in Richmond during the first week of November. Days later Lieutenant Francis Dawson, the Englishman who never quite fit in, was appointed chief of ordnance in the cavalry division of Fitzhugh Lee. Dawson had been captured on that unlucky night in September 1862 when Union cavalry, escaping from Harpers Ferry, rerouted forty of Longstreet's ordnance wagons to Pennsylvania. Dawson knew the ordnance department, having served under the tutelage of Peyton Manning, the only staff member the Britisher liked.[42]

The most important loss, however, was that of Moxley Sorrel. He had been chief of staff for three years; he knew the workings of the corps as well as the commander. At the Wilderness, Longstreet had shown his trust in Sorrel's judgment and ability when he gave the young Georgian direction of the flank attack. His performance on that day did not go unnoticed, and now with the terrible attrition among general and field officers, he was promoted to brigadier general and assigned to a brigade in Powell Hill's Third Corps. It was Sorrel, dressed in his finest uniform, who delivered the arrest order to the fiery Powell Hill in July 1862. The promotion, wrote Sorrel, "came unexpectedly," to date from October 27. "My comrades did not let me go easily," he recalled. "The night before there was a farewell party of many officers at headquarters. A goodly quantity of apple-toddy was consumed, but not to hurt, and the party, General Longstreet with us for a time, was full of feeling, touching me keenly by its spontaneous demonstration." When he rode away the next morning, part of the soul of the First Corps went with him.[43]

For Sorrel's position, Longstreet selected the Marylander Major Osmun Latrobe. Since the spring, the general had been recommending Sorrel, Latrobe, and Major John Fairfax for promotion, declaring that "these officers have been distinguished on many fields for conduct, skill, and ability, and for the faithful and zealous discharge of their duties under all circumstances." On October 31, he again renewed his effort, requesting Latrobe's and Fairfax's promotions to colonel. It was not until January 13, 1865, that the two officers were confirmed as lieutenant colonels, with Fairfax to rank from that date and Latrobe from December 19, 1864. For the final months of the war, the inner core of Longstreet's staff consisted of Latrobe, Fairfax, Peyton Manning, and Tom Goree.[44]

When Longstreet officially resumed his duties, Lee assigned him to command the forces north of the James River and Major General George Pickett's division on Bermuda Hundred, a peninsula at the confluence of the James and Appomattox rivers between Richmond and Petersburg. North of the James, the command included the infantry divisions of Charles Field and Robert Hoke, the cavalry brigade of Brigadier General Martin Gary, and the Local Defense forces and troops of the Department of Richmond under Richard S. Ewell, whose health limited his active field duties. Longstreet had approximately twenty-one thousand effectives to man twenty miles of breastworks, artillery emplacements, and forts.[45]

Operations along the Richmond-Petersburg front had settled into a stalemate by the end of October. Once the siege began in June, the Confederates faced, in Porter Alexander's words, the "inexorable necessity, military and political," of the defense of the capital and the railroad center. Grant extended his lines westward, applying pressure and seeking opportunities to rupture the Southern works. At the end of July, the Federals exploded a mine under a section of Lee's lines, tearing an enormous hole, but the resultant attack ended in a debacle. In August and September, the Union reach edged farther westward at Petersburg, toward the rail lines that connected Lee's army to supply areas in the Carolinas and Georgia. When Grant pushed his troops in that direction, he generally jabbed north of the James River and punched at Petersburg. Twice in September and October, the Yankees launched offensives against both sectors of the Southern lines.[46]

The final thrust during the last week of October ended active operations for the fall and winter. The routine along the miles of extensive works became a daily deadly ordeal of periodic artillery bombardment, of sharpshooter fire, and of occasional demonstrations or sorties. The landscape was torn and scarred, a blighted place that portended the future of warfare. For the Confederates, it meant the death of its most renowned army.[47]

The life of the Army of Northern Virginia ebbed away due to casualties and desertions. While the enemy was well fed, well clothed, and well manned, with recruits filling the ranks, the Southerners knew only shortages. For hundreds in Lee's army the suffering and the specter of final defeat proved too much. Soldiers disappeared each night, never to return to their regiments. Officers invoked measures to stanch the hemorrhaging, but few succeeded. By Christmas the signs elsewhere in the embattled nation confirmed the reality—John Hood had wrecked the Army of Tennessee at Franklin, Tennessee, and watched as it was all but destroyed at Nashville; Sherman's host had captured Savannah after leaving behind a huge blackened scar of devastation in its march from Atlanta.

With the reelection of Abraham Lincoln in November, the sword of the Union was not to be sheathed until victory.

Like Lee and the other commanders, Longstreet stayed at his post, wrestling with the burdens of staying the darkness of defeat. His right arm remained useless, but he pulled at it constantly on the advice of doctors to restore feeling. In December he told a friend: "I can now only sign my name with my left hand with great difficulty." He also may have suffered with a hernia. He attended to the needs of his men, visited the lines, filed the reports, and exchanged ideas and intelligence with Lee. On one occasion, however, his efforts elicited a sharply critical letter from Lee, who complained that his inspection reports for December indicated lax discipline and inadequate drill. The commanding general ordered that these conditions be corrected.[48]

Longstreet's assessments of the situation at Richmond and Petersburg vacillated throughout the winter months. On New Year's Day, he wrote to Lee: "I believe that we are better able to cope with him [Grant] now than we have ever been, if we will profit by our experience and exert ourselves properly in improving our organizations." A month later, on February 4, he informed Lee that he could not hold his line east of the capital with his present force. "We shall fight him [Grant] of course," Longstreet added, "as long as we have a man, but we should fight with much better heart, if we could have hope of results."[49]

In Richmond, meanwhile, Confederate authorities grasped at various proposals to save the nation. On February 3, the day before Longstreet wrote his pessimistic letter to Lee, Confederate Vice President Alexander Stephens, Assistant Secretary of War John A. Campbell, and Senator R. M. T. Hunter met with Abraham Lincoln and his secretary of state, William H. Seward, on the *River Queen* in Hampton Roads off the Virginia Peninsula. The conference brought no resolution as Lincoln and Seward demanded the restoration of the United States and the disbanding of the Confederate armies. The Southern delegation could not consent to these stipulations and reported the outcome to Jefferson Davis.[50]

Four days later Major General John C. Breckinridge replaced James Seddon as secretary of war, and Davis appointed Lee general-in-chief of all Confederate armies. Furthermore, a debate ensued over the merits of authorizing the use of slaves as soldiers with the pledge of freedom. When Lee solicited Longstreet's views, he opposed the idea because it would mean the "necessity" of abolishing slavery in the future without "materially aiding us in the present." Nevertheless, Longstreet asked Richard Ewell if the latter could raise a company of slaves in the city that could be tested as soldiers. "Their good behavior," wrote Latrobe on Longstreet's behalf, "would do much to overcome a prejudice on the minds of many adverse to their employment as troops." Both houses of the Congress eventually passed the measure, but it was too late for the Confederacy. By the end of February, Lee had already prepared retreat routes from Richmond and Petersburg for the army.[51]

During the final week of February, Longstreet became involved in negotiations that sought terms for a settlement of the conflict. Major General E. O. C. Ord, commander of the Union Army of the James, sent a note through the lines, requesting a meeting between him and Longstreet about prisoners of war and the fraternization between their troops. The two generals met the next day, discussed the matters, and then Ord proposed a "side interview." Since the politicians had failed to end the war, Ord remarked, peace must be attained by army officers. He suggested a suspension of hostilities, a meeting between Lee and Grant, and exchange visits between Louise Longstreet and Julia Grant, two old friends. Longstreet responded that he had no authority to agree to the items but would report them to Lee.[52]

That night Longstreet, Lee, Davis, and Breckinridge discussed Ord's recommendations in Richmond. They agreed to pursue the opening, and Longstreet telegraphed his wife in Lynchburg to come to the capital. Longstreet and Ord met a second time on February 28—not the 23rd, as Longstreet dated it in his memoirs—and decided that Lee should correspond with Grant. Lee wrote a letter on March 2, stating: "I propose to meet you at a convenient time and place as you may designate, with the hope that upon an interchange of views it may be found practicable to submit the subjects of controversy between the belligerent to a military convention." Longstreet read the letter before sealing it and forwarding it through the lines. Later that day Lee wrote a second letter on the subject of the exchange of prisoners. Grant replied on March 4 that the Ord-Longstreet meeting was initiated only to resolve the matter of the execution of prisoners and that he had "no authority to accede to your proposition for a conference on the subject proposed. Such authority is vested in the President of the United States alone." Grant was obeying instructions from Washington.[53]

On the day Grant replied to Lee, Abraham Lincoln was inaugurated for a second term. In his brief, eloquent address, the president offered inspiration and understanding, at one point saying, "Fondly do we hope—fervently do we pray—that this mighty scourge of war may speedily pass away." His armies and navies had already secured Wilmington, North Carolina, and Charleston, South Carolina, and William Sherman was poised to cross into North Carolina, en route to Grant's army. The Confederacy had shrunk to little more than the defenses of Richmond and Petersburg. Here Grant prepared to close the fist.[54]

The end of Confederate resistance came swiftly. Lee struck boldly on March 25 with an assault on Fort Steadman in an attempt to sever part of Grant's lines. The soldiers charged valiantly, but there were not enough of them—there never seemed to be enough—and Grant's reserves sealed the breach. Lee lost over four thousand men. A week later, on April 1, the Federals struck at Five Forks on Lee's right flank, inflicting probably another five thousand casualties and routing the Confederate force, which included George Pickett's division, a command that had walked with ghosts since July 3, 1863.[55]

When Lee learned of the disaster at Five Forks, he telegraphed Longstreet to bring Field's division by railroad to Petersburg at once. Longstreet relayed Lee's orders, instructed Ewell to fill the vacant lines with Local Defense troops, and then started with his staff toward the endangered front. They rode all night, crossing the James River on a pontoon bridge, and arrived at Lee's headquarters before daylight on April 2. An aide of the commanding general escorted Longstreet upstairs to a bedroom. Unwell, Lee remained in bed as he described the situation on the Confederate right front. Suddenly, Colonel Venable entered the room with news that the enemy was attacking. Lee and Longstreet hurried to the front of the house. In the distance, lines of skirmishers moved forward cautiously from the southwest, from the army's right front.[56]

Venable and Lieutenant General Powell Hill spurred ahead to reconnoiter. Lee and Longstreet watched intently until the morning's light revealed the soldiers' blue uniforms. The Federals had attacked along nearly the entire Confederate line around Petersburg. The Northerners came on slowly but in successive waves. Confederate resistance was valiant, hour after hour, at critical points. "Never did the superb morale of our men," Porter Alexander recalled, "shine out more beautifully than on that long day when they stood at bay in their fragments of lines before four times their numbers." Lee had warned Jefferson Davis that this day would come, and before midday he wired the president: "I see no prospect of doing more than holding our position here till night. I am not certain that I can do that."[57]

But his veterans—men who held the Bloody Lane at Sharpsburg, the stone wall at Fredericksburg, the fieldworks at Spotsylvania, and the trenches for nearly ten months at Petersburg—had enough left to give their commander one more day. At 4:30 P.M., Lee dictated retreat orders and sent telegrams to Davis and Breckinridge: "I think it absolutely necessary that we should abandon our position tonight." At eight o'clock the remnants of the once magnificent army abandoned Petersburg, crossed the Appomattox River, and turned westward. In Richmond, Davis and government officials boarded a train in the darkness. Behind them, looters ransacked, and the fires from burning military stores spread unstopped until the central city became an inferno. "It was a scene unparalleled, I believe, even among the ghostly revelations of this war," claimed an eyewitness. When Porter Alexander saw it the next morning at sunrise, he described it as "a sad, a terrible & a solemn sight. . . . The whole river front seemed to be in flames."[58]

The Confederate army marched throughout the night—the main body from Petersburg, Ewell's contingent from Richmond. As they had so frequently in the past, Lee and Longstreet rode much of the time together. Longstreet now commanded the First and Third Corps, for Powell Hill had been killed on the morning of the 2nd as he reconnoitered along the lines. When the army paused to rest and eat, Lee, Longstreet, and a few other generals shared a meal with a family. As they ate, the host reassured them that ultimate victory was theirs. Longstreet ignored the remark, but Lee replied firmly: "Whatever happens, know this, that no men ever fought better than those who have stood by me."[59]

On April 4, the Southerners recrossed to the south side of the Appomattox River and halted at Amelia Court House, where Lee expected to find rations. But there were none, and he had to send details into the countryside to forage. The army ground to a stop, losing an invaluable day to gather food. The meaning was evident as Confederate cavalry skirmished with the advance elements of Grant's army, which had been in pursuit on a parallel route since the 3rd. The delay allowed artillery crews to inspect and refit their batteries, gleaning the weak animals and their pieces from the army. About midnight, Longstreet deployed Charles Field's and Cadmus Wilcox's divisions in line to protect the wagons and other units.[60]

During the morning of the 5th, Ewell's forces from Richmond arrived at Amelia Court House. While some units resumed the march, other commands were reorganized. Shortly after midday, the entire Confederate army was on the move toward Jetersville. The Yankees, however, had been on the roads throughout the 4th and finally outdistanced the Rebels, blocking the road to the village. Union cavalry, backed by two infantry corps, sealed the route, and Lee declined battle. With Longstreet's four divisions in the lead, the Confederates swung northward around the Federals and headed for Farmville on the Southside Railroad. Longstreet pushed his weary, hungry men throughout much of the night. By late morning he had his divisions aligned for battle near Rice's Station.[61]

Longstreet held this position throughout the 6th. Lee met him here, pausing for the arrival of Ewell's command and the army's wagon train. Hours passed as Lee waited with noticeable impatience. Longstreet's troops skirmished with Union soldiers. Late in the day, Lee learned that the enemy had struck the wagon train at Sayler's Creek. He ordered Major General William Mahone's division in that direction and rode ahead. When Lee reached the crest of a hill that overlooked the stream, he saw the shattered remains of three divisions and numerous artillery batteries. "My God!" the commanding general exclaimed, as if to himself. "Has the army dissolved?" Generals Ewell, Kershaw, and Custis Lee, the general's son, were captured with hundreds of their men. Caught in a vise of Federal infantry, artillery, and cavalry they were, as Longstreet said, "crushed to fragments."[62]

Days, perhaps even hours, now measured the life of the army. About 10:00 P.M. on the 6th, the Confederates pulled back from Rice's Station and marched all night to Farmville, where they recrossed the Appomattox River. The Federals closed, and fighting flared throughout much of the day. For the first time in two days the Southerners drew rations. During the afternoon, Brigadier General William Pendleton, the army's artillery commander, spoke to Longstreet about surrender. Pendleton and a group of officers decided that it was inevitable and wanted Longstreet to approach Lee on the subject. Longstreet snapped back that the men could still whip four times their number, and as long as this was true, he would not propose surrender. "He was there to back up Lee, not to pull him down," the lieutenant general said, or something to that effect. Later, Pendleton presented the proposal to Lee and received a chilling reaction.[63]

That evening, while Lee, Longstreet, and staffs rested at a residence near the lines, a courier brought a message from Grant. The Union commander proposed a surrender of the Confederate forces, stating in part: "The results of the last week must convince you of the hopelessness of further resistance on the part of the Army of Northern Virginia in this struggle." Lee read it, said nothing, and handed it to Longstreet, who was sitting nearby. Longstreet then read his old friend's words, passed it back to Lee, and said, "Not yet." Then, without conferring with anyone, Lee wrote a reply, dismissing Grant's view of the "hopelessness of further resistance," but he asked for terms. He showed it to no one, sealed it, and gave it to a courier. "As his hand became the harder to play," Alexander noted afterward, Lee preferred "to play it more & more alone."[64]

The strain on Lee had been evident since the army began the retreat. In a postwar letter, Longstreet recounted an incident during one night's march:

> One evening, after dark, as we rode, we stopped at a little fire that some one had started, and left. While a number were hovering about it, General Lee standing near, leaning against a small tree, passed off into [illegible] slumber, and seemed so rigid I had to look a second time, to see if he had not passed into his last sleep. He was so troubled all of the march, that he had little rest, I may say no rest; though nature demanded a little quiet.[65]

The scene as Longstreet described it may have occurred on the night of April 7–8, for once again the army marched under a shield of darkness. The troops abandoned their lines north of Farmville at midnight, moving north and west. Lee's objective now was Lynchburg, a race to pass between the headwaters of the Appomattox and James rivers before the enemy barred the path. The day passed quietly for the Southerners. Strict orders had been issued to prevent straggling. By sunset the Rebels camped along the Richmond-Lynchburg Stage Road east of Appomattox Court House. Ahead of them, at Appomattox Station on the railroad, Union cavalry under Major General George A. Custer overran a Confederate detachment and seized the supply cars for Lee's army. Not far behind the horsemen, Federal infantrymen force marched to near the station.[66]

Lee established his headquarters for the night on a wooded knoll near a small stream called Rocky Run. Before midnight, Longstreet, John Gordon, and Fitzhugh Lee joined the commander for a conference. Lee had already received a second message from Grant about a surrender and had responded that he would meet with Grant at ten o'clock in the morning. Lee believed that only Union cavalry were in front, but Gordon evidently argued that infantry supported the horsemen and opposed an attack. But something had to be tried, and Lee ordered Gordon to try to break through. Longstreet would close in support, protecting the rear. If Gordon succeeded, the meeting with Grant might be unnecessary.[67]

Palm Sunday, April 9, 1865, dawned clear. Gordon's men—the majority were veterans of Stonewall Jackson's Second Corps—went forward and collided with enemy cavalry. When Union infantry replaced the troopers, the fate of Lee's army was sealed. Lee was informed and allegedly remarked: "Then there is nothing left me but to go and see General Grant, and I would rather die a thousand deaths." Confusion reigned for some time along the lines until a cessation of hostilities was secured. Although accounts conflict in details, the flamboyant Union general Custer rode into Confederate lines under a flag of truce and was escorted to Longstreet. When the two generals met, Custer said: "In the name of General Sheridan I demand the unconditional surrender of this army." Longstreet glared at the twenty-five-year-old "Boy General" and said nothing until Custer repeated his words. "I am not the commander of this army," barked Longstreet, "and if I were, I would not surrender it to General Sheridan." A Confederate officer led Custer back through the lines.[68]

Longstreet, meanwhile, had Porter Alexander select a battle line for Mahone's and Wilcox's divisions as support for Gordon. Alexander complied, and as he proudly told Longstreet after the war in a letter, "it was the *last line of battle* the Army of Northern Virginia ever formed & I remember every detail of it." Before noon, Longstreet joined several other Confederate generals in the village, where they visited with Union generals and shared the contents of a whiskey flask. Returning to Confederate lines, Longstreet met Lee in a small apple orchard, and the two friends spoke. Lee worried that Grant might demand harsh terms, but Longstreet reassured him that the Union commander would be fair. Soon, Orville E. Babcock of Grant's staff arrived to escort Lee. As the Confederate commander, dressed in full uniform with sash and sword, spurred Traveller forward, Longstreet said: "General, if he does not give us good terms, come back and let us fight it out." It was Longstreet's final counsel to Lee.[69]

Lee met with Grant in the home of Wilmer McLean. As Longstreet had predicted, Grant was generous—the Confederates had to lay down their arms in a formal ceremony and then they could go home, "not to be disturbed by United States authority so long as they observe their paroles and the laws in force where they may reside." While Colonel Charles Marshall drafted a copy of Lee's acceptance, Grant introduced Lee to the assembled officers. When Lee mentioned his men's lack of food, Grant offered to send twenty-five thousand rations through the lines. With all copies prepared and signed, Lee and Grant shook hands, and Lee rode off to inform his army.[70]

When Lee reached the battle line formed by Alexander, the artillery officer ordered his gunners to remove their hats. Somebody, however, "started a shout," according to Alexander, "& then they broke ranks, & the Infantry from their line of battle also & all crowded about him." Lee reined in Traveller, telling them that he had surrendered the army. Many in the crowd offered to continue the fight. One of them growled: "General, I wish every damned Yankee was in the bottom of hell. Don't you?" Lee remained silent and eventually guided Traveller through the throng to his headquarters. Details required his attention.[71]

Lee and Grant met a second time on the morning of the 10th and talked for about thirty minutes, with Grant asking Lee to advise the surrender of all Confederate armies. Lee declined until he consulted with President Davis, and then the two warriors separated. Afterward Longstreet, Gordon, and Pendleton rode into the village. Lee had appointed them his commissioners to prepare the terms for the formal surrender of the troops and their paroles. Rain fell as the trio halted at the McLean house. Grant was there, and when he saw Longstreet, he walked toward his former comrade, grabbed both his hands, and then embraced him. Grant offered a cigar and jokingly said: "Pete, let us have another game of brag, to recall the old days which were so pleasant to us all." Finally, the Union commander departed, and the commission began its work. The agreement was signed that evening.[72]

Confederate staff officers and unit commanders worked throughout the 10th and 11th, preparing lists of names of their men for parole and issuing orders. On the 10th, Lee wrote General Orders No. 9, his farewell address to the army. Longstreet had his staff copy letters of thanks to many of his subordinates for their dedication and service, and he signed them with his left hand. Longstreet and Lee shared a campsite together, their final one, on the night of April 11–12.[73]

The next morning Lee prepared to depart for Richmond—he would not be a witness to the final march of his army. Officers gathered at headquarters for farewells. When Lee came to Longstreet, he "warmly embraced" him, then turning to Tom Goree, who stood at Longstreet's side, he admonished, "Captain, I am going to put my old war-horse under your charge. I want you to take good care of him." With that said, Lee soon left, riding away on Traveller. He and Longstreet never saw each other again.[74]

Longstreet took his leave from his comrades later that day. The parting must have been difficult as he said farewell to Porter Alexander, Osmun Latrobe, Peyton Manning, John Fairfax, and Dorsey Cullen. Moxley Sorrel, who had been wounded in February, was not with the army. Longstreet thought he would settle in Texas and begin anew as a civilian, a life he had not known for twenty-seven years.[75]

History had a part of Longstreet now. In its hands he would not be accorded the stature he had earned on some of the conflict's greatest battlefields. He had been, as John Fairfax fairly stated years afterward, the "best tactician in the Army of Northern Virginia after Gen. Lee took command of it." John Gordon, a bitter opponent after the war, even counted him "among the great American soldiers," while Walter Taylor told a newspaperman that "no braver or stouter soldier ever marshaled his division and led them onward against the foe" than Longstreet. He was neither slow at Second Manassas or the Wilderness nor insubordinate at Gettysburg. At Sharpsburg, Fredericksburg, Chickamauga, and the Wilderness, he was a splendid warrior. Under his command, the First Corps was the "bedrock" of the army.[76]

History, however, can cast a shadow, and Longstreet's place has been darkened by Lee and the Confederacy's martyr, Stonewall Jackson. Lee was indisputably one of history's greatest chieftains. As one historian has noted, his victories and defeats "extended the life of the Confederacy beyond all reasonable expectations. That singular accomplishment is the mark of the man." Lee was a consummate organizer, preeminent strategist, and superb tactician. His intellect and moral courage, or audacity, nearly overcame his nation's limitations but did not spare him from mistakes. Lee's record must be taken as a whole—Second Manassas, Fredericksburg, Chancellorsville, and the Overland Campaign against Grant counterbalanced with Sharpsburg and Gettysburg.[77]

With his fall at Chancellorsville, Stonewall Jackson became the South's hero. In time, Lee supplanted Jackson in the "Lost Cause" pantheon, but "Old Jack" stood close at hand. Jackson was a relentless foe, a general who saw warfare in stark, unforgiving terms. His 1862 Shenandoah Campaign, his march around John Pope's Union army in the Second Manassas Campaign, and his flank march and attack at Chancellorsville were some of the war's most brilliant feats. His Second Corps was the army's lance. But Jackson's record includes his mysterious and often alibied—performance during the Seven Days Campaign and his unexplained failure to support Longstreet's counterattack at Second Manassas. Jackson may have been a genius; his death may have cost the Confederacy its independence. History still frames the Confederate effort in the East in an enduring pairing—Lee and Jackson.

The singular figure in the army who stands in history's shadow is Longstreet. To be sure, there were failures in his Confederate career—the long day at Seven Pines and his denial of responsibility; the morning of July 2 at Gettysburg; the intrigue in Tennessee after Chickamauga; and the Knoxville Campaign with its resultant melodrama of controversy and courts-martial. But he was the army's senior lieutenant, chosen by Lee; his counsel was as valued at headquarters as was Jackson's; and on no battlefield of the East can it be argued that he failed his superior. Longstreet, not Jackson, was the finest corps commander in the Army of Northern Virginia; in fact, he was arguably the best corps commander in the conflict on either side. Yet, barely fifteen months after Appomattox, Joseph Kershaw could write with resentment and prescience about the First Corps and his former leader that "the country has never known or appreciated its services and the modest virtues of its glorious chief are only rightly appreciated by his comrades and his commander."[78]

Longstreet is a disturbing presence in Lost Cause iconography. He neither viewed war as a moral absolute, like Jackson, nor accepted the effectiveness of the tactical offensive, like Lee. He advocated strategic audacity and tactical conservatism. He preferred to spare men's lives rather than test their character. An attack without strategic purpose or without the chance of tactical success violated the principles of his generalship. To Longstreet, Gettysburg was not the great "if" of Confederate history but one of its greatest mistakes. To recognize his achievements as a general and to weigh the merits of his ideas requires a reexamination of Southern icons. In the immediate postwar decades, however, when the defeated South again summoned its sons for another conflict and for history, he would be found wanting. The road from Appomattox forked in two directions.

FINAL JOURNEY

On April 13, 1865, James Longstreet reached Lynchburg, Virginia. Here his wife, Louise, and sons, Garland and Robert Lee, welcomed the weary, crippled soldier. He had one hundred dollars in United States currency with him—his share of a cache of money divided among officers and troops at Appomattox—and a vague notion that he and his family's fortune might lie in Texas. It was not much, but it was more than what awaited thousands of his former comrades, who were traveling home to destroyed farmsteads and abandoned occupations. His prospects were dimmed, however, by the opinion of doctors that he could not expect to live more than eight years because of his Wilderness wound. But the medical practitioners would be wrong—he would live nearly four more decades.[1]

Lynchburg had been a haven for the Longstreets so many times in the past, the place where they had been married, where he had healed after his wound, and where the family could always find shelter, food, and love from Louise's relatives, the large Garland clan. Although Louise may have wanted to make it their permanent home, her husband evidently never considered the idea. Lynchburg was only a temporary stopover until Louise, who was pregnant with their eighth child, was safely through the delivery. She gave birth to a son, named James, Jr., on May 31. (Their fourth son had been named James, Jr., but he had died of scarlet fever on January 26, 1862.) Less than a month later, her husband, Garland, Tom Goree, and a servant, Jim, started south.[2]

"I constituted the advance guard," Goree noted in his diary as the small party departed on June 28. He and Garland rode horseback while Longstreet followed in an ambulance, driven by Jim. The trip was slow and lengthy through the Carolinas. They sought meals and places to sleep wherever they could, and although many hosts had little to offer, they shared it with the famous general. On July 13 they arrived at Longstreet's brother William's home near Cleveland, Georgia, where they visited until month's end. Resuming the journey on July 31, they crossed the state—"the country . . . had been made almost a complete waste," Goree noted in his diary. "The fencing all destroyed and all the best houses burned"—and entered Alabama four days later.[3]

By now Tom Goree's patience must have been exhausted. He had more than fulfilled his promise to Robert E. Lee, and desiring to return to a home he had not seen in over four years, he apparently departed for Texas about this time, while Longstreet continued on to Mississippi. None of the general's staff officers had been more devoted or at his side longer than Goree. They had met on the boat to New Orleans in May 1861 and would remain lifelong friends.[4]

William accompanied his brother from Georgia and together with Garland journeyed to Canton, Mississippi, where their sister Sarah and her husband, Judge Charles B. Ames, resided. While in Mississippi, James "discharged" the family servants, and, perhaps leaving Garland with his sister, proceeded to Mobile, Alabama. From there he most likely secured passage on a steamer for New Orleans, arriving in the "Crescent City" by the end of September.[5]

New Orleans was the South's largest city and had been under Union occupation since 1862, sparing it from destruction. When and why Longstreet decided to make the city his family's home is uncertain, but upon his arrival, he found an atmosphere and business opportunity that suited him. Other ex-Confederate generals had relocated there, including P. G. T. Beauregard, John Hood, Simon Buckner, John Magruder, and Cadmus Wilcox. Two former officers of the Washington Artillery, Edward and William Owen, were organizing their own cotton brokerage firm and asked Longstreet to join them as a partner. The Owen brothers were natives of the city, with good local business connections, and Longstreet accepted.[6]

Late in October, Longstreet started back to Virginia via railroads. He returned to bring Louise and the children to New Orleans and

to secure a pardon from the government. On June 7, while he was
in Lynchburg, a Federal grand jury in Norfolk had indicted Lee and
others for treason against the United States. The likelihood of a trial
on the charges was remote at this time, but Longstreet decided to
make special application for an individual pardon as specified for
prominent Confederates in President Andrew Johnson's May 29
proclamation. He met in Washington with his good friend General-
in-Chief Ulysses S. Grant and Secretary of War Edwin Stanton. Grant
agreed to write a letter to President Johnson recommending a pardon, but when the former Confederate met with the president,
Johnson refused, saying to Longstreet: "There are three persons of
the South who can never receive amnesty: Mr. Davis, General Lee,
and yourself. You have given the Union cause too much trouble."
Like Lee, who had applied in writing earlier, Longstreet had neither
amnesty nor political rights.[7]

While in the capital, Longstreet enjoyed a brief reunion with John
Fairfax and Peyton Manning before he joined Louise and the boys
at Lynchburg. By Christmas the Longstreets were in New Orleans,
and on New Year's Day, 1866, the cotton brokerage firm of Longstreet, Owen & Company opened its office at 37 Union Street. About
this time Longstreet wrote to Lee, informing his old commander
about his prospects and enclosing his business card. Lee, who had
accepted the presidency of Washington College in Lexington, Virginia (today, Washington and Lee University), replied later in January that "I know you will do your work well, I please myself
therefore with the pleasure of your great success," closing the letter
with "wishing you all happiness & prosperity, I am with great affection."[8]

The cotton brokerage business required travel for the partners
to secure crops from farmers. Longstreet spent weeks on the road
in 1866, visiting numerous communities in Louisiana, Mississippi,
and Alabama. He offered Goree a commission of one dollar on
every "good large bale" of Texas cotton the latter could secure for
the firm. Louise, Robert Lee, and James, Jr., remained in New Orleans during his absences, while Garland attended the Virginia Military Institute in Lexington.[9]

Longstreet did not limit his business activities to the cotton trade.
On March 1 he assumed the presidency of the newly created Great
Southern and Western Fire, Marine and Accident Insurance Com-
pany with its office at 21 Carondelet Street. He welcomed the ad-

ditional income and readily managed the concerns of both businesses. He also actively sought the presidency of the Mobile and Ohio Railroad but was unsuccessful. In the spring of 1867, he endeavored to secure a stock subsidization for a proposed railroad from New Orleans, via Houston, and across Texas to Monterrey, Mexico, soliciting Grant and Philip H. Sheridan as patrons of the venture. This effort failed also, and he confined himself to the cotton and insurance businesses, which evidently provided his family with a good income. Additionally, he served as president of the Southern Hospital Association.[10]

As a businessman and citizen, Longstreet watched the turmoil and controversy engendered by Reconstruction. Like other former Confederate states, Louisiana was torn by factionalism in politics and riots in the streets. The citizenry divided over the political rights of ex-Confederates and the civil and political status of the freed blacks. Nationally, voters repudiated the policy of Johnson in the fall elections of 1866, giving control of Congress to Radical Republicans. The Radicals believed the instrument that had secured victory in the war—a powerful national government—must be wielded in the former Confederacy to guarantee the rights of the emancipated slaves. To them, the defeat of the South and the abolition of slavery under the Thirteenth Amendment provided an unprecedented opportunity to shape the country's future. Consequently, order and federal authority must be imposed on recalcitrant Southerners. In March 1867, the Radicals passed Reconstruction Acts that divided the former Confederate states, except Tennessee, into five military districts, and required each state to adopt a new constitution that provided for black suffrage and to ratify the Fourteenth Amendment, which granted citizenship to black Americans.[11]

The reaction to the measures among white Southerners was immediate and heated. In New Orleans, a city newspaper, the *Times,* solicited the views of eighteen prominent citizens. For nearly a year, publicly and privately, Longstreet urged "moderation, forebearance, and submission." Then when the editorial appeared, listing him among those individuals from whom the newspaper sought opinions, he responded with a letter, which appeared in print on March 18. "We are a conquered people," Longstreet wrote. Southerners must recognize this fact "fairly and squarely," with "but one course left for wise men to pursue, and that is to accept the terms

that are now offered by the conquerors." If "the constitutional government shall be re-established," the only course of action for
Southerners is "to comply with the requirements of the recent
Congressional legislation." He dismissed the idea that "the repre-
sentative men of a great nation could make such a pledge [of membership in Congress] in bad faith." He concluded, "Let us accept the
terms as we are in duty bound to do, and if there is a lack of good
faith, let it be upon others."[12]

Other former Rebel officers and politicians echoed Longstreet's
sentiments, not only in Louisiana but throughout the region. Gratified by the response to his views, Longstreet submitted a second
letter to the *Times,* reaffirming his previous statements, which the
newspaper printed on April 6. In New Orleans, local Republican
politicians flattered him with praise, hoping to lure the renowned
soldier into the party. In May, he attended a meeting to hear Pennsylvania Congressman W. D. "Pig Iron" Kelly and Massachusetts
Senator Henry Wilson argue for compliance with the acts. Their
speeches ignited protests and resulted in the crystallization of political parties in Louisiana. Letters increased to the city's newspapers,
opposing acceptance, and the legislature denounced the measures.[13]

Longstreet concluded, meanwhile, that the best solution was cooperation with the Republican Party in order to use the Reconstruction Acts to preserve the South and to control the black vote. Weeks
later he explained his views in a private letter: "My politics is to
save the little that is left of us, and to go to work to improve that
little as best we may." As to black suffrage, he argued:

> It is all important that we should exercise such influence over that
> vote, as to prevent its being injurious to us, & we can only do that as
> Republicans. As there is no principle or issue now that should keep
> us from the Republican party, it seems to me that our duty to our-
> selves & to all of our friends requires that our party South should
> seek an alliance with the Republican party. . . . If the whites won't do
> this, the thing will be done by the blacks, and we shall be set aside,
> if not expatriated. It then seems plain to me that we should do the
> work ourselves, & have it white instead of black & have our best
> men in public office.

To Longstreet the prospect of renewed rebellion over the Reconstruction Acts chilled him. "No one has worked more than I, nor

lost more," he concluded. "I think that the time has come for peace & I am not willing to lose more blood or means in procuring it. If there are any in the country inclined to fight the question, I hope not to be included in that number. I shall not abuse them for their views & I hope that they will not deny me the right to withdraw from the contest."[14]

Before he wrote this letter, however, Longstreet decided to make a public avowal of cooperation with the Black Republicans, as many Southerners referred to them. He evidently understood the dangers of such a statement and sought advice. His business partner, William Owen, cautioned against it, and when he spoke to John Hood about the matter, Hood said, "They will crucify you!" Longstreet even traveled to Oxford, Mississippi, to seek the views of his uncle, Augustus B. Longstreet. An astute politician in his own right, a proponent of Southern states' rights since the Nullification Crisis of 1832, the elderly Longstreet read his nephew's letter and remarked, "It will ruin you, son, if you publish it."[15]

Undeterred by the warnings, Longstreet forwarded the letter to the *Times,* where it appeared in the June 8 issue. His words were carried across the country, reprinted in many newspapers. The Northern press generally praised the contents, while Southern newspapers vilified both him and his ideas. In their indignation and fury, Southerners saw only Longstreet's argument for cooperation with the party that had emancipated the slaves and had destroyed large portions of the region, not his plan for controlling the freedmen vote. Only the black New Orleans *Tribune* denounced his views as an attempt to deny freed blacks suffrage and to restore the antebellum ruling class.[16]

The criticism, the appellation of "traitor," and the death threats surprised and confused Longstreet. He wrote to Lee, seeking the latter's endorsement, but his former commander refused to involve himself in public political disputes. A quarter of a century later he still did not grasp the spark he had tossed into the tinderbox of race relations in the South, writing to Goree: "I was anxious to keep the South out of the troubles that she has passed through since, and that was about the extent of my interest in affairs of state. For my pains I had nothing of good from them, or even appreciative expressions of sentiment." In his memoirs he dated the attacks on his and the First Corps's record in the war from the publication of the letter.[17]

His political naïveté cost him friends and business. He fled the city with his family in August, both to remove himself from the furor and his wife and children from the dangers of yellow fever and cholera. He would be away for much of the next two years. While Louise and the children stayed in Lynchburg, Longstreet traveled throughout the North, returning periodically to New Orleans. He visited New England and New York City, and was frequently in Washington. He saw Grant often and spent some time with John Fairfax at "Oak Hill," the former aide's estate located south of Leesburg, Virginia. In June 1868, Congress enacted a law granting pardons and restoring political rights to a number of Confederate officers, including Longstreet. During that autumn, Longstreet endorsed Grant's campaign for the presidency. He spent Christmas with his family in Lynchburg, traveling back and forth between there and the capital during the next two months. He was apparently in Washington to witness the inauguration of his longtime friend on March 4, 1869.[18]

Six days later, on March 10, President Grant nominated Longstreet for the position of surveyor of customs for the port of New Orleans, with an annual salary of six thousand dollars. Some opposition arose in the Senate, but the members confirmed the nomination by a vote of twenty-five to ten on April 3. Longstreet visited with Grant the following day and then left for his new job, arriving in New Orleans by the middle of the month.[19]

Although he needed a job and income, many white Southerners thought that Longstreet had committed an unpardonable sin. It was one thing to endorse support for Republican Party policies; it was altogether another matter to hold a government position and participate in the Republican rule in the South. Newspapers immediately accused Longstreet of putting self-interest over principle. He was called a scalawag, a Southerner who betrayed his native region for power and money doled out by Republicans. His old friend, West Point classmate, and fellow general Harvey Hill typified the reaction to Longstreet's appointment when he wrote in a newspaper: "Our scalawag is the local leper of the community. Unlike the carpet bagger [a Northerner], [Longstreet] is a native, which is so much the worse."[20]

Longstreet's military reputation and stature among Southerners never recovered. Explanations for the Confederate defeat were beginning to coalesce into the Lost Cause myth. According to the myth, Confederate soldiers had been vanquished by an onslaught of Northern manpower and material resources. Bravely, stoically, they had withstood Yankee aggression for four long years, and only at the end had they surrendered to the powerful foe. Religion served as the cornerstone of the myth as the cause became righteous, the living became heroes, and the fallen, martyrs. To join the Republicans, the political instrument of conquest and defeat, was to betray those who had died for the cause and those who were living under an imposed rule by the conquerors. Longstreet and those like him were even likened to Judas Iscariot. Longstreet and his family faced social ostracism, like that accorded a "leper," when they returned to New Orleans.[21]

The old warrior confronted the consequences of his actions and during the next several years became entwined in the volatile politics of Louisiana. He evidently performed the duties of surveyor of customs competently, while increasingly supporting the Republican state administration of Governor Henry C. Warmouth, a former Union officer. Warmouth rewarded Longstreet for his efforts by appointing him adjutant general of the state militia, a five-thousand-man force of both white and black troops, in May 1870. A month later Longstreet was named president of the newly organized New Orleans and Northeastern Railroad at an annual salary of three thousand dollars. It has been estimated that by year's end he was earning between ten and fifteen thousand dollars from his three positions, a very substantial sum for the times.[22]

Longstreet's involvement deepened during 1871 and 1872. The Republican Party split into two main groups—Governor Warmouth's wing and the so-called Custom House faction—with each seeking the sanction of the national party and the Grant administration. Longstreet supported Warmouth and argued the governor's position in letters and in a personal visit to Grant. The president, however, favored the anti-Warmouth group. As a reward for his efforts, Longstreet was commissioned as a major general of the state militia by Warmouth on January 8, 1872, and was assigned "to the immediate command and supervision of the entire militia, police, and all civil forces of the State of Louisiana within the City of New Orleans." Two months later, in protest to the activities of the Custom House faction, Longstreet resigned as surveyor of customs and as railroad president. In April he relinquished his post as adjutant

general of the state. By the summer of 1872, he was regarded in
Louisiana as a strong Radical Republican.[23]

The elections that fall were marked with enormous fraud, resulting in claims of victory by the Custom House Republicans of
William H. Kellogg and by the Democrats of John McEnery. The
situation became so entangled and explosive that the two boards
created to unsnarl the vote count obtained injunctions from two
different federal courts. Lieutenant Governor P. B. S. Pinchback, a
black Republican politician, became acting governor when the state
Senate impeached Warmouth. Acting with Kellogg, Pinchback appealed to Grant for support, while Warmouth maneuvered to secure McEnery's installation. On January 12, 1873, Kellogg took the
oath of office in the State House; and McEnery, in the Odd Fellows
Hall. In Washington, Congress refused to order a new election, and
Grant stated that he would recognize the Kellogg government.[24]

At the beginning of the campaign, Longstreet supported the Lib-
eral Republican movement that endorsed newspaper publisher
Horace Greeley for president and D. B. Penn for Louisiana governor. Once Penn joined the McEnery ticket as lieutenant governor,
his Republican allies, including Longstreet, backed Kellogg. Longstreet served on one of the boards that examined the returns and
was appointed by Pinchback in the interim to command of the
militia. He attended Kellogg's inauguration, and on March 5, 1873,
Longstreet assumed command of the militia and the New Orleans
Metropolitan Police Force, an organization that dated back to 1868,
and was constituted mostly of black members. That night, in the so
called Battle of the Cabildo, the Metropolitan Police Force, backed
by federal troops, repulsed an attempt by McEnery's supporters to
seize the city police stations. The next day Longstreet's policemen
occupied the Odd Fellows Hall and arrested any individual found
in the building. On the 7th, confronted by protests, Kellogg released the prisoners.[25]

Despite the official recognition of Kellogg's administration by
President Grant in a proclamation, McEnery's followers maintained
that their candidate was the legal governor of the state. Riots and
clashes cost lives, and someone attempted to assassinate Kellogg.
The Republicans held power only by the threat of intervention
by federal troops. The Democrats formed the Crescent City White
League, a military organization composed of many former Confed-

erate veterans, in June 1874. When six Republican officeholders were executed, allegedly by members of the White League on August 30, Kellogg declared martial law, and Grant ordered federal troops to be stationed throughout the city. When the Metropolitan Police Force seized cases of smuggled arms in crates labeled MACHINERY that were intended for the White League, the situation exploded into a pitched battle.[26]

On the evening of September 14, an estimated eighty-four hundred White League members advanced as an armed force on the State House. Opposing them were thirty-six hundred Metropolitan Police, city policemen, and black militia troops with two Gatling guns and a battery of artillery, under the command of Longstreet. The general had formed his line from Jackson Square to Canal Street, barricading the intersections and guarding the Customs House where Kellogg and other officials had taken refuge. When the White Leaguers approached, Longstreet rode forward to meet them and to demand that they disperse. But the rebels pulled Longstreet from his horse and opened fire. He was hit by a spent bullet and was taken to the rear as a prisoner. The White Leaguers charged, driving their opponents to the river. Longstreet's men either fled or surrendered. Total casualties amounted to thirty-eight killed and seventy-nine wounded. The White League held the center of New Orleans.[27]

On Grant's instructions, federal troops restored order on the 16th, arrested McEnery and other leaders of the opposition, and released Longstreet. The federal commander restored Kellogg to power, but the governor's authority depended entirely on the presence of the military. In the fall elections, the Democrats increased their majorities in the state legislature. With another election in 1876, Republican rule in Louisiana would be ended.[28]

Longstreet's role in the so-called White League Fight resulted in more denunciation and vilification. He had led mostly black troops against former Confederate soldiers, which to white Southerners was another indication of his betrayal of the cause. A White League officer claimed later that "it was with the greatest difficulty that I prevented the men from firing particularly at Longstreet." Shortly after the battle, he was relieved of duty with the militia, ending his active participation in the cesspool of Louisiana politics.[29]

Beginning May 30, 1873, Longstreet had been serving as president of the Levee Commission of Engineers at a yearly salary of six thousand dollars. Kellogg had appointed him to the four-year post. The commission's function was to examine existing levees and recommend the construction of new ones. The work required trudging through swamps and extensive travel throughout the state and to Washington, D.C. According to Longstreet, the labor in the swamps was "the hardest work man ever did" and caused him and his fellow commissioners serious health problems. He had returned from an inspection trip only days before the White League Fight. In the battle's aftermath, he resumed his duties with the commission, but only for a few months.[30]

Concern for his health and his family's welfare, and probably expediency, convinced Longstreet to leave New Orleans and settle in Georgia. His shoulder and arm plagued him, and he suffered from rheumatism. The city was still subjected to yellow fever epidemics, and he often relocated his family during the summer months. If nothing else good came from his years in the city, he and Louise had been blessed with two more children—a son, Fitz Randolph, born on July 1, 1869, in Lynchburg, Virginia, and a daughter, Maria Louisa, named for her mother, born on July 29, 1872, in Flint, Michigan, while Louise was visiting an aunt. In their twenty-four years of marriage, the couple had ten children, five of whom lived to adulthood.[31]

Longstreet's brother, William, who now resided near Gainesville, Georgia, had been urging James to relocate in the community, and James and his family moved there in the summer of 1875. Some residents objected to the scalawag's decision to make his home in Gainesville, but that did not deter Longstreet. On October 7 he purchased from Alvah Smith, for the sum of six thousand dollars, the Piedmont Hotel, a three-story, white-columned boardinghouse. Sometime later he acquired farmland, located two or three miles outside the town on what locals called Inspiration Point, and began construction of what a newspaperman later described as an "ordinary story-and-a-half farm house such as a northern carpenter might build." Increasingly, as the years passed, the farmhouse became Longstreet's haven.[32]

While Louise and the children remained in Gainesville, Longstreet traveled extensively during 1876 and 1877, engaged in unspecified business matters and political activities. When Republican Rutherford B. Hayes was elected president by the House of Representatives in the "disputed election" of 1876, Longstreet sought an appointment. One Republican official proposed him for secretary of the navy in Hayes's cabinet. He tried through channels to be named collector of customs in New Orleans, and when this failed, he sought the post of United States marshal for Georgia. In September 1877, however, he withdrew his application, citing "my business affairs," only to renew it two months later. Hayes, meanwhile, in an effort to conciliate his political opponents, had appointed O. P. Fitzsimmons, a Democrat, whom Longstreet had endorsed, albeit reluctantly.[33]

During these months, Longstreet frequently returned to New Orleans, serving on the board of directors of the city schools and as an ex officio administrator of the University of Louisiana (today, Tulane University). His membership on the Levee Commission expired in 1877, but he had engaged in no active work on it since 1874, with the state refusing to pay his salary for the final two years and four months. While on one visit to the city—reportedly in March 1877—he became a convert to the Roman Catholic Church, another act of apostasy in the overwhelmingly Protestant South. Longstreet wrote virtually nothing about his religious beliefs, but his conversion was sincere, and he remained a devoted Catholic until his death.[34]

Physically, Longstreet still had no use of his right arm, and he continued to seek relief at resorts with hot springs. A newspaperman who saw him during this time noted that his "beard is now grey. Soldiers who knew him during the war say that it was black and very long extending almost to his waist. He now wears the Burnside whiskers, moustache and side beard. He is said not to be so large as he was during the war and is represented as being very much changed otherwise in his present appearance."[35]

It was not until the fall of 1878 that the Hayes administration secured a job for Longstreet. On September 7, he was appointed deputy collector of internal revenue at a salary of six dollars per day. But he retained this position for only a few months, securing the postmastership of Gainesville in January 1879. The job kept him with his family and provided him with a modest steady income.[36]

It also gave him time to dabble in Georgia politics. Longstreet believed that for the Republican Party to be successful in the state it had to form a coalition with Independent Democrats, a view he would advocate for the next two decades. With the restoration of Democratic rule throughout the region—the so-called Solid South

—in 1876, the Republicans had to lure white voters and "secure cooperation from a large part of the best citizens of this section." But Longstreet's was a forlorn hope because of the Republican appeal to blacks, a tactic he preferred to use less. As he had revealed in Louisiana, Longstreet possessed little political skill or insight. A Republican leader in Georgia confided later that "the Genl. is not versed in politics...and will make blunders unless closely watched. It's too late in life for him to learn politics."[37]

His active participation in Republican politics continued to yield personal gain. On May 19, 1880, President Hayes nominated Longstreet as United States minister to Turkey, with the Senate confirming on June 14. He was a surprising choice for the diplomatic duty, and his selection generated much criticism within the country and in Europe. He accepted but delayed his departure until after the presidential campaign that fall, which resulted in the election of Republican James A. Garfield, another former Union general. Longstreet sailed from the country on November 1, arriving in Constantinople in mid-December. Louise and the children stayed in Gainesville.[38]

Sultan Abdul Hamid Khan II, a small man who preferred to wear European-styled clothing and a red fez, welcomed the new minister. Ill-suited for such service, Longstreet did not enjoy his brief tenure. He secured permission from the sultan for American archaeologists to undertake research in Turkey, a reversal of policy for Khan. It was Longstreet's only accomplishment. In April 1881 he applied for and was granted a sixty-day leave to tour Western Europe. He visited Austria, Prussia, and France, writing to his son Fitz Randolph that he hoped "before the expiration of my leave to have my recall to America."[39]

The United States government did recall him, and after returning home in late spring, he assumed the position of United States marshal for Georgia. He had sought the job for four years, and according to him, Garfield had promised it to Longstreet before he had departed for Turkey. Garfield nominated him to a four-year term on April 19, and the Senate confirmed on May 10. Longstreet posted bonds and took his oath of office in Atlanta on July 1. The next day, in Washington, Charles Guiteau, a deranged lawyer and officeseeker, assassinated Garfield, who lingered until September 19. Vice President Chester A. Arthur of New York succeeded to the presidency.[40]

Longstreet served slightly over three years as marshal, a tenure plagued by controversy and political intrigue. His predecessor, O. P. Fitzsimmons, left office under suspicion of fraud and wrongdoing. Consequently, Longstreet requested an audit of the books by the Department of Justice that eventually resulted in an investigation by a committee of the House of Representatives. An examiner uncovered "a good deal of fraud" by Fitzsimmons and his deputies, one of whom, J. M. Robinson, Longstreet had retained. Although the investigator cited Longstreet's "personal integrity," he reported that the marshal "is almost entirely without those essential and necessary qualities which constitute a business man" and recommended that the Department of Justice prosecute Fitzsimmons and some deputies, including Robinson, who alledgedly continued his illegal activities under Longstreet. The Department refused.[41]

Angered by the implication that he managed the office incompetently, Longstreet counterattacked, writing letters to congressional members and personally presenting his case to President Arthur. The controversy did not abate, however, and Longstreet had to defend not only himself but his son Garland, whom he had appointed chief deputy marshal, before a House committee. An investigator charged that Garland actually conducted the affairs of the office and "was entirely incompetent to manage the office, on account of dissolute habits and want of ability." His father was only "a figure-head," according to the report. The Democrats used the alleged misconduct in Longstreet's office and in other offices throughout the country as an issue in the presidential campaign of 1884.[42]

The politics of this campaign doomed Longstreet. Members of the Georgia Republican Party who supported Senator James G. Blaine for the party's presidential nomination began the movement for Longstreet's removal almost as soon as he entered the office. A leader of the group, John A. Bryant, coveted the marshalship, and as time passed, Bryant switched his support to Arthur, promising the incumbent a solid Georgia delegation to the national convention. Because of the investigations and Democratic exploitation of the issue, Longstreet became a liability. On July 21, Arthur requested Longstreet's resignation and then appointed Bryant to the office within days. Blaine, however, secured the nomination but lost to Democrat Grover Cleveland in the election. Longstreet, meanwhile, demanded a settlement of his accounts, which was resolved that autumn with the payment of money to him and his deputies.[43]

With a Democrat in the White House for the first time in twenty-four years, Longstreet had no prospects of another political job and went into semi-retirement in Gainesville. The next few years became some of the most pleasurable of his life. He operated the Piedmont Hotel, where the family spent the winter months. Increasingly, however, he enjoyed his time on the farm, which was "one of the delights of his life." He had the hilly ground terraced, which led local folks to refer jokingly to the farm as "Gettysburg." He raised turkeys, planted an orchard on the hill, and tended a grape vineyard. Often he could be seen in a white linen duster and broad-brimmed hat, nurturing the grapes from which he made wine that he sold to neighbors. The vineyard also attracted hungry boys who indulged themselves until the old soldier scared them off with the blast from a musket.[44]

His farm activities were restricted by his age and physical disabilities. He particularly complained in letters about the uselessness of his right arm. To Raphael Moses, his former chief of commissary, Longstreet grumbled: "My arm is paralyzed; my voice that once could be heard all along the lines is gone; I can scarcely speak above a whisper, my hearing is very much impaired, and sometimes feel as if I wish the end would come; but I have some misrepresentations of my battles that I wish to correct, so as to have my record correct before I die."[45]

On April 9, 1889—the twenty-fourth anniversary of Appomattox—disaster struck at the farm. A fire ignited in the house and destroyed the structure and its contents. Longstreet lost his uniform, sword, a sash presented to him by J. E. B. Stuart, a pair of Mexican spurs that he had worn through both wars, his Civil War relics, and his library. The loss was estimated at eight thousand dollars and was not insured. He and Louise moved into a small cottage he had previously built on the farm. Three years later another fire leveled the barn, destroying his farm implements.[46]

Months after the fire, in the autumn when the north Georgia woods turn crimson and gold, Louise became ill. The nature of the affliction is uncertain, but she died on December 29, 1889, at the age of sixty-two. She had been James's wife for over forty years, had borne ten children, grieved deeply over the loss of five of them, endured the months of separation from her husband, waited alone in the silence and darkness of nights for reports of his safety, and followed him wherever duty or desire led him. From her childhood she had witnessed the sacrifices required of a soldier's wife, and when her time came, she chose a soldier. Longstreet buried her in Alta Vista Cemetery in Gainesville.[47]

To allay his personal grief, Longstreet immersed himself in the writing of his memoirs. When the fire consumed his notes and books, he had to start from the beginning. To him the book would be a culmination of a war in private correspondence and public print that he had been waging for nearly twenty years with his opponents, most of whom were fellow officers in Lee's army. It was a struggle that Longstreet had been losing and that would taint Civil War historiography for a century.

When Longstreet was in Washington, D.C., in November 1865 seeking a pardon, he agreed to an interview with William Swinton, a former correspondent for the New York *Times*. Swinton was at work on a history of the war in the East and sought information from ex-Confederates. In the interview, Longstreet voiced criticism of the assault at Gettysburg on July 3, 1863; Swinton incorporated this in his *Campaigns of the Army of the Potomac,* published in 1866. With Lee alive, none of his officers commented publicly on Swinton's account, but then the great warrior died on October 12, 1870, in Lexington, Virginia. Within two years the public attacks on Longstreet began.[48]

Former Second Corps commander Jubal Early opened the controversy with an address at Washington College on the anniversary of Lee's birth, January 19, 1872. Early focused on Gettysburg, exonerating Lee of mistakes and accusing Longstreet of not attacking promptly on July 2, and of being responsible for the attack on the 3rd. Exactly a year later at the same site, William N. Pendleton, the army's former artillery chief and now a minister, charged Longstreet with failure to obey an order by Lee to attack at sunrise on July 2. This alleged "sunrise order" became the center of a firestorm. Pendleton either deliberately lied—Lee issued no such order—or memory failed him.[49]

At first Longstreet reacted with silence, preferring, as he said months later, "that I should bear the responsibility than to put it upon our chief." Friends and former comrades urged him to respond. It was not until the spring of 1875 in private correspondence that he demanded evidence from Pendleton and sought assistance from Lee's former staff officers—Charles Marshall, Walter Taylor, Charles Venable, and Armistead Long. By then, however, with his involvement in Louisiana politics and in the White League Fight, his wartime record had been severely damaged.[50]

"I believe that mistakes were made on both sides," Longstreet wrote in a letter in the summer of 1874, "and that I am likely to be one of those who have committed them as any one, but in order that the future students may have the benefit of our experience, I am more than willing to have a thorough investigation of all military movements and operations, and their causes, and effects." If he did not welcome the dispute, he at least did not fear a verdict.[51]

Eventually, Longstreet wrote a series of articles on the war for *Century Magazine* and the Philadelphia *Times*. Two writers with the Atlanta *Constitution,* Josiah Carter and Joel Chandler Harris, author of the Uncle Remus tales, acted as copy editors for the *Century* articles, while Henry W. Grady, a freelance journalist, edited and refined the *Times* pieces. Alexander K. McClure, editor of the *Times,* paid Grady for his services. Like his opponents, however, Longstreet made misstatements of fact and leveled unfair criticisms at others.[52]

When Longstreet turned to his memoirs in the 1890s, he sought the assistance of his surviving staff members and other officers of the First Corps. His goal in writing a book, he told Thomas Munford, an ex-Confederate cavalry general, was "to illustrate the valor of the Confederate soldier. To do him notice it should stand close by the [official] Records, in points of numbers as well as other facts." The labor consumed nearly five years. P. J. Moran, an editor at the Atlanta *Constitution* and a former Union officer who had commanded black troops during the war, served as an editor and typist on the memoirs. In fact, Moran evidently made revisions in the text, particularly the general's chapters on Sharpsburg. Longstreet expected publication by Christmas 1895, but it was delayed at the printers until early in 1896. The J. B. Lippincott Company of Philadelphia published the 690-page work.[53]

As expected, the book engendered both praise and censure. His detractors especially condemned him for his criticisms of Lee. He was also accused of shoddy research and of lacking "a facile pen." On balance, the work enjoyed a good reception and was reissued in 1908. Despite its flaws, Longstreet's book remains, as it was when first published, a classic memoir of the war.[54]

Throughout the years of political turbulence and controversy, Longstreet maintained his close association with his staff officers. Thomas Walton and Peyton Manning died before 1880. Moxley Sorrel had returned to Savannah, prospered after the war as a businessman, and written his recollections. After a number of years in Europe, Osmun Latrobe returned to Baltimore, where he served five terms as mayor. Dr. Dorsey Cullen practiced his profession and, like John Fairfax, who managed his "Oak Hill" estate, frequently had Longstreet as a guest. Porter Alexander had a varied postwar career in education, business, and government. In 1907, Alexander's excellent *Military Memoirs of a Confederate* was published.[55]

Tom Goree corresponded often with his old commander and saw him on occasion. He remained in Texas, serving for a time as state superintendent of penitentiaries. In 1875, Goree wrote a letter to Longstreet expressing sentiments that all his fellow staff members would have endorsed: "With my heart full of gratitude, I often think of you, and of your many acts of kindness shown me, and the innumerable marks of esteem and confidence bestowed upon me by you during the four long and trying years that we were together. Although we may differ in our political *opinions,* yet I have always given you credit for honesty and sincerity of purpose."[56]

Longstreet also became involved in veterans' activities as the years passed. He visited battlefields and assisted with the marking of unit locations. As a member of the Chickamauga Memorial Association, he spoke at the dedication of the Chickamauga-Chattanooga National Battlefield Park in 1895. Two years later he was a guest of Vice President Garret A. Hobart at the dedication ceremonies for the tomb of Ulysses S. Grant (who had died in July 1885) in Riverside Park, New York City. When Longstreet learned of his friend's death, he told a newspaperman that Grant "was the truest as well as the bravest man that ever lived."[57]

Most of all, Longstreet enjoyed attending Confederate ceremonies and reunions. Despite the political differences, the veteran soldiers, particularly those of the First Corps, retained their respect and affection for the general. His entrance into halls disrupted meetings, and his presence in parades halted the flow of marchers. On May 1, 1886, in Atlanta, for instance, he joined an estimated ten thousand veterans in the dedication of a monument to Senator Benjamin H. Hill, a former ally of Jefferson Davis in the Confederate Congress. Dressed in his uniform, Longstreet rode in a procession, and when the old soldiers recognized him, they emitted the Rebel yell and cheered. When he reached the platform, he approached Davis, and the two men shook hands amid louder cheering. A remarkably similar scene occurred four years later in Richmond at the dedication of Lee's statue. Such responses deeply pleased and gratified Longstreet.[58]

"Old men get lonely and must have company," Longstreet once remarked, and to the dismay and embarrassment of his children, the old widower married Helen Dortch in the governor's mansion in Atlanta on September 8, 1897. A native Georgian and devout Catholic, Helen had attended Brenau College in Gainesville and was serving as assistant state librarian at the time of her marriage. She was thirty-four years old, and Longstreet had most likely met the strong-willed woman when she was a student in Gainesville. Although she and his children never cared for each other, Helen was a devoted wife to Longstreet and became his most ardent defender after his death. She outlived him by fifty-eight years, dying in 1962.[59]

Before long the newlyweds relocated to Washington, D.C., when Longstreet secured appointment as United States Commissioner of Railroads. During the presidential campaign of 1896, he had canvassed for Republican William McKinley, and when the Union veteran won, Longstreet hoped to get the post of minister to Mexico. Instead, McKinley rewarded Longstreet with the commissioner's office. It was a choice assignment that required nominal inspection duties. Longstreet's predecessor was Wade Hampton, the former Confederate cavalry general and a bitter political foe of Longstreet. Hampton was so incensed by his failure to retain the post that he refused to assist Longstreet during the transition.[60]

While in the capital, the Longstreets resided in an apartment at 1218 Seventeenth Street, but they spent their summers on the farm in Gainesville. The limited requirements of the office permitted the couple to travel extensively on the railroads. In 1898 they visited Mexico, touring the old battlefields, and a year later they criss-crossed the western United States. Longstreet still attended reunions when his health and duties allowed and was present for McKinley's second inaugural. In 1902, with Porter Alexander, he journeyed to West Point for the hundredth anniversary of the academy. One evening, while sitting on the porch of the old West Point hotel, he saw his former cavalry commander in East Tennessee,

Joseph Wheeler, approaching. Wheeler had served in the Spanish-American War in 1898 and was dressed in the blue uniform of a general. "Joe," Longstreet allegedly remarked, "I hope that Almighty God takes me before he does you, for I want to be within the gates of hell to hear Jubal Early cuss you in the blue uniform."[61]

The summons was closer at hand than he knew. The pain from his rheumatism never ceased, and he had become so deaf that he had to use an ear horn to hear. In the summer of 1903, he was afflicted with an unspecified serious illness, and doctors were not certain he would recover. In the autumn, he traveled to Chicago for X-ray treatment of a cancerous right eye. His weight had dropped from 200 pounds to 135. By Christmas he and Helen had returned to Gainesville, and the old warrior rallied. On the morning of January 2, 1904, he visited his daughter's home in Gainesville and became gravely ill with pneumonia.[62]

The end came swiftly and mercifully. He began hemorrhaging, and "a great gush of blood" poured out of his mouth, reopening the Wilderness throat wound. He remained unconscious throughout most of the afternoon. Garland, an architect in Atlanta, and Fitz Randolph, a local farmer, joined their sister, Maria Louisa Whelchel, by his side. Robert Lee held a government job in Washington, and James, Jr., was a captain in the Thirteenth United States Cavalry, serving in the Philippine Islands. Helen was also there, and about five o'clock the soldier stirred and whispered, "Helen, we shall be happier in this post." James Longstreet was dead, six days short of his eighty-third birthday.[63]

The funeral was held on January 6, and in the estimation of an Atlanta *Constitution* reporter, was "the most impressive ceremonial ever held in Gainesville." His remains had been removed from his daughter's house on the 5th and laid in state in the courthouse until 11:00 A.M. on the 6th when the services began. A local guard unit and representatives of the Longstreet Chapter, United Daughters of the Confederacy, attended the body. Two priests and Bishop Keiley, one of the general's old soldiers, conducted the services. All the children except James attended. Once the services were concluded at the courthouse, pallbearers carried the casket to a hearse, which began the long procession to Alta Vista Cemetery. State and local dignitaries, militia units, Confederate veterans carrying flags, and other groups followed as church bells tolled.[64] At the gravesite, Bishop Keiley gave a eulogy, and the youthful warriors in the Candler and Governor's Horse Guards fired their volley. "Taps" sounded with its haunting notes.

When the news of his death had spread across the country, many newspapers had extolled his virtues as a man and his prowess as a general. But as the pallbearers prepared to lower the casket, a Confederate veteran walked to the grave. Without a word he lay part of his uniform and his enlistment papers on the lid of the coffin, and then stepped back. His comrades understood.[65]

NOTES

Works cited by author and short titles will be found in full in the bibliography. The following abbreviations are used in the notes:

ACW	*America's Civil War*
AHQ	*Alabama Historical Quarterly*
AHS	Atlanta Historical Society
ANBL	Antietam National Battlefield Library
B & L	*Battles and Leaders of the Civil War*
BU	Brown University
CCNMP	Chickamauga-Chattanooga National Military Park
CHS	Chicago Historical Society
CMH	*Confederate Military History*
CRL	Chestatee Regional Library
CSR/NA	Compiled Service Records/National Archives
CV	*Confederate Veteran*
CWM	*Civil War Magazine*
CWQ	*Civil War Quarterly*
CWTI	*Civil War Times Illustrated*
DU	Duke University
EU	Emory University
FSNMP	Fredericksburg & Spotsylvania National Military Park
GDAH	Georgia Department of Archives and History
GHQ	*Georgia Historical Quarterly*
GHS	Georgia Historical Society
GNMP	Gettysburg National Military Park
HL	Huntington Library
HSP	Historical Society of Pennsylvania
HU	Harvard University

JML   Jones Memorial Library
LC   Library of Congress
MA   *From Manassas to Appomattox*
MC   Museum of the Confederacy
MNBP   Manassas National Battlefield Park
NYHS   New York Historical Society
NYPL   New York Public Library
OR   *The War of the Rebellion: Official Records of the Union and*
               Confederate Armies
RBHPC   Rutherford B. Hayes Presidential Center
SHSP   *Southern Historical Society Papers*
TSLA   Tennessee State Library and Archives
TU   Tulane University
UG   University of Georgia
UNC   University of North Carolina
USAMHI   United States Army Military History Institute
USMAA   United States Military Academy Archives
UT   University of Texas
UTS   Union Theological Seminary
UV   University of Virginia
VHS   Virginia Historical Society
VSL   Virginia State Library
WLU   Washington and Lee University
WM   The College of William and Mary
WRHS   Western Reserve Historical Society

PREFACE

1. Longstreet–Henry B. Dawson, March 27, 1876, Dawson Papers, NYPL.

1. SOLDIER'S JOURNEY

1. Goree, *Letters,* pp. 311, 330; Washington *Post,* May 29, 30, 1890; New York *Times,* May 30, 1890.

2. Longstreet, *MA,* p. 13; Sanger and Hay, *James Longstreet,* p. 6; Mayes, *Genealogy,* p. 16; Piston, Ph.D. Diss., I, pp. 3–4.

3. Mayes, *Genealogy,* pp. 18–22; "Fitz Randolph Family History"; newspaper clipping, Longstreet Papers, CRL

4. Mayes, *Genealogy,* p. 22; Piston, Ph.D. Diss., p. 3

5. Mayes, *Genealogy,* p. 23; Piston, Ph.D. Diss., pp. 2, 3; Longstreet, *Lee and Longstreet,* p. 96.

6. Mayes, *Genealogy,* p. 24; Piston, Ph.D. Diss., p. 3; newspaper clipping, Longstreet Papers, CRL.

7. Longstreet, *MA,* p. 13; Mayes, *Genealogy,* p. 24; Piston, Ph.D. Diss., pp. 3–4.

8. Longstreet, *MA,* p. 13; Mayes, *Genealogy,* p. 24; Sanger and Hay, *James Longstreet,* p. 6; Sallie V. Odwolt–Longstreet, October 2, 1892, November 5, 1895, December 19, 1895; Mary Roper Wragg–Longstreet, Octo-

ber 31, 1895; J. M. Dent–Longstreet, December 19, 1895; John F. Dent–Longstreet, March 16, 1896; undated statement by Longstreet, Longstreet Papers, CRL.

9. Mayes, *Genealogy*, pp. 24, 25; Sanger and Hay, *James Longstreet*, p. 6.

10. Sanger and Hay, *James Longstreet*, pp. 6, 7; Piston, Ph.D. Diss., pp. 5, 6, 9.

11. Mayes, *Genealogy*, p. 25; Longstreet, *MA*, p. 15; Piston, Ph.D. Diss., pp. 5, 9.

12. Piston, Ph.D. Diss., pp. 10, 11; Longstreet, *Lee and Longstreet*, p. 98.

13. Piston, Ph.D. Diss., pp. 5, 6, 10.

14. Fitzgerald, *Judge Longstreet*, pp. 9, 11, 14, 15, 26, 28, 32; Mayes, *Genealogy*, pp. 28, 29.

15. Fitzgerald, *Judge Longstreet*, pp. 32, 36, 43; Mayes, *Genealogy*, p. 29; *CV*, 27, p. 371.

16. Fitzgerald, *Judge Longstreet*, pp. 57, 169; Piston, Ph.D. Diss., pp. 17, 18.

17. Piston, Ph.D. Diss., pp. 11, 12.

18. Ibid., pp. 12, 13.

19. Ibid., p. 13.

20. Ibid., p. 19.

21. Freehling, *Prelude, passim.*

22. Piston, Ph.D. Diss., pp. 15, 16; Mayes, *Genealogy*, p. 29.

23. Longstreet, *MA*, p. 15; Piston, Ph.D. Diss., pp. 14, 19; Mayes, *Genealogy*, p. 27; R. Chapman–J. R. Poinsett, December 23, 1837, March 30, 1838, Longstreet, Cadet Applications, USMAA.

24. Mayes, *Genealogy*, p. 31; Piston, Ph.D. Diss., pp. 15, 16, 17.

25. Piston, Ph.D. Diss., pp. 19, 19n; R. Chapman–J. R. Poinsett, December 23, 1837, March 30, 1838, Longstreet, Cadet Applications, USMAA.

26. Longstreet, Academic Record, USMAA.

27. Fleming, *West Point*, p. 96; Freeman, *R. E. Lee*, I, p. 50.

28. Piston, Ph.D. Diss., p. 22; Fleming, *West Point*, p. 46.

29. Ambrose, *Duty, Honor, Country*, p. 149.

30. Ibid., p. 154; Fleming, *West Point*, p. 92.

31. Ambrose, *Duty, Honor, Country*, p. 163; Fleming, *West Point*, p. 92.

32. Fleming, *West Point*, p. 110; Longstreet, Select List, USMAA.

33. Longstreet, *MA*, p. 17; Eliot, *West Point*, p. xxi; Warner, *Generals in Blue, passim.*

34. Longstreet, "List," USMAA; Ambrose, *Duty, Honor, Country*, p. 153; Piston, Ph.D. Diss., p. 25.

35. Longstreet, "List," USMAA; Ambrose, *Duty, Honor, Country*, p. 126; Piston, Ph.D. Diss., pp. 27, 28.

36. Hamlin, *Portrait*, p. 32; Ambrose, *Duty, Honor, Country*, p. 135.

37. Longstreet, Academic Record, USMAA; Longstreet, *MA*, pp. 15, 16.

38. Longstreet, Academic Record, USMAA; Longstreet, *MA*, p. 15; Sanger and Hay, *James Longstreet*, p. 8.

39. Longstreet, Academic Record, USMAA; Longstreet, *MA*, pp. 15–16.

40. Longstreet, Academic Record, USMAA; Ambrose, *Duty, Honor, Country,* pp. 99–102.

41. Longstreet, Academic Record, USMAA.

42. New York *Times,* July 24, 1885; Longstreet, Select List, Academic Record, USMAA; Longstreet, *MA,* p. 16; Piston, Ph.D. Diss., p. 31.

43. Piston, Ph.D. Diss., p. 30; Longstreet, *Lee and Longstreet,* pp. 100, 103.

44. Longstreet, *MA,* p. 17; *CV,* 3, p. 260; 25, p. 367; Eliot, *West Point,* p. xxi; Sanger and Hay, *James Longstreet,* p. 8; Piston, Ph.D. Diss., p. 30.

45. Longstreet, *MA,* p. 17; Grant, *Personal Memoirs,* I, p. 38; New York *Times,* July 24, 1885; Piston, Ph.D. Diss., p. 30.

46. Cullum, *Register,* II, p. 150; Piston, Ph.D. Diss., p. 33; Mayes, *Genealogy,* p. 30.

2. SOLDIER'S TRADE

1. Piston, Ph.D. Diss., p. 35; newspaper clipping, Longstreet Papers, CRL.

2. Piston, Ph.D. Diss., p. 30; Longstreet, *MA,* pp. 16, 17, 18; Sanger and Hay, *James Longstreet,* p. 9; "Garland Family," JML.

3. Longstreet, *MA,* p. 18; Grant, *Memoirs,* I, p. 45; Faeder, *CWTI,* "The Best of," 26, 6, pp. 17, 18; McFeeley, *Grant,* pp. 20–25.

4. "Garland Family," JML; Woods, *Albemarle County,* p. 200; Richmond *Times-Dispatch,* July 26, 1908.

5. "Garland Family," JML; Sanger and Hay, *James Longstreet,* pp. 12, 13; Piston, Ph.D. Diss., p. 36.

6. Piston, Ph.D. Diss., p. 36; Hamlin, *Portrait,* p. 52.

7. Piston, Ph.D. Diss., p. 37; Longstreet, *Lee and Longstreet,* p. 109.

8. Longstreet, *MA,* p. 18.

9. Piston, Ph.D. Diss., pp. 39, 40; New York *Times,* July 24, 1885.

10. Cullum, *Register,* II, pp. 150, 151; Sanger and Hay, *James Longstreet,* p. 10; Longstreet–Major E. Van Neuw, July 24, 1845, Longstreet Papers, HL; Piston, Ph.D. Diss., p. 42.

11. Piston, Ph.D. Diss., p. 44; Longstreet, *MA,* pp. 18, 19.

12. Piston, Ph.D. Diss., pp. 44, 47.

13. Longstreet, *MA,* p. 20; Longstreet, *Lee and Longstreet,* pp. 138, 141.

14. Longstreet, *MA,* p. 20; Longstreet, *Lee and Longstreet,* pp. 144, 145; Piston, Ph.D. Diss., pp. 47, 48.

15. Longstreet, *MA,* p. 21.

16. Ibid., p. 21; Bauer, *Mexican War,* p. 49.

17. Longstreet, *MA,* pp. 23, 24; Perret, *Country,* p. 150.

18. Bauer, *Mexican War,* pp. 49, 50, 52; Perret, *Country,* pp. 150, 151; Smith and Judah, *Gringos,* pp. 64, 65.

19. Perret, *Country,* pp. 151, 152; Bauer, *Mexican War,* pp. 52, 54, 57; Smith and Judah, *Gringos,* pp. 66, 67.

20. Perret, *Country,* p. 152; Bauer, *Mexican War,* pp. 59, 62; Smith and Judah, *Gringos,* p. 68.

21. Longstreet, *MA,* pp. 25–28; Longstreet, *Lee and Longstreet,* pp. 127–61.

22. Piston, Ph.D. Diss., p. 57; Perret, *Country,* pp. 152, 153.

23. Piston, Ph.D. Diss., pp. 56, 57; Smith and Judah, *Gringos,* p. 86.

24. Piston, Ph.D. Diss., p. 59; Perret, *Country,* pp. 153, 154; Bauer, *Mexican War,* p. 100.

25. Perret, *Country,* p. 154; Smith and Judah, *Gringos,* p. 86.

26. Piston, Ph.D. Diss., pp. 60, 61; Smith and Judah, *Gringos,* p. 86.

27. Piston, Ph.D. Diss., pp. 62, 63; Perret, *Country,* p. 154.

28. Piston, Ph.D. Diss., pp. 63, 64; Perret, *Country,* p. 154; Bauer, *Mexican War,* pp. 100, 101.

29. Piston, Ph.D. Diss., p. 65; Cullum, *Register,* II, p. 151.

30. Piston, Ph.D. Diss., pp. 65, 67; Perret, *Country,* pp. 154, 155.

31. Perret, *Country,* pp. 161, 162; Piston, Ph.D. Diss., p. 68.

32. Perret, *Country,* p. 164; Piston, Ph.D. Diss., p. 69.

33. Perret, *Country,* pp. 162–64.

34. Ibid., p. 164; Bauer, *Mexican War,* pp. 267, 268; Piston, Ph.D. Diss., p. 71.

35. Piston, Ph.D. Diss., pp. 72, 73.

36. Ibid., p. 74; Perret, *Country,* p. 165.

37. Perret, *Country,* p. 165; Piston, Ph.D. Diss., p. 74.

38. Piston, Ph.D. Diss., pp. 74, 75, 76; Perret, *Country,* pp. 165, 166.

39. Piston, Ph.D. Diss., p. 76; Bauer, *Mexican War,* pp. 296, 297.

40. Piston, Ph.D. Diss., pp. 77, 78; Bauer, *Mexican War,* pp. 297, 298.

41. Piston, Ph.D. Diss., pp. 77, 78; Longstreet, *Lee and Longstreet,* p. 214; Bauer, *Mexican War,* pp. 306, 307.

42. Piston, Ph.D. Diss., pp. 78, 79; Perret, *Country,* p. 166.

43. Piston, Ph.D. Diss., pp. 79, 80; Bauer, *Mexican War,* pp. 308–10; Cullum, *Register,* II, p. 151.

44. Piston, Ph.D. Diss., pp. 80, 81; Perret, *Country,* p. 165.

45. Longstreet, *Lee and Longstreet,* pp. 159, 160; Johnson, *Virginia Magazine,* "Taliaferro's Letters," 73, p. 459; Piston, Ph.D. Diss., pp. 81, 82.

46. Piston, Ph.D. Diss., p. 50; "Garland Family," JML.

47. Previous biographies of Longstreet place the wedding at St. Paul's Episcopal Church, but the contemporary accounts contradict this. "Garland Family"; Lynchburg Address Marriages," I; "Early Hist. St. Paul's," JML; Lynchburg *Virginian,* March 9, 1848.

48. Piston, Ph.D. Diss., pp. 83, 84; Longstreet–Colonel J. B. Crane, July 21, 1848, Longstreet Papers, DU; Grant, *Memoirs,* I, p. 193; New York *Times,* July 24, 1885; Faeder, "The Best of," *CWTI,* 26, 6, p. 22; *CV,* 1, p. 211.

49. Sanger and Hay, *James Longstreet,* p. 13; Longstreet, *Lee and Longstreet,* pp. 109, 110; R. L. Longstreet–F. R. Longstreet, September 3, 1947, Longstreet Papers, CRL.

50. Piston, Ph.D. Diss., pp. 84, 85, 87.

51. Ibid., pp. 85, 86.

52. Ibid., p. 87; Cullum, *Register,* II, p. 151; Longstreet–Major General George Gibson, December 12, 1850, Longstreet Papers, EU.

53. Longstreet–Major General George Gibson, January 11, 1853, Dearborn Collecton, Harvard; Longstreet Papers, CHS; Sanger and Hay, *Longstreet,* p. 13; Piston, Ph.D. Diss., pp. 88, 89; R. J. Longstreet–F. L. Longstreet, September 3, 1947, Longstreet Papers, CRL.

54. Piston, Ph.D. Diss., p. 89; Longstreet–Horace DeLano, February 25, 1852, Delano Papers, DU; Sanger and Hay, *James Longstreet,* p. 14; Cullum, *Register,* II, p. 151; R. J. Longstreet–F. R. Longstreet, September 3, 1947, Longstreet Papers, CRL.

55. "Eulogy written by Mrs. James Longstreet, Washington, D.C., 1854, Year of the Death of Her Son Willie," Longstreet Papers, CRL; Piston, Ph.D. Diss., pp. 90, 91; McMaster, *Letters,* p. 18.

56. Sanger, *Ft. Bliss,* pp. 8, 9; McCall, *New Mexico,* pp. 35, 36; Lane, *I Married,* pp. 68, 69, 73.

57. Sanger, *Ft. Bliss,* p. 9; McMaster, *Letters,* p. 18; Piston, Ph.D. Diss., pp. 93, 94.

58. Piston, Ph.D. Diss., pp. 94–97; McMaster, *Letters,* pp. 18, 19; Sanger, *Ft. Bliss,* p. 10.

59. McMaster, *Letters,* p. 19; Piston, Ph.D. Diss., pp. 100, 101; Cullum, *Register,* II, p. 151; Longstreet Papers, CHS.

60. Lane, *I Married,* pp. 45, 68, 69; Sanger, *Ft. Bliss,* p. 11; Piston, Ph.D. Diss., pp. 98, 99.

61. R. J. Longstreet–F. R. Longstreet, September 3, 1947, Longstreet Papers, CRL; Piston, Ph.D. Diss., p. 101; Sanger and Hay, *James Longstreet,* p. 14.

62. Longstreet–Major I. M. McDowell, March 29, 1858, Longstreet Papers, HSP.

63. Sanger and Hay, *James Longstreet,* pp. 14, 15; Piston, Ph.D. Diss., p. 104; Drinkard Collections, CHS; Cullum, *Register,* p. 151.

64. New York *Times,* July 24, 1885.

65. Longstreet–Uncle, November 19, 1859, A. B. Longstreet Papers, DU; Sanger and Hay, *James Longstreet,* p. 15; Piston, Ph.D. Diss., pp. 105, 106.

66. Newspaper clipping, Longstreet, CRL; *Daily National Intelligencer,* September 22, 1860, June 8, 1861; "Garland Family," JML.

67. New York *Times,* August 19, 1894.

68. Ibid; Piston, Ph.D. Diss., pp. 108, 109; Sanger and Hay, *James Longstreet,* p. 17.

69. Sanger and Hay, *James Longstreet,* pp. 16–18; Piston, Ph.D. Diss., pp. 109, 110; W. D. Longstreet–Jefferson Davis, February 22, 1861, Longstreet file, CSR/NA; R. J. Longstreet–F. R. Longstreet, September 3, 1947, Longstreet Papers, CRL.

70. Sanger and Hay, *James Longstreet,* p. 17; Piston, Ph.D. Diss., pp. 109–10; Longstreet file, CSR/NA.

71. *OR,* Series IV, 1, p. 182; Sanger and Hay, *James Longstreet,* p. 17; Piston, Ph.D. Diss., pp. 110, 111.

72. Sanger and Hay, *James Longstreet,* p. 17; Piston, Ph.D. Diss., p. 111;

Letter to Jefferson Davis, February 1861, W. D. Longstreet–Jefferson Davis, February 22, 1861, Longstreet file, CSR/NA.

73. Sanger and Hay, *James Longstreet*, p. 18; Piston, Ph.D. Diss., p. 112; Dabney H. Maury–Commander, Fort Buchanan, April 14, 1861, Letters, RG393, m. 1072, Roll 2, 580, NA.

74. Longstreet, *MA*, p. 29; Sanger and Hay, *James Longstreet*, p. 18.

75. Longstreet–Colonel L. Thomas, adjutant general, May 9, 1861, Records of the AGO, Letters Received, Main Series, File L-133 (1861), RG 94, NA.

76. Confederate Adjutant and Inspector General Records, vol. 88, p. 86, RG 109, NA.

77. Longstreet, *MA*, p. 30; New York *Times*, August 19, 1894.

3. MANASSAS

1. Longstreet, *MA*, pp. 30, 31; Sanger and Hay, *James Longstreet*, pp. 16, 18; Lane, *I Married*, p. 105; New York *Times*, August 19, 1894, Cullum, *Register*, II, p. 151.

2. Longstreet, *MA*, p. 31; Piston, Ph.D. Diss., p. 120; New York *Times*, August 19, 1894; Austerman, "Major Longstreet," *CWTI*, 20, 3, p. 32.

3. Austerman, "Major Longstreet," *CWTI*, 20, 3, p. 32; Longstreet, *MA*, p. 31.

4. Goree, *Letters*, pp. 42, 375; New York *Times*, August 19, 1894; Longstreet, *MA*, p. 32.

5. Goree, *Letters*, p. 44; Longstreet, *MA*, p. 32; Piston, Ph.D. Diss., p. 122.

6. Goree, *Letters*, p. 45; Piston, Ph.D. Diss., p. 123.

7. Longstreet, *MA*, p. 32; Goree, *Letters*, p. 46.

8. Goree, *Letters*, p. 46; Piston, Ph.D. Diss., p. 123.

9. Goree, *Letters*, p. 46; Piston, Ph.D. Diss., p. 123; Longstreet file, CRS/NA.

10. Longstreet, *MA*, p. 33.

11. *B & L*, I, pp. 196, 198; Hennessy, *First Manassas*, pp. 2, 3.

12. *B & L*, I, pp. 196, 197; Gallagher, *Fighting For*, p. 39; Hennessy, *First Manassas*, p. 3.

13. *B & L*, I, p. 196.

14. Zettler, *War Stories*, p. 59; Gallagher, *Fighting For*, p. 38; Freeman, *R. E. Lee*, I, p. xxxii.

15. Longstreet, *MA*, p. 33; Wallace, *Guide*, pp. 81, 82, 95, 100; Warner, *Generals in Gray*, pp. 63, 98, 220.

16. Longstreet, *MA*, p. 33; Daniel, *Howitzers*, p. 19; *CV*, 2, p. 291; CSR/NA; Goree, *Letters*, p. 52.

17. Goree, *Letters*, pp. 51, 52; Sorrel, *Recollections*, p. 219.

18. Longstreet file, CSR/NA.

19. Ibid.; Haskell, *Memoirs*, p. 14; Sorrel, *Recollections*, p. 172; Conolly, Diary, VHS; Dawson, *Reminiscences*, p. 128.

20. Longstreet, *MA*, p. 33; Sorrel, *Recollections*, pp. 17, 18; Crute, *Confederate Staff*, p. 123; Longstreet Papers, HL.

21. Longstreet, *MA,* p. 33; Sorrel, *Recollections,* p. 18; CSR/NA.

22. Hennessy, *First Manassas,* pp. 7, 9; *B & L,* I, p. 197.

23. Hennessy, *First Manassas,* pp. 6, 7.

24. Ibid., pp. 9, 10; *B & L,* II, p. 198; *OR,* 2, pp. 440, 478.

25. Hennessy, *First Manassas,* pp. 5, 6, 7, 8.

26. Ibid., p. 9.

27. Ibid., pp. 12–14.

28. *OR,* 51, 2, p. 172; Gallagher, *Fighting For,* p. 39; Longstreet, *MA,* pp. 33, 34; Hennessy, *First Manassas,* p. 14.

29. Longstreet, *MA,* p. 34; Hennessy, *First Manassas,* pp. 13, 18.

30. Longstreet, *MA,* p. 34; Loehr, *First Virginia,* p. 9; Hunter, "Four Years," p. 32, VHS; *CV,* 2, p. 291; Morgan, *Personal Reminiscences,* p. 51.

31. Loehr, *First Virginia,* p. 9; *CV,* 2, p. 291; Hunter, "Four Years," p. 33, VHS; Wallace, *1st Virginia,* p. 17; Chisholm Papers, NYHS.

32. Hunter, "Four Years," p. 33, VHS; Gallagher, *Fighting For,* pp. 45, 46.

33. Hunter, "Four Years," p. 33, VHS; Morgan, *Personal Reminiscences,* p. 53; Chisholm Papers, NYHS.

34. Longstreet, *MA,* p. 38; *OR,* 2, p. 461; Morgan, *Personal Reminiscences* p. 53; Chisholm Papers, NYHS.

35. Longstreet, *MA,* p. 38; *OR,* 2, pp. 461, 462; Hennessy, *First Manassas,* pp. 16, 17; Loehr, *First Virginia,* p. 9.

36. Hennessy, *First Manassas,* pp. 17, 19; Longstreet, *MA,* pp. 38–39; Goree, *Letters,* p. 57.

37. Hennessy, *First Manassas,* p. 19; *OR,* 2, p. 462.

38. Hennessy, *First Manassas,* pp. 20–22; Goree, *Letters,* p. 57; *OR,* 2, p. 462; Hunter, "Four Years," p. 36, VHS; Longstreet, *MA,* p. 39.

39. Goree, *Letters,* p. 58; Longstreet, *MA,* p. 39; *OR,* 2, p. 462; Wallace, *1st Virginia,* p. 17.

40. *OR,* 2, pp. 462, 464; Longstreet, *MA,* p. 40; Gallagher, *Fighting For,* p. 46.

41. *OR,* 2, pp. 462, 464; Squires, "Last," USAMHI; Owen, *In Camp,* pp. 1, 7, 8, 15, 27, 28; John B. Richardson–Longstreet, October 18, 1892, Longstreet Papers, EU; Wise, *Long Arm,* p. 128.

42. *OR,* 2, p. 464; Hennessy, *First Manassas,* p. 21; Morgan, *Personal Reminiscences,* pp. 56, 57, 58.

43. *OR,* 2, p. 462; Morgan, *Personal Reminiscences,* p. 60; Goree, *Letters,* p. 58; Chisholm Papers, NYHS; *CV,* 2, p. 292.

44. Hennessy, *First Manassas,* pp. 22, 23; Goree, *Letters,* p. 58; Hunter, "Four Years," p. 39, VHS; Reeve Papers, UNC; Wise Papers, DU; Gallagher, *Fighting For,* p. 47.

45. Longstreet, *MA,* p. 40.

46. *OR,* 2, pp. 445, 465.

47. Ibid., pp. 462, 463.

48. Longstreet–Uncle, August 13, 1861, Longstreet Papers, FSNMP, Vol. 136.

49. Sanger, "Was Longstreet," *Infantry Journal,* 43, p. 44; Goree, *Letters,* p. 58.

50. Hennessy, *First Manassas,* p. 27; Chisholm Papers, NYHS.

51. Owen, *In Camp,* p. 30; Hennessy, *First Manassas,* p. 28.

52. Hennessy, *First Manassas,* pp. 27, 28, 32.

53. Warner, *Generals in Gray,* p. 163; *B & L,* I, p. 245.

54. *OR,* 2, pp. 479, 480; Hennessy, *First Manassas,* pp. 34, 35; *B & L,* I, p. 202.

55. *OR,* pp. 317, 318; Hennessy, *First Manassas,* pp. 30, 35.

56. Hennessy, *First Manassas,* chapters 4–10; Symonds, *Joseph E. Johnston,* pp. 117, 119, 120; Gallagher, *Fighting For,* p. 49; Jones, *Civil War Command,* p. 34.

57. *OR,* 2, p. 543; Longstreet, *MA,* p. 44.

58. *OR,* 2, p. 543; Longstreet, *MA,* pp. 44, 45.

59. *OR,* 2, p. 543; Longstreet, *MA,* pp. 47, 48.

60. Sorrel, *Recollections,* pp. x, 7, 10, 17.

61. Ibid., p. 17.

62. *OR,* 2, pp. 519, 563; Longstreet, *MA,* p. 51; Owen, *In Camp,* p. 33.

63. Goree, *Letters,* pp. 60, 61; John Denis Keiley–Mother, July 23, 1861, Keiley Family Papers, VHS; Longstreet, *MA,* pp. 51, 52.

64. Goree, *Letters,* p. 61; Sorrel, *Recollections,* p. 20; Longstreet, *MA,* p. 52; Piston, Ph.D. Diss., p. 133.

65. Gallagher, *Fighting For,* p. 56; Longstreet, *MA,* p. 52; Morgan, *Personal Reminiscences,* p. 77; Sorrel, *Recollections,* p. 20.

66. Gallagher, *Fighting For,* p. 51; Hennessy, *First Manassas,* pp. 130–35.

67. Wood, *Reminiscences,* p. 5; Morgan, *Personal Reminiscences,* p. 80; Longstreet, *MA,* p. 564.

4. GENERALS

1. E. P. Alexander–Wife, July 31, 1861, Alexander Papers, UNC.

2. Eggleston, *Rebel's Recollections,* p. 76; Symonds, *Joseph E. Johnston,* pp. 125, 126.

3. Venable, "Reminiscences," UVA; Morgan, *Personal Reminiscences,* p. 86; Goree, *Letters,* p. 71.

4. Longstreet–Colonel Thomas Jordan, August 1, 1861, Longstreet file, CSR/NA.

5. *OR,* 2, p. 1000; Alexander Papers, UNC; Warner, *Generals in Gray,* p. 169; Wallace, *1st Virginia,* p. 18.

6. Morgan, *Personal Reminiscences,* p. 85; Goree, *Letters,* pp. 65, 66; Wallace, *1st Virginia,* p. 19.

7. Wallace, *1st Virginia,* p. 19; Stiles, *Four Years,* p. 59; Daniel, *Howitzers,* p. 36; Loehr, *First Virginia,* p. 12.

8. *OR,* 5, p. 778; Loehr, *First Virginia,* p. 13; Wallace, *1st Virginia,* p. 20; Goree, *Letters,* p. 68.

9. *OR,* 5, pp. 778–79.

10. Sears, *George B. McClellan*, pp. 89–95.

11. Ibid., chapter 5.

12. Goree, *Letters*, p. 75.

13. Ibid., p. 69; Longstreet–Colonel Thomas Jordan, July 23, 1861, Dearborn Collection, Harvard; Sorrel, *Recollections*, p. 21; Younger, *Inside*, p. 3.

14. Longstreet–J. A. Early, September 5, 1861, Longstreet Papers, HL; Longstreet–Thomas Jordan, August 27, 1861, September 25, 1861, Longstreet file, CSR/NA; Loehr, *First Virginia*, p. 14; Wise Papers, DU; "Reminiscences," Venable Papers, UVA; Gallagher, *Fighting For*, p. 66; Duggan Papers, UGA; *OR Atlas*, plate 7.

15. Longstreet–Thomas Jordan, August 22, 29, 1861, Longstreet file, CSR/NA; *OR*, 51, 1, p. 37; Goree, *Letters*, p. 76; *B & L*, I, p. 254; Wise Papers, DU; Longstreet, *MA*, chapter 4.

16. Manning file, CSR/NA; Haskell, *Memoirs*, p. 14.

17. Sorrel, *Recollections*, p. 26; Crute, *Confederate Staff Officers*, p. 124; Moses, "Autobiography," UNC, p. 51; Dawson, *Reminiscences*, p. 128.

18. Sorrel, *Recollections*, p. 30; Piston, Ph.D. Diss., p. 134; Dawson, *Reminiscences*, p. 128.

19. Longstreet file, CSR/NA; *CV*, 8, pp. 346, 347; McIntosh, Papers, UNC; Sorrel, *Recollections*, p. 29.

20. Sorrel, *Recollections*, p. 29; statement of Marcus J. Wright, November 27, 1893, Fairfax Papers, VHS; Dawson, *Reminiscences*, p. 128.

21. Moses, "Autobiography," pp. 51, 52, UNC.

22. Ibid., p. 51; Longstreet file, CSR/NA; Sorrel, *Recollections*, p. 29.

23. Goree, *Letters*, *passim*.

24. Ibid., p. 76.

25. Blackford, *Letters*, pp. 46, 47.

26. Warner, *Generals in Gray*, p. 296; Longstreet–Stuart, September 14, 1861, Longstreet Papers, HL.

27. Moses, "Autobiography," UNC.

28. Longstreet–Colonel Thomas Jordan, September 12, 1861; General Orders No. 2, Longstreet Papers, HL; *OR*, 5, pp. 181, 182; Longstreet–James Kemper, September 11, 1861, Kemper Papers, UVA.

29. Longstreet–J. E. B. Stuart, September 14, 1861; P. G. T. Beauregard–Longstreet, September 15, 1861, Longstreet Papers, HL; *OR*, 5, pp. 181, 182; Warner, *Generals in Gray*, p. 296.

30. Davis, *Jefferson Davis*, pp. 352, 353, 364, 365.

31. Haskell, *Memoirs*, p. 6; Sorrel, *Recollections*, p. 19; Gallagher, *Fighting For*, pp. 48, 49.

32. Johnston, *Narrative*, p. xiii; Gallagher, *Fighting For*, p. 49; Haskell, *Memoirs*, pp. 6–7.

33. Symonds, *Joseph E. Johnston*, pp. 5, 101; Ratchford, *Some Reminiscences*, p. 42; Freeman, *Lee's Lieutenants*, I, p. xxxviii.

34. Davis, *Jefferson Davis*, pp. 358, 359.

35. Ibid., p. 356; Johnston, *Narrative*, p. 71.

36. Davis, *Jefferson Davis*, p. 357.

37. Ibid., pp. 357, 358; Johnston, *Narrative,* pp. 71, 72.

38. Davis, *Jefferson Davis,* p. 357; Johnston, *Narrative,* p. 71; Symonds, *Joseph E. Johnston,* pp. 127–29.

39. Symonds, *Joseph E. Johnston,* pp. 128, 129; Davis, *Jefferson Davis,* p. 357; text of Johnston's September 12 letter in *OR,* 4, 1, pp. 605–8.

40. Freeman, *Lee's Lieutenants,* I, pp. 117, 118; Chesnut, *Diary,* pp. 102, 103; Moses, "Autobiography," UNC; Patterson, "Gustave," *CWTI,* 32, 3, pp. 32, 33; Davis, *Jefferson Davis,* pp. 362.

41. *B & L,* I, p. 253; Freeman, *Lee's Lieutenants,* I, p. 118; Goree, *Letters,* p. 89; New York *Herald,* February 26, 1893; Wise Papers, DU.

42. *B & L,* I, p. 254; Davis, *Jefferson Davis,* pp. 363–66; Freeman, *Lee's Lieutenants,* I, p. 118.

43. *OR,* 51, 2, p. 229; Goree, *Letters,* pp. 79, 80.

44. *OR,* 5, p. 892; 51, 2, p. 310; Longstreet file, CSR/NA.

45. Younger, *Inside,* pp. 3, 10; Wise Papers, DU.

46. Goree, *Letters,* p. 89; Wise Papers, DU; Younger, *Inside,* p. 12; Burnett, "Letters," *GHQ,* 23, 3, p. 296; Duggan Papers, UGA.

47. *OR,* 5, pp. 896, 897, 913, 914, 945, 960, 961; 51, 2, p. 368.

48. *OR,* 5, p. 961; Warner, *Generals in Gray,* pp. 136, 137, 263, 336.

49. Johnston, *Narrative,* pp. 77, 78, 81; Gallagher, *Fighting For,* pp. 60, 61; Rozier, *Granite,* p. 52; *OR,* 5, p. 1014; Chisholm Papers, NYHS.

50. Sorrel, *Recollections,* p. 31.

51. Goree, *Letters,* pp. 101, 107; Wise Papers, DU; Patterson, "Gustave," *CWTI,* 32, 3, p. 36.

52. Sorrel, *Recollections,* pp. 31, 50; Goree, *Letters,* p. 111; Warner, *Generals in Gray,* pp. 163, 314.

53. Ratchford, *Some Reminiscences,* p. 65; Wert, "Other Folks," *CWTI,* 28, 2, pp. 15, 16.

54. Wert, "Other Folks," *CWTI,* 28, 2, pp. 16, 17; Sorrel, *Recollections,* p. 54.

55. Wert, "Other Folks," *CWTI,* 28, 2, p. 17; Ratchford, *Some Reminiscences,* pp. 64, 65.

56. Goree, *Letters,* pp. 110–11.

57. Ibid., p. 110.

58. Ibid., p. 111.

59. Davis, *Jefferson Davis,* pp. 367, 368; Piston, Ph.D. Diss., p. 142; Patterson, "Gustave," *CWTI,* 32, 3, p. 33.

60. Piston, Ph.D. Diss., pp. 142–43.

61. Goree, *Letters,* pp. 121, 122.

62. Ibid., 122; Patterson, "Gustave," *CWTI,* 32, 3, pp. 33, 34; Freeman, *Lee's Lieutenants,* I, pp. 109, 121; Irving A. Buck–Lucie, January 25, 1862, Buck Papers, UNC.

5. TOWARD RICHMOND

1. Younger, *Inside,* p. 24; Longstreet, *MA,* p. 63

2. J. E. Johnston–P. G. T. Beauregard, January 24, 1862, Johnston Papers, UVA; Goree, *Letters,* p. 124.

3. J. E. Johnston–P. G. T. Beauregard, January 24, 1862, Johnston Papers, UVA; Goree, *Letters,* p. 124.

4. Goree, *Letters,* p. 129; Sanger and Hay, *James Longstreet,* p. 36.

5. R. J. Longstreet–F. R. Longstreet, September 3, 1947, Longstreet CRL; Piston, Ph.D. Diss., pp. 145, 148; Sanger and Hay, *James Longstreet,* p. 36; Goree, *Letters,* p. 129.

6. Piston, Ph.D. Diss., p. 148; Sanger and Hay, *James Longstreet,* p. 36.

7. Goree, *Letters,* pp. 129, 134; Sorrel, *Recollections,* pp. 31, 32; Chambers, *Stonewall Jackson,* p. 12.

8. Goree, *Letters,* p. 132; Johnston Papers, WM; *OR,* 5, pp. 1061, 1062; Symonds, *Joseph E. Johnston,* p. 143.

9. *B & L,* I, p. 256; Symonds, *Joseph E. Johnston,* p. 145.

10. *B & L,* I, p. 256; Goree, *Letters,* p. 143; Wise Papers, DU; Symonds, *Joseph E. Johnston,* p. 145.

11. *B & L,* I, pp. 256, 257; Johnston, *Narrative,* p. xvi; Goree, *Letters,* p. 143; Dickert, *History,* p. 91; Gallagher, *Fighting For,* p. 72.

12. *OR,* 5, pp. 526, 527; Longstreet, *MA,* pp. 64, 65; Loehr, *First Virginia,* p. 16; Gallagher, *Fighting For,* p. 73; Wise, Papers, DU.

13. Symonds, *Joseph E. Johnston,* pp. 146, 147.

14. Ibid., p. 147; Davis, *Jefferson Davis,* pp. 412, 413.

15. Symonds, *Joseph E. Johnston,* pp. 146, 147.

16. Davis, *Jefferson Davis,* p. 413; *OR,* 11, 1, p. 5.

17. *OR,* 11, 1, pp. 5, 8.

18. Davis, *Jefferson Davis,* pp. 413, 414; Symonds, *Joseph E. Johnston,* p. 148; Longstreet, *MA,* p. 65.

19. Longstreet, *MA,* p. 65; J. E. Johnston–Longstreet, February 3, 1879, Longstreet Papers, GDAH.

20. Longstreet, *MA,* p. 65; T. J. Jackson–Longstreet, April 3, 1862, Longstreet Papers, HL; *OR,* 12, 3, pp. 842–43.

21. T. J. Jackson–Longstreet, April 3, April 5, 1862, Longstreet Papers, HL; *OR,* 12, 3, pp. 842–44.

22. Symonds, *Joseph E. Johnston,* p. 148; Davis, *Jefferson Davis,* p. 414.

23. Sorrel, *Recollections,* p. 56; Gallagher, *Fighting For,* pp. 74, 75; Stiles, *Four Years,* p. 76; James Dearing–Uncle, April 28, 1862, Dearing Papers, VHS.

24. Johnston, *Narrative,* p. 114; Freeman, *Lee's Lieutenants,* I, p. 149; J. E. Johnston–G. W. Smith, January 21, 1868, Johnston Papers, WM.

25. Johnston, *Narrative,* p. 115; Longstreet, *MA,* p. 66; J. E. Johnston–Longstreet, February 3, 1879, Longstreet Papers, GDAH.

26. J. E. Johnston–G. W. Smith, January 21, 1868, Johnston Papers, WM; Johnston, *Narrative,* p. 115; Freeman, *Lee's Lieutenants,* I, pp. 150, 151.

27. Gallagher, *Fighting For,* pp. 74, 75.

28. Ibid., p. 75; Goree, *Letters,* p. 146; Sorrel, *Recollections,* p. 58; Wise, *Long Arm,* pp. 184, 188; Hill Papers, MC.

29. *OR,* 11, 3, pp. 469, 485; Symonds, *Joseph E. Johnston,* pp. 152, 153; J. E. Johnston–R. E. Lee, April 30, May 1, 1862, Lee Papers, WRHS.

30. Gallagher, *Fighting For,* pp. 77, 78, 79; D. H. Hill–Wife, May 4, 1862,

Hill Papers, USAMHI; Longstreet–R. L. Maury, March 9, 1894, Maury Papers, DU; Longstreet, *MA,* p. 67; Sorrel, *Recollections,* pp. 60, 61.

31. D. H. Hill–Wife, May 4, 1862, Hill Papers, USAMHI; *OR,* 11, 1, p. 564; Longstreet, *MA,* p. 72; Parker, Diary, WLU.

32. *OR,* 11, 1, pp. 564, 580, 587, 588; Longstreet, *MA,* pp. 68, 72.

33. C. M. Wilcox–E. P. Alexander, July 6, 1869. Alexander Papers, UNC; Goree, *Letters,* p. 710; E. Berkeley, "A Day about Williamsburg," n.d., Daniel Papers, UVA; Fleming, *Men,* p. 39.

34. *OR,* 11,1, pp. 468, 564; Smith, Diary, UVA; E. Berkeley, "A Day about Williamsburg," n.d., Daniel Papers, UVA; Hamilton, *Papers,* I, p. 193; Wood, *Reminiscences,* p. 12.

35. *OR,* 11, 1, pp. 564, 565, 585, 586, 590–93; Hamilton, *Papers,* I, p. 196; W. B. Young–Aunt, May 7, 1862, Simpson Papers, DU; Smith Diary, Freeman Papers, UVA.

36. Longstreet, *MA,* p. 74; *OR,* 2, 1, p. 570; James Keith–Eppa Hunton, July 25, 1905, Robinson Papers, UVA.

37. *OR,* 11, 1, pp. 275, 525, 602; Longstreet, *MA,* p. 75.

38. *OR,* 11, 1, pp. 565, 602, 603; Longstreet, *MA,* 77, 78; Freeman, *Lee's Lieutenants,* I, p. 191

39. *OR,* 11, 1, pp. 567, 603, 604, 607, 608; Longstreet, *MA,* p. 78; Gallagher, *Fighting For,* p. 81; Early, *Autobiographical Sketch,* pp. 69–71.

40. *OR,* 11, 1 p. 568; Freeman, *Lee's Lieutenants,* I, p. 191; *B & L,* II, p. 200.

41. *OR,* 11, 1, pp. 566, 567, 568; J. E. Johnston–Longstreet, February 3, 1879, Longstreet Papers, GDAH.

42. *OR,* 11, 1, p. 276; Longstreet, *MA,* p. 81; Theodore Fogel–Father and Mother, May 10, 1862, Fogel Papers, EU; Stiles, *Four Years,* p. 83; M. McGehee–Mrs. Montford McGehee, May 12, 1862, Polk, Badger, and McGehee Family Papers, UNC; Gallagher, *Fighting For,* p. 82.

43. *OR,* 11, 1, p. 276; Longstreet, *MA,* p. 81; Wheeler, *Sword,* pp. 223, 225.

44. Longstreet, *MA,* p. 81; Freeman, *Lee's Lieutenants,* II, p. 48.

45. Longstreet, *MA,* pp. 83, 84; Floyd, *Fortieth New York,* p. 151; *OR,* 11, 1, p. 25; *B & L,* II, p. 173; Wert, "Seven Pines," *CWTI,* 27, 6, pp. 23, 24.

46. *B & L,* II, p. 173; Wert, "Seven Pines," *CWTI,* 27, 6, p. 24.

47. Chesnut, *Diary,* p. 175.

6. A "MISUNDERSTANDING" AT SEVEN PINES

1. Longstreet, *MA,* p. 85; Alexander, *Memoirs,* p. 72; Gallagher, *Fighting For,* p. 83; Wert, "Seven Pines," *CWTI,* 27, 6, p. 24.

2. Longstreet, *MA,* p. 85, Freeman, *Lee's Lieutenants,* I, p. 220; Tanner, *Stonewall, passim.*

3. Longstreet, *MA,* pp. 85, 86; Freeman, *Lee's Lieutenants,* I, p. 221; J. E. Johnston–Longstreet, February 3, 1879, Longstreet Papers, GDAH.

4. Longstreet, *MA,* p. 87; Clark, *Histories,* II, p. 203; Wert, "Seven Pines," *CWTI,* 27, 6, p. 24.

5. Sorrel, *Recollections,* p. 64; Longstreet, *MA,* p. 88; D. H. Hill–Wife,

May 22, 1862, Hill Papers, USAMHI; John Meem–Ma, April 3, 1862, Meem Papers, VHS.

6. Longstreet, *MA,* p. 88; Gallagher, *Fighting For,* p. 84.

7. Gallagher, *Fighting For,* p. 84; Wert, "Seven Pines," *CWTI,* 27, 6, pp. 24, 25; Map, "Richmond and Vicinity," Johnston Papers, WM.

8. Gallagher, *Fighting For,* p. 85; *B & L,* II, pp. 209, 225; Wert, "Seven Pines," *CWTI,* 27, 6, pp. 25, 26.

9. Longstreet, *MA,* pp. 88, 89.

10. Ibid., pp. 89, 90; Alexander, *Memoirs,* pp. 76, 77; Smith, *Battle,* p. 23; Benjamin Huger–John Huger, June 20, 1867, Alexander Papers, UNC; Wert, "Seven Pines," *CWTI,* 27, 6, pp. 25, 26; *OR,* 11, 1, pp. 937, 938.

11. Wise Papers, DU; Brewer, *Sixty-First Regiment,* p. 24; Dickey, *103d Regiment,* p. 15.

12. D. H. Hill–Longstreet, August 27, 1879, Longstreet Papers, DU; Benjamin Huger–John Huger, June 20, 1867, Alexander Papers, UNC; Wise Papers, DU.

13. Freeman, *Lee's Lieutenants,* I, pp. 231, 231n; Smith, *Battle,* p. 178; *OR Atlas,* plate 17, 1.

14. Freeman, *Lee's Lieutenants,* I, p. 232; Alexander, *Memoirs,* p. 77; Wert, "Seven Pines," *CWTI,* 27, 6, p. 26; Smith, *Battle,* p. 169.

15. Freeman, *Lee's Lieutenants,* I, pp. 232, 233; Smith, *Battle,* p. 151; Brady, *Eleventh Maine,* p. 38; Wert, "Seven Pines," *CWTI,* 27, 6, p. 6.

16. Wert, "Seven Pines," *CWTI,* 27, 6, p. 26; Gallagher, *Fighting For,* p. 85.

17. *OR Atlas,* plate 17, 1; Map, "Richmond and Vicinity," Johnston, WM.

18. Gallagher, *Fighting For,* p. 85; Wert, "Seven Pines," *CWTI,* 27, 6, p. 26.

19. Freeman, *Lee's Lieutenants,* I, p. 234; *B & L,* II, p. 219; *OR Atlas,* plate 17, 1.

20. Benjamin Huger–John Huger, June 20, 1867, Alexander Papers, UNC; *OR,* 11, 1, p. 942; Warner, *Generals in Gray,* p. 143; Wise Papers, DU; Dowdey, *Seven Days,* p. 91.

21. *OR,* 11, 1, p. 943; Wise Papers, DU; Freeman, *Lee's Lieutenants,* I, pp. 235, 238, 239.

22. *OR,* 11, 1, p. 840; Freeman, *Lee's Lieutenants,* I, p. 239; Benjamin Huger–John Huger, June 20, 1867, Alexander Papers, UNC.

23. *OR,* 11, 1, pp. 982, 986.

24. Ibid., p. 986; Longstreet, *MA,* p. 93; Haskell, *Memoirs,* p. 40; Wise Papers, DU.

25. *OR,* 11, 1, pp. 813, 916; Reed, *101st Regiment,* p. 8; Krentzer, *Ninety-Eighth New York,* p. 66; Wert, "Seven Pines," *CWTI,* 27, 6, p. 27.

26. *OR,* 11, 1, pp. 961, 962, 963, 967; Edward Dix–Sally, June 7, 1862, Dix Letters, WLU; H. M. Talley–Mother, June 2, 1862, Talley Papers, VHS.

27. Wert, "Seven Pines," *CWTI,* 27, 6, pp. 27, 28; Thomas H. Carter–D. H. Hill, July 1, 1885, Hill Papers, VSL.

28. Longstreet–D. H. Hill, January 9, 1878, Hill Papers, VSL; Longstreet's report, Longstreet Papers, HL; Ratchford, *Some Reminiscences,* p. 65.

29. R. H. Anderson–D. H. Hill, October 26, 1867, Hill Papers, VSL; Alexander, *Memoirs,* p. 86; Longstreet, *MA,* p. 96.

30. Wert, "Seven Pines," *CWTI,* 27, 7, p. 24.

31. Warner, *Generals in Gray,* p. 155; Goree, *Letters,* pp. 100, 154.

32. Goree, *Letters,* p. 151; Wert, "Seven Pines," *CWTI,* 27, 7, pp. 24, 25.

33. Wert, "Seven Pines," *CWTI,* 27, 7, pp. 24, 25; Bond and Coward, *South Carolinians,* p. 38; Goree, *Letters,* pp. 151, 152; Freeman, *Lee's Dispatches,* p. 33.

34. Wert, "Seven Pines," *CWTI,* 27, 7, p. 25; Maurice, *Aide-de-Camp,* pp. 56, 57; Gallagher, *Fighting For,* p. 87.

35. Wert, "Seven Pines," *CWTI,* 27, 7, pp. 25, 28.

36. Ibid., pp. 22, 28.

37. Ibid., pp. 28, 29.

38. Ibid., p. 29; Gallagher, *Fighting For,* p. 88; *B& L,* II, p. 215.

39. Longstreet, *MA,* pp. 103, 104; Sanger and Hays, *James Longstreet,* p. 56; Gallagher, *Fighting For,* p. 88.

40. Longstreet, *MA,* p. 105; D. H. Hill–Longstreet, August 29, 1879, May 14, 1885, Longstreet Papers, DU; William Mahone–Longstreet, January 25, 1887, Longstreet Papers, EU.

41. William Mahone–Longstreet, January 25, 1887, Longstreet Papers, EU; D. H. Hill–Longstreet, May 14, 1885, Longstreet Papers, DU; *OR,* 11, 1, p. 986; Wert, "Seven Pines," *CWTI,* 27, 7, pp. 46, 50.

42. D. H. Hill–Longstreet, May 14, 1885, Longstreet Papers, DU; William Mahone–Longstreet, January 25, 1887; Todd, "Reminiscences," UNC; Alexander, *Memoirs,* pp. 87, 88; Wert, "Seven Pines," *CWTI,* 27, 7, pp. 46, 50.

43. Wert, "Seven Pines," *CWTI,* 27, 7, p. 50; Thomas Moore–D. H. Hill, May 11, 1885, Hill Papers, VSL.

44. Wert, "Seven Pines," *CWTI,* 27, 7, p. 50; Gallagher, *Fighting For,* pp. 83–84; Alexander, *Memoirs,* p. 77.

45. Longstreet–J. E. Johnston, June 7, 1862, Longstreet Papers, HL.

46. *OR,* 11, 1, p. 940.

47. Ibid., pp. 933–35; Smith, *Battle,* pp. 20–22.

48. *OR,* 11, 1, p. 933; Smith, *Battle,* p. 151; J. E. Johnston–D. H. Hill, June 3, 1868, January 24, 1885, Hill Papers, VSL.

49. *OR,* 11, 1, pp. 935–39; Alexander, *Memoirs,* p. 93.

50. Gallagher, *Fighting For,* pp. 88, 89.

7. "THE STAFF IN MY RIGHT HAND"

1. Freeman, *R. E. Lee,* I, *passim.*

2. Ibid., IV, pp. 175–76; Alexander, *Memoirs,* p. 111; Jones, *Civil War Command,* p. 64.

3. Freeman, *R. E. Lee,* IV, pp. 178, 179; Jones, *Civil War Command,* p. 64; Lee, *Recollections,* p. 89.

4. Sorrel, *Recollections,* p. 67; Jones, *Civil War Command,* p. 64; John Daniel–T. L. Rosser, April 16, 1901, Rosser Papers, UVA.

5. Moses, "Autobiography," pp. 58, 59, UNC.

6. Connelly, *Marble,* pp. 199, 200.

7. Longstreet, *MA,* p. 112.

8. Dowdey and Manarin, *Wartime Papers,* p. 182.

9. Ibid., p. 182.

10. Longstreet, *MA,* p. 112; R. Toombs–Longstreet, February 5, 1879, Longstreet Papers, GDAH; Sears, *George B. McClellan,* pp. 197–200.

11. Jones, *Civil War Command,* p. 154.

12. A. L. Long–Longstreet, February 27, 1870; Lafayette McLaws–Longstreet, April 9, 1879, Longstreet Papers, DU; R. Toombs–Longstreet, February 5, 1879; John B. Hood–Longstreet, March 11, 1879, Longstreet Papers, GDAH; Longstreet–A. L. Long, February 23, 1879, Long Papers, UNC; Maurice, *Aide-de-Camp,* p. 77.

13. Longstreet, *MA,* pp. 112, 113; Maurice, *Aide-de-Camp,* pp. 77, 78, 78n; Charles Marshall–A. L. Long, April 6, 1880, Long Papers, UNC; A. L. Long–Longstreet, February 27, 1870, Longstreet Papers, DU; R. Toombs–Longstreet, February 5, 1879, Longstreet Papers, GDAH; Squires, " 'Boy Officer,' " *CWTI,* 14, 2, p. 16.

14. Longstreet, *MA,* p. 112; E. V. Law–Robert N. Johnson, September 6, 1888, Law Papers, NYPL.

15. Freeman, *R. E. Lee,* II, p. 77, Maurice, *Aide-de-Camp,* p. 77; Long, *Memoirs,* pp. 161, 166; Venable, "Reminiscences," UVA; R. H. Chilton–D. H. Hill, January 1, 1868, Hill, VSL.

16. Longstreet, *MA,* p. 114; *B & L,* II, p. 396; Freeman, *R. E. Lee,* II, p. 106n; Charles Marshall–A. L. Long, April 6, 1880, Long Papers, UNC.

17. Freeman, *Lee's Dispatches,* p. 11; Sorrel, *Recollections,* p. 69.

18. Longstreet, *MA,* p. 114; Maurice, *Aide-de-Camp,* p. 79; Long, *Memoirs,* p. 167; Freeman, *R. E. Lee,* II, p. 86; A. B. Simms–Brother, June 6, 1862, Simms Family Papers, AHS; Theodore Fogel–Mother, June 20, 1862, Fogel Papers, EU.

19. Sears, *George B. McClellan,* pp. 200, 201.

20. Dowdey and Manarin, *Wartime Papers,* p. 187; *OR,* 12, 3, p. 910.

21. Thomas, *Dragoon,* pp. 112-29.

22. *OR,* 12, 2, p. 913; Freeman, *R. E. Lee,* II, pp. 104, 105.

23. Longstreet, *MA,* p. 120; Freeman, *R. E. Lee,* II, pp. 105, 106.

24. Longstreet, *MA,* p. 120; *B & L,* II, p. 396; Freeman, *R. E. Lee,* II, pp. 106, 106n; Charles Marshall–A. L. Long, April 6, 1880, Long Papers, UNC; Longstreet–J. S. D. Cullen, n.d., Robinson Papers, UVA.

25. *OR,* 11, 2, pp. 483–89; Wise, *Long Arm,* p. 204; Freeman, *R. E. Lee,* II, p. 116.

26. Gallagher, *Fighting For,* p. 98; *B & L,* II, p. 347; Stevens, *Reminiscences,* p. 45; English Combatant, *Battle-Fields,* p. 141.

27. *B & L,* II, p. 347; Maurice, *Aide-de-Camp,* p. 84; Longstreet, *MA,* p. 121; Longstreet–D. H. Hill, November 5, 1877, Hill Papers, VSL.

28. *B & L,* II, p. 347; Longstreet gives a slightly different version of the conversation in Longstreet, *MA,* pp. 121–22.

29. *B & L,* II, p. 347; Longstreet, *MA,* p. 122; Venable, "Reminiscences," UVA.

30. Dowdey and Manarin, *Wartime Papers,* pp. 198–200; Norris Collection, UVA; Maurice, *Aide-de-Camp,* pp. 86–88.

31. Conversation with Dr. W. S. Buckler, Baltimore, 1870, McIntosh Papers, VHS.

32. E. P. Alexander–Frederick Colston, February 9, 1904, Campbell-Colston Papers, UNC; Gallagher, *Fighting For,* p. 91.

33. *OR,* 11, 1, p. 756; Longstreet, *MA,* p. 122; Freeman, *Lee's Dispatches,* p. 17; Gallagher, *Fighting For,* p. 99.

34. Longstreet, *MA,* p. 122; Robertson, *A. P. Hill,* pp. 69–71.

35. Longstreet, *MA,* p. 122; Robertson, *A. P. Hill,* p. 71.

36. Gallagher, *Fighting For,* pp. 95, 100; Longstreet, *MA,* p. 122; *OR,* 11, 2, p. 756; McIntosh, "Ride on Horseback," p. 106, UNC; Robertson, *A. P. Hill,* pp. 71–76.

37. Gallagher, *Fighting For,* p. 100; Longstreet, *MA,* p. 124; Sorrel, *Recollections,* p. 74; *OR,* 11, 2, p. 491.

38. Gallagher, *Fighting For,* pp. 100, 101; *OR,* 11, 2, p. 756; Goree, *Letters,* p. 159; Freeman, *R. E. Lee,* II, pp. 138, 140, 141.

39. *OR,* 11, 2, pp. 492, 756, 757; Longstreet, *MA,* p. 126; Freeman, *R. E. Lee,* II, p. 146n.

40. Freeman, *R. E. Lee,* II, pp. 146–49; Gallagher, *Fighting For,* pp. 101, 102; E. M. Law–*Century Magazine,* April 2, 1885, Law Papers, NYPL; Longstreet, *MA,* p. 126.

41. *OR,* 11, 2, p. 757; Longstreet, *MA,* pp. 126, 127; Goree, *Letters,* p. 159; Freeman, *R. E. Lee,* II, pp. 152, 153; *CV,* 8, p. 443.

42. *OR,* 11, 2, p. 757; Longstreet, *MA,* p. 127; Freeman, *R. E. Lee,* II, pp. 153, 154; Longstreet–D. H. Hill, March 28, 1885, Hill Papers, VSL; Venable, "Reminiscences," UVA.

43. *CV,* 6, p. 472; Goree, *Letters,* p. 160; *OR,* 11, 2, p. 757; Freeman, *R. E. Lee,* II, pp. 155, 156; E. M. Law–*Century Magazine,* April 2, 1885, Law Papers, NYPL.

44. Freeman, *R. E. Lee,* II, pp. 156, 157; *OR,* 11, 2, p. 757; Longstreet, *MA,* pp. 127, 128, 129; Gallagher, *Fighting For,* p. 103; Sears, *George B. McClellan,* pp. 211, 212.

45. Faust, *Encyclopedia,* p. 296; Haskell, *Memoirs,* p. 32; Everett, *Chaplain Davis,* p. 93; Harrison, *Pickett's Men,* pp. 28, 29.

46. E. P. Alexander–Frederick Colston, April 7, 1898, Campbell-Colston Papers, UNC; Venable, "Reminiscences," UVA; Freeman, *R. E. Lee,* II, pp. 149, 150.

47. Gallagher, *Fighting For,* p. 103; Goree, *Letters,* p. 160; *OR,* 11, 2, p. 492; Taylor, *Lee,* p. 69.

48. *OR,* 11, 2, pp. 493, 494; Maurice, *Aide-de-Camp,* pp. 104, 105; Longstreet, *MA,* pp. 129, 130; Freeman, *R. E. Lee,* II, pp. 159–65; Wise Papers, DU.

49. Freeman, *R. E. Lee,* II, pp. 166, 167; Freeman, *Lee's Dispatches,* p. 21; Longstreet, *MA,* pp. 130, 131.

50. *OR,* 11, 2, p. 759; *B & L,* II, p. 399; Longstreet, *MA,* p. 131; Eckenrode and Conrad, *James Longstreet,* p. 77.

51. *B & L,* II, pp. 371, 372, 386; *OR,* 11, 2, p. 494; Longstreet, *MA,* p. 131; Sears, *George B. McClellan,* p. 217; Squires, " 'Boy Officer,' " *CWTI,* 14, 2, p. 15.

52. Longstreet, *MA,* p. 131; Taylor, *Lee,* p. 74; E. P. Alexander–Longstreet, September 29, 1902, typed copy in possession of author; Chambers, *Stonewall Jackson,* II, pp. 58, 59.

53. The fullest and best defense of Jackson on this day is in Chambers, *Stonewall Jackson,* II, pp. 57–61. Longstreet in *MA* alleged that he could have forded the river "at that season," p. 131. Also see Gallagher, *Fighting For,* pp. 105–6.

54. Freeman, *R. E. Lee,* II, pp. 177, 178, 179; *B & L,* II, p. 399; Longstreet, *MA,* p. 133.

55. *OR,* 11, 2, pp. 759, 838; *B & L,* II, pp. 399, 400; Longstreet, *MA,* p. 133.

56. *B & L,* II, p. 400; Longstreet, *MA,* p. 134; Coker, *Ninth S. C.,* p. 77; Alexander, *Memoirs,* p. 139.

57. *OR,* 11, 2, p. 759; *B & L,* II, p. 401; Longstreet, *MA,* p. 134; Sorrel, *Recollections,* p. 77.

58. *OR,* 11, 1, p. 66; pt. 2, p. 759; Goree, *Letters,* pp. 161, 162.

59. Goree, *Letters,* pp. 161, 162; Freeman, *R. E. Lee,* II, p. 186; *OR,* 11, 2, p. 759; Dowdey, *Seven Days,* pp. 298–300.

60. Goree, *Letters,* pp. 161, 162; Ambrose, *Duty, Honor,* p. 162; C. M. Wilcox–E. P. Alexander, July 6, 1869, Alexander Papers, UNC.

61. Goree, *Letters,* p. 162; *OR,* 11, 2, pp. 759, 760, 775–78; Freeman, *R. E. Lee,* II, pp. 187, 188.

62. *B & L,* II, p. 401, Longstreet, *MA,* pp. 137, 138; C. M. Wilcox–E. P. Alexander, July 6, 1869, Alexander Papers, UNC; *OR,* 11, 2, pp. 759, 838.

63. *OR,* 11, 2, pp. 759, 838; 51, 2, p. 591; *CV,* 8, p. 347; Morgan, *Personal Reminiscences,* p. 136; *B & L,* II, p. 401.

64. Longstreet, *MA,* p. 138; Dickert, *History,* p. 130; *OR,* 11, 2, p. 838.

65. *OR,* 11, 2, pp. 838, 839; Longstreet, *MA,* p. 138; Freeman, *R. E. Lee,* II, pp. 188, 189.

66. Faust, *Encyclopedia,* p. 821; Freeman, *R. E. Lee,* II, p. 192; Dowdey, *Seven Days,* p. 303.

67. Gallagher, *Fighting For,* pp. 109, 110.

68. Connelly, *Marble,* p. 204; Freeman, *R. E. Lee,* II, p. 199; *OR,* 11, 2, p. 495.

69. Chambers, *Stonewall Jackson,* II, p. 66; Freeman, *R. E. Lee,* II, p. 192; Dowdey, *Seven Days,* p. 301.

70. Detailed description of Jackson's day in Chambers, *Stonewall Jackson,* II, pp. 66–76; Vandiver, *Mighty Stonewall,* pp. 313–17; Freeman, *Lee's Lieutenants,* I, pp. 571–80; Gallagher, *Fighting For,* pp. 108, 109; Freeman, *R. E. Lee,* II, p. 194; *B & L,* II, pp. 375, 377, 381; Wade Hampton–E. P. Alexander, March 1901, T. T. Munford–Wade Hampton, March 23, 1901, Alexander Papers, UNC; Maurice, *Aide-de-Camp,* pp. 111, 112.

71. Gallagher, *Fighting For,* p. 110; Chambers, *Stonewall Jackson,* II,

pp. 70, 71; *B & L*, II, p. 389; Longstreet asserted in a letter that he sent Fairfax to Jackson the night of June 30–July 1, to tell the latter things were "at a crisis" and needed help. No other evidence corroborates this. Longstreet–E. P. Alexander, August 26, 1902, Alexander Papers, UNC.

72. Freeman, *R. E. Lee,* II, pp. 200, 201; Longstreet, *MA,* p. 142; Thompson, *Robert Toombs,* p. 192.

73. Freeman, *R. E. Lee,* II, p. 201; Longstreet, *MA,* p. 142; *B & L,* II, pp. 390, 391.

74. Freeman, *R. E. Lee,* II, p. 200; Jones, *Civil War Command,* p. 69; *OR,* 11, 2, p. 760; Longstreet, *MA,* p. 142.

75. Wise, *Long Arm,* pp. 221, 222; *B & L,* II, p. 409; Longstreet, *MA,* p. 141.

76. Stiles, *Four Years,* p. 101; Lafayette McLaws–Longstreet, November 30, 1885, Longstreet Papers, EU; D. H. Hill–R. L. Dabney, July 21, 1864, Dabney Papers, UTS.

77. *OR,* 11, 2, pp. 668, 676, 677; Longstreet, *MA,* p. 142; Freeman, *Lee's Lieutenants,* I, pp. 591, 592.

78. *OR,* 11, 2, p. 668; Longstreet, *MA,* p. 142; Lafayette McLaws–Longstreet, November 30, 1885, Longstreet Papers, EU.

79. Longstreet, *MA,* p. 143; Freeman, *Lee's Lieutenants,* I, pp. 595, 597, 598; Gallagher, *Fighting For,* p. 112; *OR,* 11, 2, p. 536.

80. Freeman, *R. E. Lee,* II, pp. 210, 211; Longstreet, *MA,* p. 144; *OR,* 11, 2, pp. 677–78, 760.

81. *OR,* 11, 2, p. 669; Freeman, *Lee's Lieutenants,* I, pp. 559, 560; Chambers, *Stonewall Jackson,* II, pp. 79, 80.

82. John Cocke–Parents, Sisters, and All, July 14, 1862, Cocke Family Papers, VHS; *OR,* 11, 2, pp. 496, 973–84.

83. Theodore Fogel–Father and Mother, August 8, 1862, Fogel Papers, EU; Todd, "Reminiscences," p. 24, UNC.

84. Brown, *Reminiscences,* p. 20; Lafayette McLaws–Longstreet, November 30, 1885, Longstreet Papers, EU; undated, untitled mss., McLaws Papers, DU.

85. D. H. Hill–R. L. Dabney, July 21, 1864, Dabney Papers, UTS; *B & L,* II, p. 394.

86. Sorrel, *Recollections,* p. 75; Douglas, *I Rode,* p. 107; Gallagher, *Fighting For,* p. 113; Stiles, *Four Years,* p. 101.

87. Freeman, *R. E. Lee,* II, pp. 222–23; Sears, *George B. McClellan,* p. 223.

88. Douglas, *I Rode,* p. 110; Jefferson Davis–William N. Pendleton, April 26, 1875, Davis Papers, WLU.

89. *OR,* 11, 2, pp. 760, 761; Longstreet, *MA,* pp. 146, 147; Taylor, *Lee,* pp. 81, 83; Longstreet–J. E. B. Stuart, July 4, 1862, Longstreet Papers, HL; R. E. Lee–Mrs. T. J. Jackson, January 25, 1866, typed copy, Lee Papers, WLU; Venable, "Reminiscences," UVA.

90. *OR,* 11, 2, p. 498; Freeman, *Lee's Lieutenants,* I, p. 605n; Jones, *Civil War Command,* p. 70; William B. Ridley–Father, July 4, 1862, Ridley Family Papers, VHS.

91. *OR,* 11, 2, pp. 497, 973–84; Gallagher, *Fighting For,* p. 104; Taylor, *Lee,* pp. 65, 74; *B & L,* II, p. 352.

92. Gallagher, *Fighting For,* pp. 96–98; on back of letter, April 7, 1898, from E. P. Alexander; Alexander-Colston, August 19, 1906, Campbell-Colston Papers, UNC; *B & L,* II, p. 395.

93. Gallagher, *Fighting For,* p. 96; on back of letter, April 7, 1898, from E. P. Alexander, Campbell-Colston Papers, UNC.

94. Gallagher, *Fighting For,* p. 96; Freeman, *Lee's Lieutenants,* I, pp. 611, 613, 614; Connelly, *Marble,* pp. 196, 197.

95. Freeman, *Lee's Lieutenants,* I, p. 663; Sorrel, *Recollections,* pp. 26, 79; *OR,* 11, 2, pp. 492, 498; Goree, *Goree Letters,* p. 164.

8. RETURN TO MANASSAS

1. Goree, *Letters,* pp. 308, 309; Robertson, *A. P. Hill,* pp. 95, 96; Freeman, *Lee's Lieutenants,* I, pp. 664, 665.

2. Goree, *Letters,* p. 309; Sorrel, *Recollections,* p. 79; Freeman, *Lee's Lieutenants,* I, pp. 664, 664n, 665, 665n.

3. Goree, *Letters,* p. 309; Sorrel, *Recollections,* p. 80; Robertson, *A. P. Hill,* p. 96; Freeman, *Lee's Lieutenants,* I, pp. 665, 666n.

4. Robertson, *A. P. Hill,* pp. 96, 97; Freeman, *Lee's Lieutenants,* I, p. 666; *OR,* 11, 3, pp. 639, 640.

5. Sorrel, *Recollections,* pp. 80, 81; Goree, *Letters,* pp. 308, 309; *OR,* 51, 2, p. 590.

6. Sorrel, *Recollections,* p. 81; Goree, *Letters,* pp. 309, 310; Robertson, *A. P. Hill,* p. 97; Freeman, *Lee's Lieutenants,* I, pp. 667, 668; *OR,* 12, 3, p. 919.

7. Dowdey and Manarin, *Wartime Papers,* p. 229; Sorrel, *Recollections,* p. 84; *OR,* 51, 2, p. 596; Longstreet, *MA,* p. 154; Longstreet–R. E. Lee, July 12, 1866, Longstreet Papers, HL.

8. Theodore Fogel–Mother, July 19, 1862, Fogel Papers, EU; A. B. Simms–Sister, July 16, 1862, Simms Family Papers, AHS; W. G. Ridley–Bettie, July 30, 1862, Ridley Family Papers, VHS.

9. Sorrel, *Recollections,* pp. 86, 87, 88; Harry Lewis–Mother, July 9, 1862, Lewis Papers, UNC.

10. Wert, "Killing Ground," *ACW,* 4, 1, pp. 18, 20.

11. Ibid., p. 18.

12. Ibid., pp. 18, 20; Freeman, *R. E. Lee,* II, p. 265.

13. *OR,* 51, 2, pp. 604–6; Longstreet, *MA,* p. 158; Theodore Fogel–Father and Mother, August 11, 1862, Fogel Papers, EU; Moxley Sorrel–Henry A. Wise, August 11, 1862, Longstreet Papers, HL; Duggan Papers, UGA; Chambers, *Stonewall Jackson,* p. 52, Gallagher, *Fighting For,* p. 128; McDonald, *Make Me,* p. 68; Douglas, *I Rode,* p. 129.

14. *OR,* 12, 3, pp. 929, 930; Maurice, *Aide-de-Camp,* p. 124; Freeman, *R. E. Lee,* II, pp. 273, 274, 281; Wert, "Killing Ground," *ACW,* 4, 2, p. 60; Dowdey and Manarin, *Wartime Papers,* p. 253.

15. Grinnan, "General Lee's," p. 21, FSNMP; Freeman, *R. E. Lee,* II,

pp. 279, 280; *OR,* 12, 3, p. 929; Dowdey and Manarin, *Wartime Papers,* pp. 252, 253; Longstreet, *MA,* p. 159.

16. Longstreet, *MA,* p. 159; Maurice, *Aide-de-Camp,* pp. 124, 125; Grinnan, "General Lee's," p. 21, FSNMP; Freeman, *R. E. Lee,* II, pp. 279, 280.

17. W. H. Taylor–Sister, August 17, 1862, Taylor, VSL; Scott, *Orange County,* pp. 195, 214; Latrobe Diary, VHS; Longstreet, *MA,* pp. 159, 166; Freeman, *R. E. Lee,* II, p. 283.

18. Longstreet, *MA,* p. 161; Thompson, *Robert Toombs,* p. 196; Sorrel, *Recollections,* p. 94; Scott, *Orange County,* p. 192; Moses, "Autobiography," p. 55, UNC.

19. Longstreet, *MA,* p. 161; Sorrel, *Recollections,* p. 94; Thompson, *Robert Toombs,* p. 197.

20. Gallagher, *Fighting For,* p. 73; Davis, *Jefferson Davis,* pp. 243–44; Moses, "Autobiography," p. 55, UNC; Bowden, "Some," p. 13, EU; Sorrel, *Recollections,* p. 53; Warner, *Generals in Gray,* pp. 306–7.

21. Thompson, *Robert Toombs,* p. 197; Longstreet, *MA,* pp. 161, 162; Sorrel, *Recollections,* pp. 94, 95; Moses, "Autobiography," pp. 54, 55, UNC.

22. Freeman, *R. E. Lee,* II, pp. 285, 286; Longstreet, *MA,* p. 160; *OR,* 12, 2, p. 726; Longstreet–T. T. Munford, November 13, 1891, Munford-Ellis Family Papers, DU; Dowdey and Manarin, *Wartime Papers,* 259–60.

23. Longstreet, *MA,* p. 161; *B & L,* II, p. 515; Scott, *Orange County,* p. 115; Grinnan, "General Lee's," p. 21, FSNMP.

24. *OR,* 12, 2, p. 563; Latrobe Diary, VHS; Theodore Fogel–Mother, August 22, 1862, Fogel Papers, EU; William H. Dobbins–Pa, September 4, 1862, Dobbins Papers, EU; Freeman, *R. E. Lee,* II, pp. 289, 290, 291.

25. *OR,* 12, 2, p. 563; Latrobe Diary, VHS; Longstreet, *MA,* p. 163; Freeman, *R. E. Lee,* II, p. 291; Duggan Papers, UGA; Owen, *In Camp,* pp. 101, 102; *CV,* 10, p. 65.

26. *OR,* 12, 2, p. 563; Latrobe Diary, VHS; Longstreet, *MA,* pp. 163, 164; Freeman, *R. E. Lee,* II, pp. 293, 294.

27. Freeman, *R. E. Lee,* II, p. 296; *OR,* 12, 2, p. 564; Latrobe Papers, VHS; "Notations, Second Manassas Report," Wilcox Papers, LC; Walton Papers, TU; Theodore Fogel–Mother, August 23, 1862, Fogel Papers, EU; Owen, *In Camp,* pp. 103–5; Longstreet, *MA,* p. 164.

28. Wert, "Return To," *ACW,* 4, 2, p. 21; Freeman, *R. E. Lee,* II, pp. 296, 297.

29. *OR,* 12, 3, p. 941; Freeman, *R. E. Lee,* II, pp. 298, 299; Maurice, *Aide-de-Camp,* p. 130.

30. *OR,* 12, 2, p. 564; Latrobe Diary, VHS; Freeman, *R. E. Lee,* II, pp. 300–301; McDonald, *Make Me,* p. 71.

31. Freeman, *R. E. Lee,* II, p. 302; Maurice, *Aide-de-Camp,* p. 130; *OR,* 12, 3, p. 941.

32. Eggleston, *Rebel's Recollections,* p. 132; Long, *Civil War Command,* p. 178; Theodore Fogel–Father and Mother, August 11, 1862, Fogel Papers, EU.

33. Gallagher, *Fighting For,* p. 130; Wert, "Killing Ground," *ACW,* 4, 2, p. 21.

34. Gallagher, *Fighting For,* pp. 130, 131; Wert, "Killing Ground," *ACW,* 4, 2, p. 21; Sorrel, *Recollections,* p. 90.

35. *OR,* 12, 2, pp. 544, 564; Duffey, Diary, VHS; Longstreet, *MA,* p. 169; Freeman, *R. E. Lee,* II, p. 306.

36. *OR,* 12, 2, pp. 546–48, 564; 12, 3, p. 945; Duffey, Diary, VHS; Latrobe Diary, VHS; Turner, "Greenlee Davidson," *CWH,* 17, p. 204; "Notations, Second Manassas Report," Wilcox Papers, LC; Wise Papers, DU; Gott, *Marshall,* p. 42.

37. Polley, *Hood's Texas Brigade,* pp. 75, 76; Durkin, *John Dooley,* p. 14; Wise Papers, DU; Joskins, Journal, MNBP; Duggan Papers, UGA; Gott, *Marshall,* p. 42; Longstreet, *MA,* p. 170; John B. Magruder–Papa, December 4, 1862, Magruder Papers, DU; Squires, "Lee's Battle Lines," USAMHI.

38. Freeman, *R. E. Lee,* II, pp. 309, 312; Sorrel, *Recollections,* Longstreet, *MA,* p. 90; Latrobe Diary, VHS.

39. Zettler, *War Stories,* pp. 97–98; Duggan Papers, UGA; Latrobe Diary, VHS; Choice, "Memoirs," MNBP; Longstreet, *MA,* p. 174; Benning Papers, UNC; Hennessy, *Historical Report,* p. 22; Young, "Antietam," MNBP.

40. Hennessy, *Historical Report,* pp. 15, 16, 23; Latrobe Diary, VHS; Longstreet, *MA,* p. 174, Theodore Fogel–Father and Mother, August 31, 1862, Fogel Papers, EU; O'Neill, "Thoroughfare Gap," *CWQ,* 6, pp. 38, 42, 43.

41. Hennessy, *Historical Report,* pp. 23–29; Longstreet, *MA,* pp. 174, 175; Freeman, *R. E. Lee,* II, p. 314; O'Neill, "Thoroughfare Gap," *CWQ,* 6, p. 43.

42. Hennessy, *Historical Report,* pp. 19, 27, 56; Longstreet, *MA,* p. 175; Wood, *Reminiscences,* p. 29; Todd, *First Texas,* p. 9.

43. Wert, "Killing Ground," *ACW,* 4, 2, pp. 21, 22.

44. Ibid.

45. Pritchard, Papers, ANBL; Philadephia *Weekly Press,* November 2, 1887; Everett, *Chaplain Davis,* p. 110; Hennessy, *Historical Report,* pp. 56, 57, 85; Longstreet, *MA,* p. 180; Durkin, *John Dooley,* p. 18.

46. McDonald, *Make Me,* p. 74; W. W. Blackford, *War Years,* p. 125; Hennessy, *Historical Report,* p. 85.

47. Venable, "Reminiscences," UVA.

48. Berkeley, "War Reminiscences," MNBP.

49. Sorrel, *Recollections,* p. 84; *CV,* 29, p. 297; Philadelphia *Weekly Press,* November 2, 1887; Longstreet, *MA,* pp. 180, 181; R. E. Lee–Fitz John Porter, October 31, 1867, copy, Lee Papers, WLU; Hennessy, *Historical Report,* pp. 123, 124.

50. Hennessy, *Historical Report,* pp. 123–26, 154; Longstreet, *MA,* p. 181; Duggan Papers, UGA; Latrobe Diary, VHS; William M. Owen–F. J. Porter, September 7, 1868, typed copy; C. M. Wilcox–F. J. Porter, June 7, 1870, typed copy, Daniel Papers, UVA; Lewis, "Account of," MNBP.

51. Freeman, *R. E. Lee,* II, p. 322; Wert, "Killing Ground," *ACW,* 4, 2, p. 23; Longstreet, *MA,* p. 181.

52. Longstreet, *MA,* p. 181; Longstreet–F. J. Porter, September 23, 1866,

typed copy; Beverly H. Robertson–F. J. Porter, June 10, 1870, typed copy, Daniel Papers, UVA; Hennessy, *Historical Report,* p. 151; Longstreet, Letter, MNBP.

53. Longstreet, *MA,* p. 182; *B & L,* II, p. 519; Hennessy, *Historical Report,* p. 151.

54. Longstreet, *MA,* p. 182; *B & L,* II, p. 519; Hennessy, *Historical Report,* pp. 151, 152.

55. Longstreet, *MA,* p. 182; *B & L,* II, p. 519; Wert, "Killing Ground," *ACW,* 4, 2, pp. 22, 23.

56. Longstreet, *MA,* p. 183; *B & L,* II, p. 519; Hennessy, *Historical Report,* pp. 146, 181, 184, 186, 190, 218; R. E. Lee–Fitz John Porter, October 31, 1867, typed copy, Lee Papers, WLU.

57. Longstreet, *MA,* p. 183; *B & L,* II, p. 519, Hennessy, *Historical Report,* p. 278.

58. Longstreet, *MA,* p. 184; *OR,* 12, 2, p. 565; Chesnut, *Diary,* p. 297; Haskell, *Memoirs,* p. 16; Everett, *Chaplain Davis,* p. 149; Ratchford, *Reminiscences,* p. 56; Polley, *Hood's Texas Brigade,* p. 204; Moses, "Autobiography," UNC.

59. *OR,* 12, 2, p. 565; Longstreet, *MA,* p. 184; Hennessy, *Historical Report,* pp. 246, 252.

60. *OR,* 12, 2, pp. 367, 565; Hennessy, *Historical Report,* pp. 234, 235, 236.

61. *OR,* 12, 2, pp. 565, 598, 605; Everett, *Chaplain Davis,* p. 113; Fletcher, *Rebel Private,* p. 37; Newspaper clipping, Sixth North Carolina, Mangum Papers, UNC; Hennessy, *Historical Report,* p. 235.

62. "Notations, Second Manassas Report," Wilcox Papers, LC; *B & L,* II, p. 520.

63. Hennessy, *Historical Report,* pp. 195, 209, 242, 243; Wert, "Killing Ground," *ACW,* 4, 2, pp. 24, 25.

64. Warner, *Generals in Blue,* pp. 379, 380; C. M. Wilcox–F. J. Porter, June [?], 1870, typed copy, Daniel Papers, UVA, R. E. Lee–Fitz John Porter, October 31, 1867, copy, February 18, 1870, Lee Papers, WLU.

65. *SHSP,* V, pp. 274–79; Freeman, *R. E. Lee,* II, p. 325; Eckenrode and Conrad, *James Longstreet,* pp. 105–6.

66. *Annals,* pp. 628–31; Fitz John Porter–Longstreet, October 30, 1892, Longstreet Papers, GDAH.

67. Longstreet, *MA,* p. 158.

68. Wood, *Reminiscences of Wood,* p. 31; Bernard, *War Talks,* p. 15; Freeman, *Lee's Dispatches,* pp. 56–58.

69. Freeman, *R. E. Lee,* II, pp. 328–30; Hennessy, *Historical Report,* p. 283; Longstreet, *MA,* pp. 185, 186.

70. Hennessy, *Historical Report,* pp. 284, 285; Shipp Diary, Shipp Family Papers, VHS; Farinholt Papers, VHS; Todd, "Reminiscences," p. 36, UNC; Duffey, Diary, VHS; William Mahone–Longstreet, March 15, 1887, Longstreet Papers, EU.

71. *SHSP,* VI, pp. 62–64; Gallagher, *Fighting For,* p. 134; Hennessy, *Historical Report,* pp. 288, 289.

72. *OR,* 51, 2, p. 613; *SHSP,* VI, p. 64; Hennessy, *Historical Report,* pp. 319, 320; Longstreet, *MA,* pp. 185, 186.

73. Wert, "Killing Ground," *ACW,* 4, 2, p. 24; Hennessy, *Historical Report,* pp. 261, 262.

74. *OR,* 12, 2, pp. 41, 41; *B & L,* II, pp. 486, 487; Hennessy, *Historical Report,* p. 262; Wert, "Killing Ground," *ACW,* 4, 2, p. 24.

75. *OR,* 12, 2, pp. 368, 646, 647; *B & L,* II, p. 524; Wert, "Killing Ground," *ACW,* 4, 2, pp. 24, 25.

76. *OR,* 12, 2, p. 607; Douglas, *I Rode,* p. 140; Longstreet, *MA,* p. 186; *Annals,* pp. 629, 630; William H. Chapman–Longstreet, August 27, 1887, Chapman Papers, VHS; Account of Samuel F. Chapman, Daniel Papers, UVA; W. H. Chapman–Walton Moore, November 22, 1922, Chapman, Virginia, Dixie Battery File, MNBP; B. W. Frobel–Longstreet, March 2, 1868, Alexander Papers, UNC; Philadelphia *Weekly Press,* November 2, 1887; CSR/NA; *B & L,* II, p. 521.

77. Longstreet, *MA,* pp. 187, 188; *B & L,* II, p. 521; Hennessy, *Historical Report,* pp. 347, 348, 349.

78. Longstreet, *MA,* p. 188; Hood, *Advance,* p. 36; Position, Corse's Report, MNBP; *B & L,* II, p. 523; Longstreet–E. P. Alexander, June 17, 1869, Alexander Papers, UNC.

79. *OR,* 12, 2, p. 565; Houghton, *Two Boys,* p. 25; *CV,* 22, p. 231; 33, p. 221.

80. *OR,* 12, 2, pp. 606, 620, 626, 628, 629; Longstreet, *MA,* 189; Hennessy, *Historical Report,* pp. 415, 450, 452–57, 490–98; Polley, *Hood's Texas Brigade,* p. 84; Todd, "Reminiscences," p. 9, UNC; B. W. Frobel–Longstreet, March 2, 1868; C. M. Wilcox–E. P. Alexander, July 6, 1869, Alexander Papers, UNC; Theodore Fogel–Father and Mother, August 31, 1862, Fogel Papers, EU; William H. Dobbins–Pa, September 4, 1862, Dobbins Papers, EU; William Mahone–Longstreet, March 15, 1887, Longstreet Papers, EU; Letter, Phillips Legion File, MNBP.

81. *OR,* 12, 2, p. 563; Longstreet, *MA,* p. 189.

82. Stevens, *Reminiscences,* p. 61; Longstreet, *MA,* p. 191; W. B. Young–Aunt, August 31, 1862, Simpson Papers, DU; Venable, "Reminiscences," UVA; Long, *Memoirs,* p. 206; Sorrel, *Recollections,* p. 96.

83. Longstreet, *MA,* pp. 191–94; Freeman, *R. E. Lee,* II, pp. 340, 341; Latrobe Diary, VHS.

84. Sears, "Getting Right," *American Heritage,* 42, 3, p. 68; W. H. Taylor–Sister, August 30, 1862, Taylor Papers, VSL; Hassler, *Pender,* p. 173; Hennessy, *Historical Report,* pp. 536–45.

85. *B & L,* II, p. 522; Newspaper interview, Gettysburg Clipping Books, 6, p. 82, GNMP; Longstreet, *MA,* pp. 197, 198; Washington *Post,* June 11, 1893.

9. "MY OLD WAR-HORSE"

1. Stillwell Diary, Fifty-third Georgia Infantry, GNMP; Robertson, "Memoirs," DU; Latrobe Diary, VHS; Longstreet, *MA,* p. 194; *OR,* 19, 1, p. 839; pt. 2, p. 602; Diary, Shipp Family Papers, VHS.

2. *OR,* 19, 1, p. 144; pt. 2, pp. 590, 591; Gallagher, *Antietam,* p. 37.

3. Dowdey and Manarin, *Wartime Papers,* pp. 293, 294; *B & L,* II, pp. 605–6.

4. Longstreet, *MA,* pp. 200, 201, 284, 288; Sears, *Landscape,* p. 66.

5. Latrobe Diary, VHS; Thomas C. Elder–Wife, September 5, 1862, Elder Papers, VHS; Jensen, *Thirty-second Virginia,* p. 83; Walton Papers, TU; *OR,* 19, 2, p. 592; Farinholt Papers, VHS; Longstreet, *MA,* p. 201; Freeman, *R. E. Lee,* II, p. 441.

6. Latrobe Diary, VHS; Douglas, *I Rode,* p. 148.

7. Longstreet–D. H. Hill, February 22, 1883, Hill, VSL; Goree, *Letters,* p. 296.

8. Longstreet, *MA,* p. 202.

9. Sorrel, *Recollections,* p. 97; McDonald, *Make Me,* p. 79; Squires, " 'Boy Officer,' " *CWTI,* 14, 2, p. 17.

10. Longstreet, *MA,* p. 202; *B & L,* II, p. 663.

11. Freeman, *R. E. Lee,* II, p. 361; Chambers, *Stonewall Jackson,* II, p. 188; Sears, *Landscape,* p. 90; D. H. Hill–R. L. Dabney, July 21, 1864, Dabney Papers, UTS; J. Chamblin–D. H. Hill, May 25, 1885, Hill Papers, VSL.

12. Longstreet–Hill, June 6, 1883, Hill Papers, VSL.

13. *B & L,* p. 663; Longstreet, *MA,* p. 289; Gettysburg Clipping Books, 6, p. 82, GNMP.

14. *OR,* 19, 1, pp. 144, 145; Sears, *Landscape,* pp. 86, 87.

15. *OR,* 19, 2, pp. 603, 604; Sears, *Landscape,* pp. 90, 91.

16. Longstreet, *MA,* p. 205; Latrobe Diary, VHS; Walton Papers, TU; *OR,* 19, 1, p. 839; Gallagher, *Fighting For,* p. 141; Sears, *Landscape,* pp. 94, 95.

17. Gallagher, *Fighting For,* p. 142; Latrobe Diary, VHS; Sears, *Landscape,* p. 96.

18. Gallagher, *Antietam,* pp. 10, 11, 36; Dowdey and Manarin, *Wartime Papers,* p. 307; J. G. Montgomery–Brother Arthur and Sister Bettie, January 9, 1863, Montgomery, Letter, vol. 161, FSNMP, Montgomery, *Howell Cobb's,* p. 68; A. B. Simms–Sister, September 4, 1862, Simms Family Papers, AHS.

19. *B & L,* II, p. 663; Sorrel, *Recollections,* p. 103; Wood, *Reminiscences,* p. 33; Robertson, "Memoirs," p. 19, DU; Gallagher, *Fighting For,* pp. 141, 142; Andrew Wardlaw–Wife, September 24, 26, 1862; Wardlaw Letters, First South Carolina File, ANBP; Theodore Fogel–Father and Mother, October 4, 1862; Fogel Papers, EU; Dowdey and Manarin, *Wartime Papers,* p. 307; Duggan Papers, UGA.

20. Theodore Fogel–Father and Mother, September 8, 13, 1862, Fogel Papers, EU; Oates, *War,* p. 153; John B. Magruder–Papa, December 4, 1862, Magruder Papers, DU; R. W. Martin–Ellen Johnson, September 8, 1862, Martin Papers, DU.

21. Gallagher, *Antietam,* pp. 42–43.

22. *OR,* 19, 2, p. 605; Williams, *Washington County,* II, pp. 326, 329; Theodore Fogel–Father and Mother, September 13, 1862; Fogel Papers, EU; Freeman, *R. E. Lee,* II, pp. 366, 367.

23. *OR,* 19, 2, pp. 590, 591; Sears, *Landscape,* Prologue.

24. Sears, *Landscape,* pp. 15–17.

25. Ibid., pp. 112–15; *B & L,* II, p. 607; D. H. Hill spent many years defending himself against charges he lost it. Jackson sent him a copy, as did Lee; it was the copy from Lee's headquarters that was lost. Some interesting letters about the controversy and defense of Hill are Charles Marshall–Hill, November 11, 1867; R. B. Marcy–Hill, May 5, 1868; S. W. Crawford–Hill, August 22, 1868, Hill Papers, VSL; D. H. Hill–R. H. Chilton, December 11, 1867, Hill Papers, MC.

26. Sears, *Landscape,* pp. 117–20; Longstreet, *MA,* p. 219.

27. Longstreet, *MA,* pp. 219, 220; *B & L,* II, p. 665; Longstreet–D. H. Hill, June 6, 1883, Hill Papers, VSL.

28. Longstreet, *MA,* pp. 219, 220; *B & L,* II, pp. 665, 666; Longstreet–D. H. Hill, June 6, 1883, Hill Papers, VSL.

29. *OR,* 19, 1, p. 839; *B & L,* II, p. 666; Longstreet, *MA,* p. 220; Wood, *Reminiscences,* p. 35; Latrobe Diary, VHS.

30. Durkin, *John Dooley,* pp. 34, 35; Hood, *Advance,* pp. 38–40; Polley, *Hood's Texas Brigade,* pp. 113, 114; Stevens, *Reminiscences,* p. 69.

31. Longstreet, *MA,* pp. 234, 235; Hood, *Advance,* p. 40; Longstreet–D. H. Hill, June 6, 1883, Hill Papers, VSL; Alexander, *Memoirs,* p. 80; Stiles, *Four Years,* p. 65.

32. D. H. Hill–Longstreet, February 11, 1885; Longstreet Papers, DU; Sears, *Landscape,* pp. 128, 129.

33. D. H. Hill–Longstreet, February 11, June 5, 1885, Longstreet Papers, DU; C. T. Zachary–D. H. Hill, August 6, 1885, Hill Papers, VSL; *OR,* 19, 1, p. 839; Longstreet, *MA,* pp. 224, 225; Wood, *Reminiscences,* p. 36; Latrobe Diary, VHS; Sears, *Landscape,* pp. 130–49.

34. Longstreet–D. H. Hill, June 6, 1883, Hill Papers, VSL; Venable, "Reminiscences," UVA; Sorrel, *Recollections,* p. 101; Longstreet, *MA,* pp. 227, 228; *OR,* 19, 1, p. 839.

35. Longstreet, *MA,* p. 227; Hood, *Advance,* p. 41; Venable, "Reminiscences," UVA; Freeman, *R. E. Lee,* II, pp. 373–75; *OR,* 19, 1, pp. 1020, 1021.

36. Dawson, *Reminiscences,* pp. 64, 65, 66; Theodore Fogel–Father and Mother, September 16, 1862, Fogel Papers, EU; Longstreet–H. Heth, November 1, 1894, Carman Papers, ANBL; Sears, *Landscape,* pp. 151–52.

37. Longstreet, *MA,* pp. 233, 234; *OR,* 19, 1, pp. 839, 840; Venable, "Reminiscences," UVA; Latrobe Diary, VHS; Longstreet–D. H. Hill, June 6, 1883, Hill Papers, VSL; Gallagher, *Antietam,* p. 55.

38. Longstreet, *MA,* pp. 233, 234; Sears, *Landscape,* pp. 161, 168, 169.

39. Gallagher, *Antietam,* p. 55; Gallagher, *Fighting For,* pp. 145–47; Longstreet, *MA,* p. 288.

40. *OR,* 19, 1, pp. 839, 840; Freeman, *R. E. Lee,* II, pp. 378, 379.

41. Freeman, *R. E. Lee,* II, pp. 379, 380; Sears, *Landscape,* p. 173.

42. Longstreet, *MA,* pp. 233, 234; Gallagher, "'Till the Sun," *CWQ,* 9, p. 57; Owen, *In Camp,* p. 138.

43. "Interpretative Planning, Piper"; Otto, "Henry Piper"; Buchanan, "Piper," ANBL; Sorrel, *Recollections,* p. 103.

44. "Interpretative Planning, Piper"; Andrews, " 'Johnny Reb,' " ANBL; Latrobe Papers, VHS; Moses, "Autobiography," p. 12, UNC.

45. Freeman, *R. E. Lee,* II, pp. 381, 382; Gallagher, *Fighting For,* p. 148; Sears, *Landscape,* p. 164; Lafayette McLaws–H. Heth, November 13, 1894, Carman Papers, ANBL; Lafayette McLaws–John Hood, May 31, 1863, typed copy, McLaws Papers, UNC.

46. Freeman, *R. E. Lee,* II, p. 382; R. E. Lee–Mrs. T. J. Jackson, January 25, 1866, typed copy, Lee Papers, WLU; Sears, *Landscape,* p. 175.

47. Sears, *Landscape,* pp. 163, 169, 170.

48. Ibid., p. 171; Longstreet, *MA,* p. 234; Freeman, *R. E. Lee,* II, pp. 382, 383.

49. *CV,* 16, p. 580; Andrews, " 'Johnny Reb,' " ANBL; Sorrel, *Recollections,* p. 103; Sears, *Landscape,* pp. 175, 294, 295; Priest, *Antietam,* pp. 331, 343.

50. Sears, *Landscape,* chapter 6; Graves, *Bedford Light,* p. 24; Freeman, *R. E. Lee,* II, pp. 387, 388.

51. Sears, *Landscape,* pp. 181, 195, 197, 202, 216, 220, 230; Stevens, *Reminiscences,* p. 75; J. A. Early–Henry Heth, November 25, 1892; G. T. Anderson—H. Heth, May 19, 1893; Lafayette McLaws–H. Heth, November 13, 1894, Carman Papers, ANBL; Lafayette McLaws–Longstreet, November 22, 1887, typed copy, Tucker Papers, UNC; Marvel, *Burnside,* p. 132; Priest, *Antietam,* pp. 318–30.

52. Gallagher, " 'Till the Sun," *CWQ,* 9, p. 58; Gordon, *Reminiscences,* p. 84.

53. *B & L,* II, p. 671; Gallagher, " 'Till the Sun," *CWQ,* 9, p. 58; D. H. Hill–Longstreet, March 12, 1885, Longstreet Papers, DU.

54. *B & L,* II, p. 671; Ratchford, *Some Reminiscences,* p. 66.

55. Ratchford, *Some Reminiscences,* p. 66.

56. Gallagher, " 'Till the Sun," *CWQ,* 9, pp. 57, 58; Priest, *Antietam,* p. 137; Sears, *Landscape,* p. 240; Lee, *Recollections,* p. 82.

57. Sears, "Antietam," *CWTI,* 26, 2, p. 31; Gallagher, " 'Till the Sun," *CWQ,* 9, pp. 58; 59; Sears, *Landscape,* pp. 236, 240; *B & L,* II, pp. 668, 669; Dinkins, *Johnnie,* p. 59.

58. Longstreet, *MA,* pp. 249, 250; Gallagher, " 'Till the Sun," *CWQ,* 9, pp. 60, 61; Sears, *Landscape,* p. 240; Priest, *Antietam,* p. 182; Smith, "Recollections," ANBL.

59. Gallagher, " 'Till the Sun," *CWQ,* 9, p. 60; Sorrel, *Recollections,* p. 106; Sears, *Landscape,* p. 241; Piston, Ph.D. Diss., pp. 171–72.

60. Sorrel, *Recollections,* p. 106; Sears, *Landscape,* pp. 247–50; Longstreet, *MA,* p. 256.

61. Sears, *Landscape,* pp. 245–47; Gallagher, " 'Till the Sun," *CWQ,* 9, p. 61; Longstreet, *MA,* p. 250; George T. Anderson–H. Heth, May 19, 1893, Carman Papers, ANBL.

62. Longstreet, *MA,* p. 241; Owen, *In Camp,* pp. 146–47; George T. Anderson–H. Heth, May 19, 1892, Carman Papers, ANBL.

63. Sorrel, *Recollections,* p. 105; Owen, *In Camp,* p. 148; *B & L,* II,

p. 669; Longstreet, *MA*, p. 250; Latrobe Diary, VHS; *CV*, II, p. 354; Buchanan, "Piper," ANBL.

64. Sears, *Landscape*, pp. 236, 240, 251–54; Longstreet, *MA*, pp. 250, 251, 253; Gallagher, " 'Till the Sun," *CWQ*, 9, p. 62; Owen, *In Camp*, pp. 147, 148; George T. Anderson–H. Heth, May 19, 1893, Carman Papers, ANBL; Smith "Recollections," ANBL.

65. Sorrel, *Recollections*, p. 108; *CV*, 27, p. 116.

66. Longstreet–E. P. Alexander, August 26, 1902, Alexander Papers, UNC; Longstreet, *MA*, p. 266.

67. Gallagher, *Fighting For*, p. 126; Marvel, *Burnside*, pp. 134–36, 140; Sears, *Landscape*, p. 276.

68. Sears, *Landscape*, pp. 277, 286–93; Latrobe Diary, VHS.

69. Priest, *Antietam*, pp. 331, 343; Sears, *Landscape*, pp. 294, 295; Douglas, *I Rode*, p. 174.

70. Priest, *Antietam*, pp. 318–30; Owen, *In Camp*, p. 148; Sorrel, *Recollections*, pp. 84, 107, 110, 111.

71. Freeman, *R. E. Lee*, II, pp. 403, 404; *B & L*, II, pp. 671, 672; Longstreet, *MA*, p. 262; Sorrel, *Recollections*, p. 108; Owen, *In Camp*, p. 157.

72. Freeman, *R. E. Lee*, II, pp. 403, 404; Sears, *Landscape*, pp. 303, 304.

73. Freeman, *R. E. Lee*, II, pp. 405, 406; *OR*, 19, 1, p. 841; Latrobe Diary, VHS; Theodore Fogel–Father and Mother, September 28, 1862, Fogel Papers, EU; Wardlaw Letters, First South Carolina File, ANBL.

74. W. H. Taylor–Sister, September 21, 1862, Taylor Papers, VSL; *OR*, 19, 1, p. 151; Sears, "Antietam," *CWTI*, 26, 2, p. 45.

75. Longstreet–J. E. Jones, February 6, 1896, Charles E. Jones Papers, DU; Gallagher, *Fighting For*, p. 92.

76. Theodore Fogel–Father and Mother, September 28, 1862, Fogel Papers, EU; Todd, "Reminiscences," p. 65, UNC; Wood, *Reminiscences*, p. 40; D. H. Hill–Longstreet, June 8, 13, 1885, Longstreet Papers, DU; Gallagher, *Antietam*, pp. 39, 44; William N. Berkeley–Wife, September 25, 1862, Berkeley Letters, ANBL; E. A. Osborne–D. H. Hill, June 18, 1895, Hill Papers, VSL; R. E. Lee–Mrs. T. J. Jackson, January 25, 1866, typed copy, Lee Papers, WLU.

77. Sears, *Landscape*, pp. 310, 311; Sears, "Getting Right," *American Heritage*, 42, 3, p. 68; Jones, *Civil War Command*, p. 96.

10. "I WILL KILL THEM ALL"

1. William Cocke–Parents and Sisters, October 7, 1862, Cocke Family Papers, VHS.

2. Thomas Elliott–Wife, September 26, 1862, Elliott Papers, DU; Jubal Early–D. H. Hill, August 2, 1885, Hill Papers, VSL; J. R. Shaffner–C. T. Pfohl, October 3, 1862, Pfohl Papers, UNC; H. M. Talley–Mother, November 9, 1862, Talley Papers, VHS.

3. Clack, Letters, Ninth Alabama File, MNBP; William Cocke–Parents and Sisters, October 7, 1862, Cocke Family Papers, VHS.

4. *OR*, 19, 1, p. 143; pt. 2, pp. 621, 639, 660, 674; Gallagher, *Fighting For*, p. 155.

5. *OR,* 19, 2, pp. 618–19; Wise, *Long Arm,* pp. 328, 333; Walton Papers, TU; Ordnance Journal, Alexander Papers, UNC; Montgomery, *Howell Cobb's,* p. 76; Owens, *In Camp,* p. 176; Everett, *Chaplain Davis,* p. 135; Gallagher, *Fighting For,* p. 155; Longstreet–J. E. Martin, October 6, 1862, Longstreet Papers, DU.

6. Freeman, *R. E. Lee,* II, p. 238; *OR,* 19, 2, pp. 633, 634, 643; Longstreet file, CSR/NA; Warner, *Generals in Gray,* p. 152.

7. Longstreet, *MA,* p. 198; George E. Pickett–LaSalle Corbell, October 11, 1862, typed copy, Inman Papers, BU.

8. New York *Times,* July 29, 1879.

9. Longstreet–J. E. Johnston, October 6, 1862, Longstreet Papers, DU.

10. Piston, Ph.D. Diss., pp. 178, 182.

11. Connelly, *Marble,* p. 208.

12. Freeman, *R. E. Lee,* II, p. 419.

13. Piston, Ph.D. Diss., p. 179.

14. D. H. Hill–R. L. Dabney, July 21, 1864, Dabney Papers, UTS.

15. Freeman, *Lee's Lieutenants,* II, pp. 253, 266, 269; Longstreet–R. H. Chilton, September 28, 1862, Longstreet Papers, CHS; Longstreet–R. H. Chilton, June 2, 1875, Longstreet Papers, MC; Longstreet file, CSR/NA; *OR,* 19, 2, pp. 698–99.

16. *OR,* 21, pp. 538–45, 1033, 1034, 1057.

17. Ibid., pp. 538–41.

18. Longstreet file, CSR/NA; Freeman, *Lee's Lieutenants,* I, p. lii; Patterson, *West Point,* p. 38; Gallagher, *Fighting For,* p. 136; Sorrel, *Recollections,* pp. 126, 127.

19. Warner, *Generals in Gray,* pp. 8–9; Sorrel, *Recollections,* p. 128.

20. Freeman, *Lee's Lieutenants,* II, p. 269; Goree, *Letters,* p. 167; Sorrel, *Recollections,* p. 127; Warner, *Generals in Gray,* p. 164; *OR,* 21, p. 540.

21. *OR,* 19, 2, p. 699; Freeman, *Lee's Lieutenants,* II, p. 269; Moses, "Autobiography," p. 58, UNC; Inman, *Soldier,* pp. 23, 24; James Dearing–Uncle, April 20, 1862, Dearing Papers, VHS.

22. *OR,* 21, p. 54; Warner, *Generals in Gray,* pp. 253, 254, 319, 320.

23. "Notations, Fredericksburg Report," Wilcox Papers, LC; Warner, *Generals in Gray,* p. 337; Freeman, *R. E. Lee,* II, pp. 418, 419; *OR,* 21, pp. 539, 540.

24. "Notations, Fredericksburg Report," Wilcox Papers, LC; R. E. Lee–C. M. Wilcox, November 12, 1862, Lee Family Papers, VHS.

25. Sorrel, *Recollections,* pp. 117, 118; *OR,* 51, 2, pp. 631, 645.

26. Moses, "Autobiography," pp. 1, 2, 49, UNC: Sorrel, *Recollections,* p. 118; Haskell, *Memoirs,* pp. 29, 30.

27. Longstreet file, CSR/NA; Piston, Ph.D. Diss., p. 196; McGee and Lander, *Rebel,* p. 27n; *OR,* 51, 2, p. 631; Moses, "Autobiography," p. 51, UNC; Latrobe Diary, VHS; Sorrel, *Recollections,* p. 118, Dawson, *Reminiscences,* p. 128.

28. *OR,* 51, 2, pp. 631, 645; Walton Papers, TU; Haskell, *Memoirs,* p. 145n.

29. *OR,* 21, p. 1046; Wise, *Long Arm,* pp. 141, 351, 757; Gallagher, *Fight-*

ing For, pp. 37, 60, 160; Warner, *Generals in Gray,* p. 3; Sorrel, *Recollections,* pp. 70, 119.

30. Sears, *George B. McClellan,* pp. 330–36; Long, *Civil War,* pp. 277–78.

31. *OR,* 19, 2, pp. 673, 675, 676; R. E. Lee–Longstreet, October 19, 1862, McLaws Papers, UNC; Freeman, *R. E. Lee,* II, p. 424.

32. *OR,* 19, 2, pp. 686, 687; Longstreet, *MA,* pp. 290, 291; Polley, *Texas,* p. 137; Walton Papers, TU; Latrobe Diary, VHS; Ordnance Journal, Alexander Papers, UNC; Moore, *Life,* p. 114; Jones, *Rebel War Clerk's,* I, p. 179; McDonald, *Make Me,* p. 92; R. E. Lee–Mary Lee, November 6, 1862, Lee Family Papers, VHS; Lee, *Recollections,* pp. 79, 81; Freeman, *R. E. Lee,* I, p. 421.

33. Sears, *George B. McClellan,* pp. 336–41; Hawkins, Statement, BU.

34. *OR,* 21, p. 1015; Ordnance Journal, Alexander, UNC; Marvel, *Burnside,* pp. 163–65.

35. *OR,* 21, pp. 550, 551; Ordnance Journal, Alexander, UNC; R. E. Lee–Longstreet, November 17, 1862, Clarke Papers, Harvard.

36. *OR,* 51, 2, pp. 647–49; Theodore Fogel–Father and Mother, November 24, 1862, Fogel Papers, EU; John B. Magruder–Papa, December 4, 1862, Magruder Papers, DU; Moore, *Life,* pp. 114–17; Longstreet, *MA,* pp. 292, 293; Ordnance Journal, Alexander, UNC; Dowdey and Manarin, *Wartime Papers,* p. 342; Sorrel, *Recollections,* pp. 125, 126.

37. Marvel, *Burnside,* pp. 166–68; *B & L,* III, p. 70; Dowdey and Manarin, *Wartime Papers,* p. 343.

38. *OR,* 21, pp. 549, 551, 552, 1021, 1027, 1034; Longstreet, *MA,* p. 293; London *Times,* January 1, 1863; Freeman, *R. E. Lee,* II, pp. 430, 431, 433.

39. Freeman, *R. E. Lee,* II, pp. 433, 438, 439; Marvel, *Burnside,* p. 179; R. W. Martin–Nellis, November 25, 1862, Martin Papers, DU.

40. *OR,* 21, pp. 545, 546, 569; Latrobe Diary, VHS; Freeman, *R. E. Lee,* II, pp. 443, 444; Marvel, *Burnside,* p. 176.

41. *OR,* 21, pp. 618, 619; Freeman, *R. E. Lee,* II, pp. 444–46; Marvel, *Burnside,* pp. 176, 177.

42. Marvel, *Burnside,* p. 177, Freeman, *R. E. Lee,* II, pp. 446, 447.

43. *OR,* pp. 569, 619; *B & L,* III, p. 75; McDonald, *Make Me,* p. 99; Latrobe Diary, VHS; Marvel, *Burnside,* p. 178.

44. Marvel, *Burnside,* pp. 179, 180; McIntosh, "A Ride on Horseback," UNC; Latrobe Diary, VHS.

45. Longstreet, *MA,* pp. 297, 299; Freeman, *R. E. Lee,* II, pp. 452, 453.

46. Longstreet, *MA,* pp. 297–99; *B & L,* III, p. 72; Dickert, *History,* p. 179.

47. Gallagher, *Fighting For,* pp. 167, 172; Whan, "Battle of Fredericksburg," pp. 91, 132; Owen, *In Camp,* p. 175; *B & L,* III, p. 79; Marvel, *Burnside,* p. 189.

48. *OR,* 21, p. 569; Hagerman, *Civil War,* pp. 123, 124; Jones, *Civil War Command,* p. 103; Moore, *Confederacy,* p. 124; *B & L,* III, p. 79.

49. Longstreet, *MA,* pp. 316, 317; Owen, *In Camp,* pp. 176, 185; Gallagher, *Fighting For,* pp. 168, 169; *B & L,* III, pp. 89, 91.

50. Longstreet, *MA,* pp. 306, 307; Latrobe Papers, VHS; Piston, Ph.D.

Diss., p. 188; Longstreet–E. P. Alexander, January 19, 1868; Longstreet Papers, DU; Alexander Papers, UNC; *B & L,* III, pp. 75, 76.

51. William B. Pettit–Wife, December 16, 1862, typed copy, Pettit Papers, UNC; *B & L,* III, p. 76.

52. Longstreet, *MA,* p. 307; Latrobe Diary, VHS; William B. Pettit–Wife, December 16, 1862, typed copy, Pettit Papers, UNC; London *Times,* January 13, 1863.

53. *OR,* 21, p. 553; Marvel, *Burnside,* pp. 186–87; marginal notes in Mary Anna Jackson, *Life and Letters of General Thomas J. Jackson,* Douglas, Personal Library, ANBL.

54. Inman, *Soldier,* p. 29; Harrison, *Pickett's Men,* p. 72; E. M. Law–E. P. Alexander, January 15, 1866, Alexander Papers, UNC; Longstreet–E. P. Alexander, January 19, 1868, Longstreet Papers, DU; Longstreet, *MA,* pp. 309, 317.

55. Whan, "Battle of Fredericksburg," pp. 144, 146, 149, 150; Marvel, *Burnside,* p. 189; Gallagher, *Fighting For,* p. 168.

56. Macon *Telegraph,* December 25, 1862; Owen, *In Camp,* p. 186; Whan, "Battle of Fredericksburg," pp. 149–51; Dickert, *History,* p. 186.

57. Whan, "Battle of Fredericksburg," pp. 152–58; Woods, "Reminiscences," vol. 127, FSNMP; *B & L,* III, p. 79; Inman, *Soldier,* p. 31; Marvel, *Burnside,* p. 190.

58. Hattaway and Jones, *How the North,* p. 307; Whan, "Battle of Fredericksburg," pp. 158–75; Marvel, *Burnside,* pp. 190, 193, 195; Blackford, *Letters,* p. 147; *B & L,* III, p. 81.

59. *OR,* 21, pp. 570, 576; *B & L,* III, pp. 91, 92, 94, 95, 115; Gallagher, *Fighting For,* pp. 176–78; Sorrel, *Recollections,* p. 131; *CV,* 22, p. 501; L. Cooper–Mother, November 9, 1862, Cooper Letters, vol. 129, FSNMP.

60. *OR,* 21, p. 581; Longstreet, *MA,* p. 315; Todd, *First Texas,* p. 12; Latrobe Papers, VHS; Morgan, *Personal Reminiscences,* p. 148; Gallagher, *Fighting For,* pp. 169, 185.

61. Longstreet, *MA,* p. 316; Oates, *War,* p. 170; Freeman, *R. E. Lee,* II, pp. 466, 467.

62. Marvel, *Burnside,* pp. 197, 198; *CV,* 16, p. 105.

63. Freeman, *R. E. Lee,* II, pp. 470, 471; Sorrel, *Recollections,* pp. 136, 137; McIntosh, "Ride on Horseback," p. 11, UNC; Jubal A. Early–D. H. Hill, August 2, 1885, Hill Papers, VSL.

64. Whan, "Battle of Fredericksburg," p. 200; Freeman, *R. E. Lee,* II, p. 471; *OR,* 21, p. 572; Philip Powers–Dearest Wife, December 17, 1862, Lewis Lehigh Collection, USAMHI; London *Times,* January 23, 1863; McIntosh, "Ride on Horseback," pp. 32, 33, UNC; Hamilton Diary, vol. 133, FSNMP; Freeman, *Lee's Lieutenants,* II, p. 385.

65. *OR,* 21, p. 571; Walton Papers, TU.

66. *OR,* 21, p. 556.

67. Freeman, *R. E. Lee,* II, p. 462.

11. INDEPENDENT COMMAND

1. Hamilton Diary, vol. 133, FSNMP.

2. Ibid.

3. Ibid.

4. Ibid.; Dawson, *Reminiscences,* pp. 86, 87.

5. Dawson, *Reminiscences,* p. 87.

6. Ibid., p. 87; Sorrel, *Recollections,* p. 123; Goree, *Letters,* p. 125; Owen, *In Camp,* p. 197.

7. Dawson, *Reminiscences,* pp. ix, x, 57, 62, 63, 83, 128; Dawson record CSR/NA.

8. Theodore Fogel–Father and Mother, December 27, 1862, February 9, 1863, Fogel Papers, EU; Lafayette McLaws–Miss Lizzie, February 18, 1863, Ewell Papers, LC.

9. R. Toombs–Longstreet, February 5, 1879, Longstreet Papers, GDAH.

10. Marvel, *Burnside,* pp. 212–17.

11. Longstreet, *MA,* pp. 323–24; London *Times,* January 23, 1863; Freeman, *R. E. Lee,* II, pp. 480–81.

12. Piston, Ph.D. Diss., pp. 178, 218, 219; Warner, *Generals in Gray,* p. 336; Connelly and Jones, *Politics of Command,* p. 58.

13. Polley, *Letters,* p. 17; Symonds, *Joseph E. Johnston,* pp. 177–80; Chesnut, *Diary,* p. 86; Longstreet–Louis T. Wigfall, November 7, 1862, Wigfall Papers, LC; Connelly and Jones, *Politics of Command,* p. x.

14. Jones, *Civil War,* p. 118; Longstreet–Louis T. Wigfall, November 7, 1862, Wigfall Papers, LC.

15. Piston, Ph.D. Diss., p. 183; Longstreet–J. E. Johnston, October 6, 1862, Longstreet Papers, DU; Symonds, *Joseph E. Johnston,* pp. 183–84.

16. Piston, Ph.D. Diss., pp. 218, 219; Connelly and Jones, *Politics of Command,* pp. 122, 123.

17. *OR,* 18, p. 959; Connelly and Jones, *Politics of Command,* p. 123.

18. Freeman, *R. E. Lee,* II, pp. 478–79; Jones, *Rebel War Clerk's,* I, p. 239; *OR,* 18, p. 872.

19. *OR,* 18, pp. 876, 883; Freeman, *R. E. Lee,* II, p. 483.

20. Lafayette McLaws–Miss Lizzie, February 18, 1863, Ewell Papers, LC; Cobb Diary, Cobb-Hunter Papers, UNC; Oates, *War,* p. 175; McDonald, *Make Me,* p. 115; Polley, *Letters,* p. 98; Theodore Fogel–Father and Mother, February 23, 1862, Fogel Papers, EU.

21. Latrobe Diary, VHS; *OR,* 18, pp. 890, 895; Cormier, *Siege,* pp. 12–14; Dowdey and Manarin, *Wartime Papers,* pp. 405–6; Jones, *Rebel War Clerk's,* I, pp. 261, 263.

22. *OR,* 18, pp. 900, 901, 903; Cormier, *Siege,* pp. 7, 13, 14.

23. *OR,* 18, pp. 896, 898, 900, 902, 903; Longstreet–S. Cooper, February 25, 1863, Longstreet Papers, HSP; Roger Pryor–Longstreet, February 27, 1863, Longstreet Papers, DU; J. E. B. Stuart–John R. Cooke, February 28, 1863, Cooke Family Papers, VHS; Cormier, *Siege,* p. 298.

24. *OR,* 18, pp. 883, 884, 903; Freeman, *R. E. Lee,* II, p. 483; Cormier, *Siege,* p. 14; "Diary," *AHQ,* 18, p. 573.

25. *OR,* 18, p. 871; Freeman, *R. E. Lee,* II, pp. 493, 494; Cormier, *Siege,* pp. 2, 3, 4, 14; Gallagher, *Fighting For,* p. 188.

26. *OR,* 18, pp. 905, 908, 918; Cormier, *Siege,* p. 298.

27. Bridges, *Lee's Maverick General,* pp. 172–74; Cormier, *Siege,* p. 47; Hill–Longstreet, March 17, 1863, Hill, *CWTI* Collection, USAMHI; *OR Atlas,* plate 117; Faust, *Encyclopedia,* p. 524.

28. Bridges, *Lee's Maverick General,* pp. 175–77; Cormier, *Siege,* pp. 47, 299; *OR,* 18, p. 931.

29. *OR,* 18, pp. 922, 923, 924.

30. Ibid., pp. 925, 927; "Diary," *AHQ,* 18, pp. 575, 576; Polley, *Texas,* pp. 142, 143.

31. *OR,* 18, pp. 926, 927.

32. Ibid.

33. Ibid., pp. 907, 933, 934, 937, 942, 943, 944, 948, 950, 953, 954; R. E. Lee–Longstreet, March 25, 1863, Longstreet Papers, HSP; R. E. Lee–Longstreet, March 30, 1863, Lee Papers, NYHS; Cormier, *Siege,* p. 300; Marvel, *Burnside,* pp. 224–26.

34. *OR,* 18, pp. 910, 933, 934, 937, 950, 959, 960; Freeman, *R. E. Lee,* II, pp. 492–95; Cormier, *Siege,* p. 43.

35. Samuel M. Bemiss–Children, April 10, 1863, Bemiss Family Papers, VHS; "Diary," *AHQ,* 18, pp. 577–78; Latrobe Diary, VHS; Wise Papers, DU; Wilson, *Confederate Soldier,* p. 106; *OR,* 18, pp. 970, 975.

36. Cormier, *Siege,* pp. 22, 24, 27, 34, 36, 37, 82.

37. Ibid., p. 22; *OR,* 18, pp. 910, 950, 958, 959, 996, 997, 999; Latrobe Diary, VHS.

38. *OR,* 18, pp. 996, 997; Latrobe Diary, VHS; "Diary," *AHQ,* 18, pp. 578–81; French, *Two Wars,* pp. 161, 162; Cormier, *Siege,* p. 288.

39. *OR,* 51, 2, p. 692; French, *Two Wars,* pp. 161, 162; Goree, *Letters,* pp. 182, 183; Cormier, *Siege,* pp. 128, 144–52.

40. *OR,* 18, pp. 326, 327, 988, 1000, 1001; 51, 2, p. 692; French, *Two Wars,* pp. 160, 162, 163, 167, 168; Cormier, *Siege,* pp. 146–47, 155–61.

41. Latrobe Diary, VHS; "Diary," *AHQ,* 18, pp. 581, 582; French, *Two Wars,* p. 166; E. P. Reeve–Wife, April 16, 1863, Reeve Papers, UNC.

42. Sorrel, *Recollections,* pp. 146–47; Cormier, *Siege,* p. 224.

43. Sorrel, *Recollections,* p. 147; Longstreet, *MA,* p. 324; *B & L,* III, p. 244; Hall, "The Spy Harrison," *CWTI,* 24, 10, pp. 21–23.

44. Latrobe Diary, VHS; *OR,* 18, p. 999; Grantham, "Letters From," *GHQ,* 40, p. 184; Moses, "Autobiography," p. 63, UNC.

45. Hendricks Account, Hampton, South Carolina, Legion File, MNBP; Latrobe Diary, VHS; *OR,* 18, pp. 956, 996; Theodore Fogel–Father and Mother, April 17, 1863, Fogel Papers, EU.

46. Moses, "Autobiography," pp. 62, 63, UNC; Latrobe Diary, VHS; Goree, *Letters,* p. 182; E. P. Reeve–Wife, April 21, 1863, Reeve Papers, UNC; Cormier, *Siege,* pp. 6, 291.

47. Freeman, *R. E. Lee,* II, pp. 507, 508; *OR,* 18, pp. 1029, 1032, 1034; Latrobe Diary, VHS; French, *Two Wars,* p. 166.

48. *OR,* 51, 2, p. 700; Latrobe Diary, VHS; Memoir from Fourth Alabama History, Alexander Papers, UNC; Wise Papers, DU; "Diary," *AHQ,* 18, pp. 582, 583; Theodore Fogel–Father and Mother, May 11, 1863, Fogel Papers, EU.

49. "Diary," *AHQ,* 18, p. 583; S. G. French–Longstreet, May 4, 1863, French Letters, BU; Latrobe Diary, VHS; James A. Seddon–Longstreet, April 16, 1875, Longstreet Papers, DU.

50. Freeman, *R. E. Lee,* II, chapters 33–35.

51. Eckenrode and Bryan, *James Longstreet,* pp. 166, 167.

52. Gallagher, *Fighting For,* p. 190; *OR,* 18, p. 1049; Cormier, *Siege,* pp. 289, 291, 292.

53. Jones, *Rebel War Clerk's,* I, p. 311; Longstreet, *MA,* p. 327; Long, *Civil War,* pp. 344–50.

54. Jones, *Rebel War Clerk's,* I, pp. 191, 192; *OR,* 25, 2, pp. 713, 720, 725, 726; Dowdey and Manarin, *Wartime Papers,* pp. 430, 434.

55. Longstreet, *MA,* p. 327; Longstreet–Lafayette McLaws, July 25, 1873, McLaws Papers, UNC.

56. Longstreet, *MA,* pp. 327, 328; *OR,* 18, p. 1050; James A. Seddon–Longstreet, April 16, 1875.

57. Longstreet, *MA,* pp. 327, 328; Davis, *Jefferson Davis,* pp. 500–502; *OR,* 18, p. 1050; Connelly and Jones, *Politics of Command,* pp. 123–27.

58. Longstreet–Lafayette McLaws, April 16, 1875, McLaws Papers, UNC; Piston, Ph.D. Diss., pp. 220–23; Connelly and Jones, *Politics of Command,* pp. 122–23; Freeman, *Lee's Lieutenants,* III, pp. 221, 222.

59. *OR,* 51, 2, pp. 704–5; Latrobe Diary, VHS.

12. COLLISION IN PENNSYLVANIA

1. Latrobe Diary, VHS; Scheibert, *Seven Months,* p. 35n; *B & L,* III, pp. 244–45.

2. Chambers, *Stonewall Jackson,* II, pp. 438–47.

3. Ibid., pp. 447, 448; Dowdey and Manarin, *Wartime Papers,* p. 484; Younger, *Inside,* p. 60.

4. Longstreet, *MA,* p. 332.

5. R. E. Lee–Charles Carter Lee, May 24, 1863, Robinson Papers, UVA; Gettysburg Clipping Books, 6, p. 128, GNMP.

6. *Annals,* pp. 415–16; Longstreet–Lafayette McLaws, July 25, 1873; McLaws Papers, UNC.

7. Longstreet, *MA,* p. 331; *Annals,* pp. 416, 417; Longstreet–Lafayette McLaws, July 25, 1873, McLaws Papers, UNC.

8. Longstreet–Louis T. Wigfall, May 13, 1863, Wigfall Papers, LC.

9. Connelly and Jones, *Politics of Command,* pp. 116–24.

10. Krick, "I Consider Him a Humbug," *CWQ,* 5, pp. 28–29; Taylor, *Four Years,* p. 91; *OR,* 27, 2, p. 308.

11. *Annals,* p. 417; Longstreet–Lafayette McLaws, July 25, 1873, McLaws Papers, UNC; Piston, Ph.D. Diss., pp. 225, 226; Krolick, "Lee and Longstreet," *CWQ,* 5, p. 34.

12. Longstreet, *MA*, pp. 329, 330; Hattaway and Jones, *How the North*, p. 384; Gallagher, *Fighting For*, p. 92.

13. *B & L*, III, pp. 246–47.

14. Freeman, *R. E. Lee*, II, pp. 19–20; Wert, "Gettysburg," *CWTI*, 27, 4, pp. 14, 16; Longstreet–John R. Cooke, May 16, 1863, Cooke Family Papers, VHS; James S. Seddon–Longstreet, April 16, 1875, Longstreet Papers, DU; J. E. Johnston–Benjamin Cheatham, December 14, 1867, Cheatham Papers, TSLA.

15. *OR*, 25, 2, p. 810.

16. Ibid.

17. Ibid., pp. 811, 840; Wert, "Gettysburg," *CWTI*, 27, 4, p. 16.

18. Washington *Post*, June 11, 1893; Haskell, *Memoirs*, pp. 16, 18; Sorrel, *Recollections*, p. 47; Eggleston, *Rebel's Recollections*, p. 136.

19. Piston, Ph.D. Diss., p. 212; Longstreet, *MA*, p. 332.

20. Lafayette McLaws–Miss Lizzie, February 18, 1863, Ewell Papers, LC; "Notations, Gettysburg Report," Wilcox Papers, LC.

21. Longstreet–Lafayette McLaws, July 25, 1873, McLaws Papers, UNC.

22. Longstreet–Lafayette McLaws, June 3, 1863, July 25, 1873, McLaws Papers, UNC.

23. Longstreet–Lafayette McLaws, July 25, 1873, McLaws Papers, UNC.

24. *OR*, 18, pp. 1063, 1066, 1071, 1073, 1085, 1088; McDonald, *Make Me*, p. 146; Freeman, *Lee's Dispatches*, pp. 74–76; Wise, *Long Arm*, pp. 419, 420; Wert, "Gettysburg," *CWTI*, 27, 4, p. 16; John W. Daniel–Father, June 4, 1863, Daniel Papers, UVA.

25. Gallagher, *Fighting For*, p. 221; *OR*, 27, 2, p. 293; Latrobe Papers, VHS; Diary, Alexander Papers, UNC; Wise Papers, DU; "Diary," *AHQ*, 18, pp. 583–84; Piston, Ph.D. Diss., p. 227.

26. Oates, *War*, p. 189; Wert, "Gettysburg," *CWTI*, 27, 4, pp. 22, 23.

27. *OR*, 27, 2, pp. 296, 357; Diary, Alexander Papers, UNC; Latrobe Diary, VHS; Duffey Diary, VHS; Gallagher, *Fighting For*, pp. 225, 226; Durkin, *John Dooley*, p. 93; Cobb Diary, Cobb-Hunter Papers, UNC; E. P. Reeve Wife, June 22, 1863, Reeve Papers, UNC; Colston, "Gettysburg," Campbell-Colston Papers, UNC; Wert, "Gettysburg," *CWTI*, 27, 4, p. 25.

28. Wert, "Gettysburg," *CWTI*, 27, 4, pp. 23, 25.

29. Diary, Shipp Family Papers, VHS; "Diary," *AHQ*, 18, p. 586; Theodore Fogel–Father and Mother, June 21, 1863, Fogel Papers, EU; Latrobe Diary, VHS; Diary, Alexander Papers, UNC; Harry Lewis–Mother, June 22, 1863, Lewis Papers, UNC; Diary of Robert James Lowry, typed copy, Brake Collection, USAMHI; Moses, "Autobiography," p. 57, UNC.

30. *OR*, 51, 2, p. 725; Maurice, *Aide-de-Camp*, p. 198; Lord, *Fremantle Diary*, p. 181; Moses, "Autobiography," p. 54, UNC; D. H. Hill–Longstreet, May 21, 1885; Longstreet–Osmun Latrobe, May 28, 1886, Latrobe Diary, VHS.

31. *OR*, 27, 3, pp. 913, 915, 923; Maurice, *Aide-de-Camp*, pp. 202–4, 207, 208; Krolick, "Lee/Stuart," *CWQ*, 2, pp. 25, 26; Longstreet–T. T. Munford, November 8, 1891, Munford-Ellis Family Papers, DU.

32. *OR,* 51, 2, p. 726; *Annals,* p. 419; Lord, *Fremantle Diary,* pp. 186–88; Diary, Alexander Papers, UNC; Diary, Kennedy Papers, UNC; Stevens, *Reminiscences,* pp. 105, 106; Green Diary, 129, FSNMP; Savannah *Morning News,* January 8, 1878; Laswell, *Rags and Hope,* p. 176; "Diary," *AHQ,* 18, p. 587.

33. Longstreet, *MA,* p. 334.

34. Powell, *Recollections,* p. 9; Diary of James B. Clifton, typed copy, Brake Collection, USAMHI; Lord, *Fremantle Diary,* pp. 190, 191, 193; Gallagher, *Fighting For,* pp. 228, 229; Sorrel, *Recollections,* pp. 168, 169; "Notations, Gettysburg Report," Wilcox Papers, LC; Freeman, *R. E. Lee,* III, p. 55.

35. Wert, "Gettysburg," *CWTI,* 27, 4, p. 26; Hagerman, *American Civil War,* p. 148; Tucker, *High Tide,* p. 55; A. S. Pendleton–Mother, June 18, 1863, Pendleton Papers, UNC; Benjamin Farinholt–Lelia Farinholt, July 3, 1863, Farinholt Papers, VHS.

36. Owen, *In Camp,* p. 242; Ross, *Cities and Camps,* p. 42; Powhatan B. Whittle–Brother, June 26, 1863, Whittle Papers, UNC; Lord, *Fremantle Diary,* pp. v, 197, 198.

37. Lord, *Fremantle Diary,* pp. 189, 192, 196, 218; Moses, "Autobiography," p. 60, UNC; Longstreet, *MA,* p. 343.

38. Lord, *Fremantle Diary,* pp. 190, 198, 198n.

39. Wert, "Gettysburg," *CWTI,* 27, 4, p. 27; *Annals,* pp. 306, 307.

40. *B & L,* III, p. 249; *Annals,* p. 418; Longstreet, *MA,* p. 333; Sorrel, *Recollections,* p. 152.

41. Longstreet, *MA,* pp. 346, 347; *Annals,* p. 419; Maurice, *Aide-de-Camp,* pp. 218, 219; *B & L,* III, p. 244; Sorrel, *Recollections,* p. 155; John W. Fairfax–Longstreet, November 12, 1877, Fairfax Papers, VHS; Moses, "Autobiography," p. 60, UNC.

42. Longstreet, *MA,* p. 383n; *OR,* 27, ?, p. 948; Longstreet Papers, UNC.

43. Gallagher, *Fighting For,* pp. 222, 230; Lord, *Fremantle Diary,* p. 199; Wert, "Gettysburg," *CWTI,* 27, 4, p. 28; *OR,* 27, 1, p. 60.

44. Wert, "Gettysburg," *CWTI,* 27, 4, p. 29; *Annals,* pp. 420, 439; London *Times,* July 29, 1863.

45. Tucker, *High Tide,* pp. 98–100.

46. McCullough Diaries, McCullough-Hotchkiss Collection, UVA; Latrobe Diary, VHS; Longstreet, *MA,* pp. 351, 352; *Annals,* p. 420; Freeman, *R. E. Lee,* III, pp. 66–67.

47. Longstreet, *MA,* pp. 357, 358; Lord, *Fremantle Diary,* pp. 201, 203.

48. Longstreet, *MA,* p. 358; Wert, "Gettysburg," *CWTI,* 27, 4, pp. 31–43; Taylor, *Four Years,* p. 95; Walter Taylor–John Daniel, July 14, 1903, Daniel Papers, UVA.

49. Longstreet gave different versions of this conversation, so the precise words are impossible to reconstruct. *B & L,* III, p. 339; *Annals,* p. 421; Longstreet, *MA,* pp. 358–59; Taylor, *Four Years,* p. 77.

50. Longstreet, *MA,* p. 358.

51. *Annals,* p. 421.

52. Connelly, *Marble,* p. 206; Taylor, *Four Years,* p. 101; Lord, *Fremantle*

Diary, p. 205; marginal note, p. 576, G. F. R. Henderson, *Stonewall Jackson, Vol II,* Douglas, ANBL.

53. Pfanz, *Gettysburg,* p. 27; Washington *Post,* June 11, 1893; Sears, "Getting Right," *American Heritage,* 42, 3, p. 66; *SHSP,* IV, p. 99; *OR,* 27, 2, pp. 307, 316.

54. *OR,* 27, 2, p. 308.

55. Longstreet, *MA,* pp. 359, 361; *Annals,* pp. 422, 439; Freeman, *R. E. Lee,* III, p. 75–76; Wert, "Gettysburg," *CWTI,* 27, 4, p. 43; Pfanz, *Gettysburg,* p. 28; A. L. Long–Longstreet, April 19, 1876; Jubal Early–A. L. Long, April 3, 1876, Long Papers, UNC; Daniel Papers, UVA; *SHSP,* V, p. 168; Tucker, *High Tide,* p. 215.

56. Lord, *Fremantle Diary,* pp. 204, 205; London *Times,* August 18, 1863; Sanger, "Was Longstreet," *Infantry Journal,* 43, p. 41; Moxley Sorrel–J. B. Walton, July 1, 1863, Walton Papers, TU; *Annals,* p. 439.

13. GETTYSBURG, JULY 2, 1863

1. Longstreet, *MA,* p. 362; Ross, *Cities and Camps,* 48; *Annals,* p. 439; Pfanz, *Gettysburg,* p. 104.

2. Freeman, *R. E. Lee,* III, p. 86; Hood, *Advance,* p. 57.

3. Longstreet–John P. Nicholson, July 15, 1877, Longstreet Papers, HL; *Annals,* p. 422.

4. Longstreet, *MA,* p. 362; *Annals,* p. 422; Samuel Johnston–Lafayette McLaws, June 27, 1892, Johnston Papers, VHS; Clarke file, CSR/NA.

5. Longstreet, *MA,* p. 362; Hood, *Advance,* pp. 56, 57; Pfanz, *Gettysburg,* p. 104; Scheibert, *Seven Months,* pp. 8, 9; Ross, *Cities and Camps,* pp. xiv, 48; Lord, *Fremantle Diary,* p. 205.

6. Hood, *Advance,* p. 57; Scheibert, *Seven Months,* p. 113; Lord, *Fremantle Diary,* p. 206; Hoole, *Lawley,* p. 206; *SHSP,* V, p. 92; London *Times,* August 18, 1863.

7. Samuel Johnston–Lafayette McLaws, July 27, 1892; Samuel Johnston–Fitz Lee, February 11, 16, 1878; Samuel Johnston–George Peterkin, December 26, [?], Johnston Papers, VHS; Pfanz, *Gettysburg,* pp. 106, 107; Greezicki, "Humbugging," *The Gettysburg Magazine,* 6, p. 64.

8. Samuel Johnston–Lafayette McLaws, June 27, 1892; Samuel Johnston–George Peterkin, December 26, [?], Johnston Papers, VHS.

9. Pfanz, *Gettysburg,* p. 107.

10. Lafayette McLaws–Samuel Johnston, June 8, 1892, Johnston Papers, VHS; Moxley Sorrel–Lafayette McLaws, January 30, 1888, McLaws Papers, UNC; Savannah *Morning News,* January 8, 1878; Pfanz, *Gettysburg,* p. 110.

11. Philadelphia *Weekly Press,* February 22, 1888; Savannah *Morning News,* January 8, 1878; Lafayette McLaws–Longstreet, June 12, 1873; McLaws, "Longstreet at Gettysburg," McLaws Papers, UNC; Pfanz, *Gettysburg,* pp. 110, 111.

12. Fitz Lee–Charles Venable, July 30, 1894, Venable Papers, UNC; *Annals,* p. 438; *CV,* 25, p. 212; Long, *Memoirs,* pp. 280–82; Pfanz, *Gettysburg,* pp. 111–12.

13. Longstreet, *MA,* pp. 364, 365; *Annals,* p. 422; *B & L,* III, p. 340; Pfanz, *Gettysburg,* pp. 112, 113, 114.

14. Sorrel, *Recollections,* p. 157; Hood, *Advance,* p. 57.

15. Longstreet–Lafayette McLaws, July 25, 1873, McLaws Papers, UNC.

16. Ibid.

17. Gallagher, *Fighting For,* pp. 233, 234; E. P. Alexander–Frederick Colston, July 22, 1903, Campbell-Colston Family Papers, UNC.

18. Gallagher, *Fighting For,* pp. 234, 277; E. P. Alexander–Frederick Colston, October 28, 1903, Campbell-Colston Family Papers, UNC.

19. *OR,* 27, pt. 2, p. 318; Gallagher, *Fighting For,* pp. 233, 234; Scheibert, *Seven Months,* p. 118; Sears, "Getting Right," *American Heritage,* 42, 3, p. 64.

20. Philadelphia *Press,* August 11, 1888; Scheibert, *Seven Months,* p. 118; Tucker, *Lee and Longstreet,* pp. 241, 242.

21. Sorrel, *Recollections,* p. 157.

22. Krolick, "Lee and Longstreet," *CWQ,* 5, pp. 38, 39; *B & L,* III, pp. 358, 359; Gallagher, *Fighting For,* pp. 235–37; Diary, Alexander Papers, UNC; *SHSP,* 5, pp. 49, 202; 6, p. 101.

23. Pfanz, *Gettysburg,* pp. 105, 112, 113; Krolick, "Lee and Longstreet," *CWQ,* 5, p. 39; Samuel Johnston–Fitz Lee, February 11, 1878, Johnston Papers, VHS.

24. Pfanz, *Gettysburg,* pp. 105, 114, 116.

25. Pfanz, *Gettysburg,* pp. 118–21; Savannah *Morning News,* January 8, 1878; McLaws, "Longstreet at Gettysburg," McLaws Papers, UNC; *OR,* 27, pt. 2, p. 358; Diary of Thomas L. Ware, Brake Collection, USAMHI.

26. Pfanz, *Gettysburg,* pp. 119–21; Savannah *Morning News,* January 8, 1878; *Annals,* pp. 422, 423; Meyers, "Kershaw's Brigade at," Kershaw's Brigade File, GNMP.

27. Samuel Johnston–McLaws, June 27, 1892, Samuel Johnston–Fitz Lee, February 11, 1878, Johnston Papers, VHS; McLaws, "Longstreet at Gettysburg," newspaper clipping, n.d., McLaws Papers, UNC; Pfanz, *Gettysburg,* p. 490n.

28. A map of the route is in Pfanz, *Gettysburg,* p. 120; Pfanz, *Gettysburg,* pp. 121, 122; Savannah *Morning News,* January 8, 1878; George W. Peterkin–William Pendleton, June 12, 1873, Pendleton Papers, UNC; Map, McLaws Papers, UNC.

29. Savannah *Morning News,* January 8, 1878.

30. Ibid.; Lafayette McLaws–Wife, July 7, 1863, McLaws Papers, UNC; Wert, "Gettysburg," *CWTI,* 27, 4, p. 47.

31. Pfanz, *Gettysburg,* pp. 151–52; *B & L,* III, pp. 332, 333; Map, McLaws Papers, UNC; Gallagher, *Fighting For,* p. 224.

32. Lafayette McLaws–Wife, July 7, 1863; "Longstreet at Gettysburg," McLaws Papers, UNC; Savannah *Morning News,* January 8, 1878; Philadelphia *Weekly Press,* February 15, 1888.

33. *B & L,* III, pp. 340–41; John Fairfax–Longstreet, November 12, 1877, Fairfax Papers, VHS; William Youngblood–Longstreet, September 5, 1893, Longstreet Papers, EU; Pfanz, *Gettysburg,* pp. 153–54, 497n.

34. Savannah *Morning News,* January 8, 1878; McLaws, "Longstreet at Gettysburg," McLaws Papers, UNC.

35. *B & L,* III, p. 359; Gallagher, *Fighting For,* pp. 237, 239; *CV,* 21, p. 434; Dickert, *History,* p. 235.

36. Pfanz, *Gettysburg,* pp. 158–63; Brake Collection, USAMHI; Hood, *Advance,* p. 57; Map, Bachelder Papers, NHHS.

37. Pfanz, *Gettysburg,* pp. 163–65; Sorrel, *Recollections,* p. 160; Hood, *Advance,* pp. 57–58; John Fairfax–Longstreet, November 12, 1877, Fairfax Papers, VHS.

38. Washington *Post,* June 11, 1893; *CV,* 23, p. 552; Ross, *Cities and Camps,* p. 52, Pfanz, *Gettysburg,* p. 165.

39. Fitzgerald, *Judge Longstreet,* p. 19.

40. Dickert, *History,* p. 234.

41. Ibid.; Wert, "Gettysburg," *CWTI,* 27, 4, pp. 47–48; Longstreet–W. Y. Ripley, July 14, 1888, Ripley Papers, DU; Bass, Letter, vol. 129, FSNMP; John Haskell–E. P. Alexander, September 7, 1901, Alexander Papers, UNC.

42. Wert, "Gettysburg," *CWTI,* 27, 4, pp. 47–51; D. M. Dubose–E. P. Alexander, August 23, 1899, Alexander Papers, UNC; Powell, *Recollections,* p. 16; Rozier, *Granite,* p. 118.

43. Gettysburg Clipping Books, 4, GNMP; Wyckoff, "Kershaw's Brigade," *Gettysburg Magazine,* 5, p. 41; *B & L,* III, pp. 334–35; Joseph B. Kershaw–John B. Bachelder, March 27, 1876, Bachelder Papers, NHHS; "Reminiscences," FSNMP, 161.

44. Longstreet, *MA,* p. 370; Tucker, *High Tide,* p. 276; Stiles, *Four Years,* p. 64; Gerald Barksdale Brigade File, GNMP; Winschel, "Barksdale's Brigade," *Gettysburg Magazine,* 1, p. 71; Krick, *Parker's Virginia Battery,* p. 174; Benjamin G. Humphreys–Lafayette McLaws, January 6, 1878, McLaws Papers, UNC.

45. Benjamin G. Humphreys–John B. Bachelder, May 1, 1876, Bachelder Papers, NHHS; Longstreet, *MA,* p. 370; Tucker, *High Tide,* p. 276; Wert, "Gettysburg," *CWTI,* 27, 4, pp. 51–52; Benjamin G. Humphreys–Lafayette McLaws, January 6, 1878, McLaws Papers, UNC; Pfanz, *Gettysburg,* p. 338.

46. Krick, *Parker's Virginia Battery,* p. 174; Goode Bryan–Lafayette McLaws, December 10, 1877, McLaws Papers, UNC; Joseph B. Kershaw–John B. Bachelder, April 3, 1876, Bachelder Papers, NHHS; *B & L,* III, pp. 334–37; Gallagher, *Fighting For,* pp. 239, 240; Colston, "Gettysburg," Campbell-Colston Papers, UNC; Busey and Martin, *Regimental Strengths,* p. 130; *OR,* 27, 1, p. 417; Wert, "Gettysburg," *CWTI,* 27, 4, p. 52.

47. London *Times,* August 18, 1863.

48. William Youngblood–Longstreet, September 5, 1893, Longstreet Papers, EU; Polley, *Hood's Texas Brigade,* p. 194.

49. Lafayette McLaws–Emily, July 7, 1863, McLaws Papers, UNC.

50. *Annals,* p. 425; Benning Papers, UNC.

51. Longstreet–Lafayette McLaws, July 25, 1873, McLaws Papers, UNC; *Annals,* p. 424.

52. William Youngblood–Longstreet, September 5, 1893, Longstreet Papers, EU; *Annals,* pp. 425, 426; Goode Bryan–Lafayette McLaws, December

10, 1877; Benjamin G. Humphreys–Lafayette McLaws, January 6, 1878, McLaws Papers, UNC; Pfanz, *Gettysburg,* chapter 16; Philadelphia *Weekly Press,* April 21, 1886.

53. *OR,* 27, pt. 2, pp. 338–40; Lafayette McLaws–Emily, July 7, 1863, McLaws Papers, UNC; *Annals,* p. 425; Pfanz, *Gettysburg,* p. 425; Latrobe Diary, VHS; Moore, *Life,* p. 153; Gallagher, *Fighting For,* p. 242; Busey and Martin, *Regimental Strengths,* pp. 31, 46, 56.

54. Wert, "Gettysburg," *CWTI,* 27, 4, pp. 54, 55.

55. Ibid., pp. 54–55; *Annals,* p. 311; Lord, *Fremantle Diary,* p. 208, *SHSP,* 5, p. 91.

56. Gallagher, *Fighting For,* p. 278; McLaws, "Longstreet at Gettysburg," McLaws Papers, UNC; Sanger and Hay, *James Longstreet,* pp. 175, 176; Sanger, "Was Longstreet," *Infantry Jounral,* 43, p. 42; Pfanz, Gettysburg, pp. 425–27.

57. *OR,* 27, pt. 2, p. 320.

14. "NEVER WAS I SO DEPRESSED"

1. Georg and Busey, *Nothing but Glory,* pp. 19, 226; James Kemper–E. P. Alexander, September 30, 1869, Dearborn Collection, HU; Harrison, *Pickett's Men,* p. 87; Inman, *Soldier,* p. 53.

2. Harrison, *Pickett's Men,* p. 88; Inman, *Soldier,* p. 53.

3. Harrison, *Pickett's Men,* pp. 88–89.

4. Shevchuk, "The Lost Hours," *Gettysburg Magazine,* 4, p. 70; Wert, "Gettysburg," *CWTI,* 27, 4, p. 56; Tucker, *Lee and Longstreet,* p. 205.

5. Tucker, *Lee and Longstreet,* pp. 197, 205, 206; Gallagher, *Fighting For,* p. 228; Sorrel, *Recollections,* pp. 153, 154, Maurice, *Aide-de-Camp,* p. 222; Longstreet, *MA,* pp. 341–43; *OR,* 27, 2, p. 321.

6. *OR,* 27, 2, p. 320; Shevchuk, "The Lost Hours," *Gettysburg Magazine,* 4, p. 71.

7. Longstreet, *MA,* p. 385; Ross, *Cities and Camps,* pp. 55, 56.

8. Longstreet, *MA,* p. 385; Gallagher, *Fighting For,* p. 244.

9. Georg and Busey, *Nothing but Glory,* pp. 19, 23; Stewart, *Pickett's Charge,* p. 21; John or William Cocke–Parents and Sister, July 11, 1863, Cocke Family Papers, VHS.

10. Longstreet, *MA,* pp. 385–86; *OR,* 27, 2, p. 359; *Annals,* p. 429; *B & L,* III, pp. 342–43; Longstreet–Lafayette McLaws, July 25, 1875, Lafayette McLaws Papers, UNC.

11. Longstreet, *MA,* pp. xxiv–xxv.

12. Longstreet–J. Van Holt Nash, October 30, 1902, copy, Taylor Papers, VSL; *Annals,* p. 429.

13. *Annals,* pp. 429, 433; Longstreet, *MA,* 387.

14. *CV,* 1, p. 246; Long, *Memoirs,* p. 288; Lord, *Fremantle Diary,* p. 210.

15. Wert, "Gettysburg," *CWTI,* 27, 4, pp. 57, 59; Busey and Martin, *Regimental Strengths,* pp. 172–79; Hassler, *Crisis,* pp. 144–45.

16. Wert, "Gettysburg," *CWTI,* 27, 4, pp. 57, 59; Gayle, Diary, Ninth Virginia Infantry File, GNMP; Georg and Busey, *Nothing but Glory,* pp. 23–

25; Harrison, *Pickett's Men,* p. 90; Isaac Trimble–John B. Bachelder, n.d., Bachelder Papers, NHHS.

17. Wert, "Gettysburg," *CWTI,* 27, 4, p. 59; Krolick, "Lee and Longstreet," *CWQ,* 5, p. 40; Gettysburg Clipping Books, 6, GNMP; Longstreet–H. Heth, February 14, 1897, Longstreet Papers, MC.

18. Coddington, *Gettysburg Campaign,* pp. 489–91.

19. Ibid., pp. 489–90; Krolick, "Lee and Longstreet," *CWQ,* 5, p. 40; *OR,* 27, pt. 2, pp. 359, 608; Harrison, *Pickett's Men,* pp. 91, 92.

20. Longstreet, *MA,* p. 388.

21. E. P. Alexander–Frederick Colston, January 14, 1895, Campbell-Colston Family Papers, UNC; Harrison, *Pickett's Men,* pp. 91–92; *Annals,* pp. 431–32; Coddington, *Gettysburg Campaign,* pp. 491–92.

22. Longstreet–H. Heth, February 14, 1897, Longstreet Papers, MC; Harrison, *Pickett's Men,* p. 91; W. H. Taylor–Sister, July 7, 1863, Taylor Papers, VSL; Dawson, *Reminiscences,* p. 96; *CV,* 34, p. 209; Edmund Berkeley–John Daniel, September 26, [?], Daniel Papers, UVA; V. A. Topscott–Robert A. Bright, January 7, 1904, Southall Papers, WM.

23. "E. P. Alexander," *CWTI,* 17, 1, p. 23.

24. Ibid.; Gallagher, *Fighting For,* pp. 244, 253, 254, 332; *B & L,* III, pp. 361, 362; Inman, *Soldier,* p. 69.

25. "E. P. Alexander," *CWTI,* 17, 1, p. 24; Coddington, *Gettysburg Campaign,* pp. 487–88.

26. Gallagher, *Fighting For,* pp. 254–55; "E. P. Alexander," *CWTI,* 17, 1, p. 24.

27. Longstreet, *MA,* p. 390; *OR,* 51, pt. 2, p. 733; C. H. C. Brown–J. B. Walton, n.d., Walton Papers, TU; Owen, *In Camp,* p. 253, Houghton, *Two Boys,* p. 34.

28. London *Times,* August 18, 1863; Wert, "Gettysburg," *CWTI,* 27, 4, p. 60; Dawson, *Reminiscences,* p. 95; James Kemper–E. P. Alexander, September 20, 1869, Dearborn Collection, HU; Lewis, "Recollections," GNMP.

29. James Kemper–E. P. Alexander, September 20, 1869, Dearborn Collection, HU.

30. Dawson, *Reminiscences,* pp. 95–96; *CV,* 27, p. 116; Gettysburg Clipping Books, 4, GNMP.

31. Blackford, *Letters,* p. 187; *Annals,* p. 430.

32. "E. P. Alexander," *CWTI,* 17, 1, p. 24.

33. Sorrel, *Recollections,* p. 48; Lord, *Fremantle Diary,* p. 197.

34. Longstreet, *MA,* p. 392; *Annals,* p. 431; Inman, *Soldier,* p. 60; Sorrel, *Recollections,* p. 162; Gallagher, *Fighting For,* p. 260.

35. Longstreet, *MA,* p. 392; Gallagher, *Fighting For,* p. 261; *OR,* 27, pt. 2, p. 360; *Annals,* p. 431; Coddington, *Gettysburg Campaign,* pp. 500–501.

36. Gallagher, *Fighting For,* p. 261; Haskell, *Memoirs,* p. 50; *OR,* 27, pt. 2, p. 360.

37. Thomas R. Friend–C. Pickett, December 10, 1894, Charles Pickett Papers, VHS; Gettysburg Clipping Books, 6, GNMP, Davis, "The Death and Burials," *Gettysburg Magazine,* 5, p. 111; Baltimore *Sun,* December 28, 1903.

38. James L. Kemper–W. H. Swallow, February 4, 1886, typed copy, Bachelder Papers, NHHS; Edmund Berkeley–John Daniel, September 26, [?], Daniel Papers, UVA; James Kemper–E. P. Alexander, September 20, 1869; Dearborn Collection, HU; *OR,* 27, pt. 1, p. 417; *B & L,* III, p. 346; R. A. Bright–Charles Pickett, October 15, 1892, Pickett Papers, VHS; Longstreet–Editor, Richmond *Times,* April 22, 1896; Johnston Papers, UVA; Longstreet, *MA,* pp. 393–95; Lord, *Fremantle Diary,* p. 212; "Notations, Gettysburg Report," Wilcox Papers, LC.

39. Wert, "Gettysburg," *CWTI,* 27, 4, pp. 61–64.

40. Ibid., pp. 64–65; *Annals,* p. 431; Lord, *Fremantle Diary,* pp. 212–15; Thomas Goree–Longstreet, May 17, 1875, Longstreet Papers, EU; Lafayette McLaws–Braxton Bragg, April 22, 1864; McLaws Papers, WRHS; "Gettysburg," McLaws Papers, DU; Sorrel, *Recollections,* pp. 163–64; Piston, Ph.D. Diss., p. 261; Philadelphia *Weekly Press,* April 21, 1886.

41. Duffey Papers, VHS; McDonald, *Make Me,* p. 158; Lord, *Fremantle Diary,* p. 219; Freeman, *R. E. Lee,* III, pp. 132–33; W. J. Kincheloe–Sister, July 10, 1863; Daniel Papers, VUA; Wert, "Gettysburg," *CWTI,* 27, 4, p. 68.

42. Wert, "Gettysburg," *CWTI,* 27, 4, pp. 66–68; London *Times,* August 18, 1863; Latrobe Diary, VHS; Diary, Alexander Papers, UNC.

43. J. F. Coghill–Pappy, Ma, and Mit, July 17, 1863, Coghill Papers, UNC; Lane, *Dear Mother,* p. 259.

44. Theodore Fogel–Sister, July 16, 1863, Fogel Papers, EU; McNeill Letters, GNMP; Fleming, *Memoir,* no page number; Rozier, *Granite Farm,* p. 115; Gettysburg Clipping Books, 6, GNMP; Kennedy Papers, UNC.

45. Freeman, *Lee's Dispatches,* p. 110.

46. Gallagher, *Fighting For,* pp. 92, 120; *OR,* pt. 2, p. 309.

47. Longstreet–Louis T. Wigfall, August 2, 1863, Wigfall Papers, LC.

48. *Annals,* p. 415.

49. Longstreet, *MA,* p. 384; other examples of his criticisms of the campaign and battle can be found in *Annals,* pp. 414–46, 619–33; *B & L,* III, pp. 244–51, 339–54.

50. E. P. Alexander–Mr. Bancroft, October 30, 1904, Longstreet Papers, DU.

51. Washington *Post,* June 11, 1893.

52. Longstreet–D. E. Sickles, September 19, 1902, typed copy, Longstreet Papers, HSP.

53. Goree, *Letters,* pp. 288–89; Thomas Goree–Longstreet, May 17, 1875; Erasmus Taylor–Longstreet, September 10, 1889, Longstreet Papers, EU; Taylor, "War Reminiscences," VHS; Longstreet–Lafayette McLaws, July 25, 1873, McLaws, UNC.

54. "Survivor of Charge Defends Longstreet," Buffalo *Evening News,* July 5, 1938, copy of clipping in author's collection.

15. "LONGSTREET IS THE MAN"

1. *CMH,* III, pp. 1200–1201; Taylor, "War Reminiscences," VHS.

2. Latrobe Diary, VHS; Sorrel, *Recollections,* p. 174.

3. Latrobe Diary, VHS; Diary, Alexander Papers, UNC; Longstreet, *MA,*

p. 431; Long, *Civil War,* pp. 388–94; Theodore Fogel–Father and Mother, July 25, August 9, 1863, Fogel Papers, EU.

4. Latrobe Diary, VHS; Freeman, *Lee's Dispatches,* pp. 122–24; *B & L,* III, p. 745; J. B. Walton–William Pendleton, August 22, 1863, Walton Papers, TU.

5. Sorrel, *Recollections,* pp. 174–75; Latrobe Diary, VHS; Lee, *Recollections,* pp. 109–10.

6. *OR,* 51, pt. 2, pp. 752–53.

7. Ibid., 29, pt. 2, pp. 639, 640.

8. Longstreet–Louis T. Wigfall, August 18, 1863, Wigfall Papers, LC; Longstreet, *MA,* p. 434.

9. Longstreet–Louis T. Wigfall, August 18, 1863, Wigfall Papers, LC.

10. Piston, Ph.D. Diss., p. 270.

11. Cozzens, *This Terrible Sound,* pp. 28–29, 59; *OR,* 51, pt. 2, p. 761.

12. Davis, *Jefferson Davis,* p. 516; Longstreet, *MA,* p. 435.

13. Longstreet–R. E. Lee, September 2, 1863, Longstreet Papers, GDAH.

14. *OR,* 29, pt. 2, p. 699.

15. Connelly, *Autumn,* p. 151; other historians who share this view of Longstreet's ambition included Freeman, *Lee's Lieutenants,* III, p. 222; Connelly and Jones, *Politics,* p. 69; Eckenrode and Conrad, *James Longstreet,* p. 220; Piston, *Lee's Tarnished Lieutenant,* p. 66.

16. Cozzens, *This Terrible Sound,* p. 59; Skoch, "A Test," *CWTI,* 25, 8, p. 14.

17. Cozzens, *This Terrible Sound,* pp. 59–60; Skoch, "A Test," *CWTI,* 25, 8, pp. 12, 14, 15; "Diary," *AHQ,* 18, p. 595; Sorrel, *Recollections,* p. 180; Taylor, *General Lee,* p. 223.

18. Latrobe Diary, VHS; *Atlanta Constitution,* April 1, 1883.

19. Latrobe Diary, VHS; Skoch, "A Test," *CWTI,* 25, 8, p. 15; *OR,* 51, pt. 2, p. 766.

20. Sword, *Embrace,* pp. 10–11, McMurry, *John Bell Hood,* pp. 75–76.

21. *OR,* 29, pt. 2, pp. 713–14.

22. Longstreet–Louis T. Wigfall, September 12, 1863, Wigfall Papers, LC.

23. Lafayette McLaws–Wife, September 19, 1863, McLaws Papers, UNC; Polley, *Hood's Texas Brigade,* pp. 198–99; Bond and Coward, *South Carolinians,* p. 83; Graves, *History,* pp. 33–34; Gallagher, *Fighting For,* pp. 286, 287.

24. Robertson, "Rails," *CWM,* 9, 6, p. 55; Houghton, *Two Boys,* p. 138; W. S. Shephard–Samuel Cooper, September 6, 1883, Benning Papers, UNC; Longstreet, *MA,* pp. 436, 437.

25. *OR,* 30, pt. 2, p. 287; Longstreet, *MA,* pp. 437–38; Sorrel, *Recollections,* p. 183; Latrobe Diary, VHS.

26. *OR,* 30, pt. 2, p. 287; Sorrel, *Recollections,* pp. 183–84; Cozzens, *This Terrible Sound,* pp. 128, 301; Longstreet, *MA,* p. 438.

27. Warner, *Generals in Gray,* p. 30; Davis, *Jefferson Davis,* p. 158.

28. Connelly, *Autumn,* pp. 70–71.

29. Ibid.

30. Ibid., pp. 71–72.

31. Ibid., chapter 8.
32. Ibid., p. 193; Lane, *Dear Mother,* p. 154; Cozzens, *This Terrible Sound,* pp. 172–73.
33. Connelly, *Autumn,* pp. 201–7.
34. Cozzens, *This Terrible Sound,* pp. 299–300; Warner, *Generals in Gray,* pp. 242–43.
35. Cozzens, *This Terrible Sound,* pp. 299–301.
36. Ibid., pp. 300–302; Sorrel, *Recollections,* p. 184; *OR,* 30, pt. 2, pp. 287–88.
37. Longstreet, *MA,* p. 439; *OR,* 30, pt. 2, pp. 288, 363; Hood, *Advance,* p. 63; Cozzens, *This Terrible Sound,* pp. 315–17.
38. *OR,* 30, pt. 2, p. 288; Cozzens, *This Terrile Sound,* pp. 315–16, 368; Connelly, *Autumn,* p. 222.
39. *OR,* 30, pt. 2, p. 288; Humphreys, "A History," Claiborne Papers, UNC; Longstreet, *MA,* p. 439; Cozzens, *This Terrible Sound,* p. 316.
40. Longstreet, *MA,* pp. 439–40; Cozzens, *This Terrible Sound,* p. 316.
41. Longstreet–E. P. Alexander, June 17, 1869, Alexander Papers, UNC; Atlanta *Constitution,* April 1, 1883.
42. Longstreet–E. P. Alexander, June 17, 1869, Alexander Papers, UNC.
43. *OR,* 30, pt. 2, p. 288; Longstreet, *MA,* pp. 445, 447; Cozzens, *This Terrible Sound,* pp. 305–10, 368–69; Connelly, *Autumn,* pp. 218–20.
44. Cozzens, *This Terrible Sound,* pp. 357–69.
45. Ibid., pp. 368–75; *OR,* 30, pt. 2, p. 288; Minnich, "Pegram's Confederate Brigade," TU.
46. Letter of Lieutenant James H. Fraser, September 26, 1863, "Southerners View," CCNMP; Cozzens, *This Terrible Sound,* p. 376.
47. Cozzens, *This Terrible Sound,* pp. 376–96, 433–34.
48. Ibid., p. 398.
49. Ibid., pp. 406–11; Theodore Fogel–Father and Mother, September 20, 1863, Fogel Papers, EU; Sorrel, *Recollections,* p. 194; Benning Papers, UNC.
50. Thomas Claiborne–James S. Fullerton, April 16, 1891, Historical Files, CCNMP; *CV,* 21, p. 302.
51. Cozzens, *This Terrible Sound,* pp. 411–12; Polley, *Hood's Texas Brigade,* p. 199; *OR,* 30, pt. 2, p. 288; Humphrey's, "A History," pp. 15, 16, Claiborne Papers, UNC.
52. Humphreys, "A History," p. 16, Claiborne Papers, UNC.
53. Cozzens, *This Terrible Sound,* pp. 9, 406–16.
54. Ibid., pp. 424–31, 434, 446–53; Humphreys, "A History," p. 17, Claiborne Papers, UNC.
55. Longstreet, *MA,* p. 450.
56. Ibid., pp. 450–51; Cozzens, *This Terrible Sound,* p. 455.
57. Longstreet, *MA,* p. 451; Sorrel, *Recollections,* p. 196.
58. Owen, *In Camp and Battle,* pp. 281–82.
59. Cozzens, *This Terrible Sound,* pp. 454–55; *OR,* 30, pt. 2, p. 289; Thomas Claiborne–James S. Fullerton, April 16, 1891, Historical Files, CCNMP.

60. Longstreet, *MA,* p. 42; Longstreet–D. H. Hill, July 5, 1884, Hill Papers, VSL.

61. The best and most detailed study of the final Confederate assaults at Chickamauga can be found in Cozzens, *This Terrible Sound,* chapters 27–30.

62. Ibid., pp. 464–66; Longstreet, *MA,* p. 453; Thomas Claiborne–James S. Fullerton, April 16, 1891, Historical Files, CCNMP.

63. Sorrel, *Recollections,* p. 192; Cozzens, *This Terrible Sound,* pp. 496–97.

64. Longstreet, *MA,* p. 455; Cozzens, *This Terrible Sound,* pp. 512–14; Connelly, *Autumn,* pp. 227–28.

65. Longstreet, *MA,* p. 461; Sorrel, *Recollections,* p. 187; *OR,* 30 pt. 2, pp. 289–90.

66. *OR,* 30, pt. 2, p. 37; Connelly, *Autumn,* p. 230.

67. Cozzens, *This Terrible Sound,* pp. 519–20; N. B. Forrest–L. Polk, September 21, 1863, Longstreet Papers, GDAH.

68. Dawson, *Reminiscences,* pp. 101–2; McLaws, "After Chickamauga," p. 50, McLaws Papers, UNC.

69. *OR,* 30, pt. 2, p. 290; Latrobe Diary, VHS.

70. London *Times,* November 24, 1863; Cozzens, *This Terrible Sound,* p. 534; Grantham, "Letters," *GHQ,* 40, p. 186; Laswell, *Rags and Hope,* p. 203.

71. Atlanta *Constitution,* April 1, 1883; Longstreet, *MA,* p. 460; *OR,* 30, pt. 2, p. 290.

72. Younger, *Inside,* pp. 115–16; London *Times,* November 24, 1863.

73. *OR,* 29, pt. 2, p. 749.

74. Eckenrode and Conrad, *James Longstreet,* p. 238; Piston, *Lee's Tarnished Lieutenant,* p. 72.

75. Tucker, "Longstreet," *CWTI,* 1, 1, p. 44.

16. "NOTHING BUT THE HAND OF GOD CAN SAVE US"

1. Sorrel, *Recollections,* p. 191; Ratchford, *Recollections,* p. 35; Mackall, *Recollections,* pp. 178–79.

2. Mackall, *Recollections,* pp. 178–79.

3. Blackford, *Letters,* p. 224.

4. *OR,* 30, pt. 2, pp. 47, 54; Connelly, *Autumn,* pp. 177–84, 236–37; Lafayette McLaws–Marcus J. Wright, June 7, 1882, McLaws Papers, UNC; Mackall, *Recollections,* p. 178.

5. *OR,* 30, pt. 4, pp. 705–6, 708; Longstreet, *MA,* p. 464; Connelly, *Autumn,* p. 237; Cozzens, *This Terrible Sound,* p. 531.

6. Longstreet, *MA,* pp. 464–65; Lafayette McLaws–Marcus J. Wright, June 7, 1882, McLaws Papers, UNC.

7. *OR,* 30, pt. 4, pp. 705–6.

8. McLaws, "After Chickamauga," p. 59, McLaws Papers, UNC.

9. Mackall, *Recollections,* p. 183; *OR,* 30, pt. 4, p. 742.

10. Longstreet, *MA,* p. 465; Longstreet–Marcus Wright, August 22, 1892,

Longstreet Papers, HL; McLaws, "After Chickamauga," p. 57, McLaws Papers, UNC.

11. Mackall, *Recollections,* pp. 181–82; Cozzens, *This Terrible Sound,* p. 532.

12. Davis, *Jefferson Davis,* pp. 518–19; Cozzens, *This Terrible Sound,* pp. 530, 532; *OR,* 30, pt. 4, p. 728.

13. Davis, *Jefferson Davis,* pp. 518–19; Longstreet, *MA,* p. 465; Jefferson Davis–B. Bragg, June 29, 1872, Dawson Papers, NYHS; Longstreet–E. P. Alexander, August 26, 1902, Alexander Papers, UNC; Mackall, *Recollections,* p. 183.

14. Longstreet–E. P. Alexander, August 26, 1902, Alexander Papers, UNC; Blackford, *Letters,* p. 221; Longstreet, *MA,* pp. 465–66.

15. Longstreet–E. P. Alexander, August 26, 1902, Alexander Papers, UNC; Longstreet, *MA,* pp. 465–66.

16. Theodore Fogel–Father and Mother, October 14, 1863, Fogel Papers, EU; Longstreet, *MA,* pp. 466–68; Longstreet–Lafayette McLaws, July 25, 1873, McLaws Papers, UNC.

17. Davis, *Jefferson Davis,* pp. 518, 521; *OR,* 30, pt. 4, p. 742; Connelly, *Autumn,* p. 254; Longstreet–D. H. Hill, July 6, 1885, Hill Papers, VSL; Jefferson Davis–B. Bragg, June 29, 1872, Dawson Papers, NYHS; Sorrel, *Recollections,* p. 192.

18. Cozzens, *This Terrible Sound,* p. 533; Davis, *Jefferson Davis,* pp. 521–22; Connelly, *Autumn,* pp. 248–53; Mackall, *Recollections,* pp. 183–84, 186.

19. Connelly, *Autumn,* pp. 160, 251; Tower, *A Carolinian,* pp. 127–28; Piston, Ph.D. Diss., p. 287.

20. Connelly, *Autumn,* p. 233.

21. Ibid., pp. 233, 255; Robertson, "Rails," *CWM,* 9, 6, p. 50; McDonough, *Chattanooga,* pp. 45–47.

22. Gallagher, *Fighting For,* p. 311; Blackford, *Letters,* p. 209; Krick, *Parker's Virginia Battery,* pp. 220, 221; Diary, Alexander Papers, UNC; *CV,* 31, p. 424; Report, Francis Dawson, January 2, 1864, Dawson file, CSR/NA.

23. *OR,* 31, 1, pp. 216, 224; Connelly, *Autumn,* p. 255; Longstreet–Lafayette McLaws, October 7, 1863, McLaws Papers, UNC.

24. *OR,* 31, 1, p. 216; Oates, *War,* pp. 270, 271; Diary, *AHQ,* 18, pp. 597–98; Gallagher, *Fighting For,* p. 301.

25. McDonough, *Chattanooga,* pp. 48–50, 58; Theodore Fogel–Father and Mother, October 14, 21, 1863, Fogel Papers, EU; Minnich, "Pegram's Confederate Brigade," p. 47, TU.

26. Longstreet, *MA,* p. 471; Connelly, *Autumn,* p. 255; Owen, *In Camp and Battle,* pp. 289–90; Longstreet–Osmun Latrobe, May 28, 1886, Latrobe Diary, VHS; R. L. Longstreet–F. R. Longstreet, September 3, 1947, Longstreet Papers, CRL.

27. McDonough, *Chattanooga,* pp. 49, 54–55.

28. Ibid., pp. 55–58.

29. Law, "Lookout Valley," Carman Papers, NYPL.

30. Ibid.; *OR,* 31, pt. 1, p. 224.

31. Law, "Lookout Valley," Carman Papers, NYPL; *OR,* 31, pt. 1, pp. 40, 78, 79, 80, 84, 224–25; "Diary," *AHQ,* 18, p. 599.

32. McLaws, "After Chickamauga," pp. 60, 61, 69; McLaws–Marcus J. Wright, June 7, 1882, McLaws Papers, UNC; McLaws–E. M. Law, fragment of letter, n.d., McLaws Papers, DU; Law, "Lookout Valley," Carman Papers, NYPL.

33. Longstreet, *MA,* pp. 471, 473, 474; Connelly, *Autumn,* pp. 256–57; McDonough, *Chattanooga,* p. 85.

34. *OR,* 31, pt. 1, p. 220; McLaws, "After Chickamauga," pp. 63, 69, McLaws Papers, UNC; Connelly, *Autumn,* pp. 257–58.

35. McDonough, *Chattanooga,* p. 85; Longstreet, *MA,* p. 474; *OR,* 31, pt. 1, 217; Connelly, *Autumn,* p. 259.

36. *OR,* 31, pt. 1, pp. 92, 93, 94, 217; Longstreet, *MA,* pp. 474, 475; Law, "Lookout Valley," Carman Papers, NYPL.

37. *OR,* 31, pt. 1, p. 217; Longstreet, *MA,* pp. 475–76; McDonough, *Chattanooga,* pp. 85–87; Connelly, *Autumn,* pp. 259–60.

38. *OR,* 31, pt. 1, pp. 114, 218 232; "Copy of a letter . . . James E. Mix, Adjutant, 137th New York," Carman Papers, NYPL; *CV,* 16, p. 638.

39. *OR,* 31, pt. 1, pp. 76, 94, 113–15, 218, 232–33; *CV,* 16, p. 638; "Copy of a letter . . . James E. Mix, Adjutant, 137th New York," Carman Papers, NYPL.

40. *OR,* 31, pt. 1, pp. 94, 225–34; D. B.–Crounse, October 29, 1863; Law, "Lookout Valley," Carman Papers, NYPL; "Diary," *AHQ,* 18, p. 599.

41. Swanson and Johnson, "Conflict," *CWH,* 31, 2, p. 106; *OR,* 31, pt. 1, pp. 219, 227–28, 232–33.

42. *OR,* 31, pt. 1, pp. 218–19; Longstreet–Lafayette McLaws, October 18, 1863, McLaws Papers, UNC.

43. Polley, *Hood's Texas Brigade,* pp. 213, 215; endorsement by McLaws on letter of Longstreet–Lafayette McLaws, October 18, 1863, McLaws Papers, UNC; *OR,* 31, pt. 1, pp. 218, 219.

44. *OR,* 31, 1, pp. 466–67; J. B. Robertson–Henry Benning, November 4, 1863, Benning Papers, UNC.

45. *OR,* 31, pt. 1, p. 455; Longstreet, *MA,* p. 481; Connelly, *Autumn,* pp. 262, 263.

46. *OR,* 31, pt. 1, pp. 455, 474; Longstreet, *MA,* pp. 484–85; Connelly, *Autumn,* p. 264.

47. *OR,* 31, pt. 1, pp. 455, 456, 474; pt. 3, p. 644; Connelly, *Autumn,* pp. 263–64; Longstreet, *MA,* pp. 481, 484–85.

48. Connelly, *Autumn,* p. 263.

49. *OR,* 31, pt. 1, p. 478; pt. 3, pp. 634, 637; Longstreet–E. P. Alexander, November 4, 1863, Dearborn Collection, HU; Diary, Alexander Papers, UNC.

17. KNOXVILLE

1. *OR Atlas,* plate 24 3; Diary, Alexander Papers, UNC; Latrobe Diary, VHS.

2. *OR,* 31, pt. 3, p. 670; Latrobe Diary, VHS; L. M. Blackford–Father, November 13, 1863, Blackford Papers, UVA.

3. Latrobe Diary, VHS; Diary, Alexander Papers, UNC; Dickert, *History,* p. 299; Longstreet, *MA,* p. 486.

4. *OR,* 31, pt. 1, p. 477; pt. 3, p. 670.

5. Ibid., pt. 1, pp. 476–77; clipping from Charleston *Courier,* December 9, 1863, Alexander Papers, UNC.

6. *OR,* 31, pt. 1, p. 476; pt. 3, p. 635.

7. Ibid., pt. 3, pp. 680, 681, 686, 687.

8. Ibid., pt. 1, pp. 288–89, 291–92, 339, 403, 671; *OR Atlas,* plate 24, 3; Marvel, *Burnside,* p. 295.

9. *OR,* 31, pt. 1, pp. 456, 457; pt. 3, p. 687; Diary, Alexander Papers, UNC.

10. Diary; clipping from Charleston *Courier,* December 12, 1863, Alexander Papers, UNC; Latrobe Diary, VHS; Duggan Papers, UG; *OR,* 31, pt. 1, p. 481; Longstreet, *MA,* pp. 488, 489.

11. Diary, Alexander Papers, UNC; Latrobe Diary, VHS; *OR,* 31, pt. 1, pp. 477, 481; L. M. Blackford–Mother, November 20, 1863, Blackford Papers, UVA; Longstreet, *MA,* p. 489; Duffey Papers, VHS.

12. Latrobe Diary, VHS; Diary, Alexander Papers, UNC; L. M. Blackford–Mother, November 20, 1863, Blackford Papers, UVA; Polley, *Letters,* p. 176; *OR,* 31, pt. 1, pp. 273, 457; Lafayette McLaws–Braxton Bragg, April 22, 1864, McLaws Papers, WRHS.

13. *OR,* 31, pt. 1, pp. 273, 340, 457, 525; Longstreet, *MA,* pp. 490–91; Lafayette McLaws–Braxton Bragg, April 22, 1864; map of Loudon-Knoxville region, McLaws Papers, WRHS.

14. Lafayette McLaws–Braxton Bragg, n.d.; Lafayette McLaws–Marcus J. Wright, June 7, 1882, McLaws Papers, UNC; Lafayette McLaws–Braxton Bragg, April 22, 1864, McLaws Papers, WRHS.

15. *OR,* 31, pt. 1, p. 477; L. M. Blackford–Mother, November 20, 1863, Blackford Papers, UVA; Report, January 2, 1864, Francis Dawson file, CSR/NA; Sorrel, *Recollections,* p. 202; Choice, "Memoirs," MNBP.

16. Lafayette McLaws–Braxton Bragg, n.d., McLaws Papers, UNC; Latrobe Diary, VHS; *OR,* 31, pt. 1, pp. 274, 458, 478, 482, 483, 525; Gallagher, *Fighting For,* p. 316; Longstreet, *MA,* p. 493; Dawson, *Reminiscences,* pp. 106–7.

17. *OR,* 31, pt. 1, pp. 458, 478, 526–27; Dawson, *Reminiscences,* p. 107; Longstreet, *MA,* pp. 493–94; Gallagher, *Fighting For,* pp. 316–17; clipping of Richmond *Dispatch,* March 8, 1896, Hotchkiss Papers, LC.

18. *OR,* 31, pt. 1, pp. 274, 458, 527.

19. Ibid., pp. 268, 458, 483, 541–42; Lafayette McLaws–Braxton Bragg, April 22, 1864, McLaws Papers, WRHS; Minnich, "Pegram's Confederate Brigade," p. 59, TU; Latrobe Diary, VHS.

20. *OR,* 31, pt. 1, pp. 267, 275, 276; *OR Atlas,* plate 48, 2; Marvel, *Burnside,* p. 315.

21. *OR,* 31, pt. 1, pp. 458–59, 479, 483, 510, 511, 514; Longstreet, *MA,* pp. 497–98; Lafayette McLaws–Braxton Bragg, n.d., McLaws Papers, UNC;

B & L, III, p. 747; Warner, *Generals in Blue,* p. 419; Marvel, *Burnside* pp. 316–17.

22. Latrobe Diary, VHS; Diary, Alexander Papers, UNC; *OR,* 31 pt. 1, p. 459; Humphreys Papers, UNC; Goode Bryan–Lafayette McLaws, December 29, 1882, McLaws Papers, UNC; Gallagher, *Fighting For,* p. 317; Seymour, *Divided Loyalties,* pp. 139, 141; *OR Atlas,* plate 48, 2.

23. *OR,* 31, pt. 3, p. 727; Latrobe Diary, VHS.

24. *OR,* 31, pt. 1, p. 459; Latrobe Diary, VHS; Diary, Alexander Papers, UNC; Gallagher, *Fighting For,* pp. 320–23; *CV,* 31, p. 425.

25. *OR,* 31, p. 1, pp. 299, 484; Longstreet, *MA,* p. 49; Lafayette McLaws–Braxton Bragg, April 22, 1864, McLaws Papers, WRHS; Seymour, *Divided Loyalties,* p. 151.

26. *OR,* 31, pt. 1, pp. 299, 306; *B & L,* III, p. 749; Longstreet, *MA,* p. 499; Seymour, *Divided Loyalties,* p. 156; Dawson, *Reminiscences,* p. 109.

27. *OR,* 31, pt. 1, pp. 459, 484; Longstreet, *MA,* p. 500.

28. *OR,* 31, pt. 1, pp. 459, 479, 531; Gallagher, *Fighting For,* p. 323; Longstreet, *MA,* pp. 500–501; *B & L,* III, p. 748; Sorrel, *Recollections,* p. 260; Diary, Alexander Papers, UNC.

29. *OR,* 31, pt. 1, pp. 460, 479; Longstreet, *MA,* p. 501; Diary, Alexander Papers, UNC; *B & L,* III, p. 748; Warner, *Generals in Gray,* pp. 176–77.

30. *OR,* 31, pt. 1, p. 460; Longstreet, *MA,* p. 501; Diary, Alexander Papers, UNC; Gallagher, *Fighting For,* p. 324.

31. *OR,* 31, pt. 1, pp. 460–61, 479, 487; Longstreet, *MA,* pp. 501, 502; Gallagher, *Fighting For,* pp. 324, 325.

32. *OR,* 31, pt. 1, p. 486.

33. Ibid., pp. 486–88.

34. Ibid., pp. 491, 492, 494.

35. Ibid., pt. 3, p. 756; statement of Micah Jenkins on Fort Sanders attack, n.d., McLaws Papers, UNC.

36. Gallagher, *Fighting For,* pp. 326–27; *OR,* 31, pt. 3, pp. 756, 757.

37. *OR,* 31, pt. 1, p. 487; *B & L,* III, p. 748.

38. *CV,* I, p. 335; *B & L,* III, p. 748; Gallagher, *Fighting For,* p. 328; statement of Captain John Storris, Phillips Legion, January 17, 1864, McLaws Papers, UNC; *OR,* 31, pt. 1, p. 490; Latrobe Diary, VHS.

39. Lafayette McLaws collected statements from the officers in his division about the assault on Fort Sanders. They contain a wealth of detail and are with his papers at UNC. Additional accounts of the assault can be found in *OR,* 31, pt. 1, pp. 270, 277, 295–99, 342, 344, 353, 356, 461, 466, 475, 479, 489–91, 495–97, 519, 521–24, 528–29, 532–33; Longstreet, *MA,* pp. 502–6; Latrobe Diary, VHS; Gallagher, *Fighting For,* pp. 326–28; *CV,* 1, p. 335; 18, p. 468; 31, p. 372; *B & L,* III, p. 749; Kilmer, "Heroic Deeds," pp. 82, 84, USAMHI; McLaws Papers, DU; Humphreys Papers, UNC.

40. Longstreet, *MA,* pp. 505–7; Latrobe Diary, VHS; Sorrel, *Recollections,* p. 205.

41. Gallagher, *Fighting For,* p. 327.

42. Lafayette McLaws–Braxton Bragg, April 22, 1864, McLaws Papers, WRHS.

43. *OR,* 31, pt. 1, p. 461; Longstreet, *MA,* pp. 506–7; Latrobe Diary, VHS; R. Ransom–Longstreet, November 28, 1863, Longstreet Papers, HSP; Gallagher, *Fighting For,* p. 328.

44. McDonough, *Chattanooga,* chapters 9–14; *OR,* 31, pt. 3, pp. 775–76.

45. *OR,* 31, pt. 1, pp. 461, 462, 546; pt. 3, pp. 758, 759; Gallagher, *Fighting For,* pp. 328, 329; Longstreet, *MA,* p. 507; Latrobe Diary, VHS.

46. *OR,* 31, pt. 1, pp. 466, 499, 500, 546; Diary, Alexander Papers, UNC; copy of General Orders No. 9, McLaws Papers, UNC; Latrobe Diary, VHS; Longstreet, *MA,* pp. 509–11; Marvel, *Burnside,* p. 330.

47. *OR,* 31, pt. 1, p. 462; Latrobe Diary, VHS; D. M. DuBose–E. P. Alexander, August 23, 1899, Alexander Papers, UNC; Humphreys Papers, UNC; Polley, *Hood's Texas Brigade,* p. 223; Krick, *Parker's Virginia Battery,* p. 239.

48. *OR,* 31, pt. 1, pp. 462–63; Longstreet, *MA,* pp. 511–12; Latrobe Diary, VHS; Diary, Alexander Papers, UNC; Theodore Fogel–Father and Mother, December 11, 1863, Fogel Papers, EU.

49. *OR,* 31, pt. 1, pp. 270, 271, 273, 278, 279, 281; Harrison, "Battle," *CWTI,* 26, 3, p. 20.

50. *OR,* 31, pt. 1, pp. 281, 473; Longstreet, *MA,* pp. 512–13.

51. *OR,* 31, pt. 1, pp. 463, 546; Longstreet, *MA,* pp. 512–13; Allardice, "Longstreet's Nightmare," *CWM,* 18, p. 40.

52. *OR,* 31, pt. 1, pp. 293, 463, 494, 495, 533–36; Latrobe Diary, VHS; Speed, "Battle," *Southern Bivouac,* II, pp. 113, 114; Harrison, "Battle," *CWTI,* 26, 3, p. 21; Graves, *History,* p. 36; Gallagher, *Fighting For,* pp. 331, 332.

53. *OR,* 31, pt. 1, pp. 341, 464; Latrobe Diary, VHS.

54. *OR,* 31, pt. 1, pp. 341, 421–22, 464; pt. 3, p. 837; Latrobe Diary, VHS; Minnich, "Pegram's Confederate Brigade," p. 62, TU; Longstreet–J. M. Martin, March 30, 1895, Longstreet Papers, EU.

55. Latrobe Diary, VHS; *OR,* 31, pt. 1, pp. 480, 508; pt. 3, p. 839; Longstreet, *MA,* pp. 520, 521; Dickert, *History,* pp. 329, 330; *B & L,* III p. 750; Dawson, *Reminiscences,* p. 110; Bond and Coward, *South Carolinians,* p. 103; Sorrel, *Recollections,* pp. 209, 210.

56. Theodore Fogel–Father and Mother, December 17, 1863, Fogel Papers, EU; Minnich, "Pegram's Confederate Brigade," p. 59, TU; E. M. Law–Isaac R. Pennypacker, April 7, 1888, Law Papers, DU; Chesnut, *Diary,* pp. 327, 336; Lafayette McLaws–Marcus J. Wright, June 7, 1882, McLaws Papers, UNC.

57. Sanger and Hay, *James Longstreet,* p. 219; Moxley Sorrel–Lafayette McLaws, December 17, 1863, Benning Papers, UNC; Goree, *Letters,* p. 199.

18. "THE IMPOSSIBLE POSITION THAT I HELD"

1. Latrobe Diary, VHS.

2. Longstreet–Lafayette McLaws, July 25, 1873, McLaws Papers, UNC.

3. *OR,* 31, pt. 1, pp. 467–69, 503–4.

4. Ibid., p. 469; Jones, *Rebel War Clerk's,* II, p. 126; McLaws file, CSR/NA.

5. McLaws file, CSR/NA; Garnett Andrews–Lafayette McLaws, February 11, 1864; McLaws Papers, UNC; L. M. Blackford–Mother, February 12, 1864, Blackford Papers, UVA; Osmun Latrobe–Micah Jenkins, February 6, 1864, Longstreet, Order and Letter Book, 1863–1865, UT.

6. *OR,* 31, pt. 1, p. 470.

7. L. M. Blackford–Mother, January 22, February 22, 1864, Blackford Papers, UVA; Polley, *Hood's Texas Brigade,* p. 225; Warner, *Generals in Gray,* pp. 262–62; Osmun Latrobe–J. B. Robertson, February 15, 1864, Longstreet, Order and Letter Book, 1863–1865, UT.

8. Longstreet–Simon Buckner, February 13, 1864; Judge Advocate–Lafayette McLaws, February 13, 1864; Lafayette McLaws–Samuel Cooper, March 19, 1864, McLaws Papers, UNC; Osmun Latrobe–Lafayette McLaws, February 14, 1864, Longstreet, Order and Letter Book, 1863–1865, UT.

9. "Note for Defence," McLaws Papers, UNC; Lafayette McLaws–Henry Benning, December 18, 1863, Benning Papers, UNC.

10. Lafayette McLaws–S. Cooper, December 29, 1863; Lafayette McLaws–Marcus J. Wright, June 7, 1882, McLaws Papers, UNC; *OR,* 31, pt. 1, pp. 501–3.

11. Lafayette McLaws–Wife, March 7, 1864; William T. Martin–Lafayette McLaws, February 10, 1864; Henry L. Benning–Lafayette McLaws, March 3, 7, 1864, McLaws Papers, UNC; Piston, Ph.D. Diss., p. 307.

12. Braxton Bragg–Lafayette McLaws, March 4, 1864, McLaws Papers, UNC; Braxton Bragg–E. T. Sykes, February 8, 1873, Claiborne Papers, UNC.

13. Braxton Bragg–Lafayette McLaws, March 4, 1864, McLaws Papers, UNC.

14. Lafayette McLaws–Wife, March 8, 1864; "Charges and Specifications against James Longstreet," n.d., McLaws Papers, UNC; Lafayette McLaws–Braxton Bragg, March 9, 1864, McLaws Papers, WRHS.

15. "Charges and Specifications against James Longstreet," n.d.; John F. Edwards–W. R. McLaws, March 13, 1864, McLaws Papers, UNC; Simon Buckner–S. Cooper, March 12, 1864, Longstreet, Order and Letter Book, 1863–1865, UT.

16. *OR,* 31, pt. 1, pp. 503–4.

17. Lafayette McLaws–Wife, March 12, 1864; John F. Edwards–W. R. McLaws, March 13, 1864; Lafayette McLaws–Marcus J. Wright, June 7, 1882; "Court-Martial Proceedings, March 16–17, 1864," McLaws Papers, UNC.

18. *OR,* 31, pt. 1, pp. 505–6; McLaws file, CSR/NA.

19. Lafayette–McLaws–Baxton Bragg, April 22, 1864, McLaws Papers, WRHS; Lafayette McLaws–Braxton Bragg, n.d. [c. April 1864]; Lafayette McLaws–Marcus J. Wright, June 7, 1882, McLaws Papers, UNC; Lafayette McLaws–Chas. Arnold, February 2, 1897, McLaws, 21, FSNMP; James Longstreet–Braxton Bragg, October 16, 1863, Dearborn Collection, HU.

20. Dickert, *History,* p. 338; Goree, *Letters,* p. 199; Oates, *War,* p. 339; Joseph Ganahl–Lafayette McLaws, September 26, 1890, McLaws Papers, UNC; Piston, Ph.D. Diss., p. 311.

21. Longstreet, *MA,* p. 548; Longstreet–Lafayette McLaws, July 25, 1875, McLaws Papers, UNC.

22. Longstreet, *MA,* pp. 524, 525; Coker, *History,* p. 138; *CV,* 6, p. 267; Graves, *History,* pp. 36–38; Houghton, *Two Boys,* p. 67; Gibson Clarke, "Reminiscences of Civil War Days," *Annals of Wyoming,* vol 15. no. 4, October 1943, copy, Brake Collection, USAMHI; Longstreet–J. E. B. Stuart, January 10, 1864, Longstreet Papers, HL; L. M. Blackford–Mother, February 5, 1864, Blackford Papers, UVA; Taylor, "War Reminiscences," VHS.

23. Graves, *History,* pp. 37, 40, 41; Coker, *History,* pp. 139, 142; Houghton, *Two Boys,* pp. 68, 69; Rozier, *Granite,* p. 158; Choice, "Memoirs," MNBP; E. R. Taylor–A. R. Lawton, January 29, 1864, Longstreet, Order and Letter Book, 1863–1865, UT.

24. Moses, "Autobiography," pp. 49–50, UNC; Blackford, *Letters,* p. 232.

25. Grantham, "Letters," *GHQ,* 40, pp. 187–88; *CV,* 26, p. 260; Blackford, *Letters,* p. 236; Theodore Fogel–Father and Mother, January 21, 1864, Fogel Papers, EU; L. M. Blackford–Mother, January 22, February 5, 12, 1864, Blackford Papers, UVA.

26. Longstreet, *MA,* pp. 525–26; Sorrel, *Recollections,* p. 212; Longstreet–Jefferson Davis, March 15, 1864, Dearborn Collection, HU.

27. Longstreet, *MA,* pp. 528, 529, 530; Sorrel, *Recollections,* pp. 212, 213; Longstreet–Jefferson Davis, March 15, 1864, Dearborn Collection, HU; Minnich, "Pegram's Confederate Brigade," p. 62, TU.

28. Longstreet, *MA,* pp. 531–39; Longstreet–Jefferson Davis, March 15, 1864, Dearborn Collection, HU; Longstreet–John Withers, January 25, 1864, C. S. A. Archives, DU; L. M. Blackford–Mother, January 17, February 13, 1864, Blackford Papers, UVA; *CV,* 30, p. 342; Diary, Latrobe Papers, VHS.

29. Longstreet, *MA,* p. 540; Longstreet–Jefferson Davis, March 15, 1864, Dearborn Collection, HU; Latrobe Diary, VHS; Longstreet–Jefferson Davis, February 20, 21, 1864, Davis Papers, DU.

30. Latrobe Diary, VHS; Longstreet, *MA,* p. 542; Sorrel, *Recollections,* p. 214; L. M. Blackford–Mother, March 3, 1864, Blackford Papers, UVA.

31. L. M. Blackford–Mother, March 3, 1864, Blackford Papers, UVA; DuBose, "Reminiscences," UNC; Moses, "Autobiography," p. 52, UNC; Sorrel, *Recollections,* p. 218.

32. Freeman, *R. E. Lee,* III, pp. 259–60; *OR,* 31, pt. 2, pp. 541, 566, 654; pt. 3, pp. 594–95; Dowdey and Manarin, *Wartime Papers,* p. 667; Longstreet–Joseph Johnston, March 3, 1864, Longstreet Papers, HL; Davis, *Jefferson Davis,* pp. 549–50; Latrobe Diary, VHS.

33. Longstreet, *MA,* p. 544; Latrobe Diary, VHS.

34. Longstreet, *MA,* pp. 540, 544.

35. Ibid., p. 544; D. B. McIntosh–Mrs. Lee, March 14, 1864, typed copy, McIntosh Papers, USAMHI.

36. Longstreet, *MA,* pp. 545–46; Freeman, *R. E. Lee,* III, p. 261; Davis, *Jefferson Davis,* pp. 548–49; Chesnut, *Diary,* p. 394; *CV,* 37, p. 98.

37. Longstreet, *MA,* pp. 546–47.

38. Longstreet–Jefferson Davis, March 15, 1864, Dearborn Collection, HU.

39. Longstreet–R. E. Lee, March 16, 1864, Longstreet—J. E. Johnston, March 16, 1864, Longstreet Papers, GDAH.

40. Latrobe Diary, VHS; Longstreet, *MA,* p. 547; Sanger and Hay, *James Longstreet,* pp. 247–49; Freeman, *R. E. Lee,* III, p. 263; Davis, *Jefferson Davis,* pp. 548–49; Dowdey and Manarin, *Wartime Papers,* p. 691.

41. Jones, *Civil War,* pp. 191–92; Piston, Ph.D. Diss., p. 319.

42. Jones, *Civil War,* p. 192; Piston, Ph.D. Diss., p. 319; *OR,* 31, pt. 3, p. 680.

43. *OR,* 31, pt. 3, p. 680.

44. Latrobe Diary, VHS; Longstreet, *MA,* pp. 547–48; Gallagher, *Fighting For,* pp. 343, 345; J. J. Webb–Father, April 16, 1864, Webb Letters, USAMHI; Longstreet–R. E. Lee, April 11, 1864, Longstreet, Order and Letter Book, 1863–1865, UT; A. B. Simms–Sister, April 24, 1864, Simms Family Papers, AHS; *Annals,* p. 631; *CV,* 26, p. 354; *OR,* 31, pt. 1, pp. 549–50.

45. *OR,* 31, pt. 2, p. 726; Warner, *Generals in Gray,* pp. 87–88.

46. *OR,* 31, pt. 2, p. 802; pt. 3, p. 583; Longstreet–Simon Buckner, March 4, 1864, Longstreet, Order and Letter Book, 1863–1865, UT.

47. *OR,* 31, pt. 3, p. 738; Freeman, *Lee's Lieutenants,* III, pp. 310–12; Gallagher, *Fighting For,* p. 337.

48. *OR,* 31, pt. 3, pp. 866, 867; Sorrel, *Recollections,* pp. 177, 203; Longstreet, *MA,* p. 566; Lafayette McLaws, letter fragment, n.d., McLaws Papers, DU.

49. Longstreet, *MA,* p. 519; Oates, *War,* pp. 338–39; Swanson and Johnson, "Conflict," *CWH,* 31, 2, p. 108.

50. *OR,* 31, pt. 1, pp. 471, 472; Longstreet–S. Cooper, March 18, 1864, Longstreet, Order and Letter Book, 1863–1865, UT; Freeman, *Lee's Lieutenants,* III, p. 304; Oates, *War,* p. 339.

51. *OR,* 31, pt. 1, pp. 472, 473, 474–75; Moxley Sorrel–E. M. Law, April 27, 1864, Longstreet, Order and Letter Book, UT.

52. *OR,* 31, pt. 1, pp. 473, 474; Oates, *War,* p. 340; Freeman, *Lee's Lieutenants,* III, pp. 338, 339.

53. Warner, *Generals in Gray,* p. 171; Gallagher, *Fighting For,* p. 349; Sorrel, *Recollections,* p. 228; Chesnut, *Diary,* pp. 58, 182; McDowell and Davis, " 'Joe Writes His Own Praise,' " *CWTI,* 1, 10, pp. 36, 37.

54. Gallagher, *Fighting For,* pp. 345, 346; Bond and Coward, *South Carolinians,* p. 133; Dickert, *History,* p. 340.

55. Gallagher, *Fighting For,* p. 346; Dickert, *History,* p. 341; A. B. Simms–Sister, May 4, 1864, Simms Family Papers, AHS.

19. TWO ROADS

1. *B&L,* IV, p. 118; Gallagher, *Fighting For,* pp. 348–49; Long, *Civil War,* p. 492; Steere, *Wilderness,* p. 46.

2. Steere, *Wilderness,* pp. 46, 73, 74; Freeman, *Lee's Dispatches,* pp. 170–71.

3. "Circular," May 1, 1864; Longstreet–W. H. Taylor, May 4, 1864; Moxley Sorrel–Charles Field and Joseph Kershaw, May 4, 1864, Longstreet, Order and Letter Book, 1863–1865, UT; Steere, *Wilderness,* pp. 54–55, 74–76; Gallagher, *Fighting For,* p. 338.

4. Longstreet, *MA,* p. 556; Steere, *Wilderness,* pp. 76–77.

5. Steere, *Wilderness,* pp. 69, 76–77.

6. Ibid., pp. 77–78, 83; Freeman, *R. E. Lee,* III, p. 273.

7. A. B. Simms–Sister, May 4, 1864, Simms Family Papers, AHS; Goree, *Letters,* p. 208; Longstreet, *MA,* pp. 556–57; Moxley Sorrel–Joseph Kershaw, May 4, 1864, Longstreet, Order and Letter Books, 1863–1865, UT; Gettysburg Clipping Books, 6, p. 6, GNMP; Gallagher, *Fighting For,* p. 350; Latrobe Diary, VHS; E. P. Alexander–Wife, May 4, 1864, Alexander Papers, UNC.

8. Charles Venable–Longstreet, July 25, 1879, Longstreet Papers, DU; Longstreet, *MA,* pp. 557–60; Steere, *Wilderness,* p. 306.

9. Longstreet, *MA,* p. 559; Latrobe Diary; Longstreet–Samuel Johnston, July 31, 1879, Johnston Papers, VHS; Gallagher, *Fighting For,* p. 350; Polley, *Hood's Texas Brigade,* p. 230; Dickert, *History,* p. 345; Moxley Sorrel–Longstreet, July 21, 1879; W. H. Taylor–Longstreet, August 15, 1879, Longstreet Papers, DU; Graves, *History,* p. 42.

10. Steere, *Wilderness,* pp. 292–95, 309–10, 319–21; Charles Venable–Longstreet, July 25, 1879, Longstreet Papers, DU.

11. Steere, *Wilderness,* pp. 328–36; Charles Venable–Longstreet, July 25, 1879, Longstreet Papers, DU; *Annals,* p. 496.

12. Charles Venable–Longstreet, July 25, 1879, Longstreet Papers, DU; *Annals,* p. 496; McIntosh, "A Ride," p. 70, UNC; Humphreys, "History," p. 2, Claiborne Papers, UNC; Ranson, "Reminiscences," *Sewanee Review,* 22, pp. 444–45; Longstreet, *MA,* p. 560; Moxley Sorrel–Longstreet, July 21, 1879, Longstreet Papers, DU.

13. Gallagher, *Fighting For,* pp. 346, 358; Laswell, *Rags and Hope,* p. 107; *CV,* III, p. 317; Charles Venable–Longstreet, October 21, 1877, Longstreet Papers, EU; Wilson, *Confederate Soldier,* p. 169; Steere, *Wilderness,* p. 350.

14. Steere, *Wilderness,* pp. 345–50; Gallagher, *Fighting For,* pp. 346, 357–58; Ranson, "Reminiscences," *Sewanee Review,* 22, p. 445; Humphreys, "History," p. 23, Claiborne Papers, UNC; Charles Venable–Longstreet, July 25, 1879, Longstreet Papers, DU.

15. Haskell, *Memoirs,* p. 63; Latrobe Diary, VHS; Piston, Ph.D. Diss., p. 324.

16. Longstreet, *MA,* p. 561; Steere, *Wilderness,* pp. 371–74.

17. Longstreet, *MA,* p. 561; Steere, *Wilderness,* pp. 344–76; Haskell, *Memoirs,* pp. 63, 64.

18. Longstreet, *MA,* p. 561; Gallagher, *Fighting For,* p. 359; Steere, *Wilderness,* p. 388; *OR,* 6, p. 842.

19. Longstreet, *MA,* p. 562; Steere, *Wilderness,* p. 392; Gallagher, *Fighting For,* p. 359; Sorrel, *Recollections,* pp. 231, 232.

20. Sorrel, *Recollections,* p. 232; Longstreet, *MA,* p. 562; Steere, *Wilderness,* pp. 392–96; Gallagher, *Fighting For,* p. 360.

21. Sorrel, *Recollections,* p. 232; Gallagher, *Fighting For,* p. 360; Longstreet, *MA,* pp. 562–63; Steere, *Wilderness,* pp. 394–404.

22. Longstreet, *MA,* p. 563; Sorrel, *Recollections,* p. 233; Steere, *Wilderness,* p. 404.

23. Longstreet, *MA,* p. 563; Sorrel, *Recollections,* p. 233; Steere, *Wilderness,* p. 405.

24. Longstreet, *MA,* p. 564; Moffett, *Letters,* p. 128; Dawson, *Reminiscences,* p. 115; David A. Weisiger–Wife, May 7, 1864, Weisiger Papers, VHS; Bond and Coward, *South Carolinians,* p. 135; Sorrel, *Recollections,* p. 287.

25. Sorrel, *Recollections,* pp. 233–34; Dawson, *Reminiscences,* pp. 115, 116, 197; Ranson, "Reminiscences," *Sewanee Review,* 22, p. 447; Longstreet, *MA,* pp. 564, 566.

26. Sorrel, *Recollections,* pp. 233–34; Dawson, *Reminiscences,* pp. 115, 116; Ranson, "Reminiscences," *Sewanee Review,* 22, p. 447; Longstreet, *MA,* pp. 564, 566.

27. Stiles, *Four Years,* p. 247.

28. Longstreet, *MA,* pp. 564, 565; Gallagher, *Fighting For,* pp. 362–63; Steere, *Wilderness,* pp. 406–46; Long, *Civil War,* p. 494.

29. Taylor, *General Lee,* pp. 236–37; Gallagher, *Fighting For,* p. 360.

30. Gallagher, *Fighting For,* pp. 360–62; Steere, *Wilderness,* pp. 398, 407–9; Helen D. Longstreet, "Battle Tested Nation's Life, Longstreet's Widow Writes," Buffalo *Evening News,* 1938, copy of newspaper clipping in author's collection.

31. Longstreet, *MA,* pp. 568–71; *SHSP,* V, pp. 184–85; Freeman, *Lee's Lieutenants,* III, pp. 441–42; Gallagher, *Fighting For,* p. 349; Bean, "Memoranda," *Virginia Magazine,* 73, pp. 477, 478; Erasmus Taylor–Longstreet, August 14, 1879, Longstreet Papers, DU; Charles Venable–Longstreet, July 25, 1879, Longstreet Papers, DU.

32. Taylor, "War Reminiscences," VHS; Longstreet, *MA,* p. 572; Latrobe Diary, VHS; *OR,* 51, pt. 2, p. 893; Goree, *Letters,* pp. 211–31; Sorrel, *Recollections,* pp. 238–39; R. Kidder Taylor–Longstreet, October 24, 1903, original letter in author's collection.

33. Wheeler, *On Fields of Fury,* pp. 182, 183; Blackford, *Letters,* pp. 261, 262.

34. Longstreet, *MA,* p. 572; Houck, "Healing Place," *CWM,* 9, 3, p. 43; Sanger and Hay, *James Longstreet,* p. 277; "Garland Family," JML; Early, *Campbell Chronicles,* p. 344; R. Kidder Taylor–Longstreet, October 24, 1903, original letter in author's collection.

35. *OR,* 40, pt. 2, pp. 661, 664; 51, pt. 2, p. 1017; "Garland Family," JML; Goree, *Letters,* p. 212; R. Kidder Taylor–Longstreet, October 24, 1903, original letter in author's collection; Longstreet file, CSR/NA.

36. Longstreet, *MA,* p. 572; Sanger and Hay, *James Longstreet,* pp. 277–78; Goree, *Letters,* pp. 213, 231.

37. R. E. Lee–Longstreet, August 29, 1864, Longstreet Papers, GDAH.

38. Symonds, *Joseph E. Johnston,* pp. 324–33.

39. Longstreet, *MA,* p. 573; Piston, Ph.D. Diss., p. 321; Chambers, *Diary,* pp. 219–20.

40. Longstreet, *MA,* pp. 573, 574; Sanger and Hay, *James Longstreet,* p. 280; *OR,* 42, pt. 3, p. 1140; Longstreet file, CSR/NA; Dawson, *Reminiscences,* p. 202; Goree, *Letters,* p. 213.

41. Longstreet–P. G. T. Beauregard, October 21, 1864, Longstreet, Order and Letter Book, 1863–1865, UT; Gallagher, *Fighting For,* p. 489; Goree, *Letters,* pp. 232–33; Owen, *In Camp and Battle,* p. 355; Dawson, *Reminiscences,* p. 202.

42. Moxley Sorrel–R. J. Moses, October 26, 1864, Longstreet, Order and Letter Book, 1863–1865, UT; Thomas Walton file; Dawson file, CSR/NA; Dawson, *Reminiscences,* p. 204.

43. Longstreet, *MA,* p. 581; Latrobe Diary, VHS; Sorrel, *Recollections,* pp. 262–64.

44. Longstreet–S. Cooper, April 22, October 31, 1864, Longstreet, Order and Letter Book, 1863–1865, UT; Latrobe Diary, VHS; Latrobe file; Fairfax file, CSR/NA.

45. *OR,* 42, pt. 1, p. 871; pt. 3, pp. 1186, 1197; Goree, *Letters,* p. 237; Longstreet, *MA,* p. 575.

46. Gallagher, *Fighting For,* pp. 491–93; 512; *OR,* 42, pt. 1, pp. 871–72.

47. Gallagher, *Fighting For,* p. 493; *OR,* 42, pt. 3, pp. 1222–24, 1257, 1258, 1260, 1265, 1267.

48. Longstreet–Reverend Dr. Hoge, December 13, 1864, Longstreet Papers, MC; Sorrel, *Recollections,* p. 262; Cullen file, CSR/NA; Osmun Latrobe–Major S. H. Carrington, Provost Marshal, January 22, 1865, Longstreet, Order and Letter Book, 1863–1865, UT; R. E. Lee–Longstreet, January 19, 1865, Fairfax Papers, VHS.

49. *OR,* 51, pt. 2, p. 1056; Longstreet–R. E. Lee, February 4, 1865, Longstreet Papers, MC.

50. Longstreet, *MA,* p. 583; Long, *Civil War,* p. 633.

51. Long, *Civil War,* pp. 642, 649; Osmun Latrobe–J. B. Kershaw, G. E. Pickett, H. L. Benning, February 16, 1865; Osmun Latrobe–R. S. Ewell, February 17, 1865, Longstreet Papers, MC; R. E. Lee–Longstreet, February 22, 1865, Lee Papers, WLU; Dowdey and Manarin, *Wartime Papers,* pp. 907–8.

52. Longstreet, *MA,* pp. 583–84; Osmun Latrobe–J. B. Kershaw, February 25, 1864, Longstreet Papers, MC.

53. Longstreet, *MA,* pp. 584–87; Longstreet–E. O. C. Ord, February 27, March 3, 1865, Longstreet Papers, MC; Latrobe Diary, VHS.

54. Long, *Civil War,* pp. 647–50.

55. Gallagher, *Fighting For,* pp. 92–93, 506–7; Freeman, *R. E. Lee,* IV, chapters 2 and 3.

56. *OR,* 46, pt. 3, pp. 1375, 1376; Osmun Latrobe–C. W. Field, April 1, 1865; Osmun Latrobe–J. B. Kershaw, April 1, 1865, Longstreet Papers, MC; Longstreet, *MA,* pp. 602–5; Atlanta *Constitution,* January 27, 1894; *Annals,* p. 633; Freeman, *R. E. Lee,* IV, pp. 41–45.

57. Longstreet, *MA,* pp. 605–6; Freeman, *R. E. Lee,* IV, pp. 45–47; *OR,* 46, pt. 3, p. 1378; Gallagher, *Fighting For,* p. 515; Jefferson Davis–Thomas Munford, May 28, 1889, Munford, "Last Days," DU.

58. Longstreet, *MA,* pp. 607, 608; Freeman, *R. E. Lee,* IV, pp. 51–56; *OR,* 46, pt. 3, p. 1379; *CV,* 24, p. 234; Dowdey and Manarin, *Wartime Papers,* pp. 925, 926; "Notations to Copy of Orders, April 2, 1865," Wilcox Papers, LC; London *Times,* April 25, 1865; Gallagher, *Fighting For,* p. 519; Sheldon, "Last March," UNC.

59. Latrobe Diary, VHS; Diary, Alexander Papers, UNC; "Diary," typed copy, McIntosh Papers, USAMHI; Longstreet, *MA,* pp. 608, 609; Davis, "Campaign," *CWTI,* 14, 1, p. 10.

60. Latrobe Diary, VHS; Diary, Alexander Papers, UNC; "Diary," typed copy, McIntosh Papers, USAMHI; Freeman, *R. E. Lee,* IV, pp. 66, 67.

61. Gallagher, *Fighting For,* pp. 520, 521; Latrobe Diary, VHS; Longstreet, *MA,* p. 610.

62. Longstreet, *MA,* pp. 612–15; Freeman, *R. E. Lee,* IV, pp. 82–85; Gallagher, *Fighting For,* pp. 521, 522.

63. Latrobe Diary, VHS; Gallagher, *Fighting For,* p. 528; Longstreet, *MA,* pp. 618, 619; Calkins, *Battles,* pp. 3, 4; Longstreet–Thomas Rosser, October 12, 1892, Rosser Papers, UVA.

64. Longstreet, *MA,* pp. 618, 619; Gallagher, *Fighting For,* p. 528; Sorrel, *Recollections,* pp. 300–302; Freeman, *R. E. Lee,* IV, pp. 103–5; Longstreet–E. P. Alexander, June 17, 1869, Alexander Papers, UNC.

65. Longstreet–Osmun Latrobe, September 1, 1892, Dawson Papers, NYHS.

66. Latrobe Diary, VHS; Diary, Alexander Papers, UNC; "Diary," typed copy, McIntosh Papers, USAMHI; *OR,* 46, pt. 3, p. 1389; Longstreet, *MA,* p. 620; Gallagher, *Fighting For,* pp. 514–28; Calkins, *Battles,* pp. 28–45.

67. Longstreet, *MA,* p. 622; Gallagher, *Fighting For,* pp. 528–30; Calkins, *Battles,* p. 55; Cauble, *Appomattox,* pp. 13–15; Freeman, *R. E. Lee,* IV, p. 114.

68. Calkins, *Battles,* pp. 57–124, has best description of action; Long, *Memoirs,* p. 421; Cauble, *Appomattox,* p. 20; the Custer-Longstreet incident is described in Goree, *Letters,* pp. 301–2, 327, numerous letters on their meeting are also in Alexander Papers, UNC; E. P. Alexander–Longstreet, December 27, 1887, Longstreet Papers, GDAH; E. P. Alexander–Longstreet, October 26, 1892, Longstreet Papers, EU.

69. E. P. Alexander–Longstreet, October 26, 1892, Longstreet Papers, EU; Longstreet, *MA,* pp. 626–27; Longstreet–E. P. Alexander, June 17, 1869, Alexander Papers, UNC; Gallagher, *Fighting For,* p. 538; Taylor Papers, VHS; Calkins, *Battles,* pp. 135–36, 212.

70. Freeman, *R. E. Lee,* IV, pp. 136–43; Calkins, *Battles,* p. 212.

71. E. P. Alexander–Longstreet, October 26, 1892, Longstreet Papers, EU; Freeman, *R. E. Lee,* IV, pp. 143–45; Goree, *Letters,* p. 302; Gallagher, *Fighting For,* p. 539.

72. Haskell, *Memoirs,* p. 98; Cauble, *Appomattox,* p. 75; New York *Times,* July 24, 1885, December 31, 1893; Gallagher, *Fighting For,* p. 541.

73. Piston, Ph.D. Diss., p. 332; Dowdey and Manarin, *Wartime Papers,* pp. 934–35; Longstreet–E. P. Alexander, April 11, 1865, Alexander Papers, UNC; Longstreet–Osmun Latrobe, April 11, 1865, Latrobe Diary, VHS; Long-

street–Thomas B. O'Brien, January 20, 1889, Association of the Army of Northern Virginia Papers, TU; Hoole, *Lawley*, pp. 120–21; Freeman, *R. E. Lee*, IV, p. 159.

74. Thomas Goree–E. P. Alexander, December 6, 1887, Alexander Papers, UNC; Freeman, *R. E. Lee*, IV, p. 159.

75. Goree, *Letters*, p. 243; Sorrel, *Recollections*, pp. 272–73.

76. John Fairfax–Joseph Bryan, August 1, 1902, Fairfax Papers, VHS; Gordon, *Reminiscences*, p. 160; New York *Times*, June 15, 1880.

77. Sears, "Getting Right," *American Heritage*, 42, 3, pp. 71–72; Freeman, *R. E. Lee*, IV, pp. 170–73.

78. Joseph Kershaw–E. P. Alexander, July 14, 1866, Alexander Papers, UNC.

20. FINAL JOURNEY

1. Goree, *Letters*, p. 243; Longstreet, *MA*, pp. 629–30; New York *Herald*, September 27, 1903; Baltimore *Sun*, January 3, 1904.

2. Goree, *Letters*, pp. 243–45; R. J. Longstreet–F. R. Longstreet, September 3, 1947, Longstreet Papers, CRL.

3. Goree, *Letters*, pp. 245–53; Sanger and Hay, *James Longstreet*, pp. 318–19.

4. Goree, *Letters*, pp. 253–55; Sanger and Hay, *James Longstreet*, pp. 319–20.

5. Goree, *Letters*, p. 255; Longstreet, *MA*, p. 638; Sanger and Hay, *James Longstreet*, p. 320.

6. Sanger and Hay, *James Longstreet*, pp. 320, 321; Longstreet, *MA*, pp. 634–35.

7. Longstreet, *MA*, pp. 632–34; Sanger and Hay, *James Longstreet*, pp. 318, 321–22; Freeman, *R. E. Lee*, IV, pp. 200–201; R. E. Lee–Josiah Tatnall, September 7, 1865, Lee Papers, DU.

8. Goree, *Letters*, p. 265; Longstreet, *MA*, pp. 635, 655; Longstreet–Osmun Latrobe, December 27, 1865, Latrobe Diary, VHS; Sanger and Hay, *James Longstreet*, pp. 321, 322, 323; R. E. Lee–Longstreet, January 26, 1866, Longstreet Papers, GDAH.

9. Sanger and Hay, *James Longstreet*, pp. 324, 325, 348; Goree, *Letters*, p. 268.

10. Goree, *Letters*, p. 272; Sanger and Hay, *James Longstreet*, pp. 323–25; Longstreet–J. L. Donaldson, January 12, 1866; Longstreet–George Thomas, January 12, 1866, Longstreet, Order and Letter Book, 1863–1865, UT; Longstreet–U. S. Grant, April 10, 1867, Longstreet Papers, CHS.

11. Sanger and Hay, *James Longstreet*, pp. 328, 329; Foner, *Reconstruction*, pp. 228–39, 271–77.

12. Sanger and Hay, *James Longstreet*, pp. 329–30; Richter, "James Longstreet," *Louisiana History*, 11, 3, pp. 216, 217.

13. Richter, "James Longstreet," *Louisiana History*, 11, 3, pp. 217–20; Piston, Ph.D. Diss., pp. 360, 361; Sanger and Hay, *James Longstreet*, pp. 330–32.

14. Piston, Ph.D. Diss., pp. 364–65.

15. Ibid., pp. 362, 363, 367.

16. Ibid., 366–69; Richter, "James Longstreet," *Louisiana History,* 11, 3, pp. 222–28; Sanger and Hay, *James Longstreet,* pp. 334–36; Longstreet, *MA,* p. 637.

17. Longstreet–R. E. Lee, June 8, 1867, Longstreet Papers, DU; Goree, *Letters,* p. 324; Longstreet, *MA,* p. 637; Sanger and Hay, *James Longstreet,* pp. 337–39.

18. Longstreet, *MA,* p. 637; Sanger and Hay, *James Longstreet,* pp. 340–45; Richter, "James Longstreet," *Louisiana History,* 11, 3, pp. 228, 229.

19. Sanger and Hay, *James Longstreet,* pp. 345, 346.

20. Ibid., pp. 345–46; Piston, Ph.D. Diss., pp. 370–75.

21. Piston, Ph.D. Diss., pp. 372–79.

22. Sanger and Hay, *James Longstreet,* pp. 349, 350; Taylor, *Louisiana,* p. 177.

23. Sanger and Hay, *James Longstreet,* pp. 352–59; Taylor, *Louisiana,* p. 229.

24. Sanger and Hay, *James Longstreet,* pp. 362–66.

25. Ibid., pp. 360–61, 363, 364–66; Taylor, *Louisiana,* pp. 177, 253–54.

26. Sanger and Hay, *James Longstreet,* pp. 366–69; Taylor, *Louisiana,* pp. 291–92; Piston, Ph.D. Diss., p. 417, *CV,* 13, p. 80; "Gen. Longstreet & The White League Fight," n.a., n.d., Longstreet Papers, CRL.

27. Taylor, *Louisiana,* pp. 293–94; Sanger and Hay, *James Longstreet,* pp. 370–71; "Gen. Longstreet & The White League Fight," n.a., n.d., Longstreet Papers, CRL.

28. Taylor, *Louisiana,* p. 294; Sanger and Hay, *James Longstreet,* pp. 371–77.

29. Sanger and Hay, *James Longstreet,* p. 374; Piston, Ph.D. Diss., p. 417.

30. "Oath of Office," Levee Commissioner of Engineers, May 30, 1863, Longstreet Papers, CRL; Sanger and Hay, *James Longstreet,* pp. 366, 367, 368, 374; Goree, *Letters,* p. 283.

31. Goree, *Letters,* p. 283; Longstreet–D. H. Hill, May 13, 1875, Hill Papers, VSL; Sanger and Hay, *James Longstreet,* pp. 348, 367, 375; R. J. Longstreet–F. R. Longstreet, September 3, 1947, Longstreet Papers, CRL.

32. Sanger and Hay, *James Longstreet,* p. 377; Piston, Ph.D. Diss., p. 470; New York *Times,* June 28, 1875; Longstreet–M. J. Fecknor, February 10, 1877, Longstreet Papers, EU; "Indenture," April 29, 1876, Longstreet Papers, CRL; newspaper clipping, n.d., Hotchkiss Papers, reel 59, frame 84, LC.

33. Sanger and Hay, *James Longstreet,* pp. 377–80; John H. Frazier–Colonel Lee, December 14, 1876; Longstreet–U. S. Grant, February 17, 1877, typed copy; F. Heiderhoff–R. B. Hayes, March 8, 1877; Longstreet–Benjamin Alvord, March 17, 1877, typed copy; John M. Harlan–President, May 25, 1877, Longstreet Papers, RBHPC; Longstreet–President Hayes, August 26, 1877, Longstreet Papers, HL.

34. Sanger and Hay, *James Longstreet,* pp. 368, 377, 379, 380; Thomas, *General,* pp. 273, 274.

35. Longstreet–R. H. Chilton, June 2, 1875, Longstreet Papers, MC; Sanger and Hay, *James Longstreet,* pp. 376–77.

36. Sanger and Hay, *James Longstreet,* p. 381; New York *Times,* July 29, 1879; Longstreet–Senator W. P. Kellogg, December 26, 1878, typed copy, Longstreet Papers, RBHPC.

37. Sanger and Hay, *James Longstreet,* pp. 383–85; Shadgett, Ph.D. Diss., pp. 130, 132; Longstreet–Senator W. P. Kellogg, December 26, 1878, typed copy, Longstreet Papers, RBHPC.

38. M. E. Thornton–R. B. Hayes, May 8, 1880, Longstreet Papers, RBHPC; Sanger and Hay, *James Longstreet,* pp. 384–85; Piston, Ph.D. Diss., p. 472.

39. Piston, Ph.D. Diss., pp. 472, 473; Sanger and Hay, *James Longstreet,* pp. 384–86; Longstreet–Fitz Randolph Longstreet, April 27, 1881, Longstreet Papers, GDAH.

40. Perros, "Letters," *GHQ,* 41, p. 301; Sanger and Hay, *James Longstreet,* pp. 386, 387; Warner, *Generals in Blue,* p. 167.

41. Perros, "Letters," *GHQ,* 41, pp. 301–2; Sanger and Hay, *James Longstreet,* pp. 390–91; Thomas, *General,* pp. 280–81; New York *Times,* December 19, 1882.

42. Perros, "Letters," *GHQ,* 41, pp. 302–8; Sanger and Hay, *James Longstreet,* pp. 393–94.

43. Sanger and Hay, *James Longstreet,* pp. 390, 394–96; Thomas, *General,* pp. 281–82.

44. Longstreet, *Lee and Longstreet,* p. 123; Piston, Ph.D. Diss., p. 556; Longstreet–Bradley T. Johnson, July 31, 1887, Johnson Papers, DU; New York *Times,* July 24, 1885, December 16, 1888.

45. Longstreet–Osmun Latrobe, February 27, 1886, Latrobe Diary, VHS; Longstreet–Charles C. Jones, Jr., June 21, 1889, Longstreet Papers, DU; Moses, "Autobiography," p. 57, UNC.

46. New York *Times,* April 16, 1889; Piston, Ph.D. Diss., p. 559; Longstreet–Thomas Munford, March 5, 1892, Munford-Ellis Papers, DU.

47. Sanger and Hay, *James Longstreet,* pp. 403, 404.

48. Tucker, "Longstreet," *CWTI,* 1, 1, p. 6; Sanger and Hay, *James Longstreet,* p. 411; Piston, Ph.D. Diss., p. 396; Connelly, *Marble Man,* pp. 83, 84.

49. Piston, Ph.D. Diss., pp. 395–97, 407–9; Sanger and Hay, *James Longstreet,* p. 412; Thomas, *General,* pp. 299–302.

50. Piston, Ph.D. Diss., pp. 415–16; Longstreet–William N. Pendleton, April 4, [14], 19, 1875, Pendleton Papers, UNC; Walter Taylor–Longstreet, April 28, 1875; Charles Marshall–Longstreet, May 7, 1875; A. L. Long–Longstreet, May 31, 1875; Charles Venable–Longstreet, n.d., Longstreet Papers, EU.

51. Longstreet–John P. Nicholson, August 15, 1874, Longstreet Papers, HL.

52. Piston, Ph.D. Diss., pp. 446, 447, 502, 503, 507; Connelly, *Marble Man,* p. 85.

53. R. E. Lee–Osmun Latrobe, June 8, 1866; Longstreet–Osmun Latrobe, February 10, 27, 1886, Latrobe Diary, VHS; Longstreet–John P. Nicholson, April 19, 1875, Longstreet Papers, HL; E. P. Alexander–Longstreet, October

26, 1892; P. J. Moran–Longstreet, February 6, 1899, Longstreet Papers, EU; Piston, Ph.D. Diss., p. 564; Krick, "I Consider Him a Humbug," *CWQ,* 5, p. 28; Longstreet–Thomas Munford, December 20, 1891, Munford-Ellis Papers, DU; Longstreet–Charles E. Jones, December 27, 1895, Charles E. Jones Papers, DU; Charles S. Arnall–John Daniel, November 30, 1904, Daniel Papers, VUA.

54. Sanger and Hay, *James Longstreet,* pp. 434–36.

55. Goree, *Letters,* p. 291; Osmun Latrobe–E. P. Alexander, September 22, 1866, Alexander Papers, UNC; New York *Times,* December 31, 1893; Sorrel, *Recollections,* pp. 304, 307.

56. Goree, *Letters,* pp. 314, 315; Thomas Goree–Longstreet, May 17, 1875.

57. Piston, Ph.D. Diss., p. 580; New York *Times,* July 24, 1885, April 27, 28, 1897; Washington *Post,* June 11, 1893; *CV,* 13, p. 396; Longstreet Papers, GHS; Longstreet–D. C. Pavey, October 18, 1895, Longstreet Papers, HL.

58. Goree, *Letters,* pp. 311, 329, 330; *CV,* 3, pp. 176, 177; 12, p. 86; Ratchford, *Some Reminiscences,* p. 69; Polley, *Letters,* p. 313; New York *Times,* December 16, 1888, May 30, 1899; Atlanta *Constitution,* January 3, 1904; Washington *Post,* May 29, 30, 1890; "Gen. Longstreet & The White League Fight," n.a., n.d., Longstreet Papers, CRL.

59. New York *Times,* September 9, 1897; Baltimore *Sun,* January 3, 1904; Alvarez, "Death," *GHQ,* 52, p. 71; Piston, Ph.D. Diss., p. 581.

60. Piston, Ph.D. Diss., p. 597; Longstreet, *Lee and Longstreet,* p. 117; Alvarez, "Death," *GHQ,* 52, p. 70; Sanger and Hay, *James Longstreet,* pp. 438–39.

61. Longstreet Papers, EU; Alvarez, "Death," *GHQ,* 52, p. 70; Longstreet, *Lee and Longstreet,* pp. 20, 21, 121, 127; Helen Longstreet–Sir, August 20, 1913, Longstreet Papers, NYPL; Piston, Ph.D. Diss., p. 582; Eliot, *West Point,* p. 222.

62. Piston, Ph.D. Diss., p. 600; New York *Herald,* September 27, 1903; Baltimore *Sun,* January 3, 1904; Longstreet My Dear Son James, February 6, 1903; Longstreet–My Dear Son Lee, October 25, 1903, Longstreet Papers, GHS; Alvarez, "Death," *GHQ,* 52, p. 71.

63. Alvarez, "Death," *GHQ,* 52, p. 71; Longstreet, *Lee and Longstreet,* pp. 109, 110; Atlanta *Constitution,* January 3, 1904; newspaper clipping, Longstreet Papers, EU.

64. Atlanta *Constitution,* January 3, 4, 7, 1904; Alvarez, "Death," *GHQ,* 52, pp. 72, 73.

65. Atlanta *Constitution,* January 3, 4, 7, 1904; Alvarez, "Death," *GHQ,* 52, pp. 72, 73; Baltimore *Sun,* January 1, 1904; Longstreet, *Lee and Long-street,* pp. 226–330.

BIBLIOGRAPHY

UNPUBLISHED SOURCES

Antietam National Battlefield Library:
    William H. Andrews, " 'Johnny Reb' at Antietam," typescript, First Georgia Infantry File
    William N. Berkeley, typescript letters, Eighth Virginia Infantry File
    Robert P. Buchanan, Piper Farm Historic Background Materials File
    Ezra Carman, Papers for Antietam Battlefield Board Maps—1908, typescript copies
    Henry K. Douglas, Personal Library (Marginal Notes)
    Interpretive Planning: II. Piper Farm File
    Betty J. Otto, Henry Piper Family Study File
    William David Henderson Pritchard Papers, Confederate Unit Folders
    Thomas Rambo, Service Record, Confederate Unit Folders
    John P. Smith, "Recollections"
    Andrew B. Wardlaw, Letters and Diary typescript, First South Carolina Infantry File
Atlanta Historical Society:
    Simms Family Papers
Brown University, The John Hay Library:
    Samuel G. French, Letter to James Longstreet, May 4, 1863
    Rush Hawkins, Statement of James Longstreet, March 16, 1870
    Arthur Crew Inman Papers
    Robert E. Lee, Letter to James Longstreet, January 25, 1863
    James Longstreet, Letter to W. P. Hopkins, March 6, 1886, Lincoln Collection
Chestatee Regional Library System, Gainesville, Georgia:
    James Longstreet Papers
Chicago Historical Society:

James Longstreet Papers
Fredericksburg and Spotsylvania National Military Park:
    Maston G. Bass, Letter, July 8, 1863
    Calhoun L. Cooper Letters
    Marcus L. Green Diary
    A. G. Grinnan, "General Lee's Movement Against Pope, August, 1862,"
        typescript copy
    Matilda Hamilton Diary, typescript copy
    G. W. C. Lee, Letter to Fitzhugh Lee, February 11, 1896
    James Longstreet, Letter to Augustus Baldwin Longstreet, August 13,
        1861, typescript copy
    Copy of Macon *Telegraph,* December 25, 1862
    Lafayette McLaws, Letter to Charles Arnall, February 2, 1897, typescript
        copy
    J. G. Montgomery, Letter, January 9, 1863
    "Reminiscences of Gettysburg by Unidentified Member of 16th Georgia
        Volunteers"
    James McClure Scott, "Confederate War Reminiscences"
    Arthur Benjamin Simms, Letter, August 23, 1864
    Charles Frederick Terrill, Letter, September 22, 1863, Typescript Copy
    Joseph White Woods, "Reminiscences"
Georgia Department of Archives and History:
    James Longstreet Papers
Georgia Historical Society:
    James Longstreet Papers
Gettysburg National Military Park, Gettysburg, Pennsylvania:
    Christopher Gayle Levin Diary, typescript copy, Ninth Virginia Infantry
        File
    G. B. Gerald, "The Battle Of Gettysburg," Waco *Daily Herald,* July 3,
        1913, Barksdale Brigade File
    Gettysburg Clipping Books
    John H. Lewis, "Recollections from 1860 to 1865," typescript copy, Ninth
        Virginia Infantry File
    Alexander McNeill, Letters, Kershaw's Brigade File
    Alonzo Meyers, "Kershaw's Brigade at Peach Orchard," *National Tri-
        bune,* January 21, 1926, Kershaw's Brigade File
    William Ross Stillwell, Diary, Fifty-third Georgia Infantry File
Harvard University, The Houghton Library:
    Autograph File: James Freeman Clarke Papers
    Frederick M. Dearborn Collection
    Charles E. Norton Papers
Rutherford B. Hayes Presidential Center, Spiegel Grove, Ohio:
    James Longstreet Papers
The Historical Society of Pennsylvania:
    James Longstreet Papers
The Henry E. Huntington Library, San Marino, California:
    James Longstreet Papers

Jones Memorial Library, Lynchburg, Virginia:
  "Early Historical Information, St. Paul's Church, 1822–1972"
  "Garland Family of Lynchburg and Their Hill"
  "Lynchburg Area Marriages 1837–1880"
Library of Congress, Washington, D.C.:
  R. S. Ewell Papers
  Jedediah Hotchkiss Papers
  Louis T. Wigfall Papers
  Cadmus M. Wilcox Papers
Manassas National Battlefield Park:
  Edmund Berkeley, "War Reminiscences And Others Of A Son Of The
     Old Dominion," typescript copy, Eighth Virginia File
  William H. Chapman, Letter, Virginia Dixie Battery File
  William Choice, "Memoirs," typescript copy, Fifth South Carolina File
  Spencer Clack, Letters, Ninth Alabama File
  J. F. Hendricks, Civil War Account, Hampton, South Carolina, Legion File
  "Joskins" Journal, transcribed, Fifth Texas File
  Letter, September 14, 1862, Athens, Georgia, *Weekly Banner,* October
     1, 1862, Phillips (Georgia) Legion File
  Charles J. Lewis, "Account of Second Manassas"
  James Longstreet, Letter regarding Second Manassas to Francis J. Lippitt,
     typescript copy
  Position, Organization, Longstreet's Corps; Corse's Report of August 30
  M. O. Young, "History of the First Brigade–Antietam"
The Museum of the Confederacy, Eleanor S. Brockenbrough Library, Rich-
     mond, Virginia:
  D. H. Hill Papers
  James Longstreet Papers
National Archives, Washington, D.C.:
  Compiled Service Records, Records Group 109
  Letters Sent by the Ninth Military Department, The Department of New
     Mexico, and the District of New Mexico, 1849–1890, Records
     Group 393
  Records of the Adjutant General's Office, Letters Received, Main Series,
     Records Group 94
New Hampshire Historical Society:
  John B. Bachelder Papers
The New York Historical Society:
  A. R. Chisholm Papers, "War of 1861–1865."
  Henry B. Dawson Papers, miscellaneous manuscripts.
  R. E. Lee Papers, miscellaneous manuscripts.
The New York Public Library Rare Books and Manuscripts Division, Astor
     Lenox and Tilden Foundations:
  Ezra Carman Papers
  Horace Greeley Papers
  E. M. Law, "Lookout Valley—Memorandum of Gen E. M. Law," Ezra
     Ayers Carman Papers

E. M. Law Papers, *Century* Collection
James Longstreet Papers, *Century* Collection
Tennessee State Library and Archives, Nashville, Tennessee:
  Benjamin Franklin Cheatham Papers
Tulane University, Howard-Tilton Memorial Library, New Orleans, Louisi-
    ana:
  Louisiana Historical Association Collection:
      Association of the Army of Northern Virginia Papers
  J. B. Walton Papers
  J. W. Minnich, "Pegram's Confederate Brigade at Chickamauga, Sept. 18–
      19–20–21, 1863," Manuscript Series No. 65, Manuscript Section
Union Theological Seminary, Richmond, Virginia:
  R. L. Dabney Papers
United States Army Military History Institute, Carlisle Barracks, Pennsyl-
    vania:
  Robert L. Brake Collection
  D. B. Easley Papers
  Daniel Harvey Hill Papers
  Daniel Harvey Hill Papers, *CWTI* Collection
  George L. Kilmer, "Heroic Deeds, Battles, Episodes, &c," Miscellaneous
      Pamphlets
  David G. McIntosh Papers, Civil War Miscellaneous Collection
  John S. Mosby Papers
  John Musser, Civil War Letters, typescript, Ronald Boyer Collection
  Philip Powers Letters, Lewis Leigh Collection
  Charles W. Squires, "The Last of Lee's Battle Line," *CWTI* Collection
  Walter Taylor, Letter to "Lucien," October 24, 1864, Lewis Leigh Collec-
      tion
  Johnson J. Webb Letters, Lewis Leigh Collection
  Nathan Woodhouse, "The Old Confederate Soldier. His Experiences
      During and After the War," Lewis Leigh Collection
United States Military Academy Archives:
  James Longstreet, "Academic Record at the United States Military Acad-
      emy, 1 July 1838—1 July 1842," typescript copy
  James Longstreet, Cadet Application Records, copies
  James Longstreet, "List of Orders Relating to Cadetship of James Long-
      street," typescript copy
  James Longstreet, "Select List of Delinquencies," typescript copy
The University of Georgia, Hargrett Rare Book and Manuscript Library:
  Ivy Duggan Papers
University of North Carolina, Southern Historical Collection:
  Edward Porter Alexander Papers
  Henry L. Benning Papers
  Irving A. Buck Papers
  Campbell-Colston Family Papers
  J. F. H. Claiborne Papers
  James E. Cobb Diary, Cobb-Hunter Papers

J. F. Coghill Papers

Frederick M. Colston, "The Campaign Of Gettysburg (as I saw it)," typed copy, Campbell-Colston Papers

William Porcher DuBose, "Reminiscences"

Mary E. Grattan Papers

Peter W. Hariston Papers, typescript reminiscences

Benjamin G. Humphreys, "A History of the Sunflower Guards," J. F. H. Claiborne Papers

Francis Milton Kennedy Diary, typescript copy

Harry Lewis Papers

Armistead L. Long Papers

James Longstreet Papers

Mangum Family Papers

David Gregg McIntosh, "A Ride On Horseback In The Summer Of 1910 Over Some Of The Battlefields Of The Great Civil War With Some Notes Of The Battles"

Lafayette McLaws Papers

Raphael J. Moses, "Autobiography"

William N. Pendleton Papers

William B. Pettit Papers

Christian Thomas Pfohl Papers

Polk, Badger, and McGehee Family Papers

Edward Payson Reeve Papers

James R. Sheldon, "Last March of the Army of 'Lee': An Address," typescript copy

Westwood A. Todd, "Reminiscences," typed copy

Glenn Tucker Papers

Charles Scott Venable Papers

Lewis N. Whittle Papers

University of Texas at Austin, Center for American History:
James Longstreet, Order and Letter Book, 1863–1865

University of Virginia, Charlottesville, Virginia:
Blackford Family Papers, #6403

Monroe F. Cockrell, "Where Was Pickett at Gettysburg?" October 1, 1949, Monroe Cockrell Collection, #3393

John Warwick Daniel Papers, #158

Dearing Family Papers, #3117

Heth-Selden Papers, #5071

Mrs. Bradley T. Johnson Journal, #5594

Clement Dixon Johnston Papers, #6693

James Lawson Kemper Papers, #4098

John Price Kepner, Diary for 1864, typescript copy, Douglas Southall Freeman Papers

Samuel Thomas McCullough Diaries, McCullough-Hotchkiss Collection, #2907

Jefferson Davis Norris Papers, #2454

Charles R. Phelps Papers, #2920

Leigh Robinson Papers, #438
Thomas Lafayette Rosser Papers, #1171
William Randolph Smith, Diary, typescript, Douglas Southall Freeman
    Papers, #5220
Charles Scott Venable, "Personal Reminiscences Of The Confederate
    War," McDowell Family Papers, #2969-A
Virginia Historical Society, Richmond, Virginia:
    Bemiss Family Papers
    Carrington Family Papers
    William Henry Chapman Papers
    Cocke Family Papers
    Thomas Conolly Diary
    Cooke Family Papers
    John W. Daniel, "Account of Gettysburg, September 23, 1863," John
        Warwick Daniel Papers
    James Dearing Papers
    Edward Samuel Duffey Diary
    Thomas C. Elder Papers
    John Walter Fairfax Papers
    Benjamin Lyons Farinholt Papers
    Alexander Hunter, "Four Years in the Ranks"
    Samuel R. Johnston Papers
    Keiley Family Papers
    Osmun Latrobe Diary 1862–1865
    Lee Family Papers
    Hunter Holmes McGuire Papers
    David G. McIntosh Papers
    John Lawrence Meem Papers
    Charles Pickett Papers
    Ridley Family Papers
    John Simmons Shipp, Diary, 1862–1864, Shipp Family Papers
    Henry M. Talley Papers
    Erasmus Taylor, "War Reminiscences of Major Erasmus Taylor, C.S.A.,
        Written For His Children"
    David Addison Weisiger Papers
Virginia State Library:
    D. H. Hill Papers
    Walter H. Taylor Papers
Washington and Lee University, Lexington, Virginia:
    Jefferson Davis Papers
    Edward Dix Letters
    Robert E. Lee Papers, Special Collections
    William P. Parker, Diary, 1861–1862, Rockbridge Historical Society Col-
        lection
Jeffry D. Wert Personal Collection
The Western Reserve Historical Society:
    Robert E. Lee Papers

Lafayette McLaws Papers, William P. Palmer Collection
George E. Pickett Papers

NEWSPAPERS

Atlanta *Constitution*
Baltimore *Sun*
London *Times*
Lynchburg *Virginian*
Macon *Telegraph*
New York *Herald*
New York *Times*
New York *Tribune*
Philadelphia *Press*
Philadelphia *Weekly Press*
Richmond *Times-Dispatch*
Savannah *Morning News*
Washington, D.C., *Daily National Intelligencer*

PUBLISHED SOURCES

Agassiz, George R., Ed. *Meade's Headquarters 1863–1865: Letters of Colonel Theodore Lyman From the Wilderness to Appomattox.* Boston: Atlantic Monthly Press, 1922.

Alexander, E. P. *Military Memoirs Of A Confederate.* Edited and with an Introduction and Notes by T. Harry Williams. Bloomington: Indiana University Press, 1962.

Allardice, Bruce L. "Longstreet's Nightmare in Tennessee," *Civil War Magazine,* vol. 18.

Alvarez, Eugene. "The Death of the 'Old War Horse' Longstreet," *The Georgia Historical Quarterly,* vol. 52, no. 1 (March 1968).

Ambrose, Stephen E. *Duty, Honor, Country: A History of West Point.* Baltimore: Johns Hopkins Press, 1966.

The Annals Of The War Written By Leading Participants North And South. Reprint edition. Dayton, Ohio: Morningside Bookshop, 1988.

Austerman, Wayne R. "Major Longstreet Goes Home," *Civil War Times Illustrated,* vol. 20, no. 3 (June 1981).

Batchelor, Benjamin Franklin. *Batchelor-Turner Letters 1861–1864. Written by Two of Terry's Texas Rangers.* Annotated by H. J. H. Rugeley. Austin, Texas: The Steck Company, 1961.

Bauer, K. Jack. *The Mexican War 1846–1848.* New York: Macmillan Publishing Co., 1974.

Bean, W. G., Ed. "Memoranda of Conversations between General Robert E. Lee and William Preston Johnston, May 7, 1868, and March 18, 1870," *Virginia Magazine of History and Biography,* vol. 73 (1965).

Bernard, George S., Ed. *War Talks of Confederate Veterans.* Reprint edition. Dayton, Ohio: Morningside Bookshop, 1981.

Blackford, Susan Leigh, Ed. *Letters From Lee's Army: On Memoirs of Life In and Out of The Army in Virginia During the War Between the States.* Paperback edition. New York: A. S. Barnes & Co., 1962.

Blackford, W. W. *War Years with Jeb Stuart.* New York: Charles Scribner's Sons, 1945.

Bond, Natalie Jenkins, and Coward, Osmun Latrobe, Eds. *The South Carolinians: Colonel Asbury Coward's Memoirs.* New York: Vantage Press, 1968.

Brady, Robert. *The Story of One Regiment, the Eleventh Maine Infantry Volunteers, in the War of the Rebellion.* New York: J. J. Little & Co., 1896.

Brewer, A. T. *History, Sixty-first Regiment, Pennsylvania Volunteers 1861–1865.* Pittsburgh, Pennsylvania: Art Engraving & Printing Co., 1911.

Bridges, Hal. *Lee's Maverick General: Daniel Harvey Hill.* Reprint edition. Gaithersburg, Maryland: Olde Soldier Books, n.d.

Brown, Phillip F. *Reminiscences of the War of 1861–1865.* Richmond, Virginia: Whittet & Shepperson, 1917.

Bruce, George A. *The Twentieth Regiment of Massachusetts Volunteer Infantry, 1861–1865.* Boston: Houghton, Mifflin & Co., 1906.

Burnett, Edmund Cody, Cont. "Letters of Barnett Handeman Cody and Others, 1861–1864," *Georgia Historical Quarterly,* vol. 23, no. 3 (September 1939).

Busey, John W., and Martin, David G. *Regimental Strengths at Gettysburg.* Baltimore: Gateway Press, 1982.

Cabell, Sears Wilson. "Longstreet at Gettysburg," Richmond *Times-Dispatch,* Sunday Magazine & Book Review, August 7, 1938.

Caldwell, J. F. J. *The History of A Brigade of South Carolinians Known First As "Gregg's," and Subsequently as "McGowan's Brigade."* Marietta, Georgia: Continental Book Co., 1951.

Calkins, Chris M. *The Battles of Appomattox Station and Appomattox Court House, April 8–9, 1865.* Lynchburg, Virginia: H. E. Howard, 1987.

Casler, John O. *Four Years in the Stonewall Brigade.* Reprint edition. Dayton, Ohio: Morningside Bookshop, 1971.

Catton, Bruce. *The Army of the Potomac: Glory Road.* Garden City, New York: Doubleday & Co., 1952.

———. *Gettysburg: The Final Fury.* Garden City, New York: Doubleday & Co., 1974.

———. *Mr. Lincoln's Army,* Garden City, New York: Doubleday & Co., 1962.

Cauble, Frank P. *The Surrender Proceedings, April 9, 1865, Appomattox Court House.* Lynchburg, Virginia: H. E. Howard, 1987.

Chambers, Henry A. *Diary of Captain Henry A. Chambers.* Edited by T. H. Pearce. Wendell, North Carolina: Broadfoot's Bookmark, 1983.

Chambers, Lenoir. *Stonewall Jackson.* New York: William Morrow & Co., 1959.

Chesnut, Mary Boykin. *A Diary From Dixie.* Edited by Ben Ames Williams. Boston: Houghton Mifflin Co., 1949.

Clark, Walter, Ed. *Histories of the Several Regiments And Battalions From*

North Carolina in the Great War, 1861–'65. Written by members of the respective commands. Reprint edition. Wendell, North Carolina: Broadfoot's Bookmark, 1982.

Coco, Gregory A. *On the Bloodstained Field: 130 Human Interest Stories from the Campaign and Battle of Gettysburg.* Hollidaysburg, Pennsylvania: Wheatfield Press, 1987.

———. *A Vast Sea of Misery.* Foreword by Kathleen George Harrison. Gettysburg, Pennsylvania: Thomas Publications, 1988.

Coddington, Edwin B. *The Gettysburg Campaign: A Study in Command.* New York: Charles Scribner's Sons, 1968.

Coker, James Lide. *History of Company G, Ninth S. E. Regiment, Infantry, S. C. Army, and of Company E. Sixth S. C. Regiment, Infantry, S. C. Army.* Reprint edition. Greenwood, South Carolina: Attic Press, 1979.

A Confederate Scout. [Cussans, John] *The Passage of Thoroughfare Gap and the . . . Assembling of Lee's Army . . . for the Second Battle of Manassas.* York, Pennsylvania: Gazette Print, 1906.

Connelly, Thomas Lawrence. *Autumn of Glory: The Army of Tennessee, 1862–1865.* Baton Rouge: Louisiana State University Press, 1971.

———. *The Marble Man: Robert E. Lee and His Image in American Society.* New York: Alfred A. Knopf, 1977.

Connelly, Thomas Lawrence, and Jones, Archer. *The Politics of Command: Factions and Ideas in Confederate Strategy.* Baton Rouge: Louisiana State University Press, 1973.

Corby, W. *Memoirs of Chaplain Life.* Notre Dame, Indiana: Scholastic Press, 1894.

Cormier, Steven A. *The Siege of Suffolk: The Forgotten Campaign, April 11–May 4, 1863.* Lynchburg, Virginia: H. E. Howard, 1989.

Cowper, Pulaski. *Extracts of Letters of Major-General Bryan Grimes to His Wife . . .* Edited by Gary W. Gallagher. Wilmington, North Carolina: Broadfoot Publishing Co., 1986.

Cozzens, Peter. *This Terrible Sound. The Battle of Chickamauga.* Chicago: University of Illinois Press, 1992.

Crute, Joseph H., Jr. *Confederate Staff Officers, 1861–1865.* Powhatan, Virginia: Derwent Books, 1982.

Cullum, George W. *Biographical Register of the Officers And Graduates of the U. S. Military Academy At West Point, N. Y., From Its Establishment, In 1802, To 1890.* Boston: Houghton, Mifflin & Co., 1891.

Cunningham, S. A., Ed. *Confederate Veteran.* 40 vols. Reprint edition. Wilmington, North Carolina: Broadfoot Publishing Co., 1988.

Daniel, Frederick S. *Richmond Howitzers In The War.* Reprint edition. Gaithersburg, Maryland: Butternut Press, n.d.

Davis, George B., et al. *The Official Military Atlas of the Civil War.* Introduction by Richard Sommers. Reprint edition. Gettysburg, Pennsylvania: National Historical Society, 1978.

Davis, Stephen. "The Death and Burial of General Richard Brooke Garnett," *Gettysburg Magazine,* no. 5 (July 1991).

Davis, W. W. H. *History of the 104th Pennsylvania Regiment, from August 22nd, 1861, to September 30th, 1864.* Philadelphia: Joseph B. Rodgers, 1866.

Davis, William C. "The Campaign to Appomattox," *Civil War Times Illustrated,* vol. 14, no. 1 (April 1975).

———. *Jefferson Davis: The Man and His Hour.* New York: HarperCollins Publishers, 1991.

Dawson, Francis W. *Reminiscences of Confederate Service, 1861–1865.* Edited by Bell I. Wiley. Baton Rouge, Louisiana: Louisiana State University Press, 1980.

"Diary of Turner Vaughan Co. 'C,' 4th Alabama Regiment, C.S.A. Commenced March 4th, 1863, and Ending February 12th, 1864," *Alabama Historical Quarterly,* vol. 18 (1956).

"A Diary on the March," *Virginia Country's Civil War,* vol. 3.

Dickert, D. Augustus. *History of Kershaw's Brigade.* Reprint edition. Dayton, Ohio: Morningside Bookshop, 1973.

Dickey, Luther S. *Eighty-fifth Regiment Pennsylvania Volunteer Infantry, 1861–1865.* New York: J. D. and W. E. Powers, 1915.

———. *History of the 103d Regiment, Pennsylvania Veteran Volunteer Infantry, 1861–1865.* Chicago: L. S. Dickey, 1910.

Dinkins, James. *1861–1865, By an Old Johnnie.* Reprint edition. Dayton, Ohio: Morningside Bookshop, 1975.

Douglas, Henry Kyd. *I Rode With Stonewall.* Chapel Hill, North Carolina: University of North Carolina Press, 1940.

Dowdey, Clifford. *Lee.* Boston: Little, Brown & Co., 1965.

———. *The Seven Days: The Emergence of Robert E. Lee.* New York: Fairfax Press, 1978.

Dowdey, Clifford, and Manarin, Louis H., Eds. *The Wartime Papers of R. E. Lee.* Boston: Little, Brown & Co., 1961.

Downey, Fairfax. *The Guns at Gettysburg.* New York: David McKay Co., 1958.

Durkin, Joseph T., Ed. *John Dooley, Confederate Soldier: His War Journal.* Notre Dame, Indiana: University of Notre Dame Press, 1963.

Early, Jubal Anderson. *Autobiographical Sketch And Narrative Of The War Between The States.* Introduction by Gary Gallagher. Reprint edition. Wilmington, North Carolina: Broadfoot Publishing Company, 1989.

Early, R. H. *Campbell Chronicles and Family Sketches Embracing the History of Campbell County, Virginia, 1782–1926.* Lynchburg, Virginia: J. P. Bell Co., 1927.

Eckenrode, H. J., and Conrad, Bryan. *James Longstreet: Lee's War Horse.* Foreword by Gary W. Gallagher. Chapel Hill, North Carolina: University of North Carolina Press, 1986.

Editors of Time-Life Books. *Lee Takes Command: From Seven Days to Second Bull Run.* Alexandria, Virginia: Time-Life Books, 1984.

Eggleston, George Cary. *A Rebel's Recollections.* Introduction by David Donald. Bloomington, Indiana: Indiana University Press, 1959.

Eliot, Ellsworth, Jr. *West Point in the Confederacy.* New York: G. A. Baker & Co., 1941.

An English Combatant. *Battle-Fields Of The South, From Bull Run To Fredericksburg.* Reprint edition. Time-Life Books, 1984.

"E. P. Alexander and Pickett's Charge," *Civil War Times Illustrated,* vol. 18, no. 1 (April 1978).

Evans, Clement A., Ed. *Confederate Military History.* Reprint edition. Dayton, Ohio: Morningside Bookshop, 1975.

Everett, Donald E., Ed. *Chaplain Davis and Hood's Texas Brigade.* San Antonio, Texas: Principia Press of Trinity University, 1962.

Faeder, Gustav S. "The Best of Friends and Enemies," *Civil War Times Illustrated,* vol. 26, no. 6 (October 1987).

Faust, Patricia L., Ed. *Historical Times Illustrated Encyclopedia of the Civil War.* New York: Harper & Row, 1986.

Fitzgerald, O. P. *Judge Longstreet: A Life Sketch.* Nashville, Tennessee: Methodist Episcopal Church, South, 1891.

Fleming, Francis P. *Memoir of Capt. C. Seton Fleming, of the Second Florida Infantry, C.S.A.* Reprint edition. Alexandria, Virginia: Stonewall House, 1985.

Fleming, Thomas J. *West Point: The Men and Times of the United States Military Academy.* New York: William Morrow & Co., 1969.

Fletcher, William Andrew. *Rebel Private Front and Rear.* Reprint edition. Washington, D.C.: Zenger Publishing Co., 1985.

Floyd, Frederick C. *History of the Fortieth (Mozart) Regiment New York Volunteers.* Boston: F. H. Gilson Co., 1909.

Foner, Eric. *Reconstruction: America's Unfinished Revolution, 1863–1877.* New York: Harper & Row, 1988.

Foote, Shelby. *The Civil War: A Narrative—Fort Sumter to Perryville.* New York: Random House, 1958.

———. *The Civil War: A Narrative—Fredericksburg to Meridian.* New York: Random House, 1963.

Ford, Andrew. *The Story of the Fifteenth Regiment Massachusetts Volunteer Infantry in the Civil War, 1861–1864.* Clinton: W. J. Coulter, 1898.

Frassanito, William A. *Gettysburg: A Journey in Time.* New York: Charles Scribner's Sons, 1975.

Frederick, Gilbert. *The Story Of A Regiment Being A Record Of The Military Services of the Fifty-Seventh New York State Volunteer Infantry in the War Of The Rebellion, 1861–1865.* Chicago: C. H. Morgan Co., 1895.

Freehling, William W. *Prelude to Civil War: The Nullification Controversy in South Carolina, 1816–1836.* Paperback edition. New York: Harper Torchbooks, 1966.

Freeman, Douglas Southall, Ed. *Lee's Dispatches: Unpublished Letters of General Robert E. Lee, C.S.A., to Jefferson Davis and the War Department of the Confederate States of America, 1862–1865.* With Additional Dispatches and Foreword by Grady McWhiney. New York: G. P. Putnam's Sons, 1957.

———. *Lee's Lieutenants: A Study in Command*. Three Volumes. New York: Charles Scribner's Sons, 1942–1944.

———. *R. E. Lee: A Biography*. Four Volumes. New York: Charles Scribner's Sons, 1934–1935.

French, Samuel G. *Two Wars: An Autobiography of General Samuel G. French*. Nashville, Tennessee: Confederate Veteran, 1901.

Gallagher, Gary W., Ed. *Antietam: Essays on the 1862 Maryland Campaign*. Kent, Ohio: Kent State University Press, 1989.

———. *Fighting for the Confederacy: The Personal Recollections of General Edward Porter Alexander*. Chapel Hill, North Carolina: University of North Carolina Press, 1989.

———. "Scapegoat in Victory: James Longstreet and the Battle of Second Manassas," *Civil War History*, vol. 34, no. 4.

———. " 'Till the Sun Goes Down or Victory Is Won': The Confederate Defense of the Sunken Road at Sharpsburg." *Virginia Country's Civil War Quarterly*, vol. 9.

Georg, Kathleen R. " 'Our Principal Loss Was in This Place': Action at the Slaughter Pen and at the South End of Houck's Ridge." *The Morningside Notes*, 1984.

Georg, Kathleen R., and Busey, John W. *Nothing but Glory: Pickett's Division at Gettysburg*. Hightstown, New Jersey: Longstreet House, 1987.

Gordon, John B. *Reminiscences Of The Civil War*. Reprint edition. Gettysburg, Pennsylvania: Civil War Times Illustrated, 1974.

Goree, Langston James, V, Ed. *The Thomas Jewitt Goree Letters, Volume I: The Civil War Correspondence*. Bryan, Texas: Family History Foundation, 1981.

Gott, John K. *High in Old Virginia Piedmont: A History of Marshall (Formerly Salem), Fauquier County, Virginia*. Marshall, Virginia: Marshall National Bank & Trust Co., 1987.

Grant, Ulysses S. *Personal Memoirs of U. S. Grant*. New York: Charles L. Webster & Co., 1885.

Grantham, Dewey W., Jr., Ed. "Letters from H. J. Hightower, a Confederate Soldier, 1862–1864," *Georgia Historical Quarterly*, vol. 40 (1956).

Graves, Joseph A. *The History of the Bedford Light Artillery*. Reprint edition. Gaithersburg, Maryland: Butternut Press, 1980.

Greezicki, Roger J. "Humbugging the Historian: A Reappraisal of Longstreet at Gettysburg," *Gettysburg Magazine*, no. 6 (January 1992).

Hagerman, Edward. *The American Civil War and the Origins of Modern Warfare: Ideas, Organization, and Field Command*. Bloomington, Indiana: Indiana University Press, 1988.

Hagood, Johnson. *Memoirs of the War of Secession From the Original Manuscripts*. Columbia, South Carolina: The State Co., 1910.

Hall, James O. "The Spy Harrison," *Civil War Times Illustrated*, vol. 24, no. 10 (February 1986).

Hamilton, J. G. deRoulhac, Ed. *The Papers of Randolph Abbott Shotwell*. Raleigh, North Carolina: North Carolina Historical Commission, 1929–1931.

Hamlin, Percy Gatling. *"Old Bald Head" (General R. S. Ewell): The Portrait of a Soldier and the Making of a Soldier: Letters of General R. S. Ewell.* Combined by Ron R. Van Sickle. Reprint edition. Gaithersburg, Maryland: Ron R. Van Sickle Military Books, 1988.

Happel, Ralph. "The Chancellors of Chancellorsville," *Virginia Magazine of History and Biography,* vol. 71, no. 3 (July 1963).

Harrison, Lowell. "Battle Beyond Knoxville," *Civil War Times Illustrated,* vol. 26, no. 3 (May 1987).

Harrison, Walter. *Pickett's Men: A Fragment of War History.* Reprint edition. Gaithersburg, Maryland: Olde Soldier Books, 1987.

Hartwig, D. Scott. "Guts and Good Leadership: The Action at the Railroad Cut, July 1, 1863." *Morningside Notes,* May 1985.

Haskell, Frank Aretas. *The Battle of Gettysburg.* Wisconsin History Commission, 1908.

Haskell, John Cheves. *The Haskell Memoirs.* Edited by Gilbert E. Govan and James W. Livingood. New York: G. P. Putnam's Sons, 1960.

Hassler, Warren W., Jr. *Crisis at the Crossroads: The First Day at Gettysburg.* University, Alabama: University of Alabama Press, 1970.

Hassler, William W., Ed. *The General to His Lady: The Civil War Letters of William Dorsey Pender to Fanny Pender.* Chapel Hill, North Carolina: University of North Carolina Press, 1965.

Hattaway, Herman, and Jones, Archer. *How the North Won: A Military History of the Civil War.* Chicago: University of Illinois Press, 1983.

Heiser, John. "Action on the Emmitsburg Road, Gettysburg, Pennsylvania, July 2, 1863." *Morningside Notes,* 1983.

Hennessy, John. *The First Battle of Manassas: An End to Innocence, July 18–21, 1861.* Lynchburg, Virginia: H. E. Howard, 1989.

———. *Historical Report on the Troop Movements for the Second Battle of Manassas, August 28 through August 30, 1862.* Denver: National Park Service, 1985.

Hood, John B. *Advance And Retreat: Personal Experiences in the United States & Confederate States Armies.* Edited and with an Introduction and Notes by Richard N. Current. Bloomington, Indiana: Indiana University Press, 1959.

Hoole, Wm. Stanley. *Lawley Covers the Confederacy.* Tuscaloosa, Alabama: Confederate Publishing Co., 1964.

Houck, Peter W. "A Healing Place," *Civil War Magazine,* vol. 9, no. 3 (May–June 1991).

Houghton, W. R. and M. B. *Two Boys in the Civil War and After.* Montgomery, Alabama: Paragon Press, 1912.

Inman, Arthur Crew, Ed. *Soldier Of The South: General Pickett's War Letters To His Wife.* Boston: Houghton Mifflin Co., 1928.

Jensen, Les. *32nd Virginia Infantry.* Lynchburg, Virginia: H. E. Howard, 1990.

Johnson, Ludwell H., Ed. "William Booth Taliaferro's Letters from Mexico, 1847–1848," *Virginia Magazine of History and Biography,* vol. 73 (1965).

Johnson, Robert Underwood, and Buel, Clarence Clough, Eds. *Battles and Leaders of the Civil War.* Reprint edition. New York: Thomas Yoseloff, 1956.

Johnston, Joseph E. *Narrative of Military Operations Directed, During The Late War Between The States.* Introduction by Frank E. Vandiver. Bloomington, Indiana: Indiana University Press, 1959.

Jones, Archer. *Civil War Command and Strategy: The Process of Victory and Defeat.* New York: Free Press, 1992.

Jones, J. B. *A Rebel War Clerk's Diary at the Confederate States Capital.* Reprint edition. New York: Time-Life Books, 1982.

Jordon, Virginia Fitzgerald, Ed. *The Captain Remembers: The Papers of Captain Richard Irby.* Nottoway County Historical Association, 1975.

Kirkland, Thomas J., and Kennedy, Robert M. *Historic Camden. Part Two: Nineteenth Century.* Reprint edition. Camden, South Carolina: Kershaw County Historical Society, 1965.

Kreutzer, William. *Notes And Observations Made During Four Years Of Service With The Ninety-Eighth N. Y. Volunteers, In The War Of 1861.* Philadelphia: Grant, Faires & Rodgers, 1878.

Krick, Robert K. " 'I Consider Him a Humbug . . .'—McLaws on Longstreet at Gettysburg," *Virginia Country's Civil War Quarterly,* vol. 5.

————. *Parker's Virginia Battery, C.S.A.* Second edition revised. Wilmington, North Carolina: Broadfoot Publishing Co., 1989.

Krolick, Marshall D. "Lee and Longstreet at Gettysburg," *Virginia Country's Civil War Quarterly,* vol. 5.

————. "Lee vs. Stuart: The Gettysburg Altercation." *Virginia Country's Civil War,* vol. 2.

Kunhardt, Philip B., Jr. *A New Birth of Freedom: Lincoln at Gettysburg.* Boston: Little, Brown & Co., 1983.

Lane, Lydia Spencer. *I Married a Soldier.* Introduction by Darlis A. Miller. Albuquerque, New Mexico: University of New Mexico Press, 1964.

Lane, Mills, Ed. *"Dear Mother: Don't grieve about me. If I get killed, I'll only be dead": Letters from Georgia Soldiers in the Civil War.* Savannah, Georgia: Beehive Press, 1977.

Laswell, Mary, Ed. *Rags and Hope: The Recollections of Val C. Giles, Four Years with Hood's Brigade, Fourth Texas Infantry, 1861–1865.* New York: Coward-McCann, 1961.

"Lee Blamed Ewell and Longstreet for His Failure in the Wilderness," *Civil War Times Illustrated,* vol. 5, no. 1 (April 1966).

Lee, Robert E. *Recollections and Letters of General Robert E. Lee.* Garden City, New York: Garden City Publishing Co., 1924.

Livermore, Thomas L. *Numbers And Losses In The Civil War In America, 1861–1865.* Reprint edition. Dayton, Ohio: Morningside House, 1986.

Loehr, Charles T. *War History of the Old First Virginia Infantry Regiment, Army Of Northern Virginia.* Reprint edition. Dayton, Ohio: Morningside Bookshop, 1970.

Long, A. L. *Memoirs Of Robert E. Lee: His Military And Personal History*. New York: J. M. Stoddard & Co., 1886.

Long, E. B., and Long, Barbara. *The Civil War Day by Day: An Almanac, 1861–1865*. Garden City, New York: Doubleday & Co., 1971.

Longstreet, Helen D. *Lee And Longstreet At High Tide: Gettysburg In The Light Of The Official Records*. Reprint edition. Wilmington, North Carolina: Broadfoot Publishing Co., 1989.

Longstreet, James. *From Manassas To Appomattox: Memoirs Of The Civil War In America*. Edited and with an Introduction and Notes by James I. Robertson, Jr. Bloomington, Indiana: Indiana University Press, 1960.

Lord, Walter, Ed. *The Fremantle Diary*. Boston: Little, Brown & Co., 1954.

Mackall, William W. *A Son's Recollections of His Father*. New York: E. P. Dutton & Co., 1930.

Marvel, William. *Burnside*. Chapel Hill, North Carolina: University of North Carolina Press, 1991.

Maurice, Frederick. *An Aide-De-Camp Of Lee*. Boston: Little, Brown & Co., 1927.

Mayes, Edward. *Genealogy Of The Family Of Longstreet*. Jackson, Mississippi: Edward Mayes, n.d.

McCall, George Archibald. *New Mexico in 1850: A Military View*. Edited and with an Introduction by Robert W. Frazer. Norman, Oklahoma: University of Oklahoma Press, 1968.

McDonald, Archie P., Ed. *Make Me a Map of the Valley: The Civil War Journal of Stonewall Jackson's Topographer*. Dallas: Southern Methodist University Press, 1973.

McDonough, James Lee. *Chattanooga: A Death Grip on the Confederacy*. Knoxville, Tennessee: University of Tennessee Press, 1984.

McDowell, John E., and Davis, William C. " 'Joe Writes His Own Praise,' " *Civil War Times Illustrated*, vol. 8, no. 10 (February 1970).

McFeely, William. *Grant: A Biography*. New York: W. W. Norton & Co., 1981.

McGee, Charles M., Jr., and Lander, Ernest M., Jr., Eds. *A Rebel Came Home: The Diary and Letters of Floride Clemson, 1863–1866*. Columbia, South Carolina: University of South Carolina Press, 1989.

McLaws, Lafayette. "After Chickamauga," *Addresses Delivered Before the Confederate Veteran Association of Savannah, Georgia, to Which Is Appended the President's Annual Report*. Savannah, Georgia: Braid & Hutton, 1898.

McMaster, Richard K., Ed. *Musket, Saber, and Missile: A History of Fort Bliss*. El Paso, Texas: Complete Printing & Letter Service, 1963.

McMurry, Richard M. *John Bell Hood and the War of Southern Independence*. Lexington, Kentucky: University Press of Kentucky, 1982.

McPherson, James M. *Ordeal by Fire: The Civil War and Reconstruction*. New York: Alfred A. Knopf, 1982.

Moffett, Mary Conner, Ed. *Letters of General James Conner, C.S.A.* Columbia, South Carolina: R. L. Bryan Co., 1950.

Montgomery, Horace. *Howell Cobb's Confederate Career.* Tuscaloosa, Alabama: Confederate Publishing Company, 1959.

Moore, Edward A. *The Story of a Cannoneer Under Stonewall Jackson.* Reprint edition. Freeport, New York: Books for Libraries Press, 1971.

Moore, Robert A. *A Life For The Confederacy.* Edited by James W. Silver. Reprint edition. Wilmington, North Carolina: Broadfoot Publishing Company, 1987.

Morgan, Claude M. "The Gettysburg Controversy," *The United Daughters of The Confederacy Magazine,* vol. 30, no. 12 (December 1967).

Morgan, W. H. *Personal Reminiscences of the War of 1861–5.* Lynchburg, Virginia: J. P. Bell Co., 1911.

Mott, Smith B. *The Campaigns of The Fifty-Second Regiment Pennsylvania Volunteer Infantry.* Philadelphia: J. B. Lippincott Co., 1911.

Muffly, J. W., Ed. *The Story of Our Regiment: A History of the 148th Pennsylvania Vols.* Des Moines, Iowa: Kenyon Printing & Mfg. Co., 1904.

Mulholland, St. Clair A. *The Story of the 116th Regiment, Pennsylvania Infantry, War of Secession, 1862–1865.* Philadelphia: F. McManus, Jr., & Co., 1899.

Nevins, Allan, Ed. *The Personal Journals of Colonel Charles S. Wainwright, 1862–1865.* New York: Harcourt, Brace & World, 1962.

Norman, William M. *A Portion of My Life.* Winston-Salem, North Carolina: John F. Blair, 1959.

Nye, Wilbur Sturtevant. *Here Come the Rebels!* Baton Rouge, Louisiana: Louisiana State University Press, 1965.

Oates, William C. *The War Between The Union And The Confederacy And Its Lost Opportunities.* Introduction by Robert K. Krick. Reprint edition. Dayton, Ohio: Morningside Bookshop, 1985.

O'Neill, Robert F., Jr. "Thoroughfare Gap: A Passage of Blood and Regrets," *Virginia Country's Civil War Quarterly,* vol. 6.

Owen, William Miller. *In Camp And Battle With The Washington Artillery Of New Orleans.* Reprint edition. Gaithersburg, Maryland: Butternut Press, n.d.

Patterson, Gerard. "Gustave," *Civil War Times Illustrated,* vol. 32, no. 3 (July-August 1992).

———. *Rebels from West Point.* New York: Doubleday and Co., 1987.

Pearce, Haywood J., Jr. "Longstreet's Responsibility on the Second Day at Gettysburg," *Georgia Historical Quarterly,* vol. 10 (1926).

Perret, Geoffrey. *A Country Made by War: From the Revolution to Vietnam —The Story of America's Rise to Power.* New York: Random House, 1989.

Perros, George P., Ed. "Letters of James Longstreet Relative to His Position of United States Marshal in Georgia," *Georgia Historical Quarterly,* vol. 41 (September 1957).

Pfanz, Harry W. *Gettysburg: The Second Day.* Chapel Hill, North Carolina: University of North Carolina Press, 1987.

Piston, William Garrett. "Lee's Tarnished Lieutenant: James Longstreet and His Image in American History," Ph.D. Dissertation, University of South Carolina, 1982.

————. *Lee's Tarnished Lieutenant: James Longstreet and His Place in Southern History.* Athens, Georgia: University of Georgia Press, 1987.

Poague, William Thomas. *Gunner with Stonewall: Reminiscences of William Thomas Poague.* Edited by Monroe F. Cockrell. Jackson, Tennessee: McCowat-Mercer Press, 1957.

Polley, J. B. *Hood's Texas Brigade: Its Marches, Its Battles, Its Achievements.* Reprint edition. Dayton, Ohio: Morningside Bookshop, 1988.

————. *A Soldier's Letters to Charming Nellie.* Introduction by Harold B. Simpson and Special Foreword by Robert K. Krick. Reprint edition. Gaithersburg, Maryland: Butternut Press, 1984.

Powell, Robert M. *Recollections of a Texas Colonel at Gettysburg.* Edited by Gregory A. Coco. Gettysburg, Pennsylvania: Thomas Publications, 1990.

Priest, John M. *Antietam: The Soldiers' Battle.* Shippensburg, Pennsylvania: White Mane Publishing Co., 1989.

Pullen, John J. *The Twentieth Maine: A Volunteer Regiment in the Civil War.* Philadelphia: J. B. Lippincott Co., 1957.

Qualfe, Milo M., Ed. *From the Cannon's Mouth: The Civil War Letters of General Alpheus S. Williams.* Detroit, Michigan: Wayne State University Press, 1959.

Ranson, A. R. H. "Reminiscences of the Civil War by a Confederate Staff Officer," *Sewanee Review,* vol. 22 (1914).

Ratchford, J. W. *Some Reminiscences of Persons and Incidents of the Civil War.* Reprint edition. Austin, Texas: Shoal Creek Publishers, 1971.

Reed, John A. *History of the 101st Regiment Pennsylvania Veterans Volunteer Infantry, 1861–1865.* Chicago: L. S. Dickey & Co., 1910.

Richter, William L. "James Longstreet: From Rebel to Scalawag," *Louisiana History,* vol. 11, no. 3 (Summer 1970).

Robertson, James I., Jr. *General A. P. Hill: The Story of a Confederate Warrior.* New York: Random House, 1987.

Robertson, William Glenn. "Rails to the River of Death: Railroads in the Chickamauga Campaign," *Civil War Magazine,* vol. 9, no. 6 (November–December 1991).

Roe, Alfred S. *The Tenth Regiment Massachusetts Volunteer Infantry, 1861–1864.* Springfield, Massachusetts: Press of the F. A. Bassette Co., 1909.

Ross, Fitzgerald. *Cities and Camps of the Confederate States.* Edited by Richard Barksdale Harwell. Urbana, Illinois: University of Illinois Press, 1958.

Round, Harold F. "The Telegraph Road," *Civil War Times Illustrated,* vol. 6, no. 3 (June 1967).

Rozier, John, Ed. *The Granite Farm Letters: The Civil War Correspondence of Edgeworth and Sallie Bird.* Foreword by Theodore Rosengarten. Athens, Georgia: University of Georgia Press, 1988.

Sanger, Donald Bridgmen. "Was Longstreet a Scapegoat?" *Infantry Journal,* vol. 43 (January-February 1936).

————. *The Story of Fort Bliss.* n.p., n.d.

Sanger, Donald Bridgmen, and Hay, Thomas Robson. *James Longstreet: I. Soldier; II. Politician, Officeholder, and Writer.* Gloucester, Massachusetts: Peter Smith, 1968.

Scheibert, Justus. *Seven Months In The Rebel States During the North American War, 1863.* Edited and with an Introduction by William Stanley Hoole. Tuscaloosa, Alabama: Confederate Publishing Company, 1958.

Scott, Kate M. *History of the One Hundred and Fifth Regiment of Pennsylvania Volunteers.* Philadelphia: New-World Publishing Company, 1877.

Scott, W. W. *A History of Orange County Virginia.* Reprint edition. Berryville, Virginia: Chesapeake Book Company, 1962.

Sears, Stephen W. "America's Bloodiest Day: The Battle of Antietam," *Civil War Times Illustrated,* vol. 26, no. 2 (April 1987).

———. *George B. McClellan: The Young Napoleon.* New York: Ticknor & Fields, 1988.

———. "Getting Right with Robert E. Lee," *American Heritage,* vol. 42, no. 3 (May-June 1991).

———. *Landscape Turned Red: The Battle of Antietam.* New York: Ticknor & Fields, 1983.

Seymour, Digby Gordon. *Divided Loyalties: Fort Sanders and the Civil War in East Tennessee.* Knoxville, Tennessee: University of Tennessee Press, 1963.

Shadgett, Olive Hall. "A History Of The Republican Party In Georgia From Reconstruction Through 1900," Ph.D. Dissertation, University of Georgia, 1962.

Shevchuk, Paul M. "The Lost Hours of 'Jeb' Stuart," *Gettysburg Magazine,* no. 4 (January 1991).

Simon, John Y., Ed. *The Personal Memoirs of Julia Dent Grant.* New York: G. P. Putnam's Sons, 1975.

Skoch, George. "A Test of Rebel Rails," *Civil War Times Illustrated,* vol. 25, no. 8 (December 1986).

Smith, Donald L. *The Twenty-fourth Michigan of the Iron Brigade.* Harrisburg, Pennsylvania: The Stackpole Company, 1962.

Smith, George Winston, and Judah, Charles. *Chronicles of the Gringos: The U.S. Army in the Mexican War, 1846–1848; Accounts of Eyewitnesses and Combatants.* Albuquerque, New Mexico: University of New Mexico Press, 1968.

Smith, Gustavus W. *The Battle Of Seven Pines.* New York: C. G. Crawford, 1891.

Smith, W. A. *The Anson Guards: Company C, Fourteenth Regiment, North Carolina Volunteers, 1861–1865.* Wendell, North Carolina: Broadfoot's Bookmark, 1978.

Sorrel G. Moxley. *Recollections Of A Confederate Staff Officer.* Edited by Bell Irvin Wiley. Jackson, Tennessee: McCowat-Mercer Press, 1958.

Southern Historical Society Papers.

Speed, Thomas. "Battle of Bean's Station, East Tennessee," *Southern Bivouac,* vol. 2 (November 1883).

Squires, Charles W. "The 'Boy Officer' of the Washington Artillery, Part I," *Civil War Times Illustrated,* vol. 14, no. 2 (May 1975).

————. " 'My Artillery Fire Was Very Destructive': The Charles W. Squires Memoir, Conclusion," *Civil War Times Illustrated,* vol. 14, no. 3 (June 1975).

Stackpole, Edward J. *They Met at Gettysburg.* Harrisburg, Pennsylvania: The Stackpole Company, 1956.

Steere, Edward. *The Wilderness Campaign.* Reprint edition. Gaithersburg, Maryland: Olde Soldier Books, 1987.

Stevens, John W. *Reminiscences of the Civil War.* Reprint edition. Powhatan, Virginia: Derwent Books, 1982.

Stewart, George R. *Pickett's Charge: A Microhistory of the Final Attack at Gettysburg, July 3, 1863.* Paperback edition. Greenwich, Connecticut: Fawcett Publications, 1963.

Stiles, Robert. *Four Years Under Marse Robert.* Reprint edition. Dayton, Ohio: Morningside Bookshop, 1977.

Stowits, George H. *History of the One Hundredth Regiment of New York State Volunteers.* Buffalo, New York: Matthews & Warren, 1870.

Swanson, Guy R., and Johnson, Timothy D. "Conflict in East Tennessee: Generals Law, Jenkins, and Longstreet," *Civil War History,* vol. 31, no. 2, (June 1985).

Sword, Wiley. *Embrace an Angry Wind.* New York: HarperCollins, 1992.

Symonds, Craig L. *Joseph E. Johnston: A Civil War Biography.* New York: W. W. Norton & Co., 1992.

Tanner, Robert G. *Stonewall in the Valley: Thomas J. "Stonewall" Jackson's Shenandoah Valley Campaign, Spring 1862.* Garden City, New York: Doubleday & Co., Inc., 1976.

Taylor, Joe Gray. *Louisiana Reconstructed, 1863–1877.* Baton Rouge, Louisiana: Louisiana State University Press, 1974.

Taylor, Walter H. *Four Years With General Lee.* Edited by James I. Robertson, Jr. Bloomington, Indiana: Indiana University Press, 1962.

————. *General Lee: His Campaigns in Virginia, 1861–1865, with Personal Reminiscences.* Reprint edition. Dayton, Ohio: Morningside Bookshop, 1975.

Thirty-fifth Annual Reunion of the Association of the Graduates of the United States Military Academy at West Point. New York. June 14th, 1904. Saginaw, Michigan: Seemann & Peters, 1904.

Thomas, Wilbur. *General James "Pete" Longstreet: Lee's "Old War Horse," Scapegoat for Gettysburg.* Parsons, West Virginia: McClain Printing Co., 1979.

Thompson, William Y. *Robert Toombs of Georgia.* Baton Rouge, Louisiana: Louisiana State University Press, 1966.

Todd, George T. *First Texas Regiment.* Notes and Introduction by Harold B. Simpson. Waco, Texas: Texian Press, 1964.

Tower, R. Lockwood. *A Carolinian Goes to War: The Civil War Narrative of Arthur Middleton Manigault.* Columbia, South Carolina: University of South Carolina Press, 1988.

Tucker, Glenn. *High Tide at Gettysburg: The Campaign in Pennsylvania.* New York: Charter Books, 1964.

————. *Lee and Longstreet at Gettysburg.* Indianapolis, Indiana: Bobbs-Merrill Co., 1968.

————. "Longstreet: Culprit or Scapegoat?" *Civil War Times Illustrated,* vol. 1. no. 1 (April 1962).

Turner Charles W., Ed. "Captain Greenlee Davidson: Letters of a Virginia Soldier," *Civil War History,* vol. 17, no. 3 (September 1971).

U. S. War Department. *The War of the Rebellion: Official Records of the Union and Confederate Armies.* 128 vols. Washington, D.C.: U. S. Government Printing Office, 1880–1901.

Vandiver, Frank E. *Mighty Stonewall.* New York: McGraw-Hill Book Co., 1957.

Wallace, Lee A., Jr. *1st Virginia Infantry.* Lynchburg, Virginia: H. E. Howard, 1985.

————. *A Guide to Virginia Military Organizations, 1861–1865.* Lynchburg, Virginia: H. E. Howard, 1986.

Ward, Joseph R. C. *History of the One Hundred and Sixth Regiment Pennsylvania Volunteers.* Philadelphia: F. McManus, Jr., & Co., 1906.

Warner, Ezra J. *Generals in Blue: Lives of the Union Commanders.* Baton Rouge, Louisiana: Louisiana State University Press, 1964.

————. *Generals in Gray: Lives of the Confederate Commanders.* Baton Rouge, Louisiana: Louisiana State University Press, 1959.

Wert, Jeffry D. "Gettysburg: The Special Issue," *Civil War Times Illustrated,* vol. 28, no. 4 (Summer 1988).

————. "I am So Unlike Other Folks," *Civil War Times Illustrated,* vol. 28, no. 2 (April 1989).

————. "Like an Avalanche: The Battle of Seven Pines. Parts I and II," *Civil War Times Illustrated,* vol. 27, nos. 6 and 7 (October and November 1988).

————. "Return to the Killing Ground," *America's Civil War,* vol. 4, no. 2 (July 1991).

Whan, Vorin E., Jr. "A Tactical Study of the Operations of the Union Army at the Battle of Fredericksburg," Master's Thesis, Pennsylvania State University, 1958.

Wheeler, Richard. *On Fields of Fury: From the Wilderness to the Crater: An Eyewitness History.* New York: HarperCollins, 1991.

————. *Sword Over Richmond: An Eyewitness History of McClellan's Peninsula Campaign.* New York: Harper & Row, 1986.

Williams, T. J. C. *A History of Washington County, Maryland.* Hagerstown, Maryland: Runk & Titsworth, 1906.

Wilson, LeGrand James. *The Confederate Soldier.* Edited by James W. Silver. Memphis, Tennessee: Memphis State University Press, 1973.

Winschel, Terrence J. "Their Supreme Moment: Barksdale's Brigade at Gettysburg," *Gettysburg: Historical Articles of Lasting Interest,* no. 1 (July 1989).

Wise, Jennings Cropper. *The Long Arm of Lee: The History of the Artillery of the Army of Northern Virginia.* Reprint edition. New York: Oxford University Press, 1959.

Wood, William Nathaniel. *Reminiscences of Big I.* Edited by Bell Irvin Wiley. Jackson, Tennessee: McCowat-Mercer Press, 1956.

Woods, Edgar. *Albemarle County in Virginia.* Bridgewater, Virginia: Green Bookman, 1932.

Worsham, John H. *One Of Jackson's Foot Cavalry.* Edited by James I. Robertson, Jr. Jackson, Tennessee: McCowat-Mercer Press, 1964.

Wray, William J. *History of the Twenty-Third Pennsylvania Volunteer Infantry, Biurey's Zowaves.* n.p. 1903–1904.

Wright, D. Giraud. *A Southern Girl in '61: The War-Time Memories of a Confederate Senator's Daughter.* New York: Doubleday, Page & Co., 1905.

Wright, James R. "Time on Little Round Top," *Gettysburg Magazine,* no. 2 (January 1990).

Wyckoff, Mac. "Kershaw's Brigade at Gettysburg," *Gettysburg Magazine,* no. 5 (July 1991).

Younger, Edward, Ed. *Inside The Confederate Government: The Diary of Robert Garlick Hill Kean.* New York: Oxford University Press, 1957.

Zettler, B. M. *War Stories and School-Day Incidents for the Children.* New York: Neale Publishing Co., 1912.

INDEX

(Page numbers in italics refer to maps.)

PHOTO CREDITS

Author's collection: 6.
Chestatee Regional Library: 30, 32, 34, 36.
Courtesy of Langston Goree: 7.
G. Moxley Sorrel, Recollections of a Confederate Staff Officer (pp. 34–35): 5.
J. Longstreet, from Manassas to Appomattox: 8, 18, 21, 25, 26, 29.
Courtesy of Jamie Longstreet Paterson: 2, 33.
U.S. Army and Military History Institute: 1, 3, 4, 9, 10, 11, 12, 13, 14, 15, 16, 17, 19, 20, 22, 23, 24, 27, 28, 31, 35.